DAVID BUSCH'S

Canon® EOS R8

GUIDE TO
DIGITAL PHOTOGRAPHY

DAVID D. BUSCH

David Busch's Canon® EOS R8
Guide to Digital Photography
David D. Busch

Project Manager: Jenny Davidson
Series Technical Editor: Michael D. Sullivan
Layout: Bill Hartman
Cover Design: Mike Tanamachi
Indexer: Valerie Haynes Perry
Proofreader: Mike Beady

ISBN: 979-8-88814-045-1
1st Edition (1st printing, November 2023)

© 2024 David D. Busch

All images © David D. Busch unless otherwise noted

Rocky Nook, Inc.
1010 B Street, Suite 350
San Rafael, CA 94901
USA

www.rockynook.com

Distributed in the UK and Europe by Publishers Group UK
Distributed in the U.S. and all other territories by Publishers Group West

Library of Congress Control Number: 2023903393

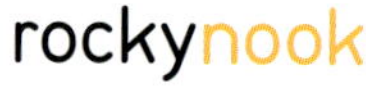

For Cathy

Acknowledgments

Thanks to everyone at Rocky Nook, including Scott Cowlin, managing director and publisher, for the freedom to let me explore the amazing capabilities of the Canon EOS R8 camera in depth. I couldn't do it without my veteran production team, including project manager, Jenny Davidson, and series technical editor, Mike Sullivan. Also, thanks to Bill Hartman, layout; Valerie Haynes Perry, indexing; Mike Beady, proofreading; Mike Tanamachi, cover design; and my agent, Carole Jelen, who has the amazing ability to keep both publishers and authors happy.

About the Author

With more than three million books in print, **David D. Busch** is the world's #1 selling digital camera guide author, and the originator of popular digital photography series like *David Busch's Pro Secrets* and *David Busch's Quick Snap Guides*. He has written more than four dozen hugely successful guidebooks and compact guides for Canon digital cameras, dozens of user guides for other camera models, as well as many popular books devoted to dSLRs, including *Mastering Digital SLR Photography, Fourth Edition* and *Digital SLR Pro Secrets*. As a roving photojournalist for more than 20 years, he illustrated his books, magazine articles, and newspaper reports with award-winning images. He's operated his own commercial studio, suffocated in formal dress while shooting weddings, and shot sports for a daily newspaper and an upstate New York college. His photos and articles have been published in magazines as diverse as *Popular Photography, Rangefinder, Professional Photographer,* and hundreds of other publications. He's also reviewed dozens of digital cameras for CNet Networks and other CBS publications. His advice has been featured on National Public Radio's *All Tech Considered.*

When About.com named its top five books on Beginning Digital Photography, debuting at the #1 and #2 slots were Busch's *Digital Photography All-In-One Desk Reference for Dummies* and *Mastering Digital Photography.* He's had as many as five of his books listed in the Top 20 of Amazon.com's Digital Photography Bestseller list—simultaneously! Busch's 300-plus other books published since 1983 include bestsellers like *Digital SLR Cameras and Photography for Dummies.*

Busch is a member of the Cleveland Photographic Society (www.clevelandphoto.org), which has operated continuously since 1887. Visit his website at http://www.canonguides.com or his Facebook group *David D. Busch Photography Guides.*

Contents

Working with Wireless Flash   217

Customizing with the Shooting Menu   237

CHAPTER 12

Customizing with the Autofocus Menu   305

CHAPTER 13

The Playback and Communication Functions Menus   321

CHAPTER 14

Set-up Menu   349

CHAPTER 15

The Custom Functions and My Menus   365

CHAPTER 16

Capturing Video   381

Preface

The new Canon EOS R8 is the company's most affordable full-frame mirrorless camera with a full range of features. With upgraded autofocus capabilities that include subject detection of people, animals, and vehicles and continuous shooting up to 40 frames per second, it's ready to capture the fastest action. Every photo enthusiast will easily master the camera's capabilities, even though the sheer number of features and options can be daunting. The only thing standing between you and pixel proficiency is the skimpy introductory booklet included in the box.

Everything you need to know is in there, somewhere, but you don't know where to start, nor how to find the information you really need to master your camera. In addition, the camera manual doesn't offer much guidance on the principles that will help you master digital photography. Nor does it really tell you much about how mirrorless shooting might differ from the kinds of digital photography you may already be used to. If you're like most enthusiasts, you're probably not interested in spending hours or days studying a comprehensive book on digital photography that doesn't necessarily apply directly to the enhanced features of your camera.

What you really need is a guide that explains the purpose and function of the camera's basic controls, available lens options, and most essential accessories from the perspective of mirrorless cameras. It should tell you how you should use them, and *why*. Ideally, there should be information about the exciting features at your disposal, how to optimize image quality, or when to use exposure modes like Aperture- or Shutter-priority, and the versatile Flexible-priority option. In many cases, you'd prefer to read about those topics only after you've had the chance to go out and take a few hundred great pictures with your new camera. Why isn't there a book that summarizes the most important information in its first two or three chapters, with lots of illustrations showing what your results will look like when you use this setting or that? This is that book.

Introduction

Only a few years ago, a full-frame digital camera *body* priced at less than $2,000 would have been unthinkable. Yet, today you can purchase the new Canon EOS R8 with a versatile RF 24-50mm f/4.5-6.3 lens, for less than $1,800. This camera is the latest entry in a burgeoning line of mirrorless cameras designed to meet the needs of a broad range of photo enthusiasts, from vlogger/content creators to the most demanding professional photographers.

As I write this, Canon offers more than two dozen different lenses and two tele-converters in your camera's native RF-mount, with more optics scheduled on the company's "lens map" projections. If you add in the dozens of existing original EF-/EF-S-mount lenses that can be used on the Canon EOS R8 with optional adapters, and full line of electronic flash units and accessories compatible with both EF-mount and RF-mount cameras, you'll see the company has built a formidable (and comprehensive) system quite quickly.

Of course, the Canon R-series cameras are not the first mirrorless interchangeable-lens cameras Canon has offered. That distinction belongs to the Canon EOS M product line, a series of consumer-oriented cameras that were truly small in size, but limited in expandability. Those cameras, targeted at amateur snapshooters, allowed Canon to develop considerable expertise in mirrorless technology. Your camera builds on what the company learned in carefully designing a new platform that fully meets the needs of a much different group: dedicated photo enthusiasts, semi-professionals, and, even, professional photographers.

Still, you may be asking yourself—*how do I use this thing?* Canon's manual is mind-numbingly dense, and online tutorials from ad-supported YouTube click-bait sites can't cover all these features in depth. Who wants to learn how to use a camera by sitting in front of a television or computer screen? Do you want to watch a movie or click on HTML links, or do you want to go out and take photos with your camera?

The large, advanced manuals Canon offers (available only online or in PDF format) are thick and filled with information, but there's really very little about *why* you should use particular settings or features. Its organization makes it difficult to find what you need. Multiple cross-references send you searching back and forth between two or three sections of the book to find what you want to know. The manual is also hobbled by black-and-white line drawings and tiny monochrome pictures that aren't very good examples of what you can do.

I've tried to make *David Busch's Canon EOS R8 Guide to Digital Photography* different from your other camera learn-up options. The roadmap sections use larger, color pictures to show you where all the buttons and dials are, and the explanations of what they do are longer and more comprehensive. I've tried to avoid overly general advice, including the two-page checklists on how to take a "sports picture" or a "portrait picture" or a "travel picture." You won't find half the content of this book taken up by generic chapters that tell you how to shoot landscapes, portraits, or product photographs. Instead, you'll find tips and techniques for using all the features of your Canon camera to take *any kind of picture* you want. If you want to know where you should stand to take a picture of a quarterback dropping back to unleash a pass, there are plenty of books that will tell you that. This one concentrates on teaching you how to select the best autofocus mode, shutter speed, f/stop, or flash capability to take, say, a great sports picture under any conditions.

Some readers who visit my blog have told me that the EOS R8 advanced photo enthusiasts don't really need the kind of basics that so many camera guides concentrate on. "Leave out all the basic photography information!" On the other hand, I've had many pleas from those who are trying to master digital photography as they learn to use their camera, and they've asked me to help them climb the steep learning curve.

Rather than write a book for just one of those two audiences, I've tried to meet the needs of both. You veterans will find plenty of information on getting the most from the camera's features and may even learn something from an old hand's photo secrets. I'll bet there was a time when you needed a helping hand with some confusing photographic topic.

Family Resemblance

If you've owned previous models in the Canon digital camera line, and copies of my books for those cameras, you're bound to notice a certain family resemblance. Canon has been very crafty in introducing upgraded cameras that share the best features of the models they replace, while adding new capabilities and options. You benefit in two ways. If you used a previous Canon camera prior to switching to the R8, you'll find that the parts that haven't changed have a certain familiarity for you, making it easy to make the transition. There are lots of features and menu choices of the camera that are exactly the same as those in the most recent models. This family resemblance will help level the learning curve for you.

Similarly, when writing books for each new model, I try to retain the easy-to-understand explanations that worked for previous books dedicated to earlier camera models, and concentrate on expanded descriptions of things readers have told me they want to know more about, a solid helping of fresh sample photos, and lots of details about the latest and greatest new features. Rest assured, this book was written expressly for you, and tailored especially for the Canon EOS R8.

Who Am I?

First, and foremost, I'm a photojournalist who made my living in the field until I began devoting most of my time to writing books. Although I love writing, I'm happiest when I'm out taking pictures, which is why I spend four to six weeks in Florida each winter as a base of operations for photographing the wildlife, wild natural settings, and wild people in the Sunshine State. In recent years, I've spent a lot of time overseas, too, photographing people and monuments. You'll find photos of some of these visual treasures within the pages of this book. You may have seen my photography articles in the late, lamented *Popular Photography* magazine. I've also written about 2,000 articles for magazines like *Rangefinder, Professional Photographer,* and dozens of other photographic publications.

In order to better understand what enthusiast photographers want to know, I regularly offer workshops and presentations on a variety of photographic topics. The questions I field often wind up as expanded explanations of those topics in books like this one.

Like all my digital photography books, this one was written by a Canon devotee with an incurable photography bug who has used Canon cameras professionally for longer than I care to admit. Over the years, I've worked as a sports photographer for an Ohio newspaper and for an upstate New York college. I've operated my own commercial studio and photo lab, cranking out product shots on demand and then printing a few hundred glossy 8 × 10s on a tight deadline for a press kit. I've served as a photo-posing instructor for a modeling agency. People have actually paid me to shoot their weddings and immortalize them with portraits. I even prepared press kits and articles on photography as a PR consultant for a large Rochester, NY company, which older readers may recall as an industry giant. My trials and travails with imaging and computer technology have made their way into print in book form an alarming number of times, including a few dozen on scanners and photography.

Like you, I love photography for its own merits, and I view technology as just another tool to help me get the images I see in my mind's eye. But, also like you, I had to master this technology before I could apply it to my work. This book is the result of what I've learned, and I hope it will help you master your Canon EOS R8.

In closing, I'd like to ask a special favor: let me know what you think of this book. If you have any recommendations about how I can make it better, visit my website at www.canonguides.com, click on the E-Mail Me tab, and send your comments, suggestions on topics that should be explained in more detail, or, especially, any typos. (The latter will be compiled on the Errata page you'll also find on my website.) You can also find me on Facebook at https://www.facebook.com/DavidBuschGuides. I really value your ideas and appreciate it when you take the time to tell me what you think! Most of the organization and some of the content of the book you hold in your hands came from suggestions I received from readers like yourself. If you found this book especially useful, tell others about it. Visit https://www.amazon.com/dp/B0BXNW4ZBX and leave a positive review. Your feedback is what spurs me to make each one of these books better than the last. Thanks!

Meet Your Canon EOS R8   1

The Canon EOS R8 *can* be incredibly easy to use right out of the box, especially if you already have some experience with digital photography. As ridiculous as it may seem, this advanced camera can be used in point-and-shoot mode simply by rotating the large Mode dial on the top-right panel to select the Program (P) label or green Scene Intelligent Auto (A+) icon. If you've charged the battery, mounted a lens, and inserted a formatted memory card (or two) into the camera, flip the power switch to On. (It's located to the right of the Mode dial, and labeled OFF, LOCK, ON.) I'll provide tips on performing these tasks later in this chapter if you need help. Otherwise, you're ready to start taking your first pictures.

As you peer through the viewfinder or examine the monitor (the rear LCD screen), the scene your camera will capture is shown, with the current shooting mode displayed in the upper-left corner of the LCD frame or bottom of the viewfinder display. Compose your image, and press the shutter release button when you're ready to take your first shot. That's all there is to it. The R8 is smart enough to produce a pretty good shot without much input from you. In this book, I'm going to help you go beyond *pretty good* to consistently great.

Although you can begin shooting as soon as you unbox your new camera, it's not a bad idea, once you've taken a few orientation pictures with your camera, to go back and review the basic operations of the R8 from the beginning—if only to see if you've missed something. This chapter will introduce new owners to the R8 and provide a review of the setup procedures for those among you who are already veteran users. I'll also help ease the more timid (even those few who have never before worked with an interchangeable-lens camera) into the basic pre-flight checklist that needs to be completed before you really spread your wings and take off. For the uninitiated, as easy as it is to use initially, your R8 *does* have some dials, buttons, and menu items that might not make sense at first but will surely become second nature after you've had a chance to review the instructions in this book.

But don't fret about wading through a manual to find out what you must know to take those first few tentative snaps. I'm going to help you hit the ground running with this chapter (or keep on running if you've already jumped right in). If you *haven't* had the opportunity to use your R8 yet, I'll help you set up your camera and begin shooting in minutes. You won't find a lot of operational detail in this chapter. Indeed, I'm going to tell you just what you absolutely *must* understand, accompanied by some interesting tidbits that will help you become acclimated. I'll go into more depth and even repeat some of what I explain here in later chapters, so you don't have to memorize everything you see. Just relax, follow a few easy steps, and then go out and begin taking your best shots—ever.

One of the challenges of writing a guidebook like this is satisfying the needs of veteran users of Canon digital SLR and mirrorless models, as well as newcomers to Canon (which now includes the hordes who jumped to the Canon mirrorless world from other camera platforms). Believe it or not, while the R8 attracts both photo enthusiasts and professional photographers, a surprising number of less experienced shooters have found the R8 appealing, too.

So, whether you're an advanced shooter looking to improve your comfort level with the features of this well-designed (yet complex) camera or are looking forward to starting from a more modest level of photographic expertise, I hope you'll find the advice I'm about to offer in this chapter useful. If you like, you can zip right through the basics, and then dive into learning a few things you probably didn't know about your R8. Canon mirrorless veterans might want to skim through the material in this chapter and move on. I promise I didn't charge you extra for it.

> **NOTE**
>
> In this book you'll find short tips labeled **My recommendation** or **My preference,** each intended to help you sort through the available options for a feature, control, or menu entry. I'll provide my preference, suitable for most people in most situations. I don't provide these recommendations for every single feature, and you should consider your own needs before adopting any of them.

First Things First

> This section helps get you oriented with all the things that come in the box with your Canon EOS R8, including what they do. I'll also describe some optional equipment you might want to have. If you want to get started immediately, skim through this section and jump ahead to "Initial Setup" later in this chapter.

The first thing to do is carefully unpack the camera and double-check the contents. At a minimum, the box should have the following:

- **Canon EOS R8 digital camera.** It almost goes without saying that you should check out the camera immediately, making sure the color LCD screen on the back isn't scratched or cracked, the memory card and battery doors open properly, and, when a charged battery is inserted and lens mounted, the camera powers up and reports for duty. Out-of-the-box defects like these are rare, but they can happen. It's probably more common that your dealer played with the camera or, perhaps, it was a customer return. That's why it's best to buy your camera from a retailer you trust to supply a factory-fresh camera.

- **Lens (optional).** At its introduction, this camera was available as a body only, and in kit configurations, such as body plus the RF 24-50mm f/4.5-6.3 IS STM lens package I purchased. Dealers were also willing to package the camera body with other lenses, such as the 24-105mm f/4L lens or more affordable 24-105mm f/4.7-7.1 zoom. Some photographers already laden with a heavy investment in Canon dSLR gear might have eschewed any RF-mount option and got one of the three available mount adapters to use with their existing lenses.

My recommendation: For an enthusiast camera at this level, the RF 24-50mm kit lens is remarkably compact and affordable, and has good sharpness. While its f/4.5 to f/6.3 maximum apertures (at the 24mm and 50mm zoom settings, respectively) are a bit on the slow side, this is a good all-around basic lens. You can't go wrong with the superb 24-105mm f/4L lens, either which compares favorably with its Canon EF-mount 24-105mm counterpart. I'll explain your lens options in more detail in Chapter 7.

- **Battery Pack LP-E17.** You'll need to charge this 7.2V, 1040mAh (milliampere hour) battery before using it. I'll offer instructions later in this chapter. It should be furnished with a protective cover, which should always be mounted on the battery when it is not inside the camera, to avoid shorting out the contacts.

- **Battery Charger LC-E17/LC-E17E.** One of these chargers, described in the "Initial Setup" section, is required to vitalize the LP-E17 battery.

- **Neck strap.** Canon provides you with a "steal me" neck strap emblazoned with your camera model. It's not very adjustable, and, while useful for showing off to your friends exactly which nifty new camera you bought, it's probably not your best option, and also can serve to alert observant unsavory types that you're sporting a higher-end model that's worthy of their attention.

  My recommendation: I never attach the Canon strap to my cameras. I generally use a plain strap and avoid holsters, slings, chest straps, or any support that dangles my camera upside down from the tripod socket and allows it to swing around too freely when I'm on the run. Give me a strap I can hang over either shoulder, or sling around my neck, and I am happy. However, you may prefer one of the alternatives available from third parties.

- **Lens accessories (if you purchased a kit).** If you purchased your camera with a lens, you'll also receive accessories, including the LF-N1 rear lens cap. The lens will also be furnished with a front lens cap of appropriate diameter and may include a case. The RF 24-105 f/4 L IS USM lens comes with a Canon E-77 II and LP1319 lens case, for example.

- **Camera cover RF-5.** The body cap keeps dust from infiltrating your camera when a lens is not mounted. Always carry a body cap (and rear lens cap). When not in use, the body cap/rear lens cap nest together for compact storage.

- **User's manuals.** Canon provides only a basic printed manual. It's small, but deceptively thick, as only about one-third of its pages are in English, with the rest of the content repeating the same information in Spanish and French. If you need a more comprehensive manual to supplement this book, you'll have to download a PDF version, available from your country's Canon website.

- **Warranty and registration card.** Don't lose these! You can register your camera by mail, although you don't really need to in order to keep your warranty in force, but you may need the information in this paperwork (plus the purchase receipt/invoice from your retailer) should you require Canon service support.

There are a few things Canon classifies as optional accessories, even though you (and I) might consider some of them essential. Here's a list of what you *don't* get in the box, but you might want to think about as an impending purchase. I'll list them roughly in the order of importance:

- **Memory card.** You'll need at least one memory card, as one is not furnished with the camera.

  My recommendation: You really need a memory card that's a *minimum* of 32GB in size, and a 64GB or larger card would be much better.

- **Extra LP-E17 battery.** Your camera's sensor and either electronic viewfinder or rear-panel LCD screen are active for long periods of time as you use your camera, so battery life may be less than what you're used to. Canon estimates you should get approximately 150 to 220 shots from a single battery when using the electronic viewfinder, and as many as 290 to 370 shots if you're working exclusively with the back-panel LCD monitor. It's easy to exceed that figure in a few hours of shooting sports at 6 fps (up to 40 fps with the electronic shutter). Batteries can unexpectedly fail, too, or simply lose their charge from sitting around unused for a week or two.

  My recommendation: Buy an extra battery (I own four, in total), keep it charged, and free your mind from worry. The LP-E17 can be charged inside the camera with the USB Power Adapter PD-E1, described in the next section, but you'll want to have a spare or two.

- **Add-on Speedlite.** Like many advanced enthusiast cameras, this camera does not include a built-in electronic flash, so you'll need an external Speedlite such as the Canon Speedlite 600EX II-RT or the flagship EL-1 (which costs $1,100!). If you're looking to cut down on the weight you carry around, consider the Canon Speedlite EL-100, which has more modest output best used for fill.

  My recommendation: Your add-on flash can function as the main illumination for your photo, or it can be softened and used to fill in shadows. If you do much flash photography at all, consider a Speedlite as an important accessory. For the most flexibility when lighting your subject, you'll need *two* flash units: one on the camera to be used as a sender (trigger), and one off-camera flash triggered wirelessly as a receiver. (The three flash units mentioned above can function in either role. Canon also offers the ST-E2 and ST-E3-RT transmitter/triggers, which can mount on the accessory shoe and serve as masters.)

- **Mount adapters.** If you already own a collection of Canon EF and EF-S lenses, Canon offers three adapters that will let you use those lenses on any R-series camera. One is a mount adapter only, a second adds a customizable control ring to your EF/EF-S lenses like those found on the RF optics themselves, while a third includes a drop-in filter carrier that lets you use a single-size filter *behind* the rear element of the EF/EF-S lens. That includes polarizers and variable neutral-density filters, and the capability works with lenses that ordinarily can't use screw-in filters at all, such as the Canon EF 11-24mm f/4L USM or Canon Tilt/Shift TS-E 17mm f/4L lenses. I'll describe the three mount adapters in more detail in Chapter 7, which deals with your full range of lens options for the EOS R8.

- **Interface Cable IFC-100U.** You can use this 1 meter/3.2-foot USB 3.0 Type-C cable to transfer photos from the camera to your computer (not recommended), to upload and download settings between the camera and your computer (highly recommended), and to operate your camera remotely using the EOS Utility software you can download from the Support page of your country's Canon website.

  My recommendation: As I'll explain later in this chapter, I don't recommend using the cable to transfer images. Direct transfer uses a lot of battery power and is potentially slower. This cable has Type-C connectors at either end—which means you'll need a Type-C-to-Type-A adapter to link to a non-Type-C computer or other device. Some generic Type-C-to-Type-A cables I've tried do not work properly, particularly with the EOS Utility (an application that allows your computer to communicate with the camera for downloading and displaying images, remote shooting, and control of camera settings). You'll need to test yours if you're trying to save a few dollars.

- **AC Adapter Kit AC-E6N.** This device is used with a *DC coupler*, the DR-E18, that replaces the LP-E17 battery and powers the camera from AC current. It is an alternative to using the PD-E1 described next.

  My recommendation: There are several typical situations where using an external power source can come in handy: when you're cleaning the sensor manually and want to totally eliminate the possibility that a lack of juice will cause the fragile shutter to spring to life during the process; when indoors shooting tabletop photos, portraits, class pictures, and so forth for hours on end; when using your camera for remote shooting as well as time-lapse photography; for extensive review of images on your television; or for file transfer to your computer. These all use prodigious amounts of power, which can be provided by an external source.

- **Remote controls.** Although the self-timer can be used to trigger your tripod-mounted camera without any vibration, it's more convenient to use a wired or wireless remote control to trip the shutter.

  My recommendation: The Canon BR-E1 wireless remote control uses Bluetooth up to a distance of about 16 feet (and doesn't require a line of sight to the camera) and is compatible with the PZ-E1 Power Zoom Adapter for remotely adjusting zoom position and movement of the EF-S 18-135mm f/3.5-5.6 IS USM lens. (That lens is an APS-C model, which doesn't cover the R8's full frame.) It also has an AF button for autofocus during video shooting. Or, you can opt for wired remotes like the Canon RS-60E remote switch.

- **HDMI cable.** You'll need an optional HDMI Type A (standard) to Type D (micro) cable if you want to connect your camera directly to an HDTV for viewing your images.

  My recommendation: I use standard HDMI micro (Type D) cables in 6- and 9-foot lengths. They work fine, and I can buy several for the price of one Canon-branded cable. Canon recommends against using cables longer than that.

Initial Setup

Many owners can skip this section, which describes basic setup steps. I'm including it at the request of ambitious photo buffs who have upgraded to this mirrorless camera after switching from a Canon dSLR, another camera brand, or an entry-level model from any manufacturer.

The initial setup of your camera is fast and easy. As I mentioned, basically, you just need to charge the battery, attach a lens, adjust the viewfinder for your vision, insert and format at least one memory card, and make a few settings. Each of these steps is easy, and if you've used a previous EOS model, you already know exactly what to do. I'm going to provide a little extra detail for those of you who are new to the Canon or digital SLR worlds.

Power Options

Your Canon EOS R8 is a sophisticated hunk of machinery and electronics, but it needs a charged battery to function, so rejuvenating the LP-E17 lithium-ion battery pack furnished with your camera should be your first step. A fully charged power source should be good for approximately 300 shots, more or less, as described above, depending on whether you're using the LCD or viewfinder to compose your shots.

All rechargeable batteries undergo some degree of self-discharge just sitting idle in the camera or in the original packaging. Lithium-ion power packs of this type typically lose a small amount of their charge every day, even when the camera isn't turned on. Li-ion cells lose their power through a chemical reaction that continues when the camera is switched off. So, it's very likely that the battery purchased with your camera is at least partially pooped out, so you'll want to revive it before going out for some serious shooting.

Several battery chargers are available for your camera. The compact LC-E17 is the charger that most owners end up using. Purchasing one of the optional charging devices offers more than some additional features: You gain a spare that can keep your camera running until you can replace your primary power rejuvenator. I like to have an extra charger in case my original charger breaks, or when I want to charge more than one battery at a time. Here's a list of your power options:

- **LC-E17.** The standard charger for the camera is the most convenient, because of its compact size and built-in wall plug prongs that connect directly into your power strip or wall socket and require no cord.
- **LC-E17E.** This is similar to the LC-E17, and also charges a single battery, but it requires a cord. That can be advantageous in certain situations. For example, if your power outlet is behind a desk or in some other semi-inaccessible location, the cord can be plugged in and routed so the charger itself sits on your desk or another more convenient spot. The cord is standard and works with many different chargers and devices (including the power supply for my laptop), so I purchased several of them and leave them plugged into the wall in various locations. I can connect my camera's charger, my laptop computer's charger, and several other electronic components to one of these cords without needing to crawl around behind the furniture. The cord draws no power when it's *not plugged into a charger.* Unhook the charger from the cord when you're not actively rejuvenating your batteries.

- **Extension Grip EG-E1.** This $79 accessory makes the camera a little easier to hold, while adding a bit of weight. It has its own tripod socket, so you can mount the combined camera/grip on a tripod or attach camera plates or L-brackets.

  My recommendation: Most will not want or need this accessory. At the time I write this, Canon has not announced a battery grip for the EOS R8, and the camera's battery chamber does not have extra contacts for a shutter release or other controls, so I do not expect to see one. Third parties sometimes develop their own grips for Canon cameras anyway, using an external cable from the grip to the remote terminal on the camera to trigger the shutter.

- **USB Power Adapter PD-E1.** Available separately, this adapter allows charging LP-E17 batteries without removing them from the camera or grip over a USB Type-C connection. Theoretically, you might be able to charge the batteries from a less-expensive adapter or power brick if it is capable of providing higher than 5V and has USB-C output. (USB-C uses a Power Delivery specification that initially provides a "profile" that delivers 5V at 2A but can "negotiate" with a device to provide up to 20V at 5A.) Ordinary USB chargers I've tried do not work and produce an Err message. (Don't panic! Turn the camera off and remove the battery for a few minutes to cancel the error message.)

  The access lamp in the lower-right corner of the camera's back panel will glow green during charging. (This is the same LED that flashes red when the camera is writing to the memory card.) When charging is finished, the lamp turns off.

Charging the Battery

When the battery is inserted into the LC-E17 charger properly, as shown in Figure 1.1 (it's impossible to insert it incorrectly), an orange Charge light begins flashing. It flashes on and off until the battery reaches a 50 percent charge, then blinks in two-flash cycles between 50 and 75 percent charged, and in a three-flash sequence until the battery is 90 percent charged, usually within about 90 minutes. In my experience, to be safe you should allow the charger to continue for about 60 minutes more, until the Full status lamp glows green steadily, to ensure a full charge. When the battery is charged, flip the lever on the bottom of the camera and slide in the battery (see Figure 1.2). To remove the battery from the camera, press the retaining button.

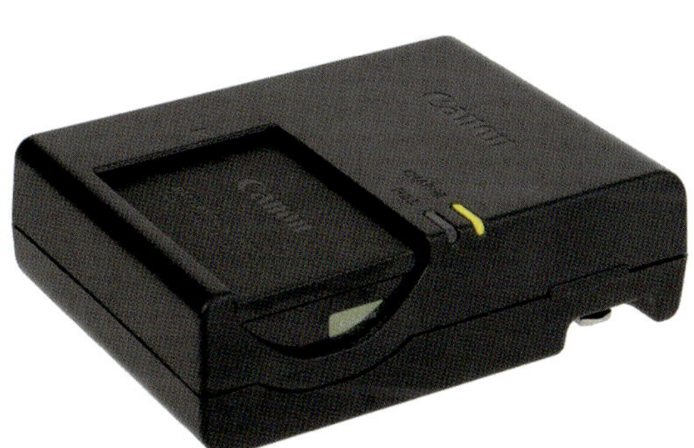

Figure 1.1 A flashing light indicates that the battery is being charged.

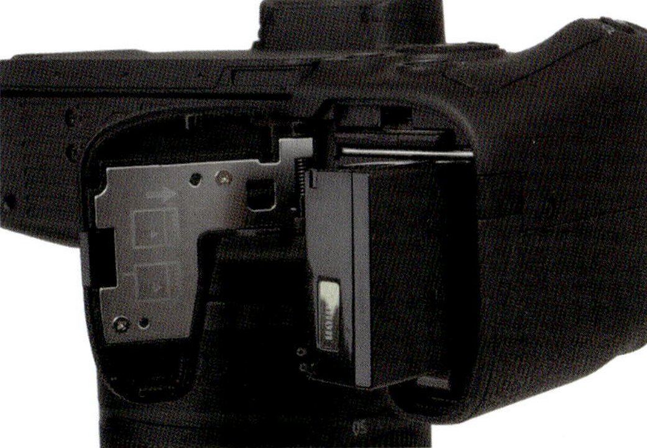

Figure 1.2 Insert the battery in the camera; it only fits one way.

Mounting a Lens

As you'll see, my recommended lens-mounting procedure emphasizes protecting your equipment from accidental damage and minimizing the intrusion of dust. If your camera has no lens attached, select the lens you want to use and loosen (but do not remove) the rear lens cap. I generally place the lens I am planning to mount vertically in a slot in my camera bag, where it's protected from mishaps, but ready to pick up quickly. By loosening the rear lens cap, you'll be able to lift it off the back of the lens at the last instant, so the rear element of the lens is covered until then.

After that, remove the body cap by rotating the cap toward the shutter release button. You should always mount the body cap when there is no lens on the camera because it helps keep dust out of the interior of the camera, where it can settle in the interior and potentially find its way onto the sensor. (While the sensor-cleaning mechanism works fine, the less dust it has to contend with, the better.) The body cap also protects the vulnerable sensor from damage caused by intruding objects (including your fingers if you're not cautious).

Once the body cap has been removed, remove the rear lens cap from the lens, set it aside, and then mount the lens on the camera by matching the raised red alignment indicator on the lens barrel with the red line on the camera's lens mount. Rotate the lens away from the shutter release until it seats securely. Set the focus mode switch on the lens to AF (autofocus) and the stabilizer switch to On. If the lens hood is bayoneted on the lens in the reversed position (which makes the lens/hood combination more compact for transport), twist it off and remount so it is facing outward. A lens hood protects the front of the lens from accidental bumps, stray fingerprints, and reduces flare caused by extraneous light arriving at the front element of the lens from outside the picture area.

Adjusting Dioptric Correction

Those of us with less than perfect eyesight can often benefit from a little optical correction in the viewfinder. Your contact lenses or glasses may provide all the correction you need, but if you are a glasses wearer and want to work without your glasses, you can take advantage of the camera's built-in dioptric adjustment, which can be varied from −4 to +1 correction. With the camera powered up, rotate the dioptric adjustment control located between the MENU button and viewfinder on the back of the camera (see Figure 1.3) while looking through the viewfinder until the indicators appear sharp.

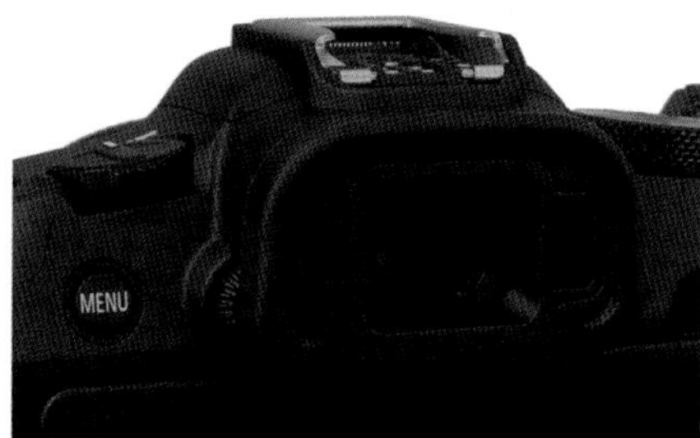

Figure 1.3 Viewfinder dioptric correction from −4 to +1 can be dialed in.

Inserting a Memory Card

You can't take photos without at least one memory card inserted in your camera, so your final step will be to insert one into the slot in the battery compartment. You should only remove the memory card when the camera is switched off, but the camera will remind you if the compartment door is opened while the camera is still writing photos to the memory card. The camera is compatible with both UHS-II and UHS-I SD cards. Close the door, and your pre-flight checklist is done! (I'm going to assume you remember to remove the lens cap when you're ready to take a picture!) When you want to remove a memory card later, press down on the card to make it pop out.

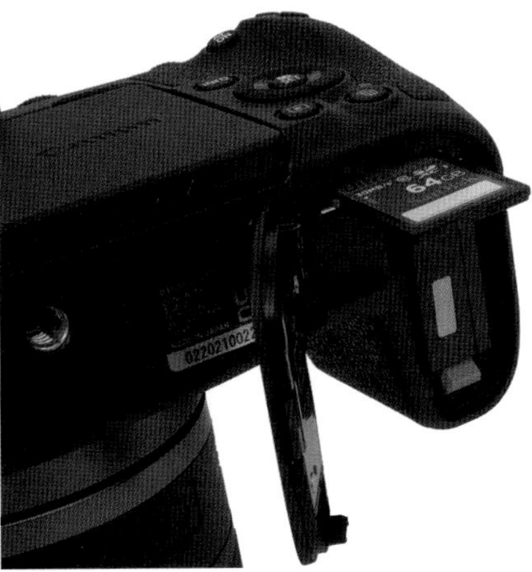

Figure 1.4 Insert the memory card in the slot with the label facing the back of the camera.

SD cards, including the latest SDXC cards, are available in speeds up to 300Mbs transfer rates with UHS-II-compliant models like the R8. Keep in mind that different vendors use different specifications for speed (both "X" factors and megabytes per second), and that *write* speed means how fast the device can transfer an image file to storage, while *read* speed (which may be emphasized because it is faster) represents how quickly the image can be transferred to your computer though a sufficiently fast connection (such as a USB 3.x card reader).

Learning Basic Navigation

The remaining setup steps require working with some of the basic controls of your camera. The R8 offers multiple ways to move through the various screens displayed in the viewfinder and on the back-panel LCD. You'll use these navigational tools to make menu selections, move focus points and zones around within the frame, and to change the area viewed during focusing and playback. This camera also has a versatile touch screen that can perform many of the same functions. For this intentionally concise Quick Start, I will stick to the basic controls suggested. I'll show you how to add the touch screen to your repertoire in Chapter 2.

Figure 1.5 shows the main navigational controls of the R8. I'll explain how to change shooting modes later. For now, let's concentrate on the navigational controls.

- **Main dial.** This wheel, located on top of the camera aft of the shutter release button, is used within menus to move from one tab to the next, within the Quick Control screen to make setting adjustments, to move a focus point horizontally, or to adjust settings such as shutter speed.
- **Quick Control dial.** The second dial positioned at the top-rear edge of the same panel, Canon could have labeled it Rear dial to differentiate the two, but stuck with Quick Control dial, abbreviated QCD. That's fine with this camera, but can cause some confusion for those who use other Canon models, as it can also be applied to a wheel on the back of the camera, or in other cases, such as the Canon R6 II, there are *two* such dials, labeled Quick Control dial 1 and Quick Control dial 2. This dial is used to move a focus point vertically, adjust settings such as aperture, or within menus to scroll among a menu tab's entries.

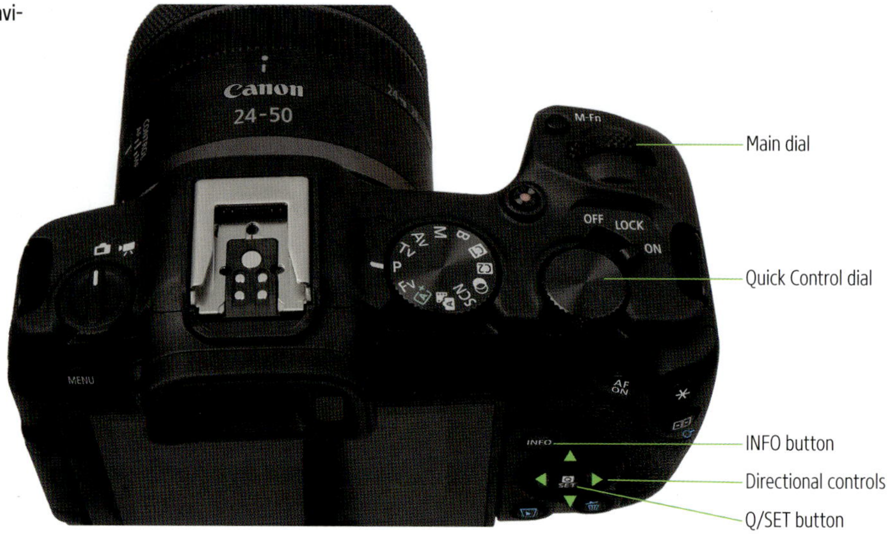

Figure 1.5 Basic navigational controls.

- **INFO button.** Located on the camera back to the right of the LCD, this button changes the type of data shown on the display, cycling among available screens when pressed repeatedly. Within menus, it is used to jump from one major main menu tab to the next (for example, from the Shooting menu to the AF menu without visiting each individual tab within the main menus).

- **Q/SET button.** In shooting mode, it accesses the Quick Control menu, which I'll describe shortly. When a menu is shown in the screen, it functions as a SET/Entry button; pressing it accesses a highlighted menu entry or function or confirms your choice or adjustment.

- **Directional buttons.** The pad of keys (Canon calls the "cross keys"), are directional buttons that provide up/down/left/right movement. Their functions overlap or duplicate the Main and Quick Control dials and the touch screen's functions, so in this book I will generally refer to all these options as "the directional controls."

Formatting a Memory Card

You can practice using the basic controls I just introduced by formatting a memory card. There are three ways to create a blank memory card for your camera, and two of them are at least partially wrong. Here are your options, both correct and incorrect:

- **Transfer (move) files to your computer.** When you transfer (rather than copy) all the image files to your computer from the memory card (either using a direct cable transfer or with a card reader, as described later in this chapter), the old image files are erased from the card, leaving the card blank. Theoretically. This method does *not* remove files that you've labeled as Protected (choosing the Protect images function in the Playback menu) nor does it identify and lock out parts of your memory card that have become corrupted or unusable since the last time you formatted the card. Therefore, I recommend always formatting the card, rather than simply moving the image files, each time you want to make a blank card. The only exception is when you *want* to leave the protected/unerased images on the card for a while longer, say, to share with friends, family, and colleagues.

- **(Don't) Format in your computer.** With the memory card inserted in a card reader or card slot in your computer, you can use Windows or Mac OS to reformat the memory card. Don't! The operating system won't necessarily arrange the structure of the card the way the camera likes to see it (in computer terms, an incorrect *file system* may be installed). The only way to ensure that the card has been properly formatted for your camera is to perform the format in the camera itself. The only exception to this rule is when you have a seriously corrupted memory card that your camera refuses to format. Sometimes it is possible to revive such a corrupted card by allowing the operating system to reformat it first, then trying again in the camera.

- **Setup menu format.** To use the recommended method to format a memory card, just follow these steps as labeled with step numbers in Figure 1.6:

  1. Press the MENU button.
  2. Press the INFO button repeatedly to move from one menu tab to the next.
  3. Rotate the Main dial to move through the menus and select the Set-up 1 menu, represented by a wrench icon.

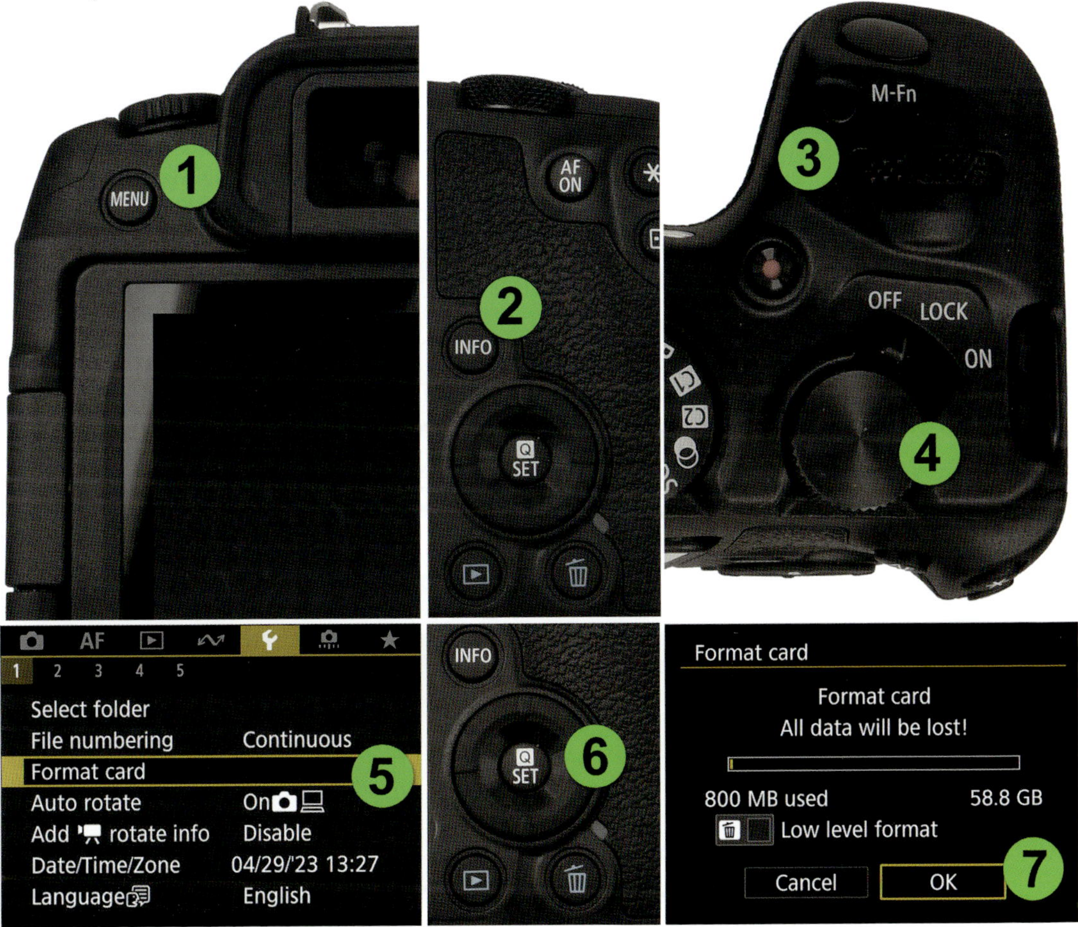

Figure 1.6 Formatting a memory card.

4. Rotate the Quick Control dial (QCD) located on top right of the camera to scroll the highlighting down within the Set-up 1 menu to the Format Card entry.

5. Press the Q/SET button to access the Format Card screen.

6. Rotate the QCD to highlight OK, and press Q/SET again to start the format.

7. You can optionally press the Trash button first to perform an extra thorough low-level "clean-up" format, which is a good idea if the card has been used many times.

Setting the Time and Date

The first time you use the camera, it may ask you to enter the time and date. (This information may have been set by someone checking out your camera on your behalf prior to sale.) Just follow these steps:

1. Press the MENU button, located in the upper-left corner of the back of the camera.

2. Rotate the Main dial (near the shutter release button on top of the camera) until the Set-up 1 menu is highlighted. It's marked by a wrench, as shown at left in Figure 1.7.

3. Rotate the QCD to move the highlighting down to the Date/Time/Zone entry.

4. Press the Q/SET button to access the Date/Time/Zone setting screen, shown at right in Figure 1.7.

5. Rotate the QCD to select the value you want to change. When the gold box highlights the month, day, year, hour, minute, or second format you want to adjust, press the Q/SET button to activate that value. A pair of up/down pointing triangles appears above the value.

6. Rotate the QCD to adjust the value up or down. Press the Q/SET button to confirm the value you've entered.

7. Repeat steps 5 and 6 for each of the other values you want to change. The date format can be switched from the default mm/dd/yy to yy/mm/dd or dd/mm/yy. You can activate/deactivate Daylight Saving Time and select a Time Zone.

8. When finished, rotate the QCD to select either OK (if you're satisfied with your changes) or Cancel (if you'd like to return to the Set-up 1 menu screen without making any changes). Press Q/SET to confirm your choice.

9. When finished setting the date and time, press the MENU button to exit.

Figure 1.7 Choose the Date/Time/Zone entry from the Set-up 1 menu and set the parameters.

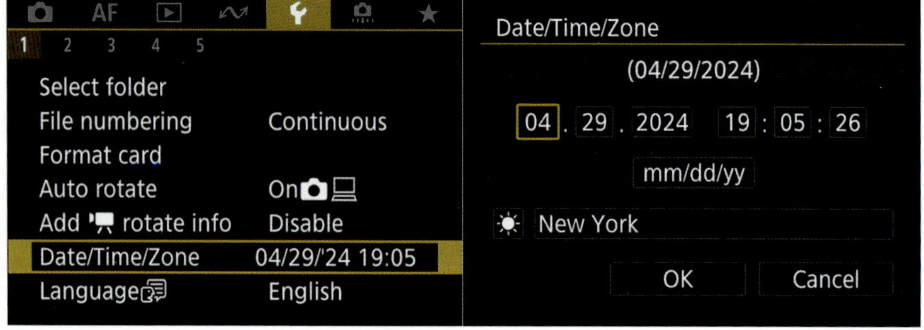

REACH OUT AND TOUCH SOMETHING

As I noted, your camera has a touch-sensitive screen that is useful for navigating menus, selecting focus points, and other functions. In many cases, you can use the buttons and dials and the touch screen almost interchangeably, but for this introductory chapter I'm going to stick to using the physical controls instead of the touch controls. There are two reasons for that. First, it's important you become comfortable using the buttons and dials, because for many functions they are faster, sometimes easier, and work reliably even when your fingers are "encumbered" (say, while you're wearing gloves). In addition, this chapter is intended primarily for those new to the Canon mirrorless world. I'll explain how to use the touch screen in Chapter 2.

Selecting a Shooting Mode

The following sections show you how to choose semi-automatic, automatic shooting, or exposure modes; select a metering mode (which tells the camera what portions of the frame to evaluate for exposure); and set the basic autofocus functions. If you understand how to do these things, you can skip ahead to "Other Settings."

Turn on the camera, and, if you mounted a lens and inserted a fresh battery and memory card, you're ready to begin. You'll need to select a shooting mode, metering mode, and focus mode. You can specify a shooting method for still photos and movies by first rotating the still/movie switch located on the top-left shoulder of the camera to either the still photo or movie positions, as seen in Figure 1.8. Then, rotate the Mode dial, located on the top-right shoulder of the camera, to the

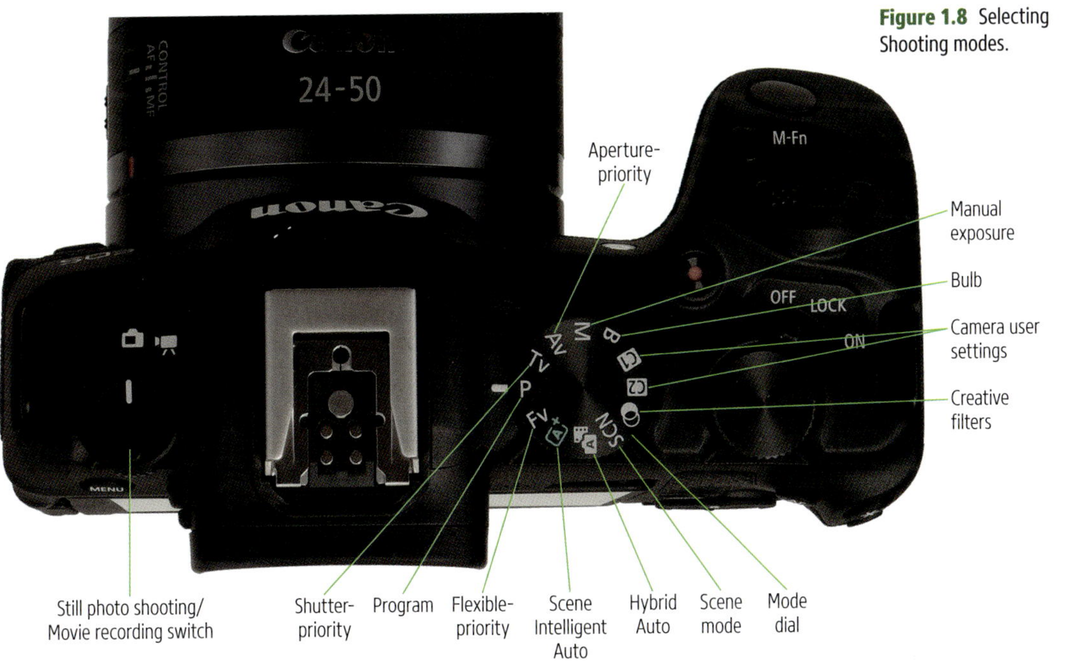

Figure 1.8 Selecting Shooting modes.

desired shooting mode. The current mode is displayed in the lower-left corner of the viewfinder or upper-left corner on the LCD screen. (You may have to press the INFO button located to the right of the LCD to activate the display.)

The camera has six *semi-automatic/manual* modes (what Canon calls Creative Zone), including Flexible-priority (Fv), Program (P), Shutter-priority (Tv), Aperture-priority (Av), Manual (M), and Bulb (B). These each allow you to provide input over the exposure and settings the camera uses. There are also two camera user settings (Custom shooting modes) that can be used to store specific groups of camera settings, which you can then recall quickly by choosing C1 or C2 as your shooting mode.

In addition to the Creative Zone modes, the R8 has what Canon calls Basic Zone modes. These modes include one fully automatic mode called Scene Intelligent Auto (A+ on the display), which makes virtually all the decisions for you (except when to press the shutter). The Special Scene (SCN) and Creative Filters positions activate additional modes. The final spot on the R8's Mode dial represents the Hybrid Auto mode, which automatically captures 2- to 4-second video clips as you take your still photos throughout the day. The video clips are combined to produce a short digest movie highlighting the still scenes you have captured. Canon has offered a somewhat similar feature called Video Snapshots for its entry-level dSLR cameras for many years, but Hybrid Auto is a relatively new feature for the EOS R mirrorless series.

You'll find a complete description of fully automatic and semi-automatic/manual modes, along with Scene and Creative Filters options, in Chapter 4, as well as Custom shooting modes in Chapter 14. Movie options are explained in detail in Chapter 16.

If you're very new to digital photography, you might want to set the camera to Scene Intelligent Auto (A+), or P (Program mode), and start snapping away. These modes will make all the appropriate settings for you for many shooting situations. Your choices are as follows:

- **A+ (Scene Intelligent Auto).** In this mode, the camera makes all the exposure decisions for you.
- **Fv (Flexible-priority).** The Fv stands for *flexible value.* This is a recently introduced exposure mode that's a combination of the four described next in this list. You can manually lock in a specific shutter speed or aperture or ISO sensitivity setting, or any combination of the three, and the other values will be set by the camera. You can also allow any or all of them to be selected automatically. You can then make your images darker or lighter using exposure compensation to override your settings.

    As its name implies, this option gives you a great deal of flexibility in choosing which settings are chosen automatically, and which are specified by you manually. I recommend that beginners not use this shooting mode until they've read my complete description of how to use it easily in Chapter 4.
- **P (Program).** This semi-automatic mode allows the camera to select the basic exposure settings, but you can still override the camera's choices to fine-tune your image.

- **Tv (Shutter-priority).** This mode (Tv stands for *time value*) is useful when you want to use a particular shutter speed to stop action or produce creative blur effects. The camera will select the appropriate f/stop for you.
- **Av (Aperture-priority).** Choose when you want to use a particular lens opening, especially to control sharpness or how much of your image is in focus. The camera will select the appropriate shutter speed for you. Av stands for *aperture value.*
- **M (Manual).** Select when you want full control over the shutter speed and lens opening, either for creative effects or because you are using a studio flash or other flash unit not compatible with the camera's automatic flash metering.
- **B (Bulb).** Choose this mode and the shutter will remain open as long as you hold down the release button. It is useful for making exposures of indeterminate length (say, you want to capture some fireworks, and leave the shutter open until a burst appears, then release the shutter after a few seconds when the light trails have been captured). The B setting can also be used to produce exposures longer than the 30 seconds (maximum) the camera can take automatically.

Making Key Settings with the Quick Control Screen

Once you've chosen your Shooting mode, as described above, you'll need to make a few key settings to specify Metering mode (which determines which areas of the frame are used to calculate exposure); AF operation (which tells the R8 *when to focus*); and AF area (which determines *what parts of the frame* to focus on). The Quick Control screen is a speedy way of making any of these three adjustments, plus seven others (for a total of 10).

The Quick Control screen comes in several variations in Shooting mode, plus an additional version that is available only when viewing your stills and videos in Playback mode. I'll explain the Playback Quick Control screen later in this chapter. First, you can learn to use the Shooting mode version, which can be accessed using one of these three methods:

- **Option 1: While looking through the viewfinder:**
  - Press the Q/SET button. The Q/SET button was shown earlier in Figure 1.5. When you press this button, a screen similar to the one shown in Figure 1.9 appears for about six seconds, waiting for your input.
  - Rotate the QCD to navigate to the icon representing the setting you'd like to adjust. Then rotate the Main dial to select one of the available options for that setting. In the example shown in Figure 1.9, Metering mode is highlighted at lower left, and the four Metering modes are arrayed along the bottom of the screen.
  - Press Q/SET to confirm.

- **Option 2: While looking at the LCD screen:**
  - The screen will display either one of several different image previews of your subject, or a graphic-based information screen. (You can cycle among these informational displays by pressing the INFO button.)
  - If the image preview is displayed, press the Q/SET button to produce the LCD version of the Quick Control screen that appears, as shown in Figure 1.9. Unlike the viewfinder version, the LCD screen displays boxes around the choices, which indicates you can tap them with the touch screen instead of using navigational controls, which you can use for Option 3, described below.
  - If you would prefer to use the graphic Quick Control screen, press the INFO button until it appears. While it's visible, press the Q/SET button to see the graphic version of the Quick Control screen, shown in Figure 1.10. Navigate to the icon of the setting you'd like to adjust with the directional buttons and then use the Main dial or the Quick Control dial while the setting is highlighted. You can also press the Q/SET button to view an adjustment screen for that setting instead. Press Q/SET to confirm.

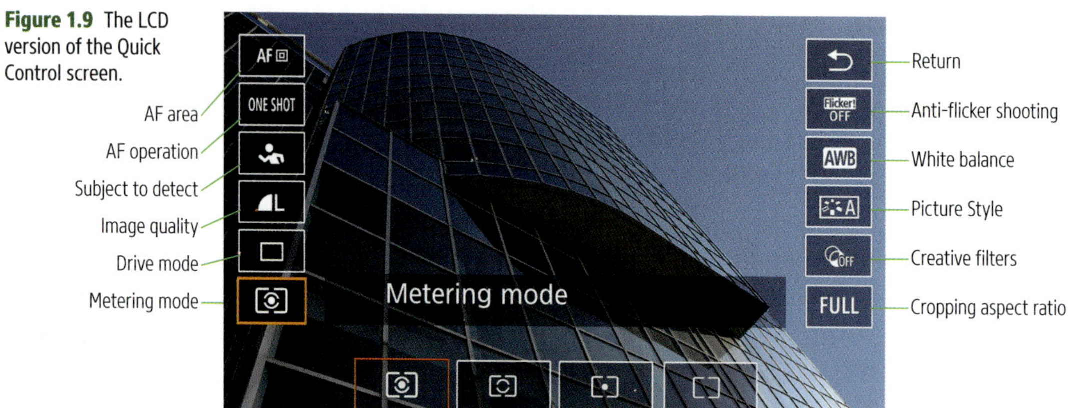

Figure 1.9 The LCD version of the Quick Control screen.

AF area
AF operation
Subject to detect
Image quality
Drive mode
Metering mode

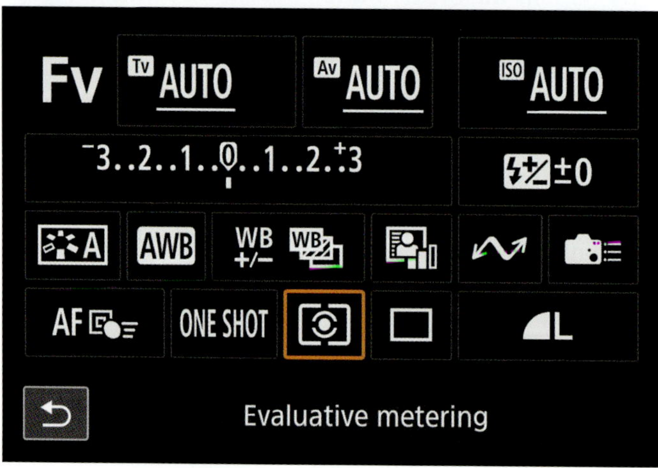

Figure 1.10 The graphic version of the Quick Control screen.

- **Option 3: When using touch controls:**
  - Access either the LCD or graphic versions of the Quick Control screen, as described in Option 2.
  - Tap the icon of the setting you want to adjust in either screen, then tap the option you want to select. Confirm and exit by tapping the "Return" arrow icon. I'll explain all your touch screen options in Chapter 2.

GETTING INFO

If at any time the expected display does not appear on the LCD screen or electronic viewfinder display in shooting or playback modes, press the INFO button several times until it is shown. One of the most frequent queries I get from new users asks why, when they follow the directions in my book, the illustrated screen isn't shown on their camera. In virtually all cases, it's because the photographer has changed the display using the INFO button on the back of the camera to the right of the viewfinder.

You can use the procedure detailed above to adjust Metering mode, AF operation, and AF area, as described in the next sections. You can also adjust the other seven default settings available from the Quick Control screen. In Shooting mode, your choices include:

- **AF area.** Choose the area of the frame that will be used to focus automatically, as described earlier in this chapter.
- **AF operation.** Choose from One-Shot AF or Servo AF modes.
- **Subject to detect.** Choose Auto, People, Animals, Vehicles, or None. I'll provide guidance on making these selections in Chapter 5.
- **Image quality.** Choose from RAW and JPEG formats and Large, Medium, and Small resolutions.
- **Drive mode.** Select Single shooting, High-speed continuous +, High-speed continuous, Low-speed continuous, Self-timer: 10 sec./remote control, Self-timer: 2 sec./remote control, or Self-timer: Continuous. You can learn more about continuous shooting in Chapter 6.
- **Metering mode.** Select the area the camera uses to collect exposure information.
- **Anti-flicker.** Counter the flickering effects of some types of illumination, as explained in Chapter 11.
- **White balance.** Select various white balance options, such as Daylight and Incandescent.
- **Picture Style.** Apply photo-enhancing parameters to your images as you shoot, as described in Chapter 11.
- **Creative filters.** Apply filters such as Grainy or Soft Focus as you capture photos, also as described in Chapter 11.
- **Cropping/Aspect ratio.** Crop your image to 1.6X (APS-C) format or change the proportions to 1:1, 4:3, or 16:9 aspect ratios.

Choosing a Metering Mode

Metering mode is the next setting you'll want to make. Note that for this and the settings that follow, the camera must be set to one of the semi-automatic and manual modes and *not* to Scene Intelligent Auto (A+). Among the four metering modes I'll describe next, the default Evaluative metering is probably the best choice as you get to know your camera. You can choose Metering mode using the Quick Control screen, as described above, or using the Metering mode entry in the Shooting 3 menu.

- **Evaluative metering.** The standard metering mode; the camera attempts to intelligently classify your image and choose the best exposure based on readings from a large number of zones within the image sensor.

- **Partial metering.** Exposure is based on a central spot, roughly 5.9 percent of the image area.

- **Spot metering.** Exposure is calculated from a smaller central spot, about 3 percent of the image area, located in the center of the frame.

- **Center-weighted averaging metering.** The camera meters the entire scene but gives the most emphasis to the central area of the frame.

You'll find a detailed description of each of these modes in Chapter 4.

Choosing a Focus Mode (AF Operation)

You can easily switch between automatic and manual focus by moving the AF/MF selector on the lens mounted on your camera (if present). If you're using a semi-automatic shooting mode, you'll still need to choose an appropriate focus mode, which Canon dubs *AF operation*. It tells the camera *when* to focus when AF is active. (You can read more on selecting focus parameters in Chapter 5.)

To set the autofocus mode, access the viewfinder or two LCD screen versions of the Quick Control display, as described above, and navigate to the AF operation (focus mode) icon. It's located immediately to the left of the Metering mode icon in the graphic Quick Control screen, and second from the top in the left column of the other two views. Choose one of these options, represented by the labels One-Shot AF or Servo AF. If the lens has been set to manual focus, neither option will be available, and an MF indicator will be shown as the icon.

- **One-Shot AF.** This mode, sometimes called *single autofocus*, locks in a focus point when the shutter button is pressed down halfway. Green boxes will appear when the image is in focus at the active focus points, or orange boxes if the camera is unable to achieve sharp focus. The focus will remain locked until you release the button or take the picture. This mode is best when your subject is relatively motionless.

- **AI Focus AF.** You may see this mode referred to as *automatic autofocus.* The camera starts to focus using One-Shot AF mode, but if your subject starts to move, it will switch to Servo AF, described next.
- **Servo AF.** This mode, sometimes called *continuous autofocus*, sets focus when you partially depress the shutter button, but continues to monitor the frame and refocuses if the camera or subject is moved. This is a useful mode for photographing sports and moving subjects.

Selecting AF Area

The Canon EOS R8 offers thousands of different selectable focus positions embedded in the sensor that you can select to calculate correct focus. (The number varies depending on shooting and autofocus mode, as I'll explain in Chapter 5.) In Scene Intelligent Auto mode, the focus point is selected automatically by the camera, using the face detection and tracking mode I'll describe shortly. In the other semi-automatic and manual exposure modes, you can allow the camera to select the focus point automatically, or you can specify which focus point should be used.

Your camera has eight different ways of specifying which of the available focus points is selected by the camera automatically, or by the user manually. I'll describe all of them in detail in Chapters 5 and 12 and will include illustrations showing the size and coverage of each of the AF methods. They are as follows:

- **Spot AF.** Allows you to manually select a single, reduced-size AF point.
- **1-point AF.** Allows you to manually select a single, slightly larger AF point, roughly three times the size of the Spot AF area.
- **Expand AF area.** You can manually select a single AF point, as well as the four points located above, below, and to the left/right of it.
- **Expand AF area: Around.** You can manually select a single AF point, as well as *up to* eight points surrounding it (above, below, left, right, and diagonally from the selected point).
- **Flexible Zone AF 1.** AF points are segregated into square-shaped zones that cover about one-sixth of the frame, and you can select which zone to use. In this Zone mode and the two that follow, the EOS camera will seek out faces, if present, and attempt to focus on them.
- **Flexible Zone AF 2 (Vertical).** AF points are segregated into larger, vertically oriented zones, and you can select which zone to use.
- **Flexible Zone AF 3 (Horizontal).** The AF points are located with a larger horizontally oriented zone that you specify.
- **Whole area AF.** The focusing area is calculated dynamically by the camera, based on subject distance; identified people, animals, or vehicles; and subject motion.

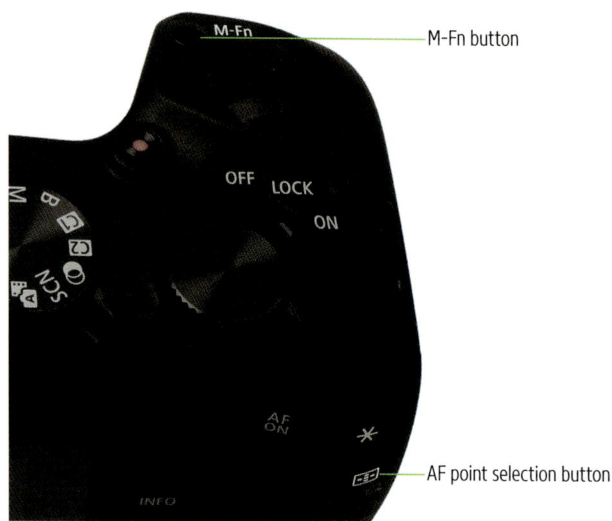

Figure 1.11 Choose AF area mode.

In addition to the Quick Control menu, the R8 offers several other ways of choosing the AF method. Here's a quick how-to on choosing the autofocus areas your camera will use:

1. **Press the AF point selection button.** It's located at the far right of the back of the camera. (See Figure 1.11.) You must press this button each time you want to change the AF area selection *mode* or when you want to select a specific AF *point* after the mode is selected.

2. **Change modes.** Within about six seconds of pressing the AF point selection button, press the M-Fn button (located on top of the camera next to the shutter release button—see Figure 1.11) repeatedly to cycle among the eight available modes.

3. **Select AF area mode.** As you press the M-Fn button the display will show each of the AF area options listed above. The highlighting will change to indicate which mode is selected. As you select the AF area, you can press the INFO button to toggle between Whole area or AF points only subject tracking in Servo AF mode, which I will explain in Chapter 5. Press Q/SET to confirm.

SIX-SECOND RULE

Many informational and settings screens will be "live" for about 6 to 14 seconds after you've pressed the relevant button. I won't repeat that information for every setting in this book; if a screen vanishes, just press the appropriate button once more.

MOVING THE AF POINT/ZONE

Once you've chosen your AF method, you can move the active focus point around the screen to a location of your choice when using any of the AF methods *except* Whole area AF. Just press the AF point selection button, as you did before, *but do not touch the M-Fn button.* Instead, simply use the Main dial to move the selected point, group of points, or zone left or right in the array, and the Quick Control dial to move the point, group, or zone up or down. Or, you can use the directional controls.

Other Settings

There are a few other options, such as white balance and using the self-timer. You can use these right away if you're feeling ambitious, but don't feel ashamed if you postpone using these features until you've racked up a little more experience with your camera.

Adjusting Settings with the M-Fn Button

The M-Fn button allows you to make several adjustments quickly, including several that aren't available from the Quick Control menu. To make these settings just follow these steps:

1. **Press the M-Fn button.** Note that you should press it *without first pressing the AF point selection button).* A screen appears with a "stack" of paired functions you can adjust.

2. **Press M-Fn repeatedly.** Cycle among the four available pairs of functions until the set you want to use is highlighted. Figure 1.12 shows the screen.

Rotate Main Dial	White Balance	Drive Mode	Flash Exposure Compensation	Picture Style
Rotate QCD	Metering Mode	AF Operation	ISO	Focus Area

3. **Make Adjustment.** Rotate the Main dial to adjust the upper parameter, or the QCD to adjust the lower parameter.

If you like, you can custom-tailor your white balance (color balance) and ISO sensitivity settings. To start out, it's best to set white balance (WB) to Auto, and ISO to ISO 100 or ISO 200 for daylight photos, and ISO 400 for pictures in dimmer light. You'll find complete recommendations for both these settings in Chapter 4.

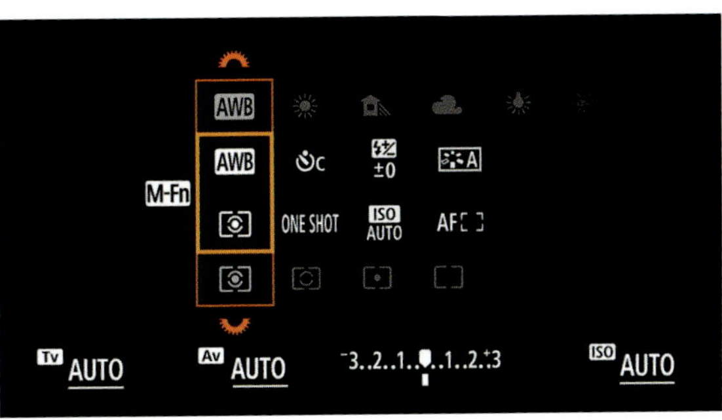

Figure 1.12 Choose a function to adjust.

Using Drive Modes and Self-Timer/Remote

You might also want to use the M-Fn button procedure to adjust Drive modes. They derive their name from the days of film shooting, when physical mechanisms were used to advance the film and provide a delay before the shutter was triggered. Your camera has seven "drive" modes, one for taking a single shot each time the shutter is pressed, three continuous shooting modes that can capture images in a range of 3 to 40 frames per second, and three self-timer/remote modes which trip the shutter after 10 seconds or 2 seconds have elapsed.

- **Single shooting.** Each time you press the shutter button down all the way, the camera takes one picture.
- **High-speed continuous shooting +.** Hold down the shutter button to capture photos at a maximum rate of 6 shots per second or 40 shots per second if you're using the electronic shutter. Shooting is slower in some picture-taking modes, as I'll explain in Chapter 6.
- **High-speed continuous shooting.** Holding down the shutter yields a rate of up to 6 shots per second with the mechanical shutter, or 20 shots per second if you're using the electronic shutter.
- **Low-speed continuous shooting.** Holding down the shutter button yields shooting at up to 3 frames per second, or 5 frames per second with the electronic shutter.
- **Self-timer: 10 sec./remote control.** The camera takes a photo 10 seconds after you press the shutter release all the way, or trigger the camera using a remote control, such as the RS-80N3. You'd use this setting when you want to have enough time to get in the picture yourself.
- **Self-timer: 2 sec./remote control.** This version takes a picture after a delay of only 2 seconds. Use it when you simply want to allow the camera to stabilize after you've pressed the shutter release, minimizing camera shake (say, for long exposures).
- **Self-timer: Continuous shooting.** After a 10-second delay, takes from 2 to 10 shots, which you can specify using the Quick Control screen or Drive mode entry of the Shooting 7 menu.

Taking a Picture

The remaining sections of the chapter guide you through taking your first pictures, reviewing them on the LCD monitor, transferring your shots to your computer, and using the Quick Control menu in Playback mode.

Just press the shutter release button halfway to lock in focus at the selected autofocus point. When the shutter button is in the half-depressed position, the exposure, calculated using the shooting mode you've selected, is also locked.

Press the button the rest of the way down to take a picture. At that instant, the shutter opens, the electronic flash (if attached and enabled) fires, and your camera's sensor absorbs a burst of light to capture an exposure. In fractions of a moment, the shutter closes, and the image you've taken is escorted off the CMOS sensor chip very quickly into an in-camera store of memory called a buffer, and the camera is ready to take another photo. The buffer continues dumping your image onto the memory card as you keep snapping pictures without pause (at least until the buffer fills and you must wait for it to get ahead of your continuous shooting, or your memory card fills completely).

Reviewing the Images You've Taken

The Canon EOS R8 has a broad range of playback and image review options. Here are the basics, as shown in Figure 1.13. I'll explain more choices, such as rotating the image on review, in Chapter 2:

- **Display image.** Press the Playback button (marked with a blue right-pointing triangle at the lower-right edge of the back of the camera just to the left of the Trash button) to display the most recent image on the LCD screen in full-screen single-image mode. If you last viewed your images using the thumbnail mode (described later in this list), the Index display appears instead.

- **View additional images.** Rotate the QCD to review additional images, one at a time. Turn it to the left to review images from most recent to oldest or toward the right to start with the last image viewed and cycle forward to the newest. You can also move among images using the directional controls or the touch screen (which I'll explain in Chapter 2).

- **Jump ahead or back.** When you're using the single-image display (not zoomed or viewing reduced-size thumbnail images), you can zip through your shots more quickly to find a specific image. Just rotate the Main dial to leap ahead or back by a variety of parameters. You can jump ahead by 1, 10, or a number of images you specify, by screens of images, by date, or by folder, and jump among movies, stills, or images that have been "protected" or assigned an image "rating." (You can mark favorite images to protect them from accidental erasure, or with one to five stars, as I'll explain when I show you how to select all these Playback options in Chapter 13.) I find the Main dial is faster.

- **View image information.** Press the INFO button repeatedly to cycle among overlays of basic image information, detailed shooting information, or no information at all.

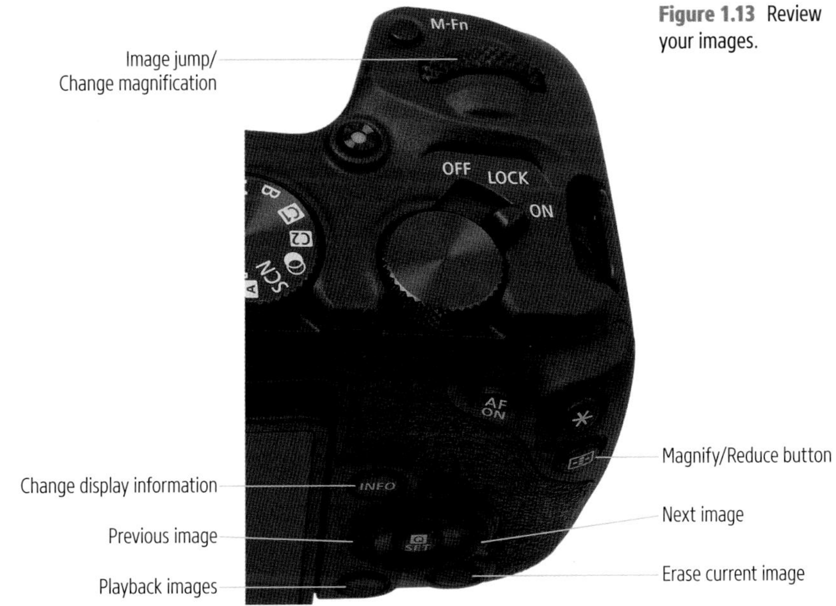

Figure 1.13 Review your images.

- **Zoom in on an image.** When an image is displayed full-screen on your LCD, press the Magnify/ Reduce button to zoom in to a magnified view. Then, rotate the Main dial clockwise to enlarge your view or counterclockwise to zoom out to full screen and to index thumbnails. Press the Playback button to exit magnified display. I'll show you how to specify how much magnification is applied (from 2X up to 10X is available) using the Playback 4 menu in Chapter 13. Pinching and spreading two fingers on the touch screen can also be used to zoom in and out, as described in Chapter 2.

- **Scroll around in a magnified image.** Press the Magnify/Reduce button, then use the directional controls to scroll around within a magnified image.

- **View thumbnail images.** You can also rapidly move among a large number of images using the Index mode described in the section that follows this list.

- **Access functions.** While reviewing pictures in full-image view, you can press the Q/SET button to produce a Quick Control screen that gives you access to many simple functions. You can protect or rate images, resize them, change the jumping method, rotate them, perform RAW image processing, enable or disable highlight alerts, search for images, and activate/deactivate AF point display. When the Quick Control screen is visible, use the directional controls to select the function to perform. I'll explain the advantages of all these options in Chapter 2.

Cruising through Index Views

You can navigate quickly among thumbnails representing a series of images using the Index mode. Here are your basic options:

- **Display thumbnails.** Press the Playback button to display an image on the color LCD screen. If you last viewed your images using Index mode, an array of images appears automatically (see Figure 1.14). If an image pops up full-screen in single-image mode, press the Magnify/Reduce button and rotate the Main dial counterclockwise to view thumbnails of 4, 9, 36, or 100 images, and back to single-image view by rotating the Main dial to the right. A few clicks will take you from magnified view to the four-image index view (and continuing to rotate counterclockwise will produce fewer/ larger index images), whereas the reverse switches to fewer index images and back to single-image mode.

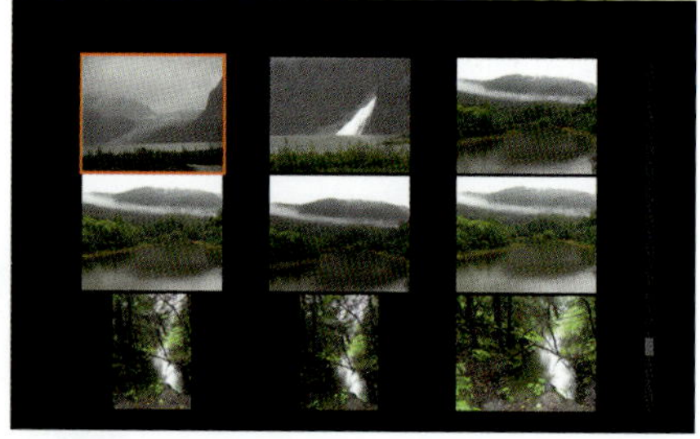

Figure 1.14 Review thumbnails of 4, 9, 36, or 100 images using Index review.

- **Navigate within a screen of index images.** In Index mode, use the directional buttons to move the highlight box around within the current Index display screen.

- **Check image.** When an image you want to examine more closely is highlighted, press the Q/SET button until the single-image version appears full screen on your LCD screen.

Transferring Photos to Your Computer

The final step in your picture-taking session will be to transfer the photos you've taken to your computer for printing, further review, or image editing. Your camera allows you to create print orders right in the camera.

For now, you'll probably want to transfer your images either by using a cable transfer from the camera to the computer or by removing the memory card from the camera and transferring the images with a card reader. The latter option is generally the best because it's usually much faster and doesn't deplete the battery of your camera. However, you can use a cable transfer when you have the cable and a computer, but no card reader (perhaps you're using the computer of a friend or colleague, or at an Internet café).

To transfer images from the camera to a Mac or PC computer using the USB cable:

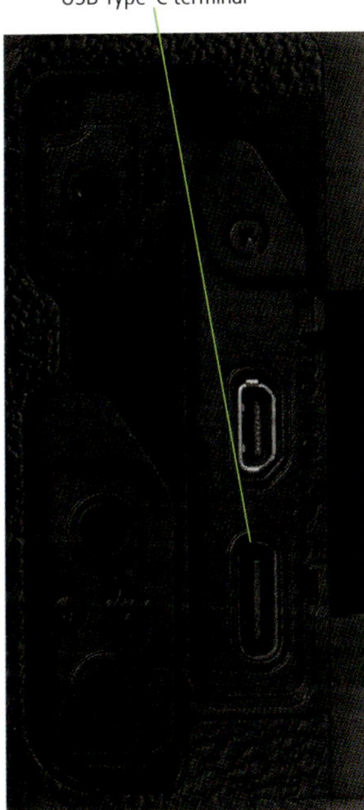

Figure 1.15 Images can be transferred to your computer using a USB cable.

1. Turn off the camera.
2. Pry back the cover that protects the camera's USB terminal, and plug the USB Type-C cable furnished with the camera into the USB terminal. (See Figure 1.15.)
3. Connect the other end of the USB cable to a USB Type-C terminal on your computer. (You may need to use an optional Type-C-to-USB-A adapter if your device lacks a USB Type-C terminal.)
4. Turn on the camera. Your installed software usually detects the camera and offers to transfer the pictures, or the camera appears on your desktop as a mass storage device, enabling you to drag and drop the files to your computer.

To transfer images from a memory card to the computer using a card reader:

1. Turn off the camera.
2. Slide open the memory card door, and press the card, which pops it up for removal.
3. Insert the memory card into your memory card reader. Your installed software detects the files on the card and offers to transfer them. The card can also appear as a mass storage device on your desktop, which you can open and then drag and drop the files to your computer.

Quick Control: Playback

The LCD version of the Quick Control menu in Playback mode is shown in Figure 1.16. As with the Shooting LCD version, you can access any of the features by tapping the icons or using the QCD to move highlighting from one icon to the next. When you've highlighted the adjustment you want to make, use the directional controls to select from the options displayed.

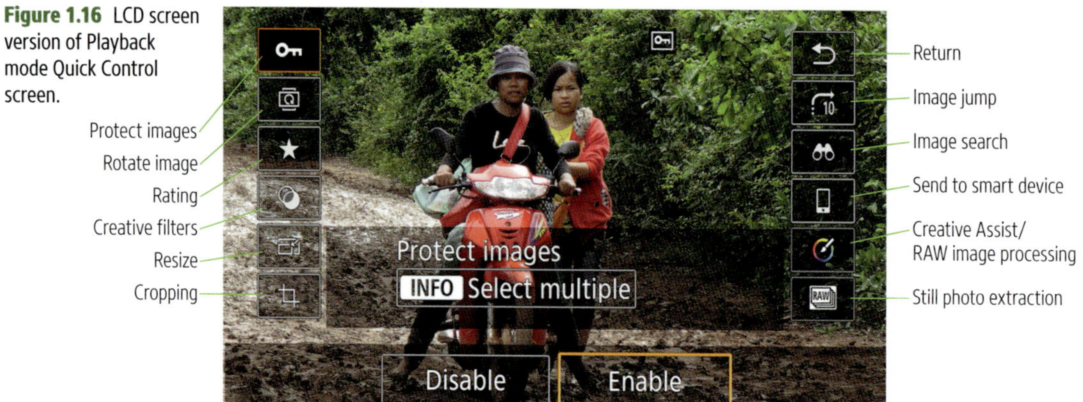

Figure 1.16 LCD screen version of Playback mode Quick Control screen.

Protect images
Rotate image
Rating
Creative filters
Resize
Cropping

Return
Image jump
Image search
Send to smart device
Creative Assist/ RAW image processing
Still photo extraction

Your choices include the following, which I will explain in detail in Chapter 13:

- **Protect images.** You can protect images or groups of images from accidental erasure (but not from a card format).

- **Rotate image.** Rotate the current image on the display in 90-degree increments.

- **Rating.** Apply one to five stars to images; these can be used to sort and search for images assigned to each rating.

- **Creative filters.** Add one of the R8's filter adjustments to an image you've already captured.

- **Resize.** Convert a full-frame Large image to Medium and Small resolutions.

- **Cropping.** You can crop, straighten, or change the aspect ratio of an image, and then save a converted copy.

- **Return.** Tap this icon to exit. It is available only in the LCD screen version of the Quick Control menu. The Q/SET button can be pressed to exit in both LCD and Viewfinder screen versions.

- **Image jump.** Jump forward or back among images during playback using leaps of 1, 10, or a specified number of images, or by date or folder name, or by movies, stills, protected, or rated image parameters.

- **Image search.** You can search for images using one *or more* search parameters, including a specific rating, specified date, selected folder/protected condition, or file type.

- **Send to smart device.** As I'll show you in Chapter 6, you can send your shots to your smart device automatically and select them using this option.

- **Creative Assist/RAW image processing.** You can perform many processing functions, such as changing brightness, contrast, and saturation using Creative Assist. You can learn more about these parameters in Chapter 13.

- **Still photo extraction from RAW Burst images.** Your R8 has a RAW Burst mode that enables fast continuous shooting of RAW images, with a Pre-Shooting option that can capture an image *before* you press the shutter release. I'll explain how to shoot RAW Bursts in Chapter 11, and how to extract still images from these bursts in Chapter 6.

Your Visual Roadmap | 2

Canon has simplified operation of your EOS R8 by providing quick access to the most frequently adjusted commands and functions through a clever use of multi-function controls, like the control ring found on RF lenses and adapters, as well as the Multi-function (M-Fn) button, Q/SET (Quick Control/SET) buttons, and the Quick Control dial. Canon says it's implemented this approach because the smaller size of the camera doesn't lend itself to the daunting number of buttons found on traditional, large digital SLRs. The design has reduced the number of dedicated controls, but still minimizes the need to delve into the sometimes-confusing thicket of conventional menus.

That's a good thing. After all, while menus are easy to *learn*, because each entry describes its function in text form, their ironic disadvantage is that they are clumsy to *use*. Even though a well-designed menu system can lead you to the right commands, they require negotiating through all the various levels with multiple steps.

Your camera's limited number of controls summon concise icon-based choices you can select with the twirl of a dial and press of a button or two. Best of all, with the customizable control ring, buttons, and menus you can tailor the camera to work the way *you* want it to, rather than succumb to the manufacturer's notion of how it *should* work.

However, even with the camera's clean, versatile design, you'll still need to learn the location, function, and application of all its parts. What you really need is a street-level roadmap that shows where everything is, and how it's used. But what Canon gives you in the comprehensive PDF user's manual is akin to a world globe with an overall view and not much information on how to use each component. Check out the Parts Names pages of the full Canon camera manuals, which offer sparse black-and-white line drawings of the camera body that show front, back, two sides, and the top and bottom of the camera. There are more than 80 callouts pointing to various buttons, dials, controls, components, and icons. If you can find the control you want in this cramped layout, you'll still need to flip back and forth among multiple pages to locate the information about them.

I originated the up-close-and-personal, full-color, street-level roadmap (rather than a satellite view) that I use in this book and my previous camera guidebooks. I provide you with many different views and lots of explanation accompanying each zone of the camera, so that by the time you finish this chapter, you'll have a basic understanding of every control and what it does. I'm not going to delve into menu functions here—you'll find a discussion of your Set-up, Shooting, and Playback menu options in Chapters 11 through 14. Everything here is devoted to the button pusher and dial twirler in you.

You'll also find this "roadmap" chapter a good guide to the rest of the book, as well. I'll try to provide as much detail here about the use of the main controls as I can, but some topics (such as autofocus and exposure) are too complex to address in depth right away. So, I'll point you to the relevant chapters that discuss things like setup options, exposure, use of electronic flash, and working with lenses with the occasional cross-reference.

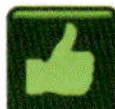

NOTE When I ask you to *press* or *tap* in this book, I mean you should press and release a button or tap the touch screen (described later). The camera will then give you some time (usually about 6 seconds, depending on the function) to make an adjustment. When I am asking you to keep a button depressed while using another control, I'll say *hold.* For many functions, the camera's exposure meters must be active; just tap the shutter release button lightly to wake them up.

Front View

The front of the camera is the face seen by your subjects as you snap away. For the photographer, though, the front is the surface your fingers curl around as you hold the camera, and there are really only a few buttons to press, all within easy reach of the fingers of your left hand, plus the shutter release button and Main dial, which are on the top/front of the hand grip. There are additional controls on the lens itself. Figure 2.1 is a view of the front of the camera with the lens detached. The other main components you need to know about are as follows:

- **Shutter release button.** Angled on top of the hand grip is the shutter release button. Press this button down halfway to lock exposure and focus (in One-Shot AF mode and Servo AF modes with non-moving subjects).

- **AF-assist beam/Self-timer lamp.** This LED flashes when needed to provide additional illumination to facilitate autofocus. This lamp also flashes when using the self-timer to mark the countdown until the photo is taken.

Figure 2.1

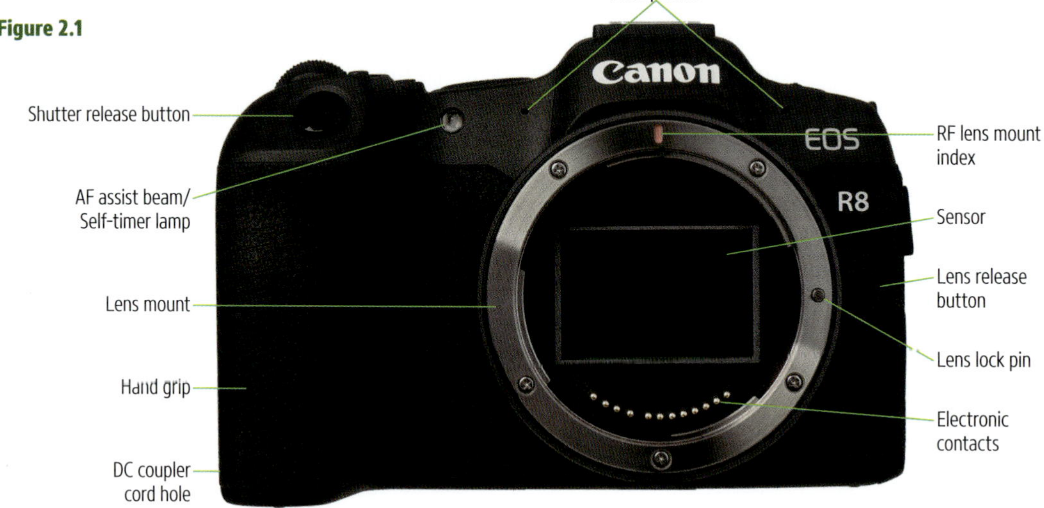

- **DC coupler cord hole.** This cover, on the outside edge of the hand grip, opens to allow the DC power cable to connect to the camera through the battery compartment.
- **Hand grip.** This provides a comfortable hand-hold, and also contains the camera's battery.
- **Depth-of-field preview button.** When pressed, stops the lens down to the aperture that will be used to take the photo, providing a preview of depth-of-field.
- **Lens mount.** This sturdy flange accepts a matching bayonet on the rear of each lens or accessory you mount on the camera.
- **Lens release button.** Press and hold this button to unlock the lens so you can rotate the lens to remove it from the camera.
- **Lens lock pin.** This pin on the lens flange retracts when the lens release button is held down to unlock the lens.
- **RF lens mount index.** Line up this mark with the matching red detent on the barrel of your RF or mount adapter lens to align it as you mount it on the camera.
- **Sensor.** The shutter is open when the camera is powered down, so you should be careful not to touch it or allow it to be touched when the lens is removed. You should be careful when manually cleaning the sensor, as described in Chapter 13.
- **Electronic contacts.** These contacts connect to matching points on the lens to allow the camera and lens to communicate electronically.
- **Microphones.** The R8 has a stereo pair of microphones located on either side of the front of the camera, slightly above the lens mount.

You'll find more controls on the side of the camera, shown in Figure 2.2. In the illustration, you can also see some of the key components of the lens that is mounted on the camera. Note that not all of the lens features are found on all lenses (e.g., there is no zoom ring on non-zoom "prime" lenses). The main elements are as follows:

- **Lens hood bayonet.** Canon offers lens hoods designed specifically for each lens; they attach to this grooved mount that rings the front of the lens, in both forward-facing and reversed positions. The hood serves to keep extraneous light, which reduces contrast and causes flare, from entering the lens. You should always use a hood when shooting, as they are your best protection from damage due to collisions and other mishaps. Filters are designed to shatter easily (that's how filter manufacturers convince you to buy more filters to "save" your lens) and are best reserved for when you want to filter something or are working in wet or dusty environments. (Lens hoods won't disintegrate into razor sharp shards of glass, either.)
- **Lens hood alignment mark.** Line up a matching indicator on your lens hood and rotate the hood to fasten it securely to the front of your lens.
- **Control ring.** This brilliant feature can be programmed to change aperture, shutter speed, ISO, and exposure compensation, as I'll explain in Chapter 14.
- **Focus ring.** Rotate this ring to focus manually or fine-tune autofocus.
- **Zoom ring.** Turn this ring to zoom in or out.

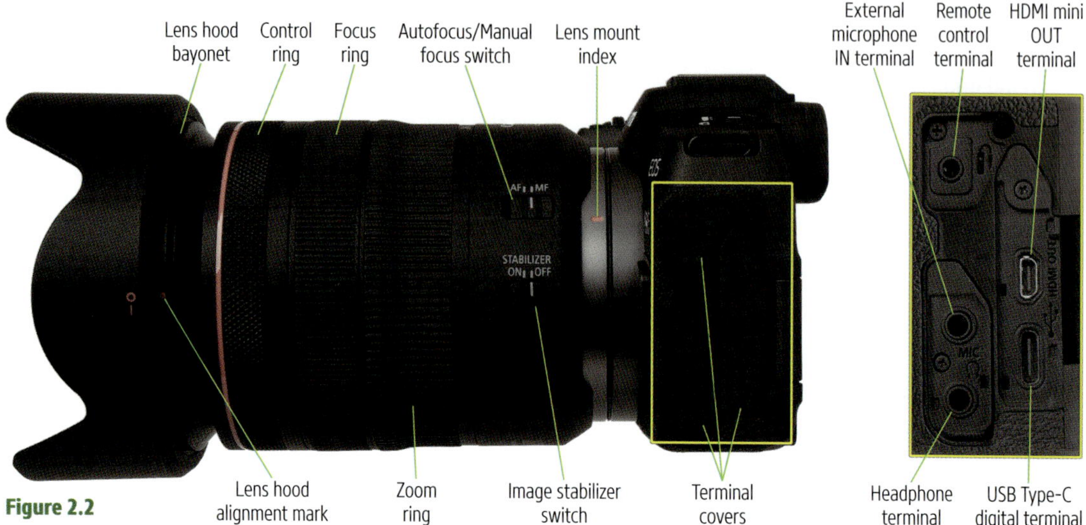

Figure 2.2

- **Image stabilizer switch.** This switch turns image stabilization on and off. You might want to disable IS when the camera is mounted on a tripod.

- **Autofocus/Manual focus switch.** Canon autofocus lenses have a switch to allow changing between automatic focus and manual focus.

- **Terminal covers.** The camera's interface terminals are behind these three rubber covers, which protect them from dust and moisture.

Several terminals are located under the terminal covers, as shown in the inset for Figure 2.2. They include:

- **USB Type-C digital terminal.** This Type-C connector accepts the supplied USB cable, which you can use to transfer photos to your computer. The terminal can be used with the Wireless File Transmitter WFT-E7 II and GPS Receiver GP-E2.

- **HDMI mini OUT terminal.** You'll need to buy an accessory cable to connect your camera to an HDMI-compatible television, video recorder, or other device, as one to fit this terminal is not provided with the camera. If you have a high-resolution television, it's worth the expenditure to be able to view your camera's output in all its glory. Any Type A (standard) to Type D (micro) HDMI cable will be compatible. Note that your camera's HDMI output is not compatible with the CEC (Consumer Electronics Control) protocol, which allows devices such as recorders and televisions to control each other.

- **Headphone terminal.** Connect headphones or other audio playback gear here. It accepts a 3.5mm stereo mini-plug.

- **Remote control terminal.** A wired remote control can be plugged in here.

- **External microphone IN terminal.** Connect an external stereo microphone with a 3.5mm stereo mini-plug here to bypass the internal stereo microphone pair when recording sound.

The Business End

The back panel of the R8 (see Figure 2.3) bristles with more than a dozen different controls, buttons, and knobs. That might seem like a lot of components to learn, but you'll find that the camera has a reasonable number of dedicated controls that make routine adjustments more quickly than a visit to a traditional menu every time you want to change a setting.

You can see the controls clustered on the upper edge of the back panel in Figure 2.4. The key buttons and components and their functions are as follows:

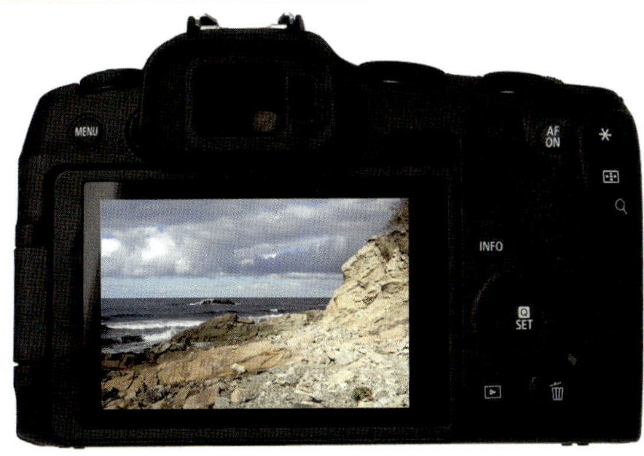

Figure 2.3

- **MENU button.** Summons/exits the menu displayed on the LCD screen or electronic viewfinder of the camera. When you're working with submenus, this button also serves to exit a submenu and return to the main menu.
- **Dioptric adjustment control.** Rotate this dial while looking through the viewfinder to make adjustments for your vision, as described in Chapter 1.
- **Viewfinder eyepiece/eyecup.** You can frame your composition by peering into the viewfinder eyepiece. It's surrounded by a soft rubber eyecup/frame that seals out extraneous light when pressing your eye tightly up to the viewfinder, and it also protects your eyeglass lenses (if worn) from scratching. The R8's electronic viewfinder has 2.36 million pixels.
- **Viewfinder sensor.** This sensor recognizes when your eye (or any other object) approaches the viewfinder eyepiece. By default, the camera switches between the two automatically, but you can configure the camera to switch only manually, using the Screen/Viewfinder Display entry in the Set-up 3 menu, as described in Chapter 13.
- **Speaker.** Sounds produced by the R8, such as audio during movie playback, emit from this monaural speaker.

Figure 2.4

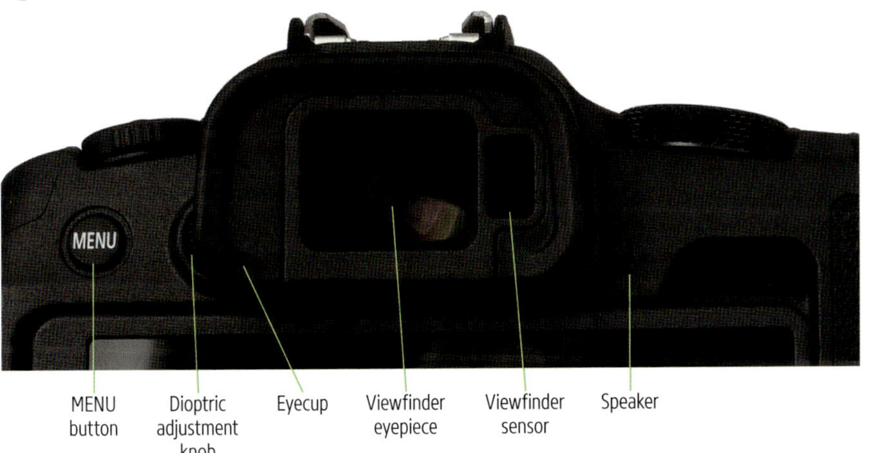

Right-Side Controls

More buttons reside on the right side of the back panel, as shown in Figure 2.5. The key controls and their functions are as follows:

- **Quick Control dial (QCD).** Used to select shooting options, such as f/stop or exposure compensation value, or to navigate through menus. It also serves as an alternate controller for some functions set with other controls, such as AF point selection.

- **AF-ON button.** Press this button to activate the autofocus system without needing to partially depress the shutter release. This control, used with other buttons, allows you to lock exposure and focus separately. Lock exposure by pressing the shutter release halfway, or by pressing the AE lock button; autofocus by pressing the shutter release halfway, or by pressing the AF-ON button. Functions of this button will be explained in more detail in Chapter 5.

- **AE/FE (autoexposure/flash exposure) lock button.** In Shooting mode, it locks the exposure or external flash exposure that the camera sets when you partially depress the shutter release button. The exposure lock indication (*) appears at lower left in the display. If you want to recalculate exposure with the shutter release button still partially depressed, press the * button again. The exposure will be unlocked when you release the shutter or take the picture. To retain the exposure lock for subsequent photos, keep the * button pressed while shooting.

  When using external flash, pressing the * button fires an extra pre-flash when you partially depress the shutter release button that allows the unit to calculate and lock exposure prior to taking the picture.

Figure 2.5

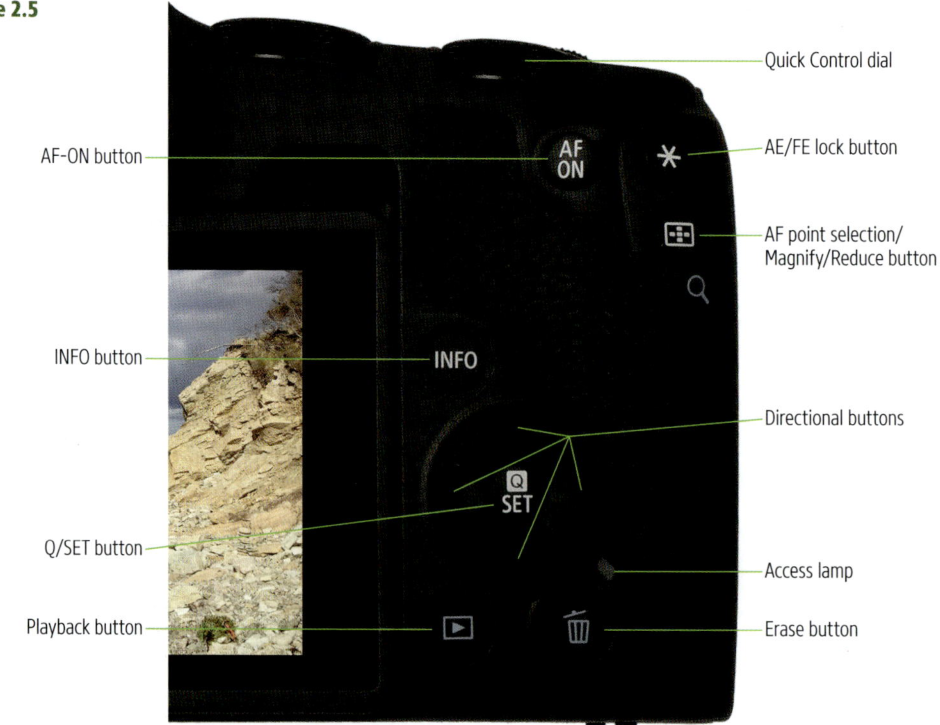

- **AF point selection button.** This button has two functions:
  - **AF area mode selection.** Press this button once, then press the M-Fn button (described shortly) repeatedly to switch among the available AF area modes, from Spot AF, 1-Point AF, Expand area AF, Expand area AF (Around), Zone AF 1, Zone AF 2, Zone AF 3, and Whole area AF. I'll describe each of these and when to use them in Chapter 5.
  - **AF point movement.** Press this button and then you can use the directional controls to move the AF point or zone around the frame in all AF area modes except Whole area AF.
- **Magnify/Reduce button.** This button has separate functions for Shooting and Playback modes.
  - **Shooting mode.** Press this button once, and *then* press the INFO button to magnify the view by 5X, 10X, and then a third time to return to 1X (full frame). (See Chapter 5 for information on setting autofocus/exposure point selection.) While the image is magnified, you can move the zoomed area using the directional buttons.
  - **Playback mode.** Press this button and release it. Then rotate the Main dial clockwise to progressively zoom in on a still image. Magnification increments from 1X to 10X are available; you can specify the *initial* magnification using the Magnification setting in the Playback 3 menu.

  Rotate the Main dial counterclockwise to zoom out to full-frame mode and then to 4-, 9-, 36-, and 100-image index views. In any index or magnified view, press Q/SET to see a full-frame view of the currently highlighted image.
- **Q/SET button.** In Shooting mode, press this button to produce the Quick Control screen, which gives you access to many adjustments and features. When you're reviewing images in Playback mode, a different Quick Control screen pops up that allows you to protect or rate images, change jump method, resize, crop, rotate, or perform other functions. When using menus and screens that involve adjustment and settings choices, this button serves as a SET/Enter control to activate or confirm your selection.
- **Directional buttons.** This pad surrounding the Q/SET button can be shifted in eight different directions when adjusting focus points, moving a zoomed area, navigating menus, and other functions.
- **Access lamp.** When lit or blinking, this lamp indicates that the memory card is being accessed.
- **Erase button.** In Playback mode, this button deletes the currently displayed image.
- **Playback button.** Displays the most recent image.
- **INFO button.** Changes the type of information displayed in shooting and playback modes. When working with menu screens, pressing it jumps from one main MENU tab to the next. It's also used within some menu screens to access additional information or options.

Mastering the Touch Screen

Your camera's versatile LCD 3.0-inch display screen is articulated so it can be positioned in multiple orientations. It is also touch sensitive for rapid selection of menu and focus options. The articulation feature makes it easy to take pictures in a variety of orientations. Using the touch screen, you can perform many routine operations, including menu navigation/selection functions, by tapping the screen. This section will show you how to best make use of those features.

Flexible View

The articulated screen offers several alternative ways of previewing and reviewing your images in ways that the electronic viewfinder can't. Here are a few to consider:

- **Selfie mode.** Swing the LCD out from the body and rotate it so the screen is pointing in the same direction as the lens. Mount the camera on a tripod, or any temporary resting place, then position yourself (alone or with a group) for a selfie. You can see the image the camera will capture before taking the shot with the self-timer or remote control. The camera can immediately display the photo, so you can review it and change poses before taking another shot, if you like.

- **Share the fun.** Even if you're not in the picture yourself, you can share the image you're about to take with your subject when the LCD is in the "selfie" position. (See Figure 2.6, left.) It works best if the camera is on a tripod. Your subject can evaluate the pose, adjust his or her hair, or turn to their "good" side before you shoot. When you move your eye to the viewfinder, the LCD preview will turn off, and you'll be able to see the image as you take the picture. Vloggers will probably use this mode to monitor their performance when shooting video or streaming using the Canon EOS Webcam Utility.

- **Waist-level view.** With the LCD swung out, you can tilt the screen back, giving you a waist-level preview of the picture you're about to take. That perspective can be especially useful when photographing low-lying subjects without needing to crouch or get down on your hands and knees. It's also useful for semi-stealth photography because you don't need to bring the camera up to your eye to compose the image. (See Figure 2.6, right.)

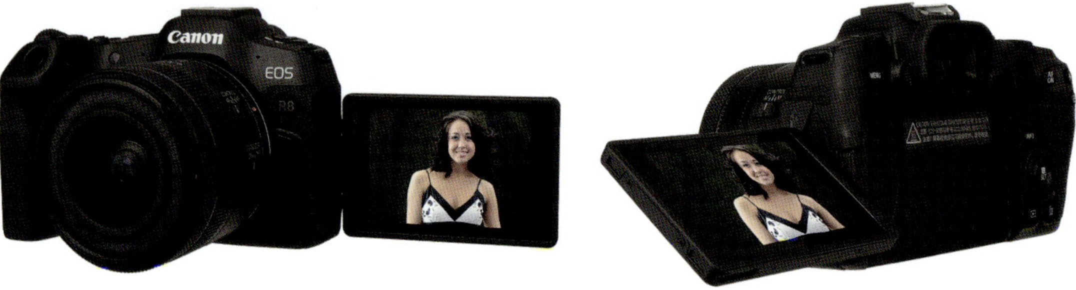

Figure 2.6 The articulated screen allows multiple views.

- **Periscope view.** The screen can pivot so it is facing completely downward so you can hold the camera over your head and shoot using a periscopic perspective. Great for shooting over crowds, particularly at parades.

- **Screen protection.** Swivel the screen so the back of the LCD is facing outward, and you've got solid protection—at least from scratches and minor impacts. Even so, I'd avoid whacking the back of the camera. But it's nice to keep your screen shielded when traveling.

Touch Operation

Of course, for many veteran shooters, some touch-friendly tasks, such as navigating through menus, may be no quicker than the button/dial procedures we are used to, and can even be more awkward for those with large fingers or those who need/want to wear gloves. However, there are several uses for the touch screen that border on outstanding as you become more accustomed to working with the camera's screen. You can even use it while viewing through the electronic viewfinder! Here are some of the things you can do:

- **Move focus point while using the EVF.** You can touch the screen with one finger and drag to move the AF point or Zone AF frame around as you preview your image through the viewfinder. You just need to activate the Touch & Drag AF feature in the AF 4 menu and choose one of several alternative methods for specifying the active area of the screen and how the point or zone moves. I'll explain how to use this feature in Chapter 5.

- **Touch focus point/shutter.** While viewing the touch screen you can specify the exact focus point (or zone) you want by tapping the screen. The camera can focus at the point you just selected, or even take a picture if you've activated the Touch Shutter feature (using an icon located at lower left on the screen). If you'd prefer to drag the point around the screen to the desired location, press the point selection button, and then swipe your finger around the touch screen to move the focus point. (See Chapter 5 for more on this.)

- **Menu navigation.** You may find some menu operations are easier to complete using the touch screen, although, as I noted, many of us may prefer using old-school dials and buttons.

- **Text entry.** If you've ever had to type in copyright information, tried to rename the My Menu tab, or performed any other text-entry operation using the camera's buttons and dials, you'll appreciate the ability to just tap on the virtual keyboard to input your data, such as photographer and copyright information. (See Figure 2.7.)

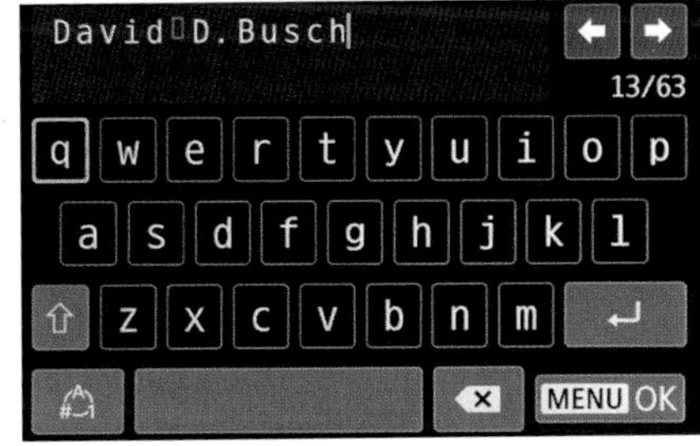

Figure 2.7 The camera's virtual keyboard makes touch typing easy.

- **Playback.** As you'll see, you can scroll through images rapidly during review, zoom in and out, and perform other functions that are much clumsier with buttons and dials—even if you've had years of experience and are adept with the traditional methods.

When you've activated the touch screen using the Touch Control entry in the Set-up 4 menu (as described in Chapter 14) you have a large range of capabilities available to you with a simple tap on the screen (represented by the green/red circles shown in Figure 2.8). Here's a quick overview of the options:

1. **Quick Control menu.** Tap the Q icon in the upper right of the screen and the Quick Control menu (which I first showed you in Figure 1.9 in the first chapter) pops up. You can adjust any of the options shown in the left and right columns in Figure 2.8.

2. **Touch shutter.** Tap here to turn the touch shutter feature on or off. When active, tapping the screen tells the camera to focus at the point you've specified and take a picture.

3. **Adjust shutter speed (or aperture).** You can adjust any parameter with a box around it. In Figure 2.8, the camera is set for Tv shooting mode (Shutter-priority), so you can tap the box displaying the current shutter speed, then rotate *either* the Main dial or Quick Control dial or use the other directional controls (left/right buttons) to change the shutter speed. In Av (Aperture-priority) mode, you can change the f/stop; in M (Manual) mode, both shutter speed and aperture will have a box around them and can be adjusted.

4. **Exposure compensation.** Tap this scale and use the dials/directional controls (or tap the scale itself) to add or subtract from the metered exposure. I'll explain exposure compensation in more detail in Chapter 4.

5. **ISO sensitivity.** Tap the ISO icon and use the dials/directional controls to select a fixed ISO setting or ISO Auto.

6. **Zoom.** Tap the magnifying glass immediately above the ISO icon to zoom in on your image.

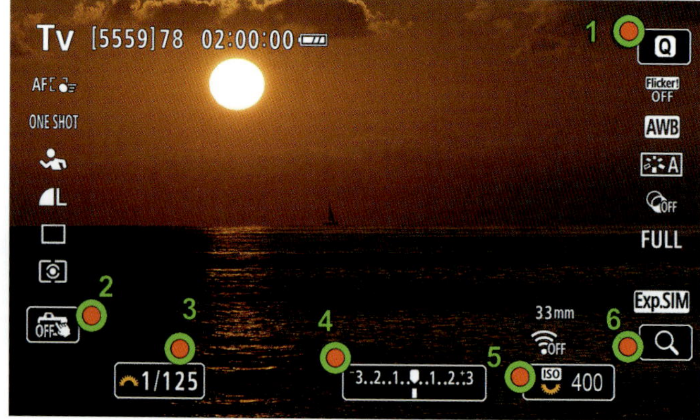

Figure 2.8 Tap any of the boxed icons to change that function's settings.

YOUR CHOICE

Throughout this book, I may not explicitly say "tap the screen," or "use the button," or "visit the menu" for every single operation. Given the large number of how-to entries in this book, that would require unnecessarily long descriptions and extra verbiage. I'm going to assume that once you master the touch screen using the information in this section, you'll make your own choice and use whichever method you prefer. I'll generally stick to using the physical controls that we're all accustomed to. But, unless I specifically say to use the touch screen or physical controls, assume I mean you can use either one.

Meaningful Gestures

I think that once you become familiar with the speed with which the touch screen allows you to make adjustments, you'll be reluctant to go back to the "old" way of doing things. The camera's touch screen is *capacitive* rather than *resistive*, making it more like the current generation of smartphones than earlier computer touch-sensitive screens. The difference is that your camera's LCD responds to the electrical changes that result from *contact* rather than the force of *pressure* on the screen itself. That means that the screen can interpret your touches and taps in more complex ways. It "knows" when you're using two fingers instead of one, and can react to multi-touch actions and gestures, such as swiping (to scroll in any direction) and pinching/spreading of fingers to zoom in and out. Since you probably have been using a smartphone for a while, these actions have become ingrained enough to be considered intuitive. Virtually every main and secondary function or menu operation can be accessed from the touch screen. However, if you want to continue using the buttons and dials, the camera retains that method of operation.

Here's what you need to know to get started:

- **Tap to select.** Tap (touch the LCD screen briefly) to select an item, including a menu heading or icon. Any item you can tap will have a frame or box around it. Figure 2.9 shows the taps needed to select a menu tab and specific entry within that menu and then make your adjustments on the screen that appears. On settings screens, tappable items will have a box around them.

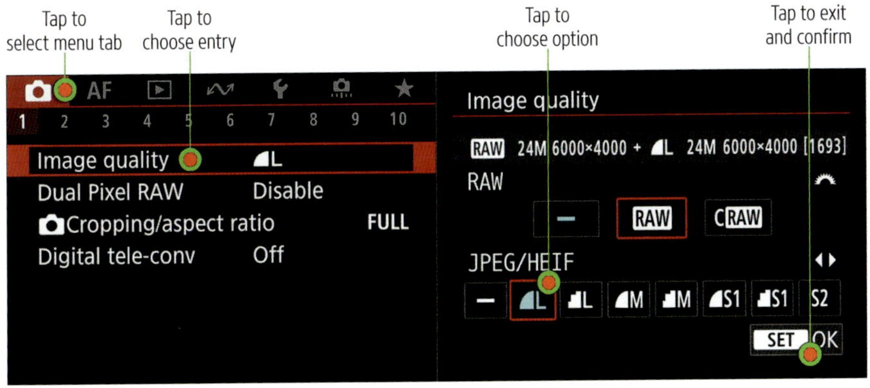

Figure 2.9 Select a menu tab and entry (left) and change settings (right).

- **Drag/swipe to select.** Many functions can be selected by touching the screen and then sliding your finger to the right or left until the item you want is highlighted. For example, instead of tapping, you can slide horizontally along the main menu's tabs to choose any Shooting, Playback, Custom, or My Menu tab. However, you can't slide vertically to choose an individual menu entry; tap the desired entry instead.

- **Drag/swipe to adjust scales.** Screens that contain a sliding scale can be adjusted by dragging. In Figure 2.10, left, the arrows show how you can drag along the scale to adjust LCD screen brightness, and at right, to add/subtract exposure compensation. You can also tap the minus/plus buttons and exit by tapping the SET/OK icon. Even when you are using the touch screen, you can still opt for the Main dial or QCD to make your changes.

- **Pinch/spread to reduce/enlarge.** During playback, you can use two fingers to "pinch" the screen to reduce/shrink the image, from, say, single-image to index view. Tap on a thumbnail to view it full size. Spread those two fingers apart to enlarge an image, to zoom in from, say, a nine-image index array to the four-image display, then to single image. If you continue spreading, you can magnify the image up to about 10X. Tap the return icon to resume single-image display. (See the arrows in the top half of Figure 2.11, left.)

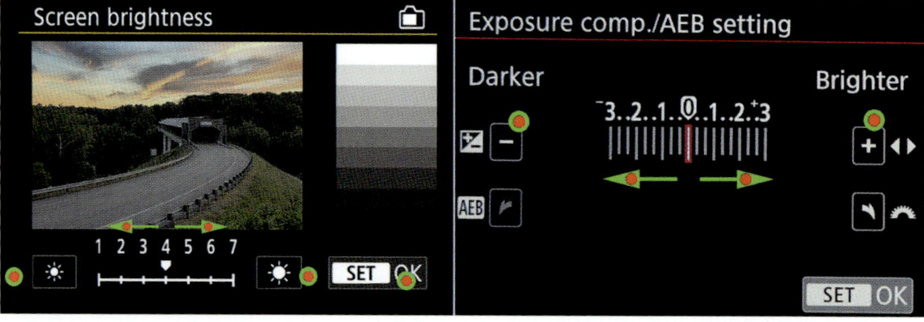

Figure 2.10 Use sliding scales or tap icons to make adjustments in screen brightness (left) and exposure compensation (right).

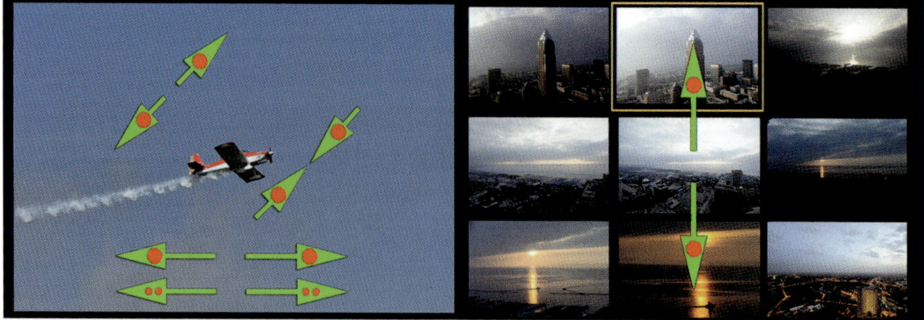

Figure 2.11 In Playback, pinch or spread fingers to magnify or reduce images (top left), and swipe/drag to move/jump among them (bottom left). You can scroll among thumbnails, too (right).

- **Drag/swipe to scroll among single images.** In Playback single-image mode, as you review your images, you can drag your finger left and right to advance from one image to another, much as you might do with a smartphone or tablet computer. Use one finger to scroll one image at a time, and two to jump using the image jump method you've chosen in the Playback 2 menu, as described in Chapter 13. The arrows at the bottom of Figure 2.11, left, represent this function.
- **Drag to scroll among thumbnails.** When viewing thumbnails, you can drag through the thumbnail screen to quickly move among sets of index images, as represented in Figure 2.11, right.
- **Fine-tune touch features.** As I'll explain in Chapter 9, you can enable or disable touch operation and change sensitivity from Standard to Sensitive in the Set-up 3 menu under the Touch Control entry. The click sound the touch feature makes can be turned on or off using the Beep setting in the Set-up 2 menu.
- **Avoid "protective" sheets, moisture, and sharp implements.** The LCD uses capacitive technology to sense your touch, rather than pressure sensitivity. LCD protectors or moisture can interfere with the touch functions, and styluses or sharp objects (such as pens) won't produce the desired results. I have, in fact, used "skins" on my camera's LCD with good results (even though the screen is quite rugged and really doesn't need protection from scratches), but there is no guarantee that all such protectors will work for you.

As I noted, the choice of whether to use the traditional buttons or touch screen is up to you. I've found that with some screens, the controls are too close together to be easily manipulated with my wide fingers. The touch screen can be especially dangerous when working with some functions, such as card formatting. In displays where the icons are large and few in number, such as the screen used to adjust LCD brightness, touch controls work just fine. Easiest of all is touch operation during Playback. It's a no-brainer to swipe your finger from side to side to scroll among images and pinch/spread to zoom out and in.

Going Topside

The top surface of the camera has its own set of frequently accessed controls. The key controls, and two additional lens control features, are shown in Figure 2.12.

- **Zoom scale.** Shows the current zoom focal length. (Only available on zoom lenses!)
- **Shutter release button.** Partially depress this button to lock in exposure and focus. Press all the way to take the picture. Tapping the shutter release button when the camera has turned off the auto-exposure and autofocus mechanisms reactivates both. When a review image is displayed on the back-panel color LCD, tapping this button removes the image from the display and reactivates the autoexposure and autofocus mechanisms.

Figure 2.12

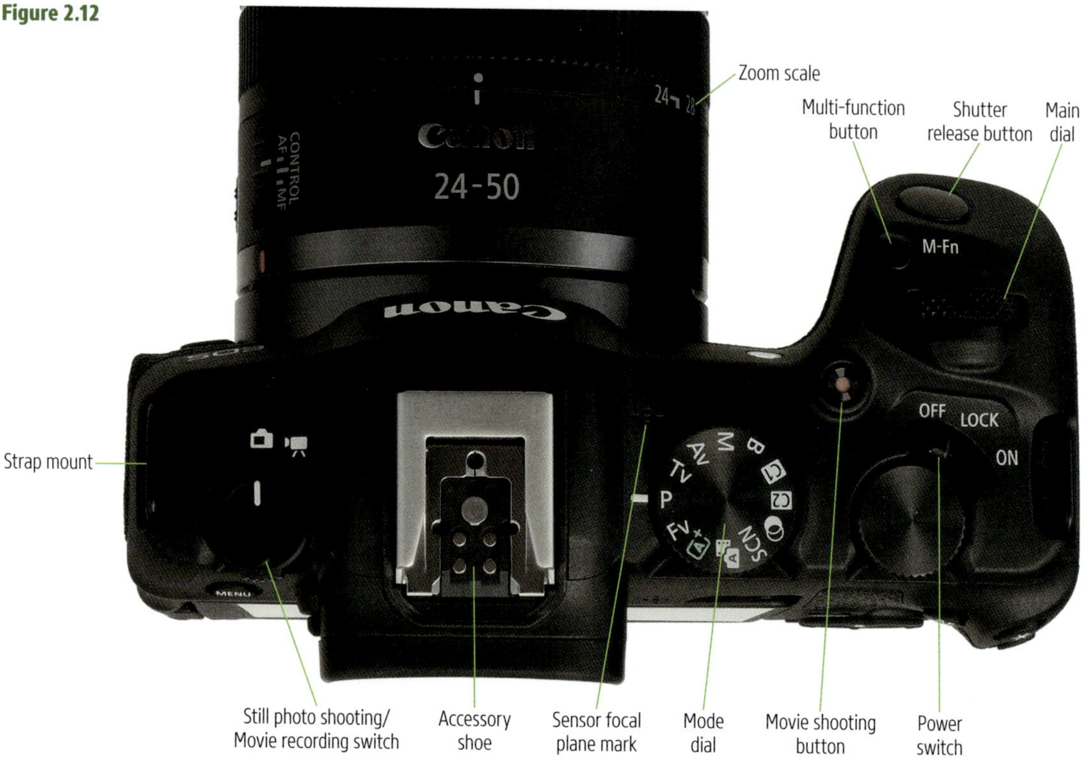

- **M-Fn button.** This multi-function button is used in two different ways:

  - **Dial functions.** By default, if you press this button alone, a pop-up horizontal list of functions will display, as seen in Figure 2.13. The display lists available functions, arranged in pairs. The default pairs are:

    - White Balance/Metering Mode
    - Drive Mode/AF Operation
    - Flash Exposure Compensation/ISO
    - Picture Style/Focus Area

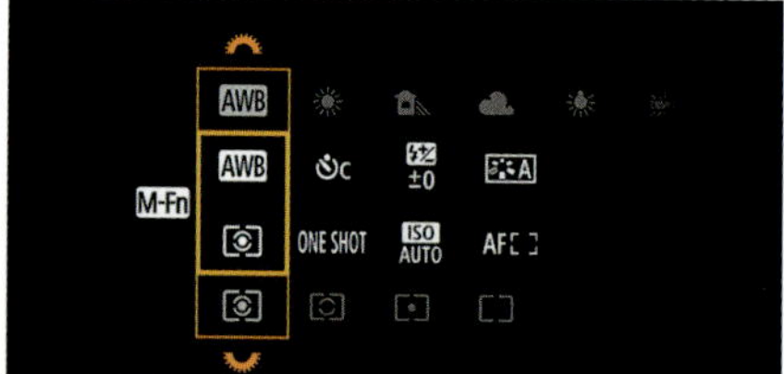

Figure 2.13 Dial functions appear when the M-Fn button is pressed.

  Once a function is highlighted you can rotate the Main dial to adjust the settings for the upper function, and the QCD to adjust the lower function. If you'd rather have different functions appear here, you can add or subtract others, as I'll describe in Chapter 15.

  - **Autofocus area selection mode.** Press the AF point selection button on the upper-right corner of the back of the camera (as described in Chapter 5). You can assign dozens of different functions to this control using the Custom Controls feature, as described in Chapter 15.

- **Main dial.** This dial is used to make many shooting settings. When settings come in pairs (such as shutter speed/aperture in Manual shooting mode), the Main dial is used for one (for example, shutter speed), while the QCD is used for the other (aperture). When an image is on the screen during playback, this dial also specifies the leaps that skip a particular number of images during playback of the shots you've already taken. Jumps can be 1 image, 10 images, 100 images, jump by date, or jump by screen (that is, by screens of thumbnails when using Index mode), date, or folder. (Jump method is selected in the Playback 6 menu, as described in Chapter 13.) This dial is also used to move among tabs when the MENU button has been pressed and is used within some menus (in conjunction with the QCD) to change pairs of settings.

- **Movie shooting button.** Press to start capturing video; press again to stop. You can redefine this button to perform any of 40 other functions if you like.

- **Still Photo Shooting/Movie Recording switch.** Selecting either Still or Movie mode gives you complete access to the still photography and movie menus, which differ slightly. However, you can capture movies even in Still mode by pressing the Movie shooting button. Only your movie options are limited.

- **Power switch.** Rotate to the far right to turn on the camera, and to the far left to turn it off. In the middle Lock position the camera is on, but certain controls can be frozen to prevent them from being changed accidentally. Move from the Lock position to unlock those controls. You can choose to lock any or all of the following: Main dial, QCD, Touch Control, or control ring. Choose which of these to lock using the Multi Function Lock entry in the Set-up 4 menu.

- **Accessory shoe.** Slide an electronic flash into this multi-purpose accessory shoe when you need an external Speedlite. A dedicated flash unit, like those from Canon, can use the multiple contact points shown to communicate exposure, zoom setting, white balance information, and other data between the flash and the camera. **Note:** Your EOS R8 has the updated Multi-Function shoe that can supply power to accessories (such as external microphones), and offers advanced communication functions found in the latest Canon EL-series Speedlites. There's more on using electronic flash in Chapters 9 and 10.

- **Sensor focal plane mark.** Precision macro and scientific photography sometimes requires knowing exactly where the focal plane of the sensor is. The symbol marks that plane.

- **Strap mount.** A neck strap fastens to this mount, with a matching mount on the other side of the camera.

- **Mode dial.** Rotate to select one of the available exposure modes and to choose one of the camera user settings.

Underneath Your Camera

There's not a lot going on with the bottom panel of your camera (see Figure 2.14).

Figure 2.14

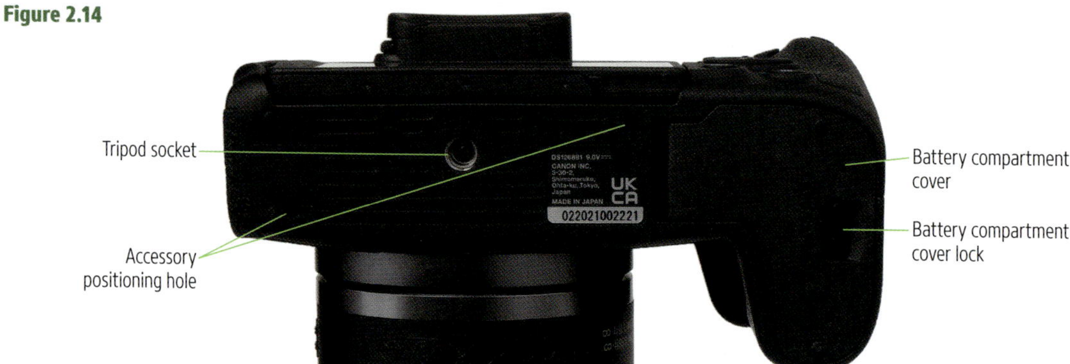

Here, you'll find the following:

- **Tripod socket.** Secures the camera to a tripod and is also used to lock on the optional Extension Grip EG-E1, an extension that some find helps the compact EOS R8 fit their hands better. (See Figure 2.15.)
- **Accessory positioning holes.** Fit matching studs on the extension grip.
- **Battery compartment cover/cover lock.** Slide the cover lock latch toward the center of the camera to open the battery compartment cover and access the LP-E17 battery. Retract the gray battery release tab to remove the battery.

To mount the EG-E1 grip, first remove the battery door. When the door is open, push down on the small black door release switch (highlighted with a green box at left in Figure 2.16), to retract the hinge pin so you can remove the battery door. You can then attach the grip, aligning the grip with the small accessory positioning holes on the other side of the tripod socket. Tighten the grip's tripod socket screw to lock the grip onto the bottom of your camera.

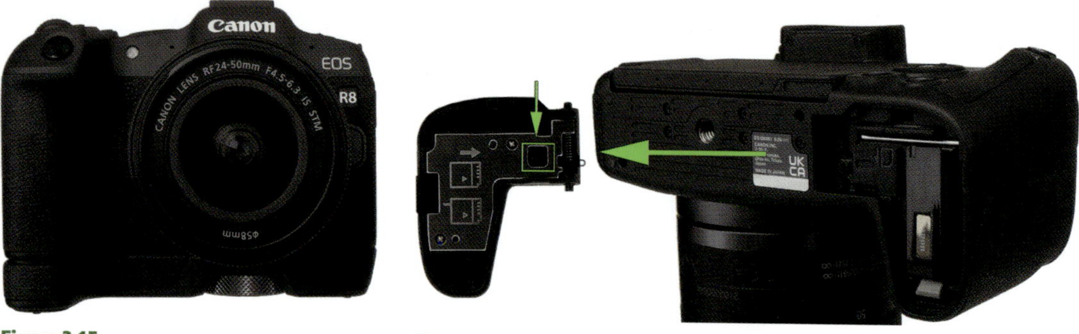

Figure 2.15   **Figure 2.16**

Recommended Settings 3

This chapter is purely optional, especially for those who are new to an advanced Canon at the level of the R8, who should skip it entirely for now, and return when they've gained some experience with this full-featured camera. This section is for the benefit of those who want to know *now* some of the most common changes I recommend to the default settings of your camera. Canon has excellent reasons for using these settings as a default; I have better reasons for changing them.

Changing Default Settings

Even if this is your first experience with a Canon digital camera, you can easily make a few changes to the default settings that I'm going to recommend, and then take your time learning *why* I suggest these changes when they're explained in the more detailed chapters of this book. I'm not going to provide step-by-step instructions for changing settings here; I'll give you an overview of how to make any setting adjustment and leave you to navigate through the fairly intuitive menu system to make the changes yourself. Or, you can jump ahead to Chapters 11 to 14 for more detailed instructions on a particular setting.

Resetting to Factory Defaults

If you want to change from the factory default values, you might think that it would be a good idea to make sure that the camera is set to the factory defaults in the first place. After all, even a brand-new camera might have had its settings changed at the retailer, or during a demo. Most of the time, however, you'll prefer to use the Reset Camera option in the Set-up 5 menu, which has two options: Basic Settings and Other Settings. Basic Settings restores the default adjustments for camera shooting functions and menu settings. Regardless of how you've set up your camera, it will be adjusted to One-Shot AF mode, Evaluative metering, Single-shot drive mode, JPEG Fine Large image quality, Automatic ISO, sRGB color mode, Automatic White Balance, Auto Lighting Optimizer Off, and Standard Picture Style. Any changes you've made to exposure compensation, flash exposure compensation, and white balance will be canceled, and any bracketing for exposure or white balance nullified. Custom white balances and Dust Delete Data will be erased.

The Other Settings option restores factory defaults for Customize Quick Controls, Shooting Information Display, Root Certificate, Communication Settings, Shooting Information Display, Custom Shooting Modes (1–3), Copyright Information, Customized Controls, Custom Functions (C.Fn), and My Menu. You'll also find a Clear Customized Settings in the Custom Functions 3 menu, which resets Customize Buttons and Customize Dials settings and Clear All Custom Functions in the Custom Functions 5 menu, all explained in Chapter 14.

The tables that follow show the settings defaults after using the Basic Settings menu resetting option. They include many (but not all) menu settings (some menu items are functions rather than settings) as well as camera settings such as Drive mode. You'll find the default values and settings options for Movie Shooting in Chapter 15.

TABLE 3.1 Still Photo Shooting Menu Defaults

Image Quality	Large, Fine	Clarity	0
Dual Pixel RAW	Disable	Shooting Creative Filters	Off
Cropping/Aspect Ratio	Full	Lens Aberration Correction	
Digital Tele-Converter	Off	Peripheral Illumination Correction	Enable
Exposure Compensation/Auto Exposure Bracketing	0	Distortion Correction	Disable
		Digital Lens Optimizer	Standard
ISO Speed Settings		Long Exposure Noise Reduction	Disable
ISO Speed	Auto	High ISO Speed Noise Reduction	Standard
ISO Speed Range	Minimum: 100	Dust Delete Data	Erased
	Maximum: 102,400	Multiple Exposure	Disable
Auto Range	Minimum: 100	RAW Burst Mode	Disable
	Maximum: 25,600	Focus Bracketing	Disable
Minimum Shutter Speed for Auto	Auto	Drive Mode	Single Shooting
HDR PQ Settings	Off	Interval Timer	Disable
HDR Mode	Off	Bulb Timer	Disable
Auto Lighting Optimizer	Standard	Silent Shutter Function	Off
Highlight Tone Priority	Off	Shutter Mode	Electronic 1st-curtain
Anti-Flicker Shooting	Disable		
High-Frequency Anti-Flicker Shooting	Off	Release Shutter Without Card	On
External Speedlite Control		IS (Image Stabilizer) Mode	
Flash Firing	Enable	Digital IS	Off
E-TTL Balance	Standard	Touch Shutter	Off
E-TTL Metering	Evaluative (Face-priority)	Image Review	2 seconds
Continuous Flash Control	E-TTL Each Shot	Review Duration	2 seconds
Slow Synchro	1/200 to 1/60 Second Auto	Viewfinder Review	Disable
Flash Function Settings	--	High-Speed Display	Off
Flash Custom Function Settings	--	Metering Timer	8 seconds
White Balance	AWB (Ambience-priority)	Display Simulation	Exposure
		Optical Viewfinder Simulated View Assist	Off
Custom White Balance	Canceled	Shooting Information Display	--
WB Shift/Bracket	0,0/+-0	Viewfinder Display Format	Display 1
Color Space	sRGB	Display Performance	Power Saving
Picture Style	Auto		

TABLE 3.2 AF Menu Defaults

AF Operation	One-Shot AF	AF Method Selection Control	M-Fn
AF Area	Whole Area AF	Multi-controller Sensitivity—AF Point Select	0
Whole Area Tracking Servo AF	On		
Subject to Detect	People	Orientation-Linked AF Point	Same for both Vertical/Horizontal
Eye Detection	Auto		
Switching Tracked Subjects	1	Limit Subject to Detect	All Selected
Servo AF	Case A (Auto)	Left/Right Eye Detection	All Enabled
One-Shot AF Release Priority	Focus-priority	MF Peaking Settings	Off
Preview AF	Disable	Level	High
Lens Drive when AF Impossible	On: Continue Focus Search	Color	Red
		Focus Guide	Off
AF-assist Beam Firing	On	Movie Servo AF Characteristics	Enable
Touch & Drag AF Settings	Disable	Lens Electronic MF	Disable after One-Shot
Positioning Method	Relative		
Active Touch Area	Right	Focus Ring Rotation	Normal: −+
Relative Sensitivity	0	RF Lens Manual Focus Ring Sensitivity	Varies with rotation speed
Limit AF Methods	All Enabled		

TABLE 3.3 Playback Menu Defaults

View From Last Seen	Enable	Playback Information Display	All Selected
Magnification		Highlight Alert	Disable
Magnification	2X	AF Point Display	Disable
Magnified Position	From Focus Point	Playback Grid	Off
Maintain Position	Disable	Move Play Count	Rec. Time
Image Jump	10 images	HDMI HDR Output	Off

TABLE 3.4 Set-up Menu Defaults

Record Function+Card/Folder Selection		Format Card	--
Still/Movies Separate	Disable	Auto Rotate	Camera+Computer
Still/Movies Record Options	Standard	Add Movie Rotate Information	Disable
Still/Movies Slot	Slot 1	Date/Time/Zone	--
Folder Name	100EOSR8	Language	Varies by Country
File Numbering	Continuous	Video System	NTSC or PAL
File Name		Help Text Size	Small
File Name	Preset unique code	Mode Guide	Enable
User Setting 1	IMG_	Feature Guide	Enable
User Setting 2	IMG+Image Size		

TABLE 3.4 Set-up Menu Defaults *(continued)*

Beep	Enable	Screen/Viewfinder Color Tone	2
Volume		Fine-Tune VF Color Tone	--
Shutter Volume	3	User Interface Magnification	Disable
Focused Beep	3	HDMI Resolution	Auto
Touch Sounds	0	Touch Control	Standard
Self-timer Volume	3	Multi Function Lock	--
Beep Per Interval Timer Exposure Taken	3	Shutter at Shutdown	Closed
Headphones		Sensor Cleaning	Off
Volume	8	Choose USB Connection App	Photo Import/ Remote Control
Audio Monitoring	Real-time	Reset Camera	--
Power Saving		Custom Shooting Mode (C1–C3)	--
Screen Dimmer	10 seconds	Battery Information	Unchanged
Screen Off	Disable	Copyright Information	Unchanged
Auto Power Off	30 seconds	Manual/Software URL	Unchanged
Viewfinder Off	1 minute	Certification Logo Display	Unchanged
Screen/Viewfinder Display	Auto 1	Firmware	Unchanged
Screen Brightness	4		
Viewfinder Brightness	Auto		

TABLE 3.5 Custom Functions Defaults

Exposure Level Increments	1/3 stop	Control Ring Direction to Set Tv/Av	– +
ISO Speed Setting Increments	1/3 stop	Switch Dials When Shooting	Off
Speed From Metering/ISO Auto	Restore Auto after metering	Customize Buttons	Erased
		Customize Dials	Erased
Bracketing Auto Cancel	On	Clear Customized Settings	N/A
Bracketing Sequence	0–+	Add Cropping Information	Off
Number of Bracketed Shots	3	Audio Compression	On
Safety Shift	Off	Default Erase Option	Cancel Selected
Same Exposure for New Aperture	Off	Release Shutter without Lens	Off
AE Lock Metering Mode after Focus	Erased	Retract Lens on Power Off	On
Set Shutter Speed Range	Erased	Add IPTC Information	Off
Set Aperture Range	Erased	Clear All Custom Functions	--
Dial Direction to Set Tv/Av	– +		

Recommended Default Changes

Although I won't be explaining how to use the menu system in detail until Chapters 11 to 14, you can make some simple changes now. These general instructions will serve you to make any of the setting changes I recommend next. It's likely that experienced photographers won't need the settings charts that follow, but I'm including some basic recommendations for those who want some guidance in shooting particular types of subjects. You'll find specific types for functions like autofocus and other features later in this book.

The camera divides its menu entries into "tabbed" sections—Shooting, Autofocus, Playback, Network, Set-up, Custom Functions, and My Menu—which, except for My Menu, each have separate pages. The available pages can vary, depending on your shooting mode, as I'll explain in Chapter 11.

To access menus, tap the MENU button. Use the Main dial to move from menu to menu, and the QCD to highlight a particular menu entry. Press the Q/SET button to select a menu item. You can also navigate with the directional controls or use the touch screen. When you've highlighted the menu item you want to work with, press the Q/SET button to select it. The current settings for the other menu items in the list will be hidden, and a list of options for the selected menu item (or a submenu screen) will appear. Or, you may be shown a separate settings screen for that entry. Within the menu choices, you can scroll up or down with the QCD; press Q/SET to select the choice you've made; and press the MENU button again to exit.

Once you've made changes for a specific type of shooting, you should store each set of parameters in one of the Custom Shooting mode user slots C1 or C2 in the Set-up 5 menu, as explained in Chapter 13. Here are some recommended settings to consider. Note that these tables don't correspond to entire menus; I'm listing only the settings that need attention. If a particular parameter is not listed, you can use a setting of your choice.

TABLE 3.6 Default, All Purpose, Sports: Outdoors, Sports: Indoors

	DEFAULT	ALL PURPOSE	SPORTS: OUTDOORS	SPORTS: INDOORS
SETTINGS				
Exposure Mode	Your choice	Your choice	Tv	Tv
Autofocus Mode	One-Shot AF	Servo AF	Servo AF	Servo AF
Drive Mode	Single Shooting	Single Shooting	Continuous Shooting	Continuous Shooting
SHOOTING MENUS				
Beep	Enable	Enable	Enable	Enable
Image Review	2 seconds	2 seconds	Off	Off
Metering Mode	Evaluative	Evaluative	Evaluative	Evaluative
Color Space	sRGB	sRGB	sRGB	sRGB
Picture Style	Standard/Auto	Auto	Standard	Standard
ISO Speed	Auto	Auto	800–3200	800–3200
ISO Speed Range	100–102,400	100–12,800	200–3200	200–12,800
Auto ISO Range	100–25,600	100–6400	200–6400	400–12,800
ISO Auto Minimum Shutter Speed	Auto	Auto	1/200	1/200
Long Exposure NR	Off	Disable	Disable	Disable
High ISO speed NR	Standard	Standard	Standard	Standard
Highlight Tone Priority	Disable	Disable	Disable	Disable
AF MENUS				
AF Assist Beam	Enable	Enable	Disable	Disable
AF Area	Whole Area AF	Whole Area AF	Whole Area AF	Zone AF

TABLE 3.7 **Stage Performances, Long Exposure, HDR, Portrait**

	STAGE PERFORMANCES	LONG EXPOSURE	HDR	PORTRAIT
SETTINGS				
Exposure Mode	Your choice	Manual/ Your choice	One-Shot	One-Shot
Autofocus Mode	One-Shot	One-Shot	One-Shot	Servo AF
Drive Mode	Continuous Shooting	Single Shooting	Continuous Shooting	Continuous Shooting
SHOOTING MENUS				
Beep	Disable	Enable	Enable	Enable
Image Review	Off	Off	Off	2 seconds
Metering Mode	Spot	Center-weighted	Evaluative	Center-weighted
Color Space	Adobe RGB	Adobe RGB	Adobe RGB	Adobe RGB
Picture Style	User—Reduce contrast, add sharpening	Neutral	Standard	Portrait
ISO Speed	800–3200	800–3200	Auto	Auto
ISO Speed Range	100–32,000	100–12,800	200–3200	200–1600
Auto ISO Range	100–12,800	100–6400	200–6400	100–3200
ISO Auto Minimum Shutter Speed	Auto	Auto	1/200	1/200
Long Exposure NR	Disable	Disable	Disable	Disable
High ISO Speed NR	Standard	Standard	Standard	Standard
Highlight Tone Priority	Disable	Disable	Disable	Disable
AF MENUS				
AF Assist Beam	Disable	Disable	Disable	Disable
AF Area	1-point AF	1-point AF	Expand AF	1-point AF

TABLE 3.8 Studio Flash, Landscape, Macro, Travel, E-Mail

	STUDIO FLASH	LANDSCAPE	MACRO	TRAVEL	E-MAIL
SETTINGS					
Exposure Mode	Manual	Av	Tv	Tv	Av
Autofocus Mode	One-Shot	One-Shot	Manual	One-Shot	One-Shot
Drive Mode	Single Shooting	Single Shooting	Single Shooting	Single Shooting	Single Shooting
SHOOTING MENUS					
Beep	Disable	Enable	Enable	Enable	Enable
Image Review	2 seconds	2 seconds	2 seconds	2 seconds	2 seconds
Metering Mode	Evaluative	Evaluative	Spot	Evaluative	Evaluative
Color Space	Adobe RGB	Adobe RGB	Adobe RGB	Adobe RGB	Adobe RGB
Picture Style	User—Reduce contrast, add sharpening	Landscape	Auto	Landscape	Auto
ISO Speed	100–400	100–1600	100–1600	Auto	Auto
ISO Speed Range	100–32,000	100–12,800	200–3200	200–1600	100–3200
Auto ISO Range	100–12,800	100–6400	200–6400	100–3200	100–6400
ISO Auto Minimum Shutter Speed	Auto	Auto	1/200	1/200	Auto
Long Exposure NR	Disable	Disable	Disable	Disable	Disable
High ISO Speed NR	Standard	Standard	Standard	Standard	Standard
Highlight Tone Priority	Disable	Enable	Disable	Enable	Enable
AF MENUS					
AF Assist Beam	Disable	Disable	Disable	Disable	Disable
AF Area	Expand AF Area	Zone AF	Manual Focus	Expand AF Area: Around	Expand AF Area
SET-UP MENUS					
Auto Power Off	1 minute	Disable	Disable	Disable	Disable
LCD Brightness	Dimmer	Dimmer	Medium	Medium	Medium

Nailing the Right Exposure | 4

As you learn to use your EOS R8 creatively, you're going to find that the right settings—as determined by the camera's exposure meter and intelligence—need to be *adjusted* to account for your creative decisions or to fine-tune the image for special situations.

For example, when you shoot with the main light source behind the subject, you end up with *backlighting*, which results in an overexposed background and/or an underexposed subject. The camera recognizes backlit situations nicely, and can properly base exposure on the main subject, producing a decent photo. Features like Highlight Tone Priority and the Auto Lighting Optimizer can fine-tune exposure to preserve detail in the highlights and shadows.

But what if you *want* to underexpose the subject, to produce a silhouette effect? Or, perhaps, you might want to use an external electronic flash to fill in the shadows on your subject. The more you know about how to use your camera, the more you'll run into situations where you want to creatively tweak the exposure to provide a different look than you'd get with a straight shot.

This chapter shows you the fundamentals of exposure, so you'll be better equipped to override the default settings when you want to or need to. After all, correct exposure is one of the foundations of good photography, along with accurate focus and sharpness, appropriate color balance, freedom from unwanted noise and excessive contrast, as well as pleasing composition. When you finish this chapter, you'll understand most of what you need to know to take well-exposed photographs creatively in a broad range of situations with the camera.

Getting a Handle on Exposure

This section explains the fundamental concepts that go into creating an exposure. If you already know about the role of f/stops, shutter speeds, and sensor sensitivity in determining an exposure, you might want to skip to the next section.

You're probably aware of the traditional "exposure triangle" of aperture (quantity of light and light passed by the lens), shutter speed (the amount of time the shutter is open), and the ISO sensitivity of the sensor—all working proportionately and reciprocally to produce an exposure. The trio is itself affected by the amount of illumination that is available. So, if you double the amount of light, increase the aperture by one stop, make the shutter speed twice as long, or boost the ISO setting 2X, you'll get twice as much exposure. Similarly, you can increase any of these factors while decreasing one of the others by a similar amount to keep the same exposure.

Working with any of the three controls involves trade-offs. Larger f/stops provide less depth-of-field, while smaller f/stops increase depth-of-field (and potentially at the same time can *decrease* sharpness through a phenomenon called *diffraction*). Shorter shutter speeds do a better job of reducing the effects of camera/subject motion, while longer shutter speeds make that motion blur more likely. Higher ISO settings increase the amount of visual noise and artifacts in your image, while lower ISO settings reduce the effects of noise. (See Figure 4.1.)

Figure 4.1 The traditional exposure triangle includes aperture, shutter speed, and ISO sensitivity.

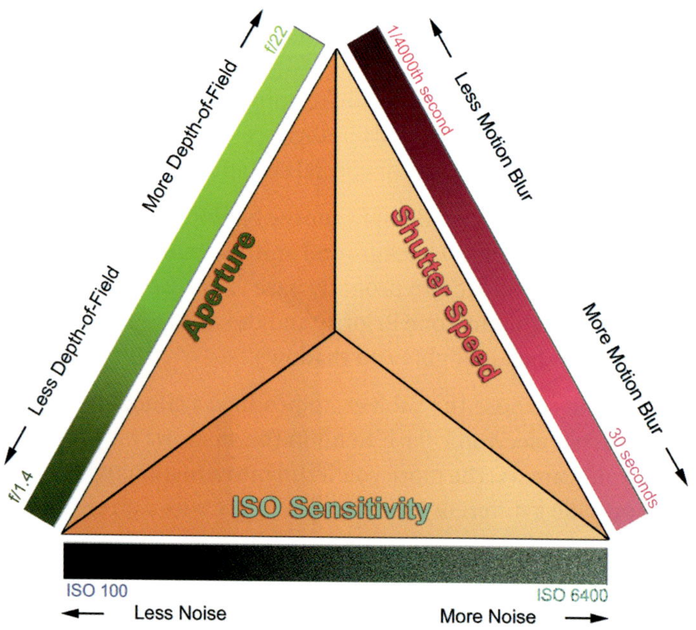

Exposure determines the look, feel, and tone of an image, in more ways than one. Incorrect exposure can impair even the best-composed image by cloaking important tones in darkness, or by washing them out so they become featureless to the eye. On the other hand, correct exposure brings out the detail in the areas you want to picture and provides the range of tones and colors you need to create the desired image. However, getting the perfect exposure can be tricky because digital sensors can't capture all the tones we can see. If the range of tones in an image is extensive, embracing both inky black shadows and bright highlights, the sensor may not be able to capture them all. Sometimes, we must settle for an exposure that renders most of those tones—but not all—in a way that best suits the photo we want to produce. You'll often need to make choices about which details are important, and which are not, so that you can grab the tones that truly matter in your image. That's part of the creativity you bring to bear in realizing your photographic vision.

For example, look at two bracketed exposures presented at top in Figure 4.2. For the image at upper left, the brightest areas, including the sky, have sufficient detail, but the shadows are cloaked in darkness. The upper-right version provides better renditions of the darker areas, but the highlights are too bright. The camera's sensor simply can't capture detail in both dark areas and bright areas in a single shot.

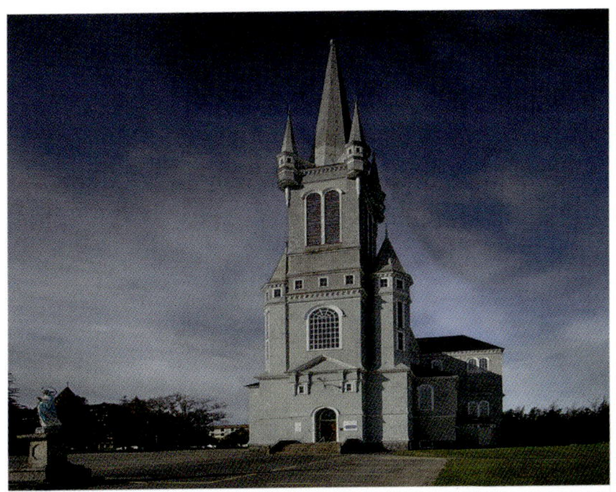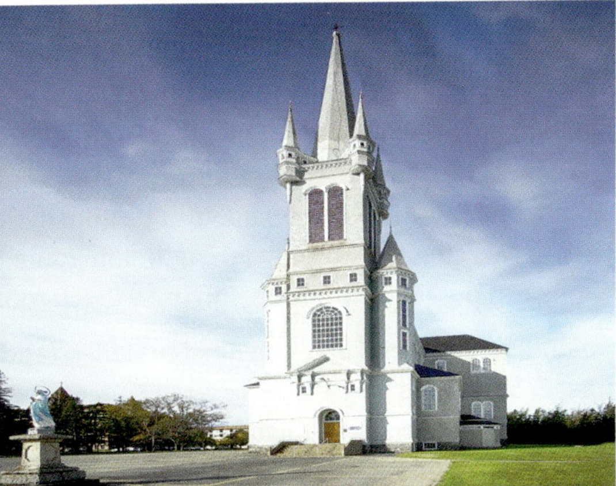

Figure 4.2 Combining the two bracketed exposures at top using HDR produces the best compromise image (bottom).

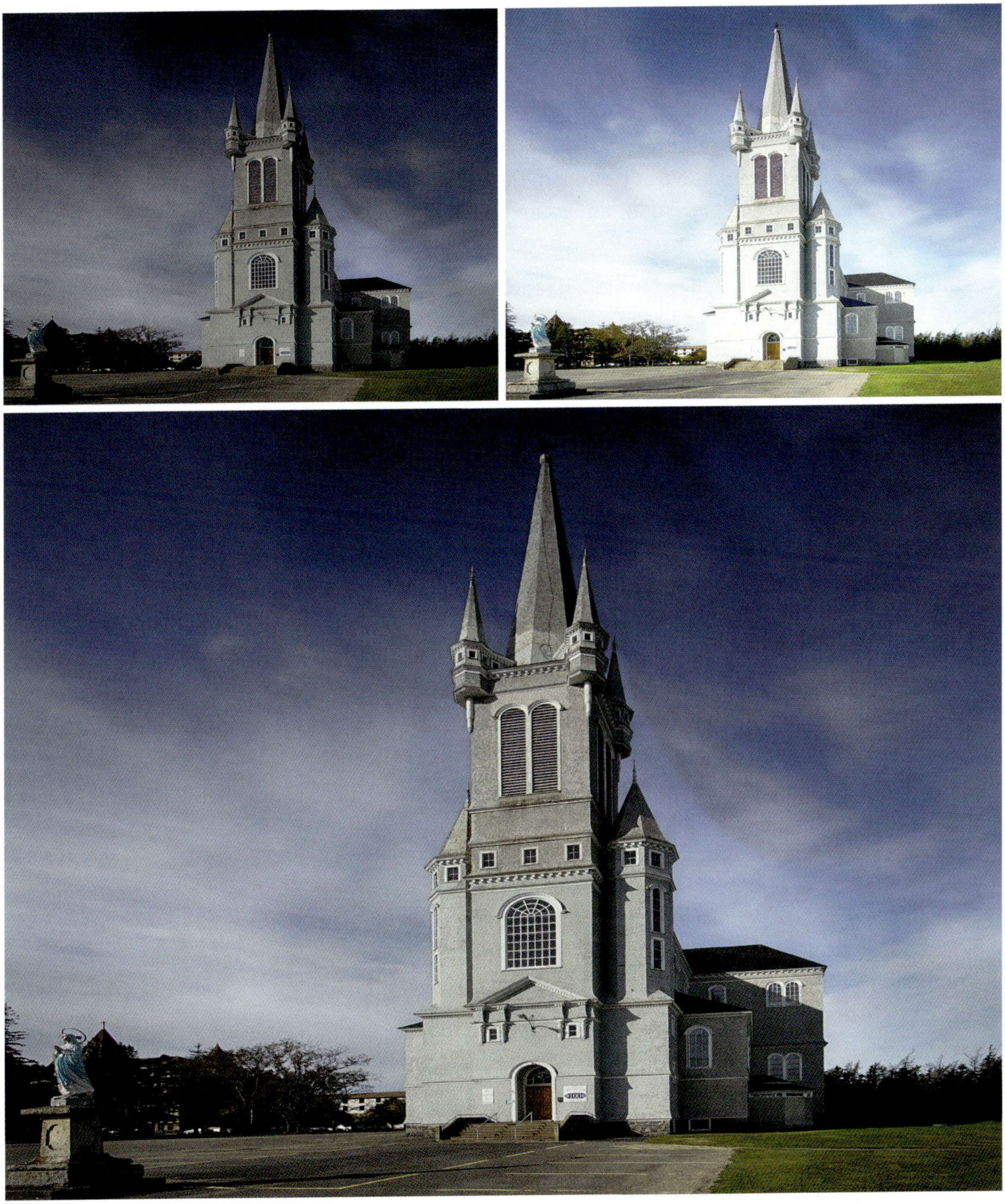

With digital camera sensors, it's tricky to capture detail in both highlights and shadows in a single image, because the number of tones, the *dynamic range* of the sensor, is limited. The solution, in this case, was to resort to a technique called High Dynamic Range (HDR) photography, in which the two upper exposures in Figure 4.2 were combined in an image editor such as Photoshop, or a specialized HDR tool like Photomatix and Aurora HDR (from www.hdrsoft.com and www.skylum.com, respectively). The resulting shot is shown at bottom in the figure. I'll explain more about HDR photography later in this chapter. For now, though, I'm going to concentrate on showing you how to get the best exposures possible without resorting to such tools, using only the features of your camera.

To understand exposure, you need to understand the six aspects of light that combine to produce an image. Start with a light source—the sun, an interior lamp, or the glow from a campfire—and trace its path to your camera, through the lens, and finally to the sensor that captures the illumination. Here's a brief review of the things within our control that affect exposure:

- **Light at its source.** Our eyes and our cameras—film or digital—are most sensitive to that portion of the electromagnetic spectrum we call *visible light.* That light has several important aspects that are relevant to photography, such as color and harshness (which is determined primarily by the apparent size of the light source as it illuminates a subject). But, in terms of exposure, the important attribute of a light source is its *intensity.* We may have direct control over intensity, which might be the case with an interior light that can be brightened or dimmed. Or, we might have only indirect control over intensity, as with sunlight, which can be made to appear dimmer by introducing translucent light-absorbing or reflective materials in its path.

- **Light's duration.** We tend to think of most light sources as continuous. But, as you'll learn in Chapter 9, the duration of light can change quickly enough to modify the exposure, as when the main illumination in a photograph comes from an intermittent source, such as an electronic flash.

- **Light reflected, transmitted, or emitted.** Once light is produced by its source, either continuously or in a brief burst, we can see and photograph objects by the light that is reflected from our subjects toward the camera lens; transmitted (say, from translucent objects that are lit from behind); or emitted (by a candle or television screen). When more or less light reaches the lens from the subject, we need to adjust the exposure. This part of the equation is under our control to the extent we can increase the amount of light falling on or passing through the subject (by adding extra light sources or using reflectors), or by pumping up the light that's emitted (by increasing the brightness of the glowing object).

- **Light passed by the lens.** Not all the illumination that reaches the front of the lens makes it all the way through. Filters can remove some of the light before it enters the lens. Inside the lens barrel is a variable-sized diaphragm that dilates and contracts to vary the size of the aperture and control the amount of light that enters the lens. You, or the camera's autoexposure system, can control exposure by varying the size of the aperture. The relative size of the aperture is called the *f/stop.*

- **Light passing through the shutter.** Once light passes through the lens, the amount of time the sensor receives it is determined by the camera's shutter, which can remain open for as long as 30 seconds (or even longer if you use the Bulb setting) or as briefly as 1/8000th second (or 1/16,000th second with the electronic shutter).

- **Light captured by the sensor.** Not all the light falling onto the sensor is captured. With the sensor found in the R8, the sites that capture the image share the front surface with other electronic components, so the photosensitive area is reduced. In addition, if the number of photons reaching a particular photosite don't pass a particular threshold, no information is recorded. Similarly, if too much light illuminates a pixel in the sensor, then the excess isn't recorded or, worse, spills over to contaminate adjacent pixels. We can modify the minimum and maximum number of pixels that contribute to image detail by adjusting the ISO setting. At higher ISOs, the incoming light is amplified to boost the effective sensitivity of the sensor.

These factors—the quantity of light produced by the light source, the amount reflected or transmitted toward the camera, the light passed by the lens, the amount of time the shutter is open, and the sensitivity of the sensor—all work proportionately and reciprocally to produce an exposure. That is, if you double the amount of light that's available, increase the aperture by one stop, make the shutter speed twice as long, or boost the ISO setting 2X, you'll get twice as much exposure. Similarly, you can increase any of these factors while decreasing one of the others by a similar amount to keep the same exposure.

F/STOPS AND SHUTTER SPEEDS

If you're *really* new to more advanced cameras (and I realize that many soon-to-be-ambitious photographers do purchase this camera as their first digital SLR), you might need to know that the lens aperture, or f/stop, is a ratio, much like a fraction, which is why f/2 is larger than f/4, just as 1/2 is larger than 1/4. However, f/2 is actually *four times* as large as f/4. (If you remember your high school geometry, you'll know that to double the area of a circle, you multiply its diameter by the square root of two: 1.4.)

Lenses are usually marked with intermediate f/stops that represent a size that's twice as much/half as much as the previous aperture. So, a lens might be marked f/2, f/2.8, f/4, f/5.6, f/8, f/11, f/16, or f/22, with each larger number representing an aperture that admits half as much light as the one before.

Shutter speeds are actual fractions (of a second), but the numerator is omitted, so that 60, 125, 250, 500, 1,000, and so forth represent 1/60th, 1/125th, 1/200th, 1/500th, and 1/1000th second. To avoid confusion, Canon uses quotation marks to signify longer exposures: 2", 2"5, 4", and so forth representing 2.0-, 2.5-, and 4.0-second exposures, respectively.

Most commonly, exposure settings are made using the aperture and shutter speed, followed by adjusting the ISO sensitivity if it's not possible to get the preferred exposure; that is, the one that uses the "best" f/stop or shutter speed for the depth-of-field (range of sharp focus) or action stopping we want (produced by short shutter speeds, as I'll explain later). Table 4.1 shows equivalent exposure settings using various shutter speeds and f/stops.

TABLE 4.1 Equivalent Exposures

SHUTTER SPEED	F/STOP	SHUTTER SPEED	F/STOP
1/30th second	f/22	1/1000th second	f/4
1/60th second	f/16	1/2000th second	f/2.8
1/125th second	f/11	1/4000th second	f/2
1/200th second	f/8	1/8000th second	f/1.4
1/500th second	f/5.6		

When the camera is set for P (Program) mode, the metering system selects the correct exposure for you automatically, but you can change quickly to an equivalent exposure by locking the current exposure (hold the shutter release button down halfway, or press the * button), and then spinning the Main dial until the desired *equivalent* exposure combination is displayed. You can use this standard Program Shift feature more easily if you remember that you need to rotate the dial toward the *left* when you want to increase the amount of depth-of-field or use a slower shutter speed; rotate to the *right* when you want to reduce the depth-of-field or use a faster shutter speed. The need for more/less DOF and slower/faster shutter speed are the primary reasons you'd want to use Program Shift. I'll explain Program mode exposure shifting options in more detail later in this chapter.

In Aperture-priority (Av) and Shutter-priority (Tv) modes (or Fv mode when you opt to choose either aperture or shutter speed manually), you can change to an equivalent exposure using a different combination of shutter speed and aperture, but only by either adjusting the aperture in Aperture-priority mode (the camera then chooses the shutter speed) or shutter speed in Shutter-priority mode (the camera then selects the aperture). I'll cover all these exposure modes and their differences later in the chapter.

Correctly Exposed

The image shown in Figure 4.3, left, represents how a photograph might appear if you inserted the patches shown at bottom left into the scene, and then calculated exposure by measuring the light reflecting from the middle gray patch, which, for the sake of illustration, we'll assume reflects approximately 12 to 18 percent of the light that strikes it. The gray patch also happens to be similar in reflectance to the background behind the subject. The exposure meter in the camera sees an object that it thinks is a middle gray, calculates an exposure based on that, and the patch in the center of the strip is rendered at its proper tonal value. Best of all, because the resulting exposure is correct, the black patch at left and white patch at right are rendered properly as well.

When you're shooting pictures with your camera, and the meter happens to base its exposure on a subject that averages that "ideal" middle gray, you'll end up with similar (accurate) results. The camera's exposure algorithms are concocted to ensure this kind of result as often as possible, barring any unusual subjects (that is, those that are backlit, or have uneven illumination). The camera has four different metering modes, each of which is equipped to handle certain types of unusual subjects, as I'll outline.

Overexposed

Figure 4.3, center, shows what would happen if the exposure were calculated based on metering the leftmost, black patch, which is roughly the same tonal value of the darkest areas of the subject's hair. The light meter sees less light reflecting from the black square than it would see from a gray middle-tone subject, and so figures, "Aha! I need to add exposure to brighten this subject up to a middle gray!" That lightens the "black" patch, so it now appears to be gray.

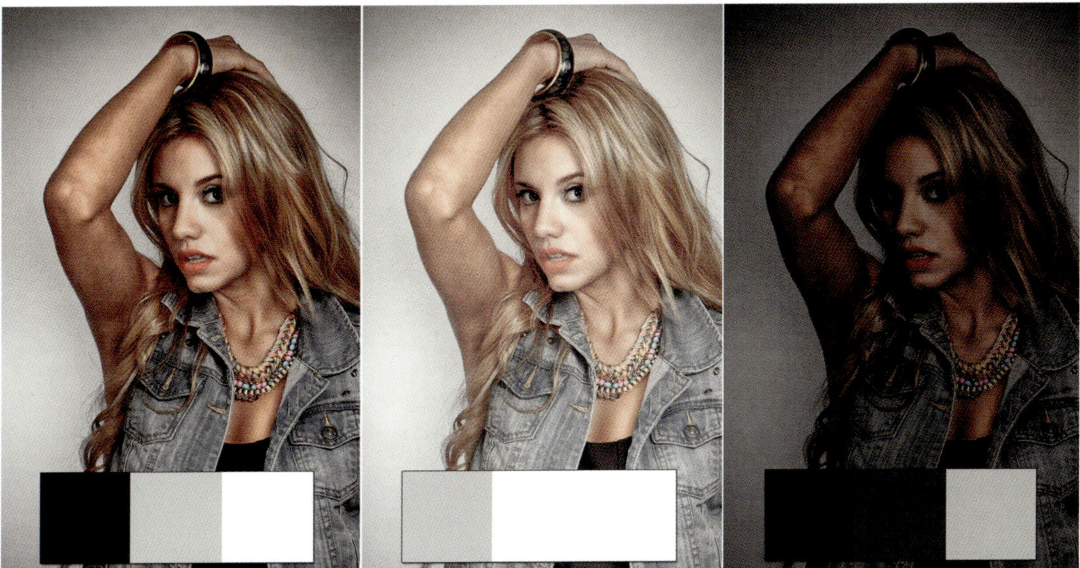

Figure 4.3 Left: When exposure is calculated based on the middle-gray tone in the center of the card, the black and white patches are rendered accurately, too. Center: When exposure is calculated based on the black square, the black patch looks gray, the gray patch appears to be a light gray, and the white square is seriously overexposed. Right: When exposure is calculated based on the white patch on the right, the photo is underexposed.

But now the patch in the middle that was *originally* middle gray is overexposed and becomes light gray. And the white square at right is now seriously overexposed and loses detail in the highlights, which have become a featureless white. Our human subject is similarly overexposed.

Underexposed

The third possibility in this simplified scenario is that the light meter might measure the illumination bouncing off the white patch, and try to render *that* tone as a middle gray. A lot of light is reflected by the white square, so the exposure is *reduced*, bringing that patch closer to a middle-gray tone. The patches that were originally gray and black are now rendered too dark. Clearly, measuring the gray patch—or a substitute that reflects about the same amount of light, such as the standard Kodak gray card sold in many photo stores—is the only way to ensure that the exposure is precisely correct. (See Figure 4.3, right.)

As you can see, the ideal way to measure exposure is to meter from a subject that reflects 12 to 18 percent of the light that reaches it. If you want the most precise exposure calculations, the solution is to use a stand-in, such as the evenly illuminated gray card I just mentioned. But, because the standard Kodak gray card reflects 18 percent of the light that reaches it and your camera is calibrated for a somewhat darker 12 percent tone, you would need to add about one-half stop *more* exposure than the value metered from the card.

In some very bright scenes (like a snowy landscape or a lava field), you won't have a mid-tone to meter. Another substitute for a gray card is the palm of a human hand (the backside of the hand is too variable). But a human palm, regardless of ethnic group, is even brighter than a standard gray card, so instead of one-half stop more exposure, you need to add one additional stop. That is, if your meter reading is 1/500th of a second at f/11, use 1/500th second at f/8 or 1/200th second at f/11 instead. (Both exposures are equivalent.)

ORIGIN OF THE 18 PERCENT MYTH

Why are so many photographers under the impression that camera light meters are calibrated to the 18 percent "standard," rather than the true value, which may be 12 to 14 percent, depending on the vendor? You'll find this misinformation in an alarming number of places. I've seen the 18 percent myth taught in camera classes; I've found it in books, and even been given this wrong information from the technical staff of camera vendors. (They should know better—the same vendors' engineers who design and calibrate the cameras have the right figure.)

The most common explanation is that during a revision of Kodak's instructions for its gray cards in the 1970s, the advice to open up an extra half stop was omitted, and a whole generation of shooters grew up thinking that a measurement off a gray card could be used as-is. The proviso returned to the instructions by 1987, it's said, but by then it was too late.

EXTERNAL METERS CAN BE CALIBRATED

The light meters built into your camera are calibrated at the factory. But if you use a handheld incident or reflective light meter, you *can* calibrate it, using the instructions supplied with your meter. Because a handheld meter, of both the reflective and incident type, *can* be calibrated to the 18 percent gray standard (or any other value you choose), my rant about the myth of the 18 percent gray card doesn't apply.

Choosing a Metering Mode

To calculate exposure automatically, you need to tell the camera *where* in the frame to measure the light (this is called the *metering mode*) and *what controls* should be used (aperture, shutter speed, or both) to set the exposure. That's called *exposure mode,* and includes Program (P), Shutter-priority (Tv), Aperture-priority (Av), Flexible-priority (Fv), or Manual (M) options, plus Scene Intelligent Auto. I'll explain all these next.

But first, I'm going to introduce you to the four metering modes. You can select any of the four if you're working with P, Tv, Av, or M exposure modes; if you're using Scene Intelligent Auto, Evaluative metering is selected automatically and cannot be changed. In Live View mode, only Evaluative and Center-weighted averaging modes can be selected.

Choose a metering mode by pressing the Q/SET button and navigating to the Metering Mode icon, which is the sixth box from the top in the left column. (See Figure 4.4.) Then use either dial to select the mode you want, and press Q/SET to confirm. Available modes include:

- **Evaluative.** The camera slices up the frame into 384 different exposure zones (a 24 × 16 matrix), shown as yellow rectangles in Figure 4.5. (Don't confuse these zones with the *autofocus* points or zones; they are different.)

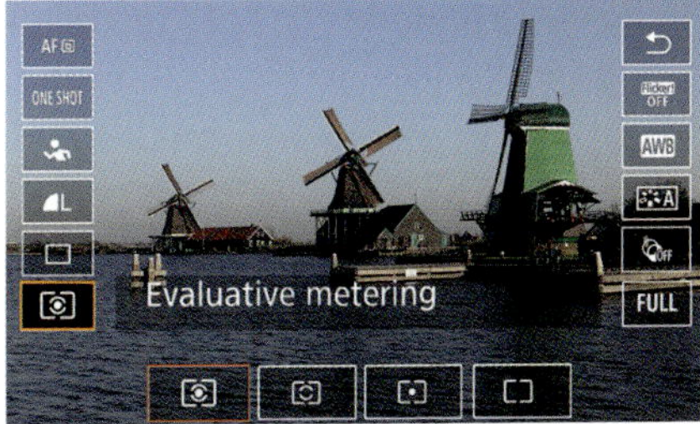

Figure 4.4 Use the Quick Control menu to choose a metering mode.

The exposure zones used are linked to the autofocus system such that as the camera evaluates the measurements, it gives extra emphasis to the metering zones that indicate sharp focus. From this data, it makes an educated guess about what kind of picture you're taking, based on examination of thousands of different real-world photos in the camera's database. For example, if the top sections of a picture are much lighter than the bottom portions, the algorithm can assume that the scene is a landscape photo with lots of sky. This mode is the best all-purpose metering method for most pictures. I'll explain how to choose an autofocus/exposure zone in the section on autofocus operation later in this chapter.

Note: Evaluative metering is sometimes described as a type of full-frame averaging. That's absolutely incorrect. The camera *intelligently* considers the differences between the measured zones and then classifies what type of scene is being evaluated before calculating an exposure. Two subjects could have exactly the same *average* illumination but require quite different exposures, depending on the location of the bright, dark, and midtone areas of the scene.

- **Partial.** This is a *faux* spot mode, using roughly 6 percent of the image area to calculate exposure, which, as you can see in Figure 4.6, is a rather large spot, represented by the larger yellow circle. Use this mode if the background is much brighter or darker than the subject, as in the figure.

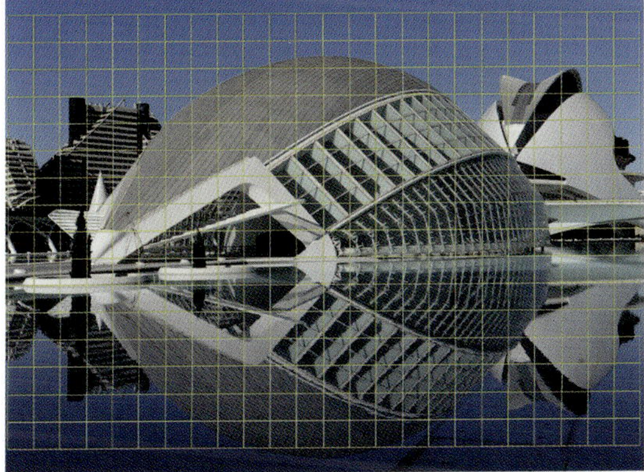

Figure 4.5 Evaluative metering uses 384 zones and is effective for interpreting evenly lit scenes.

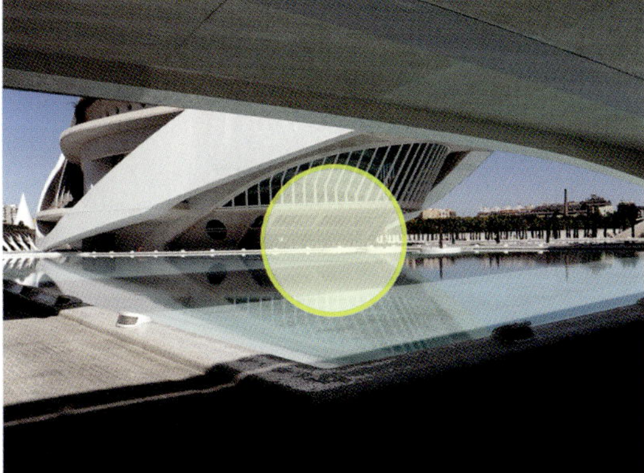

Figure 4.6 Partial metering uses a center spot that's roughly 6 percent of the frame area and is excellent for images with the most important areas in the center.

- **Spot.** This mode confines the reading to a limited area in the center of the viewfinder, as shown in Figure 4.7, making up only about 3 percent of the image. This mode is useful when you want to base exposure on a small area in the frame, such as the gray portions of the structure in the figure. If that area is in the center of the frame, so much the better. If not, you'll have to make your meter reading and then lock exposure by pressing the shutter release halfway, or by pressing the AE lock (*) button. Note that spot metering is *not* linked to the focus point.

- **Center-weighted averaging.** In this mode, the exposure meter emphasizes a zone in the center of the frame to calculate exposure, as shown in Figure 4.8, on the theory that, for most pictures, the main subject will be located in the center. Center-weighting works best for portraits, architectural photos, and other pictures in which the most important subject is located in the middle of the frame, as in the figure. As the name suggests, the light reading is *weighted* toward the central portion, but information is also used from the rest of the frame. If your main subject is surrounded by very bright or very dark areas, the exposure might not be exactly right. However, this scheme works well in many situations if you don't want to use one of the other modes.

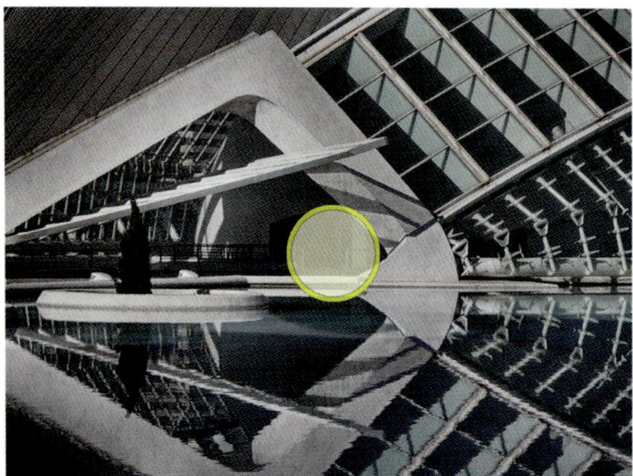

Figure 4.7 Spot metering calculates exposure based on a center spot that's roughly 3 percent of the image area and allows measuring specific areas, such as the gray portions of this structure.

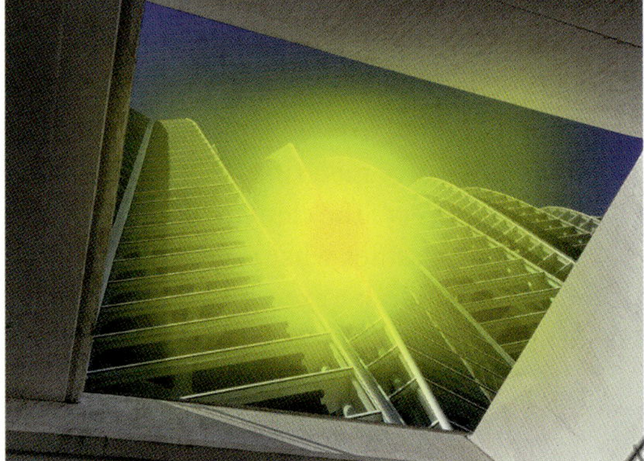

Figure 4.8 Center-weighted averaging metering calculates exposure based on the full frame but emphasizes the center area. Exposure for the example image was calculated from the large area in the center of the frame, with less emphasis on the darker surroundings.

Choosing a Shooting Mode

You'll find five semi-automatic and manual methods for choosing the appropriate shutter speed and aperture, including: Program (P), Shutter-priority (Tv), Aperture-priority (Av), and Manual (M). The fifth method, Flexible-Priority (Fv) can mimic any of the previous four. A sixth, Scene Intelligent Auto (A+), makes all the exposure calculations for you. I'll show you how to use Scene Intelligent Auto later in this chapter. To select one of these modes, just rotate the Mode dial located at the top-right side of the R8. Double-check to make sure the Shooting/Movie mode switch is set to the still photo mode. (See Figure 4.9.)

Your choice of which exposure/shooting mode is best for a given shooting situation will depend on things like your need for more/less depth-of-field, a desire to freeze action or allow motion blur, or how much noise you find acceptable in an image. (Remember that exposure triangle at the beginning of the chapter.) Each of the camera's exposure methods emphasizes one of those aspects of image capture or another.

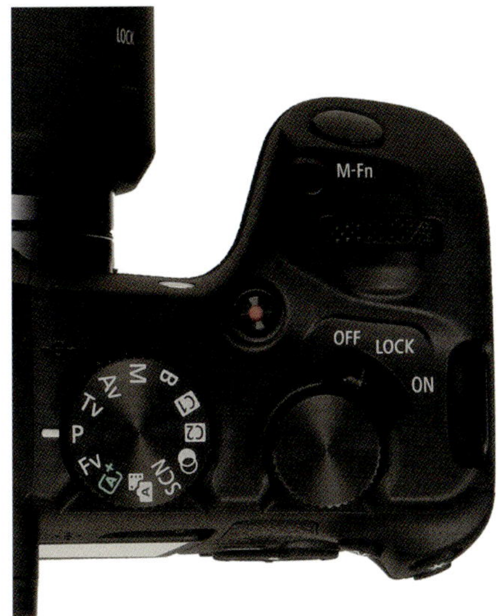

Figure 4.9 Select a Shooting mode.

Aperture-Priority Mode

In Av mode, you specify the lens opening used, and the camera selects the shutter speed. Aperture-priority is especially good when you want to use a particular lens opening to achieve a desired effect. Perhaps you'd like to use the smallest f/stop possible to maximize depth-of-field in a close-up picture. Or, you might want to use a large f/stop to throw everything except your main subjects out of focus, as in Figure 4.10. Maybe you'd just like to "lock in" a particular f/stop smaller than the maximum aperture because it's the sharpest available aperture with that lens. Or, you might prefer to use, say, f/2.8 on a lens with a maximum aperture of f/1.4, because you want the best compromise between speed and sharpness.

Aperture-priority can even be used to specify a *range* of shutter speeds you want to use under varying lighting conditions, which seems almost contradictory. But think about it. You're shooting a soccer game outdoors with a telephoto lens and want a relatively high shutter speed, but you don't care if the speed changes a little should the sun duck behind a cloud. Set your camera to Av, and adjust the aperture until a shutter speed of, say, 1/1000th second is selected at your current ISO setting. (In bright sunlight at ISO 400, that aperture is likely to be around f/11.) Then, go ahead and shoot, knowing that your camera will maintain that f/11 aperture (for sufficient DOF as the soccer players move about the field), but will drop down to 1/750th or 1/500th second, if necessary, should the lighting change a little.

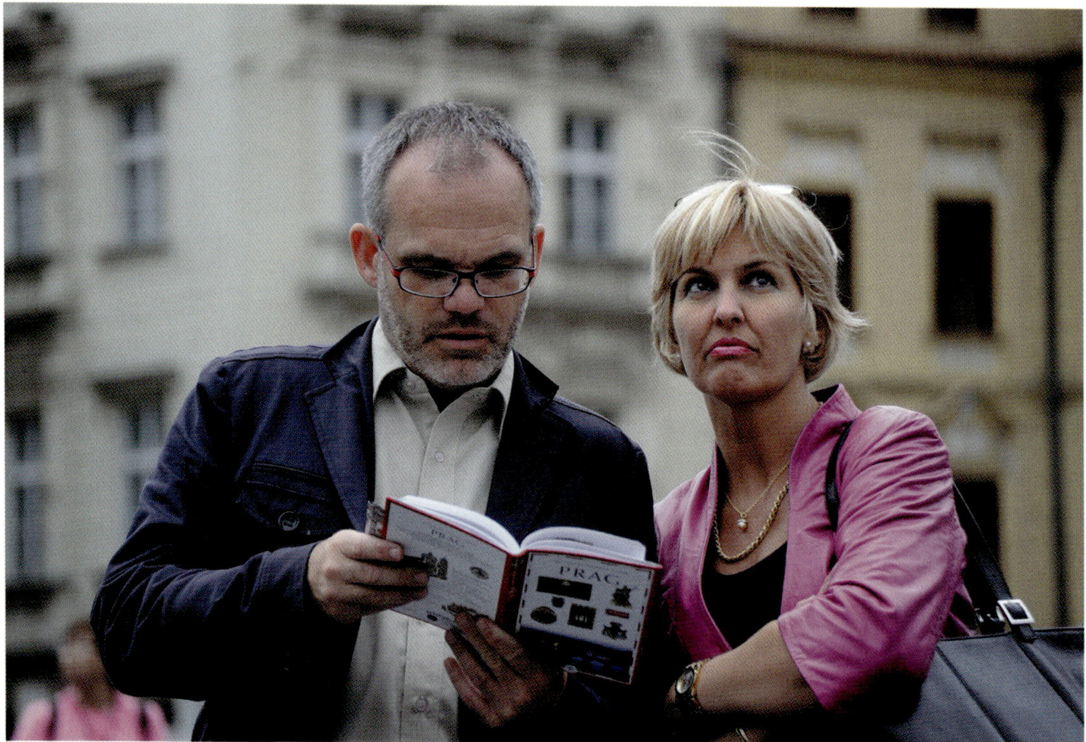

Figure 4.10 Use Aperture-priority to "lock in" a large f/stop when you want to blur the background.

If the shutter speed in the viewfinder or on the Shooting Settings screen is blinking, that indicates that the camera is unable to select an appropriate shutter speed at the selected aperture and that overexposure (the 4000 is blinking) or underexposure (the 30 shutter speed is blinking) will occur at the current ISO setting. To correct overexposure, select a smaller aperture (if available) or choose a lower ISO sensitivity. Fix underexposure conditions by choosing a larger aperture (if possible) or a higher ISO setting.

That's the major pitfall of using Av: you might select an f/stop that is too small or too large to allow an optimal exposure with the available shutter speeds. For example, if you choose f/2.8 as your aperture and the illumination is quite bright (say, at the beach or in snow), even your camera's fastest shutter speed might not be able to cut down the amount of light reaching the sensor to provide the right exposure. Or, if you select f/8 in a dimly lit room, you might find yourself shooting with a very slow shutter speed that can cause blurring from subject movement or camera shake. Aperture-priority is best used by those with a bit of experience in choosing settings. Many seasoned photographers leave their camera set on Av all the time. The Safety Shift feature can be used to automatically override your selected aperture if the camera is unable to obtain a correct exposure. Safety Shift operates even when you're using flash. I'll show you how to configure that setting in the Custom Functions 1 menu, which can also be used with P, Tv, and Fv modes, in Chapter 15.

When to use Aperture-priority:

- **General landscape photography.** Your camera has enough resolution to allow making huge, gorgeous prints, as well as smaller prints that are filled with eye-popping detail. Aperture-priority is a good tool for ensuring that your landscape is sharp from foreground to infinity, if you select an f/stop that provides maximum depth-of-field.

  If you use Av mode and select an aperture like f/11 or f/16, it's your responsibility to make sure the shutter speed selected is fast enough to avoid losing detail to camera shake, or that the camera is mounted on a tripod. One thing that new landscape photographers fail to account for is the movement of distant leaves and tree branches. When seeking the ultimate in sharpness, go ahead and use Aperture-priority, but boost ISO sensitivity a bit, if necessary, to provide a sufficiently fast shutter speed, whether shooting hand-held or with a tripod.

- **Specific landscape situations.** Aperture-priority is also useful when you have no objection to using a long shutter speed, or, particularly, *want* the camera to select one. Waterfalls are a perfect example. You can use Av mode, set your camera to ISO 100, use a small f/stop, and let the camera select a longer shutter speed that will allow the water to blur as it flows. Indeed, you might need to use a neutral-density filter to get a sufficiently long shutter speed. But Aperture-priority mode is a good start.

- **Portrait photography.** Portraits are the most common applications of selective focus. A medium-large aperture (say, f/5.6 or f/8) with a longer lens/zoom setting (in the 85mm-135mm range) will allow the background behind your portrait subject to blur. A *very* large aperture (I frequently shoot wide open with my 85mm f/1.2 lens) lets you apply selective focus to your subject's *face*. With a three-quarters view of your subject, as long as their eyes are sharp, it's okay if the far ear or their hair is out of focus.

- **When you want to ensure optimal sharpness.** All lenses have an aperture or two at which they perform best, providing the level of sharpness you expect from a camera with the resolution of the R8. That's usually about two stops down from wide open, and thus will vary depending on the maximum aperture of the lens. My 85mm f/1.2 is good wide open, but it's even sharper at f/2.8 or f/4; I shoot my 70-200mm f/2.8 wide open at concerts, but, if I can use f/4 instead, I'll get better results. Aperture-priority allows me to use each lens at its very best f/stop.

- **Close-up/Macro photography.** Depth-of-field is typically very shallow when shooting macro photos, and you'll want to choose your f/stop carefully. Perhaps you need the smallest aperture you can get away with to maximize DOF. Or, you might want to use a wider stop to emphasize your subject. Aperture-priority mode comes in very useful when shooting close-up pictures. Because macro work is frequently done with the camera mounted on a tripod, and your close-up subjects, if not living creatures, may not be moving much, a longer shutter speed isn't a problem. Aperture-priority (Av mode) can be your preferred choice.

Shutter-Priority Mode

Shutter-priority (Tv) is the inverse of Aperture-priority: you choose the shutter speed you'd like to use, and the camera's metering system selects the appropriate f/stop. Perhaps you're shooting action photos and you want to use the absolute fastest shutter speed available with your camera; in other cases, you might want to use a slow shutter speed to add some blur to a sports image that would be mundane if the action were completely frozen. Motor sports, track-and-field events, and sports like baseball particularly lend themselves to creative use of slower speeds, as you can see in Figure 4.11. Shutter-priority mode gives you some control over how much action-freezing capability your digital camera brings to bear in a particular situation.

You'll also encounter the same problem as with Aperture-priority when you select a shutter speed that's too long or too short for correct exposure under some conditions. I've shot outdoor soccer games on sunny fall evenings and used Shutter-priority mode to lock in a 1/1000th-second shutter speed, which triggered the blinking warning, even with the lens wide open.

Like Av mode, it's possible to choose an inappropriate shutter speed. If that's the case, the maximum aperture of your lens (to indicate underexposure) or the minimum aperture (to indicate overexposure) will blink. To fix, select a longer shutter speed or higher ISO setting (for underexposure), or a faster shutter speed/lower ISO setting (for overexposure), or use Safety Shift, mentioned previously.

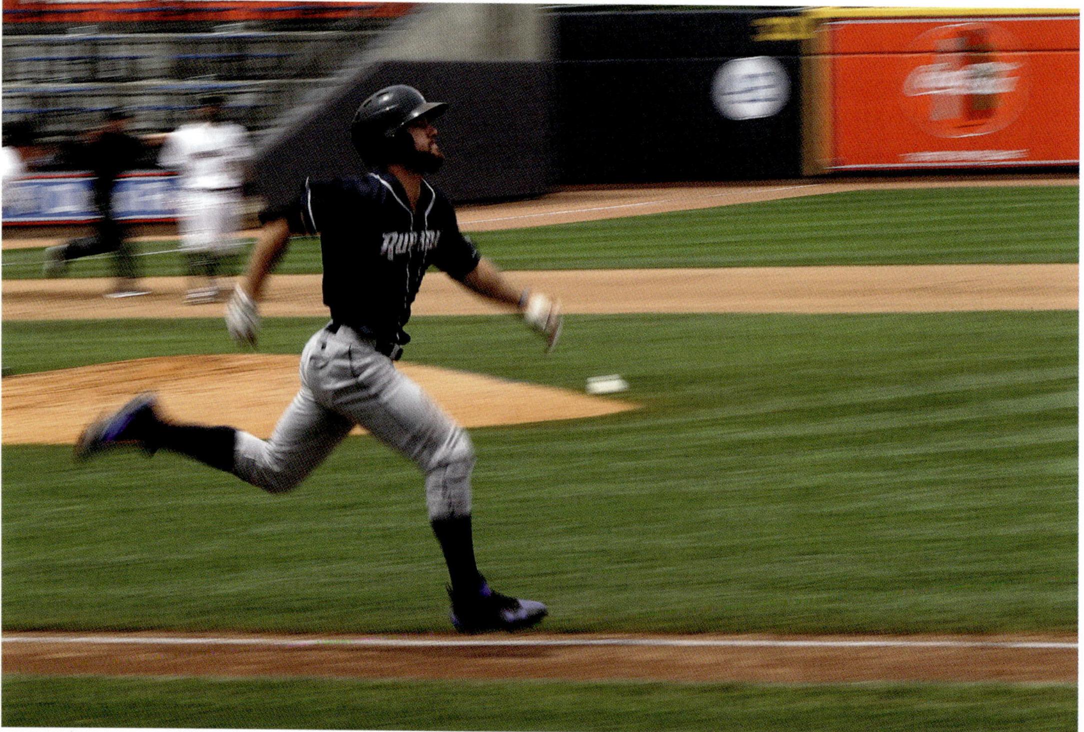

Figure 4.11 Lock the shutter at a slow speed to introduce a little blur into an action shot, seen here in this panned image of a base runner.

When to use Shutter-priority:

- **To reduce blur from subject motion.** Set the shutter speed of the camera to a higher value to reduce the amount of blur from subjects that are moving. The exact speed will vary depending on how fast your subject is moving and how much blur is acceptable. You might want to freeze a basketball player in mid-dunk with a 1/1000th-second shutter speed or use 1/200th second to allow the spinning wheels of a motocross racer to blur a tiny bit to add the feeling of motion.
- **To add blur from subject motion.** There are times when you want a subject to blur, say, when shooting waterfalls with the camera set for a one- or two-second exposure in Shutter-priority mode.
- **To add blur from camera motion when *you* are moving.** Say you're panning to follow a pair of relay runners. You might want to use Shutter-priority mode and set the camera for 1/60th second, so that the background will blur as you pan with the runners. The shutter speed will be fast enough to provide a sharp image of the athletes.
- **To reduce blur from camera motion when *you* are moving.** In other situations, the camera may be in motion, say, because you're shooting from a moving train or auto, and you want to minimize the amount of blur caused by the motion of the camera. Shutter-priority is a good choice here, too.
- **Landscape photography hand-held.** If you can't use a tripod for your landscape shots, you'll still probably want the sharpest image possible. Shutter-priority can allow you to specify a shutter speed that's fast enough to reduce or eliminate the effects of camera shake. Just make sure that your ISO setting is high enough that the camera will select an aperture with sufficient depth-of-field, too.
- **Concerts, stage performances.** I shoot a lot of concerts with my 70-200mm f/2.8 lens, and have discovered that, when the lens's built-in image stabilization is taken into account, a shutter speed of 1/180th second is fast enough to eliminate blur from hand-holding the camera with this lens, and also to avoid blur from the movement of all but the most energetic performers. I use Shutter-priority and set the ISO so the camera will select an aperture in the f/4-5.6 range.

Program AE Mode

Program mode (P) uses the camera's built-in smarts to select the correct f/stop and shutter speed using a database of picture information that tells it which combination of shutter speed and aperture will work best for a particular photo. If the correct exposure cannot be achieved at the current ISO setting, the shutter speed or aperture indicator in the viewfinder will blink, indicating under- or overexposure. You can then boost or reduce the ISO to increase or decrease sensitivity.

The camera's recommended exposure can be overridden if you want. Use the EV setting feature (described later, because it also applies to Tv and Av modes) to add or subtract exposure from the metered value. And, as I mentioned earlier in this chapter, you can change from the recommended setting to an equivalent setting (as shown in Table 4.1) that produces the same exposure but using a different combination of f/stop and shutter speed.

To accomplish this:

1. Press the shutter release halfway to lock in the current base exposure or press the AE lock button (*) on the back of the camera (in which case the * indicator will illuminate in the viewfinder to show that the exposure has been locked).

2. If the camera cannot select an appropriate exposure, the shutter speed and aperture display will blink:

   - **Underexposure.** The 30 shutter speed indicator will flash, along with the maximum (largest) aperture of the lens. (The exact number will vary, depending on which lens you are using.) To compensate, you must either use a higher ISO setting or provide additional illumination, such as electronic flash.

   - **Overexposure.** The 4000 shutter speed indicator will flash, along with the minimum (smallest available) f/stop, such as f/16, f/22, or f/32, depending on the lens you are using. You can usually compensate for this by reducing the ISO speed to a lower setting. Your scene must be *very* bright indeed to trigger overexposure at a shutter speed of 1/4000th second and the minimum ISO sensitivity setting. But if you're photographing, say, a blast furnace, and still have an overexposure situation, you can resort to a neutral-density filter or find some way to reduce the amount of illumination.

3. Once an exposure is set, you can spin the Main dial to change to a different combination of settings. Rotate left to select a longer shutter speed/smaller aperture, or to the right to choose a faster shutter speed/larger aperture.

Your adjustment remains in force for a single exposure; if you want to change from the recommended settings for the next exposure, you'll need to repeat those steps.

When to use Program mode priority:

- **When you're in a hurry to get a grab shot.** The camera will do a pretty good job of calculating an appropriate exposure for you, without any input from you.

- **When you hand your camera to a novice.** Set the camera to P, hand the camera to your friend, relative, or trustworthy stranger you meet in front of the Leaning Tower of Pisa, point to the shutter release button and viewfinder, and say, "Look through here, and press this button."

- **When no special shutter speed or aperture settings are needed.** If your subject doesn't require special anti- or pro-blur techniques, and depth-of-field or selective focus aren't important, use P as a general-purpose setting. You can still make adjustments to increase/decrease depth-of-field or add/reduce motion blur with a minimum of fuss.

Flexible-Priority Mode

Flexible-priority (Fv) takes a little getting used to, because, at least among veteran photographers, the shooting modes P, Tv, Av, and Manual (discussed later) are ingrained in our workflow. Fv almost seems counterintuitive until you've used it a few times and the realization comes that it is probably the most intuitive shooting mode of all. Flexible-priority gives you all four modes with full control of the three legs of the exposure triangle, all within a single setting.

In a nutshell, Fv, by default, acts like Program AE with Auto ISO activated. That is, the camera selects shutter speed, aperture, and ISO setting for you automatically. But you can elect to manually specify any or all of those three, and the camera's shooting mode magically transforms from P to Av, Tv, or Manual. With the mode set to Fv:

- **Tv mode.** In Fv mode, rotate the Quick Control dial until an orange icon representing the Main dial appears next to the shutter speed. You can then rotate the Main dial to manually select the shutter speed, and the aperture and ISO will continue to be changed automatically. In effect, you have Tv mode with Auto ISO.

- **Av mode.** In Fv mode, rotate the Quick Control dial until an orange icon representing the Main dial appears next to the aperture, then rotate the Main dial to manually select the f/stop. The camera behaves just like it would in Av mode with Auto ISO.

- **Manual mode.** In Fv mode, rotate the Quick Control dial to the shutter speed and aperture icons and choose a manual setting for each. Now the camera acts as if it were in Manual exposure mode with shutter speed, and the aperture and ISO will continue to be changed automatically. In effect, you have Tv mode with Auto ISO.

- **Fixed ISO.** If you want to disable Auto ISO in Fv mode, rotate the Quick Control dial to highlight the ISO icon and select a fixed ISO value of your choice with the Main dial.

- **Exposure compensation.** Highlight the exposure scale at the bottom of the screen and rotate the Main dial to add or subtract exposure compensation.

Manual Exposure Mode

Part of being an experienced photographer comes from knowing when to rely on your camera's automation (including Scene Intelligent Auto or P mode), when to go semi-automatic (with Tv or Av), and when to set exposure manually (using M). Some photographers actually prefer to set their exposure manually most of the time, as the camera will be happy to provide an indication of when its metering system judges your settings provide the proper exposure, using the analog exposure scale at the bottom of the display (see Figure 4.12).

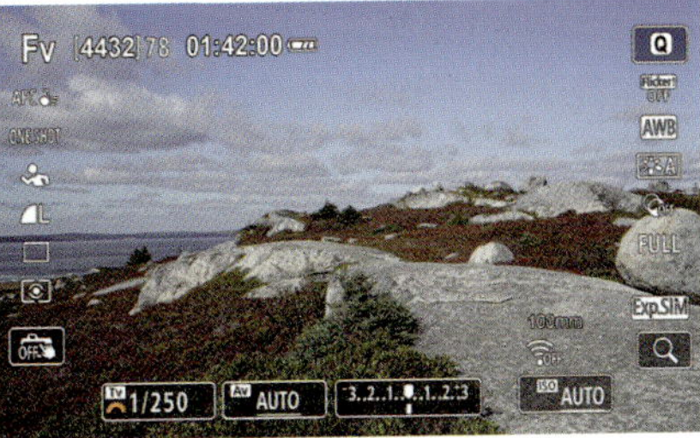

Figure 4.12 An exposure scale is shown at the bottom of the display.

Manual exposure can come in handy in some situations. You might be taking a silhouette photo and find that none of the exposure modes or EV correction features give you exactly the effect you want. For example, when I shot the ballet dancers in Figure 4.13 in front of a mostly dark background highlighted by an illuminated curtain off to the right, there was no way any of my camera's exposure modes would be able to interpret the scene the way I wanted to shoot it, even with Spot metering, which didn't have a narrow enough field-of-view from my position. So, I took a couple test exposures, and set the exposure manually using the exact shutter speed and f/stop I needed. You might be working in a studio environment using multiple flash units. The additional flash are triggered by slave devices (gadgets that set off the flash when they sense the light from another flash, or, perhaps from a radio or infrared remote control). Your camera's exposure meter doesn't compensate for the extra illumination, and can't interpret the flash exposure at all, so you need to set the aperture manually.

Because, depending on your proclivities, you might not need to set exposure manually very often, you should still make sure you understand how it works. Fortunately, the camera makes setting exposure manually very easy. Just use the Mode dial to select Manual exposure, then turn the Main dial to set the shutter speed, and the QCD to adjust the aperture. Press the shutter release halfway or press the AE lock (*) button, and the exposure scale in the viewfinder shows you how far your chosen setting diverges from the metered exposure.

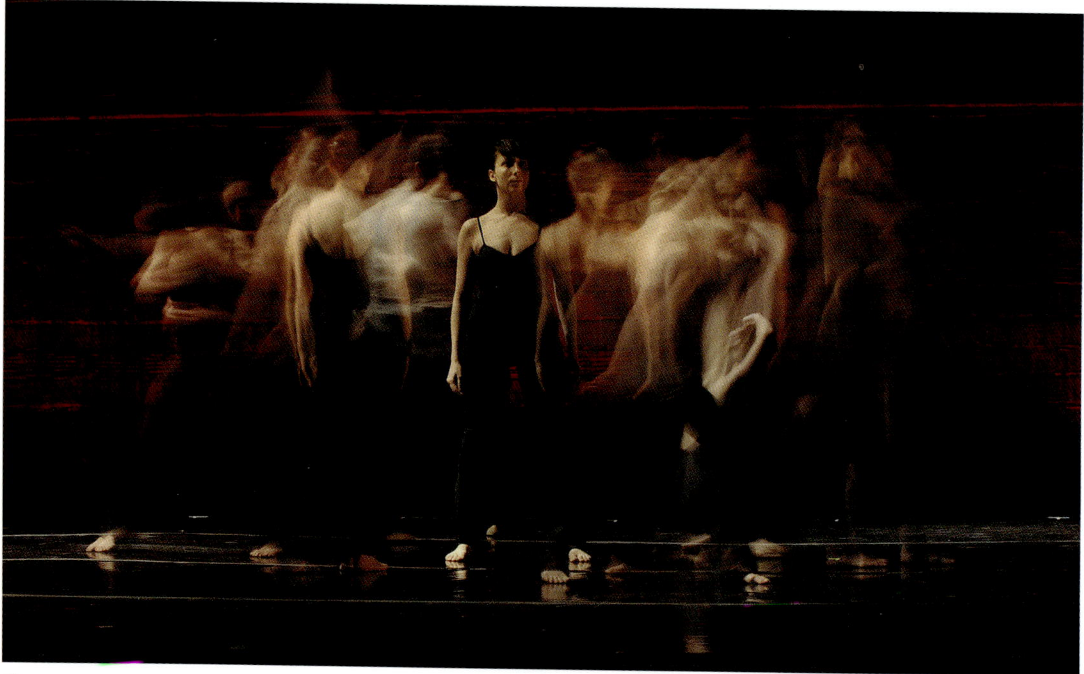

Figure 4.13 Manual exposure allows selecting both f/stop and shutter speed, especially useful when you're experimenting, as with this shot of ballet dancers.

If you activate ISO Auto, you can add or subtract exposure compensation. Just tap the exposure scale at the bottom of the touch screen, use the Quick Control screen's Exposure Compensation function in the graphical screen, or use the Exposure Compensation/AEB entry in the Shooting 2 menu.

When to use Manual exposure:

- **When working in the studio.** If you're working in a studio environment, you generally have total control over the lighting and can set exposure exactly as you want. The last thing you need is for the camera to interpret the scene and make adjustments of its own. Use M and the shutter speed, aperture, and (as long as you don't use ISO-Auto) ISO setting are totally up to you.
- **When using non-dedicated flash.** External Canon-dedicated flash units are cool, but if you're working with a non-compatible flash unit, particularly studio flash plugged into a PC/X adapter mounted on the hot shoe, the camera has no clue about the intensity of the flash, so you'll have to dial in the appropriate aperture and shutter speed manually.
- **If you're using a hand-held light meter.** The appropriate aperture, both for flash exposures and shots taken under continuous lighting, can be determined by a hand-held light meter, flash meter, or combo meter that measures both kinds of illumination. With an external meter, you can measure highlights, shadows, backgrounds, or additional subjects separately, and use Manual exposure to make your settings.
- **When you want to outsmart the metering system.** Your camera's metering system is "trained" to react to unusual lighting situations, such as backlighting, extra-bright illumination, or low-key images with murky shadows. In many cases, it can counter these "problems" and produce a well-exposed image. But what if you don't *want* a well-exposed image? Manual exposure allows you to produce silhouettes in backlit situations, wash out all the middle tones to produce a luminous look, or underexpose to create a moody or ominous dark-toned photograph.

Adjusting Exposure with ISO Settings

Another way of adjusting exposures is by changing the ISO sensitivity setting. Sometimes photographers forget about this option, because the common practice is to set the ISO once for a particular shooting session (say, at ISO 100 or 200 for bright sunlight outdoors, or ISO 800 when shooting indoors) and then forget about it. ISOs higher than ISO 100 or 200 are seen as "bad" or "necessary evils." However, changing the ISO is a valid way of adjusting exposure settings, particularly with the Canon EOS R8, which produces good results at ISO settings that create grainy, unusable pictures with some other camera models.

Indeed, I find myself using ISO adjustment as a convenient alternate way of adding or subtracting EV when shooting in Manual mode, and as a quick way of choosing equivalent exposures when in Auto or semi-automatic modes. For example, I've selected a Manual exposure with both f/stop and shutter speed suitable for my image using, say, ISO 200. I can change the exposure in one-third-stop increments by pressing the M-Fn button on top of the camera, highlighting ISO with the QCD, and then spinning the Main dial one click at a time. The difference in image quality/noise at the base setting of ISO 200 is negligible if I dial in ISO 100 to reduce exposure a little or change to ISO 400 to increase exposure. I keep my preferred f/stop and shutter speed, but still adjust the exposure.

Or, perhaps, I am using Tv mode and the metered exposure at ISO 200 is 1/500th second at f/11. If I decide on the spur of the moment I'd rather use 1/500th second at f/8, I can press the M-Fn button, select ISO with the QCD, and spin the Main dial to switch to ISO 100. Of course, it's a good idea to monitor your ISO changes, so you don't end up at ISO 1600 accidentally. ISO settings can, of course, also be used to boost or reduce sensitivity in particular shooting situations.

When not using Scene Intelligent Auto (which sets ISO automatically), the camera can set ISO speeds manually for stills. (In video mode, Auto ISO must be used in all modes except Manual exposure.) The ISO Speed Settings entry in the Shooting 2 menu allows you to specify what speeds are available and how they are used:

- **ISO speed.** This scale allows you to choose from the enabled ISO speeds, plus Auto, using a sliding scale that can be adjusted using the QCD, the multi-controller, or the touch screen. Pressing the INFO button when the scale is visible activates Auto.

- **Range for stills.** You can specify the minimum and maximum ISO sensitivity available, including "expanded" settings such as Low (ISO 50 equivalent) and H (ISO 204,800 equivalent). I find myself using this feature frequently to keep me from accidentally switching to a setting I'd rather not use (or need to avoid). For example, at concerts I may switch from ISO 1600 to 6400 as the lighting changes, and I set those two values as my minimum or maximum. Outdoors in daylight, I might prefer to lock out ISO values lower than ISO 100 or higher than ISO 800.

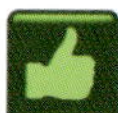

TIP The Lo and H settings enable *ISO expansion,* which may produce excessive noise, irregular colors, banding, and lower resolution. Use them with caution.

- **Auto range.** This is the equivalent "safety net" for Auto ISO operation. You can set the minimum no lower than ISO 100 and the maximum to ISO 102,400, and no further. Use this to apply your own "smarts" to the Auto ISO setting.

- **Minimum shutter speed.** You can choose whether to allow the camera to select the slowest shutter speed used before Auto ISO kicks in. The idea here is that you'll probably want to boost ISO sooner if you're using a long lens with P and Av modes (in which the camera selects the shutter speed). If you specify, for example, a minimum shutter speed of 1/200th second, if P or Av mode needs a slower shutter speed for the proper exposure, it will boost ISO instead, within the range you've specified with Auto Range.

This setting has two modes. In Auto mode, the camera decides when the shutter speed is too low. You can fine-tune this by choosing Slower or Faster on the scale (–3 to +3) that appears. Or, you can manually select the "trigger" shutter speed, from 1 second to 1/4000th second.

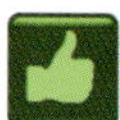

TIP By default, both the exposure level increments (size of shutter speed or f/stop changes) are in 1/3-stop jumps. In the Custom Functions 1 menu, you can set exposure level increments to 1/3 or 1/2 stops, and ISO changes to 1/3- or 1-stop increments. The larger 1-stop step for ISO allows rapid switching through ISO 100, 200, 400, 800, and so forth.

Find yourself locked out of ISO settings lower than 200 or higher than 102,400? You've probably set Highlight Tone Priority to Enable or Enhanced in the Shooting 2 menu, as described in Chapter 11.

Dealing with Visual Noise

Visual image noise is that random grainy effect that some like to use as a special effect, but which, most of the time, is objectionable because it robs your image of detail even as it adds that "interesting" texture. Noise is caused by two different phenomena: high ISO settings and long exposures.

High ISO noise commonly first appears when you raise your camera's sensitivity setting above ISO 3200. With Canon cameras, which are renowned for their good ISO noise characteristics, noise is usually fairly noticeable at ISO 6400 and above. At the H setting (ISO 204,800 equivalent), noise is usually quite bothersome, which is why those lofty sensitivity ratings are disabled by default and must be activated with ISO expansion. This kind of noise appears as a result of the amplification needed to increase the sensitivity of the sensor. Because your sensor has twice as many green pixels as red and blue pixels, such noise is typically worse in areas that have red, blue, and magenta tones, because the green signals don't have to be amplified as much to produce detail. While higher ISOs do pull details out of dark areas, they also amplify non-signal information randomly, creating noise.

A similar noisy phenomenon occurs during long time exposures, which allow more photons to reach the sensor, increasing your ability to capture a picture under low-light conditions. However, the longer exposures also increase the likelihood that some pixels will register random phantom photons, often because the longer an imager is "hot," the warmer it gets, and that heat can be mistaken for photons. There's also a special kind of noise that CMOS sensors like the one used in the R8 are potentially susceptible to. They contain millions of individual amplifiers and analog/digital (A/D) converters, all working in unison. Because all these circuits don't necessarily process in precisely the same way all the time, they can introduce something called fixed-pattern noise into the image data.

Fortunately, Canon's electronics geniuses have done an exceptional job minimizing noise from all causes in the camera. Even so, you might still want to apply the optional long exposure noise reduction that can be activated in the Shooting 5 menu. This type of noise reduction involves the camera taking a second, blank exposure, and comparing the random pixels in that image with the photograph you just took. Pixels that coincide in the two represent noise and can safely be suppressed. This noise reduction system, called *dark frame subtraction,* effectively doubles the amount of time required to take a picture, and is used only for exposures longer than one second. Noise reduction can reduce the amount of detail in your picture, as some image information may be removed along with the noise. So, you might want to use this feature with moderation. Some types of images don't require noise reduction because the grainy pattern tends to blend into the overall scene.

You can also apply noise reduction to a lesser extent using Photoshop or Canon Digital Photo Professional and when converting RAW files to some other format, using your favorite RAW converter, or an industrial-strength product like Noise Ninja (www.picturecode.com) to wipe out noise after you've already taken the picture.

Making EV Changes

Sometimes you'll want more or less exposure than indicated by the camera's metering system. Perhaps you want to underexpose to create a silhouette effect or overexpose to produce a high-key look. It's easy to use the camera's exposure compensation system to override the exposure recommendations, available in any non-automatic mode except Manual. There are three ways to make exposure value (EV) changes with the camera:

- **Display/Quick Control Dial.** When looking at the display, you can add/subtract exposure compensation +/– 3 stops by tapping the shutter release halfway (you don't have to hold it down) and then rotating the QCD. Turn clockwise to add exposure, or counterclockwise to reduce exposure. The exposure scale at the bottom of the screen will indicate the amount of exposure compensation you've dialed in.

- **Quick Control screen.** With the graphic shooting information screen displayed (see Figure 4.14), press the Q/SET button and navigate to the exposure scale. Then rotate the QCD. Rotate clockwise to add exposure, or counterclockwise to reduce exposure. (As always, you can use the touch screen to access these controls.) The exposure scale on the screen will indicate the amount of exposure compensation. You can also press Q/SET when the scale is highlighted to view the full exposure compensation/autoexposure bracketing screen, discussed next.

- **Shooting 2.** Press the MENU button and rotate the Main dial to select the Shooting 2 menu. Then highlight the Expo. Comp/AEB entry at the top. Press Q/SET to access the screen shown in Figure 4.15. Then rotate the QCD or slide a finger across the scale to select the amount of exposure compensation. The screen has helpful labels (Darker on the left and Brighter on the right) to make sure you're adding/subtracting when you really want to.

Note that this method has an advantage: you can specify automatic exposure bracketing from this screen just by rotating the Main dial. I'll explain bracketing in more detail next.

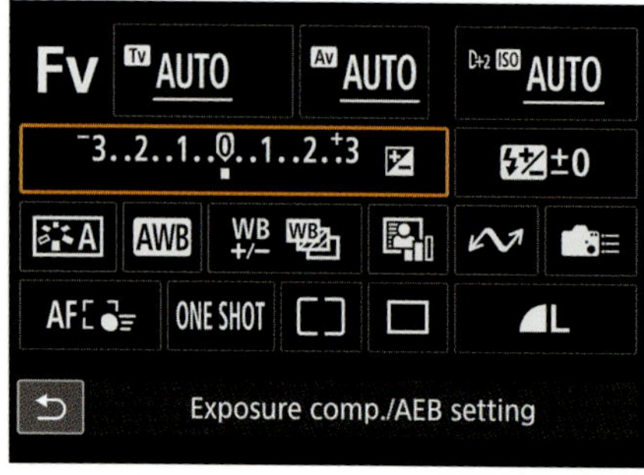

Figure 4.14 Setting exposure compensation using the Quick Control screen.

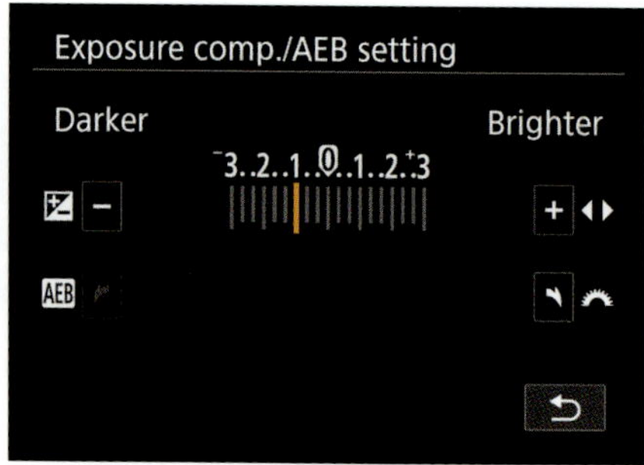

Figure 4.15 The full exposure compensation/auto exposure bracketing screen.

Bracketing Parameters

Bracketing is a method for shooting several consecutive exposures using different settings, as a way of improving the odds that one will be exactly right. Before digital cameras took over the universe, it was common to bracket exposures, shooting, say, a series of three photos at 1/125th second, but varying the f/stop from f/8 to f/11 to f/16. In practice, smaller-than-whole-stop increments were used for greater precision. Plus, it was just as common to keep the same aperture and vary the shutter speed, although in the days before electronic shutters, film cameras often had only whole-increment shutter speeds available. Figure 4.16 shows a typical bracketed series.

Today, cameras can bracket exposures much more precisely, and bracket white balance as well (using the WB Shift/Bkt entry found in the Shooting 4 menu and described in Chapter 11). While WB bracketing is sometimes used when getting color absolutely correct in the camera is important, autoexposure bracketing (AEB) is used much more often. When this feature is activated, the camera takes a series of shots, all at a different exposure value—one at the standard exposure, and the others with more or less exposure. In Av mode, the shutter speed will change, whereas in Tv mode, the aperture speed will change. The next sections will explain the parameters you can select.

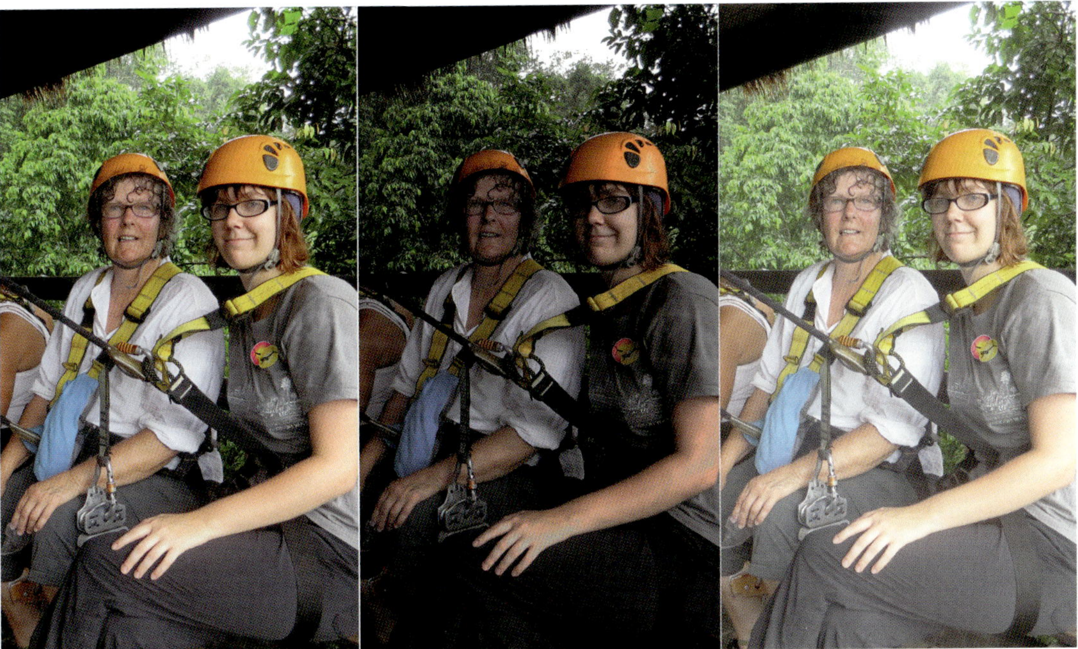

Figure 4.16 In this bracketed series, you can see metered exposure (left), underexposure (center), and overexposure (right).

Number of Exposures

In the Custom Function 1 menu, under the Number of Bracketed Shots entry, you can elect to bracket 2, 3, 5, or 7 shots:

- **2 shots.** The camera will capture one image at the *base* or standard exposure (which can be the metered exposure, or one that's more or less than the metered exposure, as I'll explain shortly). It then takes one additional shot that provides either *more* or *less* exposure relative to that "base" image. Rotate the QCD to the right to specify more exposure for the second shot, or to the left to specify less exposure. The *amount* of additional/less exposure is determined by the increment you select. (Read on! I'll tie all the parameters together in an upcoming section.)

- **3, 5, 7 shots.** The camera captures one image at the base exposure, and then two, four, or six shots bracketed around that exposure, respectively. That translates to one over/one under at the 3-shot setting, two over/two under at the 5-shot setting, and three over/three under when using the 7-shot option.

Bracketing Sequence

Also in the Custom Function 1 menu, you'll find a Bracketing Sequence entry, which allows you to specify the order in which the autoexposure bracketing series are exposed. Your choice will depend both on personal preference and what you intend to do with the bracketed shots. The options include:

- **0 − +:** The exposure sequence is standard exposure, decreased exposure, increased exposure. With this default value, your base exposure will be captured and saved first on your memory card, followed by the progressively reduced exposure images, then the shots with increased exposure. You might prefer this order if you expect your standard exposure will be the preferred image and arranged first in the queue of each bracket set and want the alternate exposures to follow.

- **− 0 +:** The sequence is decreased exposure, standard exposure, increased exposure. This order is the most logical to use if you're shooting with the intention to combine images using HDR (high dynamic range) techniques in your image editor or HDR utility. The final bracketed array is stored on your memory card starting with the most underexposed shot, and progressing to the best exposed, and then on to the overexposures. That makes it easy to use all of your bracketed shots in the HDR sequence, or to select only some of them to combine.

- **+ 0 −:** This sequence is the inverse of the last one, progressing from increased exposure to standard exposure and decreased exposure. You might prefer this order if you expect to see your best exposures on the plus side of the exposure sequence and want them to be displayed first.

Bracketing Auto Cancel

The final relevant entry in the Custom Function 1 menu is Bracketing Auto Cancel. When you activate bracketing (in the Shooting 2 menu, described shortly), the camera continues to shoot bracketed exposures until you manually turn the bracket feature off, assuming you have this setting disabled. That's a good thing. If you're out shooting a series of bracketed exposures (especially for HDR), it's convenient to have your bracket setting be "sticky" and still be active even if you turn your camera off. Some shooters like to bracket virtually *everything* and leave bracketing on routinely.

However, much of the time you'll want to turn bracketing off, and you may not want to visit the Shooting 2 menu to deactivate it manually. Set Bracketing Auto Cancel to Enable in the Custom Function 1 menu, and bracketing is cancelled when you turn the camera off, change lenses, use the flash, or change memory cards. When this setting is set to Disable, bracketing remains in effect until you manually turn it off *or use the flash*. The flash still cancels bracketing, but your settings are retained.

Increment Between Exposures

You can choose the size of the jump between each of the bracketed exposures. To do that, you'll need to visit the Expo. Comp./AEB entry in the Shooting 2 menu. There, you can select from +/– 1/3 to 3 full stops in 1/3-stop increments, by rotating the Main dial. The next section provides instructions for producing a bracketed set.

Creating a Bracketed Set

Using autoexposure bracketing is trickier than it needs to be but has been made more flexible than with some earlier models. With the R8 you are not limited to only three exposures (up to seven shots can be taken), and you can choose to bracket only overexposures or underexposures—a very useful improvement! Just follow these steps:

1. **Specify number of exposures and sequence.** Choose the number of bracketed exposures you want and the sequence in which they will be shot in the Custom Function 1 menu, as described earlier.

2. **Activate the Expo. Comp./AEB screen.** Press the MENU button and navigate to the Shooting 2 menu, where you'll find the Expo. Comp./AEB option. Press Q/SET to select this entry.

3. **Set the bracket range/increment.** Rotate the Main dial to spread out or contract the three bars to include the desired range and exposure increment you want to use. The wider the spread, the larger the increment and the larger the range of bracketed shots you'll end up with. The Main dial will allow you to set the bracket range to up to three stops on either side of the standard (middle) exposure.

   For example, in Figure 4.17, the left and right red highlighted bars are separated from the center bar by two marks, each representing 1/3rd stop, so the bracketing will produce one image at 2/3rds stop *less* than the zero point (the large center bar), one at the zero point, and one at 2/3rds stop more than that.

Figure 4.17 Use the Main dial to set the bracket range.

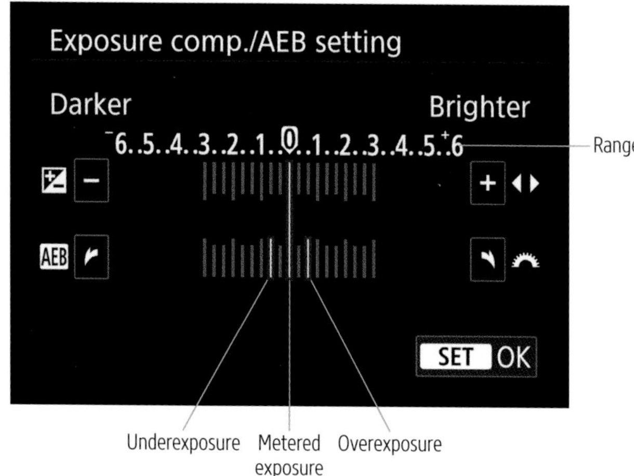

4. **Adjust zero point/standard exposure.** By default, the bracketing is zeroed around the center of the scale, which represents the correct exposure as metered by the camera. But you might want to have your three bracketed shots *all* biased toward overexposure or underexposure. Perhaps you feel that the metered exposure will be too dark or too light, and you want the bracketed shots to lean in the other direction. Use either QCD to move the bracket spread toward one end of the scale or the other. Figure 4.18 (top) shows the bracketing biased toward overexposure in one-stop increments, while in Figure 4.18 (bottom), the zero point is clustered around underexposure, also with one-stop increments.

Figure 4.18 Use the QCD to bias the bracketing toward more or less exposure, and the Main dial to set the bracket range.

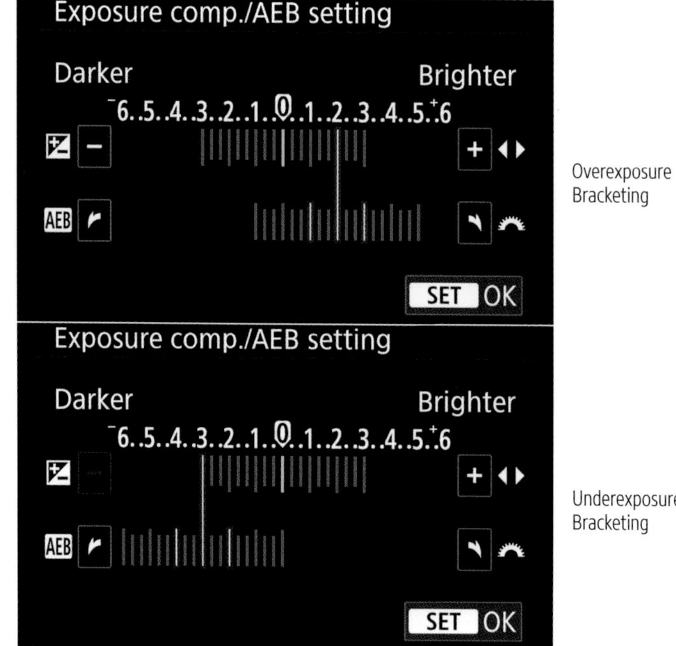

NON-BRACKETING IS EXPOSURE COMPENSATION

When the three bracket indicators aren't separated, using the QCD, in effect, adds or subtracts exposure compensation. You'll be shooting a "bracketed" set of one picture, with the zero point placed at the portion of the scale you indicated. Until you rotate the Main dial to separate the three bracket indicators by at least one indicator, this screen just supplies EV adjustment. Also, keep in mind that the increments shown will be either 1/3 stop or 1/2 stop, depending on how you've set Exposure Level Increments in the Custom Function 1 menu.

5. **Confirm your choice.** Press the Q/SET button to enter the settings.

6. **Take your photo sequence.** Press the shutter release to start capturing the bracketed sequence. The drive mode you select will determine when they are taken:

   - **Single shooting/Silent single shooting.** Press the shutter release one time for each exposure in the sequence.
   - **High-speed continuous/Low-speed continuous/Silent continuous.** You can hold down the shutter release and all the shots in the sequence will be exposed. The camera stops shooting when the series is complete.
   - **10 sec./2 sec. self-timer modes.** After the appropriate delay, all the shots in the sequence will be taken.

7. **Monitor your shots.** As the images are captured, three indicators will appear on the exposure scale in the viewfinder, with one of them flashing for each bracketed photo, showing when the base exposure, underexposure, and overexposure are taken.

8. **Turn bracketing off when done.** Bracketing remains in effect when the set is taken so you can continue shooting bracketed exposures until you use the electronic flash, turn off the camera, or return to the menu to cancel bracketing. That's true even if you have set Bracketing Auto Cancel to Enable in the Custom Function 1 menu. If bracketing were actually auto canceled each time, you'd have to respecify bracketing for each sequence you took; instead, the camera remembers your bracketing settings until you cancel manually, or until you power down or begin to use electronic flash. Only then will it automatically cancel the bracketing settings.

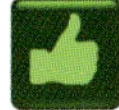 **NOTE** AEB is disabled when you're using flash, Multi Shot Noise Reduction, taking long time exposures with the Bulb setting, or if you have enabled the Auto Lighting Optimizer in the Shooting 2 menu (in which case the optimizer will probably override and nullify bracketing).

Working with HDR

High dynamic range (HDR) photography was quite the rage a few years ago, and entire books have been written on the subject. As with any fad, HDR was misused and overused, and responsible for a glut of garish, painfully unrealistic images. (I'll provide an example later in this section.) It's not really a new technique—film photographers have been combining multiple exposures for ages to produce a single image of, say, an interior room while maintaining detail in the scene visible through the windows.

Now that the thrill factor has been diminished, HDR has evolved into a functional feature that can be used tastefully to produce images that incorporate a wider range of tones without venturing into Fantasyland. As use of HDR has evolved, so have the capabilities built into cameras like the R8 to provide the tools needed to produce long-scale images.

Suppose you wanted to photograph a dimly lit street with heavy shadows punctuated by the glare of street lights and with a smattering of illuminated shop windows. Proper exposure for the darker areas of the scene might be on the order of 1/60th second at f/2.8 at ISO 200, while the brightly lit areas might require f/11 at 1/400th second. That's almost a 7 EV step difference (approximately 7 f/stops) and effectively beyond the dynamic range of any digital camera, including the EOS R8.

Until camera sensors gain much higher dynamic ranges (which may not be as far into the distant future as we think), special tricks like Active D-Lighting and HDR photography will remain basic tools. You can create in-camera HDR exposures or shoot HDR the old-fashioned way—with separate bracketed exposures that are later combined in a tool like Photomatix or Adobe's Merge to HDR Pro image-editing feature. I'm going to show you how to use both.

The camera's in-camera HDR feature is simple, flexible, and surprisingly effective in creating high dynamic range images. It's also fairly easy to use. Although it combines only three images to create a single HDR photograph, and it's not always as good as the manual HDR method, it's a *lot* faster.

Figure 4.19 shows you that typical street situation in which you might want to use HDR, a murky street in St. Augustine, Florida. None of the three bracketed exposures seen at left capture the full detail in the scene, but you can combine them manually using HDR techniques (as I'll show you later) to get the image shown at right.

Using HDR Mode

Here are some tips for using the R8's built-in feature. These guidelines also apply to manually exposed HDR sequences, as I'll explain shortly.

- **Use a tripod if possible.** Because there may be some camera movement between the continuous shots, you'll get better results if you mount the camera on a tripod. However, the R8's anti-shake capabilities can provide a good degree of compensation.
- **Moving objects may produce ghosts.** In this case, there may be some *subject* motion between shots, producing "ghost" effects. Use the built-in HDR mode's Moving Subjects option to reduce the effect.

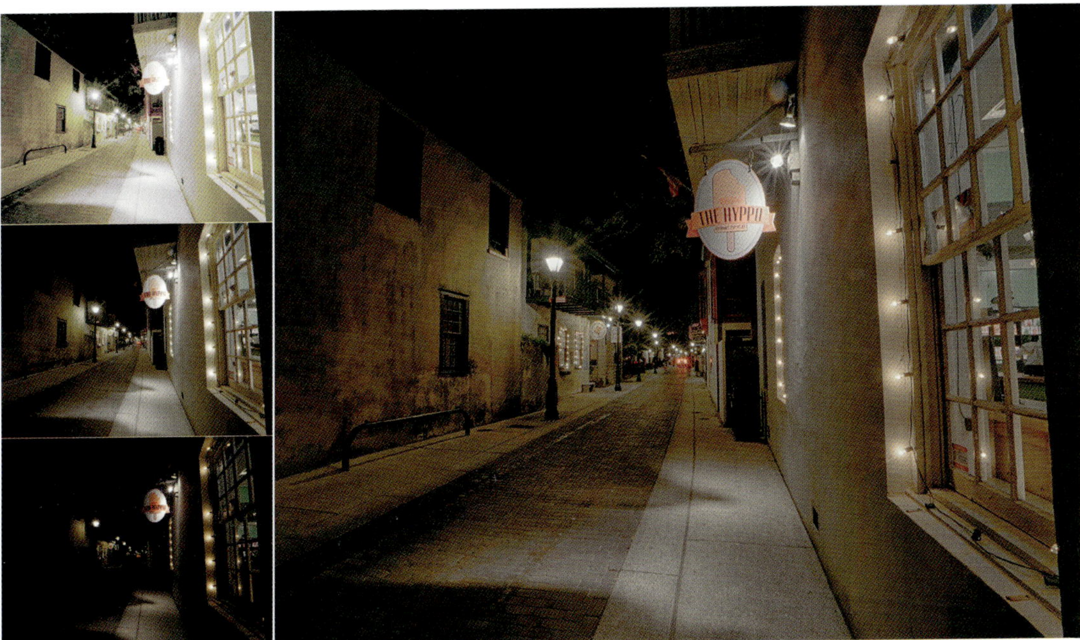

Figure 4.19 HDR combined the three images at left to produce the final version at right.

- **Misalignment.** If you *don't* use a tripod, when Auto Image Align is activated, this mode does a good job of realigning your multiple images when they are merged. However, it can't do a perfect job, particularly with repetitive patterns that are difficult for the camera's "brains" to sort out. Some misalignment is possible.

- **Shutter speeds and ISO settings may vary.** The camera brackets by adjusting the shutter speed within the increment range selected, *even if you're using Tv or M modes and have specified a shutter speed*. Changing the f/stop while shooting an HDR photo alters the focus and possibly image size, and so is not compatible with HDR. The R8 may also adjust the ISO sensitivity if necessary for proper exposure or to reduce the effects of camera shake.

- **Unwanted cropping.** Because the processor needs to be able to shift each individual image slightly in any (or all) of four directions in Auto Image Align mode, it needs to crop the image slightly to trim out any non-image areas that result. Your final image will be slightly smaller than one shot in other modes.

- **Weird colors.** Some types of lighting, including fluorescent and LED illumination, "cycle" many times a second, and colors can vary between shots. You may not even notice this when single shooting, but it becomes more obvious when using any continuous shooting mode, including HDR mode. The combined images may have strange color effects.

- **Limitations.** Images are captured in JPEG or HEIF format only, even if you've specified RAW or RAW+JPEG. Extended ISO speeds aren't available, the flash will not fire during HDR capture, and Auto Exposure Bracketing is disabled. While you can use HDR mode if Auto Lighting Optimizer has been enabled, the camera will disable it while shooting your HDR images, then re-enable it when you turn HDR mode off. Exposures may be uneven under certain types of fluorescent or LED lighting. The electronic shutter is limited to speeds of 1/8000th second or slower in HDR mode.

- **The process takes time.** Forget about firing off a large number of HDR shots in a row. After the camera captures its set of images, it takes a few seconds to process them and save your final image. Be patient.

You can locate HDR Mode in the Shooting 2 menu (see Figure 4.20, left). Press the Q/SET button, and you'll be taken to the menu shown in Figure 4.20, right.

Figure 4.20 The HDR mode menu has three top-level entries.

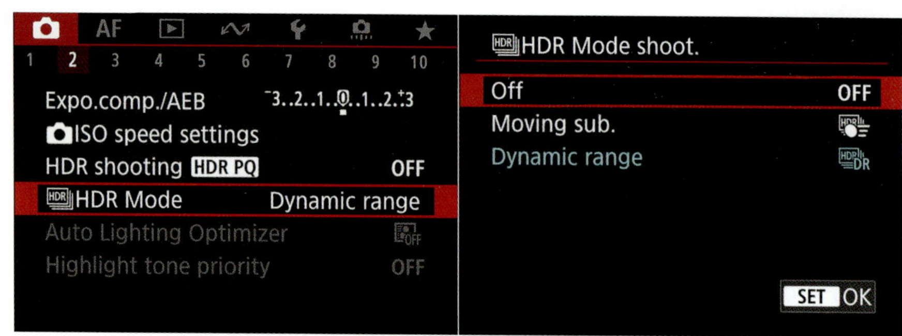

This menu has three main entries, with additional options within them:

- **Off.** Set to Disable when you do not want to produce HDR images. This will be your default setting, as HDR doesn't lend itself to every type of scene. Enable when you have a subject that can benefit from a broader dynamic range. Then choose an HDR mode, either Moving Subject or Dynamic Range, both described below.

- **Moving subject.** This mode is useful for subjects, including humans, animals, or vehicles, that won't remain motionless while the individual HDR images are captured.

- **Dynamic range.** This is your mode of choice for portraits, landscapes, table-top photography, and other scenes with subjects that won't be moving.

Moving Subject Mode

The Moving Subject mode is the easier of the two automatic HDR modes. Just select it, as shown at top left in Figure 4.21, and press SET. The screen seen at top right in Figure 4.21 appears. The only option is Limit Max Brightness, which is grayed out. It's used only if you happen to own a monitor capable of displaying an extended brightness range, as I'll explain in the next section.

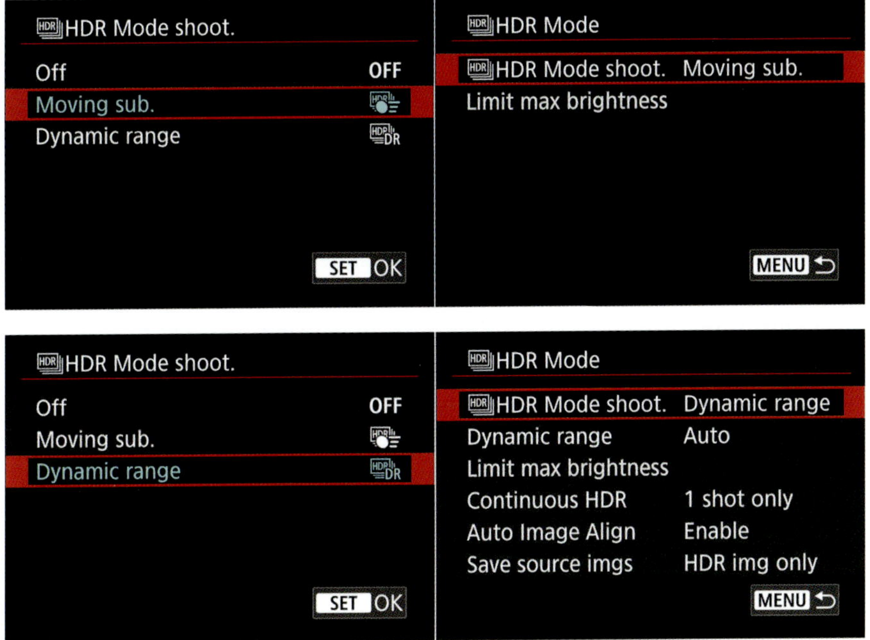

Figure 4.21 Moving Subject mode options (top); Dynamic Range mode options (bottom).

When you use this mode, the R8 will automatically attempt to counter subject motion by using higher shutter speeds and/or higher ISO sensitivity settings. With subjects in darker environments, you may see a bit of noise produced by elevated ISO settings. But keep in mind that, until recently, automatic HDR images of moving subjects were quite problematic, because the first cameras with built-in HDR modes often failed to compensate sufficiently for moving subjects and ghost images were common.

Dynamic Range Mode

This mode is more versatile and customizable, and allows you to fine-tune the settings to produce compelling HDR images of non-moving subjects, which are the traditional realm of high dynamic range photography. When you select Dynamic Range (see Figure 4.21, bottom left), the screen at bottom right appears with the following five options:

- **Dynamic range.** Here you can select the number of stops of dynamic range improvement the HDR feature will provide. (See Figure 4.22, upper left.) Choose Auto to allow the camera to examine your scene and select an appropriate EV range. As you gain experience you might want to select the range yourself, in order to achieve a particular look. You can choose +/–1, +/–2, or +/–3 EV. The higher the number, the wider the dynamic range of your HDR image.

- **Limit maximum brightness.** This entry is available only if you've enabled HDR Shooting/HDR PQ, and will be grayed out otherwise. You can disregard it if you are not using HDR PQ.

It allows you to limit the brightness of images captured using HDR PQ when they will be displayed on monitors that can't handle the format's dynamic range. If you have an HDR-compatible monitor, you can choose Disable; if not, choose 1000 nits to automatically tame your over-bright images. The term "nit" comes from the Latin word nitere, to shine, and is an unofficial, but commonly used measurement to describe the brightness of a display. Apparently, it's easier to say than "candelas per square meter," and a unit that's a better descriptor for displays than lumens (which are used for light bulbs and projectors).

- **Continuous HDR.** Choose 1 Shot Only if you plan to take just a single HDR exposure and want the feature disabled automatically thereafter, or Every Shot to continue using HDR mode for all subsequent exposures until you turn it off. (See Figure 4.22, upper right.)

- **Auto image align.** HDR images are ideally produced with the camera on a tripod, in order to reduce the ghosting effects from a series of pictures that each aren't perfectly aligned with the other. You can choose Enable to have the camera attempt to align all three HDR exposures or select Disable when using a tripod. (See Figure 4.22, lower left.) The success of the automatic alignment will vary, depending on the shutter speed used (higher is better), and the amount of camera movement (less is better!).

- **Save source images.** When the camera has finished creating its HDR image from your three shots, you can choose to save all the images on your memory card (so you can manually combine them later or perform other manipulations using your image editor). Or, you can elect to save your final HDR image only. (See Figure 4.22, lower right.) You might prefer that choice to save card space, reduce the number of images you won't be using anyway, or if you're shooting a lot of HDR and are confident that the camera's results will suit your needs.

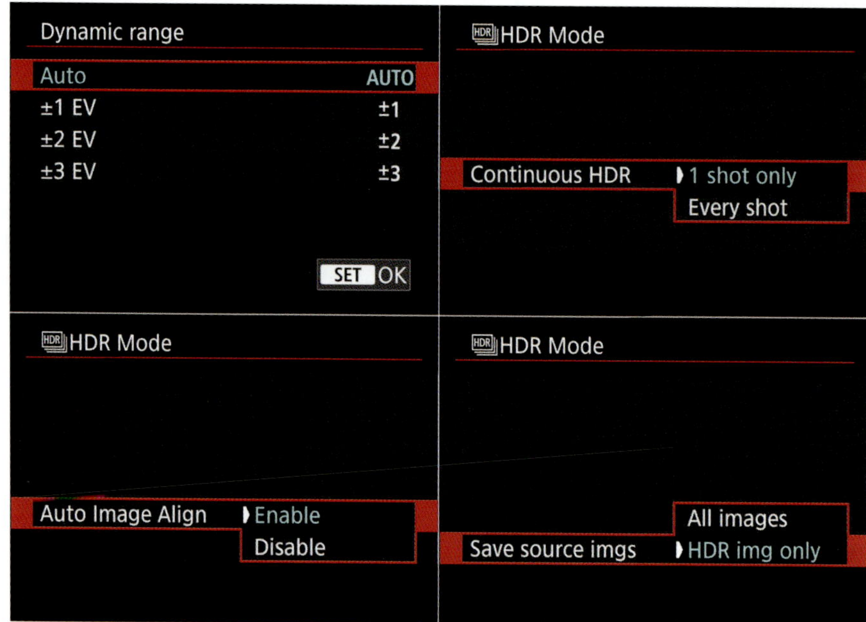

Figure 4.22 Four Dynamic Range mode options.

Bracketing and Merge to HDR

As I mentioned earlier, HDR photography was, for a while, an incredibly popular fad. Everywhere you looked there were overprocessed, garish HDR images that had little relationship to reality. I've been able to resist the temptation to overdo my landscape and travel photography (unlike the deliberately awful example I created for Figure 4.23). The phony-looking skies, the unnatural halos that appear at the edges of some objects, and the weird textures are usually a giveaway. My rule of thumb is that, if you can tell it's HDR, it's been done wrong—unless your intent was to show off what HDR can do.

Although the camera does have the built-in HDR feature I described earlier, you can usually get much better, more tasteful results if you create your high dynamic range images manually. You can use a tool such as Photoshop's Merge to HDR Pro feature, a stand-alone HDR utility, or a third-party Photoshop plug-in.

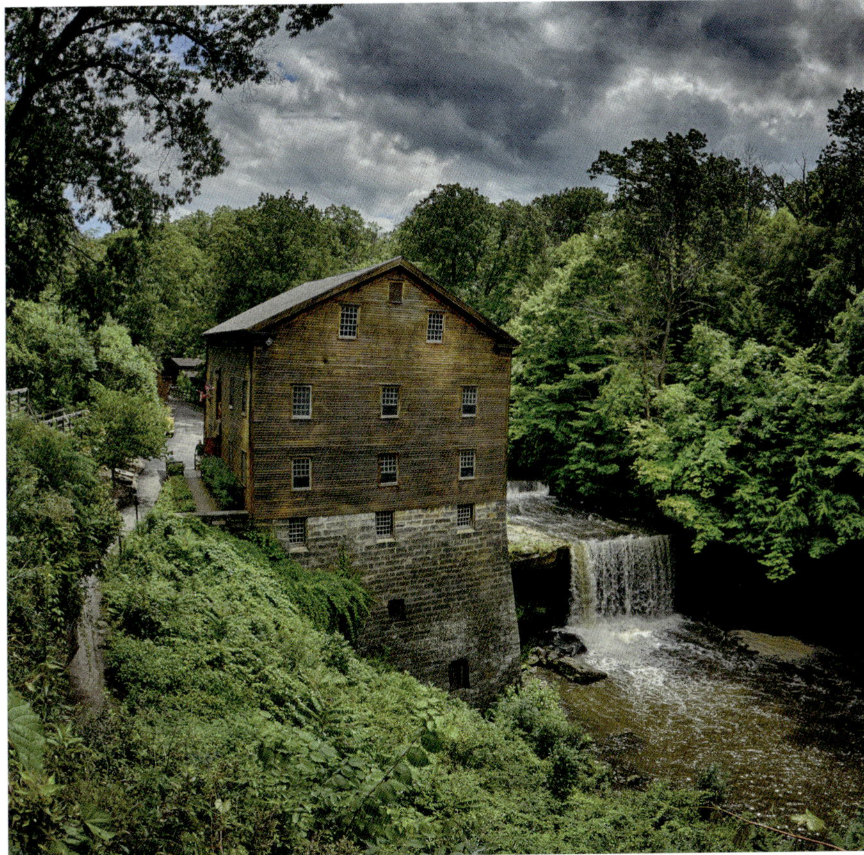

Figure 4.23 A deliberately overcooked HDR photo.

When you're using Merge to HDR Pro in Adobe Photoshop (similar functions are available in other programs, including the Mac/PC utility Photomatix [www.hdrsoft.com; free to try, $39–$99 to buy, depending on the version you select]) and Aurora HDR (www.skylum.com, available by subscription for $119 annually), you'd take and combine several pictures. As I mentioned earlier, one would be exposed for the shadows, one for the highlights, and perhaps one for the midtones. Then, you'd use the Merge to HDR command (or the equivalent in other software) to combine all of the images into one HDR image that integrates the well-exposed sections of each version. You can use the camera's bracketing feature to produce those images.

The next steps show you how to combine the separate exposures into one merged high dynamic range image. The sample images in Figure 4.24 show the results you can get from a three-shot (manually) bracketed sequence. The images should be as identical as possible, except for exposure. So, as with HDR mode, it's a good idea to mount the camera on a tripod, use a remote release, and take all the exposures at once. Just follow these steps:

1. **Set up the camera.** Mount the camera on a tripod.

2. **Choose an f/stop and Av mode.** Select an aperture that will provide a correct exposure at your initial settings for the series of bracketed shots. *And then leave this adjustment alone!* You don't want the aperture to change for your series, as that would change the depth-of-field, and, subtly, the size of some elements of the image as they move more or less out of focus. You want the camera to adjust exposure *only* using the shutter speed.

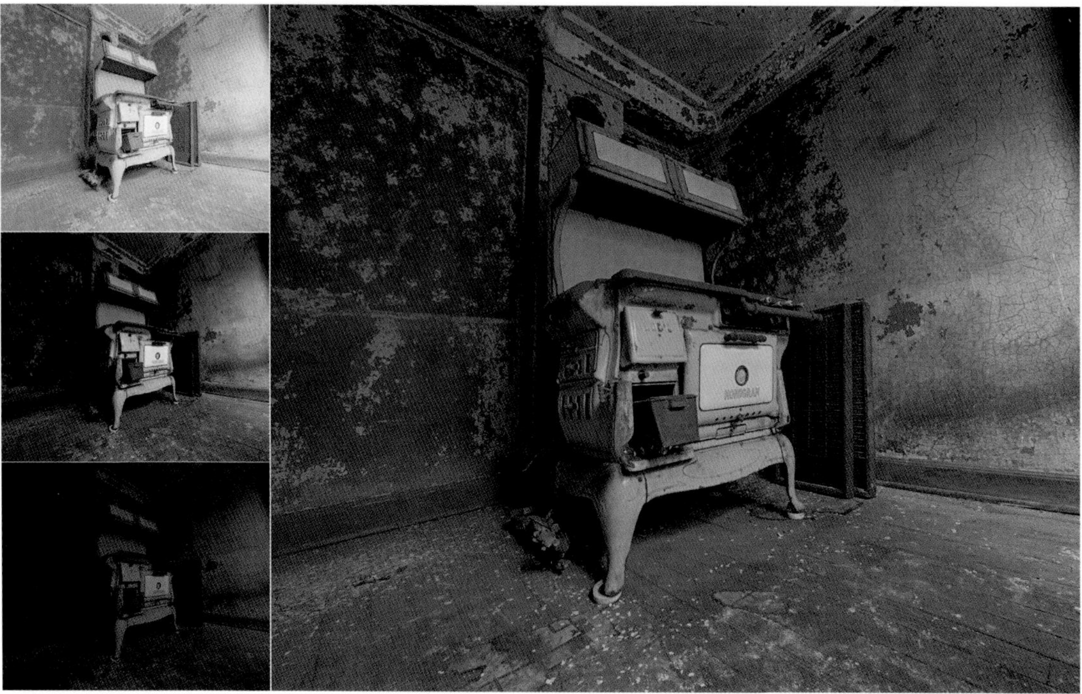

Figure 4.24 Three bracketed photos should look like this (left). The finished image is shown at right.

3. **Choose manual focus.** You don't want the focus to change between shots, so set the camera to manual focus, and carefully focus your shot.

4. **Choose RAW exposures.** Set the camera to take RAW files, which will give you the widest range of tones in your images.

5. **Set up your bracketed set.** Use the instructions earlier in this chapter to set the number of bracketed images you take, and the increment between them. After you've created your first few manual HDR photos, you'll learn to judge what increment is best (larger isn't always better). However, the more shots you have to work with, the better your results can be.

6. **Take your photos.** With the camera in continuous shooting mode, press the button on the remote (or carefully press the shutter release or use the self-timer) and take the set of bracketed exposures.

7. **Continue with the Merge to HDR Pro steps listed next.** You can also use a different program, such as Photomatix, if you know how to use it.

The next steps show you how to combine the separate exposures into one merged high dynamic range image.

1. **Copy your images to your computer.** If you use an application to transfer the files to your computer, make sure it does not make any adjustments to brightness, contrast, or exposure. You want the real raw information for Merge to HDR Pro to work with.

2. **Activate Merge to HDR Pro.** Choose File > Automate > Merge to HDR Pro.

3. **Select the photos to be merged.** Use the Browse feature to locate and select your photos to be merged. You'll note a checkbox that can be used to automatically align the images if they were not taken with the camera mounted on a rock-steady support. This will adjust for any slight movement of the camera that might have occurred when you changed exposure settings.

4. **Choose parameters (optional).** The first time you use Merge to HDR Pro, you can let the program work with its default parameters. Once you've played with the feature a few times, you can read the Adobe help files and learn more about the options than I can present in this non-software-oriented camera guide.

5. **Click OK.** The merger begins.

6. **Save.** Once HDR merge has done its thing, save the file to your computer.

What if you don't have the opportunity, inclination, or skills to create several images at different exposures, as described? If you shoot in RAW format, you can still use Merge to HDR, working with a *single* original image file. What you do is import the image into Photoshop several times, using Adobe Camera Raw to create multiple copies of the file at different exposure levels.

For example, you'd create one copy that's too dark, so the shadows lose detail, but the highlights are preserved. Create another copy with the shadows intact and allow the highlights to wash out. Then, you can use Merge to HDR to combine the two and end up with a finished image that has the extended dynamic range you're looking for. (This concludes the image-editing portion of the chapter. We now return you to our alternate sponsor: photography.)

Fixing Exposures with Histograms

While you can often recover poorly exposed photos in your image editor, your best bet is to arrive at the correct exposure in the camera, minimizing the tweaks that you have to make in post-processing. However, you can't always judge exposure just by simply looking at the preview image on your camera's display before the shot is made, nor the review image in Playback. Ambient light may make the monitor difficult to see, and the brightness level you've set for the monitor and viewfinder in the Set-up menu can affect the appearance of the image.

Instead, you can use a histogram, which is a chart shown on the camera's display that shows the number of tones that have been captured at each brightness level. Histograms are available in real time on your display as you shoot and in the review image during playback, but they are available only when enabled. I'll show you how to enable histograms and select from among the various options available for histograms in Chapter 13. To view histograms in shooting mode or playback mode, press the INFO button until a screen with the histogram appears.

Histograms come in various flavors. Photographers are generally concerned only with two types: a brightness or *luminance* histogram, which deals only with the relative overall intensity of the tones in the image (see Figure 4.25, top), and a *color* histogram that displays the intensity of each individual color channel in a particular color space (see Figure 4.25, bottom). Photographers most often work with an RGB histogram that displays values for red, green, and blue pixels in an image, but other varieties exist, such as CMYK (for cyan, magenta, yellow, and black hues) and HSL/HSV (hue, saturation, and lightness/value), which are alternate ways of representing the RGB color space.

To get you up to speed with histograms, the next few sections will deal only with the brightness/luminance histogram variety.

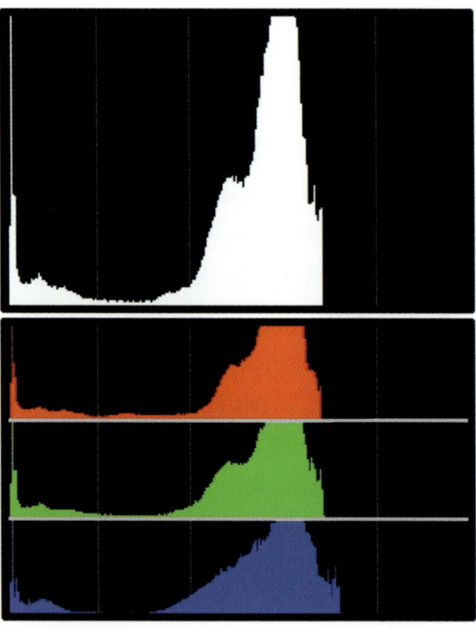

Figure 4.25 Brightness histogram (top), RGB histogram (bottom).

Tonal Range

Histograms help you adjust the tonal range of an image, the span of dark to light tones, from a complete absence of brightness (black) to the brightest possible tone (white), and all the middle tones in between. Because all values for tones fall into a continuous spectrum between black and white, it's easiest to think of a photo's tonality in terms of a black-and-white or grayscale image, even though you're capturing those tones in three separate color layers of red, green, and blue.

Because your images are digital, the tonal "spectrum" isn't really continuous: it's divided into discrete steps that represent the different tones that can be captured. Figure 4.26 may help you understand this concept. The gray steps shown range from 100 percent gray (black) at the left, to 0 percent gray (white) at the right, with 20 gray steps in all (plus white).

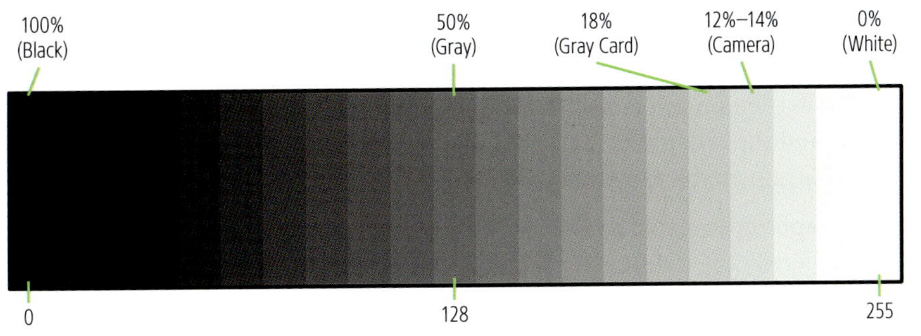

Figure 4.26 A tonal range from black (left) to white (right) and all the gray values in between.

Along the bottom of the chart are the digital values from 0 to 255 recorded by your sensor for an image with 8 bits per channel. (8 bits of red, 8 bits of green, and 8 bits of blue equal a 24-bit, full-color image.) Any black captured would be represented by a value of 0, the brightest white by 255, and the midtones would be clustered around the 128 marker. The actual information captured may be "finer" and record, say, 0 to 4,094 for an image captured when the camera is set to 14 bits per channel for a RAW file (see Chapter 11 for more detail on that option).

Grayscale images (which we call black-and-white photos) are easy to understand. Or, at least, that's what we think. When we look at a black-and-white image, we think we're seeing a continuous range of tones from black to white, and all the grays in between. But, that's not exactly true. The blackest black in any photo isn't a true black, because *some* light is always reflected from the surface of the print, and if viewed on a screen, the deepest black is only as dark as the least-reflective area a computer monitor can produce. The whitest white isn't a true white, either, because even the lightest areas of a print absorb some light (only a mirror reflects close to all the light that strikes it), and, when viewing on a computer monitor, the whites are limited by the brightness of the display's LCD or LED picture elements. Lacking darker blacks and brighter, whiter whites, that continuous set of tones doesn't cover the full grayscale tonal range.

The full scale of tones becomes useful when you have an image that has large expanses of shades that change gradually from one level to the next, such as areas of sky, water, or walls. Think of a picture taken of a group of campers around a campfire. Since the light from the fire is striking them directly in the face, there aren't many shadows on the campers' faces. All the tones that make up the *features* of the people around the fire are compressed into one end of the brightness spectrum—the lighter end.

Yet, there's more to this scene than faces. Behind the campers are trees, rocks, and perhaps a few animals that have emerged from the shadows to see what is going on. These are illuminated by the softer light that bounces off the surrounding surfaces. If your eyes become accustomed to the reduced illumination, you'll find that there is a wealth of detail in these shadow images.

This campfire scene would be a nightmare to reproduce faithfully under any circumstances. If you are an experienced photographer, you are probably already wincing at what is called a *high-contrast* lighting situation. Some photos may be high in contrast when there are fewer tones, and they are all bunched up at limited points in the scale. In a low-contrast image, there are more tones, but they are spread out so widely that the image looks flat. Your digital camera can show you the relationship between these tones using a *histogram*.

Histogram Basics

Your camera's histograms are a simplified display of the numbers of pixels at each of 256 brightness levels, producing an interesting "mountain range" shape in the graph. Although separate charts may be provided for brightness and the red, green, and blue channels, when you first start using histograms, you'll want to concentrate on the brightness histogram.

Each vertical line in the graph represents the number of pixels in the image for each brightness value, from 0 (black) on the left to 255 (white) on the right. The vertical axis measures that number of pixels at each level.

Although histograms are most often used to fine-tune exposure, you can glean other information from them, such as the relative contrast of the image. Figure 4.27, top, shows a generic histogram of an image having normal contrast. In such an image, most of the pixels are spread across the image, with a healthy distribution of tones throughout the midtone section of the graph. That large peak at the right side of the graph represents all those light tones in the sky. A normal-contrast image you shoot may have less sky area, and less of a peak at the right side, but notice that very few pixels hug the right edge of the histogram, indicating that the lightest tones are not being clipped because they are off the chart.

With a lower-contrast image, like the one shown in Figure 4.27, center, the basic shape of the previous histogram will remain recognizable, but gradually will be compressed together to cover a smaller area of the gray spectrum. The squished shape of the histogram is caused by all the grays in the original image being represented by a limited number of gray tones in a smaller range of the scale.

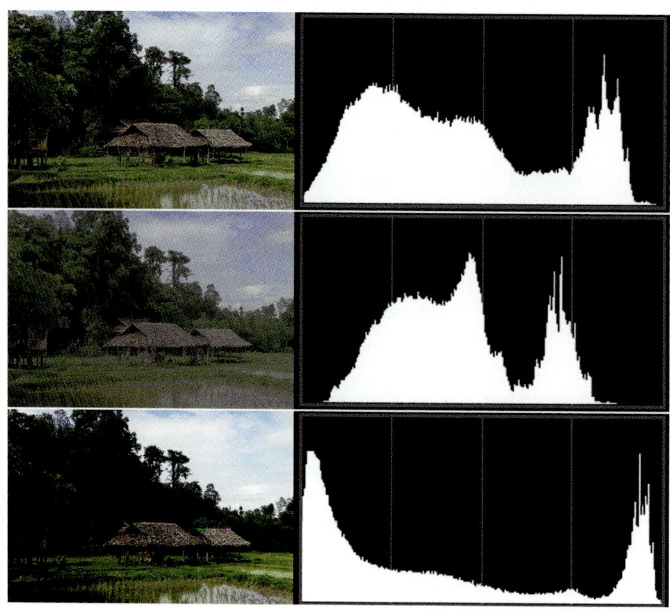

Figure 4.27 Top: This image has fairly normal contrast, even though there is a peak of light tones at the right side representing the sky. Center: This low-contrast image has all the tones squished into one section of the grayscale. Bottom: A high-contrast image produces a histogram in which the tones are spread out.

Instead of the darkest tones of the image reaching into the black end of the spectrum and the whitest tones extending to the lightest end, the blackest areas of the scene are now represented by a light gray, and the whites by a somewhat lighter gray. The overall contrast of the image is reduced. Because all the darker tones are actually a middle gray or lighter, the scene in this version of the photo appears lighter as well.

Going in the other direction, increasing the contrast of an image produces a histogram like the one shown in Figure 4.27, bottom. In this case, the tonal range is now spread over the entire width of the chart, but, except for the bright sky, there is not much variation in the middle tones; the mountain "peaks" are not very high. When you stretch the grayscale in both directions like this, the darkest tones become darker (that may not be possible) and the lightest tones become lighter (ditto). In fact, shades that might have been gray before can change to black or white as they are moved toward either end of the scale.

The effect of increasing contrast may be to move some tones off either end of the scale altogether, while spreading the remaining grays over a smaller number of locations on the spectrum. That's exactly the case in the example shown. The number of possible tones is smaller, and the image appears harsher.

Understanding Histograms

The important thing to remember when working with the histogram display in your camera is that changing the exposure does *not* change the contrast of an image. The curves illustrated in the previous three examples remain exactly the same shape when you increase or decrease exposure. I repeat: The proportional distribution of grays shown in the histogram doesn't change when exposure changes; it is neither stretched nor compressed. However, the tones as a whole are moved toward one end of the scale or the other, depending on whether you're increasing or decreasing exposure. You'll be able to see that in some illustrations that follow.

So, as you reduce exposure, tones gradually move to the black end (and off the scale), while the reverse is true when you increase exposure. The contrast within the image is changed only to the extent that some of the tones can no longer be represented when they are moved off the scale.

To change the *contrast* of an image, you must do one of four things:

- **Change the camera's contrast setting** using the menu system. You'll find these adjustments in your camera's Picture Style options in the Shooting 4 menu, as explained in Chapter 11.
- **Use your camera's shadow-tone and highlight "boosters."** Auto Lighting Optimizer and Highlight Tone Priority, also discussed in Chapter 11, can help you adjust contrast.
- **Alter the contrast of the scene itself,** for example, by using a fill light or reflectors to add illumination to shadows that are too dark.
- **Attempt to adjust contrast in post-processing** using your image editor or RAW file converter. You may use features such as Levels or Curves (in Photoshop, Photoshop Elements, and many other image editors) or work with HDR software to cherry-pick the best values in shadows and highlights from multiple images.

Of the four of these, the third—changing the contrast of the scene—is the most desirable, because attempting to fix contrast by fiddling with the tonal values is unlikely to be a perfect remedy. However, adding a little contrast can be successful because you can discard some tones to make the image more contrasty. However, the opposite is much more difficult. An overly contrasty image rarely can be fixed because you can't add information that isn't there in the first place.

What you *can* do is adjust the exposure so that the tones *that are already present in the scene* are captured correctly. Figure 4.28, top, shows the histogram for an image that is badly underexposed. You can guess from the shape of the histogram that many of the dark tones to the left of the graph have been clipped off. There's plenty of room on the right side for additional pixels to reside without having them become overexposed. So, you can increase the exposure (either by changing the f/stop or shutter speed, or by adding an EV value) to produce the corrected histogram shown in Figure 4.28, center.

Conversely, if your histogram looks like the one shown in Figure 4.28, bottom, with bright tones pushed off the right edge of the chart, you have an overexposed image, and you can correct it by reducing exposure. In addition to the histogram, the camera has its Highlights option, which, when activated, shows areas that are overexposed with flashing tones (often called "blinkies") in the review screen. Depending on the importance of this "clipped" detail, you can adjust exposure or leave it alone. For example, if all the dark-coded areas in the review are in a background that you care little about, you can forget about them and not change the exposure, but if such areas appear in facial details of your subject, you may want to make some adjustments.

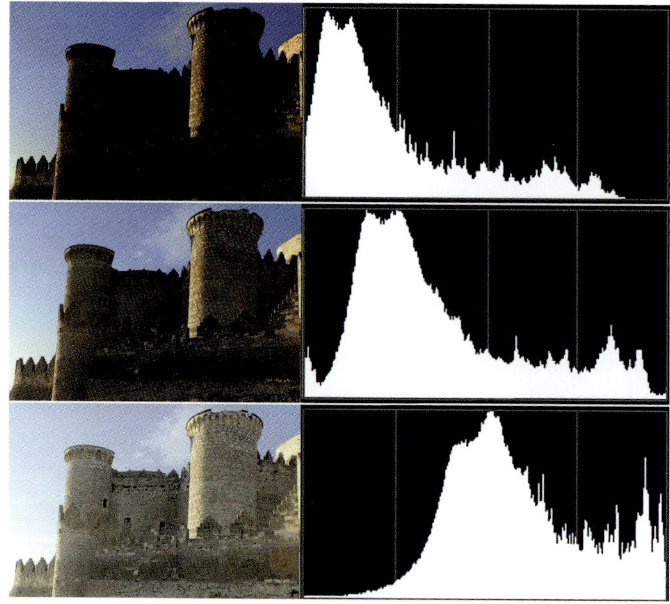

Figure 4.28 Top: A histogram of an under-exposed image may look like this. Center: Adding exposure will produce a histogram like this one. Bottom: A histogram of an overexposed image will show clipping at the right side.

In working with histograms, your goal should be to have all the tones in an image spread out between the edges, with none clipped off at the left and right sides. Underexposing (to preserve highlights) should be done only as a last resort, because retrieving the underexposed shadows in your image editor will frequently increase the noise, even if you're working with RAW files. A better course of action is to expose for the highlights, but, when the subject matter makes it practical, fill in the shadows with additional light, using reflectors, fill flash, or other techniques rather than allowing them to be seriously underexposed.

A traditional technique for optimizing exposure is called "expose to the right" (ETTR), which involves adding exposure to push the histogram's curve toward the right side *but not far enough to clip off highlights.* The rationale for this method is that extra shadow detail will be produced with a minimum increase in noise, especially in the shadow areas. It's said that half of a digital sensor's response lies in the brightest areas of an image, and so require the least amount of amplification (which is one way to increase digital noise). ETTR can work, as long as you're able to capture a satisfactory amount of information in the shadows.

Exposing to the Right

It's easier to understand exposing to the right if you mentally divide the histogram into fifths (unfortunately, the camera's histogram uses quarters instead). And, for the sake of simplicity and smaller numbers, assume you're shooting in 14-bit RAW. Any 14-bit image can record a maximum of 16,383 different tones per channel. However, each fifth of the histogram does *not* encompass 3,277 tones (one-fifth of 16,383).

Instead, the right-most fifth, the highlights, shown in Figure 4.29, accounts for about half of the captured tones. Moving toward the left, the next fifth represents one-quarter, followed by one-eighth, and one sixteenth of the available levels. In the left-most section where the deepest shadows reside,

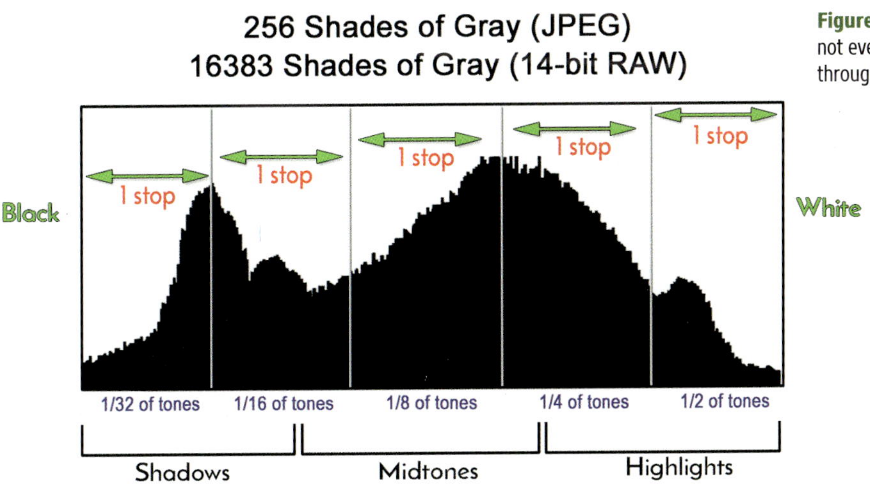

Figure 4.29 Tones are not evenly allocated throughout a histogram.

only about 512 different tones are captured. So, when processing your RAW file, there are only about 500 tones to recover in the shadows, which is why boosting/amplifying them increases noise. (The effect is most noticeable in the red and blue channels; your sensor's Bayer array has twice as many green-sensitive pixels as red or blue.)

Instead, you want to add exposure—as long as you don't push highlights off the right edge of the histogram—to brighten the shadows. Because there are roughly 8,000 tones available in the highlights, even if the RAW image *looks* overexposed, it's possible to use your RAW converter's Exposure slider (such as the one found in Adobe Camera Raw) to bring back detail captured in that surplus of tones in the highlights. This procedure is the exact opposite of what was recommended for film of the transparency variety—it was fairly easy to retrieve detail from shadows by pumping more light through them when processing the image, while even small amounts of extra exposure blew out highlights. (Note: I've rounded the numbers a bit for simplicity.) You'll often find that the range of tones in your image is so great that there is no way to keep your histogram from spilling over into the left and right edges, costing you both highlight and shadow detail. Exposing to the right may not work in such situations. A second school of thought recommends *reducing* exposure to bring back the highlights, or "exposing to the left." You would then attempt to recover shadow detail in an image editor, using tools like Adobe Camera Raw's Exposure slider. But remember, above all, that this procedure will also boost noise in the shadows, and so the technique should be used with caution. In most cases, exposing to the right is your best bet.

Dealing with Channels

The more you work with histograms, the more useful they become. One of the first things that histogram veterans notice is that it's possible to overexpose one channel even if the overall exposure appears to be correct. For example, flower photographers soon discover that it's really, really difficult to get a good picture of a red rose, like the one shown at left in Figure 4.30. The exposure looks okay—but there's no detail in the rose's petals. Looking at the histogram (see Figure 4.30, right)

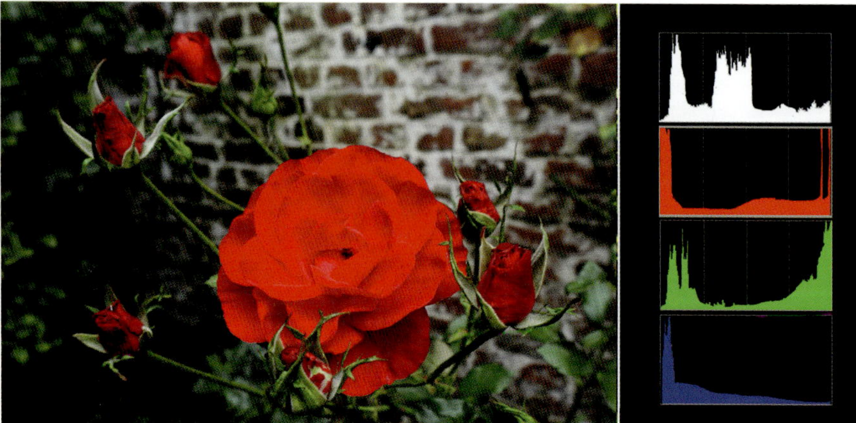

Figure 4.30 It's common to lose detail in bright red flowers because the red channel becomes overexposed even when the other channels are properly exposed (left). The RGB histograms show that both the red and green channels are overexposed, with tones extending past the right edge of the chart (right).

shows why: the red channel is blown out. If you look at the red histogram, there's a peak at the right edge that indicates that highlight information has been lost. In fact, the green channel has been blown, too, and so the green parts of the flower also lack detail. Only the blue channel's histogram is entirely contained within the boundaries of the chart, and, on first glance, the white luminance histogram at top of the column of graphs seems fairly normal.

Any of the primary channels—red, green, or blue—can blow out all by themselves, although bright reds seem to be the most common problem area. More difficult to diagnose are overexposed tones in one of the "in-between" hues on the color wheel. Overexposed yellows (which are very common) will be shown by blowouts in *both* the red and green channels. Too-bright cyans will manifest as excessive blue and green highlights, while overexposure in the red and blue channels reduces detail in magenta colors. As you gain experience, you'll be able to see exactly how anomalies in the RGB channels translate into poor highlights and murky shadows.

The only way to correct for color channel blowouts is to reduce exposure. As I mentioned earlier, you might want to consider filling in the shadows with additional light to keep them from becoming too dark when you decrease exposure. In practice, you'll want to monitor the red channel most closely, followed by the blue channel, and slightly decrease exposure to see if that helps. Because of the way our eyes perceive color, we are more sensitive to variations in green, so green channel blowouts are less of a problem, unless your main subject is heavily colored in that hue. If you plan on photographing a frog hopping around on your front lawn, you'll want to be extra careful to preserve detail in the green channel, using bracketing or other exposure techniques outlined in this chapter.

Discovering Basic Zone Modes

I'm going to finish this chapter with descriptions of the Basic Zone exposure settings: Scene Intelligent Auto, Special Scene, and Creative Filter modes. As I noted earlier in the chapter, these modes give you little control over many settings, but are fast and fun to use when you want the camera to do more of the thinking. They are especially useful when you suddenly encounter a picture-taking opportunity and don't have time to decide exactly which Creative Zone mode you want to use. Instead, you can spin the Mode dial to Scene Intelligent Auto (with the green A+ icon), or to the SCN position, where you can choose an appropriate SCN mode, and fire away, knowing that at least you have a fighting chance of getting a good or usable photo. Or, you can select a Creative Filter to add a special effect automatically.

Basic Zone modes are also helpful when you're just learning to use your Canon EOS R8. Once you've learned how to operate your camera, you'll probably prefer one of the Creative Zone modes that provide more control over shooting options.

Scene Intelligent Auto Mode

On first consideration, including an exposure mode with almost no user options might seem counterintuitive on a camera as advanced as the R8, because it essentially transforms a sophisticated pro/enthusiast camera into a point-and-click snapshooter. Delve deeper, and you'll discover that there is method in Canon's madness, and that Scene Intelligent Auto is a lot more than a less versatile version of Program mode. The key is the *intelligent* part of the mode's nomenclature.

With P mode (discussed earlier in this chapter), only the shutter speed and aperture are determined by the camera. You can change the metering mode, autofocus mode, white balance, and virtually all other settings. In Scene Intelligent Auto mode, the camera will analyze your scene, even to the extent of evaluating whether or not your subject is static or moving, and then intelligently choose optimum settings without any input from you. The settings the camera has to work with include:

- **ISO speed.** The camera will choose an ISO sensitivity automatically.
- **Picture Style.** The A (automatic) Picture Style is active, and the camera will choose appropriate settings. Note that if you have made changes to the Auto Picture Style (I'll show you how to do that in Chapter 11), they will be ignored in Scene Intelligent Auto.
- **White balance.** White balance is set automatically and cannot be changed.
- **Auto Lighting Optimizer.** Always active in Scene Intelligent Auto mode.
- **Color space.** Forced to sRGB.
- **Autofocus.** The camera selects either One-Shot AF or Servo AF when you press the shutter release button halfway. You cannot switch from one to the other manually. AF point selection is always automatic, and the AF-assist beam is activated if needed. You can turn Eye Detection on or off by pressing the Q/SET button, highlighting the AF Method icon, and pressing the INFO button.
- **Metering mode.** Evaluative metering is always used.

When you rotate the Mode dial to the A+ position, the screen shown at left in Figure 4.31 appears. Choose OK, and the view seen at right in the figure appears on the touch screen. In the upper-left corner, an icon will be shown that indicates the scene mode the camera has chosen (in this case, Portrait).

Figure 4.31 Using Scene Intelligent Auto.

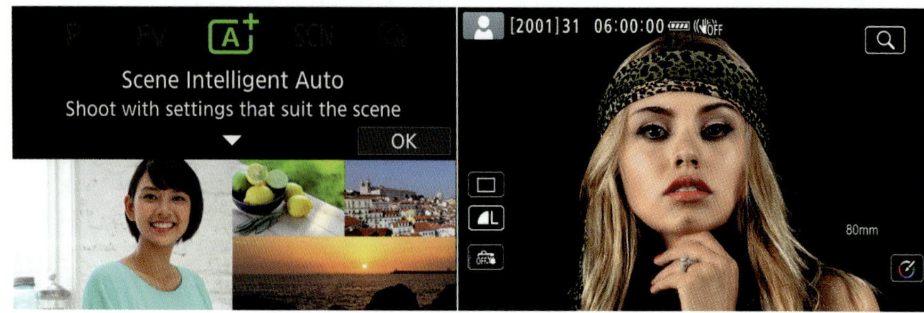

Arrayed along the left side are icons representing the settings you can adjust using the touch screen:

- **Drive mode.** Tap the icon to choose from single shooting, three continuous shooting speeds, and self-timer modes with delays of 2 or 10 seconds, plus a continuous self-timer mode that directs the camera to take from 2 to 10 individual shots after the timer has elapsed.
- **Image quality/size.** Tap the icon to select among your RAW, JPEG, and other image size options, including Movie Recording Size.
- **Touch Shutter (Enable/Disable).** When Touch Shutter is enabled, you can tap on a person's face or some other subject within the frame and take a picture.
- **Manual focus.** In addition to the three parameters listed above, Manual focus can be chosen by toggling the AF/MF switch on the lens barrel (if present).
- **Creative Assist.** At the lower-right corner of the screen, you'll see the focal length/zoom setting of the lens, and an icon that lets you summon Creative Assist, which I'll describe in the next section.

The reason this mode is called Scene Intelligent is that the camera is able to make a fairly accurate guess about whether your subject fits into one of its Special Scene categories (discussed shortly), and automatically apply that Scene mode as if you'd chosen it yourself. An icon representing the scene selected appears at the upper-left corner of the display.

Things that you *can* choose in Scene Intelligent Auto mode include:

- **Manual focus.** Manual focus can be chosen by toggling the AF/MF switch on the lens to Manual.
- **Touch focus.** You can tap on a person's face or some other subject within the frame, using the touch screen.
- **Drive mode.** You use the Quick Control screen to choose from single shooting, high-/low-speed continuous shooting, silent single shooting, silent continuous shooting, and 10 sec./2 sec. self-timer modes.
- **Image quality/size.** Press the Q/SET button to select among your RAW, JPEG, and other image size options, including Movie Recording Size.

Some specific Shooting menu options are available from the truncated four-tab menu system offered in Scene Intelligent Auto mode; there are also two Autofocus menu tabs. The available choices are described in more detail in Chapters 11 and 12.

Creative Assist

Scene Intelligent Auto has a Creative Assist feature, similar to the one found in Playback mode, which lets you apply certain effects to images as you capture them. To invoke this feature while using A+, tap the Creative Assist icon at lower right on the touch screen, or press the Q/SET button. A scrollable list, shown in the top row of Figure 4.32, appears. It has icons representing Presets, plus seven Settings you can apply, as described below:

- **Presets.** Highlight the first icon in the row to access a scrollable array of 11 Preset effects. They include Vivid, Soft, Warm, Cool, Green, Shine, Lime, Peach, B&W, Blue, and Purple. (See Figure 4.32, second row.)

- **Settings.** There are seven more icons located to the right of the Preset icon. Each represents a different parameter you can adjust: Background Blur, Brightness, Contrast, Saturation, Color Tone 1, Color Tone 2, and Monochrome.

  Each of the seven can be individually fine-tuned. For example, Background Blur can be set from Blurred to Auto to Sharp. Brightness can be adjusted from Darker to Brighter, as seen at left and right (respectively), at the bottom of Figure 4.32. The Color Tone 1 (Blue/Amber bias), Color Tone 2 (Magenta/Green bias), and Monochrome (Black-and-White, Sepia, Blue, Purple, Green) add specific hues to your scene.

  Any parameters you set here are lost when you change to another shooting mode or turn off the camera. To preserve them for a future session, enable the Retain Creative Assist Data entry of the Shooting 4 menu. **Note:** This entry appears *only* when the Mode dial is set to the SCN position! Then, in the settings screen, press the INFO button to register those adjustments as Presets. Up to three sets can be stored and will appear as User 1, User 2, and User 3 in the Presets array. Once all three are filled, you can only save a new set by overwriting one of the existing User slots.

Figure 4.32 Presets and special effects (top); available Presets (center); typical effects adjustments (bottom).

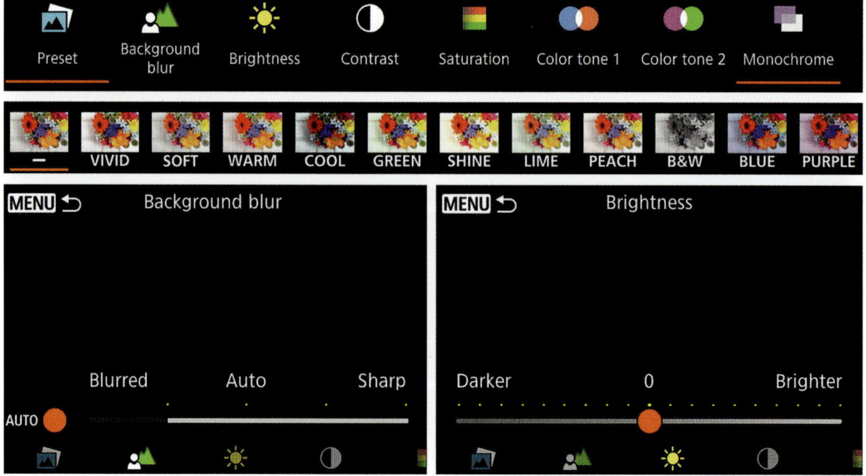

In practice, the Creative Assist options allow you to apply changes to the look of your image in a variety of ways, ranging from brightness and contrast, richness of the colors, and amber/blue or green/magenta color bias. You can also adjust "background" blur, which is simply a way of saying varying the depth-of-field to make the background sharper or blurrier. However, keep in mind that Background Blur can't be used with electronic flash.

Special Scene Mode

The SCN position on the Mode dial activates the R8's Special Scene mode, which includes a roster of 13 subject categories that really do cover a broad range of the most typical kinds of things you'll be photographing. If the Mode Guide has been activated in the Set-up 2 menu, the introductory screen shown at the left center of Figure 4.33 appears. Press Q/SET to choose one of the Scene modes arrayed in the figure.

If the Mode Guide is disabled, just press the Q/SET button and rotate the Main dial to cycle through the available Scene modes. Your choices include:

- **Portrait.** This mode tends to use wider f/stops and faster shutter speeds, providing blurred backgrounds and images with no camera shake. If you hold down the shutter release, the R8 will take a continuous sequence of photos, which can be useful in capturing fleeting expressions in portrait situations. Skin tones and hair are portrayed in a softer, more flattering way.

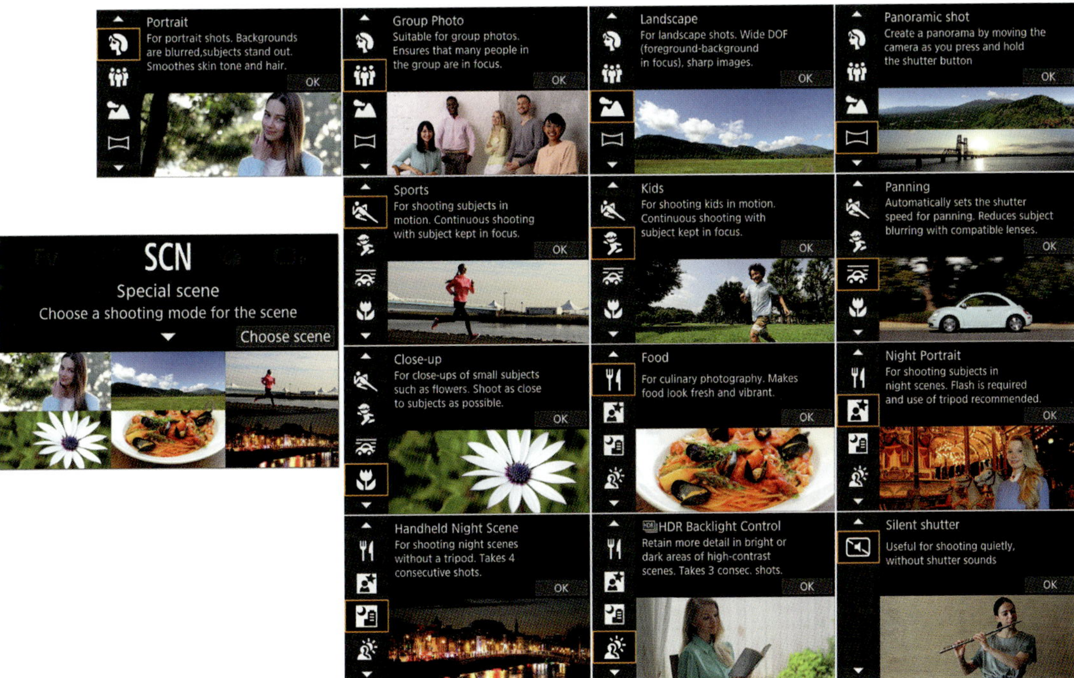

Figure 4.33 Special Scene modes.

- **Group Photo.** For best results, use a wide-angle lens to increase depth-of-field. This mode will attempt to maximize the range of sharpness so you can capture images in which the folks in front and those standing in the back of a group are all in focus.

- **Landscape.** The R8 tries to use smaller f/stops for more depth-of-field, and boosts saturation slightly for richer colors. The built-in flash is disabled, but an attached and powered-up external Speedlite *will* fire.

- **Panoramic Shot.** You can create a wide-screen panorama by rotating the camera during the exposure, as directed by on-screen prompts.

- **Sports.** In this mode, the R8 tries to use high shutter speeds to freeze action, switches to continuous shooting to allow taking a quick sequence of pictures with one press of the shutter release, and uses AI Servo AF to continually refocus as your subject moves around in the frame. You can find more information on autofocus options in Chapter 5.

- **Kids.** This mode applies continuous focusing to follow the movement of frenetic children, and continuous shooting to grab a continuous stream of still photos. Skin tones are adjusted to look vibrant and healthy. You can place the center AF point in the viewfinder over your main subject and press the shutter release halfway. The R8 will refocus as required to track the child's motion, and you'll hear a beep that indicates that refocusing is taking place. If the camera cannot achieve sharp focus, the focus confirmation indicator in the viewfinder will blink.

- **Panning.** This mode adds a feeling of motion by using a slow shutter speed that allows some blurring as you rotate the camera to follow a moving subject.

- **Close-Up.** This mode is similar to the Portrait setting, with wider f/stops to isolate your close-up subjects, and high shutter speeds to eliminate the camera shake that's accentuated at close-focusing distances. However, if you have your camera mounted on a tripod or are using an image-stabilized (IS) lens, you might want to use the Creative Zone Aperture-priority (Av) mode instead, so you can specify a smaller f/stop with additional depth-of-field.

- **Food.** Rich colors and higher contrast in this mode make your food pictures look vivid and appetizing.

- **Night Portrait.** Combines flash with ambient light to produce an image that is mainly illuminated by the flash, but the background is exposed by the available light. This mode uses longer exposures, so a tripod, monopod, or IS lens is a must.

- **Handheld Night Scene.** In this mode, the R8 takes four continuous shots and combines them to produce a well-exposed image with reduced camera shake.

- **HDR Backlight Control.** The R8 takes three continuous shots at different exposures and combines them to produce a single image with improved detail in the highlights and shadows.

- **Silent Shutter.** Uses the electronic shutter to capture an image virtually noiselessly, because the mechanical shutter is not used.

Creative Filters

One useful feature of the R8 is the ability to apply Creative Filters to images *as you take the picture*. However, you can also apply these effects to images you've already taken using the Playback Creative Filters entry in the Playback 2 menu (as I'll describe in Chapter 13). The advantage of applying the filters as you shoot is that you can preview their effect before shooting during live view; the advantage of applying them to a shot that you've already taken is that the modified image is saved alongside the original, which is not changed.

You can apply any of these Creative Filters when using the optical viewfinder (although you can't preview the effects) and when shooting using live view with the LCD screen. Just rotate the Mode dial to the Creative Filters position, located between the SCN and C1 positions. If the Mode Guide is enabled, press the Q/SET button, and you can scroll through a list that includes Grainy B/W, Soft Focus, Fish-eye Effect, Water Painting Effect, Toy Camera Effect, Miniature Effect, and HDR Art (Standard, Vivid, Bold, and Embossed), as seen in Figure 4.34. If the Mode Guide is disabled, press the Q/SET button and rotate the Main dial to select a filter from the Quick Control screen.

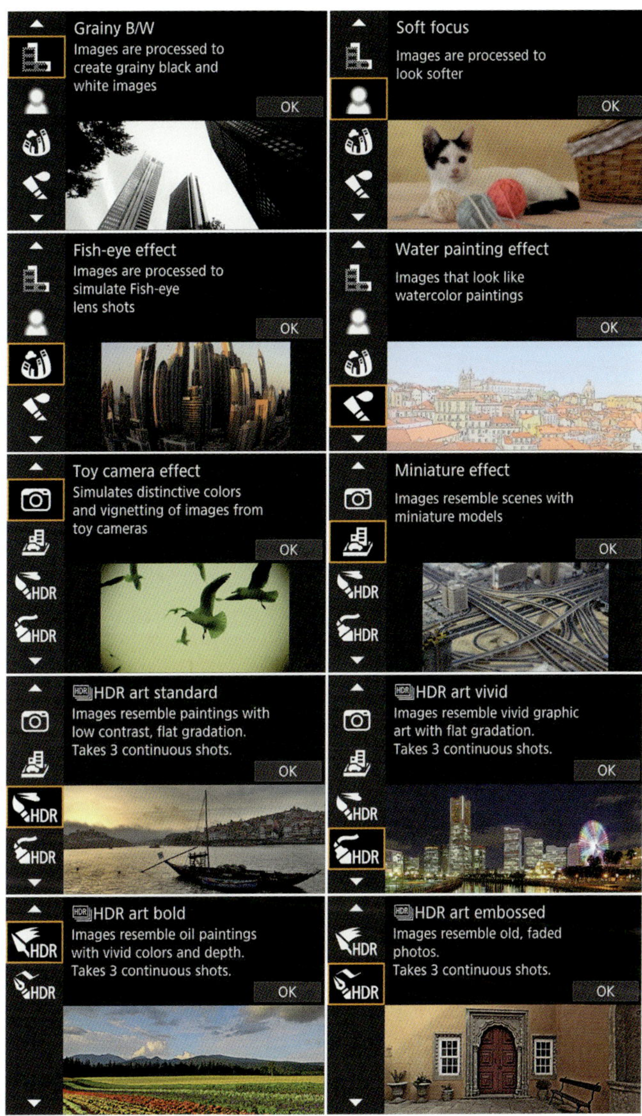

Figure 4.34 Creative Filters.

Each filter has adjustments available. Five of the six choices allow you to modify the effect by pressing the up directional button and pressing left/right controls to increase/decrease parameters: Grainy B/W (Contrast), Soft Focus, Fish-eye (Strength of the effect), Water Painting (Color Density), and Toy Camera (Warm, Neutral, Cool color tone). All of them, except the four HDR choices, allow you to specify Drive mode and Built-in Flash controls. (The HDR modes only allow Drive mode changes.)

SPECIAL HDR EFFECTS

The HDR filters generate four different special effects (see Figure 4.35):

- **Art Standard.** Offers a great deal of highlight and shadow detail, but with lower overall contrast and outlines accentuated, making the image look more like a painting. Saturation, bold outline, and brightness are adjusted to the default levels, and tonal range is lower in contrast.

- **Art Vivid.** Similar to Art Standard, but the saturation is boosted to produce richer colors, and the bold outlines are not as strong, producing a poster-like effect.

- **Art Bold.** Even higher saturation than Art Vivid, with emphasized edge transitions, producing what Canon calls an "oil-painting" effect.

- **Art Embossed.** Reduces saturation, darker tones, and lower contrast, and gives the image a faded, aged look. The edge transitions are brighter or darker to emphasize them.

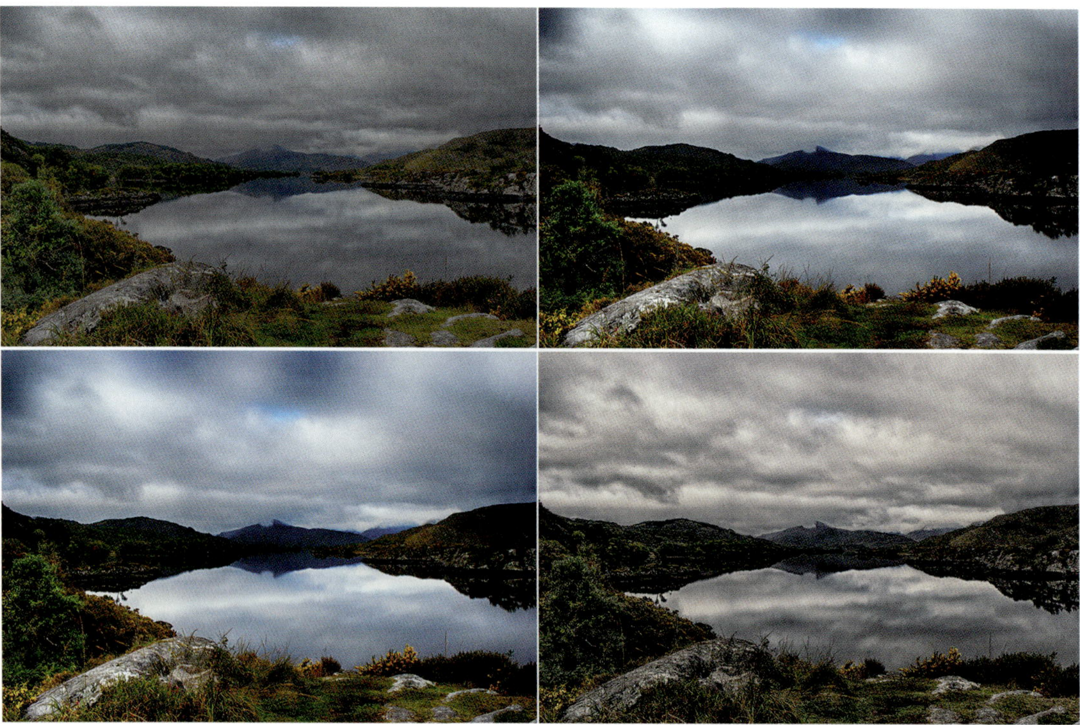

Figure 4.35 Top row (left to right): Art Standard, Art Vivid; bottom row: Art Bold, Art Embossed.

Mastering the Mysteries of Focus

5

Modern digital cameras like the EOS R8 can identify potential subject matter, lock in on human faces (if present), and automatically focus faster than the blink of an eye. Usually. Of course, sometimes autofocus will zero in on the *wrong* subject, become confused by background patterns, or be totally unable to follow a fast-moving target like a bird in flight. While autofocus *has* come a long way, it's still a work-in-progress that relies heavily on input from the photographer. Your Canon EOS R8 can calculate and set focus for you quickly and with a high degree of accuracy, but you still need to make a few settings that provide guidance on three of the four Ws of autofocus: *what, where,* and *when.* Your decisions in how you apply those choices supplies the fourth W: *why.* This chapter will provide you with everything you need to put all four to work.

Auto or Manual Focus?

Advances in autofocus technology have given photographers the confidence to rely on AF most of the time. For the average subject, the EOS R8 will do an excellent job of evaluating your scene and quickly focusing on an appropriate subject. Interestingly enough, however, the switch to mirrorless technology has actually revived interest in old-school manual focus. I'll show you how to use the EOS R8's manual focus aids later in this chapter, but meanwhile you can consider the five reasons why manual focus is being used more by creative photographers these days:

- **WYSIWYG.** *What you see* (in the viewfinder or LCD monitor) *is what you get,* in terms of sharp focus. When focusing manually, you're evaluating the exact same sensor image that will be captured when you press the shutter release. Traditional single-lens reflex (SLR) cameras use a mirror to direct the image to a separate focusing screen (when not in live view mode), which can be coarser, not as bright, and possibly out of alignment.

- **WYSIWYW.** Focusing manually can mean that *what you see is what you want,* that is, *you* can select the precise plane of focus you desire for, say, a macro photo or portrait, rather than settle for what the camera *thinks* you want. Your camera doesn't have any way of determining, for certain, what subject you *want* to be in sharp focus. It can't read your mind (at least, not yet). Left to its own devices, the camera may select a likely object—often the closest one—and lock in focus with lightning speed, even though the subject is not the one that's the center of interest of your photograph.

- **Less confusion.** Canon has given us faster and more precise autofocus systems, with many more options, and it's common for the sheer number of these choices to confuse even the most advanced photographers. If you'd rather not wade through the AF alternatives for a given shot, switch to manual focus and shoot. You won't have to worry about whether the camera locks focus too soon, or too late.

- **Focus aids.** You can zoom in on the sensor image as you focus manually and use a feature called *manual focus peaking,* which Canon also refers to as "outline emphasis" to accentuate in-focus areas with distinct colored outlines. The EOS R8 also has a "focus guide" that helps you judge how much out of focus the image is, and which direction you need to focus to achieve a sharp image. I'll explain all these options later.

- **More lenses.** All mirrorless cameras—and not just the Canon EOS R-series—have had a limited number of lenses available when they were introduced. But fortunately, the reduced flange-to-sensor distance (which I'll explain in more detail in Chapter 7) offers plenty of room to insert an adapter that allows mounting an extensive number of existing lenses, including those from manufacturers other than Canon. Many of those third-party optics are inexpensive manual focus lenses, or lenses intended for other camera platforms which function only in manual focus on the R-series models. A whole generation of photographers who grew up using nothing but autofocus have discovered that focusing manually is a reasonable tradeoff for access to this wide range of optics.

How Focus Works

Simply put, focus is the process of adjusting the camera so that parts of our subject that we want to be sharp and clear are, in fact, sharp and clear. We allow the camera to focus for us, automatically, or we can rotate the lens's focus ring manually to achieve the desired focus. Manual focusing is especially problematic because our eyes and brains have poor memory for correct focus. That's why your eye doctor conducting a refraction test must shift back and forth between pairs of lenses and ask, "Does that look sharper—or was it sharper before?" in determining your correct prescription. Too often, the slight differences are such that the lens pairs must be swapped multiple times.

Similarly, manual focusing involves jogging the focus ring back and forth as you go from almost in focus, to sharp focus, to almost focused again. The little clockwise and counterclockwise arcs decrease in size until you've zeroed in on the point of correct focus. What you're looking for is the image with the most contrast between the edges of elements in the image.

The autofocus mechanism, like all such systems found in modern cameras, also evaluates these increases and decreases in sharpness, but it is able to remember the progression perfectly, so that autofocus can lock in much more quickly and, with an image that has sufficient contrast, more precisely. Unfortunately, while the camera's focus system finds it easy to measure degrees of apparent focus at each of the focus points in the viewfinder, it doesn't really know with any certainty *which object* should be in sharpest focus. Is it the closest object? The subject in the center? Something lurking *behind* the closest subject? A person standing over at the side of the picture? Using autofocus effectively involves deciding exactly what to focus on.

Learning to use the autofocus system is easy, but you do need to fully understand how the system works to get the most benefit from it. Once you're comfortable with autofocus, you'll know when it's appropriate to use the manual focus option, too.

As the camera collects focus information from the sensors, it then evaluates it to determine whether the desired sharp focus has been achieved. The calculations may include whether the subject is moving, and whether the camera needs to "predict" where the subject will be when the shutter release button is fully depressed, and the picture is taken. The speed with which the camera is able to evaluate focus and then move the lens elements into the proper position to achieve the sharpest focus determines how fast the autofocus mechanism is. Although your R8 will almost always focus more quickly than a human eye, there are types of shooting situations where that's not fast enough. For example, if you're having problems shooting a sport with many fast-moving players because the autofocus system manically follows each moving subject, a better choice might be to switch autofocus modes, or shift into manual and prefocus on a spot where you anticipate the action will be, such as a goal line or soccer net.

Autofocus is generally achieved using two different technologies called contrast-detection autofocus (CDAF) and phase-detection autofocus (PDAF). I'm going to provide a quick overview of contrast detection first, and then devote much of the rest of this chapter to the complexities of the phase-detection system.

Contrast Detection

This is a slower, but potentially more accurate mode, best suited for static subjects, and was originally the only kind of autofocus available for mirrorless cameras and for dSLRs when shooting in their live view and movie modes. The recent innovation of adding phase-detection pixels to the sensor itself converted contrast detection from a main system into a fine-tuning option for designers creating a hybrid system that used both. I'm going to give you a brief overview of how contrast detection works, which will help you appreciate Canon's sophisticated PDAF system.

Contrast detection is very easy to understand, and is illustrated by Figure 5.1, a close-up of some weathered wood. At top in the figure, the transitions between the edges found in the image are soft and blurred because of the low contrast between them. Whether the edges are horizontal, vertical, or diagonal doesn't matter in the least; the focus system looks only for contrast between edges, and those edges can run in any direction at all.

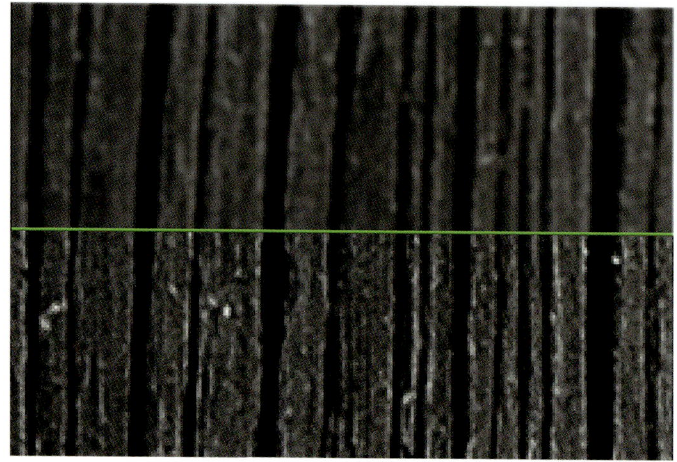

Figure 5.1 Focus in contrast-detection mode evaluates the increase in contrast in the edges of subjects, starting with a blurry image (top) and producing a sharp, contrasty image (bottom).

At the bottom of Figure 5.1, the image has been brought into sharp focus, and the edges have much more contrast; the transitions are sharp and clear. Although this example is a bit exaggerated so you can see the results on the printed page, it's easy to understand that when maximum contrast in a subject is achieved, it can be deemed to be in sharp focus. Although achieving focus with contrast detection is generally quite a bit slower, there are several advantages—and disadvantages—to this method:

- **Works with more image types.** Any subject that has edges will work with CDAF.

- **Focus on any point.** With contrast detection, any portion of the image can be used to focus: you don't need dedicated AF sensors. Focus is achieved with the actual sensor image, so focus point selection is simply a matter of choosing which part of the sensor image to use. It's easy to move the focus frame around to virtually any location.

- **Potentially more accurate.** Contrast detection is clear-cut. The camera can clearly see when the highest contrast has been achieved, as long as there is sufficient light to allow the camera to examine the image produced by the sensor. However, some "hunting" may be necessary. As the camera seeks the ideal plane of focus, it may overshoot and have to back up a little, then re-correct if the new focus plane is not optimal. However, once CDAF settles on the ideal focus plane, the results are generally very accurate. Contrast detection is an excellent way of fine-tuning focus that has been achieved through PDAF.

Phase Detection

The phase-detection pixels in the sensor split incoming photons arriving from opposite sides of the lens into two parts, forming a pair of images, exactly like the rangefinders used for surveying and in rangefinder-focusing cameras like the venerable Leica M series. The dual images are separated when out of focus, and then gradually brought together to achieve sharp focus, as shown from top to bottom in Figure 5.2.

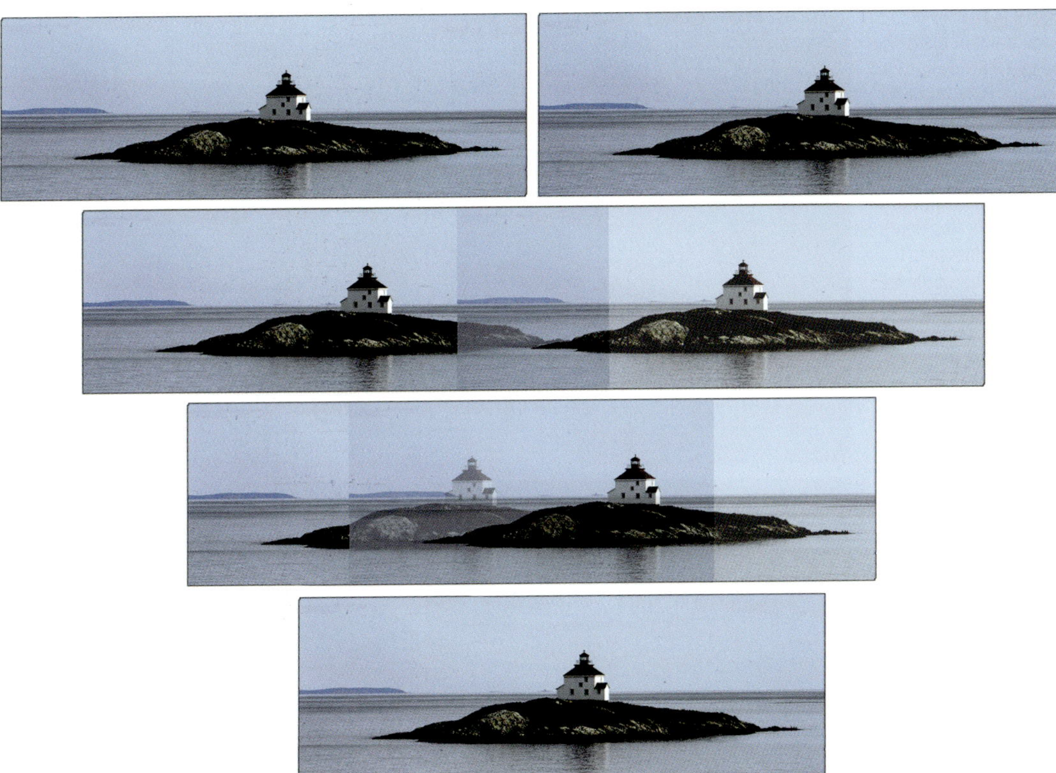

Figure 5.2 In phase detection, parts of an image are split in two and compared (top). When the image is in focus, the two halves of the image align, as with a rangefinder (bottom).

This process tells the camera when the image pair are "in phase" and aligned. The rangefinder approach of phase detection calculates exactly how out of focus the image is, and in which direction (focus is too near, or too far) thanks to the amount and direction of the displacement of the split image. The camera can quickly and precisely snap the image into sharp focus and match the lines.

The PDAF sensors are all *line sensors,* horizontally oriented, which means they work best with features that transect the sensor either perpendicularly or at an angle, as visualized in Figure 5.3, top. It's easy to detect when the two halves of the vertical lines of the weathered wood—actually a 19th century outhouse—are aligned. However, when the same sensor is asked to measure focus for, say, horizontal lines that don't split up quite so conveniently, or, in the worst case, subjects such as the sky (which may have neither vertical nor horizontal lines), focus can slow down drastically, or even become impossible. One such scenario is pictured in Figure 5.3, bottom left. A possible solution is to incorporate vertically oriented AF sensors, which can easily focus horizontal subject matter (see Figure 5.3, bottom right). The line sensors arranged perpendicularly to each other are called "crosstype" sensors.

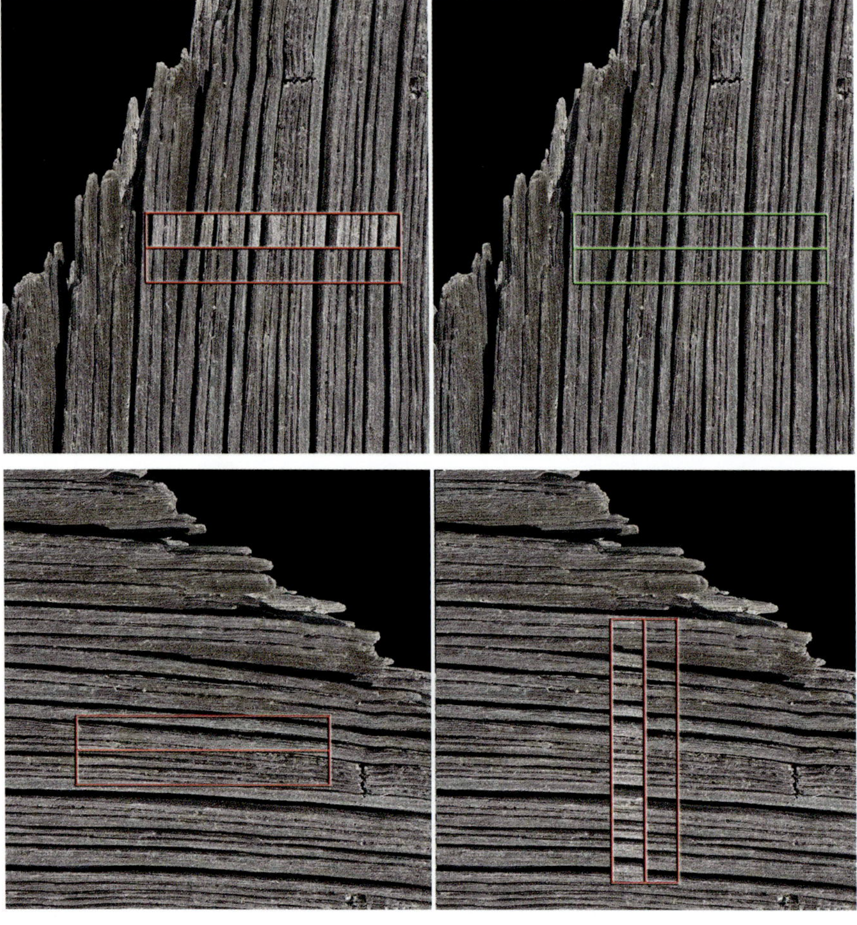

Figure 5.3 When an image is out of focus, the split lines don't align precisely (top left). Using phase detection, the camera is able to align the features of the image and achieve sharp focus quickly (top right). Horizontal lines aren't ideal for horizontally oriented sensors (bottom left) and require vertically oriented AF sensors (bottom right).

However, the R8 includes no cross-type sensors, as those types of PDAF pixels are difficult (expensive) to embed in today's image sensors. Canon feels that the high density of AF positions virtually insures that the line sensors will still find enough detail crossing the sensor at an angle conducive to autofocus. There are 1,053 individual focus zones on the sensor, and a maximum of 4,897 *positions* within the frame that can be used to focus. More on that later.

In typical competing cameras, a given sensor pixel must be either a PDAF detector or an imaging pixel—not both. But Canon's Dual Pixel technology means that any given sensor can include *both* an AF sensor and an imaging photo diode and perform both tasks, so they have fewer limitations on the placement and number of PDAF detectors included in a sensor like the one found in your R8. I'll tell you more about the Dual Pixel technology later in this chapter.

Of course, as with any rangefinder-like function, phase-detection accuracy is better when the "base length" between the two images is larger. (Think back to your high school trigonometry; you could calculate a distance more accurately when the separation between the two points where the angles were measured was greater.) For that reason, phase-detection autofocus is more accurate with larger (wider) lens openings—especially those with maximum f/stops of f/2.8 or better—than with smaller lens openings and may not work at all when the f/stop is smaller than f/8. As I noted, comparisons can be calculated very quickly.

AF Pixel Layout

Because of the flexibility of the Dual Pixel technology, Canon has been able to spread the AF area to fill nearly 100 percent of the vertical frame, and about 100 percent of the horizontal area, when working with RF (native) lenses. EF-mount lenses attached using a mount adapter may not produce that full coverage; Canon says some may provide only 80 percent horizontal coverage.

This very broad coverage of phase-detect pixels provides several significant advantages for mirrorless cameras like the R8. The separate non-sensor-based PDAF systems of traditional dSLRs typically cover a much smaller area of the frame and may have only a few hundred AF points (at most), compared with the 1,000-plus available with your R8. Canon's PDAF system has many of the strengths formerly the province of contrast-detection AF technology:

- **Works with all image types.** Because it has so many AF point positions on the sensor it's unlikely that the area being examined will lack the edges needed to achieve sharp focus.
- **Focus on any point.** While contrast detection can examine virtually any position on the sensor, the large number of AF points on the sensor means it, too, is capable of using almost any area of the sensor to focus, and you can, of course, move the 1-point AF point almost anywhere you please.
- **Just as accurate.** The large number of PDAF points means that it can be virtually as accurate as contrast detection, and without the hunting and slowness.

Figure 5.4 is my rough approximation of the layout of the autofocus pixels, based on Canon's descriptions. At top left, the blue squares represent the location of the 1,053 AF zones available with the R8. As I noted, they cover virtually 100 percent of the frame, and are arranged in a 39 × 27–zone array.

At bottom left, the green squares represent the *positions you can select* using the directional controls. These also cover roughly 100 percent of the frame. There are 4,897 positions (in an 83 × 59 array). Those figures don't mean that your camera has almost 5,000 phase-detect pixels. That humongous figure and the green squares just enumerate the locations you can use to specify your focus point using 1-point AF. When the camera is choosing an AF area, it will use the smaller number of sections of the sensor, roughly represented by the blue squares. At right in Figure 5.4 you can see the layout of the AF pixels and available selectable AF positions overlaid.

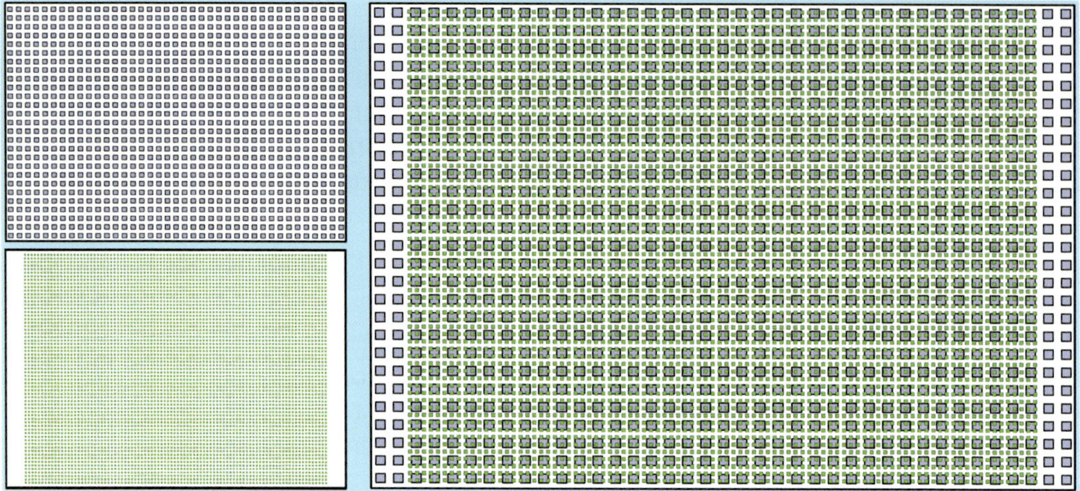

Figure 5.4 The layout of the autofocus system.

Dual Pixel CMOS AF

Understanding contrast and phase detection helps you appreciate the marvel that is Canon's Dual Pixel CMOS AF system. Used while shooting both stills and movies, as I've noted, it works much more quickly than traditional contrast-detection systems.

The sensor's pixel array includes special pixels that provide the same type of split-image rangefinder phase-detection AF that all PDAF modules use. The most important aspect of the system is that it doesn't rob the camera of any imaging resolution. It would have been possible to place AF sensors *between* the pixels used to capture the image, but that would leave the sensor with less area with which to capture light. Keep in mind that CMOS sensors, unlike earlier CCD sensors, have more on-board circuitry which already consumes some of the light-gathering area. Microlenses are placed above each photosensitive site to focus incoming illumination on the sensor and to correct for the oblique angles from which some photons may approach the imager. (Older lenses, designed for film, are the worst offenders in terms of emitting light at severely oblique angles; newer "digital" lenses do a better job of directing photons onto the sensor plane with a less "slanted" approach.)

With the Dual Pixel CMOS AF system, the same photosites capture both image and autofocus information. Each pixel is divided into two photodiodes, facing left and right when the camera is held in horizontal orientation (or above and below each other in vertical orientation; either works fine for autofocus purposes). Each pair functions as a separate AF sensor, allowing a special integrated circuit to process the raw autofocus information before sending it on to the digital image processor, which handles both AF and image capture. For the latter, the information grabbed by *both* photodiodes is combined, so that the full photosensitive area of the sensor pixel is used to capture the image.

While traditional contrast detection frequently involves frustrating "hunting" as the camera continually readjusts the focus plane trying to find the position of maximum contrast, adding Dual Pixel CMOS AF phase detection allows the camera to focus smoothly, which is important for speed, and essential when shooting movies (where all that hunting is unfortunately captured for posterity). Movie autofocus tracking is improved, allowing shooting movies of subjects in motion.

Dual Pixel RAW Focus Adjustments

An interesting adjunct to the dual pixel autofocus approach is the EOS R8's ability to save Dual Pixel RAW image files, which allow including the rangefinder-like focus information in RAW files. With Digital Photo Professional, Dual Pixel RAW files can be manipulated to provide focus microadjustment during post-processing, adjust bokeh (the out-of-focus regions of a photograph in both foreground and background), reduce flare and ghosting effects, and make sharpness adjustments. The important thing to keep in mind is that while Dual Pixel CMOS AF is active whenever you are using autofocus, *only* the files captured in Dual Pixel RAW mode can be manipulated.

My guides emphasize getting great pictures *in the camera,* rather than through post-processing, so I generally don't cover software tools like the EOS Utility or Digital Photo Professional in any detail. However, most of you will be curious about the focus enhancements that the Dual Pixel RAW format makes possible with Digital Photo Pro, so I'll provide a brief overview here. A more complete discussion of what you can do with this format can be found in the Digital Photo Professional PDF manual available for download from your country's Canon website.

Dual Pixel RAW is a special double-size RAW format that can be manipulated in an image editor (as I write this, only Digital Photo Pro has that capability) to make microadjustments to the focus plane, slightly improve bokeh effects, and make corrections to ghosting and flare and sharpness. When activated, Dual Pixel RAW saves, in effect, two different RAW files (and takes twice as long to do so), combined into a single file on your memory card. One half contains information from both sets of pixels (call them Sets A+B) while the other half includes information only from the pixels in Set B.

To use Dual Pixel RAW, you must select RAW or C RAW or RAW+JPEG/HEIF or C RAW+JPEG/ HEIF as your Image Quality, and then enable the dual-pixel feature in the Shooting 1 menu. You cannot use Dual Pixel RAW if you want to shoot multiple exposures, or use automatic HDR, the electronic shutter, or One-Touch image quality. The two highest continuous speeds (H+ and H) are not available.

We're primarily concerned with the focus plane microadjustment feature here. Dual Pixel RAW doesn't improve the resolution of your image: those 24-megapixel split pairs don't give you 48 megapixels of resolution. What the Dual Pixel RAW file does do is make use of the sensor's phase-detection information.

What you *can* do is make very small adjustments in the plane of focus, amounting to just a few millimeters in front of or behind the original plane. This is similar to what Lytro's *light field photography* did before the company closed in 2018 (Google it for more information), although on a reduced scale. These are *micro* adjustments. As a practical matter, a portrait photographer who discovers that an image captured wide open with a portrait-friendly lens or focal length that has been focused on the subject's eyelashes, can move the plane of focus back to the eyes instead.

You'll locate Start Dual Pixel RAW Optimizer in the Tools menu of Digital Photo Pro, with an image area and tool palette like the one shown in Figure 5.5. There are four palettes, and you can activate *only one of them* (plus sharpness) at a time for a particular image by putting a checkmark in the box at upper left of the palette you want to work with. Your options include:

- **Image microadjustment.** You can zoom in and out from 100 percent to 400 percent to view the focus plane changes you're making in real time. You'll generally use some level of zoom because, as I noted, the adjustments are very small. A vertical slider lets you move the focus plane toward the front or back of your subject, in increments of five. You can also specify the strength of the adjustment from 1 to 10. Figure 5.6 shows a zoomed-in view of a Dual Pixel RAW image that has had its focal plane moved to the maximum forward and backward positions.

- **Bokeh shift.** You can shift background or foreground "bokeh" left or right, again in values of 1–5 in either direction. Click the Select Area button and you can drag an area the adjustment is applied to. I've found the effect to be very subtle.

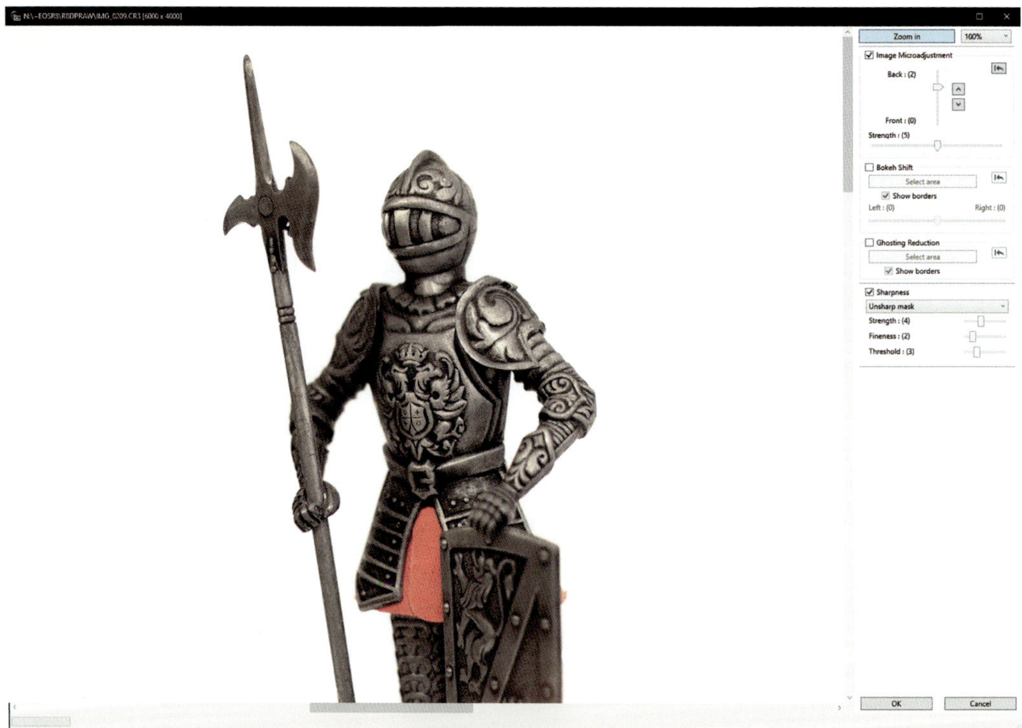

Figure 5.5 Four palettes are available in the Dual Pixel RAW pane.

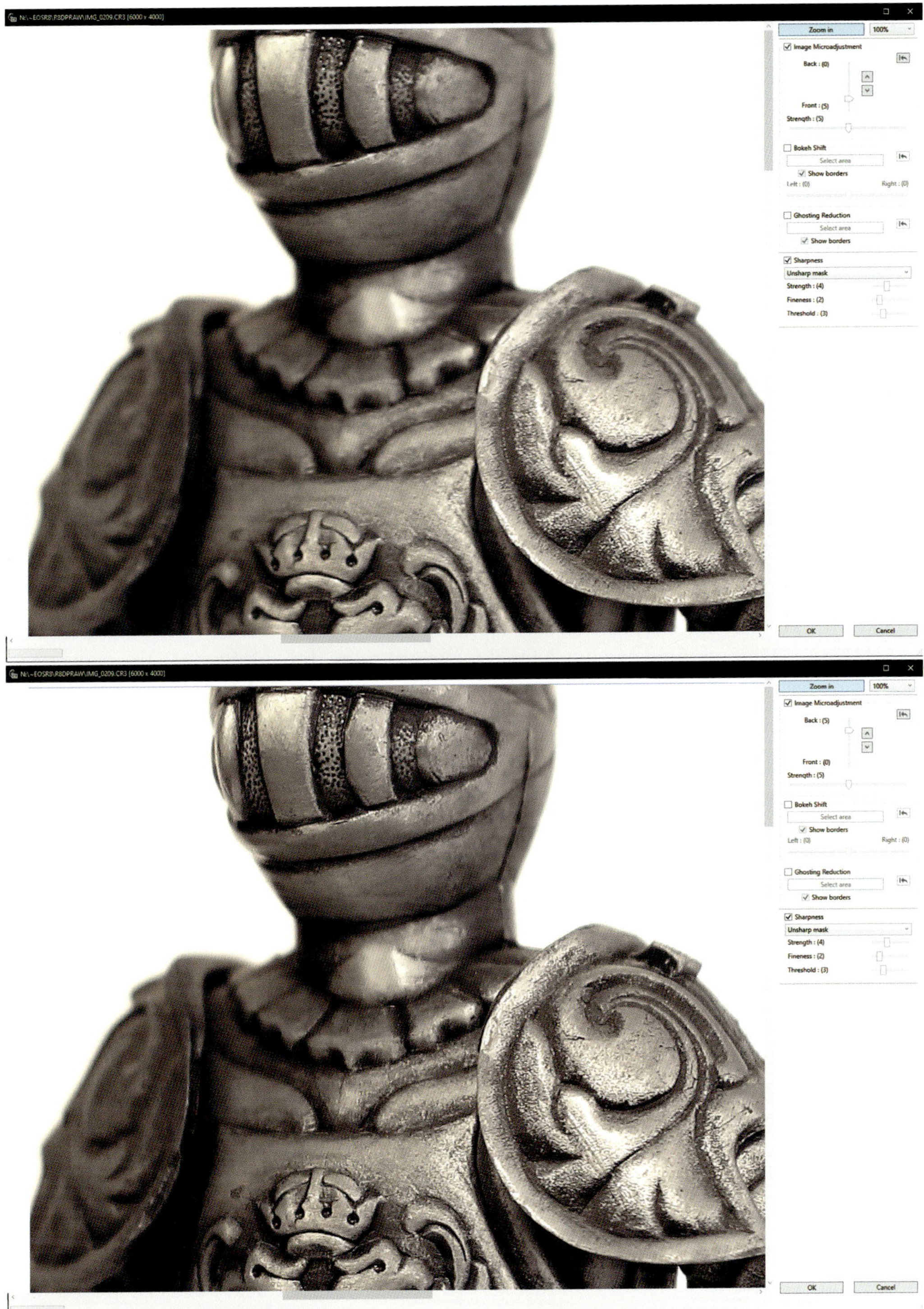

Figure 5.6 Focus plane the maximum amount forward (top) and back (bottom).

- **Ghosting reduction.** Reduces ghosting superimposed on your subject and flare from bright light sources in the frame. You can select the area affected, but not the amount of correction. Because flare may differ from the light gathered from one side of the lens or the other, the Dual Pixel RAW feature can be an effective way of detecting it and making corrections.
- **Sharpness.** This feature allows you to adjust overall sharpness or apply an unsharp mask to the image, either alone or in conjunction with the other effects of this tool. Strength, fineness, and threshold can be applied in a manner similar to most other image-processing sharpeners, including Canon's in-camera Picture Controls.

As you might expect, any adjustments you make to a Dual Pixel RAW file are implemented *only* in the file you save from Digital Photo Professional; the original RAW file remains untouched, so you're free to play around with this feature as much as you like.

Canon notes that the effects produced can vary depending on the particular lens in use, shooting conditions, and whether the camera is held in vertical or horizontal orientations. For example, the tool is most effective if the lens is used at its maximum aperture. That makes sense, because depth-of-field is less when the lens is wide open, so adjustments in focus plane, bokeh, sharpness, and perhaps ghosting/flare will be more obvious.

Circles of Confusion and Focus

You know that increased depth-of-field brings more of your subject into focus. But more depth-of-field also makes autofocusing (or manual focusing) more difficult because the contrast is lower between objects at different distances. This is an added factor *beyond* the rangefinder aspects of lens opening size in phase detection. An image that's dimmer is more difficult to focus with any type of focus system, phase detection, contrast detection, or manual focus.

So, focus with a 200mm focal length may be easier in some respects than at a 28mm focal length (or zoom setting) because the longer lens has less apparent depth-of-field. By the same token, a lens with a maximum aperture of f/1.8 will be easier to autofocus (or manually focus) than one of the same focal length with an f/4 maximum aperture, because the f/4 lens has more depth-of-field *and* a dimmer view. That's yet another reason why lenses with a maximum aperture smaller than f/5.6 can give your autofocus system fits—increased depth-of-field joins forces with a dimmer image that's more difficult to focus using phase detection.

To make things even more complicated, many subjects aren't polite enough to remain still. They move around in the frame, so that even if the camera is sharply focused on your main subject, it may change position and require refocusing. An intervening subject may pop into the frame and pass between you and the subject you meant to photograph. You (or the camera) have to decide whether to lock focus on this new subject or remain focused on the original subject. Finally, there are some kinds of subjects that are difficult to bring into sharp focus because they lack enough contrast to allow the AF system (or our eyes) to lock in. Blank walls, a clear blue sky, or other subject matter may make focusing difficult.

If you find all these focus factors confusing, you're on the right track. Focus is, in fact, measured using something called a *circle of confusion.* An ideal image consists of zillions of tiny little points,

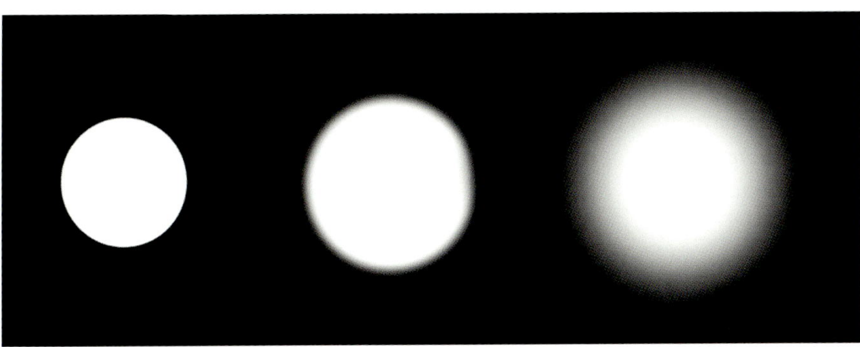

Figure 5.7 When a pinpoint of light (left) goes out of focus, its blurry edges form a circle of confusion (center and right).

which, like all points, theoretically have no height or width. There is perfect contrast between the point and its surroundings. You can think of each point as a pinpoint of light in a darkened room. When a given point is out of focus, its edges decrease in contrast and it changes from a perfect point to a tiny disc with blurry edges (remember, blur is the lack of contrast between boundaries in an image). (See Figure 5.7.)

If this blurry disc—the circle of confusion—is small enough, our eyes still perceives it as a point. It's only when the disc grows large enough that we can see it as a blur rather than a sharp point that a given point is viewed as out of focus. You can see, then, that enlarging an image, either by displaying it larger on your computer monitor or by making a large print, also enlarges the size of each circle of confusion. Moving closer to the image does the same thing. So, parts of an image that may look perfectly sharp in a 5 x 7–inch print viewed at arm's length, might appear blurry when blown up to 11 x 14 and examined at the same distance. Take a few steps back, however, and it may look sharp again.

To a lesser extent, the viewer also affects the apparent size of these circles of confusion. Some people see details better at a given distance and may perceive smaller circles of confusion than someone standing next to them. For the most part, however, such differences are small. Truly blurry images will look blurry to just about everyone under the same conditions.

Technically, there is just one plane within your picture area, parallel to the back of the camera (or sensor, in the case of a digital camera), that is in sharp focus. That's the plane in which the points of the image are rendered as precise points. At every other plane in front of or behind the focus plane, the points show up as discs that range from slightly blurry to extremely blurry until the out-of-focus areas become one large blur that de-emphasizes an unattractive textured white background.

In practice, the discs in many of these planes will still be so small that we see them as points, and that's where we get depth-of-field. Depth-of-field is just the range of planes that include discs that we perceive as points rather than blurred splotches. The size of this range increases as the aperture is reduced in size and is allocated roughly one-third in front of the plane of sharpest focus, and two-thirds behind it. The range of sharp focus is always greater behind your subject than in front of it.

REMINDER

The following sections concisely describe the important settings you'll need to use your camera's manual focus and autofocus features. You'll find in-depth descriptions of all AF menu entries in Chapter 12.

Working with the AF System

Now that you understand the basics of how the autofocus system works, it's time to jump into the actual settings and options you have at your disposal. To achieve tack-sharp focus every time, you'll need to master focus modes (*when* to evaluate a scene and lock in focus) and focus area selection (you or the camera decides *what* to focus on).

AF Operation

The AF Operation focus modes tell the camera *when* to evaluate and lock in focus. They don't determine *where* focus should be checked; that's the function of other autofocus features. Focus modes tell the camera whether to lock in focus once, say, when you press the shutter release halfway (or use some other control, such as the AF-ON button), or whether, once activated, the camera should continue tracking your subject and, if it's moving, adjust focus to follow it.

The R8 has manual focus, plus magnified (up to 10X manual focus), and three AF modes: One-Shot AF (also known as single autofocus), Servo AF (continuous autofocus), and AI Focus AF (which switches from One-Shot AF to Servo AF if a stationary subject begins moving.) I'll explain all of these in more detail later in this section. Choosing the right autofocus mode and the way in which focus points are selected is your key to success. Using the wrong mode for a particular type of photography can lead to a series of pictures that are all sharply focused—on the wrong subject.

To save battery power in still photography mode, focus doesn't initiate until you partially depress the shutter release or other defined AF-ON button (unless you've activated Preview AF in the AF 3 menu). But, autofocus isn't some mindless beast out there snapping your pictures in and out of focus with no feedback from you after you press that button. There are several settings you can modify that return at least a modicum of control to you. Your first decision should be whether you select One-Shot AF, AI Focus AF, or Servo AF. While using one of the non-auto modes, use the Q/SET button to summon the Quick Control menu and navigate to AF Operation (second from the top in the left column). Then spin the Main dial to cycle among One-Shot AF, AI Focus AF, or Servo AF. (The AF/M switch on the lens must be set to AF before you can change autofocus mode.)

One-Shot AF

In this mode, also called *single autofocus,* focus is set once and remains at that setting until the button is fully depressed, taking the picture, or until you release the shutter button without taking a shot. This mode is best for subjects that are not moving around a great deal. So, for non-action photography, this setting is usually your best choice, as it minimizes out-of-focus pictures (at the expense of spontaneity). The drawback here is that you might not be able to take a picture at all while the camera is seeking focus; you're locked out until the autofocus mechanism is happy with the current setting. One-Shot AF/single autofocus is sometimes referred to as *focus-priority* for that reason. Because of the small delay while the camera zeroes in on correct focus during focus-priority operation, you might experience slightly more shutter lag. This mode uses less battery power than the other autofocus modes.

When sharp focus is achieved, the selected focus point will flash green in the viewfinder and the camera will beep (unless you've disabled Beep in the Set-up 2 menu). If you're using Evaluative metering, the exposure will be locked at the same time. By keeping the shutter button depressed halfway, you'll find you can reframe the image while retaining the focus (and exposure) that's been set. You can also use the AE lock/FE lock button to retain the exposure calculated from the center AF point while reframing. If the camera cannot achieve focus, the focus point will turn orange, and taking a picture is not possible even if the shutter release is pressed down all the way.

However, you may find yourself deciding to take a picture quickly without enough time to lock in focus with a half-press of the shutter release. If that happens frequently, and "getting the shot" is more important than "getting sharp focus," you can switch from focus-priority to release-priority using the One-Shot AF Release Priority entry in the AF 3 menu. The camera will henceforth go ahead and take a picture when the shutter release is pressed down all the way, even if sharp focus isn't confirmed.

AI Focus AF

This mode, sometimes called *automatic autofocus*, switches between One-Shot AF and Servo AF, depending on whether your subject is stationary or moving. It selects the mode when you depress the shutter release halfway, or when shooting continuously.

Servo AF

This mode, also known as *continuous autofocus*, is the mode to use for sports and other fast-moving subjects and is often used with continuous shooting modes. Once the shutter release is partially depressed, the camera sets the focus on the point that's selected (by the camera or by you manually), but continues to monitor the subject, so that if it moves or you move, the lens will be refocused to suit. When focus is achieved, the AF point turns blue; there is no Beep signal however, as it would be intrusive if there was a chirp each time refocusing occurred.

As you might expect, focus and exposure aren't really locked until you press the shutter release button down all the way to take the picture. You'll find that Servo AF produces the least amount of shutter lag of any autofocus mode: press the button and the camera fires. It also uses the most battery power, because the autofocus system operates as long as the shutter release button is partially depressed. If you're using Scene Intelligent Auto mode, the camera switches automatically to Servo AF if it detects subject movement.

You'll often see continuous autofocus referred to as *release-priority,* because that's the way it has been traditionally used. In that mode, if you press the shutter release down all the way while the system is refining focus, the camera will go ahead and take a picture, even if the image is slightly out of focus. Servo AF uses a technology called *predictive AF,* which allows calculating the correct focus if the subject is moving toward or away from the camera at a constant rate. It uses either the automatically selected AF point or the point you select manually to set focus.

Note that release-priority mode does *not* result in many out-of-focus images. It simply means that a picture will be taken even if the camera has not *confirmed* sharp focus. Your image may very well be sharply focused at the moment of exposure, or, perhaps, close enough.

AF Area

What Canon dubs the AF area is actually a feature that specifies *which areas of the frame* are used to collect autofocus information. There are eight *AF area modes* you can use to select the initial point or zone of points (with variations on what additional points will also be deployed, if needed). For each of these you can also enable or disable *subject tracking* (just press the INFO button while selecting an AF method), which tells the R8 (not you) to select a subject (people, animals, or vehicles) to track and follow. I'll explain subject tracking later in this chapter.

Switching among the AF modes is easy: press the AF selection button on the upper-right corner of the camera's back panel (just below the * button), and then press the M-Fn button repeatedly while the available modes cycle on the display. As I noted, while you're selecting an AF area, you can press the INFO button to enable/disable subject tracking.

You can also access the AF area entry in the AF 1 menu. Should you generally use only a few of the available total modes, Canon gives you the ability to "hide" the others using the Limit AF Methods entry in the AF 4 menu. I'll describe the parameters and use of each of these entries in Chapter 12.

USING THE TOUCH SCREEN

The Touch & Drag AF entry in the AF 1 menu allows you to specify moving the AF point or Zone AF frame by tapping the screen or dragging the point/zone on the screen to a new location. In addition to using the touch screen to position the AF point, you can actually take a picture by tapping the screen by activating the Touch Shutter using an icon that appears in the lower-left corner of the screen in shooting mode. The same icon can be used to disable the feature.

Spot AF

In this mode, you can zero in and focus on a small box displayed on the screen (see Figure 5.8). This focus area can be moved in tiny increments to nearly any location on the screen using directions described in the "Moving the Focus Point" sidebar that follows. Just keep in mind that you must press the AF point selection button *first* to enable moving the focus point with any of these controls. (Figure 5.4 showed the selectable positions.)

This precision can be too much of a good thing, however; camera movement (as when shooting hand-held, especially with a front-heavy long lens) and subject movement can easily move the focus spot away from your primary subject. This mode may be your best choice when you want to focus precisely on a subject that is surrounded by fine detail. It is most practical for scenes where you want to focus on a certain point, but your subject may be moving slowly. Position the active focus point with the controls. You can use Spot AF for everyday shooting where precision is needed, and the subject contains sufficient detail within the area covered by the sensor. If such a small area of your subject is a bit amorphous, you'll want to use one of the selection modes described next, which allow the AF system to take into account surrounding focus points as well as the manually selected point.

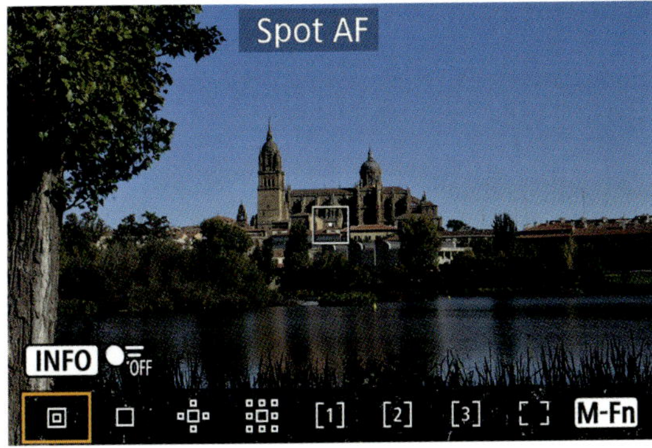

Figure 5.8 Focus on a single area within the frame.

Figure 5.9 Focus on a slightly larger area within the frame.

MOVING THE FOCUS POINT

Once you've selected a Focus Area, you can move the active focus point around the screen, in all modes except Whole area AF.

- **Press the AF point selection button.** To enable movement of the focus point, you *must* press this button first. When you're satisfied with the position of the point, press the button again to lock it in.
- **Move point within frame.** You can use the directional buttons to move the focus point. If you want to move in one orientation only, it may be easier to just rotate the Main dial to make horizontal adjustments, or the QCD to move the point vertically.
- **Recenter.** If you want to return the point to the center of the screen, press the Trash button.

1-Point AF

In this mode, you can zero in and focus on a box that is roughly 3X larger displayed on the screen (see Figure 5.9). When speed is important, but you still want to specify the focus location with some degree of precision, this option is probably your best choice. I use it for sports when I want to be able to single out specific players who are not moving a great deal (say, an infielder covering third base).

Expand AF Area

In this mode, the focus point you select is used, along with the points immediately above, below, and to either side of it (until the manually selected point reaches the edge of the array and one or more of the additional points scroll off). (See Figure 5.10.) This mode is better for moving objects, because the larger effective zone makes it easier to track subjects that are moving within the frame. As the subject moves outside the area defined by the selected focus point, three to four of the surrounding focus points can pick up and track the movement. In One-Shot AF mode, the manually selected focus point and expanded point used will be displayed.

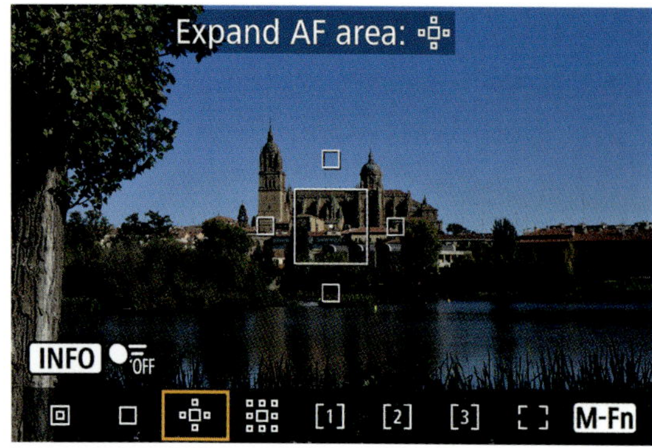

Figure 5.10 A larger AF area when using Expand AF area allows autofocus of moving subjects.

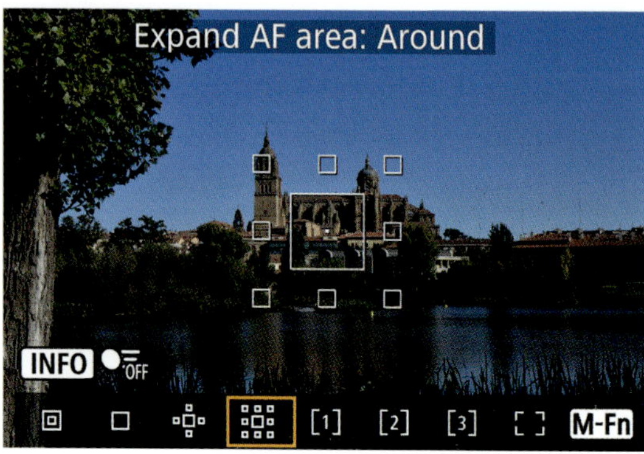

Figure 5.11 Four additional focus points are active in this mode.

Expand AF Area: Around

This mode is similar to the one above, except that the eight points adjacent to the manually selected point are included in the focusing array. It is slightly better for subjects that don't contain a lot of detail at the manually selected focus point, and the additional points surrounding the initial focus point improve your results. This mode is also better for larger moving objects, even though it offers a bit less precision. As always, while the active points are shown in the center of the frame in the figure, you can move the active area around while viewing the display. (See Figure 5.11.)

Flexible Zone AF 1

This is a zone-oriented point selection method, in which the AF points are divided in a zone, a square covering roughly one-sixth of the frame. When you move the focus "point" using the controls, you are actually simply moving the zone from one position to the next within the frame. This mode works well when you know the approximate area where your subject will reside and want to cover a particular zone. (See Figure 5.12.) This mode usually focuses on the nearest subject, and so lacks the precision of the other AF methods described so far.

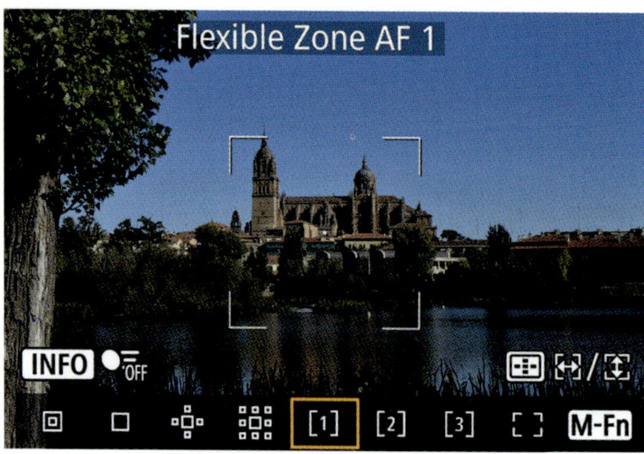

Figure 5.12 Flexible Zone AF 1 uses a larger focus area.

RESIZING ZONES

Your three zone options are called Flexible because you can resize them at will, making them larger or smaller to suit your particular subject. Press the AF point selection button, the M-Fn button, and then the AF point selection button again. Then you can make the zone wider using the Main dial or taller with the QCD. Press the Q/SET button to confirm. To revert back to the original size, repeat the sequence above, then press the INFO button to reset.

Flexible Zone AF 2 (Vertical)/Flexible Zone AF 3 (Horizontal)

These last two methods use large rectangular zones oriented in the vertical and horizontal directions, although, as I mentioned above, you can resize them vertically or horizontally to suit your needs. Each might be useful for tall subjects (basketball action) or wide areas (motor sports or boat racing). The appropriate AF points within the frame will be selected automatically, generally from among those covering the closest subject. Both methods will search for and focus on any faces detected within the frame. (See Figures 5.13 and 5.14.)

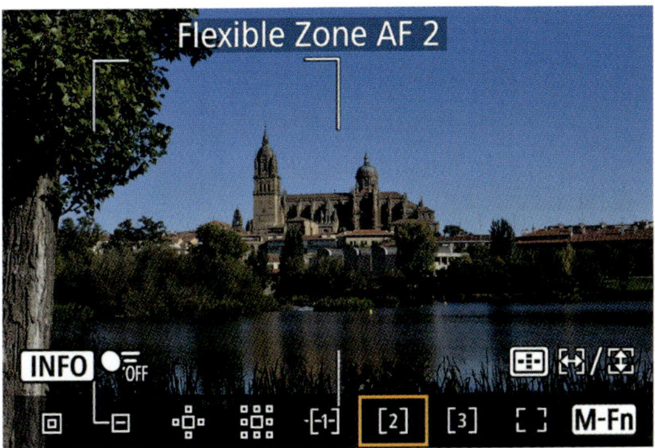

Figure 5.13 Flexible Zone AF 2 (Vertical).

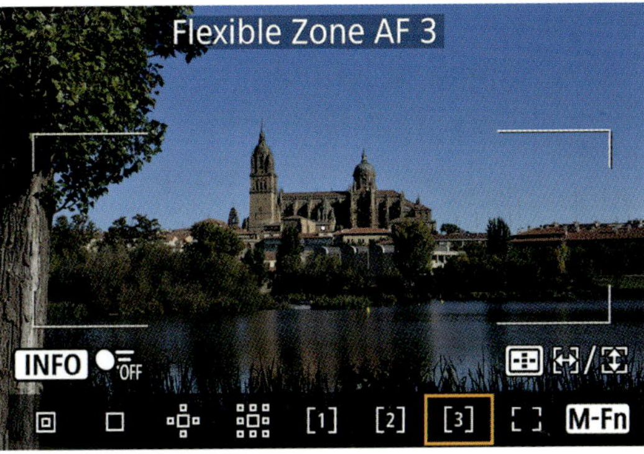

Figure 5.14 Flexible Zone AF 3 (Horizontal).

Whole Area AF

In this mode, the R8 chooses the focus area for you, using the entire frame. It's particularly effective for subjects that are moving so rapidly that choosing a focus area or zone yourself would be difficult (or futile). I use this method a lot for sports. (See Figure 5.15.) When this mode and Subject Tracking are active, you can quickly select a face or eye by tapping the screen.

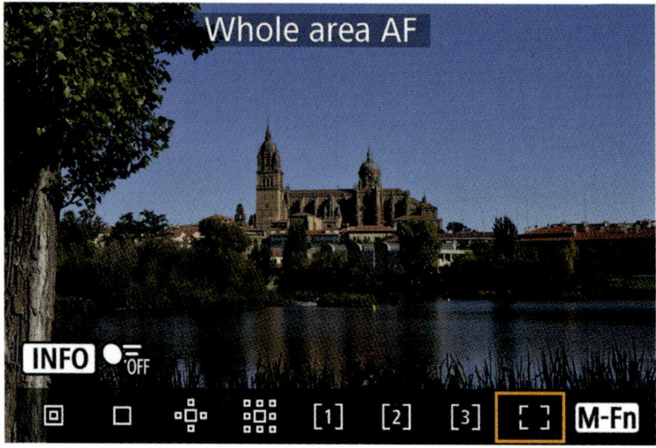

Figure 5.15 Whole area AF.

Orientation Linked AF Point

You'll often find that a particular AF method may be better for certain types of subjects in one orientation, but not as advantageous in another. For example, when I shoot basketball from behind the baseline under the basket, I take quite a few shots in vertical orientation and use Expand AF area with the focus area centered around the basket at the "top" of the vertical frame when I rotate the camera 90-degrees clockwise. But, a few seconds later I may return the camera to horizontal orientation to cover two or more players jockeying for position at the foul line. Luckily, the EOS R8 lets me specify a *different* AF method for each orientation. Even better, I can choose to have separate AF areas and focus points for each orientation, or keep the same AF method but specify different points alone. That is, I can use, say, Expand AF area for both, but position the *focusing point* in a different location in each orientation, as shown at top and bottom in Figure 5.16.

Figure 5.16 Orientation-linked AF areas and points.

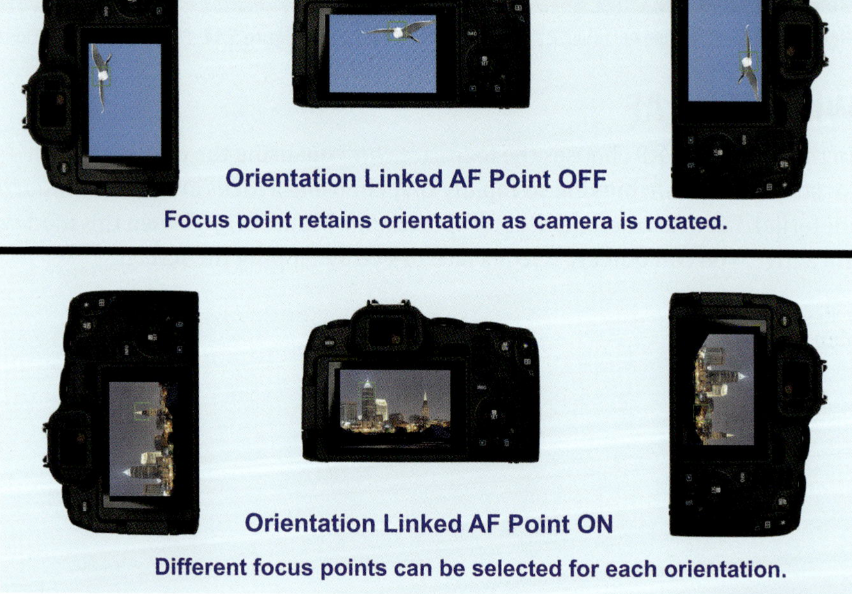

You'll find this option in the AF 4 menu's Orientation Linked AF Point entry, seen in Figure 5.17. In practice, there are three different orientations for the camera: rotated counterclockwise, horizontal, and rotated clockwise. No one generally shoots with the camera held horizontally, but upside down, so that odd position isn't separately accounted for. Within the entry there are these choices:

- **Same for both vertical and horizontal (default).** The AF area selection mode *and* the AF point or zone position that you select manually are used for both vertical and horizontal images.

- **Separate AF points: Area + Point.** The AF area mode and position of the AF point can be set in tandem for each of the camera's three orientations.

  - **Camera held horizontally.** This orientation assumes that the camera is positioned so the viewfinder/shutter release are on top.

  - **Camera held vertically** with the grip/shutter release above the viewfinder.

  - **Camera held vertically** with the viewfinder above the grip/shutter release.

- **Separate AF points: Point only.** The AF area mode remains the same regardless of camera orientation, but you can specify a different AF point position in manual point selection modes for each of three orientations. The specified point will remain in force even if you switch from one manual selection mode to another.

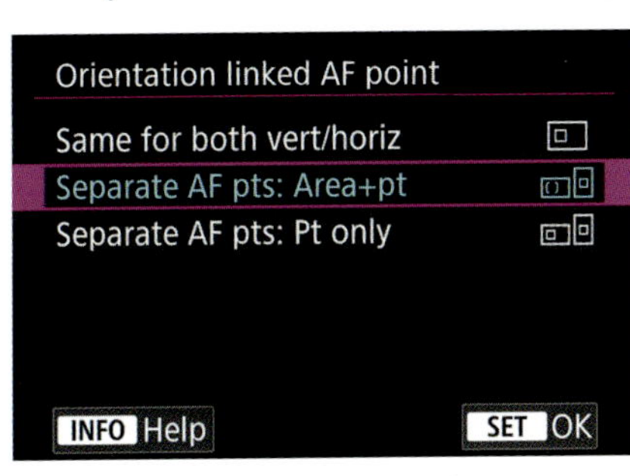

Figure 5.17 Choose orientation settings.

Subject Tracking

By default, your EOS R8 uses a variety of criteria to focus on a particular subject. The camera will tend to favor the nearest object, and take into account subject motion, so it can predict where to focus next. The current focus area is displayed in green if using One-Shot AF mode, and in blue if AF operation is set to Servo AF. If you want to see the focus areas being used, just press the shutter release button halfway. This is particularly helpful when using the Flexible Zone or Whole area AF options, because they cover such a large amount of frame real estate.

As I mentioned earlier, when using any of the AF methods, you can activate subject tracking, which means in Servo AF mode, once you press the shutter release halfway, the camera will lock in on that subject and follow it as the subject (or your camera) changes position. You're given quite a few options, with four entries in the AF 1 menu devoted to tracking parameters, highlighted in Figure 5.18.

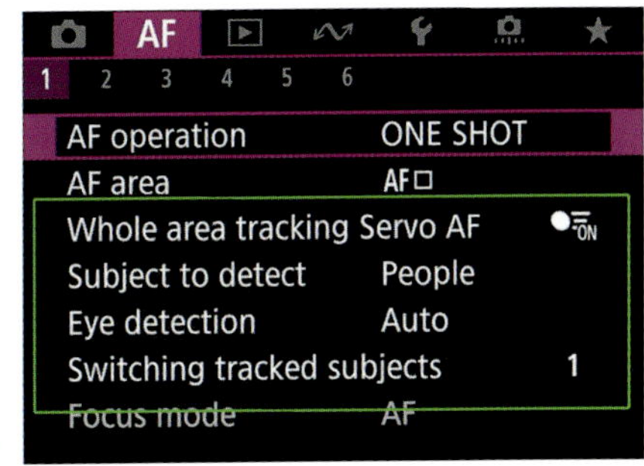

Figure 5.18 Subject Tracking settings.

Your options are:

- **Whole area tracking Servo AF.** While Whole area AF can usually correctly identify and focus on your subject, you might want to use another AF area mode better suited to a specific type of subject. That might be the case when your subject is located in a particular area of the frame and not likely to move. This entry allows you to choose an AF area for use with stationary subjects, and switch automatically to Whole area AF only when Servo AF is active.

  - **On.** Switches to Whole area tracking if AF operation is set to Servo AF and tracking is enabled. If AF operation is set to One-Shot AF or AI Focus, the area specified in the AF area entry is used instead.

  - **Off.** The area specified with the AF area entry above will be used consistently for One-Shot, AI Focus, or Servo focus methods.

- **Subject to detect.** Choose People, Animals, Vehicles, or None. The camera can look for specific types of subjects, although you can override this setting by using the touch screen to select the subject to be tracked.

  - **People.** The camera will look for faces or heads first, then try to track their torso or, last, some other parts of their body. Very large or small faces, or those that are partially hidden (say, by a hat) or extremely bright or dark may not be detected.

  - **Animals.** The R8 can recognize a variety of dogs, cats, and birds and tries to detect their faces (if the creature is close to and facing the camera) or bodies. In all cases, the tracking frame shows the animal's body. Note that the camera may also detect people in the frame, but prioritizes animals. That will help you get photos of the prizewinners at the next Westminster Kennel Club Dog Show, rather than their owners.

  - **Vehicles.** This setting is great for motor sports fans who want to capture the action as it unfolds. The camera looks for both two- and four-wheeled vehicles, as well as people, but prioritizes the vehicle. Bicycles and non-competition motor vehicles (e.g., your brother-in-law's SUV) may not be detected. Dust and dirt kicked up at motocross events may also confuse the tracking system. You can press the INFO button *while choosing Vehicles* to enable or disable spot detection of typical key details of vehicles, such as headlights, wheels, etc. Spot detection can be useful for finding a particular vehicle if there aren't too many overlapping.

  - **None.** This general-purpose setting tells the R8 to look for subjects using the current composition you've framed as an indicator of what you're interested in following. No tracking frames are displayed. While faces may be found, eyes are not detected in this mode.

- **Eye detection.** The eyes may or may not be the windows to the soul, but sharp eyes are usually a key to a pleasing picture of a person or animal. So, Canon gives you the option to enable eye detection. The process takes a bit of extra time, so you might want to disable it when getting any picture at all is more important than having the eyes sharply focused. If you're using Whole area AF, you can select an eye by tapping the screen. In this screen you can select:
  - **Disable.** Eye detection is not used.
  - **Auto.** The R8 will select which detected eye to focus on.
  - **Right Eye/Left Eye.** You can choose which eye to prioritize. This can be useful when the subject's face is turned away slightly from the camera. You will usually want to focus on the eye closest to the camera, and you can choose the appropriate eye here.
- **Switching tracked subjects.** This option determines how quickly the camera switches from one subject to another when the initial tracked subject moves out of the frame or moves behind an obstruction (say, a referee runs along the sideline between you and a player you're tracking). You may "lose" your tracking, too, if the subject turns away from the camera or their appearance is otherwise altered (for example, a standing person crouches down).

  If necessary, the R8 can switch to a new subject, with the amount of delay set using this option. Your choices include:
  - **Initial-priority.** With this setting, the camera will do its best to track the initial subject for as long as possible, even when other subjects intervene.
  - **On subject.** The R8 will attempt to track the initial subject, but will switch to other subjects, if necessary, after a shorter delay.
  - **Switch subject.** The camera more readily switches to another subject. You might want to use this setting at a basketball game, where the ball is passed around from person to person frequently.

Working with Tracking

Here are the key points you need to keep in mind when using subject tracking once you've selected Focus Operation, Focus Area, and Subject to Track parameters.

- **One-Shot/Servo.** The EOS R8 can automatically find subjects and track them in both One-Shot and Servo modes if you've enabled tracking by pressing the INFO button when you select your AF area mode.

  In both cases a tracking frame will appear in the frame highlighting the currently selected subject. In One-Shot mode, focus will lock in on the tracking frame when you press the shutter release and hold it down. In Servo mode, focus will continue to change as the camera or subject moves.

- **Focus Area.** In all focus area modes except for Whole area AF, you specify the location of the active focus points, whether they are a spot, area around a spot, or a zone. The R8 can track subjects whether they are located within your active focus area or not; however, it cannot *focus* on the tracked subject unless the subject is within the active focus area.

  You may need to move the focus area to the location where your subject is likely to reside. Press the AF point selection button and use the directional buttons to move the focus area (or the Trash button to re-center it), as described earlier. If you're using Whole area AF, you don't have to worry about this.

- **Tracking Frame.** If the subject being tracked is *outside* the active focus area, the tracking frame will be displayed in gray. Once you move the focus area to the subject or reframe the image so the subject is within (or very near) the focus area, the tracking frame will turn white. The size of the tracking frame may vary, depending on the subject.

- **Setting Focus.** Once tracking begins, you can reframe the image and the camera will keep the tracking frame on your subject as long as the subject remains within the image area. If the subject leaves the image area, the camera will look for a new subject to track.

  Press the shutter release halfway to commence focusing. In One-Shot mode the tracking frame will turn green and you will hear a beep. In Servo mode, the tracking frame will turn blue indicating focus is achieved, and will remain blue as the camera refocuses while the subject and/or camera move. If the tracking frame turns orange instead, the camera was unable to focus on the subject (most likely because the subject was closer than the lens's minimum focusing distance).

- **Whole Area AF.** If you've selected Whole area AF instead of one of the other AF area modes, a double tracking frame will appear. If you feel a need to be able to turn on Whole area AF quickly, you can define a button to do this using the Customize Buttons entry in the Custom Functions 3 menu, described in Chapter 15.

Manual Focus

As I mentioned at the beginning of this chapter, manual focus is being used more frequently than before in the modern autofocus era, thanks to the large variety of manual focus lenses available for Canon EOS R-series cameras, and the great manual focusing aids those cameras provide. You can switch from autofocus to manual focus (if an AF lens is mounted) simply by sliding the AF/MF switch on the lens to the MF position, allowing you to set the focus yourself.

There are some advantages and disadvantages to this approach. While your batteries will last longer in manual focus mode, it will take you longer to focus the camera for each photo, a process that can be difficult. Canon does give you a great deal of help in focusing manually.

Magnified View

You can check focus with magnified views of either 5X or 10X by pressing the Magnify/Reduce button in all modes. That includes autofocus modes as well, should you want to fine-tune the focus plane your camera arrives at.

Just press the Magnify/Reduce button once or twice to zoom in, or a third time to return to non-magnified view. In autofocus mode, the magnification is centered on the AF point when using Spot AF, 1-point AF, Expand AF area, Expand AF area: Around, and Zone AF Large Zone: Vertical or Large Zone: Horizontal. AF is performed in magnified display if you press the shutter button down halfway in Spot AF and 1-point AF.

In other modes, AF is performed after restoring normal display. In Servo AF mode, the camera returns to normal view for focusing. Continuous AF and Movie Servo AF are not available in magnified view. Focus may be more difficult when magnified due to shake.

When zoomed in, whether in AF or MF mode, use the directional controls to move the magnified area. Press the Trash button to center the magnified area in the middle of the frame. (See Figure 5.19.)

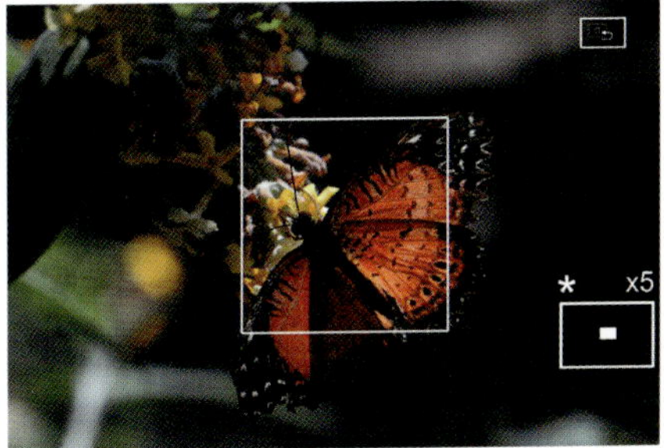

Figure 5.19 Magnified views can be used when focusing manually.

Focus Peaking

You can also use MF Peaking in the AF 5 menu to emphasize the outlines of your image with a contrasting color. In Chapter 12, I will show you how to choose a color (from red, yellow, or blue) so areas that are in focus appear outlined in that hue. (See Figure 5.20.) You can also select how much peaking is used (from High, Medium, or Low) to get effects like that seen in Figure 5.21. Peaking is not shown during magnified display.

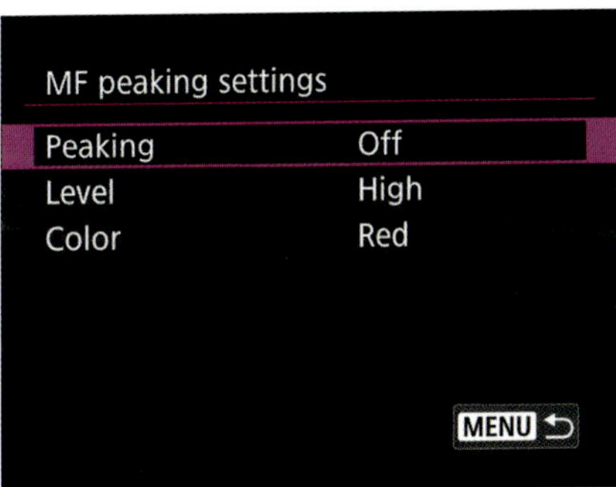

Figure 5.20 Focus peaking options.

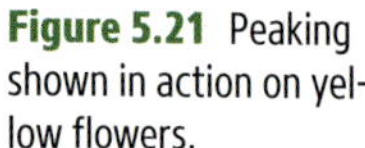

Figure 5.21 Peaking shown in action on yellow flowers.

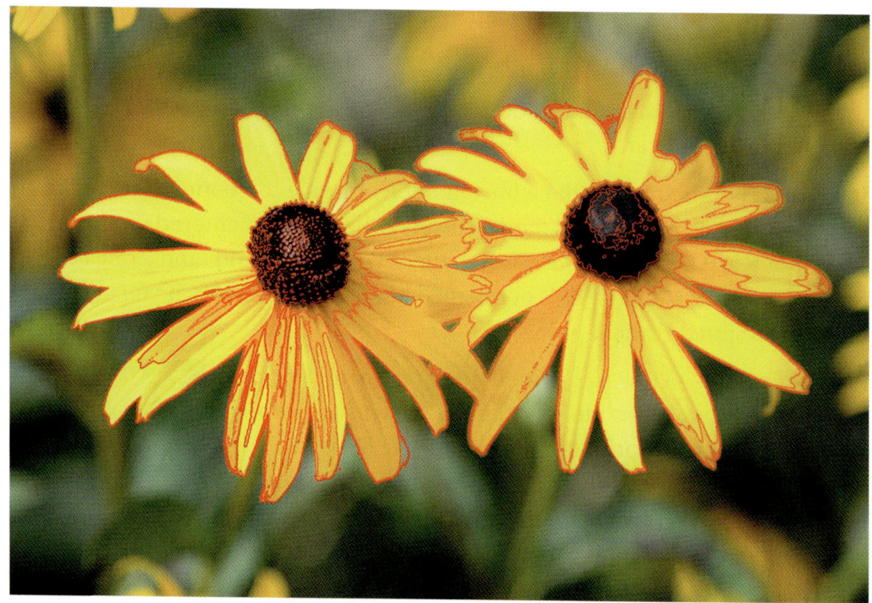

Focus Guide

The Focus Guide, activated in the AF 5 menu, is a sensational tool that can speed up manual focus dramatically. Because the human brain has difficulty remembering which version of an image is "sharpest," it's often necessary to jog the focus ring back and forth in arcs of decreasing size until you're sure that your subject is in sharp focus.

Focus Guide is your focus "memory." When enabled, it displays an on-screen icon overlay that indicates whether the current focal plane is too close, too far, or just right. Best of all, the tool is smart enough to look for particular types of subjects and erect a focus frame around them to show exactly which part of the frame is being used to optimize manual focus. It will perform that magic if Subject to Detect in the AF 1 menu is set to Auto or People *and* Eye Detection is set to Auto, Left Eye, or Right Eye.

Figure 5.22 illustrates what the readouts might look like with a typical human subject:

- **Focus set too close.** As seen in the top row of Figure 5.22, when focusing too close with a human subject, a frame appears around one eye. Tap the AF point selection button and then use the directional controls to move the frame to another location. You might want to do that if your subject is non-human (the frame will appear in gray in the lower-left corner of the screen if no human is identified).

  An array of three triangles will be set far apart, as shown at top left, if focus is much too close. The two outer triangles will point toward the center of the focus frame, and will gradually become closer together as you focus back, as seen at top right.

- **Focus set too far.** If you've set focus *beyond* your subject, the outer pair of triangles will be spread far apart and pointing upward (see Figure 5.22, center left). They'll draw together as you bring the focus plane forward (see Figure 5.22, center right).

- **Correct focus.** When focus is correct, the focus frame will turn green and a single pair of upward/downward triangles will align (see Figure 5.22, bottom).

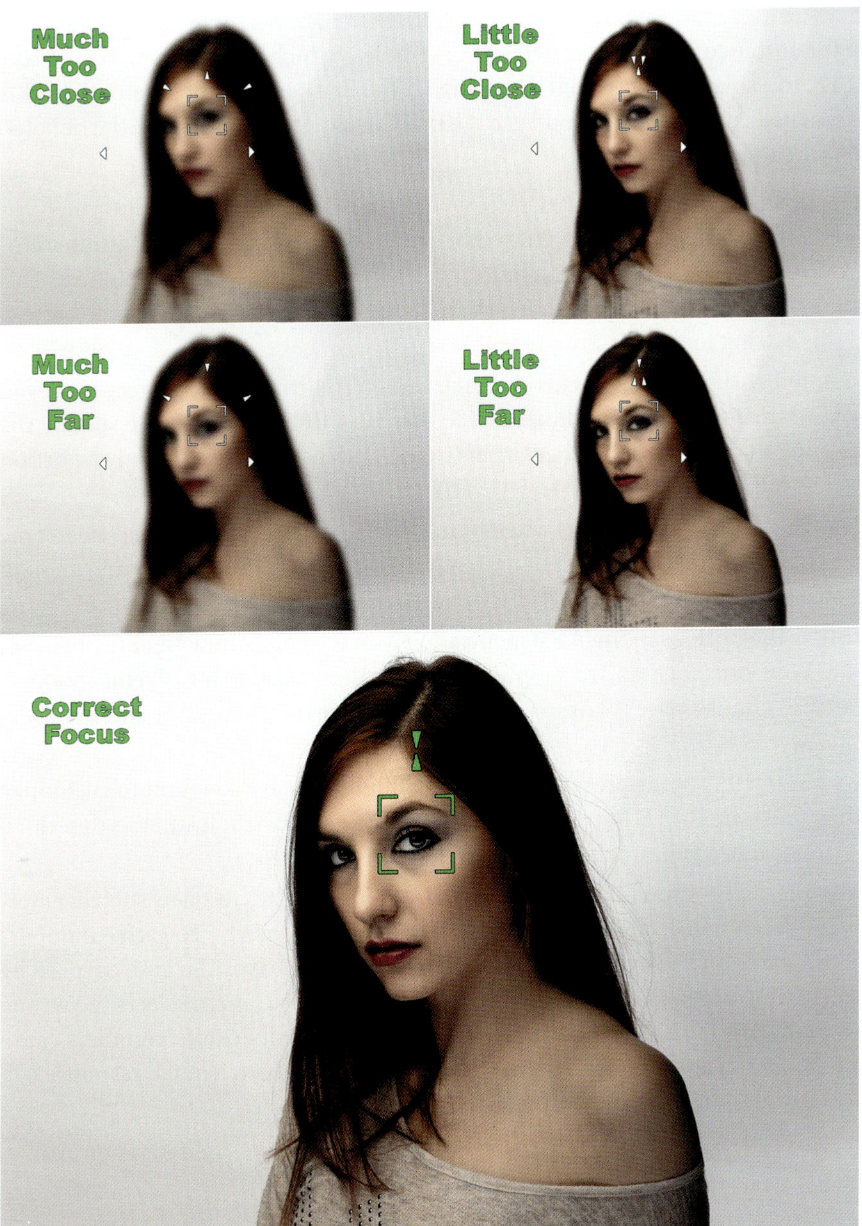

Figure 5.22 Using the Focus Guide.

If you've moved the guide frame, press Q/SET to lock it at that location. You can restore it to the center by pressing the Trash button. The guide frame can also be moved by tapping the touch screen. The Focus Guide may not operate consistently when using smaller f/stops, the display is magnified, or when using digital zoom.

Fine-Tuning Your Autofocus

The options available for autofocus can be overwhelming at times, which is why I'm devoting this chapter, and Chapter 12, to explaining them. I'm covering all the key concepts of autofocus in this chapter. Most of what you need to know to find and use the individual options is found in the bulleted list below. Your options include:

- **Preview AF.** The camera will constantly refocus, even when using One-Shot mode, until you press the shutter release halfway. Then, focus in One-Shot AF mode locks, and will continue refocusing in Servo AF mode, until you press the shutter release all the way to take a picture. This setting's pre-focus activity can speed up AF as you take pictures, at the expense of some battery drain. You'll find this setting in the AF 3 menu.

- **Touch & Drag.** As I noted earlier, you can use the touch screen to position the focus point even while composing your image in the viewfinder. In Chapter 12, I'll show you how to specify the most useful positioning method, and whether the entire LCD screen is active, or only a portion of the panel is used. This entry is located in the AF 4 menu.

- **AF-assist beam firing.** This setting determines when bursts from a compatible external electronic flash or the camera's built-in LED are used to emit a pulse of light that helps provide enough contrast to focus on a subject. You'll find this entry in the AF 3 menu.

- **Servo AF characteristics.** The options in the AF 2 menu allow you to specify how tracking behaves in Servo AF mode. Four preset cases are supplied with settings suitable for several shooting situations. You can also choose Case A (Auto), which allows the camera to adapt automatically to moving subjects.

You can adjust two parameters of the preset cases. Just highlight the case you want to customize and press SET. Then press the RATE button and highlight one of the two adjustments described next. Press Q/SET once more and use the directional controls to adjust:

- **Tracking sensitivity.** This determines how quickly the AF system switches to a new subject entering the focus area. Your choices are −2 (Locked On) to +2 (Responsive). Negative numbers allow you to retain focus on the original subject even if it briefly leaves the area covered by the focus points, making tracking easier. The drawback is that if the camera selects the wrong subject, there is a longer delay before the correct subject is captured. Positive numbers cause the AF system to more quickly switch to a new subject. However, such a quick response can cause the camera to focus on the wrong subject.

- **Acceleration/deceleration tracking.** This parameter determines how the AF system responds to sudden acceleration, deceleration, or stopping. Your choices are 0 (for subjects that move at a constant speed) to 2 (for faster reactions to subjects that suddenly change speed). Lower values can cause the camera to be "fooled" if a subject that was moving consistently suddenly stops; focus may change to the position where the subject *would* have been if it'd kept moving. A higher value may cause inconsistent focus with subjects that move at a constant speed.
- **When focus is difficult.** Low-contrast scenes and dim light levels can give the autofocus system fits. This is often the case with long telephotos or lenses with a relatively small maximum aperture. The Lens Drive When AF Impossible setting (AF 3) can tell the camera either to keep trying to focus, or to stop.
- **Limit AF methods.** If you don't use every AF method, you can make them invisible in the selection screen, so that switching among the ones you do use is faster. As described in Chapter 12, you can enable any or all methods, or have only one or two available. The 1-point AF mode cannot be disabled. These options are found in the AF 4 entry.

Back-Button Focus

Back-button focus is a tool you can use to separate two functions that are commonly locked together—exposure and autofocus—so that you can lock in exposure while allowing focus to be attained at a later point, or vice versa. It's a *good* thing, although using back-button focus effectively may require you to unlearn some habits and acquire new ways of coordinating the action of your fingers.

As you have learned, the default behavior is to set both exposure and focus (when AF is active) when you press the shutter release down halfway. When using One-Shot AF mode, that's that: both exposure and focus are locked and will not change until you release the shutter button or press it all the way down to take a picture and then release it for the next shot. In Servo AF mode, exposure is locked and focus set when you press the shutter release halfway, but the system will continue to refocus if your subject moves for as long as you hold down the shutter button halfway. Focus isn't locked until you press the button down all the way to take the picture.

What back-button focus does is *decouple* or separate the two actions. You can retain the exposure lock feature when the shutter is pressed halfway, but assign autofocus to a different button. So, in practice, you can press the shutter button halfway, locking exposure, and reframe the image if you like (perhaps you're photographing a backlit subject and want to lock in exposure on the foreground, and then reframe to include a very bright background as well).

But, in this same scenario, you *don't* want autofocus locked at the same time. Indeed, you may not want to start AF until you're good and ready, say, at a sports venue as you wait for a ballplayer to streak into view in your viewfinder. With back-button focus, you can lock exposure on the spot where you expect the athlete to be and activate AF at the moment your subject appears by pressing the AF-ON button. That's where the learning of new habits and mind-finger coordination comes in. You need to learn which back-button focus techniques work for you, and when to use them.

Back-button focus lets you avoid the need to switch from One-Shot AF to Servo AF when your subject begins moving unexpectedly. You retain complete control. It's great for sports photography when you want to activate autofocus precisely based on the action in front of you. It also works for static shots. You can press and release your designated focus button, and then take a series of shots using the same focus point. Focus will not change until you once again press your defined back button.

Want to reframe after focus is achieved? Use back-button focus to zero in focus on that location, then reframe. Focus will not change. Don't want to miss an important shot at a wedding or on a photo-journalism assignment? If you're set to *focus-priority* your camera may delay taking a picture until the focus is optimum; in *release-priority* there may still be a slight delay. With back-button focus you can focus first and wait until the decisive moment to press the shutter release and take your picture. The camera will respond immediately and not bother with focusing at all.

Here are some things to consider when using back-button focus:

- **Great for unwanted subjects in action photography.** Earlier in this chapter I talked about using the tracking sensitivity settings to minimize the camera locking onto an intervening object (in football, that might be a yard line marker, another player, or a ref) during an action shot. With back-button focus, you can not only initiate focus whenever you want, you can *pause* focus temporarily by releasing the back button and then pressing it again when the intervening subject is no longer in the frame.

- **Exact timing of focus.** Sports and action photographers also like the ability of back-button focus to allow them to focus at a decisive moment. Perhaps you're shooting a scenic waterscape when a playful dolphin suddenly begins a series of leaps a few yards from you. You can lock exposure with a half-press of the shutter button, and then frame the area in which you think the dolphin may next appear. At the right moment, press the back button to focus on the creature quickly and the shutter button to take the picture. (See Figure 5.23.) Or, you may be shooting a football game and following the action through the viewfinder, seeking a subject to capture. You decide to capture an image of a wide receiver reaching out for the ball. Frame the receiver in the view-finder and press the back button to lock in focus, and then press the shutter release all the way to actually take the picture.

- **Reframing.** As I mentioned earlier, you can lock focus with the back button, then release the but-ton and reframe before taking the picture with the shutter release button. The camera will not refocus when the shutter button is pressed.

- **Fine-tuning focus.** Many Canon lenses allow you to fine-tune focus even when the lens is set for autofocus. With those lenses, you can go ahead and initiate autofocus using the back button; then, if you want to fine-tune focus manually, release the button and rotate the focusing ring. The camera will not refocus when you press the shutter release button, and you won't have to switch the lens' AF/MF switch to Manual. This technique works particularly well for macro photography, which often benefits from precise manual focusing on the exact plane that you want to be sharpest. Go ahead and pre-focus using the autofocus feature, then release the back button and manually set your focus. It's faster than focusing entirely in manual focus mode.

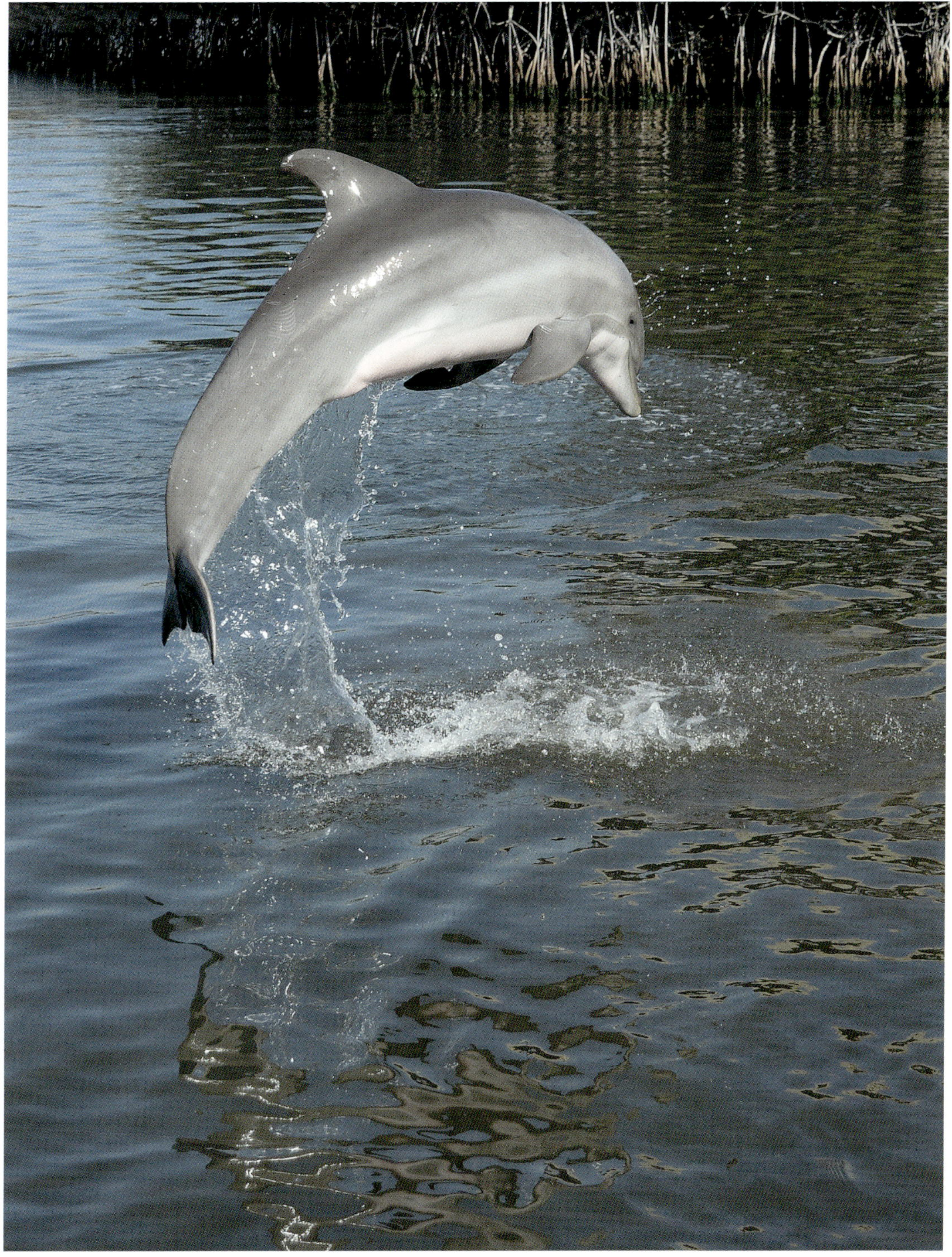

Figure 5.23 Back-button focus is great for timing the exact moment of focus.

Activating Back-Button Focus

The R8 implements back-button focus slightly differently from some other cameras, because they don't allow you to assign AF Start (only) to a button like the AF-ON button. When you press AF-ON, the camera focuses *and* meters. But there's a way to work around that.

The easiest way to activate back-button focus is to make a quick trip to the Customize Buttons entry in the Custom Functions 3 menu, as described in Chapter 15. Once you've activated this feature, you press the shutter release down halfway to lock exposure and press the AF-ON button when you're ready to autofocus. Here's what you need to do:

1. **Redefine the shutter release button.** In Customize Buttons, highlight the Shutter Button entry, as shown at left in Figure 5.24. Press Q/SET.

2. **Choose Metering Start.** When selected, pressing the shutter release button down all the way meters and locks exposure, but *not* autofocus, as the shutter is tripped. Press Q/SET to confirm. (See Figure 5.24, right.)

3. **Select Back Button.** The default value for the AF-ON button works fine. When you press the AF-ON button, autofocus will initiate *and* metering will be performed, continuously updating both until you release the button. When the shutter release button is pressed, metering will take place and the exposure will be locked. If you want to lock exposure before the picture is taken, press the AE lock (*) button.

   Alternatively, you can define some other button with the Metering and AF Start function and use that for back-button focus instead if you find it more comfortable to access with your thumb.

4. **Turn off continuous focus.** You'll be using One-Shot AF with back-button focus, and you'll also want to turn off Preview AF in the AF 3 menu.

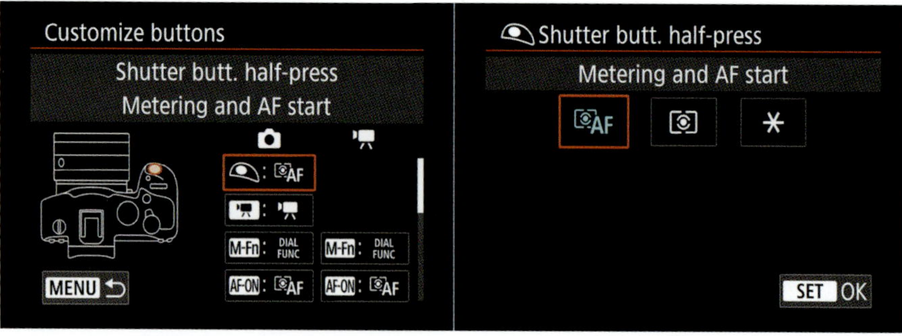

Figure 5.24 Activating back-button focus.

Advanced Techniques 6

Y ou can happily spend your entire shooting career using the techniques and features already explained in this book. Great exposures, sharp pictures, and creative compositions are all you really need to produce great shot after great shot. But, those with enough interest in getting the most out of their R8 will be interested in going beyond those basics to explore some of the more advanced techniques and capabilities of the camera. Capturing the briefest instant of time and transforming common scenes into the unusual with lengthy time exposures and working with Panorama capture are all tempting avenues for exploration. So, in this chapter, I'm going to offer longer discussions of some of the more advanced techniques and capabilities that I like to put to work.

Continuous Shooting

The continuous shooting mode reminds me how far digital photography has brought us. The first accessory I purchased when I worked as a sports photographer many years ago was a motor drive for my film SLR. It enabled me to snap off a series of shots in rapid succession, which came in very handy when a fullback broke through the line and headed for the end zone. Even a seasoned action photographer can miss the decisive instant when a crucial block is made, or a baseball superstar's bat shatters and pieces of cork fly out. Continuous shooting simplifies taking a series of pictures, either to ensure that one has more or less the exact moment you want to capture or to capture a sequence that is interesting as a collection of successive images. Digital cameras have reusable "film," so if you waste a few dozen shots on non-decisive moments, you can erase them and shoot more. Save only the best shots, like the series shown in Figure 6.1.

To use the continuous shooting mode, press the Q/SET button and navigate to the Drive icon, which is the fifth from the top in the left column. You can also access Drive mode from the M-Fn button's Dial Functions; press the M-Fn button until the Drive mode is highlighted, then rotate the Main dial to select. In both cases, you can choose from three continuous shooting settings, at speeds shown in Table 6.1.

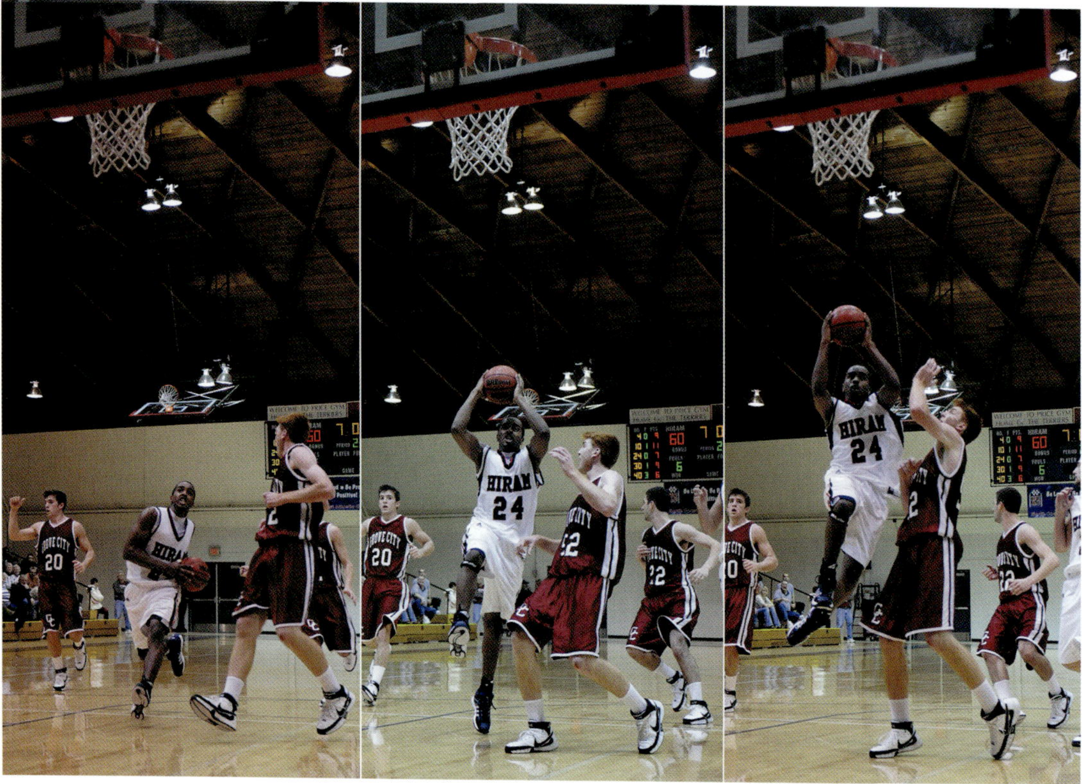

Figure 6.1 Continuous shooting allows you to capture an entire sequence of exciting moments as they unfold.

TABLE 6.1 Continuous Shooting Speeds

DRIVE MODE	ELECTRONIC 1ST-CURTAIN SHUTTER	ELECTRONIC SHUTTER
High-speed continuous+	6.0 fps	40 fps
High-speed continuous	6.0 fps	20 fps
Low-speed continuous	3.0 fps	5.0 fps

Actual frames per second may be reduced when flicker control is enabled, you're using Dual Pixel RAW, you've activated Servo AF, or when you're working with electronic flash. Other factors can come into play when shooting in high-speed mode, which is also affected by many shooting settings, including shutter speed, aperture, autofocus mode, or even the type of lens you are using. A cold or nearly dead battery can also reduce shooting speeds.

When you partially depress the shutter button, a number representing the maximum number of shots you can take at the current quality settings is displayed. In the viewfinder, that number is located to the left of the battery status indicator at lower right, immediately above the Possible Shots value. On the LCD screen, the maximum burst is located to the immediate right of the Possible Shots indicator at upper left.

The display shows a maximum of 99 shots remaining; it's possible that the camera can take more than that, so the 99 will remain lit until the actual number remaining drops below that value. When the internal buffer is full, a "BUSY" indicator will be shown. When the internal buffer fills, the camera will stop capturing images until enough pictures have been written to the memory card to allow shooting to resume. As you might expect, the number of continuous shots you can fire off before that happens varies with the format you choose and the write speed of your card. For that reason, a fast memory card is a good idea.

The reason the size of your bursts is limited by the buffer is that continuous images are first shuttled into the camera's internal memory, then doled out to the memory card as quickly as they can be written to the card. Technically, the camera takes the RAW data received from the digital image processor and converts it to the output format you've selected—either JPG or RAW/DPRAW or both—and deposits it in the buffer ready to store on the card.

This internal "smart" buffer can suck up photos much more quickly than the memory card and, indeed, some memory cards are significantly faster or slower than others. Table 6.2 provides Canon estimates of the maximum continuous burst you can expect at the Large image size when using electronic 1st-curtain and electronic shutters with standard SDXC (UHS-I) and fast (UHS-II) memory cards. The table assumes you'll be shooting at a maximum 6 fps rate with electronic 1st-curtain shutter and 40 fps with the electronic shutter.

TABLE 6.2 Maximum Bursts: H+ Continuous Shooting

IMAGE QUALITY	ELECTRONIC 1ST-CURTAIN: UHS-I	ELECTRONIC 1ST-CURTAIN: UHS-II	ELECTRONIC SHUTTER: UHS-I	ELECTRONIC SHUTTER: UHS-II
JPEG/HEIF	1000+	1000+	120	120
RAW	85	1000+	51	56
RAW+JPEG	70	570	50	54
RAW+HEIF	69	87	35	42

In all cases, you'll get the best results when using a shutter speed of 1/500th second and the widest opening of the lens. However, when One-Shot AF is active, the camera will focus only once at the beginning of the sequence, and then use that focus setting for the rest of the shots in the burst. If your subject is moving, you can use Servo AF instead, at a slightly slower continuous frame rate.

Setting High ISO Speed Noise Reduction to High also limits the length of your continuous burst. You'll also see a decrease if lens aberration correction is active, or you have the camera set to do white balance bracketing. (In such cases, the camera stores multiple copies of each image snapped, slowing down the burst rate.) Anti-flicker shooting and Dual Pixel RAW also reduce the continuous shooting speed. While you can use flash in continuous mode, the camera will wait for the flash to recycle between shots, slowing down the continuous shooting rate.

BURSTS NOT JUST FOR ACTION

I often use continuous shooting mode even when I'm not busy shooting action. As I've mentioned before, bursts make sense when you're shooting HDR or bracketing. But here's a technique you might not have thought of—continuous shooting can give you sharper images!

When I'm photographing concerts, I enjoy greater mobility by not using a monopod (and a tripod would be even more of a ball-and-chain, even if not forbidden by the venue). I'm generally shooting at around 1/180th second, which is usually fast enough to eliminate blur from the performers' motion. IS has no effect on stopping *their* movement, of course, and it does a fairly good job of eliminating camera/photographer shake. However, I invariably find that if I shoot in continuous, one of the middle frames in a sequence will be sharpest. Even the most seasoned photographer will add a little bump to the camera when they squeeze (not stab) the shutter release.

More Exposure Options

In Chapter 4, you learned techniques for getting the *right* exposure, but I haven't explained all your exposure options just yet. You'll want to know about the *kind* of exposure settings that are available to you. There are options that let you control when the exposure is made, or even how to make an exposure that's out of the ordinary in terms of length (time or bulb exposures). The sections that follow explain your camera's special exposure features, and even discuss a few it does not have (and why it doesn't).

A Tiny Slice of Time

Exposures that seem impossibly brief can reveal a world we didn't know existed. In the 1930s, Dr. Harold Edgerton, a professor of electrical engineering at MIT, pioneered high-speed photography using a repeating electronic flash unit he patented called the *stroboscope*. As the inventor of the electronic flash, he popularized its use to freeze objects in motion, and you've probably seen his photographs of bullets piercing balloons and drops of milk forming a coronet-shaped splash.

Electronic flash freezes action by virtue of its extremely short duration—as brief as 1/50,000th second or less. You can read more about using electronic flash to stop action in Chapter 9.

Of course, the camera is fully capable of immobilizing all but the fastest movement using only its shutter speeds, which range all the way up to 1/8000th second (or 1/16,000th second with the electronic shutter in Tv or M mode). Indeed, you'll rarely have need for such a brief shutter speed in ordinary shooting. If you wanted to use an aperture of f/2.8 at ISO 100 outdoors in bright sunlight, for some reason, a shutter speed of 1/8000th second would more than do the job. You'd need a faster shutter speed only if you moved the ISO setting to a higher sensitivity (but why would you do that?). Under less than full sunlight, 1/8000th second is more than fast enough for any conditions you're likely to encounter.

Most sports action can be frozen at 1/2000th second or slower, and for many sports a slower shutter speed is actually preferable—for example, to allow the wheels of a racing automobile or motorcycle, or the propeller on a classic aircraft to blur realistically.

But if you want to do some exotic action-freezing photography without resorting to electronic flash, the top shutter speed is at your disposal. Here are some things to think about when exploring this type of high-speed photography:

- **You'll need a lot of light.** High shutter speeds cut very fine slices of time and sharply reduce the amount of illumination that reaches your sensor. To use 1/4000th second at an aperture of f/6.3, you'd need an ISO setting of 800—even in full daylight. To use an f/stop smaller than f/6.3 or an ISO setting lower than 800, you'd need *more* light than full daylight provides. (That's why electronic flash units work so well for high-speed photography when used as the sole illumination; they provide both the effect of a brief shutter speed and the high levels of illumination needed.)

- **Don't combine high shutter speeds with electronic flash.** You might be tempted to use an electronic flash with a high shutter speed. Perhaps you want to stop some action in daylight with a brief shutter speed and use electronic flash only as supplemental illumination to fill in the shadows. Unfortunately, under most conditions you can't use flash in subdued illumination at any shutter speed faster than 1/200th second in electronic 1st-curtain mode (flash cannot be used at all in electronic shutter mode). That's the fastest speed at which the camera's focal plane shutter is fully open: shorter speeds are produced by exposing only a small portion of the sensor at a time as the shutter curtains move down the sensor plane. As a result, the flash will expose only the small portion of the sensor exposed by the resulting slit during its duration. (Check out "Avoiding Sync-Speed Problems" in Chapter 9 if you want to see how you *can* use shutter speeds shorter than 1/200th second with certain Canon Speedlites, albeit at much-reduced effective power levels.)

Working with Short Exposures

You can have a lot of fun exploring the kinds of pictures you can take using very brief exposure times, whether you decide to take advantage of the action-stopping capabilities of your external electronic flash or work with the faster shutter speeds. Here are a few ideas to get you started:

- **Take revealing images.** Fast shutter speeds can help you reveal the real subject behind the façade, by freezing constant motion to capture an enlightening moment in time. Legendary fashion/portrait photographer Philippe Halsman used leaping photos of famous people, such as the Duke and Duchess of Windsor, Richard Nixon, and Salvador Dali to illuminate their real selves. Halsman said, "*When you ask a person to jump, his attention is mostly directed toward the act of jumping and the mask falls so that the real person appears.*" Try some high-speed portraits of people you know in motion to see how they appear when concentrating on something other than the portrait. (See Figure 6.2.)

Figure 6.2 When your subjects leap, the real person inside emerges.

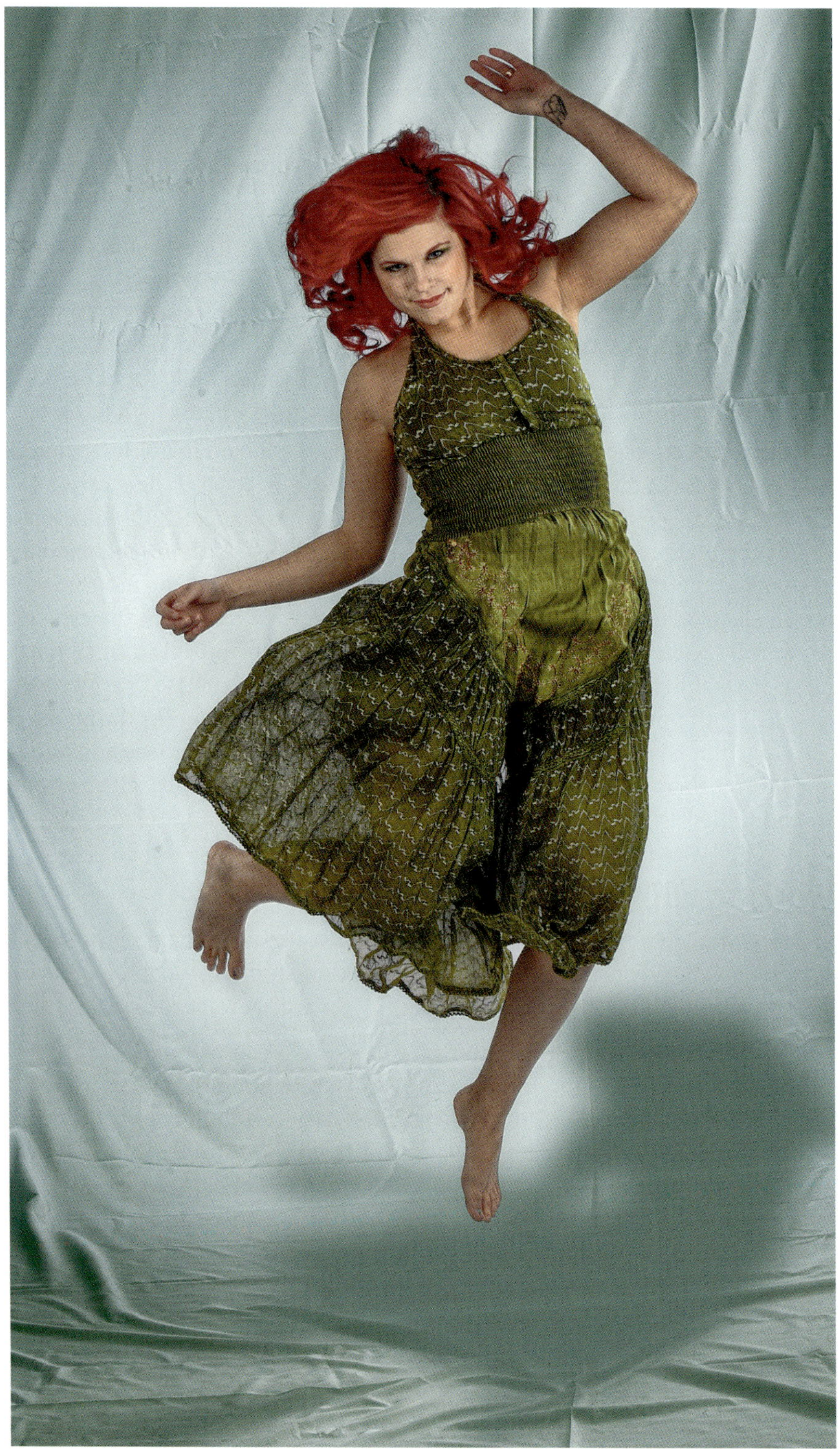

- **Create unreal images.** High-speed photography can also produce photographs that show your subjects in ways that are quite unreal. A helicopter in mid-air with its rotors frozen makes for an unusual picture. Figure 6.3 shows a pair of pictures. At top, a shutter speed of 1/1000th second virtually stopped the rotation of the chopper's rotors, while the bottom image, shot at 1/200th second, provides a more realistic view of the blurry blades as they appeared to the eye.

- **Capture unseen perspectives.** Some things are *never* seen in real life, except when viewed in a stop-action photograph. Edgerton's balloon bursts were only a starting point. Freeze a hummingbird in flight for a view of wings that never seem to stop. Or, capture the splashes as liquid falls into a bowl, as shown in Figure 6.4. No electronic flash was required for this image (and wouldn't have illuminated the water in the bowl as evenly). Instead, a clutch of high-intensity lamps, a couple blue gels, and an ISO setting of 1600 allowed the camera to capture this image at 1/2000th second.

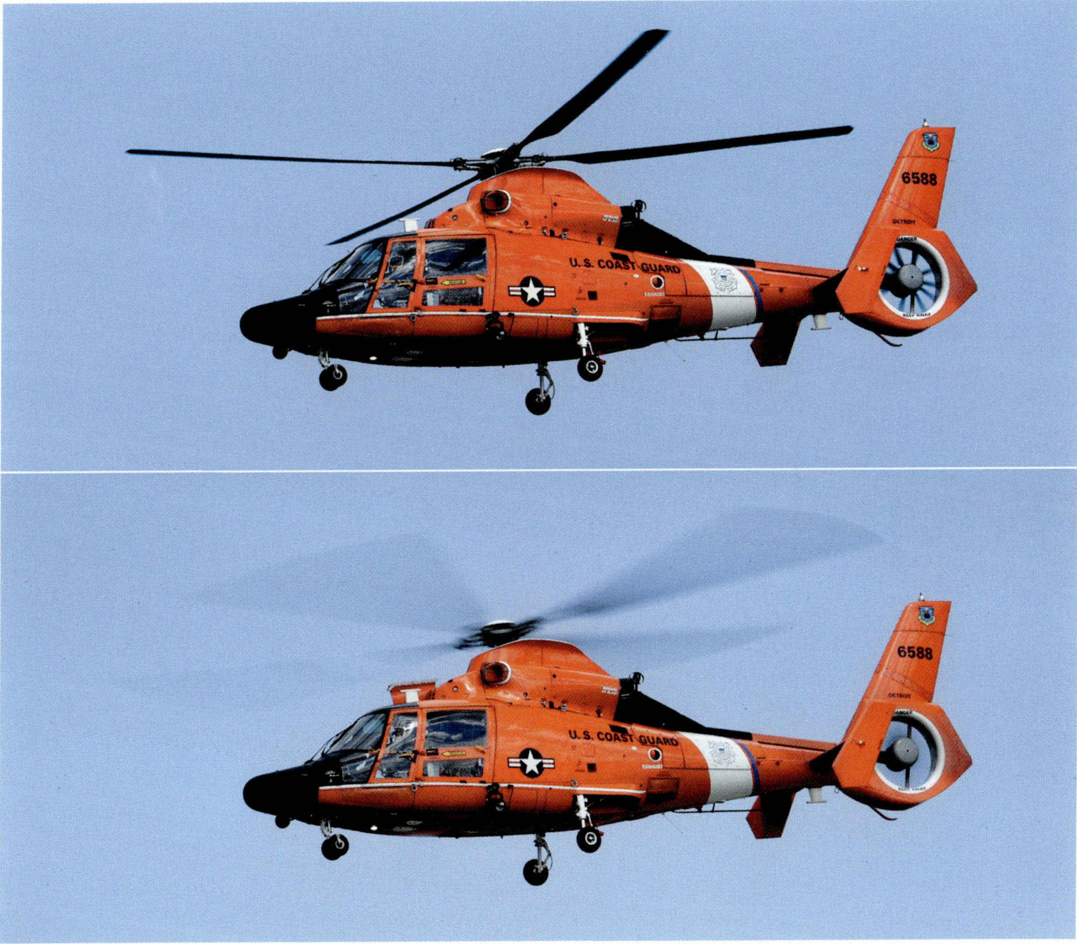

Figure 6.3 Top: the chopper's blades are frozen at 1/1000th second; bottom: a more realistic blurry rendition at 1/200th-second shutter speed.

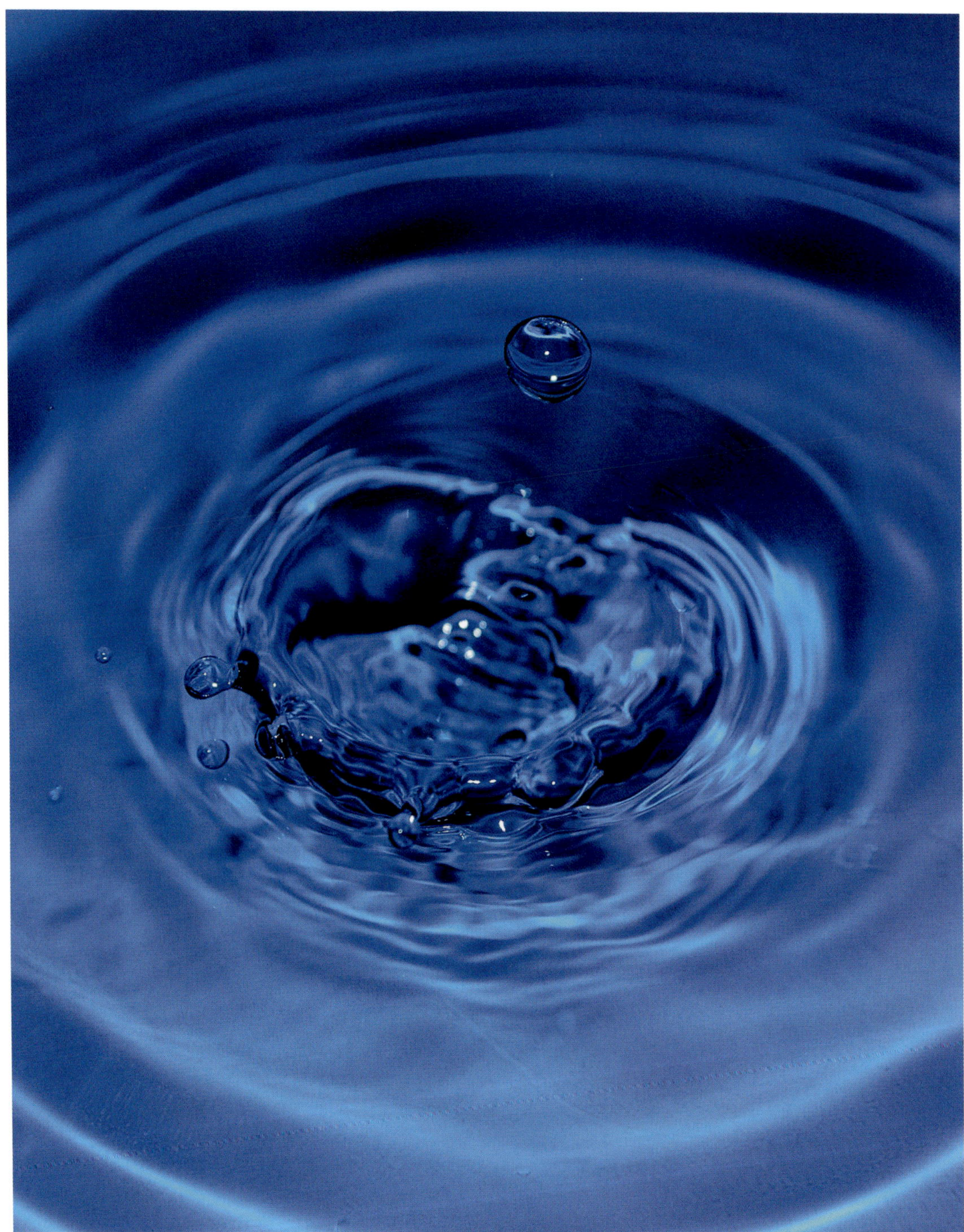

Figure 6.4 A large amount of artificial illumination and an ISO 1600 sensitivity setting allowed capturing this shot at 1/2000th second without use of an electronic flash.

- **Vanquish camera shake and gain new angles.** Here's an idea I mentioned earlier in this chapter that's so obvious it isn't always explored to its fullest extent. A high enough shutter speed can free you from the tyranny of a tripod, making it easier to capture new angles, or to shoot quickly while moving around, especially with longer lenses. I tend to use a monopod or tripod for almost everything when I'm not using an image-stabilized lens, and I end up missing some shots because of a reluctance to adjust my camera support to get a higher, lower, or different angle. If you have enough light and can use an f/stop wide enough to permit a high shutter speed, you'll find a new freedom to choose your shots. I have a favored 500mm lens that I use for sports and wildlife photography, almost invariably with a tripod, as I don't find the "reciprocal of the focal length" rule particularly helpful in most cases. (I would *not* hand-hold this hefty lens with a 1/500th-second shutter speed under most circumstances.) However, at 1/2000th second or faster, and with a sufficiently high ISO setting (I recommend ISO 800 to 1600) to allow such a speed, it's entirely possible for a steady hand to use this lens without a tripod or monopod's extra support, and I've found that my whole approach to shooting animals and other elusive subjects changes in high-speed mode.

Long Exposures

Longer exposures are a doorway into another world, showing us how even familiar scenes can look much different when photographed over periods measured in seconds. At night, long exposures produce streaks of light from moving, illuminated subjects like automobiles or amusement park rides. Extra-long exposures of seemingly pitch-dark subjects can reveal interesting views using light levels barely bright enough to see by. At any time of day, including daytime (in which case you'll often need the help of neutral-density filters, which reduce the amount of light passing through the lens, to make the long exposure practical), long exposures can cause moving objects to vanish entirely, because they don't remain stationary long enough to register in a photograph.

Three Ways to Take Long Exposures

There are actually three common types of lengthy exposures: *timed exposures, bulb exposures,* and *time exposures.* Your camera offers all three. Because of the length of the exposure, all of the following techniques should be used with a tripod to hold the camera steady:

- **Timed exposures.** These are long exposures from 1 second to 30 seconds, measured by the camera itself. To take a picture in this range, simply use Manual or Tv modes and use the Main dial to set the shutter speed to the length of time you want, choosing from preset speeds of 1.0, 1.5, 2.0, 3.0, 4.0, 6.0, 8.0, 10.0, 15.0, 20.0, or 30.0 seconds (if you've specified 1/2-stop increments for exposure adjustments) or 1.0, 1.3, 1.6, 2.0, 2.5, 3.2, 4.0, 5.0, 6.0, 8.0, 10.0, 13.0, 15.0, 20.0, 25.0, and 30.0 seconds (if you're using 1/3-stop increments). The advantage of timed exposures is that the camera does all the calculating for you. There's no need for a stopwatch. If you review your image on the LCD and decide to try again with the exposure doubled or halved, you can dial in the correct exposure with precision. The disadvantage of timed exposures is that you can't take a photo for longer than 30 seconds.

- **Bulb exposures.** This type of exposure is so-called because in the olden days the photographer squeezed and held an air bulb attached to a tube that provided the force necessary to keep the shutter open. Traditionally, a bulb exposure is one that lasts as long as the shutter release button is pressed; when you release the button, the exposure ends. To make a bulb exposure, set the mode to B. Then, press the shutter to start the exposure, and press it again to close the shutter.

- **Time exposures.** This is a setting found on some cameras to produce longer exposures. It's actually an enhancement of the Bulb exposure feature. With the R8's mode set to Bulb, locate the Bulb Timer setting in the Shooting 7 menu. Press Q/SET, and in the screen that pops up, highlight Enable. Press the INFO button, and a screen appears that will allow you to set an exposure time of up to 99 hours, 59 minutes, and 59 seconds. You'll rarely need extra-long exposures (unless you're shooting continuous star trails), but many exposures longer than 30 seconds are quite useful. For example, many star photographers shoot multiple one-minute exposures (any longer than that, and the star pinpoints become blurs) and then merge them together to get a different kind of sky photograph.

  When using this type of Bulb exposure, you can press the shutter release button, go off for a few minutes, and come back to take your next shot (assuming your camera is still there). The disadvantages of this mode are exposures must be timed manually, and with shorter exposures, it's possible for the vibration of manually opening and closing the shutter to register in the photo. For longer exposures, the period of vibration is relatively brief and not usually a problem—and there is always the release cable option to eliminate photographer-caused camera shake entirely.

Working with Long Exposures

Because your camera can produce such good images at longer exposures, and there are so many creative things you can do with long-exposure techniques, you'll want to do some experimenting. Get yourself a tripod or another firm support and take some test shots with long exposure noise reduction both enabled and disabled using the entry in the Shooting 5 menu, as explained in Chapter 11 (to see whether you prefer low noise or high detail) and get started. Here are some things to try:

- **Make people invisible.** One very cool thing about long exposures is that objects that move rapidly enough won't register at all in a photograph, while the subjects that remain stationary are portrayed in the normal way. That makes it easy to produce people-free landscape photos and architectural photos at night or, even, in full daylight if you use a neutral-density filter (or two or three) to allow an exposure of at least a few seconds. At ISO 100, f/22, and a pair of 8X (three-stop) neutral-density filters, you can use exposures of nearly two seconds; overcast days and/or more neutral-density filtration would work even better if daylight people-vanishing is your goal. They'll have to be walking *very* briskly and across the field of view (rather than directly toward the camera) for this to work. At night, it's much easier to achieve this effect with the 20- to 30-second exposures that are possible, as you can see in Figure 6.5.

- **Create streaks.** If you aren't shooting for total invisibility, long exposures with the camera on a tripod or monopod can produce some interesting streaky effects, as you can see in Figure 6.6. You don't need to limit yourself to indoor photography, however. Even a single 8X ND filter will let you shoot at f/22 and 1/6th second in full daylight at ISO 100.

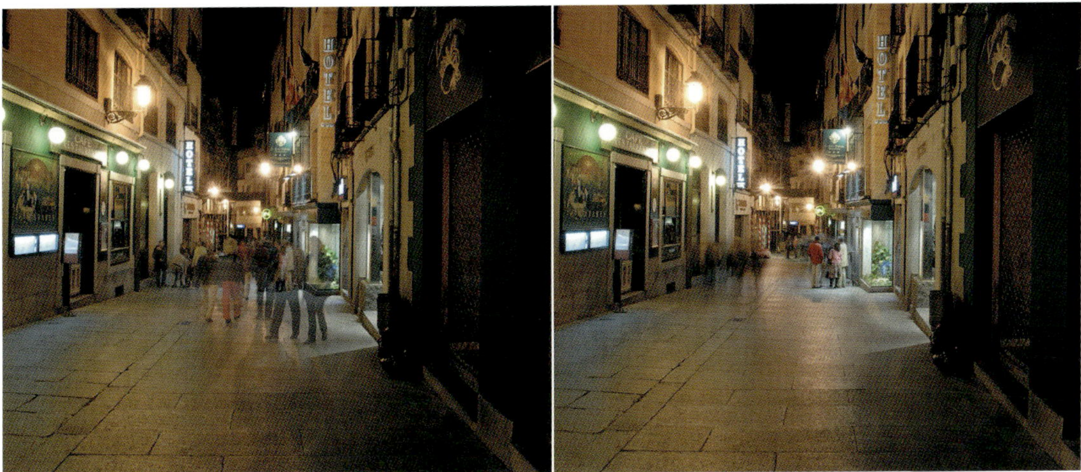

Figure 6.5 This alleyway is thronged with people, as you can see in this two-second exposure using only the available illumination (left). With the camera still on a tripod, a 30-second exposure rendered the passersby almost invisible (right).

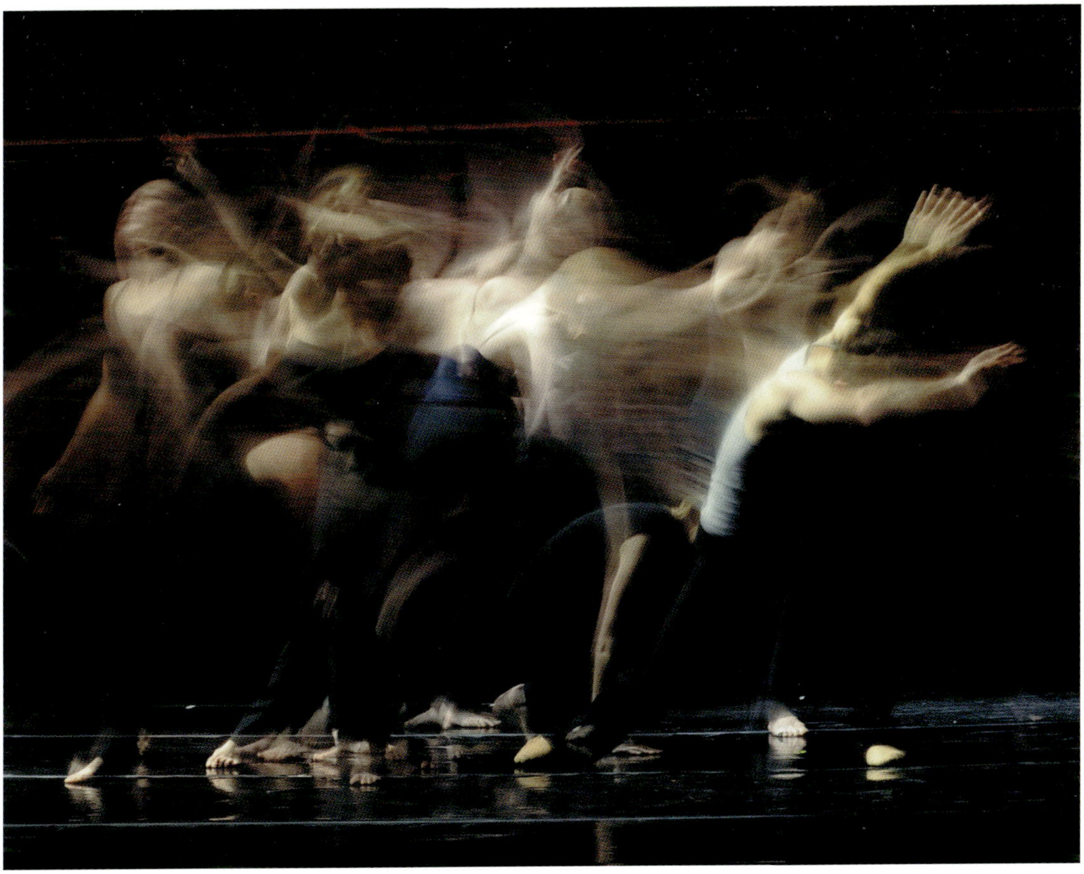

Figure 6.6 These dancers produced a swirl of movement during the 1/8th-second exposure.

- **Produce light trails.** At night, car headlights and taillights and other moving sources of illumination can generate interesting light trails. Your camera doesn't even need to be mounted on a tripod; hand-holding for longer exposures adds movement and patterns to your trails. If you're shooting fireworks (preferably with a tripod), a longer exposure of several seconds may allow you to combine several bursts into one picture. Or, you can record the movement of an amusement park ride, as shown in Figure 6.7.

- **Blur waterfalls, etc.** You'll find that waterfalls and other sources of moving liquid produce a special type of long exposure blur, because the water merges into a fantasy-like veil that looks different at different exposure times, and with different waterfalls. Cascades with turbulent flow produce a rougher look at a given longer exposure than falls that flow smoothly. Although blurred waterfalls have become almost a cliché, there are still plenty of variations for a creative photographer to explore, as you can see in Figure 6.8.

- **Show total darkness in new ways.** Even on the darkest nights, there is enough starlight or glow from distant illumination sources to see by, and, if you use a long exposure, there is enough light to take a picture, too. Figure 6.9 shows Florence, Italy, late at night.

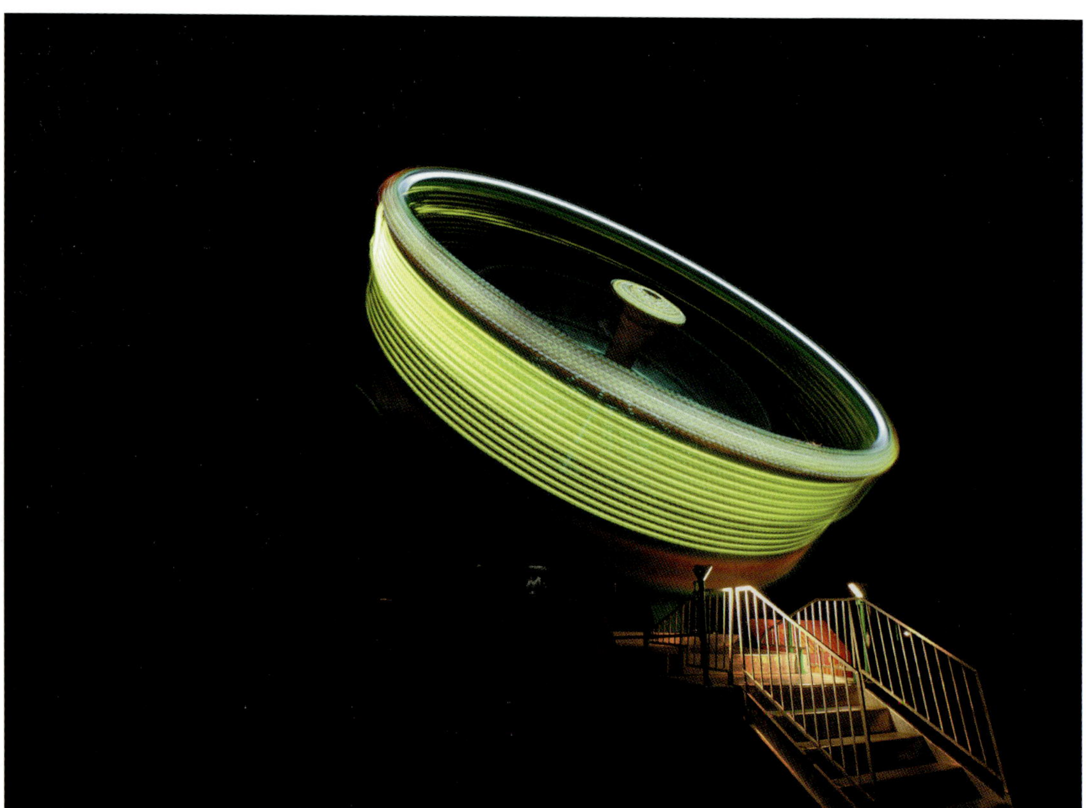

Figure 6.7 A long exposure of several seconds allows capturing the movement of this thrilling amusement park ride.

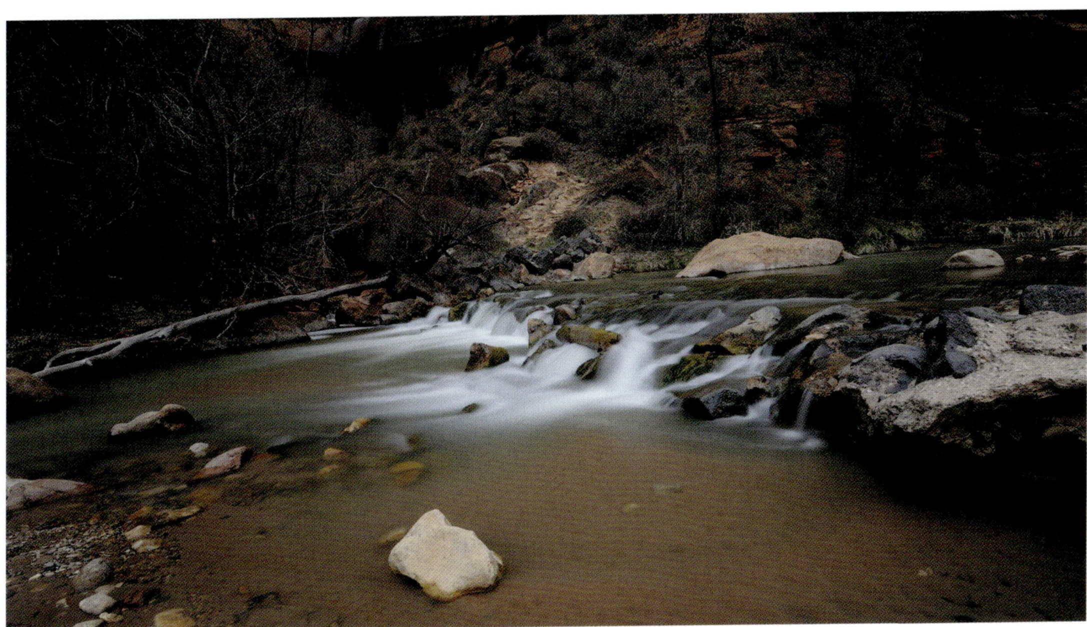

Figure 6.8 A 1/4-second exposure blurred the falling water.

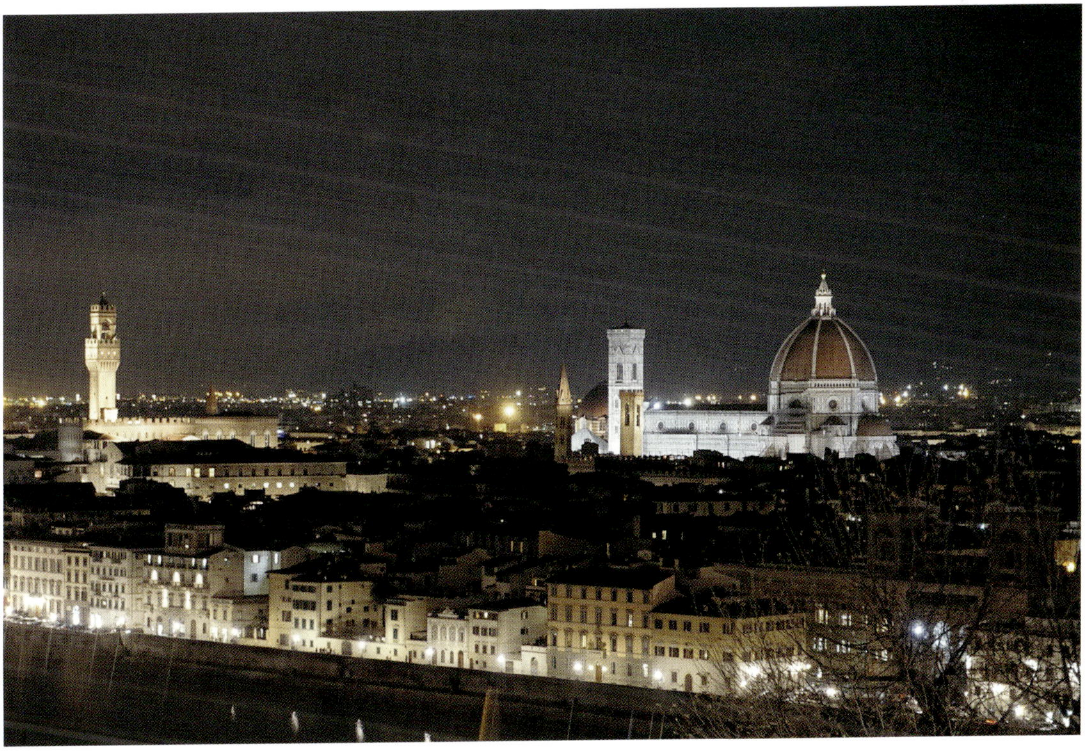

Figure 6.9 A 20-second exposure revealed this view of Florence, Italy.

Delayed Exposures

Sometimes it's desirable to have a delay of some sort before a picture is actually taken. Perhaps you'd like to get in the picture yourself and would appreciate it if the camera waited 10 seconds after you press the shutter release to actually take the picture. Maybe you want to give a tripod-mounted camera time to settle down and damp any residual vibration after the release is pressed to improve sharpness for an exposure with a relatively slow shutter speed. It's possible you want to explore the world of time-lapse photography. The next sections present your delayed exposure options.

Self-Timer

The built-in self-timer has 10-second and 2-second delays, plus an additional mode that will shoot continuously for 10 seconds for a number of shots that you specify. (Explained in Chapter 11.) Activate the timer using the Drive option in the Q menu, rotating the Main dial to select the drive modes. Press the shutter release button halfway to lock in focus on your subjects (if you're taking a self-portrait, focus on an object at a similar distance and use focus lock). When you're ready to take the photo, continue pressing the shutter release the rest of the way. The lamp on the front of the camera will blink slowly for eight seconds (when using the 10-second timer) and the beeper will chirp (if you haven't disabled it in the Set-up 2 menu, as described in Chapter 11). During the final two seconds, the beeper sounds more rapidly, and the lamp remains on until the picture is taken.

This is something you might want to do if you're shooting close-ups, landscapes, or other types of pictures using the self-timer, to trip the shutter in the most vibration-free way possible. Forget to bring along your tripod, but still want to take a close-up picture with a precise focus setting? Set your digital camera to the self-timer function, then put the camera on any reasonably steady support, such as a fence post or a rock. When you're ready to take the picture, press the shutter release. The camera might teeter back and forth for a second or two, but it will settle back to its original position before the self-timer activates the shutter. The self-timer remains active until you turn it off—even if you power down your camera—so remember to turn it off when finished.

Time Lapse and Interval Photography

Who hasn't marveled at interval stills, shot moments or minutes apart to document an event, or wasn't enrapt by a time-lapse movie of a flower opening, a series of shots of the moon marching across the sky, or one of those extreme interval or time-lapse photography productions showing something that takes a very, very long time, such as a building under construction.

You probably won't be shooting such construction shots, unless you have a spare camera you don't need for a few months (or are willing to go through the rigmarole of figuring out how to set up your camera in precisely the same position using the same lens settings to shoot a series of pictures at intervals). However, other kinds of time-lapse photography are entirely within reach.

For Figure 6.10, I pointed my camera out my office window in Florida, hoping to use Interval Timing Shooting to catch some manatees. I left the camera running for hours, capturing the three images shown in the figure. I've also used interval shooting for HDR images of sunsets. Typically, I aim the camera at the horizon and set it to shoot a three-shot bracket with a 3.0-stop increment. Then, I set the interval time to capture an image every 10 seconds.

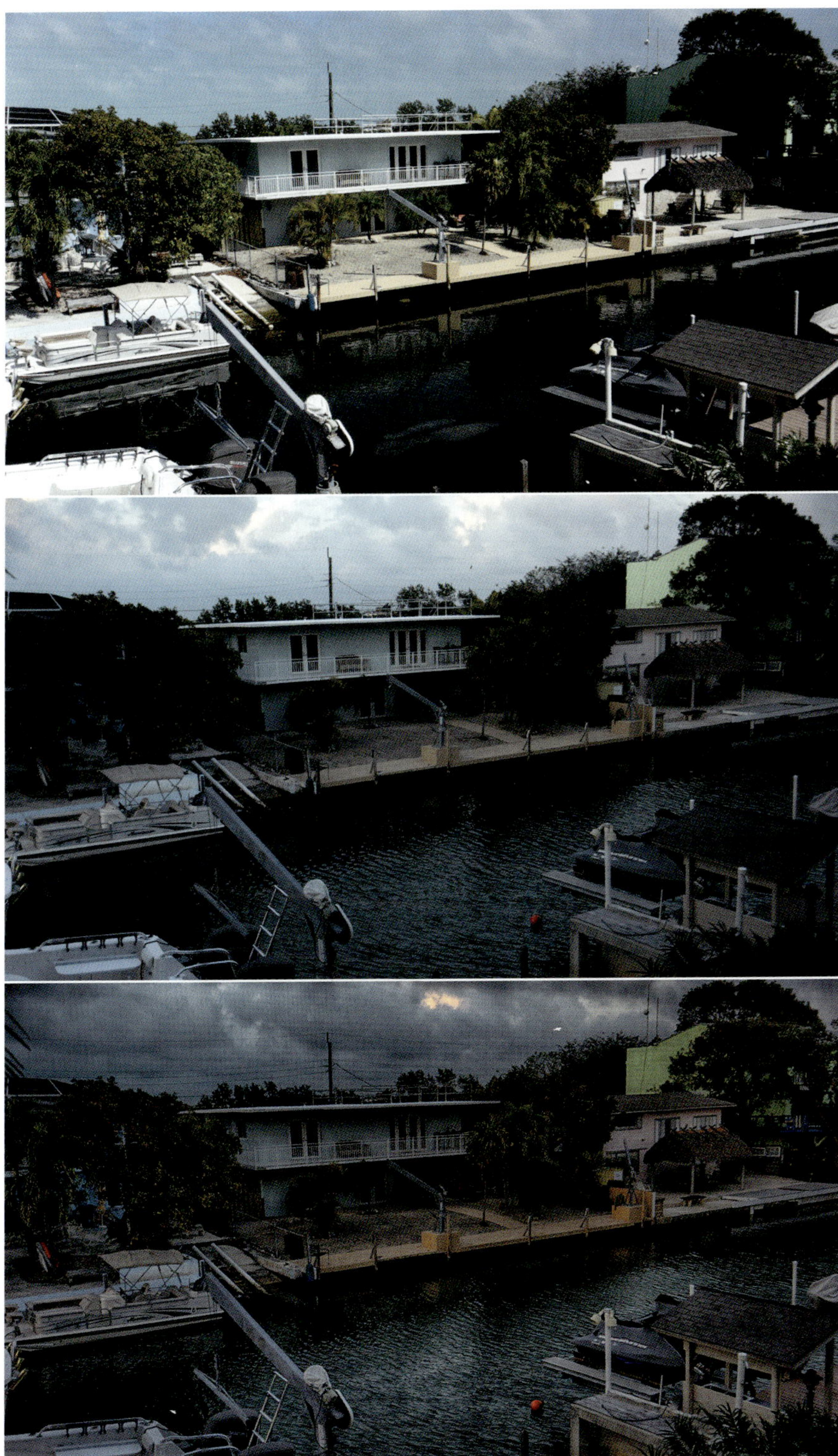

Figure 6.10 One of my time-lapse photos captured a mother manatee and her calf swimming by (top); the other exposures produced interesting variations on a static scene.

The built-in features allow you to shoot interval sequences and time-lapse movies easily. Before I explain how to use these features, here are a few things to keep in mind:

- **Use AC power.** If you're shooting a long sequence, consider connecting your camera to an AC adapter, as leaving the camera on for long periods of time will rapidly deplete the battery. The optional Canon DC Coupler DR-E6 and AC Adapter AC-6N are perfect for this application. While shooting time-lapse movies, auto power off will not take place.

- **Disabled functions.** While capturing time-lapse movies, shooting and menu functions and playback are disabled, and output to HDMI (both monitor and recorder) is disabled. You can't shoot time-lapse movies if digital zoom is enabled, and sound and time codes are not recorded. Autofocus is disabled during time-lapse recording (to avoid focus changing between shots). When using Movie Tv mode with the R8, the aperture is fixed and exposure is adjusted by changing the ISO, again, to avoid focus/depth-of-field changes.

- **Make sure you have enough storage space.** Unless your memory card has enough capacity to hold all the images you'll be taking, you might want to change to a reduced resolution to maximize the image count. At 4K and FHD, a 256GB memory card will accommodate a 72-minute recording at 4K, and 6 hours, 19 minutes at FHD.

- **Protect your camera.** If your camera will be set up for an extended period of time (longer than an hour or two), make sure it's protected from weather, earthquakes, animals, young children, Keyser Söze, innocent bystanders, and theft.

- **Vary intervals.** Experiment with different time intervals. You don't want to take pictures or frames too often or less often than necessary to capture the changes you hope to image in your movies or still series. If a scheduled shot is not possible (say, the time required to write to the card exceeds the shooting interval), it will be skipped.

Using Interval Photography

This next section will tell you everything you need to know to capture images using the camera's built-in intervalometer. To set up interval timer shooting, just follow these steps:

1. **Access feature.** Choose Interval Timer from the Shooting 7 menu. The screen shown in Figure 6.11 appears.

2. **Activate interval timer.** Highlight Enable and press INFO. The Adjust Interval/Shots screen pops up.

3. **Choose interval.** Highlight Interval and chose the elapsed time between exposures, up to 99 hours, 59 minutes, and 59 seconds. The interval cannot be shorter than the shutter speed; for example, you cannot set one second as the interval if the images will be taken at two seconds or longer. If the camera is unable to take a scheduled image because it is busy doing something else (for example, saving the last exposure), the shot will be skipped.

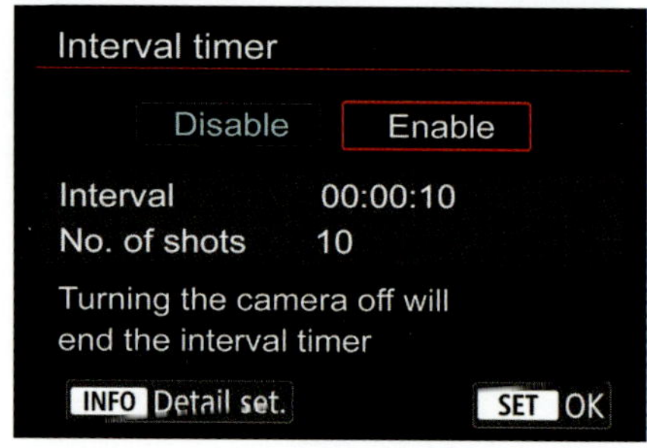

Figure 6.11 Interval timer shooting options.

4. **Select number of shots.** You can choose the number of individual shots that will be taken, from 1 to 99. Photography will stop when the specified number of exposures are captured. If you want the camera to continue shooting until you stop it (or the memory card fills, or your camera is stolen), enter 00.

5. **Confirm.** Highlight OK. The interval and number of shots will be displayed in the Shooting 6 menu. You can calculate the total time elapsed by multiplying the interval times the number of shots. For example, with the maximum elapsed time of almost 100 hours, it will take more than 400 days to shoot 99 individual exposures. In practice, your sequence should be a bit shorter than that.

6. **Start sequence.** Press the shutter release all the way to begin capturing your interval sequence.

Here are some additional tips for interval shooting:

- **Extra shots.** Even while interval shooting is underway you can take a picture by pressing the shutter release. You can even change shooting settings, access menus, and playback images, except for the last five seconds before the next scheduled interval shot is taken.

- **Shooting flexibility.** You can activate Auto Exposure or White Balance Bracketing, specify Multiple Exposures, or shoot HDR images during interval shooting. Instructions for these features are found in Chapter 11.

- **Saving power.** The camera automatically powers down after eight seconds but will wake up again about one minute before the next scheduled shot. You can keep the camera "awake" by setting Auto Power Off under the Power Saving entry in the Set-up 3 menu to Disable.

Star Trails

Star trails are another great application for both long exposures and interval shooting. You can shoot the night sky using long exposures with your camera mounted on a tripod. However, because of the rotation of the Earth, longer exposures will record the apparent motion of the celestial objects through the sky, producing a light trail. If you use a very, very long exposure, the light trail will record as continuous streaks, centered around the Polaris (the North Star) in the northern hemisphere and Sigma Octantis (which is, unfortunately, too dim to be easily seen with the naked eye) in the southern hemisphere. If you activate Extended Shutter Speeds, you can record night shots as long as 15 minutes.

Such long exposures can result in excessive noise and sensor overheating, so it's more common for photographers to take a series of individual exposures and combine them to produce a single star trail image. If you want your stars to appear as reasonably sharp points, you'll need to keep the exposure short enough that their movement in the sky isn't apparent. Fortunately, there's a simple formula you can use to calculate that exposure time, the "500 Rule." Divide 500 by the focal length of your lens to determine the longest exposure (in seconds) before stars start to produce a blurred trail. For example, with a 50mm lens, the longest exposure would be 10 seconds (500 divided by 50). Capturing the complete canopy of stars generally requires a wider viewing perspective. With the 16mm wide-angle setting, exposures could be as long as roughly 30 seconds.

For Figure 6.12, I set my camera to ISO 200, and used a basic exposure of 30 seconds at f/5.6. I selected an interval of 32 seconds and 170 total exposures, which totals about 90 minutes. Noise reduction was off. Then, I followed these steps, using Photoshop:

1. **Transfer files to a folder.** Select a folder on your computer and copy all your files to that location.
2. **In Photoshop:** Choose Files > Scripts > Load Files into Stack.
3. **Browse to folder.** Click the Browse button and navigate to the folder where your images are stored.
4. **Click OK.** Photoshop will create a file with one layer for each of your captured images.
5. **Select All layers.** Then click Layer Blending Options from the Layers palette and choose Lighten.
6. **Flatten image.** You'll want to flatten your image (the multi-layer file will be huge!). You'll end up with an impressive star trail image.

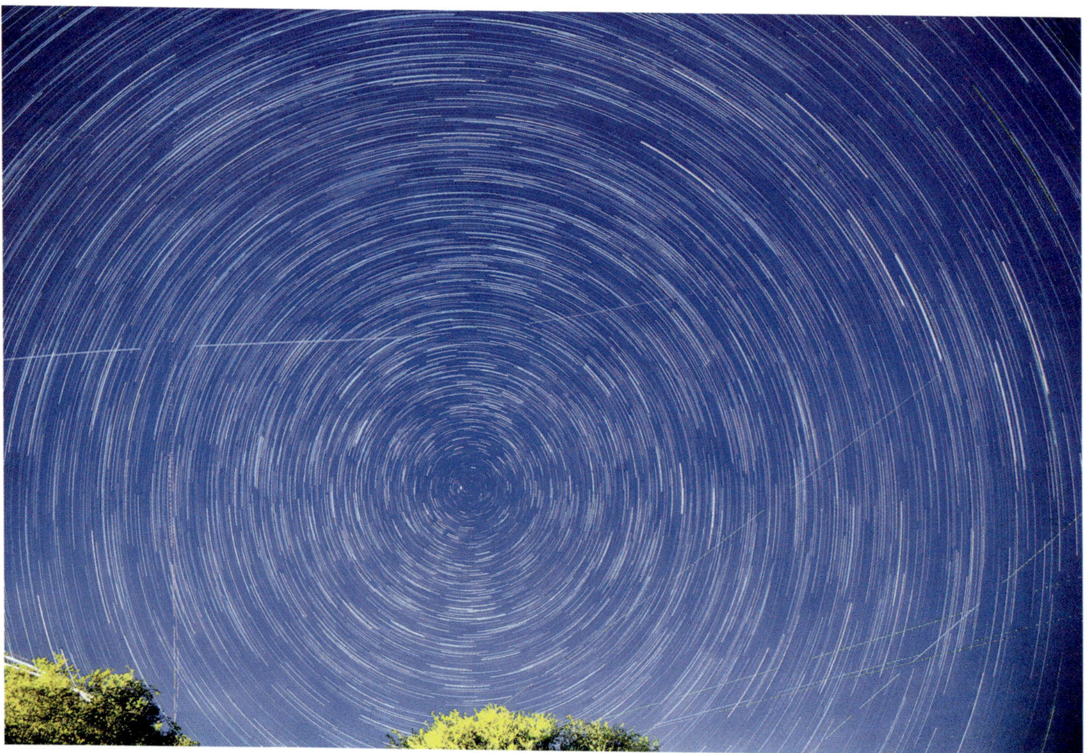

Figure 6.12 Capturing a star trail.

Time-lapse Movies

The time-lapse movie facility is actually a still photography mode that shoots images at intervals you specify, and then stitches them together automatically to create an MP4-format movie in Full HD (1920 × 1080) and 4K formats (3840 × 2160) at a playback rate of 30/25 fps (NTSC/PAL). To create a time-lapse movie, just follow these steps:

1. **Switch to Movie mode.** Even though time-lapse clips are a series of stills, you must be in Movie mode to access the feature. Even though individual images are still photographs, no stills are stored; they are converted to a movie file even if you take only one shot in time-lapse mode.

2. **Navigate to the Movie Shooting 6 menu.** Select Time-lapse Movie and press Q/SET.

3. **Choose Enable.** Highlight Time-lapse and press Q/SET. Choose Enable (see Figure 6.13, top left).

4. **Specify interval and number of shots.** The options shown in Figure 6.13, top right, and bottom left, appear in the main Time-lapse menu. You can choose the interval between shots, from 2 seconds up to 99 hours, 59 minutes, and 59 seconds, and the total number of shots (from 2 to 3600) to take in the sequence. The expected elapsed time for the entire sequence is shown near the bottom of the screen.

5. **Choose movie recording size.** The screen for the R8 is shown in Figure 6.13, lower right, with 4K and FHD options.

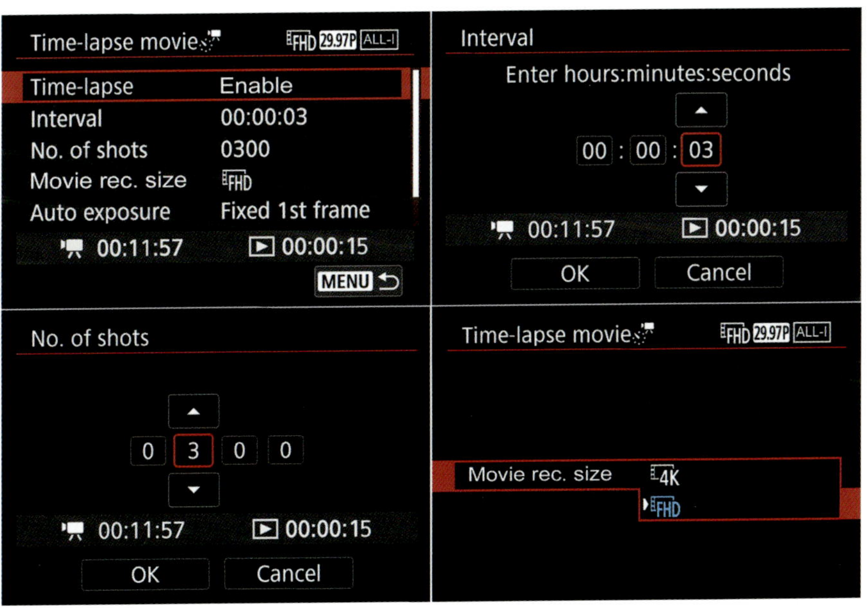

Figure 6.13 Enable/disable and check settings on this screen.

6. **Select exposure setting.** Highlight Auto exposure and press Q/SET. You can then choose:
   - **Fixed 1st frame.** Metering takes place and the exposure is set for the first frame and used for all subsequent frames. You'd use this setting when you want the exposure to remain constant, even if lighting changes.
   - **Each frame.** Metering is performed for each shot in the sequence. A time-lapse movie of a city skyline from dawn to dusk will reflect the correct exposure for each stage of the day.

7. **Screen Auto Off.** Choose this setting to specify whether you want each captured image to be displayed.
   - **Disable.** The sensor image will be displayed at all times during capture, except during the moment of exposure. The screen will eventually turn off roughly 30 minutes after shooting started.
   - **Enable.** The screen turns off 10 seconds after shooting begins. This gives you a chance to monitor the first shot, so you'll know the scene is framed and exposed as you intend.

8. **Specify beeper.** You'll need to scroll down to see this option. After setting Screen Auto Off, you can enable or disable the Beep As Image Taken feature to provide feedback that the sequence is still underway. Because the electronic shutter is used, there is no other indicator that an exposure has been made.

9. **Confirm.** When finished setting each parameter, highlight OK and press Q/SET to confirm.

10. **Exit menu and test settings.** Press MENU to exit the menu system. A message appears on the LCD monitor advising you to make your exposure settings and press the shutter release to take a test shot. Note that you can use a range of shutter speeds from 1/4000th to 30 seconds (in Tv and Manual mode on the R8). If you've selected a speed slower than 1/60th second, when capture ends, the camera will change to a shutter speed allowable for movie shooting.

11. **Exit setup.** When satisfied with your exposure settings, press OK to exit the setup screen.

12. **Take test shot.** Press the *shutter button* (not Movie button) to take a test shot, which will be created as a JPEG Large image.

13. **Start time-lapse.** When ready to begin, press the *Movie button* to commence your time-lapse movie. You can cancel by pressing the shutter button completely or Movie button.

14. **Turn on screen (optional).** You can check your settings by pressing the INFO button to turn the screen on or off.

15. **Stop capture.** While the time-lapse movie is recording, you can return to the Time-lapse menu setting and switch to Disable. When time-lapse shooting ends, the settings are cleared, and the camera resumes normal Movie shooting mode.

Shooting Panoramas

You can now shoot interesting panorama images with your EOS R8, just like you've been doing for years with your smartphone. The technique requires a little practice to execute smoothly and accurately, but I'm going to provide some useful tips, and even show you how to shoot panos with your camera held vertically.

The Panorama feature is one of the Special Scene modes and is accessed using the SCN position on the Mode dial. It gives you four options for the direction in which the camera will prompt you to pan: right, left, up, or down. The camera actually is processing the image pieces you have already captured *as you continue to shoot,* so you have to select one of these directions so the camera will know ahead of time how to perform this processing of the many JPEGs you'll shoot while panning. Within seconds of finishing the capture, all your shots will be aligned and stitched together into the final panorama photo. The default, right, is probably the most natural way to sweep the camera horizontally, at least for those of us who read from left to right. The up/down panning directions can be used to produce vertically oriented panoramas with the camera held horizontally, say, in the unlikely event you're photographing Burj Kalifa from ground level. However, a more reasonable scenario is to rotate the camera ninety degrees and pan horizontally to produce a conventional panorama with a different aspect ratio. I'll explain this quirky option shortly.

I spend many weeks shooting scenics, and have spent a lot of time taking panoramas with this camera. While the process is simple in concept, it can be frustrating in execution, chiefly because it's easy for your "sweeping" motion to be too fast or too slow, and you may be 80 percent through the process when the camera informs you that your movement was at the wrong pace. I'll show you a step-by-step procedure that will help you minimize the frustration.

You'll need to be prepared for the huge file sizes of the images produced. While the EOS R8 captures 24MP still images, its panoramas consist of parts of many individual shots stitched together to produce much larger files. Some image-editing programs and hardware combinations may have trouble handling them. Photoshop can work with them as Large Document Format (.PSB) files, but you may end up wanting to resize your panoramas to more manageable resolutions, especially for printing.

Watch out for subjects that move. If something is in motion as you sweep the camera, you may get multiple renditions of that subject. Potentially, this can be a creative effect if used, say, to follow a bicycle rider. Also beware of collateral "damage" from cropping. Don't include very important information at the very top and bottom of your frames (when shooting in left/right mode, for example). Because you probably won't hold the camera perfectly level as you pan, the camera will automatically try to align your images as they are stitched together, and the "excess" image above and/or below is cropped out to produce a seamless image. Subjects that vary greatly in brightness don't photograph well in panoramas, and dark subjects may mean the shutter speed is so long that your subject will blur as you pan.

The first step after you've selected a subject is to get set up to shoot your panorama. Just follow these steps:

1. **Select Panorama.** Rotate the Mode dial to the SCN position. If the mode guide is enabled in the Set-up 2 menu, the scene guide will appear with the Choose Scene option, and you can press Q/SET to select Panorama as your Special Scene, as shown in Figure 6.14, upper left.

   If mode guide is disabled, press the Q/SET button, and choose Panorama. Note that in either case, the next time you rotate the Mode dial to SCN, the last Special Scene you selected will already be chosen.

2. **View initial screen.** The initial panorama screen, shown in Figure 6.14, upper right, appears. It shows the masked area that will be captured during panning. Some of the image area will be clipped off at top and bottom. The stitching algorithm needs extra pixels above and below the panned area to account for slight up and down and tilt movements of the hand-held camera as you rotate the camera. Other indicators on the screen include:

   - **Motion warning.** The "waving hand" icon appears at the top to warn you that lens stabilization is not used during panning.

   - **Horizontal orientation.** The horizontal line can be used to line up with horizontal features in your subject, guiding you to rotate the camera smoothly without tilting.

Figure 6.14 Capturing a panorama.

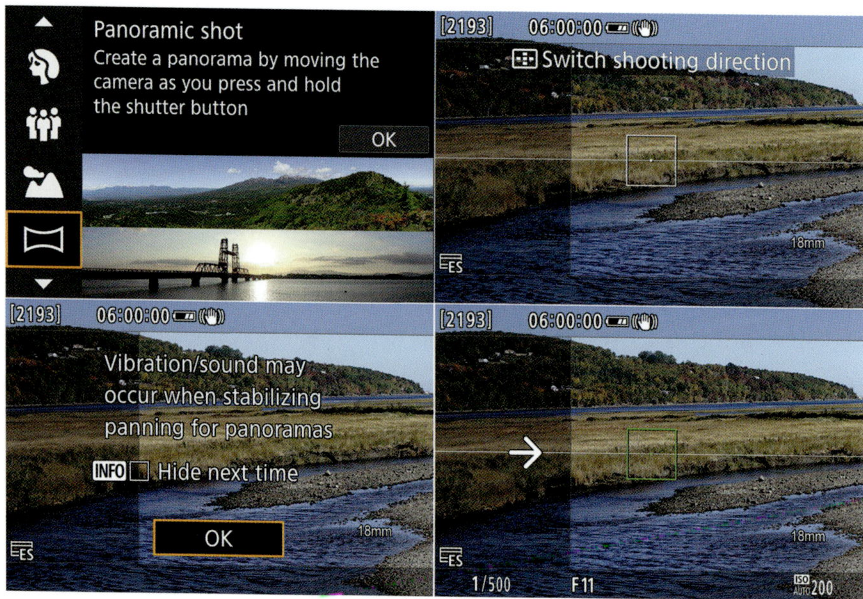

- **Current focus point.** The focus point shows where the camera will focus as the panning procedure begins. It is white, and it turns to red if the camera is unable to focus, then turns green to indicate focus is achieved and panning can begin.
- **ES icon.** Reminds you that the electronic shutter will be used to capture the individual images.
- **Current focal length.** Panoramas are most easily captured using wide-angle lenses or zoom settings. The current focal length is displayed at lower right.

3. **Choose shooting direction.** Press the AF point selection button repeatedly to cycle among the left/right/up/down shooting directions. A vibration warning screen, like the one at lower left in Figure 6.14, may appear.

4. **Take your position.** Plant your feet firmly such that the center of your picture is straight in front of you. Keep the camera as near to your body as practical, so that the rotation point as your body twists is as close as possible to the sensor plane. Technically, the pivot point should be located underneath the center point of the lens, but it's easier to use the back of the camera as a reference.

5. **Set focus and exposure.** Lock focus and exposure before you start shooting, as the camera doesn't adjust once capture begins.

6. **Twist and shout.** With your feet securely anchored, twist your body as far as you can toward the angle you'll use for the beginning of the exposure. That is, if you choose Right, twist as far as you can to the right.

7. **Shoot and Unwind.** While viewing through the electronic viewfinder, begin shooting, slowly "untwisting" to pan the camera until you're facing forward again. Use the guides and masked area to frame your image as you pan. (See Figure 6.14, lower right.)

8. **Speed kills.** Continue twisting smoothly toward the finish position. It's important to keep a constant speed.

9. **View your progress.** As you shoot, the camera will provide a highlighted view of the area currently being captured, as it takes a series of overlapping shots. An arrow is shown on the screen to indicate the direction you should be moving.

10. **Follow through.** If you rotate too slowly or too quickly, a message that the camera could not shoot the panorama will appear, advising you to move more slowly or more quickly. However, the partial panorama you shot will be saved.

11. **Cross the finish line.** You'll finish twisted all the way in the opposite direction from your initial position. When you have successfully captured a panorama, the screen will blank for a few seconds while the camera stitches your exposures together. It will then display your finished shot.

12. **View your results.** The preview shows a reduced-size version of the entire panorama; press the center button to see a scrolling display of the entire shot.

Left/Right vs. Up/Down Panning

As I mentioned earlier, you can hold the camera in the horizontal orientation and pan to the left, right, or up or down. The latter two aren't really practical, however (try it!). Instead, rotate the camera 90 degrees to vertical orientation and then choose Up or Down, which, in that position, involves left/right panning relative to the horizon. What you end up with is a "taller" pano, which may be suited for subjects that aren't worthy of the very broad vista horizontally oriented panning produces. Figure 6.15 shows a comparison. At top is a conventional panorama shot left to right with the camera held horizontally. At bottom, a different scene is shown; the camera was rotated 90 degrees and panned left to right in that orientation.

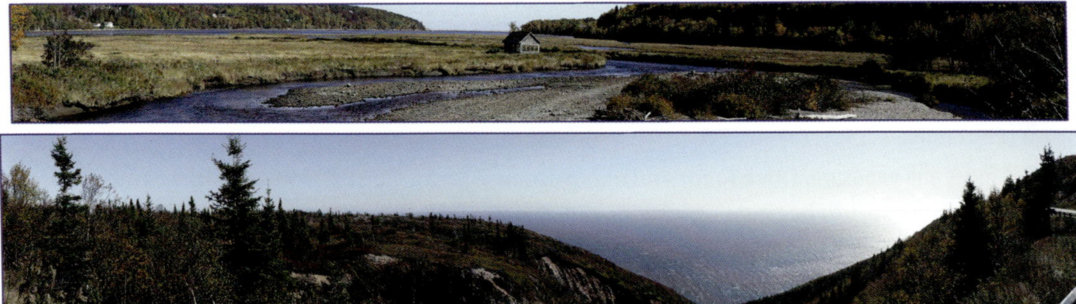

Figure 6.15 Pan with the camera held horizontally (top); camera rotated for a vertical panorama (bottom).

It's not an overstatement to say that Canon has built its reputation on its expertise in lenses. Since the company began producing its own optics for Canon cameras in mid-1947, it has pioneered many innovations, including the world's first 10X zoom lens, the first lenses to include optical image stabilization, and the first super-telephoto lens to include a built-in tele-extender.

Potential compatibility with older EF and EF-S lenses is part of what makes the RF mount so interesting and exciting. Canon has officially sold more than 150 million lenses in RF or EF mount, and millions more are available from third parties like Laowa, Tamron, Sigma, Tokina, and other companies. A large number of them are compatible with your new camera, thanks to the mount adapters I'll be discussing later in this chapter.

So, introducing the brand-new RF-mount for Canon's first full-frame mirrorless cameras offered little risk for Canon. The company wisely announced EF-to-RF-mount adapters at the same time as the first two R-series cameras and lenses were introduced. The availability of these adapters was essential to the success of the new series of cameras. After all, even if you did not own any Canon lenses when you purchased your camera, you probably will consider both types as you expand your optical horizons, because RF mount and legacy lenses work seamlessly with your camera. A vast number of affordable pre-owned EF/EF-S-mount lenses are available from sources like www.keh.com.

Your First Lenses

The R8 is frequently purchased with a lens, such as the compact Canon RF 24-50mm f/4.5-6.3 IS STM kit lens (available separately for $299), or the more versatile Canon RF 24-105mm f/4L IS USM lens (about $1,300 if purchased separately). The more affordable Canon RF 24-105mm f/4-7.1 IS is another option at about $399. Here's an overview of this trio:

- **Canon RF 24-50mm f/4.5-6.3 IS STM.** This lens covers the wide-angle-to-standard zoom range, exchanging telephoto reach for extraordinary compactness. It makes a great walk-around lens outdoors and for vlogging, as its f/4.5-6.3 maximum aperture can be limiting under low-light conditions. It does have built-in Optical Image Stabilization to further enhance your low-light shooting abilities by providing up to 4.5 stops of shake correction. It also supports Movie Digital IS. (See Figure 7.1.)

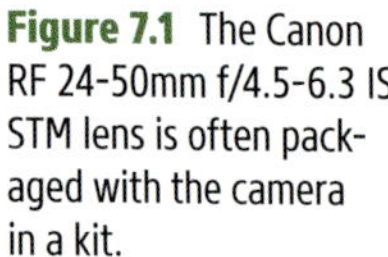

Figure 7.1 The Canon RF 24-50mm f/4.5-6.3 IS STM lens is often packaged with the camera in a kit.

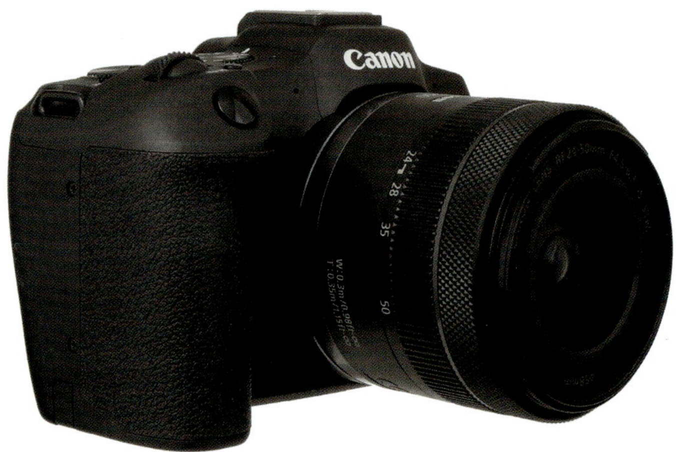

- **Canon RF 24-105mm f/4L IS USM.** One key difference is that this L lens has a constant f/4 maximum aperture that does not change as you zoom in and out. It offers quick, accurate, and almost silent autofocusing that's almost noise-free when shooting video. Canon's so-called "Nano USM" AF system includes both ring-type and STM-focusing motors. (I'll explain different AF motors later in this chapter.) The optical image stabilization system provides up to five stops of anti-shake compensation. A rounded 9-blade circular aperture produces incredible bokeh (creamy background blur), and Canon's Super Spectra coating does a superior job of reducing flare and ghost images. This lens compares favorably with Canon's legendary EF-mount version with roughly the same optical specifications but is significantly smaller and lighter.

- **Canon RF 24-105mm f/4-7.1 IS.** This budget lens has a variable maximum aperture, effectively an f/4 at the 24mm setting, but providing almost two stops less light at 105mm. Like most lenses, it performs best when closed down an f/stop or two, meaning you might be shooting indoor portraits at f/11 when zooming in. It also has a five-stop image stabilizer, so you may be able to compensate with slower shutter speeds. A single STM motor is reasonably fast and quiet, and the rounded 7-blade diaphragm does offer pleasing bokeh. If you're on a tight budget, this optic makes a versatile first lens.

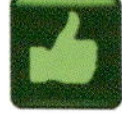

TIP Throughout this chapter, I'm going to use the current Canon manufacturer-suggested list price (MSRP) when it's available. (I'll use the Canon store price if it's not.) You should know that many lenses are available for less at the Canon store for your country or at retailers, and that prices can (and will) change throughout the life of this book.

As a step up from the 24-50mm kit lens, you can't go wrong with either 24-105mm optic. Many photographers, especially old-school film shooters, prefer working with prime (fixed focal length) lenses as much as they can, and may prefer a "normal" lens, which can be had in both pricey and affordable configurations, including the RF 50mm f/1.2L USM ($2,299 MSRP) or the Canon RF 50mm f/1.8 STM lens ($199).

So, depending on which category you fall into, you'll need to make a decision about what lens to buy, or decide what other kind of lenses you need to fill out your complement of Canon optics. This section will cover "first lens" concerns, while later in the chapter we'll look at "add-on lens" considerations. When deciding on your initial lens purchases, there are several factors you'll want to consider:

- **Cost.** You might have stretched your budget a bit to purchase your camera, so you might want to keep the cost of your add-on lenses fairly low. Even if you already own many EF/EF-S optics, I don't recommend buying only a body and trying to work only with legacy lenses and a mount adapter, even though that would be the lowest-cost way of building a fledgling system. The RF 35mm f/1.8 Macro IS STM lens will set you back only $499, and some retailers are packaging it in a kit. But if you need multiple focal lengths and want to cut costs, one of the 24-105mm lenses is the best way to go.

- **Built-in image stabilization.** Because the R8 lacks in-body image stabilization (IBIS), you'll want to award extra points to any lens that has IS included as part of its lens design.

- **Zoom range.** If you have only one lens, you'll want a fairly long zoom range to provide as much flexibility as possible. Again, I think the two 24-105mm lenses are your best bet, but the awesome RF 28-70mm f/2L has a useful, but much more limited zoom range, and is saddled with a $3,000 price tag. The RF 24-240mm f/4-6.3 IS USM ($899) has the longest zoom range among announced lenses.

- **Adequate maximum aperture.** You'll want an f/stop of at least f/3.5 to f/4 in any lens you buy to allow shooting under fairly low-light conditions. The thing to watch for is the maximum aperture when the lens is zoomed to its telephoto end. With lenses that have a variable rather than constant maximum aperture, you may end up with no better than an f/6.3 or f/7.1 as your largest f/stop. That's indeed the case with the budget 24-50mm kit lens, one of the 24-105mm lenses, and the RF 24-240mm f/4-6.3 optic. Small maximum apertures are not ideal, but you can often live with them.

- **Image quality.** Your starter lens should have good image quality because that's one of the primary factors that will be used to judge your photos.

- **Size matters.** A good walking-around lens is compact in size and light in weight. My favorite, the 24-105mm f/4 isn't tiny, but having it mounted on the camera most of the time isn't a burden, either. Considering its image quality and zoom range, I think it's worth every ounce.

- **Fast/close focusing.** Your first lens should have a speedy autofocus system (which is where the ultrasonic motor/USM or STM found in nearly all moderately priced lenses is an advantage). Close focusing (to 12 inches or closer) will let you use your basic lens for some types of macro photography.

Canon RF-Mount Lenses

If you don't own many EF/EF-S lenses or want to use RF-mount optics as much as possible, you should pay attention to Canon's RF "lens road map," and its periodic updates, which lists current and announced lenses that are available or in development. I'm going to provide a quick overview, based on what we know now.

Zoom Lenses

Zooms are the most popular choice for most; they cover a range of focal lengths and reduce the need to change to a different lens or move closer or farther from your subject. While zoom lenses often don't equal their fixed-focal length ("prime") counterparts in sharpness, the difference is often not obvious for many applications, or when the lenses are stopped down to their optimum apertures. Although some zoom lenses may seem expensive, keep in mind that a single $2,000 lens may replace four or five (or more) prime lenses that would cost much more and take up more space in your camera bag.

- **RF 14-35mm f/4L IS USM.** At $1,500, this lens seems costly until you compare it with its premium RF 15-35mm f/2.8L stablemate described next. If you don't need an f/2.8 maximum aperture, you'll find this zoom well-suited for a variety of landscape, architecture, and nature applications.

- **RF 15-35mm f/2.8L IS USM.** As the wide-angle anchor of Canon's trinity of f/2.8 RF lenses, this $2,400 lens is suitable for everything from landscape photography to architecture to street shooting. It has its own built-in image stabilization system for better control of camera shake, making it the perfect tool for low-light conditions under which longer shutter speeds may be necessary. The lens includes Canon's Nano USM system that combines USM and STM motors (mentioned earlier) for fast and quiet focusing. Like all Canon "premium" L lenses, it has a weather-resistant design that keeps dust and moisture out in challenging environments. When combined with the 24-70mm f/2.8L and 70-200mm f/2.8L lenses, you have an awesome trio of (not-cheap) optics that can cover most photo opportunities.

- **RF 15-30mm f/4.5-6.3 IS STM.** Coming down from the price stratosphere, this $550 optic may be the best choice for R8 owners who need a versatile wide-angle lens and can give up a fast maximum aperture. A big plus: 1:2 magnification and a 5.1-inch minimum focus distance. I expect many R8 owners on a budget to flock to this lens.

- **RF 24-70mm f/2.8L IS USM.** Next up is another premium lens with a $2,400 price tag. It overlaps the 15-35mm zoom slightly in the 24-35mm range but extends all the way to short telephoto at 70mm. If you don't need an ultra-wide viewpoint, this lens can do a lot of what its wider cousin can handle, plus provide a flattering perspective for full-length or head-and-shoulders single or group portraits. It includes the hybrid Nano USM AF system, weather resistance, and image-stabilization features found in the other members of the Canon "trinity."

- **RF 28-70mm f/2L USM.** If you need even more speed, this $3,100 lens has a useful focal length from modest wide-angle to short telephoto and a fast f/2 constant aperture, which means you can use it for everything from architecture and street photography to indoor sports and portraiture. It focuses down to about 1.28 feet and has nine rounded diaphragm blades for excellent bokeh (defocused highlights). Like other RF lenses, this optic's customizable control ring lets you adjust exposure settings, including shutter speed, aperture, ISO, and exposure compensation without removing your hands from the lens. It's hefty at more than three pounds, and that wide aperture calls for expensive 95mm filters. There's no image stabilization, which can be a drawback in low-light situations where you'll be using longer shutter speeds.

- **RF 24-50mm f/4.5-6.3 IS STM.** Described above as your basic kit lens.

- **RF 24-105mm f/4L.** I described this lens earlier. There's not much more to add. It features full-time manual focus adjustments in One-Shot mode. It focuses down to roughly 18 inches for close-up work, uses "standard" 77mm filters, and has the configurable control ring.

- **RF 24-105mm f/4-7.1 IS.** This lens was also detailed above. It's simpler in construction (16 elements in 14 groups), which helps account for its modest cost, but can function well as a walk-around lens.

- **RF 24-240mm f/4-6.3 IS USM.** I'm always wary of extreme zooms, which tend to embrace a broad range of focal lengths, while being a master of none. But given the optical design flexibility the new RF mount offers, this lens could be a winner, especially at its $899 price. It's heavy at 1.65 pounds and obviously is quite slow (f/6.3) at the 240mm zoom setting. The built-in IS is valuable even though the R8 has in-body stabilization, because lenses typically do a better job at handling pitch movement (lens tilting up or down) and yaw (rotations from side to side). I'll explain image stabilization in more detail later in this chapter.

- **RF 70-200mm f/2.8L IS USM.** This is the third member of the RF trinity, a fast, versatile short-to-medium telephoto lens with a fast f/2.8 constant aperture and that innovative dual-motor Nana USM autofocus mechanism. Like other lenses in the trinity you can make manual focus corrections at all times. There are three IS modes: standard single-shot mode, panning-optimized (which compensates for up-and-down motion as you pan from side to side), and a mode that activates stabilization only during the exposure itself (avoiding the disconcerting effect of the lens making corrections while you're framing a shot). A rotating tripod collar helps sports photographers (in particular) who may be using a monopod or tripod. This advanced lens comes at a price, and that price is about $2,700.

- **RF 70-200mm f/4L IS USM.** Since the lenses in Canon's top-line trinity will set you back $7,300, you may be tempted to cut some corners. In that case, if you can live with an f/4 maximum aperture, this $1,600 lens can save you $1,100. Fortunately, you're not giving up a lot more than the f/stop, as this optic is still an L lens, has the dual Nano USM autofocus system, and 5-stop image stabilization that can coordinate with the in-body image stabilizer to up the anti-shake ante to what Canon claims is 7.5 stops.

- **RF 100-400mm f/5.6-8.** This is one of the least expensive lenses you can buy for an RF-mount camera that qualifies as a medium-to-long telephoto lens. Priced at $650, it's excellent for outdoor work and quite sharp stopped down to f/11 or f/16. It's actually more versatile than Canon's 600mm f/11 and 800mm f/11 budget lenses described later.

- **RF 100-500mm f/4.5-7.1L IS.** While other vendors of mirrorless cameras lagged a bit in providing super-telephoto lenses for their offerings, Canon has stepped up to the plate quickly with this impressive $2,900 lens. It's compatible with Canon's Extender RF 1.4x and RF 2x teleconverters, too, giving you 140-700mm and 200-1000mm equivalent zooms with a loss of one and two f/stops, respectively. The zoom ring has "torque" adjustments to fine-tune the handling of the lens for those who want to zoom fast, slow, somewhere in between, or to lock the focus ring completely. A window in the lens hood gives you access to your polarizer or split/graduated neutral-density filter so they can be adjusted with the hood attached. This lens is a hefty three pounds and measures eight inches in length.

Prime Lenses

Prime lenses are designed to be especially sharp at their fixed focal length, and many are even superb wide open. Such lenses are typically faster, too. While zoom lenses may have an f/2.8 (or smaller) maximum aperture, prime lenses are often more than one or two stops faster at f/1.8 or f/1.4. Indeed, Canon is famed for its excellent f/1.2 optics. Prime lenses also offer some optical design tradeoffs: those willing to accept relatively slow f/11 *fixed* apertures can buy Canon's remarkably compact and affordable RF 600mm f/11 ($799) and RF 800mm F/11 ($999) lenses. Here are some of your options:

- **RF 5.2mm f/2.8L Dual Fisheye 3D VR.** If you have to ask why you would want this $2,000 lens, then you probably don't need it. It is the world's first digital interchangeable lens that can capture stereoscopic 3D 180-degree VR imagery to a single image sensor. It's intended for creating high-resolution virtual reality video (the kind you need a headset to view) for immersive entertainment, tourism, training, education, and storytelling. I'm listing it for completeness, but it's really best suited for full-frame models.

- **RF 16mm f/2.8 STM.** This is an affordable $300 super-compact wide angle for interiors, architecture, and street photography for prime lens aficionados. If focuses down to 5.1 inches for macro work, and vloggers love its wide-angle perspective.

- **RF 24mm f/1.8 Macro IS STM.** This is probably a better lens for those interior, architecture, and street photography applications, but it costs twice as much at $600. It also has a maximum aperture that's twice as fast, making it more useful for low-light applications. It focuses down to 5.5 inches and provides a half life-size magnification for close-up work.

- **RF 28mm f/2.8 STM.** This is a $300 "pancake" style lens that those looking for a super-compact lens will like for stealth shooting or when size and weight are important considerations. It retracts when not in use making it even smaller. It focuses down to 9.1 inches.

- **RF 35mm f/1.8 Macro IS STM.** This inexpensive lens ($500) is not an L lens, but it has a lot to offer, including a fast maximum aperture, which, combined with image stabilization, makes it a great lens for low-light street photography. You'll find the control ring especially useful for changing exposure settings on-the-fly in stealth shooting situations. As a macro lens, it has close focusing down to about 6.7 inches for half life-size reproduction. The quiet STM motor is smooth and accurate, making it especially suitable for video. It's a lightweight lens, too, at about 11 ounces and measuring about 3 × 2.5 inches when mounted. (See Figure 7.2.)

- **RF 50mm f/1.2L USM.** At $2,300, this lens is pricey for a fixed focal length ("prime") lens, but it has exquisite image quality, even wide open at f/1.2. It has the customizable control ring and weather-resistant sealing found in typical Canon L-series lenses. While this normal lens has no image stabilization of its own, your camera's in-body stabilization works fine and the fast f/1.2 maximum aperture allows you to use faster shutter speeds in many situations. It weighs about 2 pounds and uses the standard 77 filter size.

- **RF 50mm f/1.8.** You've probably heard the term "nifty fifty" to describe 50mm lenses, generally applied to direct appreciation to a versatile, often under-used focal length prime. Priced at around $200, this lens has a lot going for it in addition to a low price. It's f/1.8 maximum aperture is fast enough for available-light work, and it's a compact 2.7 × 1.6 inches and 5.6 ounces. This lens makes a good macro lens, focusing down to less than a foot, and will give great close-up results when mounted on extension tubes offered by third-party vendors. While you're building your collection of zoom lenses, you should consider having this lens in your bag as a backup.

- **RF 85mm f/2 Macro IS.** At $600, this lens has excellent image quality and built-in optical image stabilization, which combines with the camera's in-body IS to provide optimal anti-shake correction that is especially useful for close-up photography. It has the customizable control ring and a minimum focus distance of 1.15 feet.

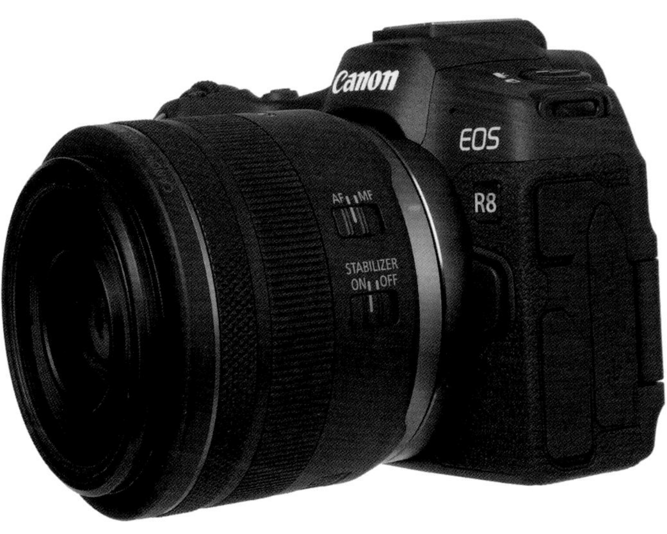

Figure 7.2 Canon RF 35mm f/1.8 Macro IS STM lens.

- **RF 85mm f/1.2L USM.** Every Canon photographer I come in contact with who does fashion or portrait photography owns the EF-mount 85mm f/1.2 lens. This RF version is a virtual cream machine in terms of background bokeh, is sharp enough wide open to allow stunning selective focus effects, and can focus close enough for tight face-only portraiture. The price is $2,800.

- **RF 85mm f/1.2L USM DS.** The $3,100 price is likely to be no barrier for those seeking the ultimate portrait lens. It includes Canon's defocus smoothing technology, a coating technology which provides even better bokeh, and, possibly, the ability to adjust the effect as you shoot. While the soft look in the out-of-focus regions in an image is gorgeous, this lens retains sharpness in the in-focus areas of the frame, giving you unmatched subject separation with the background. Sharpness is still retained on the in-focus portions for noticeable subject separation from the background.

   The three-dimensional quality and improved bokeh is strongest at f/1.2. With apertures of f/3.2 or smaller, however, this lens's performance is similar to that of the non-DS version. So, to get your money's worth for the extra $700, you should be planning on working at wide apertures with this lens. The only drawback is that the special coating reduces transmission of light by about 1.3 stops.

- **RF 100mm f/2.8L IS USM Macro.** Announced early in 2021, the longer focal length of this $1,200 lens, compared with that of the 85mm f/2 Macro IS, lets you put a little extra distance between you and your close-up subject. That's useful for skittish creatures, such as insects, and to provide a more natural perspective. This short telephoto also can serve as a portrait lens.

   The most important feature of this lens is the spherical aberration control ring. It's used to provide manual control of the lens's bokeh, which is the appearance of out-of-focus highlights. Oddly enough, a lens that had perfect correction for spherical aberration would have terrible bokeh, with the out-of-focus discs having an unpleasant gradation outward along its radius. "Good" bokeh is considered to be defocused discs that blend smoothly into the background.

   With the SA control ring in its central, neutral position, the lens will provide a normal, sharp image. Rotating left or right adjusts lens groups independently, which affects the shape of both the foreground and background bokeh while adding a soft-focus effect. By visually evaluating the look as you rotate the ring, you can choose between a soft dreamy look and enhanced, contrasty bokeh discs with sharp edges. You'll want to use this ring with the lens aperture set to its widest.

- **RF 400mm f/2.8L IS USM.** This $12,000 lens fit an enormous hole in Canon's super-telephoto lineup, which lacked a fast pro-level sports and wildlife lens. Expect it to leave a massive hole in your wallet, as well.

- **RF 600mm f/11 IS STM.** What do you have to give up to acquire a super-telephoto lens for $799? Only a variable aperture and a great deal of weight. Yes, this compact long lens has a fixed f/11 aperture, so all your exposure adjustments must be made using shutter speed and ISO settings. It includes a control ring so you can make these adjustments by rotating a control on the lens itself. If you need even more telephoto, Canon's optional RF 1.4x and RF 2x teleconverters give you a boost to 840mm f/16 and 1200mm f/22, respectively.

Optical image stabilization in the lens is almost mandatory for a lens of this length, and is included, along with a fast STM stepping motor for speedy autofocus. It weighs about two pounds and is less than 11 inches long when extended and 7.9 inches when collapsed.

- **RF 600mm f/4L IS USM.** How much are three extra stops of speed—and a variable aperture—worth? Would you believe $13,000? This lens is a mainstay among well-heeled landscape and sports photographers, prized for its extra speed and impressive image quality. Add a 1.4X tele-converter and you have an 840mm f/5.6 super-telephoto that easily outperforms Canon's "budget" option, described next.

- **RF 800mm f/11.** Priced $200 higher than the 600mm f/11 at $999, this lens big brother has the same fixed f/11 aperture, image stabilization, and STM autofocus motor. With teleconverters, you can achieve focal lengths of 1120mm and 1600mm, almost certainly with the camera mounted on a tripod. Hand-held use is practical at fast shutter speeds. I recommend using at least 1/2000th second, which means you'll need a sensitivity setting of ISO 1000 in bright daylight.

- **RF 800mm f/5.6L IS.** If you sell your car right now, you might be able to afford the down payment on this $17,000, seven-pound beast. Its introduction does demonstrate that Canon is serious about the R-series camera lineup. Like its 600mm sibling, the lens is collapsible and surprisingly compact for an 800mm lens. It weighs in at 2.77 pounds and is less than 11 inches in length when collapsed and a tad less than 14 inches when extended to its full length. The lens hood for both the 600mm and 800mm lenses is optional.

- **RF 1200mm f/8L IS.** I'll bet you thought the RF 800mm f/5.6 lens described above was outrageously priced, right? Well, for only $3,000 *more* ($20,000 total) you can get on the waiting list for this monster. Its big selling points are that it's lightweight, at only 7 pounds, and compact, at 6.6 × 21.1 inches. If 1200mm is a bit disappointing, you can mount it on Canon's Extender RF 1.4x ($500) to obtain a 1680mm f/11 ultra-telephoto lens.

Using Adapted Lenses

As I noted at the beginning of the chapter, Canon wisely elected to provide the ability to use legacy EF and EF-S lenses with full compatibility with image stabilization, autofocus, and autoexposure. The keys to using your existing lenses (or new EF-mount optics you decide to purchase because no RF equivalent is available) are three mount adapters, which I'll describe shortly.

The adapters are your entry to relatively inexpensive, high-quality EF lenses, which have been in production since 1987 and are easily found in excellent condition on the used market. (I own a large number of EF lenses that I bought from keh.com in Smyrna, Georgia.) Perhaps you need a fast 50mm lens and aren't ready to pay the $2,000 tariff on the RF model. The 50mm f/1.8 II EF lens is available in Excellent-Plus condition at keh.com for less than $100. Lenses that don't date back to the EOS dark ages, like the current model 75-300mm f/4-5.6 III lens pictured (at the 75mm zoom position at left and extended to 300mm at right) in Figure 7.3 are available brand new for less than $200. Usable lenses don't have to empty your wallet.

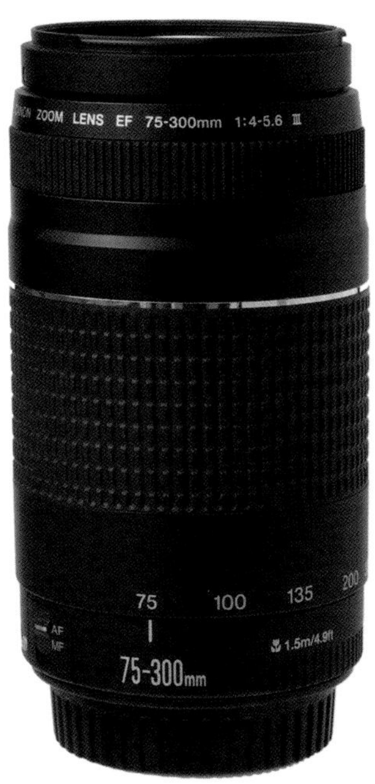

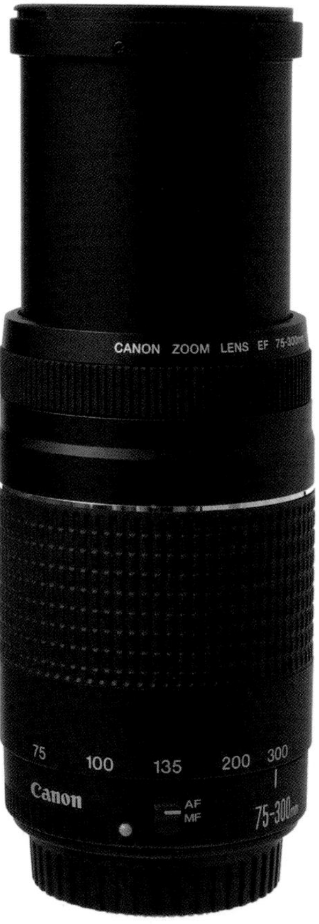

Figure 7.3 Canon offers affordable telephoto zooms like this 75-300mm lens, shown in retracted (left) and extended (right) positions.

Of course, Canon's own RF-mount lenses are likely to be more compact and optimized for mirrorless use, when compared to adapted lenses. Figure 7.4 shows the R8 with the Canon EF version of its 24-105mm f/4 optic (top) and the RF version at bottom.

Even if you currently own no Canon optics at present, you can't ignore the value of using adapted lenses. It's certain that lenses that some photographers absolutely must have will be slow in coming to the RF system or may be prohibitively expensive. So, you may want to purchase an EF lens to get the features you need, or because the EF equivalent can be had for much, much less in the used equipment market. For example, Canon's array of perspective control (TS-E) tilt-shift lenses may be moderately easy to release in RF-mount configurations, because those lenses are manual focus and would not require re-engineering to incorporate AF features. However, demand for such specialized optics is likely to be low enough that any RF perspective control optics may be very slow in coming. While TS-E lenses are not cheap, they are available from time to time in excellent condition, used.

Another example might be Canon's EF 8-15mm f/4L Fisheye USM zoom lens. This autofocus lens would be more difficult to convert to RF-mount, would probably enjoy only modest popularity, and is readily available as an EF lens for $1,250 or less (used). If you need one of these, why wait for an RF version—just grab the EF fisheye zoom, mount it with an adapter, and start shooting. The mount adapters also let you, for the first time, safely attach an EF-S lens to a full-frame model. The rationale is partially flawed—the R8 produces a lower-resolution 10MP image in crop mode. Because the registration distance is a scant 20mm, there is plenty of room to insert other third-party adapters aft of other vendors' zoom and prime lenses, too.

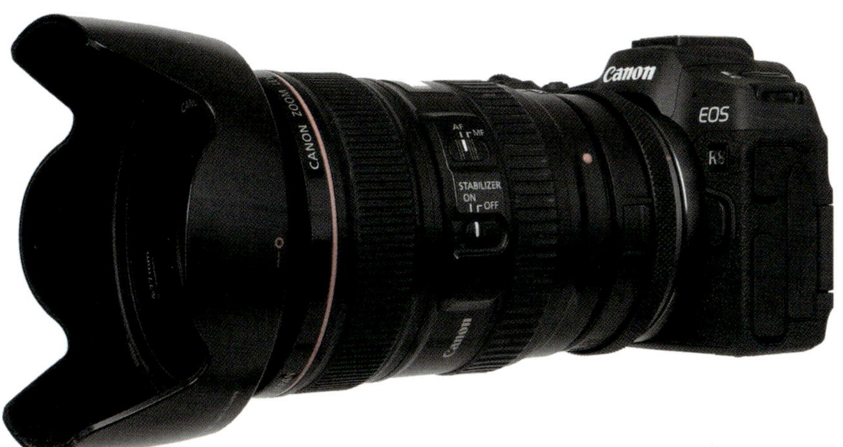

Figure 7.4 Canon EF (top) and RF (bottom) versions of its popular 24-105mm f/4 lenses.

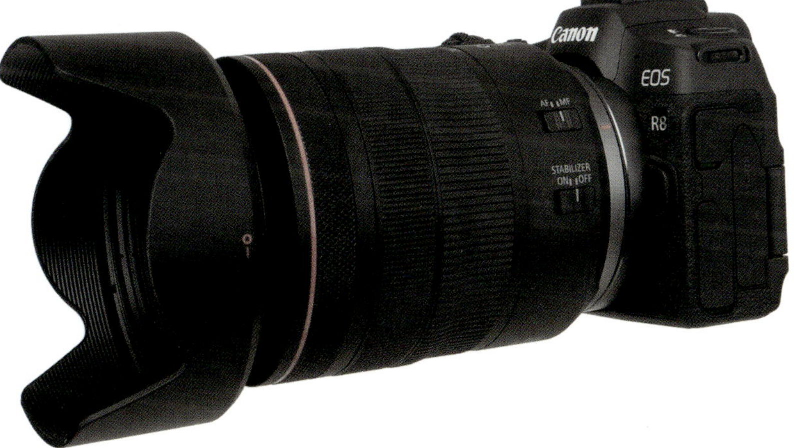

Canon RF-Mount Adapters

Canon has introduced four mount adapters, each with different attributes. Your choices are as follows:

- **Mount Adapter EF-EOS R.** This bare-bones adapter costs just $99, and it has several useful characteristics. It's lightweight (four ounces) but made of metal and its exterior design matches that of EF lenses. (Third-party adapters may include plastic or poorly machined parts and look ugly.) It's dust- and water-resistant, and like the other mount adapters, has all the electrical contacts you need for smooth operation of your EF and EF-S lenses.

- **Control Ring Mount Adapter EF-EOS R.** Priced at a modest $199, this version is the one you should definitely opt for, as it includes a control ring like that found on RF-mount lenses. Once you use the control ring, you won't want to do without it. It's only a fraction heavier than the basic adapter at 4.6 ounces. (See Figure 7.5.)

- **Drop-in Filter Mount Adapter EF-EOS R.** You can purchase this adapter with either a circular polarizing filter ($299) or a variable neutral-density (ND) filter ($399). A thumb wheel on the filter holder allows rotating the filter to achieve the desired amount of polarization or neutral density. The ND filter can reduce light reaching the sensor by 1.5 to 9 f/stops (ND3 to ND500), although, like all the variable neutral-density filters I've used, color tinges and density irregularities can be a problem. Canon says these effects are noticeable at ND250 settings or higher. The advantage of using drop-in filters is clear (so to speak): while a large number of EF lenses take standard 77mm filters, some require 82mm or 95mm filters (or larger) or may not accept filters at all. With this adapter every legacy-mount lens you use can work with the same polarizer or ND filter.

Figure 7.5 Canon RF mount adapter.

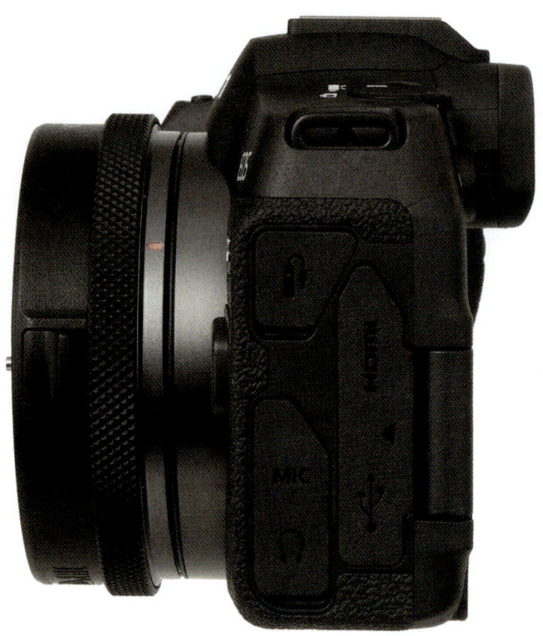

- **Mount Adapter EF-EOS R 0.71x.** This newer adapter is intended for Canon video cameras, like the EOS C70 Cinema Camera. Like the other three adapters, this $599 version allows mounting EF lenses, but includes optical elements that reduce the effective focal length by 0.71x and increase the effective maximum aperture by one stop. That is, an EF 50mm f/1.2 lens "becomes" a 35mm f/0.95 lens in terms of field of view and exposure settings. For R8 owners, that's not generally a feature that is much-needed, because both EF and RF wide-angle lenses are readily available.

  However, Canon's cinema models with the RF mount use the Super 35 format, which is virtually identical to your camera's APS-C mode. To achieve a super-wide view, such cameras would need a 10mm lens to produce the same perspective as a full-frame camera's 16mm lens. With this adapter, roughly the same field of view is provided by 24mm focal length. Canon recommends video shooters use the adapter with lenses like the EF 16-35mm f/2.8L III USM (resulting in an 11-25mm f/2 zoom) or EF 24-70mm f/2.8L II USM (producing a 17-85mm f/2 lens).

Image Stabilization and You

Image stabilization/vibration reduction can take many forms, and Canon has expertise in all of them. No amount of image stabilization can eliminate blur from moving subjects, but you should find yourself less tied to a tripod when using longer lenses, or when working with wide-angle lenses under dim lighting conditions than in the past. If you're taking photos in venues where flash or tripods are forbidden, you'll find the image-stabilization feature invaluable. The available forms include:

- **Electronic (Movie) IS.** This is available with the EOS R8 and also is used in video cameras. It involves shifting pixels around from frame to frame so that pixels that are not moving remain in the same position, and portions of the image that *are* moving don't stray from their proper path.

- **Optical image stabilization (OIS).** This feature is built into many EF and RF lenses and involves lens elements that shift in response to camera movement, as detected by motion sensors included in the optics. Including lenses with OIS in your kit is a plus because of the extra protection from blur caused by camera shake. The results can be spectacular. You can expect a minimum 4.5-stop improvement from image stabilization technology. That is, a photograph taken at 1/30th second should have the same sharpness (at least in terms of resistance to camera shake) as one shot at 1/750th second.

- **In-body image stabilization (IBIS).** This technology, available in Canon's higher-end mirrorless models, adjusts the position of the sensor carriage itself along five different axes to counteract movement. IBIS will integrate with OIS to provide several more stops of stabilization with a compatible camera and lenses.

When working with image stabilization, here are some things you should keep in mind:

- **Image stabilization doesn't stop action.** Unfortunately, no stabilization is a panacea to replace the action-stopping capabilities of a faster shutter speed. If you need to use 1/1000th second to freeze a high jumper in mid-air, neither type of image stabilization achieves the desired effect at a longer shutter speed.

- **Image stabilization works best with wider focal lengths.** However, IS is most *needed* at longer focal lengths. The adjustments required to compensate for camera movement are smaller with wide-angle lenses. With a lens having, say, a 24-105mm zoom range, you'll probably discover that your anti-shake results are better at 24mm than at 105mm.

  Longer focal lengths require much more correction and, to make things worse, tend to magnify any camera/lens movement. That magnification tends to make IS more useful with telephoto lenses. Longer primes and zooms are thus perfect candidates for lens-based IS, and, because of their physical length, are able to detect pitch and yaw motion well.

- **Stabilization might slow you down.** The process of adjusting the lens to counter camera shake takes time, just as autofocus does, so you might find that image stabilization adds to the lag between when you press the shutter and when the picture is actually taken. In a situation where you want to capture a fleeting instant that can happen suddenly, image stabilization might not be your best choice. However, Canon's implementation is so speedy this will not be a concern most of the time.

- **Give image stabilization a helping hand.** When you simply do not want to carry a tripod all day and you'll be relying on the IS system, brace the camera or your elbows on something solid, like the roof of a car or a piece of furniture. Remember that an inexpensive monopod can be quite compact when not extended; many camera bags include straps that allow you to attach this accessory. Use a monopod for extra camera-shake compensation. Brace the accessory against a rock, a bridge abutment, or a fence and you might be able to get blur-free photos at surprisingly long shutter speeds. When you're heading out into the field to photograph wild animals or flowers and want to use longer exposures and think a tripod isn't practical, at least consider packing a monopod.

What Lenses Can Do for You

A sane approach to expanding your lens collection is to consider what each of your options can do for you and then choose the type of lens that will really boost your creative opportunities. Here's a guide to the sort of capabilities you can gain by adding a lens (using an adapter, if necessary) to your repertoire.

- **Wider perspective.** A 24-70mm or 28-70mm lens can serve you well for moderate wide-angle-to-medium telephoto shots. Now you find your back is up against a wall and you *can't* take a step backward to take in more subject matter. Or, you might find yourself just behind the baseline at a high school basketball game and want an interesting shot with a little perspective distortion tossed in the mix. If you often want to make images with a super wide field of view, a wider lens is in your future.

- **Bring objects closer.** A long focal length brings distant subjects closer to you, allows you to produce images with very shallow depth-of-field, and avoids the perspective distortion that wide-angle lenses provide.

- **Bring your camera closer.** Many Canon lenses, such as the RF 35mm f/1.8 Macro use the Macro designation because they focus closer than most. If you need to get more magnification, use a dedicated macro lens or extension tubes.

- **Look sharp.** Many lenses, particularly Canon's L lineup, are prized for their sharpness and overall image quality. Your run-of-the-mill lens is likely to be plenty sharp for most applications at the optimum aperture (usually f/8 or f/11), but the very best optics are definitely superior.

- **More speed.** Your basic lens might have the perfect focal length and sharpness for sports photography, but the maximum aperture may be small at telephoto focal lengths, such as f/5.6 or f/6.3 at the far end. That makes the RF-mount lenses with a very wide aperture (small f/number) a prime choice (so to speak) for low-light photography when you can get close to the action; that's often possible at an amateur basketball or volleyball game. You don't need to spend huge sums; the $200 RF 50mm f/1.8 has enough speed for most dim environments.

Using Wide-Angle Lenses

To use wide-angle prime lenses and wide zooms, you need to understand how they affect your photography. Here's a quick summary of the things you need to know:

- **More depth-of-field (apparently).** With a wide-angle lens, you usually include a full scene in an image; any single subject is not magnified very much, so the depth-of-field will be quite extensive. You'll find a wide-angle lens helpful when you want to maximize the range of acceptable sharpness in a landscape, for example.

- **Stepping back.** Wide-angle lenses have the effect of making it seem that you are standing farther from your subject than you really are. They're helpful when you don't want to back up—or can't because of impediments—to include an entire group of people in your photo, for example.

- **Wider field of view.** While making your subject seem farther away, as implied above, a wide-angle lens also provides a more expansive field of view, including more of the scene in your photos.

- **More foreground.** As background objects appear further back than they do to the naked eye, more of the foreground is brought into view by a wide-angle lens. That gives you extra emphasis on the area that's closest to the camera. So, wide-angle lenses are great when you want to emphasize that lake in the foreground, but problematic when your intended subject is located farther in the distance.

- **Super-sized subjects.** The tendency of a wide-angle lens to emphasize objects in the foreground while de-emphasizing objects in the background can lead to a kind of size distortion that may be more objectionable for some types of subjects than others. Shoot a bed of flowers up close with a 16mm or shorter focal length, and you might like the distorted effect of the nearby blossoms looming in the photo. Take a shot of a family member with the same lens from the same distance, and you're likely to get some complaints about that gigantic nose in the foreground.

- **Perspective distortion.** This type of distortion occurs when you tilt the camera so the plane of the sensor is no longer perpendicular to the vertical plane of your subject. As a result, some parts of the subject are now closer to the sensor than they were before, while other parts are farther away. This is what makes buildings, flagpoles, or NBA players appear to be leaning over backward.

- **Steady cam.** You'll find that it is easier to get photos without blur from camera shake when you hand-hold a wide-angle lens at slower shutter speeds than it is with a telephoto lens. And, thanks to image stabilization, you can take sharp photos at surprisingly long shutter speeds at a long focal length without using a tripod.

Avoiding Potential Wide-Angle Problems

Wide-angle lenses have a few quirks that you'll want to keep in mind when shooting so you can avoid falling into some common traps. Here's a checklist of tips for avoiding common problems:

- **Symptom: converging lines.** Unless you want to use wildly diverging lines as a creative effect, it's a good idea to keep horizontal and vertical lines in landscapes, architecture, and other subjects carefully aligned with the sides, top, and bottom of the frame. To prevent undesired perspective distortion, you must take care not to tilt the camera. If your subject is very tall, like a building, you may need to shoot from an elevated position (like a high level in a parking garage) so you won't need to tilt the lens upward. And if your subject is short, like a small child, get down to a lower level so you can get the shot without tilting the lens downward.

- **Symptom: lines that bow outward.** Some wide-angle lenses cause straight lines to bow outward, an effect called barrel distortion; you'll see the strongest effect at the edges. Most fisheye (or *curvilinear*) lenses produce this effect as a feature of the lens; it's much more obvious than with any other type of lens. You can minimize barrel distortion simply by framing your photo with some extra space all around, so the edges where the bowing outward is most obvious can be cropped out of the picture. The Lens Correction feature can help reduce this problem, too.

- **Symptom: light and dark areas when using a polarizing filter.** You should be aware that polarizers work best when the camera is pointed 90 degrees away from the sun and have the least effect when the camera is oriented 180 degrees from the sun. The polarizing effect may be much milder at the edges so the sky in those areas will be much lighter in tone (less polarized). The solution is to avoid using a polarizing filter in situations where you'll be including the sky with lenses that have an actual focal length of less than about 28mm.

Using Telephoto and Tele-Zoom Lenses

Telephoto lenses also can have a dramatic effect on your photography. Here are the most important things you need to know. In the next section, I'll concentrate on telephoto considerations that can be problematic—and how to avoid those problems.

- **Selective focus.** Long lenses have reduced depth-of-field, a shallow range of acceptably sharp focus, especially at wide apertures (small f/numbers); this is useful for selective focus to isolate your subject. You can set the widest aperture to create shallow depth-of-field or close it down (to a small f/number) to allow more of the scene to appear to be in acceptably sharp focus.

- **Getting closer.** Telephoto lenses allow you to fill the frame with wildlife, sports action, and candid subjects. A long lens can help you capture memorable moments while retaining enough distance to stay out of the way of events as they transpire.

- **Reduced foreground/increased compression.** Telephoto lenses have the opposite effect of wide angles: they reduce the importance of things in the foreground by squeezing everything together. This so-called *compressed perspective* makes objects in the scene appear to be closer than they are to the naked eye. You can use this effect as a creative tool.

- **Accentuates camera shakiness.** Telephoto focal lengths hit you with a double whammy in terms of camera/photographer shake. The lenses themselves are bulkier, more difficult to hold steady, and may even produce a barely perceptible seesaw rocking effect when you support them with one hand halfway down the lens barrel. As they magnify the subject, they amplify the effect of any camera shake. It's no wonder that image stabilization is especially popular among those using longer lenses.

Avoiding Telephoto Lens Problems

Many of the "problems" that telephoto lenses pose are really just challenges and not that difficult to overcome. Here is a list of the most common picture maladies and suggested solutions:

- **Symptom: flat faces in portraits.** Head-and-shoulders portraits of humans tend to be more flattering when a focal length of 50mm to 85mm is used. Longer focal lengths compress the distance between features like the nose and ears, making the face look wider and flat. (Conversely, a wide-angle lens will make the nose look huge and ears tiny if you move close enough for a head-and-shoulders portrait.) So, avoid using a focal length much longer than about 60mm with your camera unless you're forced to shoot from a greater distance. (Use a wide-angle lens only when shooting three-quarters/full-length portraits, or group shots.)

- **Symptom: blur due to camera shake.** Because a long focal length amplifies the effects of camera shake, make sure the image stabilization is not turned off. Then, if possible, use a faster shutter speed; that may mean that you'll need to set a higher ISO to be able to do so, or use a tripod.

- **Symptom: color fringes.** Chromatic aberration is the most pernicious optical problem found in telephoto lenses. There are others, including spherical aberration, astigmatism, coma, curvature of field, and similarly scary-sounding phenomena. You may be able to correct the fringing in your favorite RAW conversion tool or image editor or the camera's Lens Compensation feature.

- **Symptom: lines that curve inward.** Pincushion distortion is common in photos taken with many telephoto lenses; lines, especially those near the edges of the frame, bow inward like the pin-cushion your grandma might have used. Like chromatic aberration, it can be partially corrected using tools like Photoshop's Lens Correction filter (or a similar utility in some other software).

- **Symptom: low contrast from flare.** Lenses are often furnished with lens hoods for a good reason: to minimize the amount of stray light that will strike the front element causing flare or a ghost image of the diaphragm containing the aperture.

Mastering Light   8

The key tool we use to create and shape our images is light itself, in all its many forms and textures. Indeed, it's said that Sir John Herschel coined the term "photography" from the Greek words for "writing with light" in a paper read before the Royal Society in March 1839. Our dependence on the qualities of the light we use to produce our images is absolute. An adept photographer knows how to compensate for too much or too little illumination, how to soften harsh lighting to mask defects, or increase its contrast to evoke shape and detail. Sometimes, we must adjust our cameras for the apparent "color" of light, use a brief burst of it to freeze action, or filter it to reduce glare.

The many ways we can work with light deserve three full chapters in this book. This chapter introduces using *continuous* lighting (such as daylight, incandescent, LED, or fluorescent sources). I'll cover the brilliant snippets of light we call *electronic flash,* in Chapters 9 and 10.

Light That's Available

You'll often hear the term *available light,* meaning the ambient light at a scene, including whatever illumination is present outdoors during the day or at night, and that provided by lighting fixtures, windows, and other sources. In practice, available light includes any sort of illumination that's available, and can include supplementary lighting added by the photographer in the form of additional lamps, reflectors, or studio continuous light sources.

For our purposes, available light is exactly what you might think: uninterrupted illumination that is available all the time during a shooting session. Daylight, moonlight, and the artificial lighting encountered both indoors and outdoors count as continuous light sources (although all of them can be "interrupted" by passing clouds, solar eclipses, a blown fuse, or simply by switching a lamp off). Indoor continuous illumination includes both the lights that are there already (such as incandescent lamps or overhead fluorescent lights indoors) and fixtures you supply yourself, including photoflood lamps or reflectors used to bounce existing light onto your subject.

Continuous lighting differs from electronic flash, which illuminates our photographs only in brief bursts. Flash, or "strobe" light is notable because it can be much more intense than continuous lighting, lasts only a moment, and can be much more portable than supplementary incandescent sources. It's a light source you can carry with you and use anywhere. There are advantages and disadvantages to each type of illumination.

Here's a quick checklist of pros and cons:

- **Lighting preview—Pro: continuous lighting.** With continuous lighting, thanks to the real-time sensor image preview through the viewfinder or LCD screen, if you've opted to enable Exposure Simulation in the Display Simulation entry of the Shooting 9 menu, you'll always know exactly what kind of lighting effect you're going to get—including color balance—and, if multiple lights are used, how they will interact with each other. If the natural light present in a scene is perfect for the image you're trying to capture, you'll know immediately.

- **Lighting preview—Con: electronic flash.** With electronic flash, unless you have a modeling light built into the flash, the general effect you're going to see may be a mystery until you've built some experience, and you may need to review a shot, make some adjustments, and then reshoot to get the look you want.

- **Exposure calculation—Pro: continuous lighting.** Your camera has no problem calculating exposure for continuous lighting, because it remains constant and can be measured directly from the light reaching the sensor.

- **Exposure calculation—Con: electronic flash.** Electronic flash illumination doesn't exist until the flash fires, and so can't be measured by the exposure sensor at the moment of exposure. Instead, the light must be measured by metering the intensity of a *pre-flash* triggered an instant *before* the main flash, as it is reflected back to the camera and through the lens.

- **Evenness of illumination—Pro/con: continuous lighting.** Of the continuous light sources, daylight, in particular, provides illumination that tends to fill an image completely, lighting up the foreground, background, and your subject almost equally. Shadows do come into play, of course, so you might need to use reflectors or fill in additional light sources to even out the illumination further.

- **Evenness of illumination—Con: electronic flash.** Electronic flash units are subject to the *inverse square law*, which dictates that as a light source's distance increases from the subject, the amount of light reaching the subject falls off proportionately to the square of the distance. In plain English, that means that a flash or lamp that's twelve feet away from a subject provides only one-quarter as much illumination as a source that's six feet away (rather than half as much). This translates into relatively shallow "depth-of-light." I'll discuss this aspect again in Chapter 9.

- **Action stopping—Pro: electronic flash.** When it comes to the ability to freeze moving objects in their tracks, the advantage goes to electronic flash. The brief duration of electronic flash serves as a very high "shutter speed" when the flash is the main or only source of illumination for the photo. Your shutter speed may be set for 1/200th second during a flash exposure, but if the flash illumination predominates, the *effective* exposure time will be the 1/1000th to 1/50,000th second or less duration of the flash, as you can see in Figure 8.1, because the flash unit reduces the amount of light released by cutting short the duration of the flash. The only fly in the ointment is that, if the ambient light is strong enough, it may produce a secondary, "ghost" exposure, as I'll explain in Chapter 9.

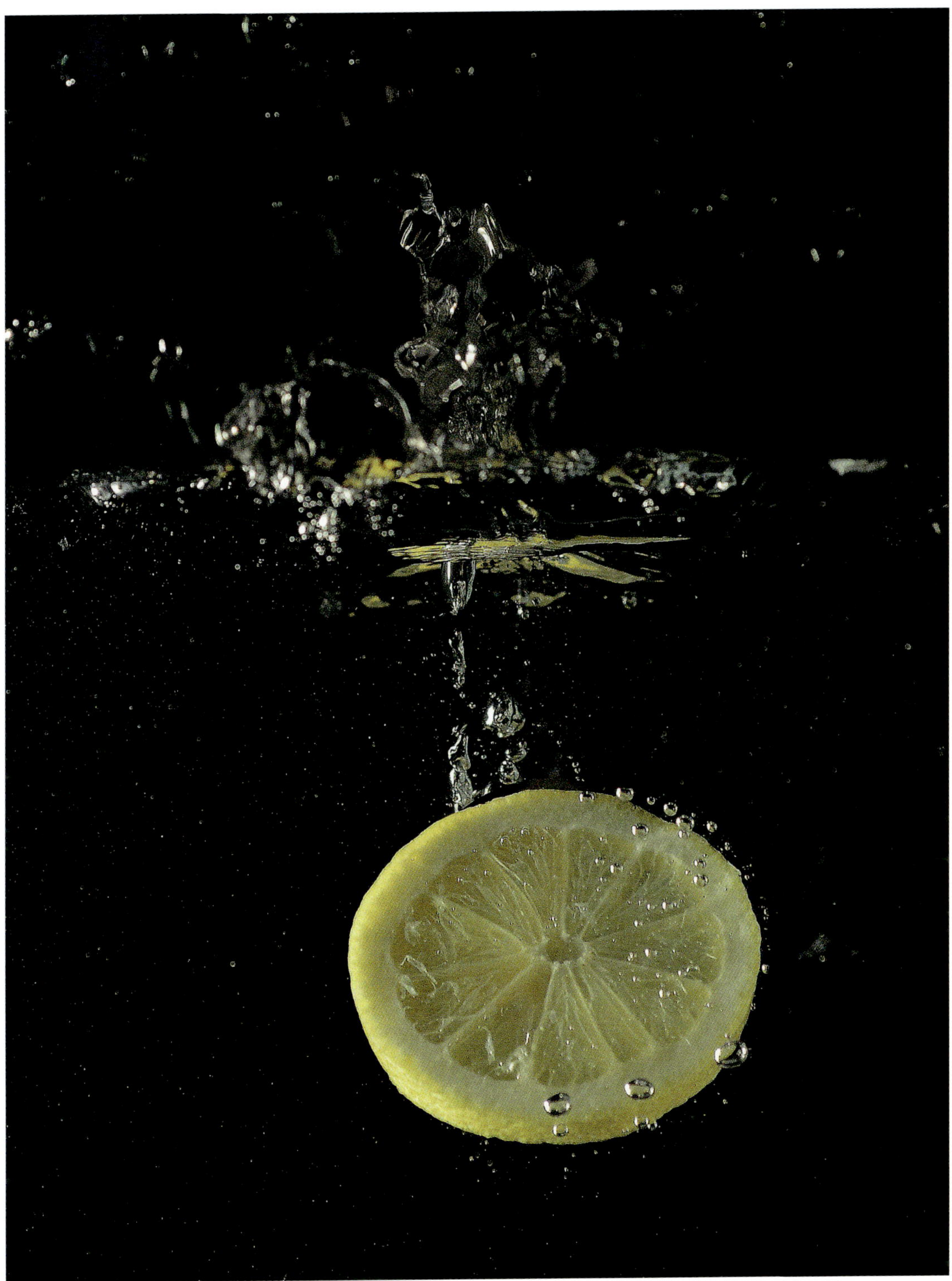

Figure 8.1 Electronic flash can freeze almost any action.

- **Action stopping—Con: continuous lighting.** Action stopping with continuous light sources is completely dependent on the shutter speed you've dialed in on the camera. And the speeds available are dependent on the amount of light available and your ISO sensitivity setting.
- **Cost—Pro: continuous lighting.** Incandescent, fluorescent, or LED lamps are generally much less expensive than electronic flash units, which can easily cost several hundred dollars.
- **Cost—Con: electronic flash.** Electronic flash units aren't particularly cheap. The lowest-cost dedicated flash designed specifically for the Canon EOS cameras is about $150 (the EL-100), and it is probably not powerful enough for an advanced camera like the R8. Such basic units are limited in features and intended for those with entry-level cameras. Plan on spending some money to get the features that a sophisticated electronic flash offers.
- **Flexibility—Pro: electronic flash.** Electronic flash's action-freezing power allows you to work without a tripod in the studio (and elsewhere), adding flexibility and speed when choosing angles and positions. Flash units can be easily filtered, and, because the filtration is placed over the light source rather than the lens, you don't need to use high-quality filter material.
- **Flexibility—Con: continuous lighting.** Because the typical lamp is not as bright as electronic flash, the slower shutter speeds required mean that you may have to use a tripod more often, especially when shooting portraits.

Continuous Lighting Basics

While continuous lighting and its effects are generally much easier to visualize and use than electronic flash, there are some factors you need to take into account, particularly the color temperature of the light, how accurately a given form of illumination reproduces colors (we've all seen the ghastly looks human faces assume under mercury-vapor lamps outdoors), and other considerations.

One important aspect is color temperature. Of course, color temperature concerns aren't exclusive to continuous light sources, but the variations tend to be more extreme and less predictable than those of electronic flash, which output relatively consistent daylight-like illumination.

Living with Color Temperature

In practical terms, color temperature is how "bluish" or how "reddish" the light appears to be to the digital camera's sensor. Indoor illumination is quite warm, comparatively, and appears reddish to the sensor. Daylight, in contrast, seems much bluer to the sensor. Our eyes (our brains, actually) are quite adaptable to these variations, so white objects don't appear to have an orange tinge when viewed indoors, nor do they seem excessively blue outdoors in full daylight. Yet, these color temperature variations are real, and the sensor is not fooled. To capture the most accurate colors, we need to take the color temperature into account in setting the color balance (or *white balance*)—either automatically using the camera's intelligence or manually using our own knowledge and experience.

While Canon has been valiant in its efforts to smarten up the camera's ability to adjust for color balance automatically, an entire cottage industry has developed to provide us additional help, including gadgets like the ExpoDisc filter/caps and their ilk (www.expoimaging.com), which allow the camera's add-on external custom white balance measuring feature to evaluate the illumination that passes through the disc/cap/filter/Pringle's can lid, or whatever neutral-color substitute you employ. (A white or gray card also works.) When it comes to zeroing in on the exact color temperature for a scene, your main tools will be custom white balances set using neutral targets like the ExpoDisc, and adjustment of RAW files when you import photos into your image editor.

The only time you need to think in terms of actual color temperature is when you're making adjustments using the Color Temp. setting in the White Balance entry of the Shooting 4 menu, as I'll describe in Chapter 11. It allows you to dial in exact color temperatures, if known. You can also shift and bias color balance along the blue/amber and magenta/green axes, and bracket white balance.

In most cases, however, the Auto setting in the Shooting menu's White Balance entry will do a good job of calculating white balance for you. Auto can be used as your choice most of the time. Use the preset values or set a custom white balance that matches the current shooting conditions when you need to.

Remember that if you shoot RAW, you can specify the white balance of your image when you import it into Photoshop, Photoshop Elements, or another image editor using Adobe Camera Raw, or your preferred RAW converter. While color-balancing filters that fit on the front of the lens exist, they are primarily useful for film cameras, because film's color balance can't be tweaked as extensively as that of a sensor.

White Balance Bracketing

When using WB bracketing, the camera takes a single shot, and then saves multiple JPEG copies, each with a different color balance. It's not necessary to capture multiple shots, as the raw information retrieved from the sensor for the single exposure is used to generate the multiple different versions.

Access the WB Shift/Bkt. entry in the Shooting 4 menu, rotate the QCD to the right to bracket one, two, or three increments in the blue/amber direction (see Figure 8.2, left), or to the left to bracket one, two, or three increments in the magenta/green direction. Once you have set blue/amber or magenta/green bias orientations, you can use the up/down directional buttons to shift a bracket to provide greater bias in any of the two orientations. Figure 8.2, right, shows a bracketing sequence along that blue/amber axis that is shifted in the blue and green directions. It's unlikely you'll need such fine-tuning; making images bluer/yellower or more green/magenta will usually suffice.

Making these adjustments are the only times you're likely to be confused by a seeming contradiction in how color temperatures are named: warmer (more reddish) color temperatures (measured in degrees Kelvin) are the *lower* numbers, while cooler (bluer) color temperatures are *higher* numbers. It might not make sense to say that 3,400K is warmer than 6,000K, but that's the way it is. If it helps, think of a glowing red ember contrasted with a white-hot welder's torch, rather than fire and ice.

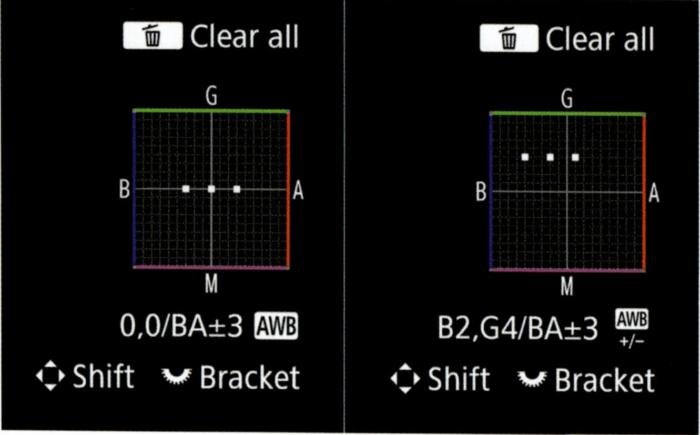

Figure 8.2 White balance bracketing can be done along the amber/blue axis (left) or green/magenta axis. Bias can be shifted, as well (right).

The confusion comes from physics. Scientists calculate color temperature from the light emitted by a mythical object called a black body radiator, which absorbs all the radiant energy that strikes it, and reflects none at all. Such a black body not only *absorbs* light perfectly, but it *emits* it perfectly when heated (and since nothing in the universe is perfect, that makes it mythical).

At a particular physical temperature, this imaginary object always emits light of the same wavelength or color. That makes it possible to define color temperature in terms of actual temperature in degrees on the Kelvin scale that scientists use. Incandescent light, for example, typically has a color temperature of 3,200K to 3,400K. Daylight might range from 5,500K to 6,000K. Each type of illumination we use for photography has its own color temperature range—with some cautions.

Daylight

Daylight is produced by the sun, and so is moonlight (which is just reflected sunlight). Daylight is present, of course, even when you can't see the sun. When sunlight is direct, it can be bright and harsh. If daylight is diffused by clouds, softened by bouncing off objects such as walls or your photo reflectors, or filtered by shade, it can be much dimmer and less contrasty.

Daylight's color temperature can vary quite widely. It is highest in temperature (most blue) at noon when the sun is directly overhead, because the light is traveling through a minimum amount of the filtering layer we call the atmosphere. The color temperature at high noon may be 6,000K. At other times of day, the sun is lower in the sky and the particles in the air provide a filtering effect that warms the illumination to about 5,500K for most of the day. Starting an hour before dusk and for an hour after sunrise, the warm appearance of the sunlight is even visible to our eyes when the color temperature may dip to 5,000K to 4,500K, as shown in Figure 8.3.

Because you'll be taking so many photos in daylight, you'll want to learn how to use or compensate for the brightness and contrast of sunlight, as well as how to deal with its color temperature.

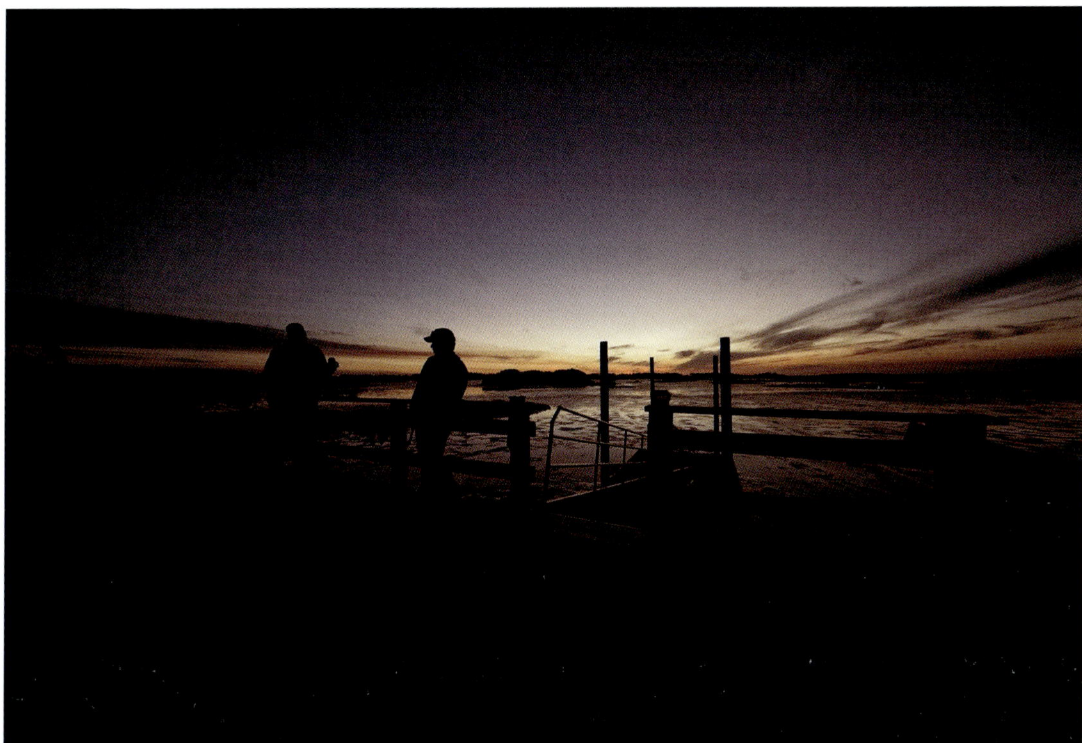

Figure 8.3 At dawn and dusk, the color temperature of daylight may dip as low as 4,500K.

Incandescent/Tungsten/Halogen Light

The term *incandescent* or *tungsten/halogen illumination* is usually applied to the direct descendents of Thomas Edison's original electric lamp. Such lights consist of a glass bulb that contains a vacuum, or is filled with a halogen gas, and contains a tungsten filament that is heated by an electrical current, producing photons and heat. Tungsten-halogen lamps are a variation on the basic light bulb, using a more rugged (and longer-lasting) filament that can be heated to a higher temperature, housed in a thicker glass or quartz envelope, and filled with iodine or bromine ("halogen") gases. The higher temperature allows tungsten-halogen (or quartz-halogen/quartz-iodine, depending on their construction) lamps to burn "hotter" and whiter. Although popular for automobile headlamps today, they've also been used for photographic illumination.

Although incandescent illumination isn't a perfect black body radiator, it's close enough that the color temperature of such lamps can be precisely calculated and used for photography without concerns about color variation (at least, until the very end of the lamp's life). As I noted earlier, the color rendering index of such lamps tends to be very high, so you need to account only for the color temperature.

Of course, old-style tungsten lamps are on the way out, at first replaced either by compact fluorescent lights (CFL) or newer, more energy-efficient (and expensive) tungsten and halogen lights, and, eventually, by LED illumination. It appears that LED illumination is on track to supplant all of these for most applications in the near future. The other qualities of this type of lighting, such as contrast, are dependent on the distance of the lamp from the subject, type of reflectors used, and other factors.

Fluorescent Light/LEDs

Fluorescent light has some advantages in terms of illumination, but some disadvantages from a photographic standpoint. This type of lamp generates light through an electro-chemical reaction that emits most of its energy as visible light, rather than heat, which is why the bulbs don't get as hot. The type of light produced varies depending on the phosphor coatings and type of gas in the tube. So, the illumination fluorescent bulbs produce can vary widely in its characteristics.

That's not great news for photographers. Different types of lamps have different "color temperatures" that can't be precisely measured in degrees Kelvin, because the light isn't produced by heating. Worse, fluorescent lamps have a discontinuous spectrum of light that can have some colors missing entirely. A particular type of tube can lack certain shades of red or other colors (see Figure 8.4),

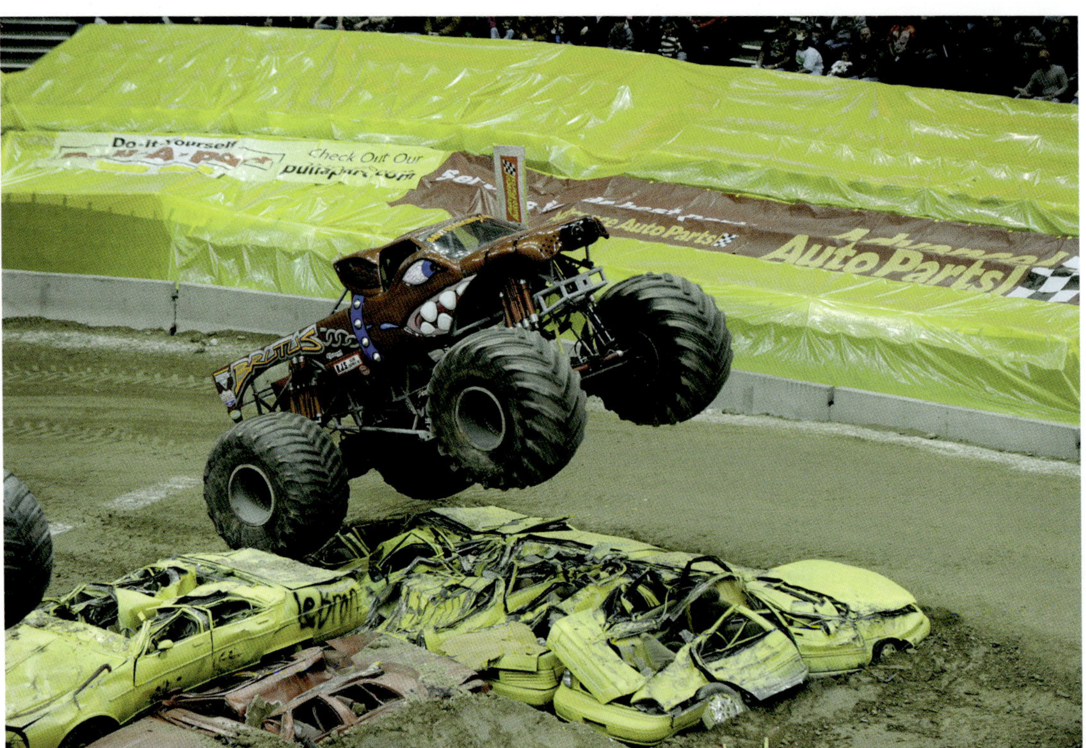

Figure 8.4 The uncorrected fluorescent lighting adds a distinct greenish cast to this image when exposed with a daylight white balance setting.

which is why fluorescent lamps and other alternative technologies such as sodium-vapor illumination can produce ghastly looking human skin tones. Their spectra can lack the reddish tones we associate with healthy skin and emphasize the blues and greens popular in horror movies.

LED light sources have almost entirely replaced CFLs for all illumination and photographic applications, particularly for movie shooting, which uses compact units that clip onto the camera and provide a continuous beam of light to fill in shadows indoors or out, and/or to provide the main illumination when shooting video inside. Several vendors have introduced LED studio lights that are bright enough for general-purpose shooting. It's become obvious that LED illumination will soon become the most widely used continuous light source. They've already made dramatic inroads in the automotive industry for taillights, headlights, and interior illumination. Innovations like the Lume Cube 2, a brilliant $90 waterproof variable-brightness LED lamp that can be triggered wirelessly, will find broader use. (See Figure 8.5.)

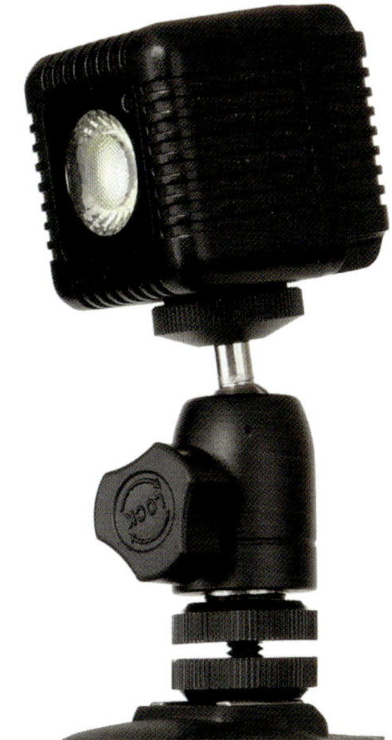

Figure 8.5 The Lume Cube 2.

Color Rendering

Faithful color rendition goes beyond color temperature. So-called "white" light is produced by a spectrum of colors that, when added together, provide the neutral color needed for accuracy. Artificial light sources don't necessarily offer the same balanced spectrum found in sunlight. Some portions of the spectrum may be deficient or truncated or include gaps with certain wavelengths missing entirely. Astronomers use their knowledge of which elements absorb which colors of light to calculate the makeup of distant stars using spectrographs. In photography, the analysis of spectra is used to calculate the color rendering index, which measures how accurately colors are presented.

All artificial light sources have a color rendering index (CRI). That figure is calculated by rating eight different colors on a scale of 0 to 100, based on how natural the color looks compared to a perfect or "reference" light source at a particular color temperature. A CRI of 80-plus is considered acceptable; for critical applications like photography, a CRI higher than 93 is best. Incandescent and halogen bulbs typically have a CRI of 100 compared to a reference light source at the same color temperature. Some sodium-vapor lamps earn a horrid 0 rating. Standard LED lamps are rated at 83, although some can have CRIs as high as 98. Many types of fluorescent lights fall into the CRI 50–75 range.

Vendors, such as GE and Sylvania, may provide the color rendering index on the packaging. Daylight fluorescents and deluxe cool white fluorescents suitable for photography might have a CRI of about 79 to 95, which is perfectly acceptable for most photographic applications. Less desirable are warm white fluorescents, which may have a CRI of 55. White deluxe mercury-vapor lights are even less suitable with a CRI of 45, while low-pressure sodium lamps can vary from CRI 0 to 18. If you're using such a source not intended for photography, such as many fluorescent lamps, it may be worth your while to determine its color rendering index before you shoot, as the R8's color balance settings cannot compensate for wavelengths that are entirely absent from a particular type of illumination.

Electronic Flash Basics

Until you delve into the situation deeply enough, it might appear that serious photographers have a love/hate relationship with electronic flash. You'll often hear that flash photography is less natural looking, and that the built-in flash in most cameras should never be used as the primary source of illumination because it provides a harsh, garish look. Indeed, many advanced cameras, like the R8, don't have a built-in flash at all. Available ("continuous") lighting is praised, and built-in flash photography seems to be roundly denounced.

In truth, however, the bias is against *bad* flash photography, the kind produced when you clamp a flash on top of the camera and point it directly at your subject. In that mode, you'll often end up with well-exposed (thanks to Canon's e-TTL II metering system), but *harshly lit* images. Yet, in other configurations, flash has become the studio light source of choice for pro photographers, because it's more intense (and its intensity can be varied to order by the photographer), freezes action, frees you from using a tripod (unless you want to use one to lock down a composition), and has a snappy, consistent light quality that matches daylight. (While color balance changes as the flash duration shortens, some Canon flash units can communicate to the camera the exact white balance provided for that shot.) And even pros will cede that an external flash has some important uses as an adjunct to existing light, particularly to illuminate dark shadows using a technique called *fill flash*. Moreover, creative photographers can use an external Speedlite in remarkably creative ways, especially in wireless and multiple flash modes (which I'll explain in Chapter 10).

But electronic flash isn't as inherently easy to use as continuous lighting. As I noted in Chapter 8, electronic flash units are more expensive, don't show you exactly what the lighting effect will be (unless you use a second, relatively continuous source called a *modeling light* for a preview), and the exposure of electronic flash units is more difficult to calculate accurately.

How Electronic Flash Works

The bursts of light we call electronic flash are produced by a flash of photons generated by an electrical charge that is accumulated in a component called a *capacitor* and then directed through a glass tube containing xenon gas, which absorbs the energy and emits the brief flash. For a typical external flash, such as the Speedlite 600EX II-RT, the full burst of light lasts about 1/1000th of a second and provides enough illumination to shoot a subject 12 feet away at f/16 using the ISO 100 setting.

Because the duration of the burst is so brief, if the external flash is the main source of illumination, the effective exposure time is short, typically 1/1000th to 1/50,000th second, freezing a moving subject dramatically, as shown in Figure 9.1. These short bursts can also be repeated, producing multiple-exposure/stroboscopic effects, as described later in this chapter.

An electronic flash is triggered at the instant of exposure, during a period when the sensor is fully exposed by the shutter. The camera has a vertically traveling shutter. Conventional cameras have traditionally had two physical curtains. The first curtain opens and moves to the opposite side of the frame, at which point the shutter is completely open. The flash can be triggered at this point (so-called *first-curtain sync*), making the flash exposure. Then, after a delay that can vary from 30 seconds to 1/200th second, a second curtain begins moving across the sensor plane, covering up the sensor again. If the flash is triggered just before the second curtain starts to close, then *second-curtain sync* is used. In both cases, though, a shutter speed of 1/200th second is the maximum that can be used to take a photo (unless you're using high-speed sync, discussed later in this chapter).

With your EOS R8, Canon has dispensed entirely with that physical *first* curtain. Instead, when the exposure begins, the preview image you've been watching on the LCD or electronic viewfinder is *dumped,* so the sensor is essentially blank, just as if it had been covered by a physical first curtain. Then, the sensor goes active again (as when the physical first curtain had dropped in cameras that used one) and begins recording the image.

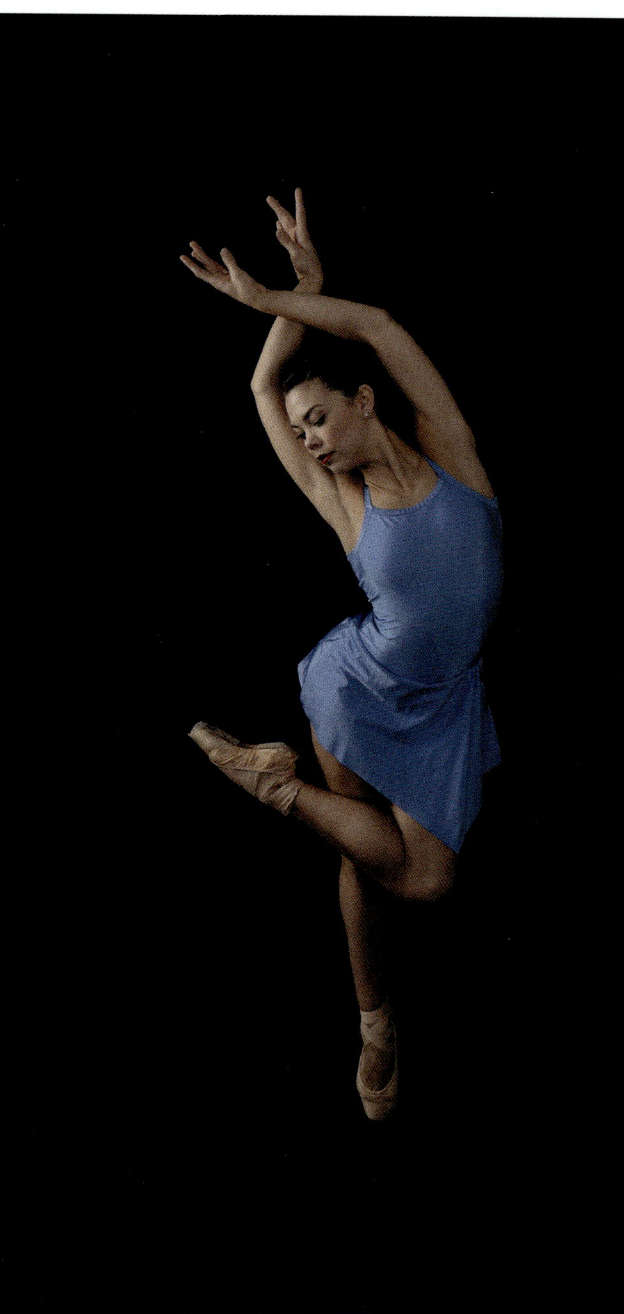

Figure 9.1 An external flash placed to the left and slightly in front of the dancer produced a brief burst that froze her en pointe.

Your camera's default flash sync mode is *electronic first-curtain sync.* As with all first-curtain sync modes, the flash is triggered at the instant that the sensor is completely exposed. The shutter then remains open for that additional length of time (from 30 seconds to 1/200th), and the second (physical) curtain begins to move downward, covering the sensor once more.

Your camera's electronic first-curtain sync shutter mode will work for you well for most shots. However, the R8 has an *all-electronic shutter* which dispenses with the physical second curtain as well, using electronic functions to both start and end the exposure. You can switch between the two modes using the Shutter Mode entry of the Shooting 7 menu, as described in Chapter 11. **Note:** *Electronic flash is disabled when using the electronic shutter.*

If you have an electronic flash mounted on your R8 and powered up, you can switch from electronic first-curtain sync to an alternate mode, *second-curtain sync.* When this sync mode is activated, the flash is triggered *after* the main exposure is over, just before the second (physical) curtain begins to move downward.

Ghost Images

The difference between triggering the flash when the shutter just opens, or just when it begins to close might not seem like much. But whether you use electronic first-curtain sync (the default setting) or second-curtain sync (an optional setting) can make a significant difference to your photograph *if the ambient light in your scene also contributes to the image.* You can set either of these sync modes in the Shooting 3 menu, under External Speedlite control, where you'll find the Flash Function setting option, shown at left in Figure 9.2. When you select it, you can choose First-curtain synchronization, Second-curtain synchronization, or High-speed synchronization (which I'll discuss later in this chapter). (See Figure 9.2, right.)

Here's how first-curtain and second-curtain sync differ. At faster shutter speeds, there isn't much time for the ambient light to register, unless it is very bright. It's likely that the electronic flash will provide almost all the illumination, so first-curtain sync or second-curtain sync isn't very important. However, at slower shutter speeds, or with very bright ambient light levels, there is a significant difference, particularly if your subject is moving, or the camera isn't steady.

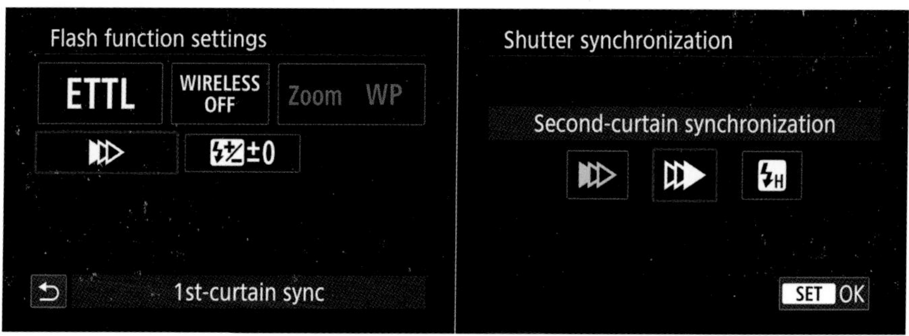

Figure 9.2 From the Flash Functions Settings screen (left), choose shutter synchronization (right).

In any of those situations, the ambient light will register as a second image accompanying the flash exposure, and if there is movement (camera or subject), that additional image will not be in the same place as the flash exposure. It will show as a ghost image and, if the movement is significant enough, as a blurred ghost image trailing in front of or behind your subject in the direction of the movement.

As I noted, when you're using electronic first-curtain sync, the flash's main burst goes off the *instant the shutter is activated* to begin capturing the image. (A pre-flash used to measure exposure in auto flash modes fires *before* the shutter "opens.") This produces an image of the subject on the sensor. Then, the shutter remains open for an additional period, as described earlier. If your subject is moving, say, toward the right side of the frame, the ghost image produced by the ambient light will generate a blur on the right side of the original subject image, making it look as if your sharp (flash-produced) image is chasing the ghost. For those of us who grew up with lightning-fast superheroes who always left a ghost trail *behind them*, that looks unnatural (see Figure 9.3).

So, Canon uses second-curtain sync to remedy the situation. You can specify second-curtain sync *only* when using shutter speeds of 1/30th second or slower. If you change to a shutter speed of 1/40th second or faster, the R8 switches back to electronic first-curtain sync *even if you've specified second-curtain sync.* In the alternate mode, the shutter "opens," as before. The shutter remains open for its designated duration, and the ghost image forms. If your subject moves from the left side of the frame to the right side, the ghost will move from left to right, too. *Then,* about 1.5 milliseconds before the second shutter curtain closes, the flash is triggered, producing a nice, sharp flash image *ahead* of the ghost image. Voilà! We have monsieur *Speed Racer* outdriving his own trailing image.

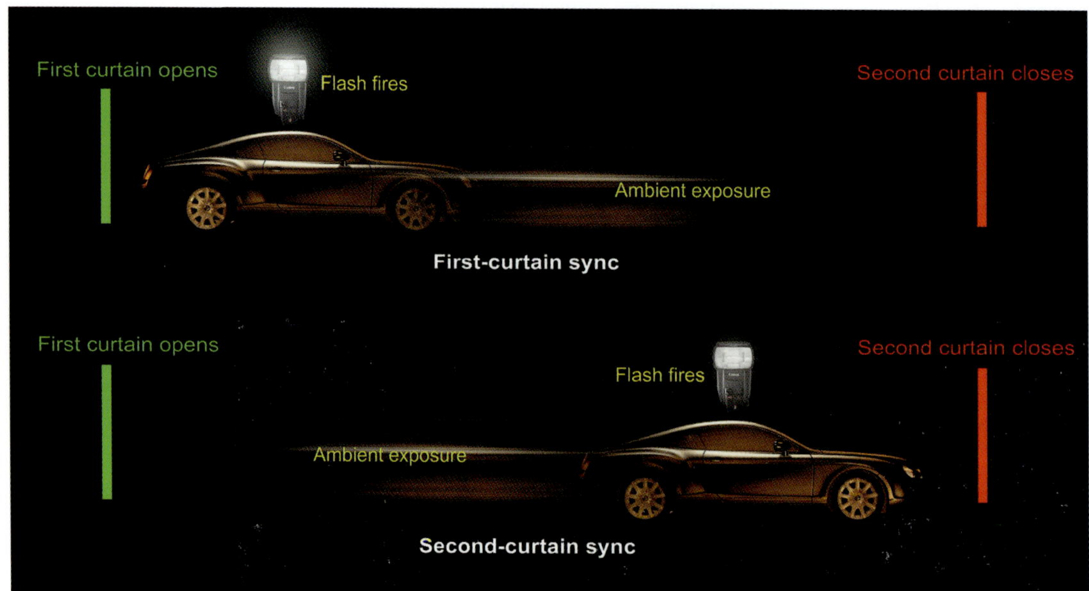

Figure 9.3 First-curtain sync produces an image that trails in front of the flash exposure (top), whereas second-curtain sync creates a more "natural-looking" trail behind the flash image (bottom).

Avoiding Sync-Speed Problems

Using a shutter speed faster than the 1/200th-second sync speed can cause problems. Triggering the electronic flash only when the shutter is completely open makes a lot of sense if you think about what's going on. To obtain shutter speeds faster than the sync speed, only part of the sensor is exposed at one time, effectively providing a briefer exposure. If the flash were to fire during the time when the second curtain partially obscured the sensor, only the exposed portion of the sensor will receive any illumination. You end up with a photo like the one shown in Figure 9.4.

Note that the band across the bottom of the image is black. That's a shadow of the second (physical) shutter curtain, which had started to move when the flash was triggered. Sharp-eyed readers will wonder why the black band is at the *bottom* of the frame rather than at the top, where the second curtain begins its journey. The answer is simple: your lens flips the image upside down and forms it on the sensor in a reversed position. You never notice that, because the camera is smart enough to show you the pixels that make up your photo in their proper orientation. But this image flip is why, if your sensor gets dirty and you detect a spot of dust in the upper half of a test photo, if cleaning manually, you need to look for the speck in the *bottom* half of the sensor.

Ordinarily, you don't have to worry about this sync-speed problem. That's because if you're using a "smart" (dedicated) flash, the camera knows that a strobe is attached, and remedies any unintentional goof in shutter speed settings. If you happen to set the shutter to a faster speed in Fv, Tv, or M mode, the camera will automatically adjust the shutter speed down to the sync speed. In Av, P, or Scene Intelligent Auto modes where the exposure system selects the shutter speed, it will never choose a shutter speed higher than the sync speed when using flash. In P mode, shutter speed is automatically set between 1/60th and 1/200th second when using flash.

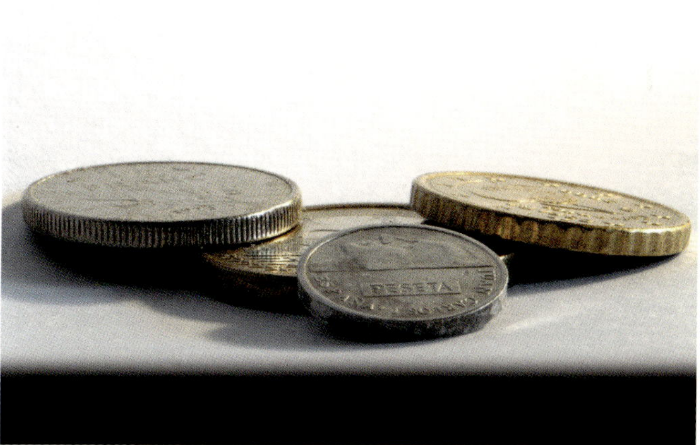

Figure 9.4 If a shutter speed faster than 1/200th second is used, you can end up photographing only a portion of the image.

But when using a non-dedicated flash, such as a studio unit plugged into a PC/X adapter (an accessory that fits into the flash shoe and provides a "dumb" flash connector), the camera has no way of knowing that a flash is connected, so shutter speeds faster than 1/200th second can be set inadvertently. Note that you can use a feature called *high-speed sync* that allows shutter speeds faster than the sync speed with certain external dedicated Canon flash units. When using high-speed sync (HSS), the flash fires a continuous series of bursts at *reduced power* for the entire exposure, so that the duration of the illumination is sufficient to expose the sensor as the slit moves. High-speed sync is set using the controls on the attached and powered-up compatible external flash. I'll explain HSS later.

Determining Exposure

Calculating the proper exposure for an electronic flash photograph is a bit more complicated than determining the settings by continuous light. The right exposure isn't simply a function of how far away your subject is (which can be calculated based on the autofocus distance that's locked in just prior to taking the picture). Various objects reflect more or less light at the same distance so, obviously, the camera needs to measure the amount of light reflected back and through the lens. Yet, as the flash itself isn't available for measuring until it's triggered, there is nothing to measure.

The solution is to fire the flash multiple times. The initial shot is a pre-flash that can be analyzed, then followed by a main flash that's given exactly the calculated intensity needed to provide a correct exposure. If the main flash is serving as a sender to trigger off-camera flash units, additional coded pulses can convey settings information to the receiver flashes and trigger their firing. Of course, if *radio* signals rather than optical signals are in play, the sequences may be different. I'll cover various radio and optical wireless flash modes in Chapter 10; this chapter just explains the basics.

Because of the need to abbreviate or quench a flash burst in order to provide the optimum exposure, the primary flash may be longer for distant objects and shorter for closer subjects, depending on the required intensity. This through-the-lens evaluative flash exposure system is called E-TTL II, and it operates whenever you have attached a Canon dedicated flash unit.

Guide Numbers

Guide numbers, usually abbreviated GN, are a way of specifying the power of an electronic flash in a way that can be used to determine the right f/stop to use at a particular shooting distance and ISO setting. In fact, before automatic flash units became prevalent, the GN was actually used to do just that. A GN is usually given as a pair of numbers for both feet and meters that represent the range at ISO 100. For example, consider the Canon Speedlite 270EX II. The 270EX II has a GN of 89 at ISO 100. That guide number applies when the flash is set to the 50mm zoom setting (so that the unit's coverage is optimized to fill up the frame when using a 50mm focal length on a *full-frame* camera body). (The effective guide number is just 72 when the flash is mounted on a "cropped" sensor camera like the Canon EOS R7 or R10.) If you're using the 270EX II set to the 28mm zoom position, the light spreads out more to cover the wider area captured at that focal length, and the guide number of the unit drops to 79.

Of course, the question remains, what can you *do* with a guide number, other than to evaluate relative light output when comparing different flash units? In theory, you could use the GN to calculate the approximate exposure that would be needed to take a photo at a given distance. To calculate the right exposure at ISO 100, you'd divide the guide number by the distance to arrive at the appropriate f/stop. (Remember that the shutter speed has no bearing on the *flash* exposure; the flash burst will occur while the shutter is wide open and will have a duration of *less* than the time the shutter is open.)

Again, using the 270EX II as an example, at ISO 100 with its GN of 89, if you wanted to shoot a subject at a distance of 11 feet, you'd use f/8 (89 divided by 11). At approximately 16 feet, an f/stop of f/5.6 would be used. Some quick mental calculations with the GN will give you any particular electronic flash's range. You can easily see that the 270EX II would begin to peter out at about 32 feet, where you'd need an aperture of roughly f/2.8 at ISO 100. Of course, in the real world you'd probably bump the sensitivity up to a setting of ISO 400 so you could use a more practical f/5.6 at that distance.

You should use guide numbers as an *estimate* only. Other factors can affect the relative "power" of a flash unit. For example, if you're shooting in a small room. Some light will bounce off ceilings and walls—even with the flash pointed straight ahead—and give your flash a slight boost, especially if you're not shooting extra-close to your subject. Use the same flash outdoors at night, say, on a football field, and the flash will have less relative power, because helpful reflections from surrounding objects are not likely.

So, today, guide numbers are most useful for comparing the power of various flash units. You don't need to be a math genius to see that an electronic flash with a GN of, say, 197 (like the 600EX II-RT) would be *a lot* more powerful than that of the 270EX II. You could use f/12 instead of f/5.6 at 16 feet. That's slightly more than two full f/stops' difference. As the owner of an R8, we can safely assume you'll be using one of the more powerful flash units in the Canon line (or perhaps a similar unit from a third-party vendor).

Getting Started with Electronic Flash

The accessory flash is one of the most useful add-ons you can have. I'll include detailed explanations of your flash settings options later in the chapter. This section will get you started quickly.

When you're using Scene Intelligent Auto, P, Av, Tv, Fv, B, or Manual exposure modes, attach the flash and turn it on. The behavior of the external flash varies, depending on which exposure mode you're using:

- **Scene Intelligent Auto.** When set to this mode, the flash will fire automatically, if it is attached and powered up.
- **P.** In Program mode, the exposure process is fully automated, giving you subtle fill flash effects in daylight, and fully illuminating your subject under dimmer lighting conditions. The camera selects a shutter speed from 1/60th to the sync speed and sets an appropriate aperture.

- **Av.** In Aperture-priority mode, you set the aperture as always, and the camera chooses a shutter speed from 30 seconds to the sync speed. Use this mode with care, because if the camera detects a dark background, it will use the flash to expose the main subject in the foreground, and then leave the shutter open long enough to allow the background to be exposed correctly, too. If you're not using an image-stabilized lens, you can end up with blurry ghost images even of non-moving subjects at exposures longer than 1/30th second, and if your camera is not mounted on a tripod, you'll see these blurs at exposures longer than about 1/8th second even if you are using IS.

  To disable use of a slow shutter speed with flash, access the Slow Synchro option in the External Speedlite Control entry in the Shooting 3 menu and change from the default setting (1/200-30sec. auto) to either 1/200-1/60sec. auto or 1/200sec. (fixed).

- **Tv.** When using flash in Tv mode, you set the shutter speed from 30 seconds to 1/200th second, and the camera will choose the correct aperture for the correct flash exposure. If you accidentally set the shutter speed higher than 1/200th second, the camera will reduce it to 1/200th second when you're using the flash.

- **Fv.** In this mode, you can specify shutter speed, aperture, and ISO sensitivity either manually or automatically, and the camera will adjust the remaining parameters. That means when using flash, the camera will behave as if it were in Program mode (if you don't choose a shutter speed or aperture manually), or Tv mode (if you select only a shutter speed), or Av mode (if you choose only the aperture), or M mode (if you select both).

- **M/B.** In Manual or Bulb exposure modes, you select both shutter speed and aperture. The camera will adjust the shutter speed to the sync speed if you try to use a faster speed with a flash. The E-TTL II system will provide the correct amount of exposure for your main subject at the aperture you've chosen (if the subject is within the flash's range, of course). In Bulb mode, the shutter will remain open for as long as the release button on top of the camera is held down, or the release of your remote control is activated. If you use the Bulb timer, you can specify long exposures.

Flash Exposure Compensation and FE Lock

If you want to lock flash exposure for a subject that is not centered in the frame, you can use the FE lock button (the * button) to lock in a specific flash exposure. Just center the viewfinder on the subject you want to correctly expose and press the * button. The pre-flash fires and calculates exposure. The camera remembers the correct exposure until you take a picture, and the FEL indicator, a lightning bolt with an * next to it in the lower-left corner of the display, is your reminder. If you want to recalculate your flash exposure, just press the * button again. When you're ready to shoot, recompose your photo and press the shutter down the rest of the way to take the picture.

You can also manually add or subtract exposure, without needing to touch the flash. When using any of the exposure modes *except* Scene Intelligent Auto (that is, Program AE, Aperture-priority, Shutter-priority, Flexible-priority, or Manual), you can access flash exposure compensation (FEC) as illustrated in four different ways, with three of them illustrated in Figure 9.5.

- **Set FEC on the flash.** Consult your Speedlite manual to see if you can set flash exposure compensation on the flash. See the sidebar which follows. Note that when you specify FEC on the flash, you cannot change it using the camera's controls.

- **Press the INFO button.** If you've enabled the Shooting Information screen, display it by pressing the INFO button until the screen appears. (See Figure 9.5, upper left.) Then press the Q/SET button, highlight the FEC icon at the right side of the second row of the Quick Control screen, then use the Main dial or QCD to make the adjustment.

- **Quick Control screen.** After you've summoned the Quick Control screen and highlighted the FEC icon, as described above, you can press Q/SET to produce the sliding scale shown at upper right in Figure 9.5. You might want to do this if you preferred to use the touch screen to make your adjustments or needed the extra legibility the larger screen provides.

- **Access External Speedlite Control.** Find it in the Shooting 3 menu, press Q/SET, and, if your flash is attached and powered up, select Flash Function settings. Then navigate to the Flash Exposure Compensation icon in the second row of the screen, as shown in Figure 9.5, lower left. Then press Q/SET to access the touch-screen friendly sliding scale seen in Figure 9.5, lower right.

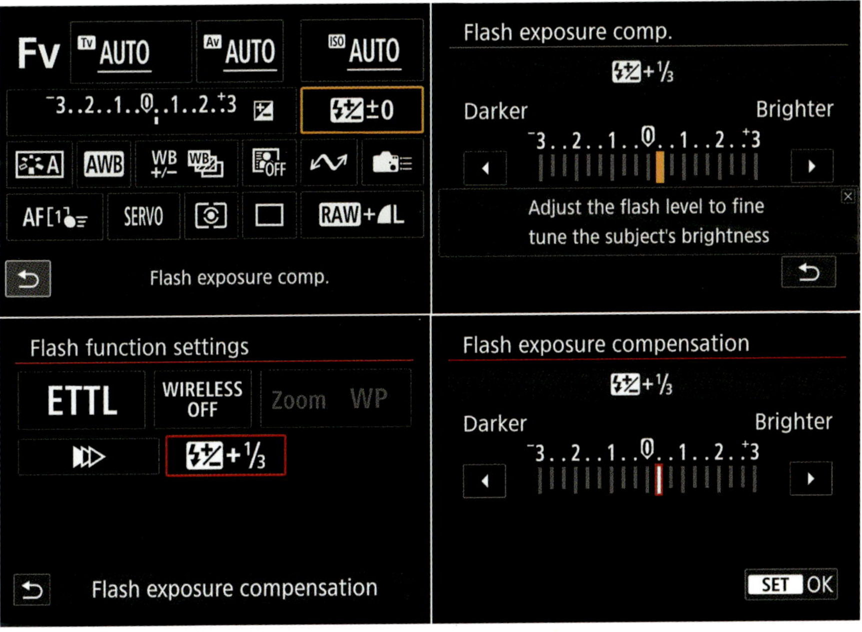

Figure 9.5 Four ways of setting flash exposure compensation.

SETTING FEC ON THE FLASH

While setting flash exposure compensation within the camera is usually most convenient, with some Canon Speedlites (such as the 600EX II-RT), you can set exposure compensation on the external flash instead. With the 600EX II-RT, in ETTL, M, or MULTI modes, press the #2 button to highlight the +/- FEC indicator, then rotate the flash's Select dial to set the specific amount. Press the Select/SET button to confirm your choice.

   If you want to avoid accidentally changing the FEC value on the flash, say, while making other adjustments, use either flash unit's C.Fn-13 setting (not to be confused with the camera's own Custom Functions). When set to the default, 0, rotating the Select dial specifies the amount; change to 1, instead, and you must *first* press the Select/SET button before rotating the dial.

Flash exposure compensation can work in tandem with non-flash exposure compensation, so you can adjust the amount of light registered from the scene by ambient light even while you're tweaking the amount of illumination absorbed from your flash unit. As with non-flash exposure compensation, the compensation you make remains in effect for the pictures that follow, and even when you've turned the camera off, remember to cancel the flash exposure compensation adjustment by reversing the steps used to set it when you're done using it.

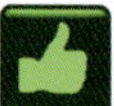

TIP If you've enabled the Auto Lighting Optimizer in the Shooting 2 menu, it may cancel out any EV you've subtracted using flash exposure compensation. Disable the Auto Lighting Optimizer if you find your images are still too bright when using flash exposure compensation.

Flash Range

The illumination of the external flash varies with distance, focal length, and ISO sensitivity setting:

- **Distance.** The farther away your subject is from the camera, the greater the light fall-off, thanks to the inverse square law discussed in Chapter 8. Keep in mind that a subject that's twice as far away receives only one-quarter as much light, which is two f/stops' worth. (See Figure 9.6.)

- **Focal length.** A non-zooming flash "covers" only a limited angle of view, which doesn't change. So, when you're using a lens that is wider than the default focal length, the frame may not be covered fully, and you'll experience dark areas, especially in the corners. As you zoom in using longer focal lengths, some of the illumination is outside the area of view and is "wasted." (This phenomenon is why some external flash units, such as the 600EX II-RT or EL-1, automatically "zoom" to match the zoom setting of your lens to concentrate the available flash burst onto the actual subject area.)

- **ISO setting.** The higher the ISO sensitivity, the more photons captured by the sensor. So, doubling the sensitivity from ISO 100 to 200 produces the same effect as, say, opening up your lens from f/8 to f/5.6.

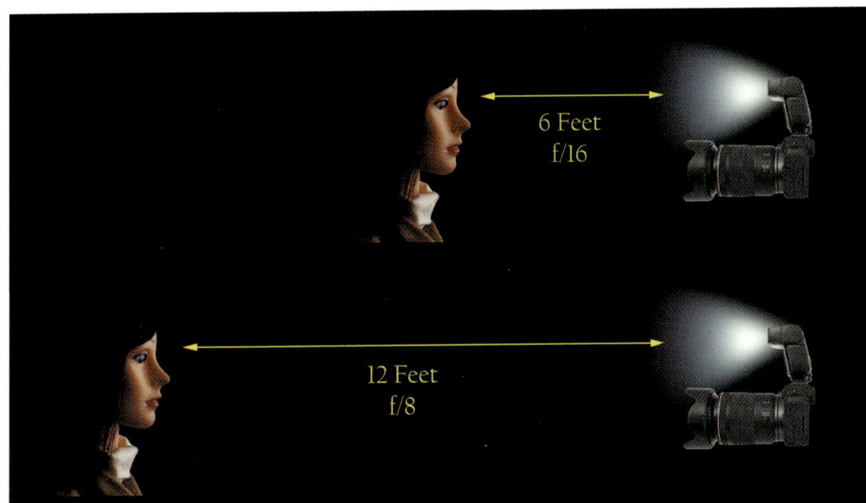

Figure 9.6 Because of the inverse square law, a subject that's twice as far away receives two stops, worth less illumination.

External Speedlite Control

The Shooting 3 menu's External Speedlite control menu offers seven options, plus Clear Settings (six are shown in Figure 9.7). The next sections will explain your choices, which are also discussed in Chapter 11.

Flash Firing

This menu entry has two options: Enable and Disable. It can be used to activate or deactivate any attached external electronic dedicated flash unit. When disabled, the flash cannot fire even if you have an accessory flash attached and turned on. However, you should keep in mind that the AF-assist beam can still be used. If you want to disable that, too, you'll need to turn it off using the AF-Assist Beam Firing entry in the AF 3 menu.

E-TTL Balance

As I explained in the "Ghost Images" section earlier in this chapter, when using flash your image is always comprised of two different exposures: one by the ambient illumination and a second exposure from the flash. These dual exposures are a problem only when your subject is moving, and the ambient illumination produces that "ghost" image in addition to the static image recorded by the flash.

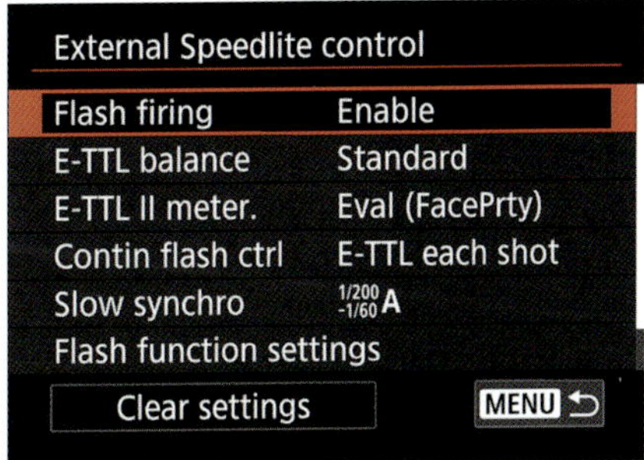

Figure 9.7 The External Speedlite control menu has several options, plus Clear Settings.

At other times, ambient illumination can be useful, lighting up the background area that is too far from the flash to be lit evenly. This entry allows you to specify how the camera mixes ambient and flash illumination by using slower shutter speeds, when useful, to allow ambient light to fill in those backgrounds. You can choose Standard (the default), which gives Speedlite and existing illumination equal weight. With the Ambience Priority setting, the existing light dominates, and the flash is used as fill light to brighten shadows. If you don't care about the background, or are concerned about ghost images with subjects that aren't stationary, choose Flash Priority instead. The Speedlite becomes the main light source, illuminating both your subject and the background. This mode may work best under dim lighting conditions in which not much ambient illumination is available.

E-TTL II Metering

When you're using E-TTL II mode, you can specify whether the camera uses Evaluative (Matrix) or Average metering modes for the electronic flash exposure meter. A third option, Evaluative (Face-priority) gives extra exposure emphasis to faces detected in a scene. Both types of Evaluative metering intelligently look at selected areas in the scene and compares its measurements to a database of typical scene "layouts" to calculate exposure, while Average calculates flash exposure by reading the entire scene. Your choice becomes active when you select E-TTL II as your flash mode, using the entry listed first on this menu screen, and described in more detail in the next section.

Continuous Flash Control

You can use flash when shooting continuously and use this entry to control whether the camera re-calculates exposure before every shot (choose E-TTL Each Shot), or uses the exposure determined for the first exposure in a sequence for all subsequent photos (choose E-TTL 1st Shot). The last option is useful when you want the highest continuous shooting speed and works best when you are not recomposing between shots. That's because if you reframe (or if your subject moves) the exposure may change, and the first shot setting may be less than optimal.

Slow Synchro

You can select the flash synchronization speed that will be used when working in Aperture-priority mode. In Aperture-priority mode when using flash, you specify the f/stop to be locked in. The exposure is then adjusted by varying the output of the electronic flash (rather than by adjusting the shutter speed, which is the norm with non-flash images). Because the primary exposure comes from the flash, the main effect of the shutter speed selected is on the *secondary* exposure from the ambient light within the scene.

The 1/200-30 second Auto option is your best choice under most conditions. The camera will choose a shutter speed that balances the flash exposure and available, ambient light. The 1/200-1/60 Auto setting locks out slower shutter speeds, preventing blur from camera/subject movement in the secondary ("ghost") exposure. However, the background may be rendered dark, if the flash is not strong enough to illuminate it. The 1/200th-second (fixed) setting further reduces the chance of getting those blurry ghosts, but there is more of a chance the background will be dark.

Here are your options:

- **1/200-30 second auto.** The camera selects the shutter speed from 30 seconds to 1/200th second; however, high-speed sync (HSS) can also be activated at the flash.

- **1/200-1/60 auto.** Only shutter speeds from 1/200th to 1/60th second will be used. This locks out shutter speeds slower than 1/60th second and is useful when you want to avoid blur in the secondary, ambient-light exposure due to subject movement and/or camera shake. The camera will always expose the main subject correctly using the flash, but, as noted earlier, the unavailability of slower shutter speeds may mean that the camera is unable to balance the flash with ambient illumination, making the background too dark. HSS is not possible in Av mode with this setting.

- **1/200 sec. (fixed).** A shutter speed of 1/200th second will be used with flash at all times. Use this setting when you want to make sure that the highest flash sync speed is used, minimizing the possibility of blur in the secondary, ambient-light exposure. As with the previous setting, using a fixed 1/200th-second shutter speed may cause the background to appear darker because less of the ambient light can be used to balance the exposure. HSS is not possible in P or Av modes with this setting.

Flash Function Settings

This entry (see Figure 9.8) provides access to functions that may differ between different flash units. Because the available features may vary, you can't access this screen unless the Speedlite you'll be using is attached and powered up; the camera needs to know what flash it is working with to properly display this submenu. It has six sections that can be used to adjust flash mode, wireless functions, zoom head coverage, shutter sync, flash exposure compensation, and flash exposure bracketing.

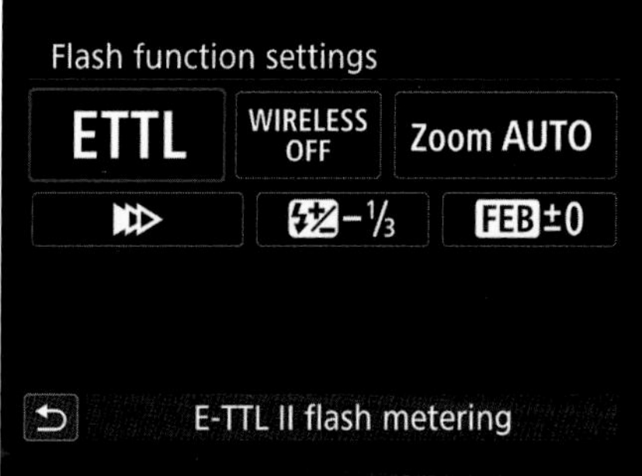

Figure 9.8 The entries in the Flash Function Settings screen.

- **Flash mode.** This entry offers several choices, depending on the modes your flash offers (check your Speedlite's manual to see the full list of specialized flash modes for your unit):

  - **E-TTL.** This E-TTL II is the standard mode for EX-series Speedlites.

  - **M.** This Manual flash can be used to set a fixed flash output, from full power (1/1) to 1/128th power.

  - **MULTI.** This MULTI flash is used to produce stroboscopic effects.

- **External Auto/External Manual.** Some flash units include a metering sensor on the flash itself. When you specify either of those choices, through-the-lens (E-TTL II) metering is disabled, and the flash's external sensor will be used to measure exposure instead. You'll find in most cases that E-TTL II metering is more accurate, and preferable for applications like balanced fill flash outdoors or balancing ambient light and flash indoors when using Av or Tv modes.

  While these external metering modes are often considered obsolete, some find them useful, say, when removing the flash from the camera to illuminate backgrounds or other objects—including macro subjects—from an angle. The Speedlite still needs to be connected with a cable, such as the Canon OC-E3, but you can position the flash anywhere the cable can stretch to.

  With External A, when you take a photo, the flash output is adjusted according to the aperture and ISO speed you've chosen. Press the shutter release halfway to see the effective flash range. With External M, you must manually tell the flash unit the aperture and ISO speed set on the camera. This manual mode allows connecting the Speedlite to the camera using a "dumb" PC/X terminal or adapter. The main reason you might want to use this type of connection is because PC/X cables are available in much longer lengths than the "intelligent" OC-E3 cable. It's a stretch, but this feature is available if you need it.

- **CSP.** If your flash offers the continuous shooting priority mode, the flash output will be automatically decreased by one stop, ISO sensitivity is set to Auto, and Safety FE is automatically enabled. These adjustments allow you to shoot continuously if you need to and conserve your flash's battery power in both continuous and single-shot modes. Because of the adjustments the camera makes for you in this mode, you should check your ISO settings after you stop using the flash and reset them to your preferred values if necessary.

- **Wireless functions.** Functions vary, depending on the attached Speedlite. If you're not working with wireless flash, your only choice is Wireless: OFF. If you do want to use an attached flash (or a flash trigger unit) as a sender flash, multiple additional options may appear, such as Wireless: Optical Transmission; Wireless: Radio Transmission; and, with either of those two, additional functions, such as mode, channel, firing group, and other options become available. These options are explained in Chapter 10.

- **Zoom.** When using a compatible (zoomable) flash, select this entry and press the Q/SET button. Then, you can rotate the Quick Control dial to choose Auto (the flash zooms to the correct setting based on information about focal length supplied to the flash by the camera) or 24mm, 28mm, 35mm, 50mm, 70mm, 80mm, or 105mm (available with the older 580EX II) plus 135mm and 200mm (with the 600EX II-RT and EL-1).

- **Flash exposure compensation.** If you'd rather adjust flash exposure using a menu than with the Quick Control screen, you can do that here. Select this option with the Q/SET button, then dial in the amount of flash EV compensation you want using the Quick Control dial. The EV that was in place before you started to make your adjustment is shown as a blue indicator, so you can return to that value quickly. Press Q/SET again to confirm your change, then press the MENU button twice to exit. Keep in mind that using this entry overrides any flash exposure compensation you might set with any flash function settings.

- **Flash exposure bracketing (FEB).** This option is available with flash units that support Flash Exposure Bracketing. It operates similarly to regular exposure bracketing, discussed in Chapter 4. Highlight this entry, press SET, and you can rotate the QCD, or use the directional controls to specify up to four stops of compensation over/under the metered exposure for a set of three flash pictures.

If you enable wireless flash, additional options appear in this menu. I'll cover these in more detail in Chapter 10:

- **Channel.** All flashes used wirelessly can communicate on one of four channels. This setting allows you to choose which channel is used. Channels are especially helpful when you're working around other Canon photographers; each can select a different channel so one photographer's flash units don't trigger those of another photographer.

- **Sender flash firing.** You can enable or disable use of the external flash as the sender controller for the other wireless flashes. When set to enable, the attached external flash is used as the sender.

- **Flash firing group.** Multiple flash units can be assigned to a group. This choice allows specifying which groups are triggered, A/B, A/B plus C, or All. The 600EX-RT/600EX II-RT and EL-1 offer additional groups when using radio control mode, Groups D and E.

- **A:B fire ratio.** If you select A/B or A/B plus C, this option appears, and allows you to set the proportionate outputs of Groups A and B, in ratios from 8:1 to 1:8.

- **Group C exposure compensation.** If you select A/B plus C, this option appears, too, to the right of the Fire Ratio icon, allowing you to set flash exposure compensation separately for Group C flashes.

Flash C.Fn Settings

This menu entry produces a screen that allows you to set any available Custom Functions in your flash, *from the camera.* The functions available will depend on the C.Fn settings included in the flash unit. The EL-100 has only two Custom Functions, while the more top-of-the-line models EX600 II-RT and EL-1, each have 23 Custom Functions (see Figure 9.9). To set flash Custom Functions, rotate the QCD to choose the C.Fn number to be adjusted, then press SET. Rotate the QCD again to choose from that function's options, then press Q/SET again to confirm.

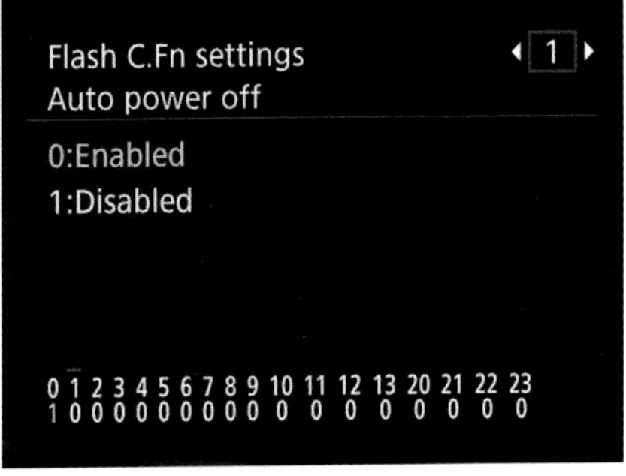

Figure 9.9 Custom Functions for your Speedlite can be set from the camera's Flash C.Fn menu.

Clear Settings

Select this menu entry, located at the bottom of the screen, and you'll be asked if you want to change all the flash settings to their factory default values. You have two choices: Clear Flash Settings (the settings internal to the camera) and Clear All Speedlite C.Fn's, which returns all the *attached* Speedlite's Custom Function settings to their factory defaults. The only exception is C.Fn-0: Distance Indicator Display, which will remain at its set value.

Using Flash Settings

This section includes some tips for using the available Flash settings.

When to Disable Flash Firing

There are a few applications where I always disable my flash and AF-assist beam, even though my camera won't fire an attached flash without my intervention anyway. Some situations are too important to take chances.

- **Venues where flash is forbidden.** I've discovered that many No Photography signs actually mean "No Flash Photography," either because those who make the decisions feel that flash is distracting, or they fear it may potentially damage works of art. Tourists may not understand the difference between flash and available-light photography or may be unable to set their camera to turn off the flash. One of the first phrases I learn in any foreign language is "Is it permitted to take photos if I do not use flash?" Fortunately, the word "flash" has come to mean camera electronic flash in many languages, and quite a few tongues have adopted the English expression "OK," too. So "OK (sin, sans, senza, sem) flash?" usually works in Spanish, French, Italian, and Portuguese, respectively, with no problem. A polite request, while brandishing an advanced camera like the R8 (which may indicate you know what you are doing), can often result in permission to shoot away.

- **Venues where flash is ineffective anyway.** We've all seen the concert goers who stand up in the last row to shoot flash pictures from 100 yards away. I tend to not tell friends that their pictures are not going to come out, because they usually come back to me with a dismal, grainy shot (actually exposed by the dim available light) that they find satisfactory, just to prove I was wrong.

- **Venues where flash is annoying.** If I'm taking pictures in a situation where flash is permitted, but mostly supplies little more than visual pollution, I'll disable or remove it from the camera entirely. Concerts or religious ceremonies may *allow* flash photography, but who needs to add to the blinding bursts when you have a camera that will take perfectly good pictures at ISO 3200? Of course, I invariably see one or two people flashing away at events where flash is not allowed, but that doesn't mean I am eager to join in the festivities.

More on Flash Modes

In choosing Flash mode, you have up to four main choices. The available modes are E-TTL II, the standard mode for EX-series Speedlites; Manual flash, which you can use to set a fixed flash output, from full power (1/1) to 1/128th power; MULTI flash, used to produce stroboscopic effects; and high-speed sync.

E-TTL II

You'll leave Flash mode enabled most of the time. In this mode, the camera fires a pre-flash prior to the exposure, and measures the amount of light reflected to calculate the proper settings. As noted earlier, when you've selected the E-TTL II flash mode, you can also choose Evaluative, Evaluative (Face-priority), or Average metering methods. If you select Manual flash or MULTI flash, that option is removed from the menu.

Manual Flash

Use this setting when you want to specify exactly how much light is emitted by the flash, and don't want the E-TTL II exposure system to calculate the f/stop for you. When you activate this option, a new entry appears in the Flash Func. Setting menu, with a sliding scale from 1/1 (full power) to 1/128th power. (The EL-1 has 14 stops worth of manual power variations, up to 1/8192nd power.) Highlight the scale and press the Q/SET button. You can then rotate the QCD and choose any of the settings. (Only 1/4, 1/2, 1/1, and the intermediate settings between them appear when 1/1 is chosen; view the other power settings by rotating the QCD counterclockwise.) A blue dot appears under the 1/1 setting, and a white dot appears under your new setting, a reminder that you've chosen something other than full power.

Here are some situations where you might want to use manual flash settings:

- **Close-ups.** You're shooting macro photos and the E-TTL II exposure is not precisely what you'd like. You can dial in exposure compensation or set the output manually. Close-up photos are problematic, because the power of the flash may be too much (choose 1/128th power or a higher setting with the EL-1, to minimize the output), or the reflected light may not be interpreted accurately by the through-the-lens metering system. Manual flash gives you greater control.

- **Fill flash.** Although E-TTL II can be used in full daylight to provide fill flash to brighten shadows or add a catchlight to a human subject's eyes, using manual flash allows you to tweak the amount of light being emitted in precise steps. Perhaps you want just a little more illumination in the shadows to retain a dramatic lighting effect without the dark portions losing all detail. Again, you can try using exposure compensation to make this adjustment, but I prefer to use manual flash settings. (See Figure 9.10.)

- **Action stopping.** The lower the power of the flash, the shorter the effective exposure. Use 1/128th power in a darkened room (so that there is no ambient light to contribute to the exposure and cause a "ghost" image) and you can end up with a "shutter speed" that's the equivalent of 1/50,000th second!

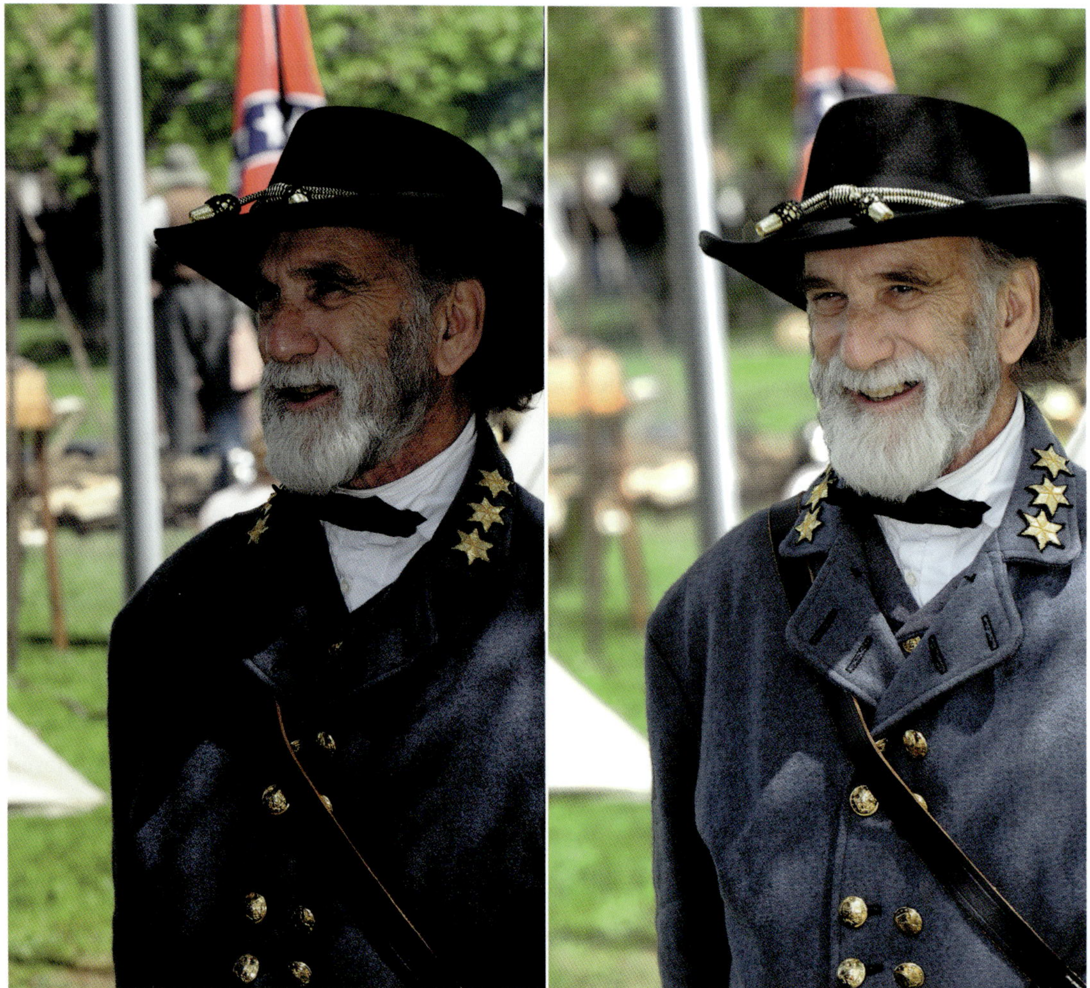

Figure 9.10 You can fine-tune fill illumination by adjusting the output of your camera's flash manually.

MULTI Flash

The MULTI flash setting makes it possible to shoot cool stroboscopic effects, with the flash firing several times in quick succession. You can use the capability to produce multiple images of moving objects, to trace movement (say, your golf swing). When you've activated MULTI flash, three parameters appear on the Flash Function Setting menu, as shown in Figure 9.11. They include:

- **Flash output.** Similar to the Flash Output option in Manual mode, you can choose the intensity of each individual flash in your multiple flash sequence, from 1/4 to 1/128th power (the 1/1 and 1/2 power settings are not available).

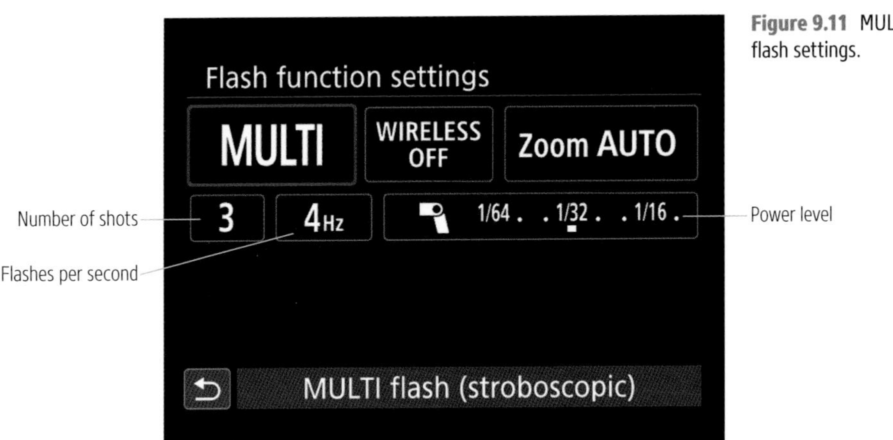

Figure 9.11 MULTI flash settings.

- **Frequency.** This figure specifies the number of bursts per second. With the external flash, you can choose (theoretically) 1 to 199 bursts per second (or up to 500 bursts per second with the EL-1). The actual number of flashes produced will be determined by your flash count (which turns off the flash after the specified number of flashes), flash output (higher output levels will deplete the available energy in your flash unit), and shutter speed.

- **Flash count.** This setting determines the number of flashes in a given burst and can be set from 1 to 30 flashes.

These factors work together to determine the maximum number of flashes you can string together in a single shot. The exact number will vary, depending on your settings and your Speedlite model. Here are some guidelines you can use:

- **Power level.** As you cut the power from 1/4 to 1/128th (and beyond), the output of the flash drops dramatically, and so does the maximum distance you can shoot at any particular f/stop. The 1/4 power setting, the most powerful setting available with MULTI flash, will give you the greatest flash range in this mode. With your sensitivity set to ISO 1600, your flash will allow you to photograph a subject at 10 feet using f/8 and one-quarter power. (If you remember the discussion of guide numbers from earlier in this chapter, the flash would have an effective GN of 80 at ISO 1600.)

If you wanted to use the 1/16th power setting instead, you'd need to use f/4 to account for the reduced output of the flash. By the time you dial down to 1/128th power, your flash has a feeble guide number of about 14 (at ISO 1600!), so to shoot at f/4 you'd be able to locate your subject *no farther* than 3.5 feet from the camera.

The output level also determines the maximum number of flashes that are possible before the charge stored in your flash's capacitor is depleted. The capacitor partially recharges itself as you shoot, so the number of flashes also varies by the flashes-per-second rate. At the 1Hz (one flash per second) rate and 1/4 power, you can expect about 6 to 7 flashes before the Speedlite's power poops out. By the time you reach 10Hz (10 flashes per second) and higher, the unit can crank out no more than two flashes per second at 1/4 power.

Logically, as output levels decrease, more flashes can be pumped out in a given time period. At 1/128th power, you can expect as many as 100 flashes at the 1Hz rate, and up to 40 consecutive flashes at the 20Hz to 199Hz frequency.

- **Flashes per second.** Cycles per second are, by convention, measured using an increment called *Hertz*. The more flashes you want during the time the shutter is open, the higher the rate you must select. You can select rates of 1Hz to 199Hz, or 1 to 199 flashes per second (or up to 500 flashes per second with the EL-1), plus "- -" (more on that later). To maximize the number of flashes in a second, you'll also need to choose the lowest power output level that you find acceptable. The flash unit can emit a lot more fractional 1/128th power bursts in a given period of time than it can more robust (relatively) 1/4 power bursts.

  When you choose "- -" for your frequency, the flash will continue firing until the shutter closes, or its internal storage is depleted. (In any case, you should not use the MULTI flash feature for more than 10 consecutive pictures. At that point, you should allow the flash to "rest" for at least 15 minutes. But don't worry, the unit will shut down automatically to avoid overheating.)

  I like to shoot "strobing" flash pictures in dark rooms against a dark backdrop and use a long exposure to capture multiple images in a single frame, like the (yet another) plummeting fruit example seen in Figure 9.12.

- **Number of shots.** Choose the number of flashes, from 1 to 30, that you want in your multiple exposure, given the output and flash frequency constraints described above.

High-Speed Sync

High-speed sync is a special mode that allows you to synchronize a compatible external flash at all shutter speeds, rather than just 1/200th-second and slower. The entire frame is illuminated by a series of continuous bursts as the shutter opening moves across the sensor plane, so you do *not* end up with a horizontal black band, as shown earlier in Figure 9.4.

HSS is especially useful in three situations, all related to problems associated with high ambient light levels:

- **Eliminate "ghosts" with moving images.** When shooting with flash, the primary source of illumination may be the flash itself. However, if there is enough available light, a secondary image may be recorded by that light (as described under "Ghost Images" earlier in this chapter). If your main subject is not moving, the secondary image may be acceptable or even desirable. But if your subject is moving, the secondary image creates a ghost image.

  High-speed sync gives you the ability to use a higher shutter speed. If ambient light produces a ghost image at 1/200th second, upping the shutter speed to 1/500th or 1/1000th second may eliminate it.

  Of course, HSS *reduces* the amount of light the flash produces. If your subject is not close to the camera, the waning illumination of the flash may force you to use a larger f/stop to capture the flash exposure. So, while shifting from 1/200th second at f/8 to 1/500th second at f/8 *will* reduce ghost images, if you switch to 1/500th second at f/5.6 (because the flash is effectively less intense), you'll end up with the same ambient light exposure. Still, it's worth a try.

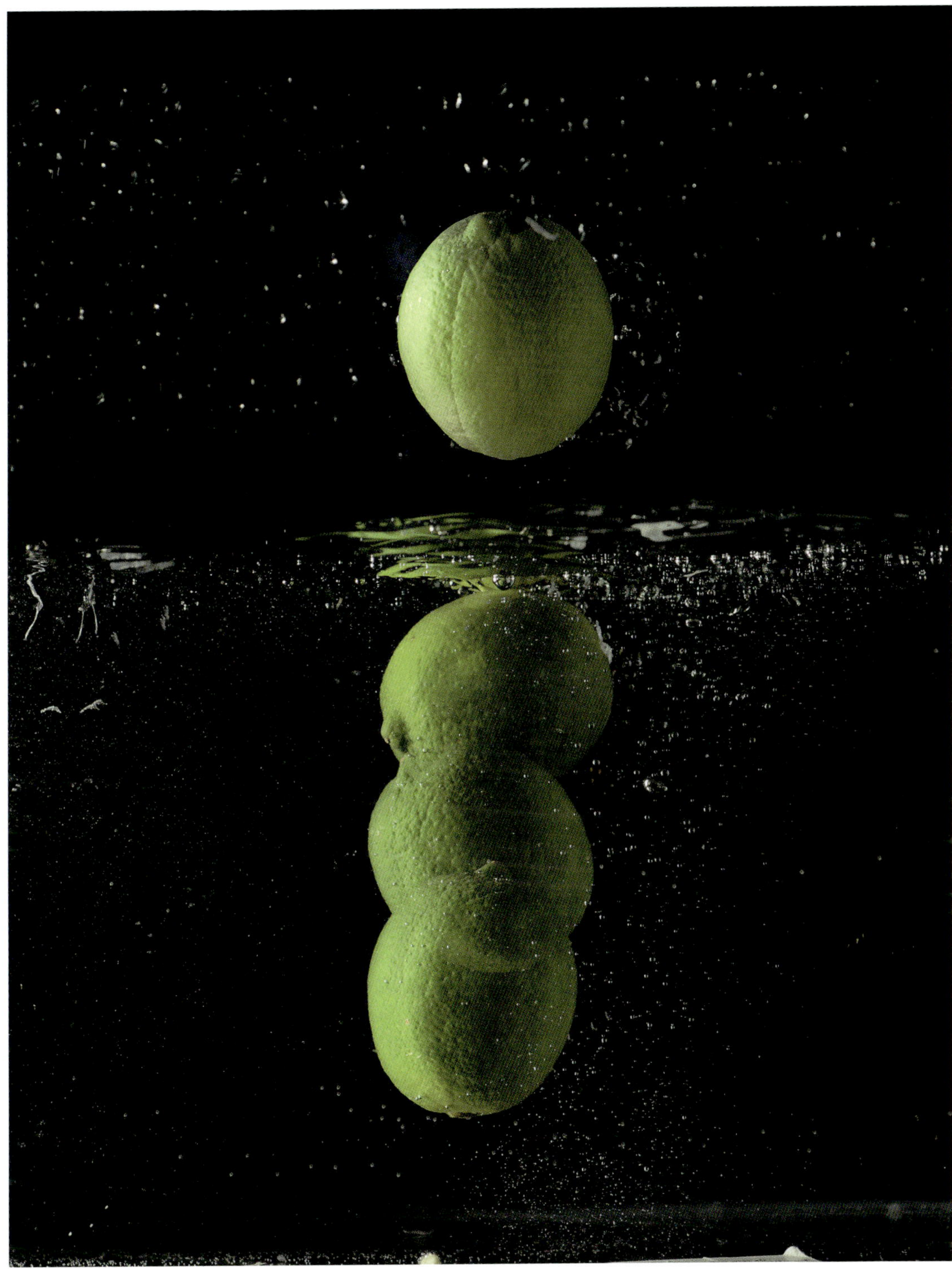

Figure 9.12 Four bursts during the exposure yielded this exciting photo of a drowning lime.

- **Improved fill flash in daylight.** The camera can use an attached flash unit to fill in inky shadows—both automatically and using manually specified power ratios, as described earlier in this chapter. However, both methods force you to use a 1/200th-second (or slower) shutter speed. That limitation can cause three complications.

  First, in very bright surroundings, such as beach or snow scenes, it may be difficult to get the correct exposure at 1/200th second. You might have to use f/16 or a smaller f/stop to expose a given image, even at ISO 100. If you want to use a larger f/stop for selective focus, then you encounter the second problem—1/200th second, for example, won't allow apertures wider than f/8 or f/5.6 under many daylight conditions at ISO 100. (See the discussion of fill flash with Aperture-priority in the next bullet.)

  Finally, if you're shooting action, you'll probably want a faster shutter speed, if at all possible, under the current lighting. That's because, in fill-flash situations, the ambient light (often daylight) provides the primary source of illumination. For many sports and fast-moving subjects, 1/500th second, or faster, is desirable. HSS allows you to increase your shutter speed and still avail yourself of fill flash. This assumes that your subject is close enough to your camera that the fill flash has some effect; forget about using fill and HSS with subjects a dozen feet away or farther. The flash won't be powerful enough to have much effect on the shadows.

- **When using fill flash with Aperture-priority.** The difficulties of using selective focus with fill flash, mentioned earlier, become particularly acute when you switch to Av exposure mode. Selecting f/5.6, f/4, or a wider aperture when using flash is guaranteed to create problems when photographing close subjects, particularly at ISO settings higher than ISO 100. If you own a compatible external flash unit, HSS may be the solution you are looking for.

To use high-speed sync, just follow these steps:

1. **Attach the flash.** Mount/connect the external flash on the camera, using the hot shoe or a dedicated flash cable. (HSS cannot be used in wireless radio mode with the 600EX II-RT, nor with a flash linked through the PC terminal.)

2. **Power up.** Turn the flash and camera on.

3. **Select HSS in the camera.** Set the Flash Function setting *in the camera* to HSS as the camera's sync mode.

4. **Choose HSS on the flash.** Activate HSS (FP flash) on your attached external flash. With the older (but still common) Speedlite 580EX II, press the High-speed sync/Sync button on the back of the flash unit (it's the second from the right under the LCD). If you're using the 600EX II-RT, press the #4 function button (of the array under the LCD) until the HSS icon appears on the LCD. With the EL-1, push the flash's joystick vertically and select HSS from the menu that appears.

5. **Confirm HSS is active.** The HSS icon will be displayed on the flash unit's LCD, and at bottom left in the camera's viewfinder. If you choose a shutter speed of 1/200th second or slower, the indicator will not appear in the viewfinder, as HSS will not be used at slower speeds.

6. **View minimum/maximum shooting distance.** Choose a distance based on the maximum shown in the line at the bottom of the flash's LCD display (from 0.5 to 18 meters).

7. **Shoot.** Take the picture. To turn off HSS, press the button on the flash again. Remember that you can't use MULTI flash or Wireless flash when working with high-speed sync.

Using External Electronic Flash

Once the capacitor is charged, the burst of light that produces the main exposure can be initiated by a signal from the camera that commands the internal or connected flash units to fire. External strobes can be linked to the camera in several different ways:

- **Camera-mounted/hardwired external dedicated flash.** Units offered by Canon or other vendors that are compatible with Canon's lighting system can be clipped onto the accessory "hot" shoe on top of the camera or linked through a wired system such as the Canon Off-Shoe Camera Cord OC-E3 or equivalent third-party cable.

- **Wireless dedicated flash.** A compatible unit can be triggered by signals produced by a pre-flash (before the main flash burst begins), which offers two-way communication between the camera and flash unit. The triggering flash can be an external flash unit in sender mode, or a wireless non-flashing accessory, such as the Canon Speedlite Transmitter ST-E2 optical unit and the radio-controlled wireless trigger, the Speedlite Transmitter ST-E3-RT, which each do nothing but "talk" to the external flashes. You'll find more on this mode in Chapter 10.

- **Wired, non-intelligent mode.** If you connect a flash to a PC/X adapter attached to the hot shoe, you can use non-dedicated flash units, including studio strobes, through a non-intelligent camera/flash link that sends just one piece of information, one way: it tells a connected flash to fire. There is no other exchange of information between the camera and flash. The PC/X connection can be used to link the camera to studio flash units, manual flash, flash units from other vendors that can use a PC cable, or even Canon-brand Speedlites that you elect to connect to the camera in "unintelligent" mode.

- **Infrared/radio transmitter/receivers.** Another way to link flash units to the camera is through third-party wireless infrared or radio *transmitters*, like a PocketWizard, Radio Popper, or the Paul C. Buff CyberSync trigger. These are generally mounted on the accessory shoe of the camera and emit a signal when the camera sends a command to fire through the hot shoe. The simplest of these function as a wireless dumb (PC/X-type) connector, with no other communication between the camera and flash (other than the instruction to fire). However, sophisticated units have their own built-in controls and can send additional commands to the receivers when connected to compatible flash units. I use one to adjust the power output of my Alien Bees studio flash from the camera, without the need to walk over to the flash itself.

- **Simple receiver connection.** In the days before intelligent wireless communication, the most common way to trigger off-camera, non-wired flash units was through a *receiver* unit. These can be small external triggers connected to the remote flash (or built into the flash itself) and set off when the receiver's optical sensor detects a burst initiated by the camera itself. When it "sees" the main flash (from the camera-attached external flash, or another flash), the receiver flash units are triggered quickly enough to contribute to the same exposure. The main problem with this type of connection—other than the lack of any intelligent communication between the camera and flash—is that the receiver may be fooled by any pre-flashes that are emitted by the other strobes, and fire too soon. Modern receiver triggers have a special "digital" mode that ignores the pre-flash and fires only from the main flash burst.

Canon offers a broad range of accessory electronic flash units for the camera. They can be mounted to the flash accessory shoe or used off-camera with a dedicated cord that plugs into the flash shoe to maintain full communications with the camera for all special features. (Non-dedicated flash units, such as studio flash, can be connected using a PC/X adapter.) They range from the Speedlite EL-1, Speedlite 600EX II-RT, and Speedlite 580EX II, which can correctly expose subjects up to 24 feet away at f/11 and ISO 200, to the 270EX II, which is good out to 9 feet at f/11 and ISO 200. (You'll get greater ranges at even higher ISO settings, of course.) There are also two electronic flash units specifically for specialized close-up flash photography.

I power my Speedlites with Panasonic Eneloop AA nickel–metal hydride batteries. These are a special type of rechargeable battery with a feature that's ideal for electronic flash use. The Eneloop cells, unlike conventional batteries, don't self-discharge over relative short periods of time. Once charged, they can hold onto most of their juice for a year or more. That means you can stuff some of these into your Speedlite, along with a few spares in your camera bag, and not worry about whether the batteries have retained their power between uses. There's nothing worse than firing up your strobe after not using it for a month and discovering that the batteries are dead.

Speedlite EL-1

It may be an oversimplification to call the new Canon Speedlite EL-1 the flagship of the company's electronic flash lineup. At $1,100, such a quantum leap above the previous top-line Canon strobe, the Speedlite 600EX-RT II, probably belongs in a separate category, along with the professional users who can afford this flash. It's really nothing like what we've seen before in a Speedlite from Canon. (See Figure 9.13.)

Start with the battery. Instead of AA cells, EL-1 uses a new LP-EL battery ($110) that looks a lot like the LP-E17NH battery that powers the camera and can be revitalized in the same LC-E6 charger. The new power source allows a lightning-fast 0.9-second recycling time at full power, which means continuous shooting at about one frame per second is possible. An active cooling system helps keep the flash from overheating during rapid-fire shooting of up to 170 frames. You can expect up to 335 flashes with a guide number of 60/197 meters/feet.

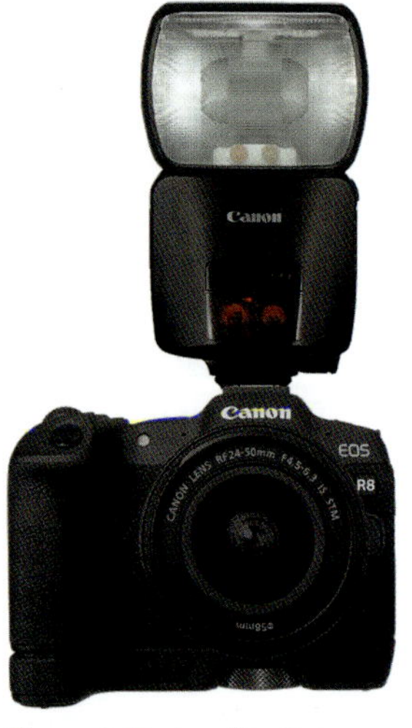

Figure 9.13 Speedlite EL-1.

The EL-1's controls are new, using a command dial and joystick to navigate a new, faster menu system. The flash head swivels 180 degrees, allows bounce flash at angles up to 120 degrees, and has built-in panels (for "white card" fill and catchlights) and wide-angle adjustment. Pro-level weather sealing can withstand extreme environments, and there's an LED modeling light that can be adjusted for brightness and color temperature. As I mentioned earlier, manual flash power settings extend to the equivalent of 14 f/stops—to 1/8192nd power. There's a "memory" option to recall your settings when you switch from auto to manual mode and back again.

Some 13 Custom Functions of the EL-1 can be set using the External Flash C.Fn Setting menu. Additional Personal Functions can be specified on the flash itself. The functions include:

C.Fn-00   Distance indicator display (Meters/Feet)

C.Fn-01   Auto power off (Enabled/Disabled)

C.Fn-02   Modeling flash (Enabled-DOF preview button/Enabled-test firing button/Enabled-both buttons/Disabled)

C.Fn-03   FEB Flash exposure bracketing auto cancel (Enabled/Disabled)

C.Fn-04   FEB Flash exposure bracketing sequence (Metered > Decreased > Increased Exposure/Decreased > Metered > Increased Exposure)

C.Fn-08   AF-assist beam firing (Enabled/Disabled)

C.Fn-10   Receiver auto power-off timer (60 minutes/10 minutes)

C.Fn-11   Cancellation of receiver unit auto power off by sender unit (within 8 hours/within 1 hour)

C.Fn-12   Flash recycling on external power (Use internal and external power/Use only external power)

C.Fn-13   Flash exposure metering setting button (Speedlite button and dial/Speedlite dial only)

C.Fn-21   Light distribution (Standard, Guide number priority, Even coverage)

C.Fn-22   LCD panel illumination (On for 12 seconds, Disable, Always on)

C.Fn-23   Receiver flash battery check (AF-assist beam/Flash lamp, Flash lamp only)

The Personal Functions available include the following:

P.Fn-01   LCD panel display contrast (Five levels of contrast)

P.Fn-02   LCD panel illumination color: Normal (Green, Orange)

P.Fn-03   LCD panel illumination color: Sender (Green, Orange)

P.Fn-04   LCD panel illumination color: Receiver (Green, Orange)

P.Fn-05   Color filter auto detection (Auto, Disable)

P.Fn-06   Wireless button toggle sequence (Normal > Radio > Optical, Normal < > Radio, Normal < > Optical)

P.Fn-07   Flash firing during linked shooting (Disabled, Enabled)

P.Fn-08   Modeling lamp (Brightness, Color)

P.Fn-09   Modeling lamp (Lit time)

Many other features—including zoom head and custom functions—match those of the Speedlite 600EX II-RT, described next.

Speedlite 600EX-RT/600EX II-RT

This former flagship of the Canon accessory flash line (about $500) has the same 197 guide number as the EL-1 and costs half as much. It has a manual/automatic zoom flash head that covers the full frame of lenses from 24mm wide angle to 200mm telephoto. (There's a flip-down, wide-angle diffuser that spreads the flash to cover a 14mm lens's field of view, too.) All angle specifications given by Canon refer to full-frame sensors, but this flash unit automatically converts its field of view coverage to accommodate the 1.6X crop factor. The latest 600EX II-RT has improved continuous flash firing rates (up to 2X faster with an optional CP-E4N battery pack).

The 600EX-RT/II-RT share basic features with the discontinued (but still widely used) 580EX II, described next, so I won't repeat them here, because the typical veteran Canon owner is more likely to own multiple Speedlites.

The killer feature of this series is the wireless two-way radio communication between the camera and this flash (or ST-E3-RT wireless controller and the flash) at distances of up to 98 feet. You can link up to 15 different flash units with radio control, using *five* groups (A, B, C, D, and E), and no line-of-sight connection is needed. (You can hide the flash under a desk or in a potted plant.) With the latest Canon cameras having a revised "intelligent" hot shoe, a second 600EX-RT/600EX II-RT can be used to trigger a *camera* that also has a 600EX-RT/600EX II-RT mounted, from a remote location. That means you can set up multiple cameras equipped with multiple flash units to all fire simultaneously! For example, if you were shooting a wedding, you could photograph the bridal couple from two different angles, with the second camera set up on a tripod, say, behind the altar.

> **600EX (NON-RADIO)**
>
> If you see references to a 600EX model (non-RT), you'll find that a version with the radio control crippled is sold only outside the USA in countries where obtaining permission to use the relevant radio spectrum is problematic.

The 600EX II-RT maintains backward compatibility with optical transmission used by earlier cameras. If you're looking for a high-end flash unit and don't need radio control, I still recommend the Speedlite 580EX II (described next), which is still widely available and is the most-used high-end flash Canon has ever offered.

Remember that with the 600EX II-RT, you can't use radio control and some other features unless you own at least *two* radio-controlled Speedlites, such as an EL-1, 600EX II-RT, or 430EX III-RT (described later), or one EL-1 or 600EX II-RT plus the ST-E3-RT, which costs about $300. Radio control is possible only between a camera that has a radio-capable flash or ST-E3-RT in the hot shoe, and an additional radio-capable flash or ST-E3-RT.

Some 18 Custom Functions of the 600EX II-RT can be set using the External Flash C.Fn Setting menu. Additional Personal Functions can be specified on the flash itself. The functions include:

C.Fn-00   Distance indicator display (Meters/Feet)

C.Fn-01   Auto power off (Enabled/Disabled)

C.Fn-02   Modeling flash (Enabled-DOF preview button/Enabled-test firing button/Enabled-both buttons/Disabled)

C.Fn-03   FEB Flash exposure bracketing auto cancel (Enabled/Disabled)

C.Fn-04   FEB Flash exposure bracketing sequence (Metered > Decreased > Increased Exposure/Decreased > Metered > Increased Exposure)

C.Fn-05   Flash metering mode (E-TTL II/E-TTL/TTL/External metering: Auto/External metering: Manual)

C.Fn-06   Quickflash with continuous shot (Disabled/Enabled)

C.Fn-07   Test firing with autoflash (1/32 / Full power)

C.Fn-08   AF-assist beam firing (Enabled/Disabled)

C.Fn-09   Auto zoom adjusted for image/sensor size (Enabled/Disabled)

C.Fn-10   Receiver auto power-off timer (60 minutes/10 minutes)

C.Fn-11   Cancellation of receiver unit auto power off by sender unit (within 8 hours/within 1 hour)

C.Fn-12   Flash recycling on external power (Use internal and external power/Use only external power)

C.Fn-13   Flash exposure metering setting button (Speedlite button and dial/Speedlite dial only)

C.Fn-20   Beep (Enable/Disable)

C.Fn-21   Light distribution (Standard, Guide number priority, Even coverage)

C.Fn-22   LCD panel illumination (On for 12 seconds, Disable, Always on)

C.Fn-23   Receiver flash battery check (AF-assist beam/Flash lamp, Flash lamp only)

The Personal Functions available include the following. Note that you can set the LCD panel color to differentiate at a glance whether a given flash is functioning in sender or receiver mode.

P.Fn-01   LCD panel display contrast (Five levels of contrast)

P.Fn-02   LCD panel illumination color: Normal (Green, Orange)

P.Fn-03   LCD panel illumination color: Sender (Green, Orange)

P.Fn-04   LCD panel illumination color: Receiver (Green, Orange)

P.Fn-05   Color filter auto detection (Auto, Disable)

P.Fn-06   Wireless button toggle sequence (Normal > Radio > Optical, Normal < > Radio, Normal < > Optical)

P.Fn-07   Flash firing during linked shooting (Disabled, Enabled)

Speedlite 580EX II

If you were using Canon cameras prior to purchasing your R8, you might already own this deposed flagship of the Canon accessory flash line. Despite the introduction of several newer models, this unit is still one of the most widely used Canon Speedlites, popular because of its relatively lower price and wide availability. The 580EX II is powerful, with a GN of 190, and a manual/automatic zoom flash head that covers the full frame of lenses from 24mm wide angle to 105mm telephoto, as well as 14mm optics with a flip-down diffuser.

Like the 600EX II-RT, this unit offers full swivel, 180 degrees in either direction and has its own built-in AF-assist beam. Powered by economical AA-size batteries, the unit recycles in 0.1 to 6 seconds, and can squeeze 100 to 700 flashes from a set of alkaline batteries.

The 580EX II automatically communicates white balance information to your camera, allowing it to adjust WB to match the flash output. You can even simulate a modeling light effect: When you press the depth-of-field preview button on the R8, the 580EX II emits a one-second burst of light that allows you to judge the flash effect. If you're using multiple flash units with Canon's wireless E-TTL system, this model can serve as a master/sender flash that controls the receiver units you've set up (more about this later) or function as a receiver itself.

It's easy to access all the features of this unit, because it has a large backlit LCD panel on the back that provides information about all flash settings. There are 14 Custom Functions that can be controlled from the flash, numbered from 00 to 13. These functions are (the first setting is the default value):

C.Fn-00	Distance indicator display (Meters/Feet)
C.Fn-01	Auto power off (Enabled/Disabled)
C.Fn-02	Modeling flash (Enabled-DOF preview button/Enabled-test firing button/Enabled-both buttons/Disabled)
C.Fn-03	FEB Flash exposure bracketing auto cancel (Enabled/Disabled)
C.Fn-04	FEB Flash exposure bracketing sequence (Metered > Decreased > Increased Exposure/Decreased > Metered > Increased Exposure)
C.Fn-05	Flash metering mode (E-TTL II/E-TTL/TTL/External metering: Auto/External metering: Manual)
C.Fn-06	Quickflash with continuous shot (Disabled/Enabled)
C.Fn-07	Test firing with autoflash (1/32 / Full power)
C.Fn-08	AF-assist beam firing (Enabled/Disabled)
C.Fn-09	Auto zoom adjusted for image/sensor size (Enabled/Disabled)
C.Fn-10	Receiver auto power-off timer (60 minutes/10 minutes)
C.Fn-11	Cancellation of receiver unit auto power off by sender unit (within 8 hours/within 1 hour)
C.Fn-12	Flash recycling on external power (Use internal and external power/Use only external power)
C.Fn-13	Flash exposure metering setting button (Speedlite button and dial/Speedlite dial only)

Speedlite EL-5

The newest addition to the growing EL line of Speedlites, the EL-5 is, at $399, more affordable than the top-tier EL-1, but still has a full list of features, including ability to function as a radio sender or receiver, a rechargeable lithium-ion battery pack, and a modeling lamp to accompany its hefty 197 Guide number. You can expect 350 full-power bursts per charge. It can be triggered continuously for up to 95 flashes in a row, and so is well suited for fast-moving shoots. You can control its settings remotely using the Canon Camera Connect app.

One caveat: It uses the newer multi-function shoe introduced with the initial EOS R mirrorless cameras and cannot be used with older cameras, such as Canon's dSLR models, that use a different hot shoe design, without the AD-E1 multi-function shoe adapter.

Speedlite 470EX-AI

If you don't want to work with your flash detached from the camera, the Speedlite 470EX-AI (about $370) makes the most of on-camera flash, thanks to an Auto Intelligent (AI) bounce function. The flash itself can evaluate the distance and position of nearby walls or ceiling, the focus distance to your subject, and then calculate the optimal bounce angle, and swivel itself into position automatically. It maintains that bounce angle even as you rotate the camera from vertical to horizontal. Just tap the shutter release twice and the flash will reposition its flash head. The feature can be used in full-auto mode, or you can choose a bounce angle yourself (from 0 to 120 degrees of tilt, and plus/minus 180 degrees of rotation).

The flash has a useful 154 guide number, a zoom head with coverage of 24-105mm, and a diffuser that extends flash coverage to 14mm. Although it can't be used as a wireless sender flash, it can be triggered optically by any Canon sender flash or controller.

Speedlite 430EX III-RT

This less pricey electronic flash (available for less than $300) is an affordable replacement for the 580EX II for those who don't need the beefy power of the older Speedlite. It also makes radio control wireless triggering available to those who can't afford the 600EX-RT's price tag. The 430EX III-RT has automatic and manual zoom coverage from 24mm to 105mm, and the same wide-angle pullout panel found on the 600EX-RT/600EX II-RT that covers the area of a 14mm lens on a full-frame camera, and automatic conversion to the cropped frame area of the APS-C format. The 430EX III-RT also communicates white balance information with the camera and has its own AF-assist beam. Compatible with Canon's wireless E-TTL system, it makes a good receiver unit, but it cannot serve as a sender flash. It, too, uses AA batteries, and offers recycle times of 0.1 to 3.7 seconds for 200 to 1,400 flashes, depending on subject distance.

This long-overdue replacement for the 430EX II has as its biggest selling point the ability to communicate either optically (as a receiver) with any compatible sender flash or by radio transmission (as either sender or receiver) with other RT flashes, including the 600EX RT. Previously, you needed either two of the expensive 600EX RT/600EX II-RT units or one 600EX RT/600EX II-RT and an ST-E3-RT trigger to use radio communications.

The Canon Speedlite 430EX III-RT offers a sophisticated set of features, including an LCD panel that allows you to navigate the unit's menu and view its status. These features, along with powerful output and automatic zoom means this unit has more in common with Canon's high-end Speedlites than it does with the 320EX or the 270EX II. The Speedlite 430EX III-RT is compatible with E-TTL II and earlier flash technologies. It can serve as a receiver unit in an optical wireless configuration. The Speedlite 430EX III-RT has a guide number of 43/141 (meters/feet) at ISO 100, at 105mm focal length.

Speedlite 320EX

This $249 flash (see Figure 9.14, left) has a GN of 105. Lightweight and more pocket-sized than the 430EX III-RT and 600EX-RT, this bounceable (both horizontally and vertically) flash has some interesting features, including a built-in LED video light that can be used for shooting movies with the R8, or as a modeling light or even AF-assist beam when shooting with live view. Canon says that this efficient LED light can provide up to four hours of illumination with a set of AA batteries. It can be used as a wireless receiver unit, and it has a flash-release function that allows the shutter to be triggered remotely with a two-second delay.

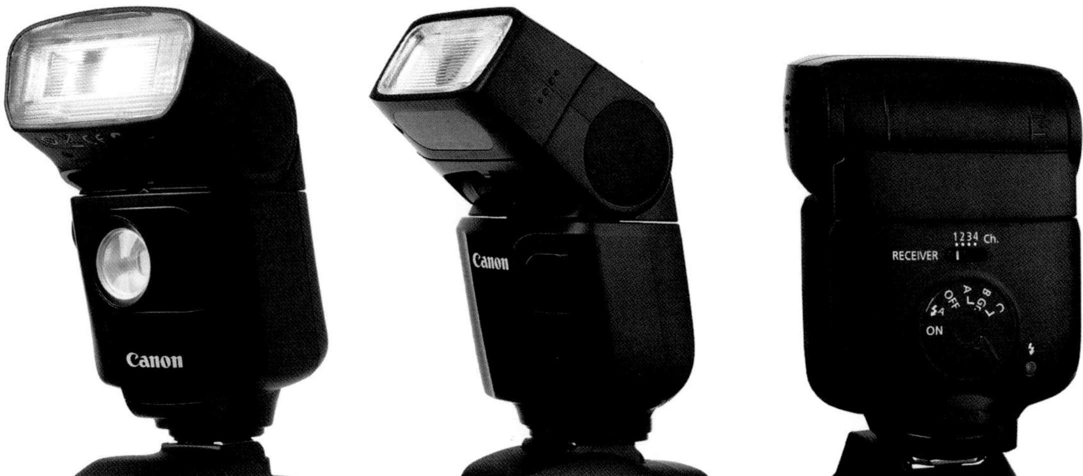

Figure 9.14 The Speedlite 320EX has a built-in video lamp (left). The EL 100 is Canon's most versatile low-cost Speedlite (center and right).

Speedlite EL-100

I got this compact little flash when it was first introduced and have grown especially fond of it. At $150, it's clearly the high-value bargain flash among Canon Speedlites, because it does so many things you don't expect from such an inexpensive unit. If you want to keep your kit's weight reasonable, the EL-100 has most of what you really need, with the only cost being total light output.

It's pleasantly small at about 2.5 × 3.6 × 2.8 inches and weighs less than eight ounces with two AA batteries. (See Figure 9.14, center.) The flash head rotates 180 degrees and pivots up and down from zero to 90 degrees, so you can easily bounce light off a nearby wall or ceiling. (Keep in mind that bounce flash really soaks up a strobe's illumination, and the EL-100 has a guide number of only 85 at ISO 100 when using the 50mm flash coverage setting to begin with.) It recycles in less than six seconds, and signals that it's ready to go with a flash-ready indicator.

The EL-100's controls are simplicity itself; there is no LCD and a plethora of buttons or dials. One switch labeled Receiver allows you to choose Channels 1–4, a rotating dial chooses Off, On, Auto Flash (which allows the camera to decide whether to use flash or not), and assigns the flash to Groups A, B, or C for wireless applications. There's also a flash Test button. That's it. (See Figure 9.14, right.)

The number of flash modes available make this unit quite versatile. You can use E-TTL, Manual, MULTI, or CSP modes using External Flash Functions settings described earlier. In wireless mode, it can serve as an optical sender or receiver, and access the ratio and exposure compensation options described earlier, including light ratio controls and separate Group C exposure compensation. Its burst will normally fill the frame captured by a 24mm lens or zoom setting, but you can adjust it for a 50mm focal length, which gives the unit a bit more range.

The EL-100 can clearly be a strong choice for someone who's already working with a variety of Canon equipment. But any creative photographer can enjoy the Speedlite EL-100 as the highly competent tool it is. In the right hands, it can brighten shots with precision, help you evade overexposure, and enable you to be ready to take on challenging lighting circumstances. And with how simple it is to use, it's not hard to find the right hands to use the EL-100.

I like this unit as an on-camera flash for fill light outdoors, and to trigger wireless Speedlights optically (in such cases, you may not want an extra-powerful flash mounted on the camera anyway). The EL-100 is an economical choice for both functions.

Speedlite 270EX II

The Canon Speedlite 270EX II is designed to work with compatible EOS cameras utilizing E-TTL II and E-TTL automatic flash technologies. This flash unit is entirely controlled from the camera, making it as simple to use as a built-in flash. Its options can be selected and set via the camera's menu system. The 270EX II can also be used as an off-camera receiver unit when controlled by a sender Speedlite, transmitter unit, or a camera with an integrated Speedlite transmitter. One interesting feature of this unit is that it is also a remote-control transmitter, allowing you to wirelessly release the shutter on cameras compatible with certain remote-controller units. The Speedlite 270EX II has a guide number of 27/89 (meters/feet) at ISO 100, with the flash head pulled forward.

This $170 ultra-compact unit is Canon's entry-level Speedlite, and suitable for owners who want a simple strobe for occasional use, without sacrificing the ability to operate it as a wireless receiver unit. With its modest guide number, it provides a little extra pop for fill-flash applications. It has vertical bounce capabilities of up to 90 degrees, and it can be switched between Tele modes to Normal (28mm full-frame coverage) at a reduced guide number of 72.

The 270EX II functions as a wireless receiver unit triggered by any Canon EOS unit or flash (such as the 430EX III-RT) with a sender function. It also has the new flash release function with a two-second delay that lets you reposition the flash. There's a built-in AF-assist beam, and this 5.5-ounce, 2.6 × 2.6 × 3–inch unit is powered by just two AA-size batteries.

Close-Up Lites

Canon has offered three *lites*, especially suitable for close-up photography: the Macro Ring Lite MR-14EX/EX II and Macro Twin Lite flash MD-26EX-RT. As you might guess from their names, these lites are especially suitable for close-up, or macro photography, because they provide a relatively shadowless illumination. It's always tricky photographing small subjects up close, because there often isn't room enough between the camera lens and the subject to position lights effectively. Ring lites, in particular, especially those with their own modeling lamps to help you visualize the illumination you're going to get, mount around the lens at the camera position, and help solve many close-up lighting problems.

But, in recent years, the ring lite has gone far beyond the macro realm and is now probably even more popular as a light source for fashion and glamour photography. The right ring lite, properly used, can provide killer illumination for glamour shots, while eliminating the need to move and reset lights for those shots that lend themselves to ring lite illumination. As you, the photographer, move around your subject, the ring lite moves with you.

One of the key drawbacks to ring lites (whether used for macro or glamour photography) is that they are somewhat bulky and clumsy to use (they must be fastened around the camera lens itself, or the photographer must position the ring lite, and then shoot "through" the opening or ring). That means that you might not be moving around your subject as much as you thought and will, instead, mount the ring lite and camera on a tripod, studio stand, or other support.

Another drawback is the cost. The MR-14EX/MR-14EX II and MR-26EX-RT close-up lites are priced in the $550 and $989 range, respectively. You have to be planning a *lot* of macro or fashion work to pay for one of those. Specialists take note. I tend to favor a third-party substitute for close-up photography, the Alien Bees ABR800 Ringflash. It's priced at about $400, and, besides, it integrates very well with my other Alien Bees studio flash units.

Working with Wireless Flash 10

As I mentioned in the last chapter, one of the chief objections to the use of electronic flash is the stark, flat look of direct/on-camera flash. But as flash wizard Joe McNally, author of *The Hotshoe Diaries*, has proven, small flash units can produce amazingly creative images when used properly.

The key to effective flash photography is to get the flash off the camera, so its illumination can be used to paint your subject in interesting and subtle ways from a variety of angles. But, sometimes, using a cable to liberate your flash from the accessory shoe isn't enough. Nor is the use of just a single electronic flash always the best solution. What we really have needed is a way to trigger one—or more—flash units wirelessly, giving us the freedom to place the electronic flash anywhere in the scene and, if our budgets and time allow, to work in this mode with multiple flashes.

Wireless Evolution

Most Canon "enthusiast"-level cameras with a built-in flash include internal wireless triggering capabilities using the on-camera flash. Because more advanced cameras like the R8 don't have a flash to serve as a wireless sender (master), we must rely on using other flash units or add-ons to trigger our Speedlites wirelessly. Fortunately, most users of this camera are advanced photographers and can generally abide the equipment requirements that accompany useful wireless capabilities.

It's not possible to cover every aspect of wireless flash in one chapter. There are too many permutations involved. For example, you can use an external flash, or the ST-E2 optical transmitter (or ST-E3-RT and ST-E10 radio transmitters) as the sender. You may have one external "receiver" flash or use several. It's possible to control all your wireless flash units as if they were one multi-headed flash, or you can allocate them into "groups" that can be managed individually. You may select one of several "channels" to communicate with your strobes (or any of multiple wireless IDs when using radio-controlled units like the EL-1, EL-5, or 600EX II-RT). These are all aspects that you'll want to explore as you become used to working with the amazing wireless capabilities.

What I hope to do in this chapter is provide the introduction to the basics that you won't find in the other guidebooks, so you can learn how to operate the wireless capabilities quickly, and then embark on your own exploration of the possibilities.

Elements of Wireless Flash

Here are some of the key concepts to electronic flash and wireless flash that I'll be describing in this chapter. Learn what these are, and you'll have gone a long way toward understanding how to use wireless flash. You need to understand the various combinations of flashes that can be used, how they can be controlled individually and together, and why you might want to use multiple and off-camera flash units. I'm going to address all these points in this section.

Flash Combinations

Your attached on-camera external flash can be used alone, or, if it has the capability to serve as a *master or controller flash* (not all Canon Speedlites do), now called *sender* in Canonspeak, in combination with other, external *remote* or *slave* flash units (now called *receivers* by Canon). Here's a quick summary of the permutations available to you:

- **On-camera flash used alone.** Your on-camera flash can function as the only flash illumination used to take a picture. In that mode, the flash can provide the primary illumination source (the traditional "flash photo") with the ambient light in the scene contributing little to the overall exposure. (See Figure 10.1, left.) Or, the on-camera flash can be used in conjunction with the scene's natural illumination to provide a balanced lighting effect. (See Figure 10.1, center.) In this mode, the flash doesn't overpower the ambient light, but, instead, serves to supplement it. Finally, the on-camera flash can be used as a "fill" light in scenes that are illuminated predominantly by a natural main light source, such as daylight. In this mode, the flash serves to brighten dark shadows created by the primary illumination, such as the glaring daylight in Figure 10.1, right.

- **On-camera flash used simultaneously with off-camera flash.** You can use the off-camera flash as a *main light* and supply *fill light* from the on-camera flash to produce interesting effects and pleasing portraits.

- **On-camera flash used as a trigger only for off-camera flash.** Use the on-camera wireless flash controller to command single or multiple Speedlites for studio-like lighting effects, without having the flash contribute to the 8 exposure itself.

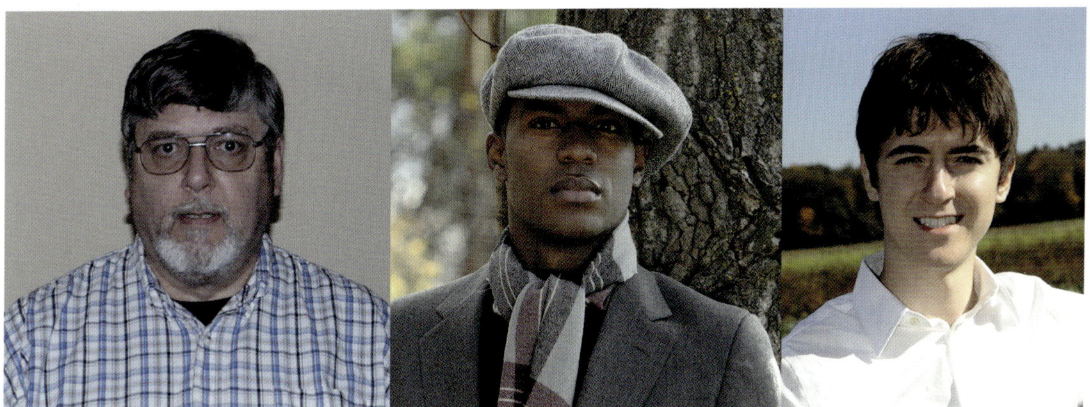

Figure 10.1 On-camera flash alone (left), as a supplement (center), and for fill flash (right).

Controlling Flash Units

There are multiple ways of controlling flash units, both through direct or wired connections and wirelessly. Here are the primary methods used:

- **Direct connection.** The on-camera flash, of course, is directly connected to the camera, and triggered electronically when a picture is taken. External flash units can also be controlled directly by linking them to a camera with a dedicated flash cord that in turn attaches to the accessory hot shoe, such as the Canon OC-E3 EOS Dedicated TTL off-camera shoe cord.

  When used in these modes, the camera has full communication with the flash, which can receive information about zoom lens position, correct exposure required, and the signals required to fire the flash. You can also plug a non-dedicated strobe, such as studio flash units, into an adapter plugged into the R8's hot shoe. Either PC/X connection is "dumb" and conveys no information other than the signal to fire.

- **Dedicated wireless optical signals.** In this mode, external flash units communicate with the camera through a pre-flash, which is used to measure exposure prior to the "real" flash burst an instant later. The pre-flashes can also wirelessly send information from the camera to the flash unit, to determine the duration of the burst to achieve the desired exposure. The pulses also can be used to adjust zoom head position (if the flash has that feature). In the case of Canon flash units, the pre-flash information is sent and received as visible light, sent so quickly just before the main burst that you may not be able to distinguish them from the "real" flash.

- **Dedicated wireless infrared signals.** Some devices, such as the Canon ST-E2 Speedlite Transmitter, can communicate with dedicated flash units through infrared signals—much like the remote control of your television. (And, also like your TV remote, the IR signal can bounce around the room somewhat, but you more or less need a line-of-sight connection for the communication to work properly.) (See Figure 10.2, left, for front and back views.) The transmitter attaches to the accessory shoe or is connected to the accessory shoe through a dedicated cable. It was an option for wireless flash for Canon cameras prior to the EOS 7D (and later models with an in-camera

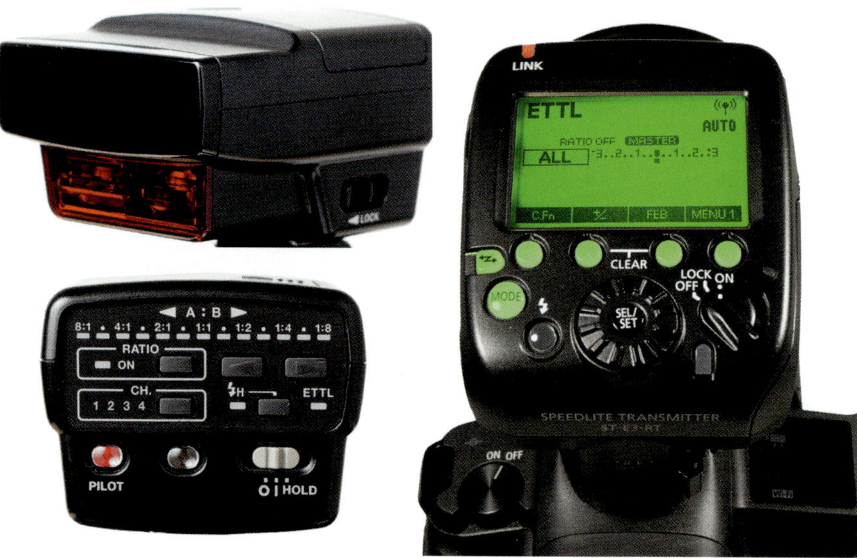

Figure 10.2 The ST-E2 infrared transmitter (left) and ST-E3-RT radio transmitter (right).

wireless controller), as well as for Canon cameras that have no flash unit at all (such as the EOS 1D and 5D series). Although the ST-E2 is expensive, it's still less expensive than using a unit like the 600EX II as an optical sender/controller, particularly when on-camera flash is not desired. However, the EL-100 flash, priced at about $150, may be an even better budget choice as a controller, because it gives you the option to use it as a conventional on-camera or off-camera flash.

- **Canon and third-party IR and radio transmitters.** The EL-1, EL-5, 600EX-RT/600EX II-RT, 430EX III-RT, ST-E10, and ST-E3-RT from Canon can communicate as sender units using radio signals. The EL-1, 600EX-RT, and 600EX II-RT can also serve as a sender optical flash, and as a radio or optical receiver, while the 430 EX III-RT and EL-5 function as a receiver only in optical mode. The ST-E3-RT, shown at right in Figure 10.2, functions *only* as a radio trigger and cannot communicate with flashes that recognize only optical signals. It's priced at about $300. A less expensive option is the ST-E10, at around $120. There were some problems maintaining a link to the camera with this transmitter when it was first introduced, but Canon should have a fix by the time this book is published.

In addition, some excellent wireless flash controllers that use IR or radio signals to operate external flash units are available from sources like Godox, PocketWizard, and RadioPopper. One advantage some of these third-party units have is the ability to dial in exposure/output adjustments from the transmitter mounted on the accessory shoe of the camera.

- **Optical receiver units.** A relatively low-tech/low-versatility option is to use optical receiver units that trigger the off-camera flash units when they detect the firing of the main flash. Receiver triggers are inexpensive, but dumb: they don't allow making any adjustments to the external flash units and are not compatible with the E-TTL II exposure system. Moreover, you should make sure that the receiver trigger responds to the *main* flash burst only, rather than a pre-flash, using a so-called *digital* mode. Otherwise, your receiver units will fire before the main flash, and not contribute to the exposure.

Why Use Wireless Flash?

Canon's wireless flash system gives you a number of advantages that include the ability to use directional lighting, which can help bring out detail or emphasize certain aspects of the picture area. It also lets you operate multiple strobes; with many models that can be four flash units in each of three groups, or twelve in all (although most of us won't own 12 Canon Speedlites). With the EL-1, 600EX-RT/600EX II-RT, and 430EX III-RT, which also have radio control in addition to optical transmission, you can control many more flash units optically, but only 15 radio-controlled Speedlites, in five different groups.

You can set up complicated portrait or location lighting configurations. Since the two top Canon Speedlites pump out a lot of light for a shoe-mount flash, a set of these units can give you near studio-quality lighting. Of course, the cost of these high-end Speedlites approaches or exceeds that of some studio monolights—but the Canon battery-powered units are more portable and don't require an external AC or DC power source.

Key Wireless Concepts

There are three key concepts you must understand before jumping into wireless flash photography: channels, groups, and flash ratios. Here is an explanation of each:

- **Channels.** Canon's wireless flash system offers users the ability to determine on which of four possible channels the flash units can communicate. (The pilots, ham radio operators, or scanner listeners among you can think of the channels as individual communications frequencies.) When using optical transmission, the channels are numbered 1, 2, 3, and 4, and each flash must be assigned to one of them. Moreover, in general, each of the flash units you are working with should be assigned to the *same* channel, because the receiver Speedlites will respond *only* to a sender flash that is on the same channel.

  When using the EL-1, 600EX-RT, or 430EX III-RT in radio control mode, or the ST-E3-RT and ST-E10 transmitters, there are 15 different channels, plus an Auto setting that allows the flash to select a channel. In addition, you can assign a four-digit Wireless Radio ID that further differentiates the communications channel your flashes use.

  The channel ability is important when you're working around other photographers who are also using the same system. Photojournalists, including sports photographers, encounter this situation frequently. At any event populated by a sea of "white" lenses, you'll often find photographers who are using Canon flash units triggered by Canon's own optical or (now) radio control. Third-party triggers from PocketWizard or RadioPopper are also popular, but Canon's technology remains a mainstay for many shooters.

  Each photographer sets flash units to a different channel so as to not accidentally trigger other users' strobes. (At big events with more than four photographers using Canon flash and optical transmission, you may need to negotiate.) I use this capability at workshops I conduct where we have two different setups. Photographers working with one setup use a different channel than those using the other setup and can work independently even though we're at opposite ends of the same large room.

There is less chance of a channel conflict when working with radio control and all radio-compatible Canon flash units. With 15 channels to select from, and almost 10,000 wireless radio IDs to choose from, any overlap is unlikely. (It's smart not to use a radio ID like 0000, 1111, 2222, etc., to avoid increasing the chances of conflicts. I use the last four digits of my mother-in-law's social security number.) Remember that you must use either all optical or all radio transmission for all your flash units; you can't mix and match.

- **Groups.** Canon's wireless flash system lets you designate multiple flash units in separate groups. There can be as many as three groups with earlier Speedlites like the 580EX II, and newer models like the EL-100, labeled A, B, and C.

  With the EL-1, EL-5, 600EX-RT, 430EX III-RT, and ST-E3-RT/ST-E10 transmitters, up to five groups (A, B, C, D, and E) can be used with as many as 15 different flash units. All the flashes in all the groups use the exact same *channel* and all respond to the same sender controller, but you can set the output levels of each group separately. So, Speedlites in Group A might serve as the main light, while Speedlites in Group B might be adjusted to produce less illumination and serve as a fill light. It's convenient to be able to adjust the output of all the units within a given group simultaneously. This lets you create different styles of lighting for portraits and other shots.

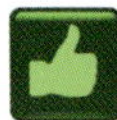

> **TIP** It's often smart to assign flash units that will reside to the left of the camera to the A group, and flashes that will be placed to the right of the camera to the B group. It's easier to adjust the comparative power ratios because you won't have to stop and think where your groups are located. That's because the adjustment controls in the *menus* are always arranged in the same A-B-C left-to-right alignment.
>
> For example, if your A group is used as a main light on the left, and the B group as fill on the right, you intuitively know to specify more power to the A group, and less output to the B group. Reserve the C group (if used) to some other purpose, such as background or hair lights.

- **Flash ratios.** This ability to control the output of one flash (or set of flashes) compared to another flash or set allows you to produce lighting *ratios*. You can control the power of multiple off-camera Speedlites to adjust each unit's relative contribution to the image, for more dramatic portraits and other effects.

Which Flashes Can Be Operated Wirelessly?

A particular Speedlite can have one of two functions. It can serve as a *sender* flash that's capable of triggering other compatible Canon units that are on the same channel. Or, a Speedlite can be triggered wirelessly as a receiver unit that's activated by a sender, with full control over exposure through the camera's eTTL flash system. The second function is easy: all current and many recent Canon shoe-mount flash, including the EL-1, 600EX-RT, 580EX II, 470EX AI, 430EX II, 430EX III, 430EX III-RT, EL-100, 320EX, and 270EX II can be triggered wirelessly. In addition, some Speedlites have the ability to serve as a sender flash.

I'm not going to discuss older flash units in this chapter; if you own one, particularly a non-Canon unit, it may or may not function as a receiver. For example, the early Speedlite 380EX lacked the wireless capabilities added with later models, such as the 420EX, 430EX, 430EX II, 430EX III, and 430EX III-RT.

Here's a quick rundown of current flash capabilities:

- **Canon Speedlite EL-1 or 600EX-RT/600EX II-RT.** These top-of-the-line flashes can function as a sender flash when physically attached to any Canon EOS model, using either optical or radio transmission, and can be triggered wirelessly by another sender flash, such as a compatible EOS model, another EL-1, 600EX-RT/600EX II-RT, or 580EX II, or the ST-E2/ST-E3-RT transmitters.

- **Canon Speedlite EL-5.** This newer flash can function as a sender (in radio mode only) and as a receiver when using both optical and radio technology.

- **Canon Speedlite 580EX II.** This discontinued, but still widely used flash can function as a sender flash when physically attached to any Canon EOS model and can be triggered wirelessly by an optical (not radio) transmission from another sender flash from a compatible EOS camera, another 580EX II, a 600EX-RT, 600EX II-RT, 430EX III-RT, or the ST-E2 transmitter. (The ST-E3-RT transmitter operates in radio mode only.)

- **Canon Speedlite 470EX AI.** This flash can function only as an optical receiver when used off-camera. It cannot serve as a sender.

- **Canon Speedlite 430EX III.** This sibling of the radio-compatible version described next cannot function as a sender but can be used as a receiver when working with optical triggering technology.

- **Canon Speedlite 430EX III-RT.** This newer flash can function as a sender (in radio mode only) and as a receiver when using both optical and radio technology.

- **Canon Speedlite 430EX II.** This discontinued flash cannot function as a sender, but can be triggered wirelessly by a sender flash, including a compatible EOS camera, a Speedlite 600EX-RT/580EX II, or the ST-E2 transmitters.

- **Canon Speedlite 320EX.** This flash can be triggered wirelessly by a sender flash, including a compatible EOS camera, a 600EX-RT/600EX II-RT, 580EX II, or the ST-E2 transmitter.

- **Canon Speedlite 270EX II.** This flash can be triggered wirelessly by a compatible camera's sender flash, a 600EX-RT/600EX II-RT, 580EX II, or the ST-E2 transmitter in optical mode.

- **Canon Speedlite EL-100.** This flash can be triggered wirelessly by a compatible camera's sender flash, a 600EX-RT/600EX II-RT, 580EX II, or the ST-E2 transmitter in optical mode and serve as a sender to trigger other flashes.

You can use any combination of compatible flash units in your wireless setup. You can use an attached 600EX-RT/600EX II-RT, 580EX II, 430EX III-RT, EL-100, or ST-E2/ST-E3-RT/ST-E10 as a sender, with any number of 600EX-RT, 580EX II, 470EX AI, 430EX III, 430EX III-RT, EL-100, 430EX II, 320EX, or 270EX II units (or older compatible Speedlites not discussed in this chapter) as wireless receivers. I'll get you started assigning these flash to groups and channels later on.

Setting Up a Sender/Controller Flash

The first step in working with wireless flash is to set up one unit (either a flash or controller) as the sender. You can mount a Speedlite EL-100, 580EX, 580EX II, EL-1, EL-5, or 600EX-RT/600EX II-RT to your camera, which can serve as the sender unit, transmitting E-TTL II optical signals to one or more off-camera Speedlite receiver units. The sender unit can have its flash output set to "off" so that it controls the remote units with the pre-flash but omitting the main flash so the sender unit does not contribute any illumination of its own to the exposure. This is useful for images where you don't want noticeable flash illumination coming in from the camera position. The next sections explain your options for setting up a sender unit for fully automatic, E-TTL II exposure. You can also use manual exposure instead of E-TTL II automatic exposure in wireless mode. Setting up your sender flash for manual operation is beyond the scope of this introductory wireless chapter.

Using a Speedlite as an Optical Sender

Here are the steps to follow with the on-flash controls to set up and use compatible Speedlites as a camera-mounted sender unit for automatic exposure. (The EL-100 is set up as a sender using the Flash Function settings rather than controls on the flash; when you activate Wireless functions, Channel, Group, and Flash Ratio adjustments become available.) For each individual flash unit described below, check your flash's manual if you have any questions about particular button location.

EL-1

1. Press the joystick on the flash to the left to select flash functions.
2. Highlight Optical (lightning bolt symbol on the flash LCD) sender using the joystick or by rotating the Select dial.
3. Press the joystick vertically to confirm.
4. Use the menu system to control and make changes to RATIO, output, and other options on the sender and receiver units.

600EX-RT/600EX II-RT

1. Press the Wireless button repeatedly until the LCD panel indicates you are in optical wireless sender mode.
2. Press MODE to cycle through the ETTL, M, and Multi modes.
3. Use the menu system to control and make changes to RATIO, output, and other options on the sender and receiver units.

580EX II

1. Press and hold the ZOOM button to bring up the wireless options. Use the Select dial to cycle through the OFF, SENDER on, and RECEIVER on options. Select and confirm SENDER on.
2. Press MODE to cycle through the ETTL, M, and Multi modes.

3. Press the ZOOM button repeatedly to cycle through the following options: Flash zoom, RATIO, CH., and flash emitter ON/OFF. Use the Select dial and Select/SET button to make any changes to these options.

4. Use the Select/SET button to select and confirm the output power settings when using Manual and Multi modes, or to use FEC or FEB when in ETTL mode.

580EX

1. Slide the OFF/SENDER/RECEIVER wireless switch near the base of the unit to SENDER.

2. Press MODE to cycle through the ETTL, M, and Multi modes.

3. Press the ZOOM button repeatedly to cycle through the following options: Flash zoom, RATIO, CH., and flash emitter ON/OFF. Use the Select dial and Select/SET button to make any changes to these options.

4. Use the Select/SET button to select and confirm the output power settings when using Manual and Multi modes, or to use FEC or FEB when in ETTL mode.

Using the ST-E2 Transmitter as Sender

Canon's Speedlite Transmitter (ST-E2) is mounted on the camera's hot shoe and provides a way to control one or more Speedlites and/or units assigned to Groups A and B. The ST-E2 does not provide any flash output of its own and will not trigger units assigned to Group C. It has the following features and controls:

- **Transmitter.** Located on the top front of the unit, the transmitter emits E-TTL II pulses through an infrared filter.

- **AF-assist beam emitter.** Just below the transmitter, the AF-assist beam emitter works similarly to the Speedlite 430EX II and higher models.

- **Battery compartment.** The ST-E2 uses a 6.0V 2CR5 lithium battery. The battery compartment is accessed from the top of the unit.

- **Lock slider and mounting foot.** The lock slider is located on the right side of the unit when facing the front. Sliding it to the left lowers the lock pin in the mounting foot (located on the bottom of the unit) to secure it to the camera's hot shoe.

- **Back panel.** The rear of the unit features several indicators and controls:
  - **Ratio indicator.** A series of red LED lights indicating the current A:B ratio setting.
  - **Flash ratio control lamp.** A red LED that lights up when flash ratio is in use.
  - **Flash ratio setting button.** Next to the flash ratio control lamp. Press this button to activate flash ratio control.
  - **Flash ratio adjustment buttons.** Two buttons with raised arrows (same color as buttons) pointing left and right. Use these to change the A:B ratio setting.
  - **Channel indicator.** The channel number in use (1–4) glows red.

- **Channel selector button.** Next to the channel indicator. Press this button to select the communication channel.
- **High-speed sync (FP flash) indicator.** A red LED that glows when high-speed sync is in use.
- **High-speed sync button.** Press this button to activate/deactivate high-speed sync.
- **ETTL indicator.** A red LED that glows when E-TTL II is in use.
- **Off/On/HOLD switch.** Slide this switch to turn the unit off, on, or on with adjustments disabled (HOLD). The ST-E2 will power off after approximately 90 seconds of idle time. It will turn back on when the shutter button or test transmission button is pressed.
- **Pilot lamp/Test transmission button.** This lamp works similarly to the Speedlite pilot lamp/test buttons. The lamp glows red when ready to transmit. Press the lamp button to send a test transmission to the receiver units.
- **Flash confirmation lamp.** This lamp glows green for about three seconds when the ST-E2 detects a good flash exposure.

Here are the steps to follow to set up and use the ST-E2 transmitter (shown previously at left in Figure 10.2) as a camera-mounted sender unit:

1. Mount the ST-E2 unit on your camera.
2. Make sure both the ST-E2 unit and your camera are powered on.
3. Make sure the receiver units are set to E-TTL II, assigned to the appropriate group(s), and that all units are operating on the same channel.
4. If you'd like to set a flash ratio between Groups A and B, press the flash ratio setting button and flash ratio adjustment buttons to select the desired ratio. Press the high-speed sync button to use high-speed sync (often helpful with outdoor shooting).

Using the Speedlite EL-1 as Radio Sender

The Speedlite EL-1 can serve as the sender unit when mounted to your camera, transmitting radio signals to one or more off-camera Speedlite EL-1, 430EX III-RT, or 600EX-RT/600EX II-RT receiver units. The sender unit can have its flash output set to "off" so that it controls the remote units without contributing any flash output of its own to the exposure. This is useful for images where you don't want noticeable flash illumination coming in from the camera position. Just follow these steps:

1. Press the joystick on the flash to the left to select flash functions.
2. Highlight Radio (wireless antenna symbol on the flash LCD) sender using the joystick or by rotating the Select dial.
3. Press the joystick vertically to confirm.
4. Use the menu system to control and make changes to RATIO, output, and other options on the sender and receiver units.

Using the Speedlite 600EX-RT/600EX II-RT as Radio Sender

The Speedlite 600EX-RT/600EX II-RT can serve as the sender unit when mounted to your camera, transmitting radio signals to one or more off-camera Speedlite 600EX-RT/600EX II-RT receiver units. The sender unit can have its flash output set to "off" so that it controls the remote units without contributing any flash output of its own to the exposure. This is useful for images where you don't want noticeable flash illumination coming in from the camera position.

Here are the steps to follow to set up and use a Speedlite 600EX-RT/600EX II-RT as a camera-mounted sender unit for radio wireless E-TTL II operation:

1. Mount the Speedlite 600EX-RT/600EX II-RT to your camera.

2. Make sure the 600EX-RT sender units, receiver units, and the camera are powered on.

3. Set the camera-mounted unit to radio wireless SENDER mode. Press the Wireless button until the LCD panel indicates you are on radio wireless sender mode.

4. Set the receiver 600EX-RT/600EX II-RT or 430EX III-RT units to radio wireless RECEIVER mode. For each 600EX-RT unit, press the Wireless button until the LCD panel indicates you are on radio wireless receiver mode. For each 430EX III-RT receiver, press the left directional key and rotate the Select dial until Receiver appears on the LCD. Then press the Select button to confirm.

5. Confirm that all units are set to E-TTL II, assigned to the appropriate group(s), and that all units are operating on the same channel and ID number. The LINK lamps on all units should glow green.

Using the Speedlite 430EX III-RT as Radio Sender

The Speedlite 430EX III-RT can serve as a radio sender unit to trigger another 430EX III-RT or a 600EX-RT flash. Just follow these steps:

1. Press the left directional key on the Select dial. It's marked with a lightning bolt symbol.

2. Rotate the Select dial until SENDER appears on the LCD.

3. Press the Select button in the center of the Select dial.

4. Set any 600EX-RT or 430EX III-RT units that you will be using as receivers to the Receiver mode.

   - For the 600EX-RT, press the Wireless button until the LCD panel indicates you are in radio wireless receiver mode.

   - For any 430EX III-RT receivers, press the left directional key and rotate the Select dial until Receiver appears on the LCD. Then press the Select button to confirm.

5. Repeat Step 4 for any additional receiver units.

6. When sender and receivers are communicating, the LINK lamps on all units will glow green.

Using the ST-E3-RT or ST-E10 as a Radio Sender

The ST-E3-RT and ST-E10 transmitters can be mounted to the camera's hot shoe and used as a sender controller to one or more receiver Speedlite 600EX-RT units. The ST-E3-RT/ST-E10 and the 600EX-RT share essentially the same radio control capabilities except that the ST-E3-RT/ST-E10 do not produce flash, provide AF-assist, or otherwise emit light and are therefore incapable of optical wireless transmission.

The layout of the ST-E3-RT's control panel is virtually identical to the 600EX-RT. So is the menu system and operation, except that, as stated earlier, it will only operate as a radio wireless transmitter. (The ST-E10 has only a Menu button. When you press it, the Flash Function Settings screen on the R8 appears.) Here are the steps to follow to set up and use the ST-E3-RT transmitter as a camera-mounted sender unit for radio wireless E-TTL II operation:

1. Mount the ST-E3-RT unit on your camera.
2. Make sure both the ST-E3-RT unit and your camera are powered on.
3. Set the receiver 600EX-RT or 430EX III-RT units to radio wireless RECEIVER mode. For each 600EX-RT unit, press the Wireless button until the LCD panel indicates you are on radio wireless receiver mode. For each 430EX III-RT receiver, press the left directional key and rotate the Select dial until Receiver appears on the LCD. Then press the Select button to confirm.
4. Confirm that all units are set to E-TTL II, assigned to the appropriate group(s), and that all units are operating on the same channel and ID number. The LINK lamps on all units should glow green.

The ST-E3-RT controls receiver units as described earlier in the section, "Using the Speedlite 600EX-RT/600EX II-RT as Radio Sender."

Setting Up a Receiver Flash

The whole point of working wirelessly is to have a sender flash/controller trigger and adjust one or more receiver flash units. So, once you've defined your sender flash, the next step is to switch your remaining Speedlites into receiver mode. That's done differently with each particular Canon Speedlite.

- **Speedlite EL-1.** Use the joystick on the flash as described above and choose Optical Receiver or Wireless Receiver.
- **Speedlite 600EX-RT/600EX II-RT.** Press the Wireless button repeatedly until the LCD panel indicates that the unit is in optical wireless receiver mode or radio wireless receiver mode. In this mode, the 600EX-RT is assigned a flash mode by the sender transmitter, either a flash or ST E2 or ST-E3-RT.
- **Speedlite 580EX II.** Press and hold the ZOOM button until the wireless setting options appear. Use the Select dial and Select/SET button to select and confirm that wireless is on and in receiver mode.

- **Speedlite 430EX III/430EX III-RT.** For each 430EX III-RT receiver, press the left directional key and rotate the Select dial until Receiver appears on the LCD. Then press the Select button to confirm.

- **Speedlite 430EX II.** Press and hold the ZOOM button for two seconds or more until the wireless setting options appear. Use the Select dial and Select/SET button to select and confirm that wireless is on and in receiver mode.

- **Speedlite 320EX.** This flash has an On/Off/Receiver switch at the lower left of the back panel. In Receiver mode, you can use the flash's C.Fn-10 setting to tell the unit to power down after either 10 or 60 minutes of idle time. That can help preserve the 320EX's batteries. The unit's C.Fn-11 setting can be set to allow the sender transmitter to "wake" a sleeping 320EX after your choice of within 1 hour or within 8 hours. Note that the C.Fn settings of the 320EX and 270EX II (described next) can be set only while the Speedlites are connected to the camera with the hot shoe.

- **Speedlite 270EX II.** This flash has an Off/Receiver/On switch. If left on and idle, the 270EX II will power itself off after approximately 90 seconds. C.Fn-1 can be used to disable auto power off. As with the 320EX, in Receiver mode, you can use the flash's C.Fn-10 setting to tell the unit to power down after either 10 or 60 minutes of idle time. The unit's C.Fn-11 setting can be set to allow the sender transmitter to "wake" a sleeping unit after your choice of within 1 hour or within 8 hours.

- **Speedlite EL-100.** Using this flash as a remote is ridiculously easy. Set the Receiver switch on the back of the unit to the same channel used by the sender and rotate the Mode dial to the appropriate Group (usually A).

Choosing a Channel

In optical mode, Canon's wireless flash system can work on any of four channels, so if more than one photographer is using the Canon system, each can set his gear to a different channel so they don't accidentally trigger each other's strobes. You need to be sure all of your gear is set to the same channel. Selecting a channel is done differently with each particular flash model. The EL-100 is the easiest in this regard: just slide the Receiver switch to the Channel you want to use.

The ability to operate flash units on a particular channel isn't really important unless you're shooting in an environment where other photographers are also using the Canon wireless flash system. If the system only offered one channel, then each photographer's wireless flash controller would be firing every Canon flash set for wireless operation. By having four channels available, the photographers can coordinate their use to avoid that problem. Such situations are common at sporting events and other activities that draw a lot of shooters.

It's always a good idea to double-check your flash units before you set them up to make sure they're all set to the same channel, and this should also be one of your first troubleshooting questions if a flash doesn't fire the first time you try to use it wirelessly.

You do this as follows:

1. **Set flash units to the channel you want to use for all your groups.** Before you use the camera's controls to configure your flash exposures, you must first make adjustments on the external Speedlite. Each flash unit may use its own procedure for setting that strobe's channel. Consult your Speedlite's manual for instructions. With the 580EX II, press the Zoom button repeatedly until the CH. indicator blinks, then rotate the Control dial to select Channel 1, 2, 3, or 4. Press the Control dial center button to confirm. With the 600EX-RT/600EX II-RT, press Fn Button 4 until Menu 2 appears, then press Fn Button 1 to select a channel. The EL-1 allows you to set the channel (plus groups, and all other settings) from the integrated LCD menu on the flash itself using the joystick and Select wheel.

2. **Activate wireless operation.** From the External Speedlite Control entry in the Shooting 3 menu, navigate to the Flash Function Settings choice, Flash Functions. Highlight the second icon from the left in the top row (as seen in Figure 10.3, left) and press SET. Then choose Wireless: Optical Transmission from the screen that appears (see Figure 10.3, right). Press Q/SET to confirm and exit.

3. **Navigate to the camera's channel selection option.** Navigate to the Channel Setting (highlighted in red at left in Figure 10.4) and push the Q/SET button.

Figure 10.3 You can choose the Channel, Groups, and other parameters from the Flash Functions Settings screen (left); activate wireless functions (right).

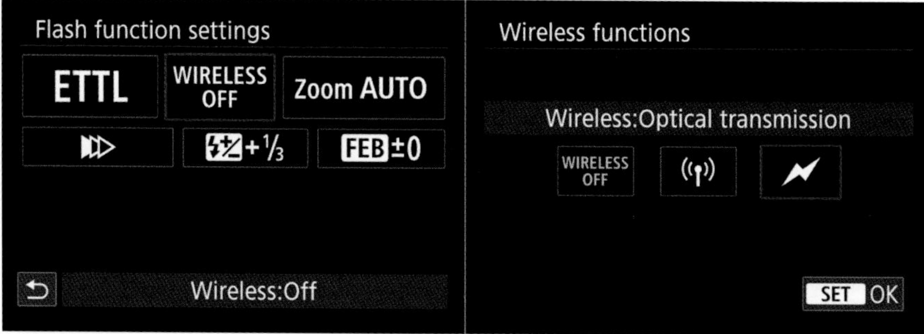

Figure 10.4 Selecting an optical channel.

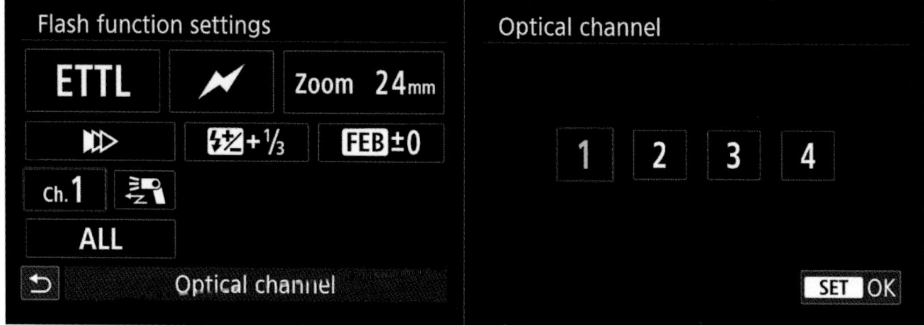

4. **Select the channel your flashes are set to.** You can then use the QCD to cycle the channel number from 1 to 4. (Figure 10.4, right.)

5. **Enable/disable sender flash firing.** The icon to the immediate right of the Channel Setting icon shown in Figure 10.4 allows you to enable or disable firing of the sender flash. When disabled, the sender flash will still control external flashes wirelessly with a pre-flash burst but won't contribute to the exposure. This is useful if you want all the illumination to come from your receiver flash units, such as when shooting close-up or macro images, or when you're simulating a studio flash setup with Speedlites.

6. **Double-check to make sure your off-camera flash units are set to the appropriate channel.** Your wireless flash units must be set to the same channel as the camera's wireless flash controller; otherwise, the Speedlites won't fire.

Working with Groups

With what you've already learned, you can shoot wirelessly using your camera's on-camera flash and one or more external flash units. All these strobes will work together with the camera for automatic exposure using E-TTL II exposure mode. You can vary the power ratio between your on-camera flash and the external units. As you become more comfortable with wireless flash photography, you can even switch the individual external flash units into manual mode and adjust their lighting ratios manually.

But there's a lot more you can do if you've splurged and own two or more compatible external flash units. Canon wireless photography lets you collect individual strobes into *groups* and control all the Speedlites within a given group together. You can operate as few as two strobes in two groups or three strobes in three groups, while controlling more units if desired. You can also have them fire at equal output settings (A+B+C mode) versus using them at different power ratios (A:B or A:B C modes). Setting each group's strobes to different power ratios gives you more control over lighting for portraiture and other uses.

This is one of the more powerful options of the EOS wireless flash system. I prefer to keep my Speedlites set to different groups normally. I can always set the power ratio to 1:1 if I want to operate the flash units all at the same power. If I change my mind and need to make adjustments, I can just change the wireless flash controller and then manipulate the different groups' output as desired.

Canon's wireless flash system works with a number of Canon flashes and even some third-party units. I routinely mix a 600EX-RT, 600EX II-RT, 580EX II, 550EX, and 420EX. I control these flash units either with the on-camera external flash or using a Canon ST-E2 Speedlite Transmitter.

The ST-E2 is a hot-shoe mount device that offers wireless flash control for a wide variety of Canon wireless-flash-capable strobes and can even control flash units wirelessly for high-speed sync (HSS) photography. (HSS is described in Chapter 9.) The ST-E2 can only control two flash groups though.

Here's how you set up groups (for flashes other than the EL-100, which has Group positions on its Mode dial):

1. **Set flash units to the group you want to assign them to.** Each flash unit may use its own procedure for setting that strobe's group. Consult your Speedlite's manual for instructions.

2. **Navigate to the camera's group selection option.** From the External Speedlite Control entry in the Shooting 3 menu, navigate to the Flash Function Settings choice. Highlight the Group setting. It's located just below the Channel and Sender Flash Firing options and reads ALL at left in Figure 10.5. Push the Q/SET button.

3. **Select the group configuration you want.** You can then use the QCD to cycle to select ALL, A:B, or A:B C. If you're using the 600EX-RT/600EX II-RT in radio control mode, you can also activate Groups D and E. (See Figure 10.5, right.)

4. **Double-check to make sure your flash units are set to the appropriate channel.** Your wireless flash units must be set to the same channel as the camera's wireless flash controller; otherwise, the Speedlites won't fire.

Figure 10.5 Selecting a group.

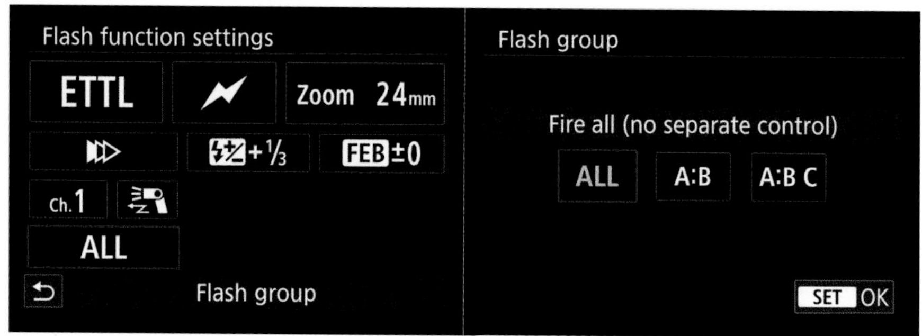

Ratio Control

By default, all the flashes in each group will fire at full power. However, for more advanced lighting setups, you can select lighting ratios.

Your on-camera sender flash and your wireless receiver flash units have their own individual *oomph*—how much illumination they put out. This option lets you choose the relationship between these units, a *power ratio* between your on-camera flash and your wireless flash units—the relative strength of each. That ability can be especially useful if you want to use the on-camera flash for just a little fill light, while letting your off-camera units do the heavy work.

Having the ability to vary the power of each flash unit or group of flash units wirelessly gives you greater flexibility and control. Varying the light output of each flash unit makes it possible to create specific types of lighting (such as traditional portrait lighting, which frequently calls for a 3:1 lighting ratio between main light and fill light) or to use illumination to highlight one part of the photo while reducing contrast in another.

Lighting ratios determine the contrast between the main light (sometimes called a "key" light) and fill light. For portraiture, usually the main light is placed at a 45-degree angle to the subject (although there are some variations), with the fill-in light on the opposite side or closer to the camera position. Choosing the right lighting ratio can do a lot to create a particular look or mood. For instance, a 1:1 ratio produces what's known as "flat" lighting. While this is good for copying or documentation, it's not usually as interesting for portraiture. Instead, making the main light more powerful than the fill light creates interesting shadows for more dramatic images. (See Figure 10.6.)

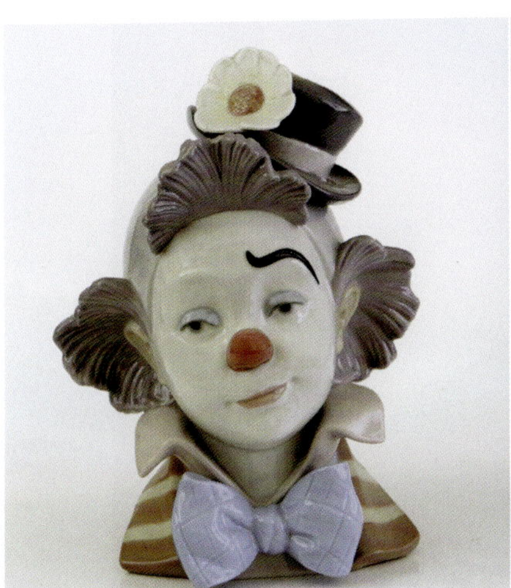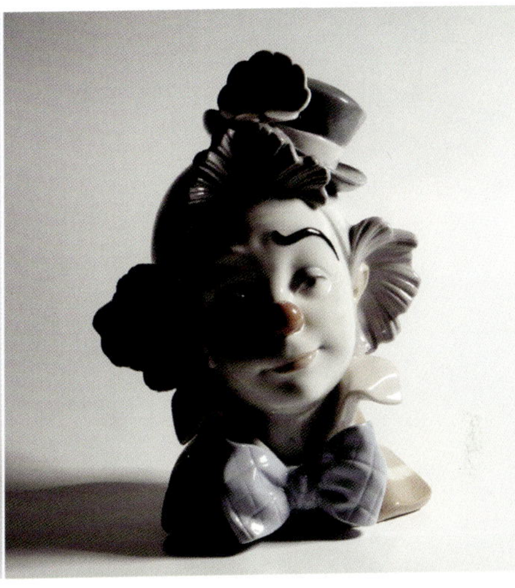

Figure 10.6 More dramatic lighting ratios produce more dramatic-looking illumination.

By selecting the power ratio between the flash units, you can change the relative illumination between them. Figure 10.7 shows a series of four images with a single main flash located at a 45-degree angle off to the right and slightly behind the model. The on-camera flash at the camera provided illumination to fill in the shadows on the side of the face closest to the camera. The ratio between the two Speedlites flash was varied using 2:1 (upper left), 3:1 (upper right), 4:1 (lower left), and 5:1 (lower right) ratios.

Here's how to set the lighting ratio between the sender flash and additional external wireless flash units:

1. **Navigate to the camera's Flash Group selection option.** With wireless flash already activated, visit the External Speedlite Control entry in the Shooting 3 menu, then navigate to the Flash Function Settings choice. Navigate to the Flash Group choice at the lower left of the screen as described above, and push the Q/SET button.

2. **Choose Group Configuration.** As noted earlier, you can select ALL, A:B, or A:B C. If you're using the 600EX-RT/600EX II-RT in radio transmission mode, you can also select Groups D and E. Press Q/SET to confirm.

3. **Access A:B ratio.** If you've chosen A:B C, a screen like the one shown in Figure 10.8, upper left appears. Use the QCD to navigate to the A:B Ratio Control option, highlighted in red at left in Figure 10.8. Then press the Q/SET button. (If you selected A:B instead, the screen will be slightly different.)

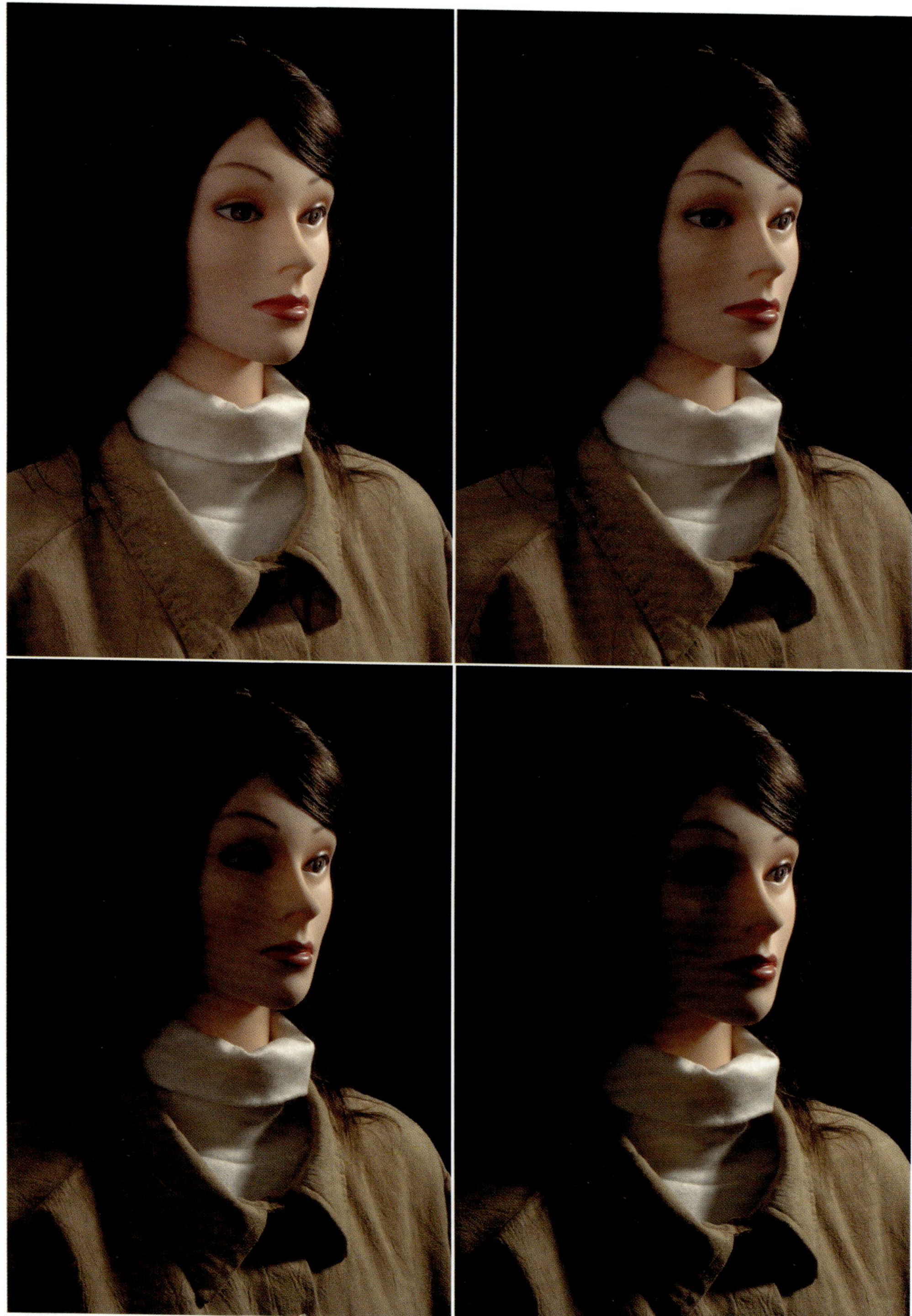

Figure 10.7 The main light (to the right and behind the model) and fill light (at the camera position) were varied using 2:1 and 3:1 (top row, left to right) as well as 4:1 and 5:1 (bottom row, left to right) ratios.

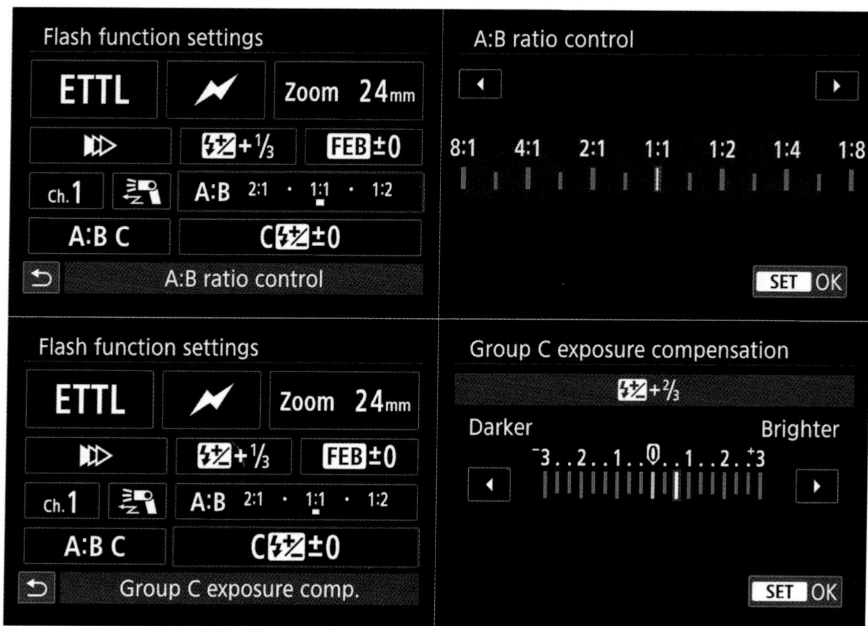

Figure 10.8 Select your Group Configuration.

4. **Choose A to B ratio.** The screen shown at upper right in Figure 10.8 appears. Select the output of the A group relative to the B group. You can specify the A group to be up to 8X more powerful than B (at left on the scale), or for the A group to supply as little as 1/8th the output of the B group (at right on the scale). If you selected A:B (rather than A:B C), you're finished and can press the MENU button to confirm and exit.

5. **Choose C ratio.** If you chose A:B C, you can now separately specify the ratio between the C group and the A:B group ratio defined in Steps 3 and 4. Highlight the C Exposure Compensation area, shown at lower left in Figure 10.8, and press Q/SET.

6. **Apply Group C compensation.** To adjust the relative output of the C group, you don't use ratios. Instead, you select exposure compensation from –3 to + 3 stops, as seen at lower right in Figure 10.8. In effect, the R8 will adjust the output of the C group flash(es) so they are up to 1/8th as powerful (–3 stops) to 8X more powerful (+3 stops) in comparison.

7. **Confirm.** Press Q/SET to confirm your C group ratio, and then MENU to exit.

I know all these adjustments can be confusing. But here's a summary of how the various basic Group Configurations work:

- **ALL.** All groups will fire at the power level set at the flash unit itself. That may be full power, or you may have set individual flashes to fire at some other power level. It's usually simpler to set your flashes at full power and allow the sender to control their output.

- **A:B.** In this configuration, you can specify the ratio of the power levels of Groups A and B, as described in Steps 3 and 4 above.

- **A:B C.** In this Group configuration, you can specify the power ratio between Groups A and B, but *not* the output of Group C flashes. Those are controlled only using Flash Exposure Compensation, as outlined in Steps 5–7.

Remote Release Function/Linked Shooting

The EL-1, EL-5, 600EX-RT/600EX II-RT Speedlites, and ST-E3-RT/ST-E10 transmitters have a remote release function, which allows you to use a receiver unit to trigger your camera by remote control when using *radio transmission* mode. EOS cameras released since 2012 can be triggered in this way through the intelligent hot shoe, using an EL-1, 600EX-series flash, or ST-E3-RT/ST-E10 transmitter mounted on the camera, and the receiver EL-1, 600EX-RT, or 600EX II-RT off camera as the remote trigger. The remote release/linked shooting features operate within a perimeter of about 33 feet.

Check your transmitter/flash menu for a more complete explanation, but setup is relatively simple. The EL-1 allows you to choose REL (Release), located between the TEST and MODEL options in the bottom row of the flash's LCD screen. On the 600EX-series, press the Menu 2 button on the unit which will be used as a remote/receiver flash and choose REL (release). Thereafter, a release signal is sent from the receiver to the sender/controller flash on the camera, and the camera will be triggered to take a picture and fire all the remote units. Remote release can be triggered only when autofocus can be achieved and is performed only using Single Shooting, regardless of the camera's drive mode.

Linked shooting is also possible and allows triggering the shutter of a receiver unit *camera* by linking it to a sender unit camera. You can then trigger all the camera and flash units simultaneously. Each camera must have a flash that supports radio transmission wireless shooting, or you can use the ST-E3-RT/ST-E10 transmitters on one or more of the receiver cameras. You're better off using manual focus when triggering multiple cameras, because if even one camera is unable to achieve autofocus, linked shooting with that camera is disabled.

You'll need to set the flash/transmitter on the sender camera as the sender of the multi-camera array, and the receiver flash/transmitters to linked receiver mode. On each receiver ST-E3-RT/ST-E10, you'll need to press the Wireless/Linked Shooting button until Linked Shot appears. (The button is located on the left edge of the back panel, labeled with a double-headed lightning bolt icon, as shown earlier in Figure 10.2.) On the sender transmitter, press the button again to make it the sender. Note that each time you switch a unit from receiver to sender modes, any other units that had been set as "sender" will automatically switch to receiver mode. The Link light (at the top left of the back panel) of the receiver and sender units should be lit green.

Setting up the sender/receiver Speedlites is similar. The 600EX-series flash have their own Wireless/Linked Shooting button in roughly the same location on their back panels. Press that button and rotate the large Select dial until Linked Shot appears, then press the Select/SET button. Use the control wheel to set each flash as Sender or Receiver, then press the Select/SET button.

Then press the button again to set the "sender" unit of the linked shooting configuration. When the Channel and ID are specified and ready, the Link lamp on the receiver unit(s) will illuminate in green. Then, point the remote/receiver flash used as a trigger at the front of the camera/sender flash within 16 feet of the camera, and press the remote control button on the side of the flash. During the two-second delay, you can then point the flash in a different direction (as is likely, because you're probably using this feature to illuminate the scene, not the camera). That's the real reason for the two-second delay, by the way: giving you the ability to reposition the "remote" release flash.

11

Customizing with the Shooting Menu

This chapter and the next four will help you sort out the settings you can make to customize how your camera uses its features, shoots photos, displays images, and processes the pictures after they've been taken. I'm not going to waste a lot of space on some of the more obvious menu choices. For example, you can probably figure out that the Touch Shutter option in the Shooting 8 menu deals with whether the Touch Shutter option is enabled or disabled. In this chapter, I'll devote no more than a sentence or two to the blatantly obvious settings and concentrate on the more confusing aspects of setup, such as Automatic Exposure Bracketing.

This chapter discusses the nine Shooting menu pages used for still photography. I'll save discussion of the tenth, which lists movie options exclusively, for Chapter 16, where I've collected all the basic video capture information and settings. For now, let's start off with a general overview of the menus found on the EOS R8.

Anatomy of the Menus

Your menus are divided into seven major tabs: Shooting, Autofocus, Playback, Wireless, Set-up, Custom Functions, and My Menu. Each tab consists of one or more separate pages, with each page's listings shown as a separate screen with no scrolling.

The tabs are color-coded: red for Shooting, magenta for Autofocus, blue for Playback, violet for Communication Functions/wireless, amber/yellow for Set-up, brown for Custom Functions, and green for My Menu. The currently selected menu tab's icon is white within a background corresponding to its color code. A lineup immediately underneath shows the page numbers available. The current screen's number is highlighted. All the inactive menus are gray and dimmed.

TABS VS PAGES

By main *menu tab*, I am referring to the color coded groups described above: Shooting, Autofocus, Playback, Wireless, Set-up, Custom Functions, and My Menu. When I mention a *menu page*, I am talking about the individual listings within a tab, such as Shooting 1, Shooting 2, and so forth.

The menus are easy to use, too. Just press the MENU button and use these controls:

- **Jump between tabs.** Press the INFO button to jump from one main tab to the next, meaning from the Shooting menu tab to the Autofocus tab to the Playback tab, rather than from one page to the next within a main tab.

  Highlighting will always move from the current page on the current tab to *the most recently accessed page* and *the most recently accessed entry* of the next main tab. For example, if you've highlighted an entry on the Shooting 3 page and press the INFO button, you'll jump to whichever page you last used in the AF (autofocus) menu, with the particular entry you last used in that page highlighted.

- **Move from page to page.** Once you have moved to a main menu tab you want, to move continuously from page to page within that tab, rotate the Main dial or press the left/right directional controls. If, for example, you were viewing the AF 3 menu, subsequent clicks to the right would take you to the AF 4, AF 5, AF 6, and then onward to Playback 1, Playback 2, etc. Rotate to the left to reverse your movement. Forward and reverse movement wraps around, too; the Shooting 1 menu is located immediately after the last My Menu entry. As with whole-tab jumps, the most recently used entry on each page visited is highlighted. This is convenient if you use particular entries frequently.

- **Scroll among page entries.** When a given page is active, rotate the QCD or use the up/down directional controls to scroll among the entries on that page.

Tapping the MENU button brings up a typical menu like the one shown in Figure 11.1. (If the camera goes to "sleep" while you're reviewing a menu, you may need to wake it up again by tapping the shutter release button.) Different menu tabs are provided, depending on the shooting mode, shown in Table 11.1:

TABLE 11.1 Available Menus

MODES	AVAILABLE MENU TABS
Bulb, M, Tv, Av, Fv, P modes	Shooting 1–10, AF 1–6, Playback 1–4, Network 1–2, Set-up 1–5, Custom Functions 1–5, My Menu 1
Scene Intelligent Auto/Hybrid Auto/Scene Modes/Color Filters	Shooting 1–5, AF 1–5, Playback 1–4, Network 1–2, Set-up 1–5
Movie mode	Shooting 1–4, AF 1–4, Playback 1–4, Network 1–2, Set-up 1–5, Custom Functions 1–5

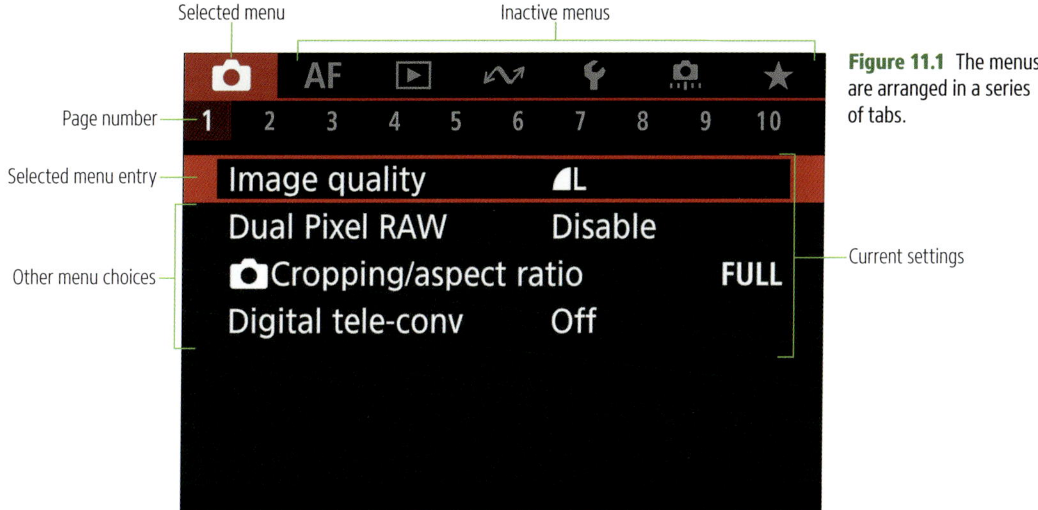

Figure 11.1 The menus are arranged in a series of tabs.

Here are the things to watch for as you navigate the menus:

- **Menu tabs.** In the top row of the menu screen, the menu that is currently active will be high-lighted as described earlier. The numbers within the tab let you know if you are in, say, Set-up 1, Set-up 2, Set-up 3, or another tab. Just remember that the red camera icons stand for still and movie shooting options; the blue right-pointing triangles represent playback options; the yellow wrench icons stand for set-up options; the brown camera icons represent Custom Functions; and the green star stands for personalized menus defined for the star of the show—you.

- **Selected menu item.** The currently selected menu entry within a given tab will have a black background and will be surrounded by a box the same hue as its color code.

- **Other menu choices.** The other menu items visible on the screen will have a dark gray background.

- **Current settings.** The current settings for visible menu items are shown in the right-hand column, until one menu entry is selected (by pressing the Q/SET key). Current settings aren't appropriate for some menu entries which are actually functions (for example, the Protect Images or Print options in the Playback 1 and 2 screens), so the right column is left blank.

When you've moved the menu highlighting to the menu item you want to work with, press the Q/SET button to select it. The current settings for the other menu items in the list will be hidden, and a list of options for the selected menu item (or a submenu screen) will appear. Or, you may be shown a separate settings screen for that entry. Within the menu choices, you can scroll up or down with the QCD. Press Q/SET to select the choice you've made and press the MENU button again to exit.

Shooting Menu Options

You'll find that the Shooting menu options are those that you access second-most frequently. You might make such adjustments as you begin a shooting session, or when you move from one type of subject to another. Canon makes accessing these changes very easy.

This section explains the options of the Shooting menus in still photography mode and how to use them. The options you'll find in these red-coded menus include:

Shooting 1

- Image Quality
- Dual Pixel RAW
- Cropping/Aspect Ratio
- Digital Tele-converter

Shooting 2

- Exposure Compensation/ AEB (Automatic Exposure Bracketing)
- ISO Speed Settings
- HDR Shooting [HDR PQ]
- HDR Mode
- Auto Lighting Optimizer
- Highlight Tone Priority

Shooting 3

- Anti-flicker Shooting
- High-Frequency Anti-flicker Shooting
- External Speedlite Control
- Metering Mode

Shooting 4

- White Balance
- Custom White Balance
- WB Shift/Bkt
- Color Space
- Picture Style
- Clarity
- Digest Type (Hybrid Auto mode only)
- Retain Creative Assist Data (Scene Intelligent Auto mode only)
- Shooting Creative Filters

Shooting 5

- Lens Aberration Correction
- Long Exposure Noise Reduction
- High ISO Speed Noise Reduction
- Dust Delete Data

Shooting 6

- Multiple Exposure
- RAW Burst Mode
- Focus Bracketing

Shooting 7

- Drive Mode
- Interval Timer
- Bulb Timer
- Silent Shutter Function
- Shutter Mode
- Release Shutter Without Card

Shooting 8

- IS (Image Stabilizer) Mode
- Customize Quick Controls
- Touch Shutter
- Image Review
- High-Speed Display
- Metering timer

Shooting 9

- Display Simulation
- Optical Viewfinder Simulated View Assist
- Shooting Information Display
- Viewfinder Display Format
- Display Performance

Image Quality

Options: Resolution: Large (default), Medium, Small 1, Small 2; JPEG/HEIF Compression: Fine (default), Normal; JPEG (default), RAW, or RAW+JPEG/HEIF

My preference: Resolution: Large; JPEG Compression: Fine; RAW+JPEG

This is the first entry in the Shooting 1 menu (shown in Figure 11.1). You can choose the image quality settings used to store files. You have these choices when selecting a quality setting:

- **Resolution.** The number of pixels captured determines the absolute resolution of the photos you shoot. Your choices include Large/RAW/C-RAW: 6000 × 4000 pixels (24MP); Medium: 3984 × 2656 pixels (11MP); Small 1: 2976 × 1984 pixels (5.9MP); Small 2: 2400 × 1600 pixels (3.8MP)

- **JPEG/HEIF compression.** To reduce the size of your image files and allow more photos to be stored on a given memory card, the camera uses compression to squeeze the images down to a smaller size. This compacting reduces the image quality a little, so you're offered your choice of Fine compression and Normal compression. The symbols help you remember that Fine compression (represented by a quarter-circle) provides the smoothest results, while Normal compression (signified by a stair-step icon) provides "jaggier" images. The Small 2 (S2) file option has no quality option icon, but it is Fine quality. I'll explain the difference between JPEG and HEIF in the next section.

- **JPEG/HEIF, RAW, or both.** You can elect to store only JPEG/HEIF versions of the images you shoot or you can save your photos as uncompressed, loss-free RAW files, which consume about four times as much space on your memory card. Or, you can store both at once as you shoot. Many photographers elect to save *both* a JPEG and a RAW file, so they'll have a JPEG or HEIF version that might be usable as-is, as well as the original "digital negative" RAW file in case they want to do some processing of the image later. You'll end up with two different versions of the same file: one with a JPG extension and one with the CR3 extension that signifies a Canon RAW file.

To choose the combination you want, access the menus, scroll to Image Quality, and press the Q/SET button. A screen similar to the one shown in Figure 11.2 will appear with two rows of choices. (If you've enabled HDR recording in the Shooting 2 menu, HEIF will appear instead of JPEG in the lower row.)

Spin the Main dial to choose from: — (no RAW), RAW, or C RAW. Rotate the QCD to select one of the JPEG/HEIF choices: — (no JPEG/HEIF), Large, Medium, or Small in Fine or Normal compression (represented by smooth and stepped icons, respectively), plus Small 2 (with Fine

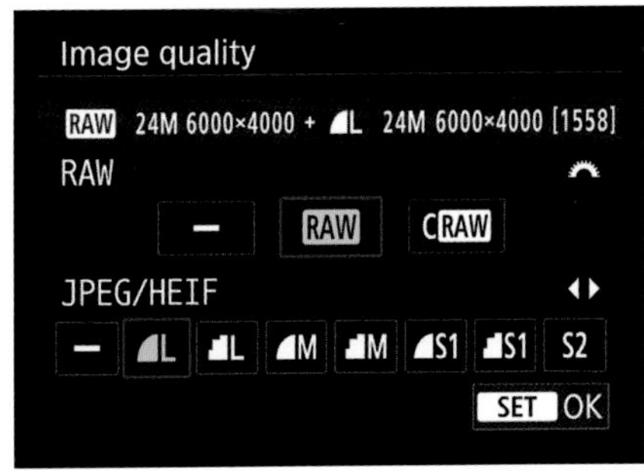

Figure 11.2 Choose your resolution, amount of compression, and file format from this screen.

compression), at the resolutions listed above. A red box appears around the currently selected choice. If you choose — for both RAW and JPEG/HEIF, then JPEG/HEIF Fine will be used. As always, when you've highlighted your selection, press Q/SET to confirm.

Why so many choices? There are some limited advantages to using the Medium and Small resolution settings, Normal JPEG/HEIF compression setting, and the more compressed C-RAW format. They all allow stretching the capacity of your memory card so you can shoehorn quite a few more pictures onto a single memory card. That can come in useful when on vacation and you're running out of storage, or when you're shooting non-critical work that doesn't require full resolution. The Small 2 setting can be useful for photos taken for real estate listings, web page display, photo ID cards, or similar non-critical applications.

For most work, using lower resolution and extra compression is often false economy. You never know when you might need that extra bit of picture detail. Your best bet is to have enough memory cards to handle all the shooting you want to do until you have the chance to transfer your photos to your computer or a personal storage device.

However, reduced image quality can sometimes be beneficial if you're shooting sequences of photos rapidly, as the camera is able to hold more of them in its internal memory buffer before transferring to the memory card. Still, for most sports and other applications, you'd probably rather have better, sharper pictures than longer periods of continuous shooting.

HEIF vs. JPEG

Unless you're using an iPhone and are deep into its features, you probably don't know much about the relatively recent HEIF format. The Apple's iOS 11 operating system for its smart devices was the first consumer product to use the HEIF format. Canon was the first digital camera company to support it, with Sony following thereafter.

In a nutshell, HEIF images use an advanced compression scheme to produce files with higher image quality that may be only half the size of JPEGs, and have more features, including transparency and 16-bit color. The downside is that, as I write this, no browser supports it natively, and many software applications as well as operating systems like Windows 10 and Android need updates to accommodate HEIF. Macs need macOS High Sierra or later to interpret HEIF images. If you're using a recent iPhone with HEIF, it can convert your images to JPEG automatically when you export them but will use the format to deploy special features internally (say, for Live images).

So, while HEIF will eventually replace JPEG (last updated in 1994) the transition will take many years. The good news is that you can create them now with your R8. When you enable HDR Shooting using the HDR PQ Settings entry of the Shooting 2 menu, the Image Quality menu will display HEIF at the bottom of the screen shown in Figure 11.2 instead of JPEG. In addition, the Playback 4 menu has an option for converting HEIF to JPEG so you can use your files with applications that can't yet handle HEIF. I'll explain the HDR Shooting [HDR PQ] entry later in this chapter, and cover HEIF to JPEG conversion in Chapter 13.

JPEG/HEIF vs. RAW

You'll sometimes be told that RAW files are the "unprocessed" image information your camera produces, before it's been modified. That's nonsense. RAW files are no more unprocessed than camera film is after it's been through the chemicals to produce a negative or transparency. A lot can happen in the developer that can affect the quality of a film image—positively and negatively—and, similarly, your digital image undergoes a significant amount of processing before it is saved as a RAW file. Canon even applies a name (DIGIC X) to the digital image processing (DIP) chip used to perform this magic.

A RAW file is more like a film camera's processed negative. It contains all the information, captured in 14-bit channels per color (and stored in a 16-bit space), with no compression, no sharpening, and no application of any special filters or other settings you might have specified when you took the picture. Those settings are *stored* with the RAW file so they can be applied when the image is converted to a form compatible with your favorite image editor. However, using RAW conversion software such as Adobe Camera Raw or Canon's Digital Photo Professional, you can override those settings and apply settings of your own. You can select essentially the same changes there that you might have specified in your camera's picture-taking options.

RAW exists because sometimes we want to have access to all the information captured by the camera, before the camera's internal logic has processed it and converted the image to a standard file format. RAW doesn't save as much space as JPEG. What it does do is preserve all the information captured by your camera after it's been converted from analog to digital form. Of course, the RAW format preserves the *settings* information.

So, why don't we always use RAW? Although some photographers do save only in RAW format, it's more common to use either RAW plus one of the JPEG/HEIF options or just shoot JPEG/HEIF and avoid RAW altogether. That's because having only RAW files to work with can significantly slow down your workflow. While RAW is overwhelmingly helpful when an image needs to be fine-tuned, in other situations working with a RAW file, when all you really need is a good-quality, untweaked image, consumes time that you may not want to waste. For example, RAW images take longer to store on the memory card, and require more post-processing effort, whether you elect to go with the default settings in force when the picture was taken, or just make minor adjustments.

Thus, those who depend on speedy access to images or who shoot large numbers of photos at once may prefer JPEG over RAW or HEIF. Wedding photographers, for example, might expose several thousand photos during a bridal affair and offer hundreds to clients as electronic proofs for possible inclusion in an album or transfer to a CD or DVD. These wedding shooters, who want JPEG images as their final product, take the time to make sure that their in-camera settings are correct, minimizing the need to post-process photos after the event. Given that their JPEGs are so good (in most cases thanks, in large part, to the pro photographer's extensive experience), there is little need to get bogged down shooting RAW or the conversion headaches of HEIF this early in the game.

JPEG was invented as a more compact file format that can store most of the information in a digital image, but in a much smaller size. JPEG predates most digital SLRs and was initially used to squeeze down files for transmission over slow dialup connections. Even if you were using an early dSLR with 1.3-megapixel files for news photography, you didn't want to send them back to the office over a modem (Google it) at 1,200 bps.

But, as I noted, JPEG (and now HEIF) provides smaller files by compressing the information in a way that loses some image data. Even though HEIF is gradually seeing more use, JPEG remains a viable alternative because it offers several different quality levels. At the highest-quality Fine level, you might not be able to tell the difference between the original RAW file or an HEIF image and the JPEG version. You've squeezed the image significantly without losing much visual information at all. (See Figure 11.3.)

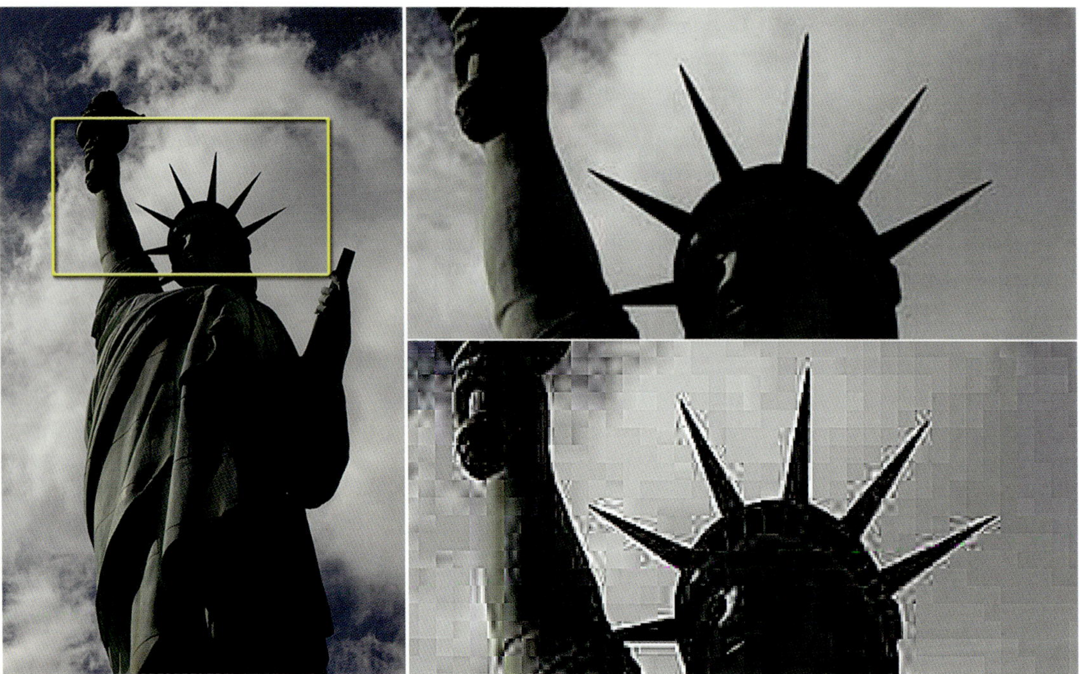

Figure 11.3 Original image (left). Low compression yields the best image (upper right); at very high compression, pixelation and artifacts rear their ugly heads (lower right).

In my case, I shoot virtually everything at RAW+JPEG Fine. I'm currently not bothering with HEIF much, at least until my software catches up with it. (Adobe didn't add support for HEIF in Photoshop for Windows until December 2020.) Most of the time, I'm not concerned about filling up my memory cards, as I usually have a minimum of five fast 64GB or 128GB memory cards with me. If I think I may fill up all those cards on a trip, I usually have a laptop with me and can transfer photos to that device. As I mentioned earlier, when shooting sports, I'll shift to JPEG Fine (with no RAW file) to squeeze a little extra speed out of my continuous shooting mode, and to reduce the need to wade through eight-photo bursts taken in RAW format. On the other hand, on my last trip to Europe, I took only RAW (instead of my customary RAW+JPEG) photos to fit more images onto my laptop, as I planned on doing at least some post-processing on many of the images for a travel book I was working on.

Dual Pixel RAW

Options: Enable, Disable (default)

My preference: Disable unless this special format is needed

Dual Pixel RAW is a special RAW format that can be manipulated in an image editor to make micro-adjustments to the focus plane, slightly improve bokeh effects (the smoothness of the out-of-focus areas of the image), and make corrections to ghosting and flare. Dual Pixel RAW files also offer the opportunity for advanced users to recover up to one additional stop in the highlights, and to adjust virtual lighting. In effect, the camera saves two different RAW files: one containing information from both sets of pixels (call them Sets A+B) while the other contains only the pixels in Set B. The software can then process each subset separately. I explained Dual Pixel Raw more completely in Chapter 5, which deals primarily with autofocus, but offers explanations of the other features of the format.

To use Dual Pixel RAW, you must select RAW, C RAW, or RAW+JPEG as your Image Quality, and then enable the Dual Pixel feature here. This feature is not available if you want to shoot multiple exposures, use automatic HDR, or One-Touch image quality. Larger lens apertures increase the amount and effect of available corrections, and continuous shooting will be slower when using DPR. High-speed continuous shooting is not available at all.

I explained how to manipulate Dual Pixel RAW files in Chapter 5. As I noted earlier, I don't spend a lot of time explaining how to use software in this book, but you can learn more about processing these files in Canon's Digital Photo Professional manual and other white papers available on their websites.

Cropping/Aspect Ratio

Options: FULL (default), 1.6X, 1:1, 4:3, 16:9; Shooting area display: Masked, Outlined
My preference: FULL

Your camera allows you to crop images in the camera. Instead of the full sensor frame of 36mm × 24mm, you can select a 1.6X APS-C crop (with a 3:2 crop ratio that's the same as the FULL setting), or aspect ratios of 1:1 (square), 4:3, or 16:9 (which corresponds to high-definition/ultra-high-definition movie frames). You can also choose whether the shooting area is displayed within the frame—either outlined with blue lines or masked so that only the current crop or aspect ratio is displayed.

The 1.6X crop is significant, because the R8 can also use APS-C-format RF-S lenses (designed for crop-sensor models like the EOS R7 and R8), and, when equipped with an EF/EF-S mount adapter, use APS-C format EF-S lenses. You can use the 1.6X crop to increase the telephoto "reach" of RF and EF lenses (with adapter), giving you a 3744 × 2496-pixel, 9.3MP image. If you are using an RF-S or EF-S lens, then the 1.6X crop is chosen automatically and the other aspect ratios are not available.

If you've selected the 1.6X crop or have mounted an RF-S/EF-S lens, the image is magnified so the cropped portion fills the display, as the APS-C aspect ratio of 3:2 is identical to that of the full-frame image. A 1.6X indicator is displayed in the frame. For other aspect ratios, press the INFO button and choose either Masked or Outlined for the Shooting Area display. When masked, only the captured image area will be shown on the display; with Outlined, the full frame is shown, but the shooting area is marked with blue lines. Choose Outlined if you want to be able to see the parts of your subject outside the actual capture area.

If you've chosen a specific crop and then shoot in RAW format, the RAW image will be captured at the full 6000 × 4000-pixel resolution, but when the RAW image is played back, the cropped image area will be indicated by lines, and only that area will be shown when displaying a slide show (described in Chapter 13). The relative resolutions are listed in Table 11.2 and the crop/aspect ratio options are shown in Figure 11.4.

TABLE 11.2 Aspect Ratio Image Sizes

SIZE RATIO	JPEG/ HEIF LARGE RAW/ C RAW	JPEG/ HEIF MEDIUM	JPEG/ HEIF SMALL 1	JPEG/ HEIF SMALL 2	RAW/ C RAW
3:2	6000 × 4000 (24MP)	3984 × 2656 (10.6MP)	2976 × 1984 (5.9MP)	2400 × 1600 (3.8MP)	6000 × 4000 (24MP)
1.6X	3744 × 2496 (9.3MP)	—	—	2400 × 1600 (3.8MP)	3744 × 2496 (9.3MP)
1:1	4000 × 4000 (16MP)	2656 × 2656 (7.1MP)	1984 × 1984 (3.9MP)	1600 × 1600 (2.6MP)	—
4:3	5328 × 4000 (21.3MP)	3552 × 2664 (9.5MP)	2656 × 1992 (5.3MP)	2112 × 1600 (3.4MP)	—
16:9	6000 × 3368 (20.2MP)	3984 × 2240 (8.9MP)	2976 × 1680 (5MP)	2400 × 1344 (3.2MP)	—

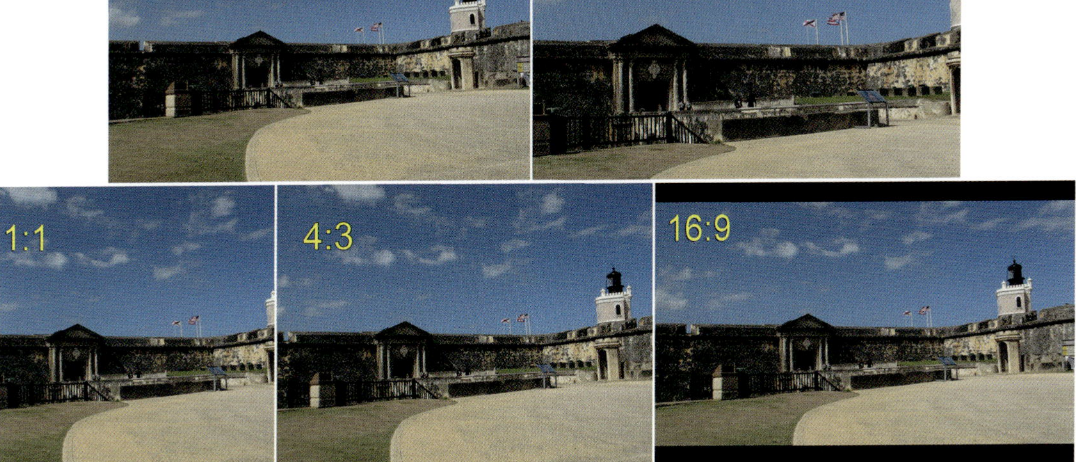

Figure 11.4 Crop/Aspect Ratio options.

Digital Tele-converter

Options: Off (default); Full frame: 2.0X, 4.0X; APS-C: 3.2X, 6.4X

My preference: Off

This is essentially another crop mode, which you can use independently of the cropping/aspect ratio feature described above, or, at your option, apply *on top of* those settings, giving you, effectively, increased magnification. The proportions of the image remain the same, but are magnified 2X or 4X for the 3:2, 1:1, 4:3, and 16.9 aspect ratios, and by 3.2X and 6.4X when using the R8's 1.6X crop mode. The difference between the two features can be summed up like this:

- **Cropping/Aspect ratio entry.** The image is not magnified when using the 3:2, 1:1, 4:3, or 16.9 aspect ratios; the only change is to *crop out* some of the image at left and right sides with the 1:1 and 4:3 proportions, and from the top and bottom of the frame with the 16:9 aspect ratio. The 1.6X option "magnifies" the image by filling the frame with an APS-C-sized section of the center using the same 3:2 aspect ratio as the FULL setting. Those crops were shown earlier in Figure 11.4.

- **Digital tele-converter.** The frame is cropped using the cropping/aspect ratio proportions you have selected, producing a 2X or 4X "magnified" version of images captured in 3:2, 1:1, 4:3, or 16.9 aspect ratios. If you've selected the 1.6X crop in the Cropping/Aspect Ratio entry, the magnification is 3.2X or 6.4X, instead. Figure 11.5 illustrates the effects of the digital tele-converter.

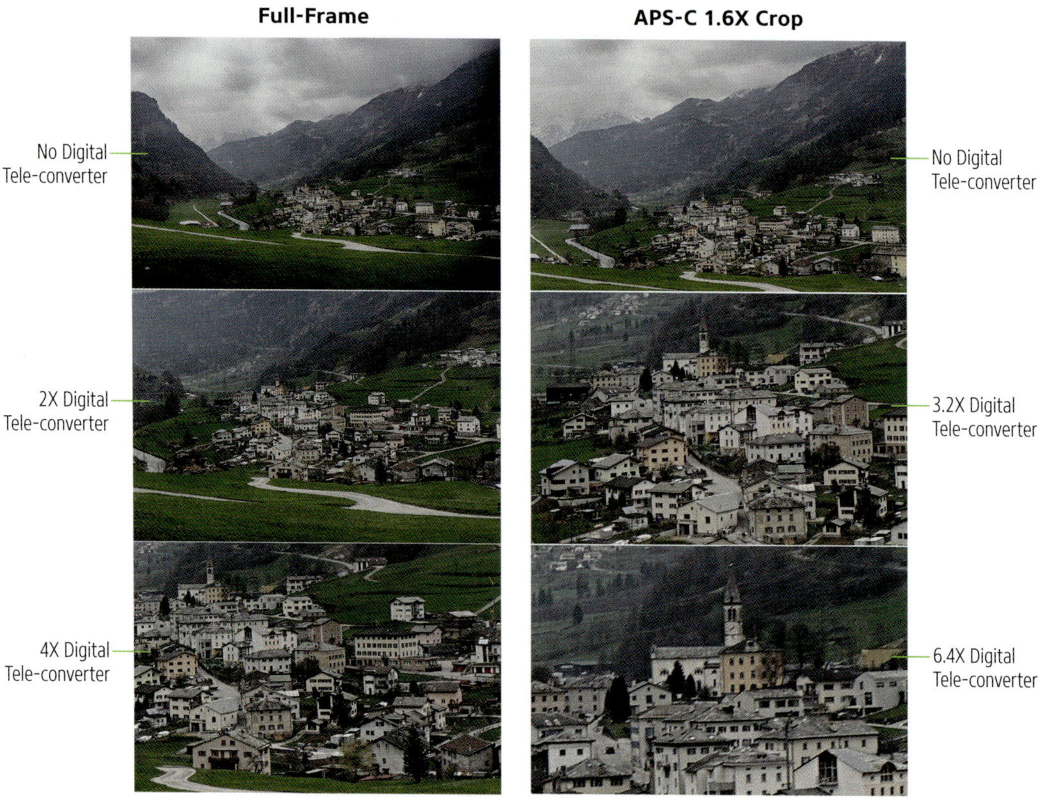

Full-Frame   **APS-C 1.6X Crop**

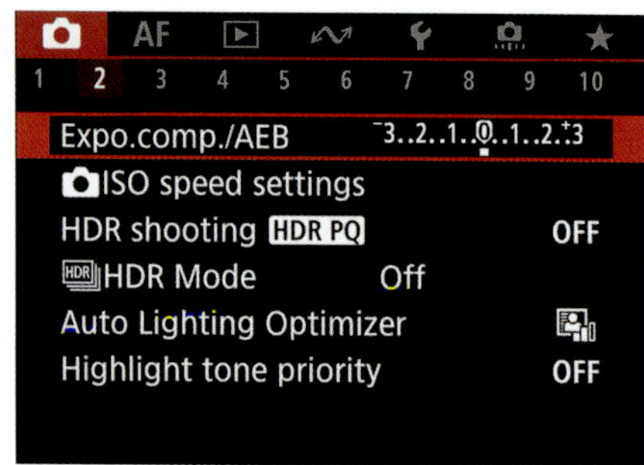

No Digital Tele-converter

2X Digital Tele-converter

4X Digital Tele-converter

No Digital Tele-converter

3.2X Digital Tele-converter

6.4X Digital Tele-converter

Figure 11.5 Left column: Full frame: No digital tele-converter, 2X, and 4X magnifications (top to bottom). Right column: APS-C (1.6X crop): No digital tele-converter, 3.2X, 6.4X magnifications (top to bottom).

Exposure Compensation/Automatic Exposure Bracketing

Options: Exposure Comp/Auto Exposure Bracketing

My preference: N/A

The first entry on the Shooting 2 menu is Expo. Comp./ AEB, or exposure compensation and automatic exposure bracketing. (See Figure 11.6.) As you learned in Chapter 4, exposure compensation increases or decreases exposure from the metered value. You can set it from this screen, or, in Fv, P, Tv, or Av modes by simply pressing the shutter release halfway and then rotating the QCD to add or subtract exposure. A plus/minus exposure compensation indicator scale is displayed while compensation is in effect.

Figure 11.6 Exposure compensation/AEB is the first entry in the Shooting 2 menu.

Exposure bracketing using the AEB feature is a way to shoot several consecutive exposures using different settings, to improve the odds that one will be exactly right. Automatic exposure bracketing is also an excellent way of creating the base exposures you'll need when you want to combine several shots to create a high dynamic range (HDR) image. (You'll find a discussion of HDR photography in Chapter 4, too.)

To activate automatic exposure bracketing, select this menu choice, then rotate the Main dial to spread or contract the three lines beneath the scale until you've defined the range you want the bracket to cover, which can be up to plus/minus three stops from the base exposure, as shown in Figure 11.7. Then, use the QCD (or left/right directional controls) to move the bracket set right or left, moving the base exposure point from the metered (0) value and biasing the bracketing toward underexposure (rotate left) or overexposure (rotate right).

When AEB is activated, the bracketed shots will be exposed in this sequence: metered exposure, decreased exposure, increased exposure. You'll find more information about exposure bracketing in Chapter 4.

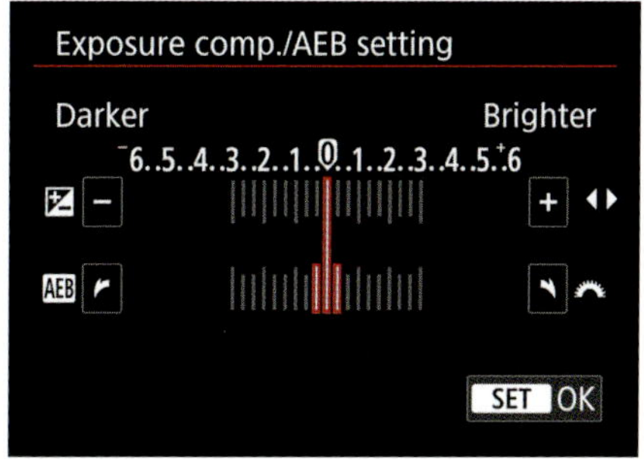

Figure 11.7 Set the range of the bracketed exposures.

ISO Speed Settings

Options: ISO Speed, ISO Speed Range, Auto Range, Minimum Shutter Speed
My preference: N/A

Use this entry to select a specific ISO speed for still photography using a conventional menu instead of the Quick Control menu; or to limit the range of ISO settings and shutter speeds that the camera selects automatically. In Basic Zone modes like Scene Intelligent Auto, ISO is set automatically. The four subentries, shown in Figure 11.8, include:

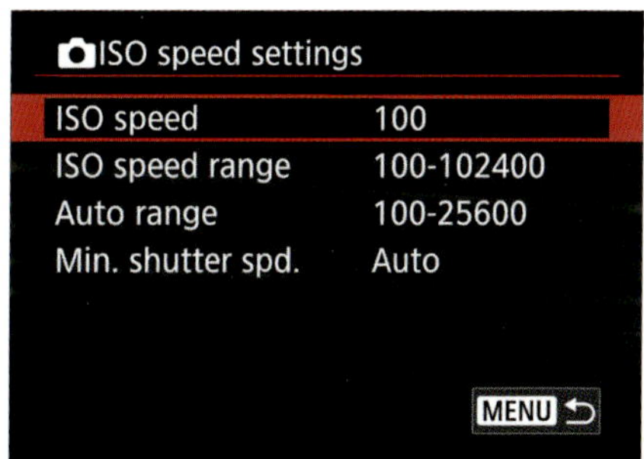

Figure 11.8 ISO Speed Setting options.

- **ISO Speed.** This scale allows you to choose from the enabled ISO speeds, plus Auto, using a sliding scale that can be adjusted using the QCD, left/right directional controls, or the touch screen. Press INFO when the scale is visible to activate Auto. If you frequently use a particular ISO setting, you can register it, and then select that speed by tapping an icon on the screen. I'll show you how to register an ISO setting shortly.

- **ISO Speed Range.** You can specify the minimum and maximum ISO sensitivity available. The default range is ISO 100 to ISO 102,400. But you can expand that range here to enable Low (ISO 50 equivalent) and H (ISO 204,800 equivalent). I find myself using this feature frequently to keep me from accidentally switching to a setting I'd rather (or need to) avoid. For example, at concerts I may switch from ISO 1600 to 6400 as the lighting changes, and I set those two values as my minimum or maximum. Outdoors in daylight, I might prefer to lock out ISO values lower than ISO 100 or higher than ISO 800.

- **Auto Range.** This is the equivalent "safety net" for Auto ISO operation. You can set the minimum no lower than ISO 100 and the maximum to ISO 102,400 in one-stop increments. Use this to apply your own "smarts" to the Auto ISO setting. These settings will also act as the minimum and maximum speeds for ISO Safety Shift.

- **Minimum Shutter Speed.** You can choose whether to allow the camera to select the slowest shutter speed used before Auto ISO kicks in. The idea here is that you'll probably want to boost ISO sooner if you're using a long lens with P and Av modes (in which the camera selects the shutter speed). If you specify, for example, a minimum shutter speed of 1/200th second, if P or Av mode needs a slower shutter speed for the proper exposure, it will boost ISO instead, within the range you've specified with Auto Range.

This setting has two modes: Auto (Standard) mode and Manual mode. In Auto (Standard) mode, the camera decides when the shutter speed is too low, using the reciprocal of the lens focal length. That is, if a 200mm focal length is being used, Auto (Standard) will start to boost the ISO sensitivity when the shutter speed dips below 1/200th second. You can fine-tune this by rotating the Main dial to choose Slower or Faster on the scale (–3 to +3) that appears in Auto (Standard) mode. Each increment is equivalent to one stop of shutter speed.

In Manual mode, you can rotate the Main dial to manually select the "trigger" shutter speed, from 1 second to 1/4000th second.

However, if you've handicapped the camera by locking out some of the highest ISO settings using the Auto ISO range entry described above, if an appropriate ISO setting is not available, the camera will *override this setting* and use a shutter speed lower than the minimum you specify anyway. The camera assumes (rightly or wrongly) that your upper ISO boundary is more important than your lower shutter speed limit. The lesson here is that if you really, really want to enforce a minimum shutter speed when using Auto ISO, make sure your upper limit is high enough. Note that the Minimum Shutter Speed setting is ignored when using flash, which may need a specific shutter speed for proper sync.

HDR Shooting [HDR PQ]

Options: Disable (default), Enable

My preference: N/A

This entry enables capturing high dynamic range (HDR) images in HEIF and RAW formats conforming to the Perceptual Quantization (PQ) specification. (PQ is a non-linear electro-optical transfer function that allows the display of HDR images using highly verbose scientific terminology.) Expanded ISO speeds (L or H) are not available with HDR Shooting enabled. HDR images are most accurately viewed on an HDR-compatible monitor and some scenes may have a different appearance when viewed in the camera or on a non-HDR-compliant monitor. Canon recommends enabling Highlight Tone Priority (discussed shortly) when you've enabled HDR capture.

You can specify how HDR images are displayed during Playback with the HDMI HDR Output entry of the Playback menu, as described in Chapter 13.

HDR Mode

Options: Off, Moving Subject, Dynamic Range

My preference: N/A

I described using HDR mode in detail in Chapter 4 and won't repeat that information here. To recap, when you access this menu entry, a screen like the one shown at left in Figure 11.9 appears, with three choices: Off, Moving Subject, and Dynamic Range. The default is Off, and is used when you don't want to capture. When you select Moving Subject or Dynamic Range, other options are available:

- **Moving Subject.** You'll specify Moving Subject when shooting scenes containing motion. In this mode, the R8 will capture three images using different exposures and combine them to produce an HDR image. Because your subjects are moving, it will use faster shutter speeds in an attempt to decrease the amount of time *between* shots while *freezing* the action as much as possible. That mode reduces any ghost images that would result from individual images that are slightly blurred and displaced (due to subject motion) at slower shutter speeds.

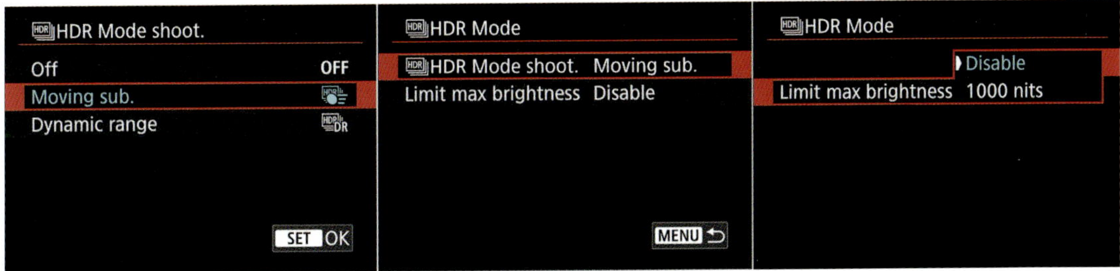

Figure 11.9 HDR Mode Moving Subject options.

In Moving Subject mode, you have one option: Limit Maximum Brightness, as seen at center in Figure 11.9. The option can be disabled or set to limit brightness to 1000 nits, as discussed in more detail shortly. (See Figure 11.9, right.)

- **Dynamic Range.** If you are shooting landscapes or other non-moving subjects, you can choose this option instead of Moving Subject. (See Figure 11.10, left.) Because the scene doesn't contain motion, the camera has a greater range of exposure settings it can use to capture the individual HDR frames. Slower shutter speeds can be used and any camera motion countered by aligning the images while processing the HDR image.

When you select Dynamic Range five options appear on the HDR Mode screen, as seen in Figure 11.10, center. Those five include:

- **Dynamic Range.** You can select the number of stops of dynamic range improvement the HDR feature will provide. (See Figure 11.10, right.) Choose Auto to allow the camera to examine your scene and select an appropriate EV range. As you gain experience you might want to select the range yourself, in order to achieve a particular look. You can choose +/− 1, 2, or 3 EV. The higher the number, the wider the dynamic range of your HDR image.

- **Limit Maximum Brightness.** This entry is available only if you've enabled HDR Shooting/HDR PQ, so you can disregard it if you are not using HDR PQ. It allows you to limit the brightness of images captured using HDR PQ when they will be displayed on monitors that can't handle the format's dynamic range. If you have an HDR-compatible monitor, you can choose Disable; if not, choose 1000 nits to automatically tame your over-bright images. The term "nit" comes from the Latin word nitere, to shine, and is an unofficial, but commonly used measurement to describe the brightness of a display. Apparently, it's easier to say than "candelas per square meter," and a unit that's a better descriptor for displays than lumens (which are used for light bulbs and projectors).

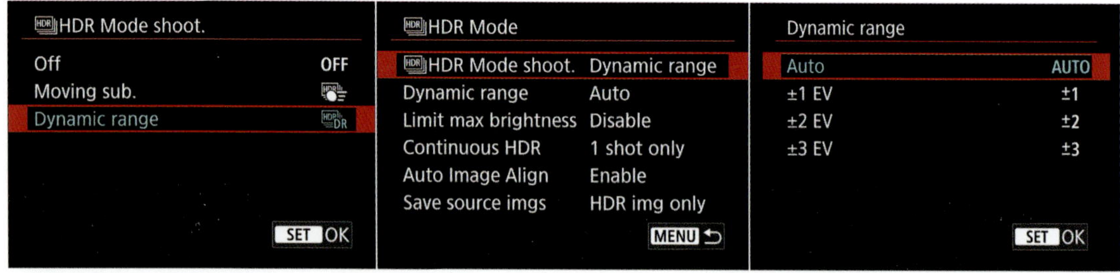

Figure 11.10 HDR Mode Dynamic Range options.

- **Continuous HDR.** Choose 1 Shot Only if you plan to take just a single HDR exposure and want the feature disabled automatically thereafter, or Every Shot to continue using HDR mode for all subsequent exposures until you turn it off.

- **Auto Image Align.** HDR images are ideally produced with the camera on a tripod, in order to reduce the ghosting effects from a series of pictures that each aren't perfectly aligned with the other. You can choose Enable to have the camera attempt to align all three HDR exposures or select Disable when using a tripod. The success of the automatic alignment will vary, depending on the shutter speed used (higher is better), and the amount of camera movement (less is better!).

- **Save Source Images.** When the camera has finished creating its HDR image from your three shots, you can choose to save all the images on your memory card (so you can manually combine them later or perform other manipulations using your image editor). Or, you can elect to save your final HDR image only. You might prefer that choice to save card space, reduce the number of images you won't be using anyway, or if you're shooting a lot of HDR and are confident that the camera's results will suit your needs.

Auto Lighting Optimizer

Options: Disable, Low, Standard (default), High, Disabled in Manual or Bulb modes

My preference: Disable

The Auto Lighting Optimizer provides a partial fix for images that are too dark or flat. Such photos typically have low contrast, and the Auto Lighting Optimizer improves them—as you shoot—by increasing both the brightness and contrast as required. The feature can be activated in Program, Aperture-priority, Shutter-priority, and Flexible-priority modes. You can select from four settings: Standard (the default value, which is always selected when using Basic Zone modes), plus Low, High, and Disable. (See Figure 11.11.) Press the INFO button to add/remove a checkmark icon that indicates the Auto Lighting Optimizer is disabled during manual exposure. Since you're likely to be specifying an exposure in Manual and Bulb mode, you probably don't want the optimizer to interfere with your settings, so disabling the feature is the default. **Note:** Auto Lighting Optimizer is not available when HDR Mode is set to Moving Subject or Dynamic Range.

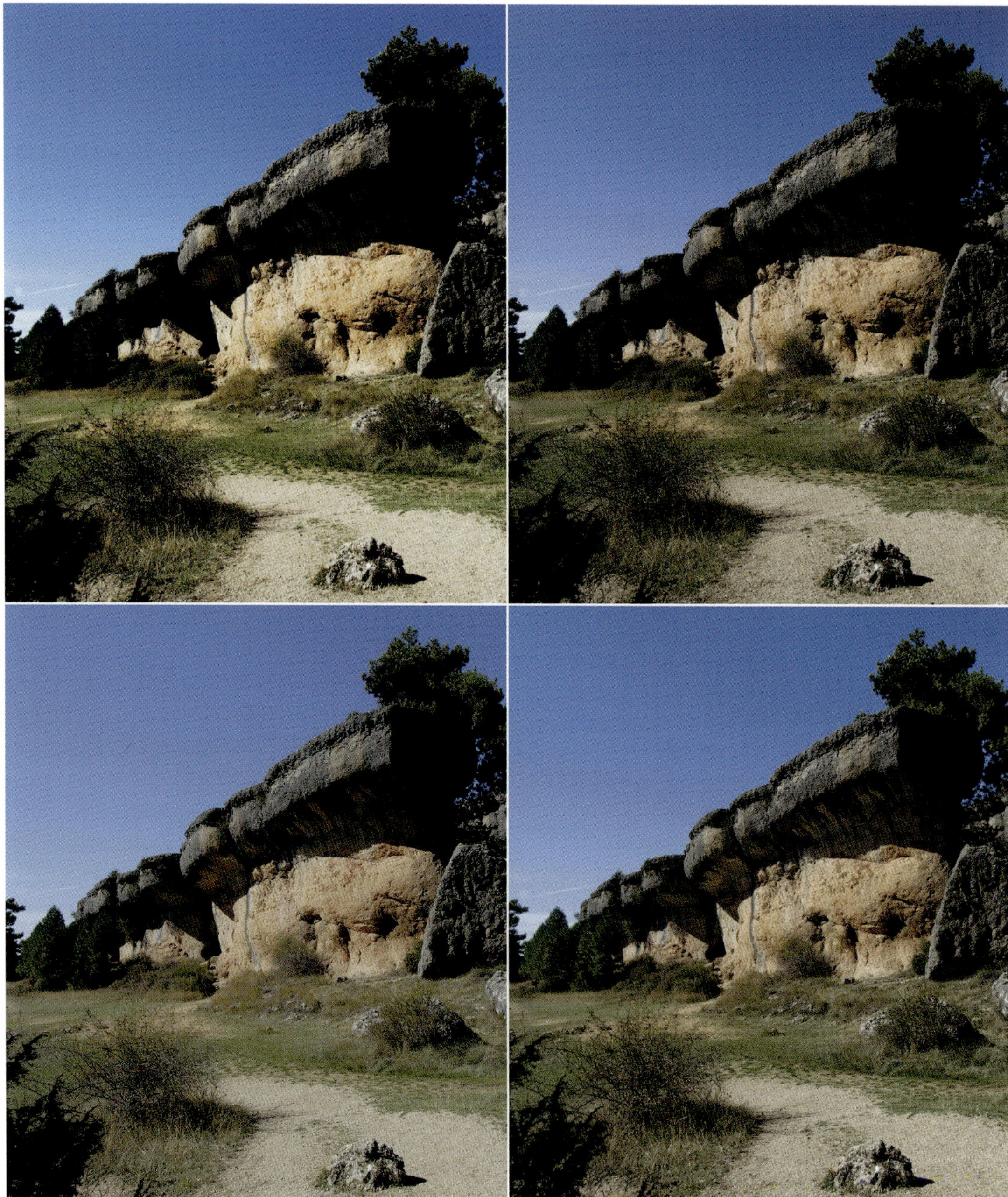

Figure 11.11 Auto Lighting Optimizer can brighten dark, low-contrast images, giving them a little extra snap and brightness. You can choose Disable (upper left), Standard (upper right), Low (lower left), or High (lower right).

Highlight Tone Priority

Options: Disable/OFF (default), Enable D+, Enhanced D+2
My preference: Disable

This setting concentrates the available tones in an image from the middle grays up to the brightest highlights, in effect expanding the dynamic range of the image at the expense of shadow detail. You'd want to activate this option when shooting subjects in which there is lots of important detail in the highlights, and less detail in shadow areas. Highlight tones will be preserved, while shadows will be allowed to go dark more readily (and may exhibit an increase in noise levels). Bright beach or snow scenes, especially those with few shadows (think high noon, when the shadows are smaller) can benefit from using Highlight Tone Priority. **Note:** Highlight Tone Priority is not available when HDR Mode is set to Moving Subject or Dynamic Range. Your choices include:

- **Disable/OFF.** The normal dynamic range is applied.
- **Enable D+.** Highlight areas are given expanded tonal values, while the tones available for shadow areas are reduced. The ISO 100 sensitivity setting is disabled and only ISO 200 and above settings are possible. The expanded L and H ISO speeds are disabled. You can tell that this restriction is in effect by viewing the D+ icon shown in the viewfinder, on the ISO Selection screen, and in the shooting information display for a particular image. Image noise may slightly increase as the camera manipulates the image.

  Canon recommends the D+ setting when shooting HDR PDQ. You can activate/deactivate it for that mode by pressing the Q/SET button to add a checkmark to the option in the Highlight Tone Priority screen.

- **Enhanced D+2.** More aggressive preservation of overexposed highlights. Use this with caution, as your images can be changed rather drastically. This setting is not available when shooting movies.

Anti-Flicker Shooting

Options: Enable, Disable (default)
My preference: Disable, unless shooting under flickering light source

This is the first entry in the Shooting 3 menu. (See Figure 11.12.) Novice sports photographers often ask me why shots they take in certain gymnasiums or arenas have inconsistent exposure, wildly varying color, or banding. The answer is that certain types of artificial lighting have a blinking cycle that is imperceptible to the eye, but which the camera can capture. This setting, when enabled, detects the light source's blinking frequency (it's optimized for 100Hz to 120Hz [cycles per second]), and takes the picture at the moment when the flicker has the least effect on the final image. It cannot be used in live view or movie shooting.

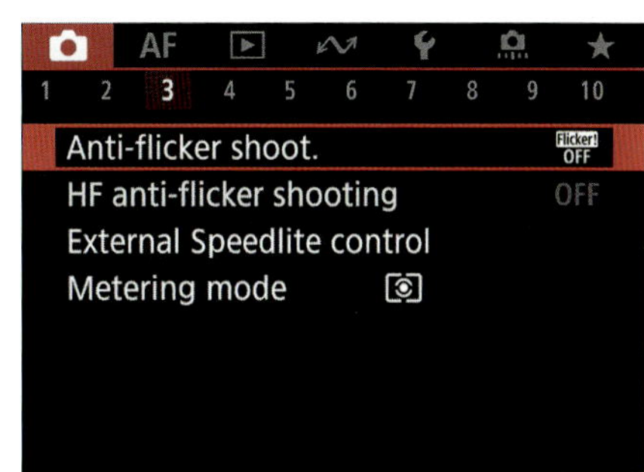

Figure 11.12 The Shooting 3 menu.

You may experience a slight shutter release time lag as the camera "waits" for the proper instant, and your continuous shooting speed may be reduced, which makes this setting a necessary evil for sports and other activities involving action. Your results may vary when using P or Av modes, because the shutter speed can change between shots as proper exposure requires. You're better off using Tv or M mode, so the shutter speed remains constant.

If you want to detect flicker manually, once this feature is enabled, you can press the Q/SET button, choose Anti-Flicker Shooting from the Quick Control menu, and press the INFO button. The camera will tell you whether or not flicker has been detected.

Anti-Flicker is disabled when using Basic Zone modes, and may not work as well with dark backgrounds, a bright light within the image area, when using wireless flash, and under other shooting conditions. Canon recommends taking test shots to see how effective the feature is under the light source you are working with.

High-Frequency Anti-Flicker Shooting

Options: Enable, Disable (default); Manual Setting, Auto Detecting

My preference: Disable, unless shooting under flickering high-frequency light source

You've been living with flickering artificial illumination all your life, and never noticed it. Old-fashioned incandescent lights using 60Hz (Hertz) circuits flicker at 100 to 120 cycles per second, but change their intensity only by about 10 percent. That's generally not enough to cause discomfort or affect photography.

Other types of artificial illumination have enough variation in intensity to cause banding, and the Anti-Flicker Shooting entry described above does a good job with those sources. However, some newer types of lighting, including higher-quality LED lamps, flicker with lower intensities and much higher frequencies, and require more advanced correction. This setting allows fine-tuning the shutter speed so that it syncs up with the cycle of flickering light sources to reduce or eliminate those undesirable banding effects. You have two options. Just follow these steps:

For Auto Detecting:

1. **Choose Shooting mode.** Rotate the Mode dial to one of the modes that allow you to specify a shutter speed, M or Tv.

2. **Select shutter speed.** Choose your preferred shutter speed. The Auto Detecting feature will calculate a speed that is close to that setting.

3. **Choose Auto Detecting.** The camera can automatically detect flickering at 50.0Hz to 2011.2Hz.

4. **Hold camera steady.** A Detect Flicker? message will appear. You'll need to hold the camera steady to make sure the frequency is detected accurately. Choose OK to proceed.

5. **Camera looks for flicker.** The screen will display a screen: Detecting.

6a. No flicker found. If this display is shown, the light source does not flicker, and you may exit and try the alternatives that follow this list.

6b. Flicker found xxxx.hz flicker. If this display is shown, the camera will make a suggestion, such as Change shutter speed to 1/1002.1?

7. Accept or reject selection. You can highlight No, Yes (the default) to confirm, or select the third choice, Yes (Move to Tv Settings). The latter switches to Manual Setting, described next.

If Auto Detecting does not discover any flickering, or if the suggested shutter speed still produces banding, you can try to use the auto detect feature again. Sometimes, a second or third try will be successful. You can also rotate the camera about 90 degrees and try again. Flicker detection is sometimes confused by scenes with repetitive patterns, very bright or dark scenes, moving subjects, flashing light sources, and lower frequency flickering. Rotating the camera can sometimes improve auto detecting.

SHUTTER SPEEDS: AUTOMATIC DETECTION

The range of shutter speeds used for automatic high-frequency flicker reduction is limited by your choice of shutter mode:

- **Electronic first-curtain shutter:** 1/50.0–1/512.0 second.
- **Electronic shutter:** 1/50.0–1/2048.0 second.
- **Movie recording:** 1/50.0–1/2048.0 second.

Manual adjustments may end up being your best bet. Just follow these steps:

For Manual Setting:

1. Choose Shooting mode. Rotate the Mode dial to one of the modes that allow you to specify a shutter speed, M or Tv.

2. Select shutter speed. Choose your preferred shutter speed.

3. Choose manual setting. The camera can automatically detect flickering at 50.0Hz to 2011.2Hz, and a setting screen will appear with an adjustment beginning with a shutter speed close to the preferred speed you have set. Figure 11.13 shows the viewfinder version of the screen. The LCD version is similar, but adds touch controls.

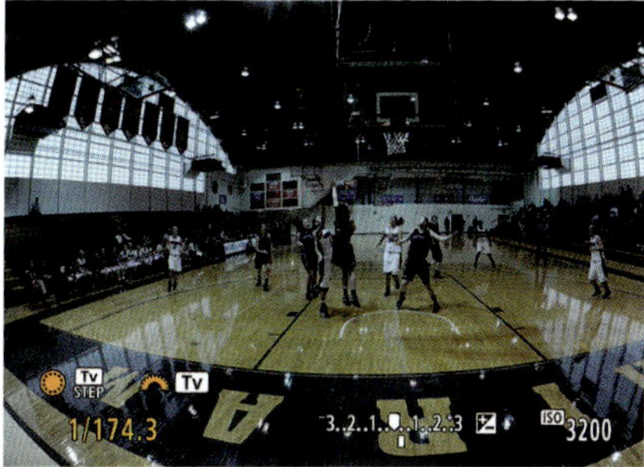

Figure 11.13 Manually fine-tuning shutter speeds for high-frequency anti-flicker correction.

4. **View scene.** As you look at the scene, review different areas of the image to visually spot banding.

5. **Adjust shutter speed.** You can use the QCD and the Main dial to adjust the shutter speed until visual banding disappears.

   - **QCD.** When you rotate this dial, the camera tries automatic detection at various alternate shutter speeds. Rotating clockwise will try higher shutter speeds, increasing the initial speed by 2X, 3X, 4X, and so forth; rotating counterclockwise reduces the shutter speed by 1/2X, 1/3X, 1/4X, and so on.

   - **Main dial.** As banding decreases, you can fine-tune the shutter speed in small increments by rotating the Main dial to the right or left.

6. **If banding remains.** Try rotating the camera 90 degrees or try automatic detection.

SHUTTER SPEEDS: MANUAL SETTING

The range of shutter speeds used for manual frequency flicker reduction is also limited by your choice of shutter mode:

- **Electronic first-curtain shutter:** 1/50.0–1/2048.0 second.
- **Electronic shutter:** 1/50.0–1/8192.0 second.
- **Movie recording:** 1/50.0–1/8192.0 second.

HDR Mode cannot be set to Dynamic Range when this feature is used. Canon recommends setting Custom Function 2: Same Exposure for New Aperture to ISO Speed, so the shutter speed will remain the same. When using this feature flash sync is limited to 1/181.0 second or slower. Manual safety shift adjusts only the aperture, and leaves your fine-tuned shutter speed alone.

External Speedlite Control

Options: Flash Firing, E-TTL Balance, E-TTL II Metering, Continuous Flash Control, Slow Synchro, Flash Function Settings, Flash Custom Function Settings, Clear Settings

My preference: N/A

This multi-level menu entry includes settings for controlling the accessory EL/EX series Speedlites attached to the camera (see Figure 11.14). I provided in-depth coverage of how you can use these options in Chapters 9 and 10 but will list the main options here for reference.

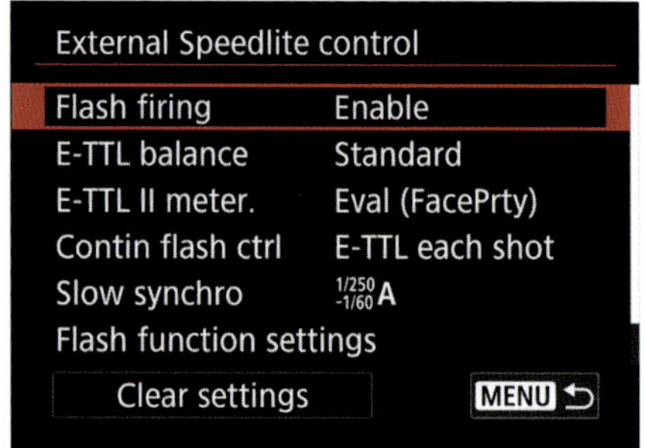

Figure 11.14 The External Speedlite Control menu entry.

Flash Firing

Use this option to enable or disable the attached electronic flash. Choose Enable, and the flash fires normally when it's attached to the camera and powered up. Select Disable, and the flash itself will not fire, but the AF-assist beam emitted by the unit will function normally. You might want to use the latter option when you prefer to shoot under low levels of existing light, but still need the autofocusing boost the flash's AF beam provides.

E-TTL Balance

This is an important feature that gives you extra control over how the illumination of the flash and ambient light are mixed to provide the overall exposure. Your choices include Standard (the default), which gives Speedlite and existing illumination equal weight. Specify Ambience-priority, and the existing light is dominant, with the flash being used as fill light to brighten the shadows. Choose Flash-priority instead, and the Speedlite becomes the main light source, illuminating both your subject and the background. This mode may work best under dim lighting conditions in which not much ambient illumination is available.

E-TTL II Metering

You can choose Evaluative (Matrix) or Average metering modes for the electronic flash exposure meter. Evaluative looks at selected areas in the scene to calculate exposure and is the best choice for most images because it attempts to interpret the type of scene being shot; Average calculates flash exposure by reading the entire scene, and it is possibly a good option if you want exposure to be calculated for the overall scene. If your scene includes faces, you can select a third option, Evaluative (Face-priority), which bases exposure on faces in the scene. This process takes a bit of extra time, so continuous shooting speeds may be slower in this mode. However, it's more likely that your flash's recycling time will be the dominant factor in selecting a continuous shooting speed.

Continuous Flash Control

This entry also has an effect on continuous shooting with a Speedlight. You can select E-TTL Each Shot, in which case the camera will meter your scene before every exposure in a continuous sequence. Choose E-TTL 1st Shot instead and the exposure determined for the first shot will be used for subsequent shots. Use that option when you want the highest continuous shooting speed; it obviously works best when you are not recomposing between shots. Indeed, subject movement may result in a change in optimal exposure, so that first shot setting may turn out to be incorrect.

Slow Synchro

You can select the flash synchronization speed that will be used when working in Av (Aperture-priority) or P (Program) exposure modes. There are three choices:

- **1/200 to 30 seconds Auto.** The shutter speed is set automatically from 1/200th second to 30 seconds. High-speed sync can be used.
- **1/200 to 1/60 second Auto.** The shutter speed is set automatically from 1/200th second to 1/60th second. Slower shutter speeds are locked out. This setting reduces ghost images (as explained in Chapter 9) but backgrounds may be darker.
- **1/200 (fixed).** Shutter speed is fixed at 1/200th when using flash. High-speed sync is not available.

Normally, in Aperture-priority mode when using flash, you specify the f/stop to be locked in. The camera then adjusts exposure by varying the output of the electronic flash. In Program mode, the camera chooses the f/stop. Because the primary exposure comes from the flash, the main effect of the shutter speed selected is on the secondary exposure from the ambient light remaining on the scene.

Flash Function Settings

There is a total of six basic choices for this menu screen if you're not using the optical or wireless transmission options, plus Clear Settings. The additional options are not shown unless you're working in wireless flash mode. All these are explained in Chapters 9 and 10.

- **ETTL Flash mode.** This entry allows you to choose from automatic exposure calculation (E-TTL II), manual flash exposure, multi (repeating) flash, or Continuous Shooting Priority (CSP). The latter setting, which increases flash output and ISO speed each by one stop, uses less battery power and enables the camera to use flash when shooting continuously.
- **Wireless functions/Firing ratio controls.** These choices include Mode, Channel, Firing Group, and other options, such as Wireless Radio ID, used only when you're working in wireless mode to control a wireless-capable external flash. If you've disabled wireless functions, the other options don't appear on the menu. I covered these options in Chapter 10, which is an entire chapter dedicated to using the wireless shooting capabilities.
- **Zoom.** Use this to select a flash zoom head setting to adjust coverage area of compatible Speedlites.
- **Shutter sync.** You can choose first-curtain sync, which fires the pre-flash used to calculate the exposure before the shutter opens, followed by the main flash as soon as the shutter is completely open. This is the default mode, and you'll generally perceive the pre-flash and main flash as a single burst. Alternatively, you can select second-curtain sync, which fires the pre-flash as soon as the shutter opens, and then triggers the main flash in a second burst at the end of the exposure, just before the shutter starts to close. (If the shutter speed is slow enough, you may clearly see both the pre-flash and main flash as separate bursts of light.) This action allows photographing a blurred trail of light of moving objects with sharp flash exposures at the beginning and the end of the exposure. This type of flash exposure is slightly different from what some other cameras produce using second-curtain sync. I explained how it works in Chapter 9.

If you have an external compatible Speedlite attached, you can also choose high-speed sync, which allows you to use shutter speeds faster than 1/200th second, using the External Flash Function Setting menu.

- **Flash exposure compensation.** Select this option with the Q/SET button, then dial in the amount of flash EV compensation you want using the QCD. The EV that was in place before you started to make your adjustment is shown as a blue indicator, so you can return to that value quickly. Press Q/SET again to confirm your change, then press the MENU button twice to exit.
- **Flash exposure bracketing.** Use these settings to specify options for adjusting the output of your unit when using bracketing with your compatible electronic flash.

Flash Custom Function Settings

Many external Speedlites from Canon include their own list of Custom Functions, which can be used to specify things like flash metering mode and flash bracketing sequences, as well as more sophisticated features, such as modeling light/flash (if available), use of external power sources (if attached), and functions of any slave unit attached to the external flash. This menu entry allows you to set an external flash unit's Custom Functions from your camera's menu. The exact functions available will vary by flash unit. For example, with the Speedlite 320EX, only Custom Functions 1 (Auto Power Off), 6 (Quick Flash with Continuous Shot), 10 (Slave Auto Power Off Timer), and 11 (Slave Auto Power Off Cancel) are available. With high-end units, like the Speedlite 600EX-RT II, a broader range of choices (described in Chapter 9) are at your disposal.

Clear Settings

This entry allows you to zero-out any changes you've made to your external flash's settings and Custom Functions settings and return them to their factory default settings. The exception is C.Fn-00 Distance Indicator Display (if available for your flash). That setting remains as adjusted until you change it yourself. Note that a flash's Personal Functions (P.Fn) cannot be set or reset from the camera; you must use the Speedlite's controls instead.

Metering Mode

Options: Evaluative, Partial, Spot, Center-weighted Averaging

My preference: N/A

This entry is just a menu-based way of selecting the metering mode, as discussed elsewhere in the book. It resides here primarily to give you an option to assign this function to a custom key if you want to access it in an additional way that suits your needs.

White Balance

Options: Auto (default), Daylight, Shade, Cloudy, Tungsten, White Fluorescent, Flash, Custom, Color Temperature

My preference: N/A

This is the first entry in the Shooting 4 menu. (See Figure 11.15.) If automatic white balance or one of the six preset settings available (Daylight, Shade, Cloudy, Tungsten, White Fluorescent, or Flash) aren't suitable, you can set a custom white balance using the Custom menu option or a specific color temperature value. The screen shown at left in Figure 11.16 is basically similar to the one that pops up when you select White Balance from the Quick Control screen. If you choose the "K" entry, you can select an exact color temperature from 2,500K to 10,000K using the Main dial.

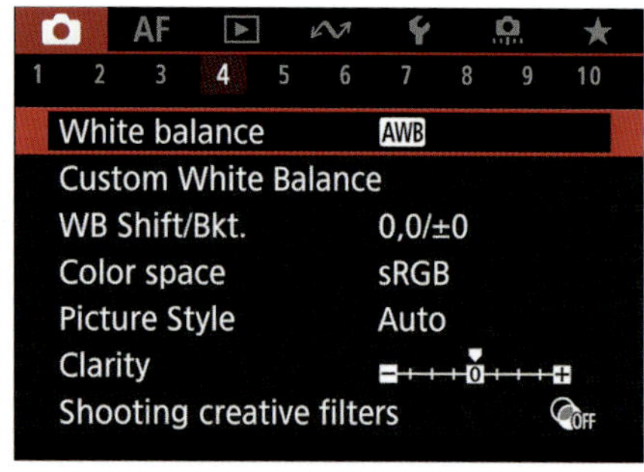

Figure 11.15 The Shooting 4 menu.

Of course, unless you own a specialized tool called a color temperature meter, you probably won't know the exact color temperature of your scene. However, knowing the color temperatures of the preset options can help you if you decide to tweak them by choosing a different color temperature setting. The values used are as follows, with two options available for Auto:

- **Auto (AWB).** 3,000K–7,000K. Press the INFO button when this is selected to toggle between Ambience-priority (to keep warm color under tungsten light) or White-priority (to produce neutral whites even under tungsten illumination). (See Figure 11.16, right.)
- **Daylight.** 5,200K
- **Shade.** 7,000K
- **Cloudy.** 6,000K
- **Tungsten.** 3,200K
- **White Fluorescent.** 4,000K
- **Flash.** 6,000K
- **Custom.** 2,000K–10,000K
- **Color temperature.** 2,500K–10,000K (settable in 100K increments)

Figure 11.16 White balance presets can be chosen here (left). Ambience- or White-priority can be set for Auto White Balance (right).

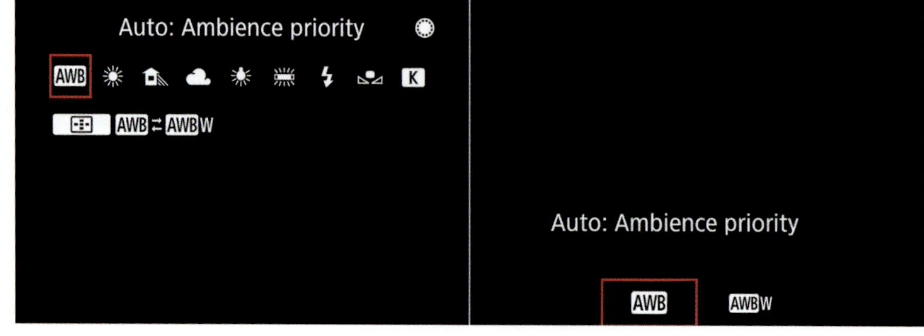

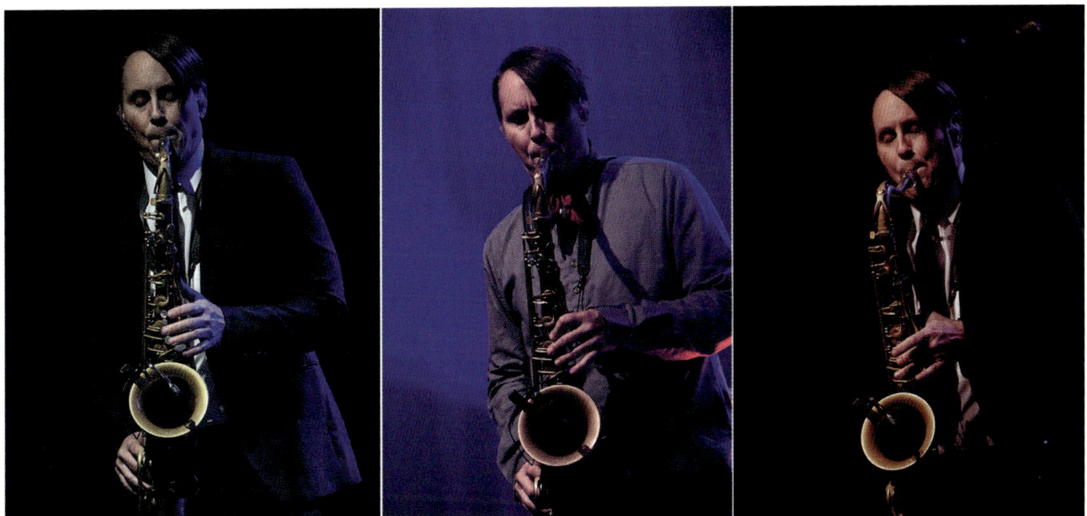

Figure 11.17 Adjusting color temperature can provide different results of the same subject at 3,400K (left), 5,000K (center), and 2,800K (right).

Choosing the right white balance can have a dramatic effect on the colors of your image, as you can see in Figure 11.17.

The problem with the available presets (Daylight, Shade, etc.) is that you have only six of them, and in any given situation, all of them are likely to be wrong—strictly speaking. The good news is that they are likely to be only a *little bit* wrong. The human eye is very adaptable, so in most cases you'll be perfectly happy with the results you get if you use Auto or choose a preset that's in the white balance ballpark.

But if you absolutely must have the correct color balance or are frequently dissatisfied with the color balance when using Auto or one of the presets, you can always shoot RAW and adjust the final color balance in your image editor when converting the .cr3 file. Or, you can use a custom white balance procedure, described next.

Custom White Balance

Options: White balance setting

My preference: N/A

If automatic white balance or one of the preset settings (Daylight, Shade, Cloudy, Tungsten, White Fluorescent, or Flash) aren't suitable, you can set a custom white balance using this menu option. The custom setting you establish will then be applied whenever you select Custom using the White Balance menu.

To set the white balance to an appropriate color temperature under the current ambient lighting conditions, focus manually (with the lens set on MF) on a plain white or gray object, such as a card or wall, making sure the object fills the spot metering circle in the center of the viewfinder. Then, take a photo. Next, press the MENU button and select Custom White Balance from the Shooting 4 menu. Rotate the QCD until the reference image you just took appears and choose Q/SET to store the white balance of the image as your Custom setting. Only compatible images that can be used to specify a custom white balance will be shown on the screen. Custom white balance images are marked with a custom icon and cannot be removed (although they can be replaced with a new custom white balance image).

Using an ExpoDisc

As I mentioned in Chapter 8, many photographers prefer to use a gadget called an ExpoDisc, from ExpoImaging, Inc. (www.expoimaging.com), which fits over (or attaches to) the front of your lens and provides a diffuse neutral (or semi-neutral) subject to measure with your camera's custom white balance feature. ExpoDiscs cost $75 to $100 or so, depending on the filter size of your lens, but many just buy the 77mm version and hold it in front of their lens. (There's a strap attached, so you won't lose it.) Others have had mixed success using less-expensive alternatives (such as the lid of a Pringles can). ExpoImaging also makes ExpoCap lens caps with similar diffusing features, and you can leave one of them on your lens at all times (at least, when you're not shooting).

There are two models, the standard ExpoDisc Neutral, and a Portrait model that produces a slightly warmer color balance suitable for portraits. The product produces the best results when you use it to measure the *incident light*; that is, the light falling onto your subject. In other words, instead of aiming your camera at your subject from the shooting position, take the time (if it's possible) to position yourself at the subject position and point your ExpoDisc-equipped lens toward the light source that will illuminate the scene. (However, don't point your camera directly at the sun! Aim at the sky instead.)

I like to use the ExpoDisc in two situations:

- **Outdoors under mixed lighting.** When you're shooting outdoors, you'll often find that your scene is illuminated by direct sunlight as well as by open shade, full shade, or a mixture of these. A custom white balance reading can help you zero in on the correct color balance in a situation that's hard to judge visually.

- **When using studio flash.** It's a nasty secret that many studio flash units change color temperature when you adjust the power slider to scale down the output. Perhaps your 1600ws (watt second) flash puts out too much light to allow you to use a larger f/stop for selective focus. So, you dial it down to 1/4 power. That will likely change the color temperature of the unit slightly, particularly when compared to your 800ws fill light, which you've reduced to *half* power. You can use the ExpoDisc to measure the color temperature of your main light at its new setting or aim it between two lights to obtain an average reading. The result will probably be close enough to the correct color temperature to satisfy most studio shooters.

White Balance Shift/Bracketing

Options: WB bias and WB bracketing

My preference: N/A

White balance shift allows you to dial in a white balance color bias along the blue/amber dimensions, and/or magenta/green scale. In other words, you can set your color balance so that it is a little bluer or yellower (only), a little more magenta or green (only), or a combination of the two bias dimensions. You can also bracket exposures, taking several consecutive pictures each with a slightly different color balance biased in the directions you specify.

The process is a little easier to visualize if you look at Figure 11.18. The center intersection of lines BA and MG (remember high school geometry!) is the point of zero bias. Move the point at that intersection using the directional controls to locate it at any point on the graph using the blue/amber and magenta/green coordinates. The amount of shift will be displayed in the SHIFT box to the right of the graph.

White balance bracketing is like white balance shifting, only the bracketed changes occur along the bias axis you specify. This form of bracketing is like exposure bracketing, but with the added dimension of hue. Bias bracketing can be performed in any JPEG- (or HEIF-) only mode. You

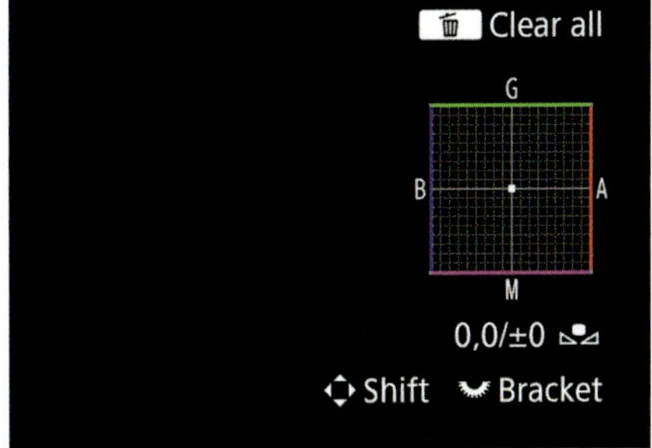

Figure 11.18 Use the QCD to specify color balance bracketing using magenta/green bias or to specify blue/amber bias.

can't use any RAW format or RAW+JPEG format because the RAW files already contain the information needed to fine-tune the white balance and white balance bias.

When you select WB SHIFT/BKT, the adjustment screen appears. First, you rotate the QCD to set the range of the shift in either the magenta/green dimension (rotate to the left to change the vertical separation of the three dots representing the separate exposures) or in the blue/amber dimension by rotating to the right. Use the left/right directional controls to move the bracket set around within the color space, and outside the MG or BA axes.

In most cases, it's easy to determine if you want your image to be more green, more magenta, more blue, or more amber, although judging your current shots on the LCD screen can be tricky unless you view the screen in a darkened location so it will be bright and easy to see. Bracketing was covered in Chapter 4.

Color Space

Options: sRGB (default), Adobe RGB

My preference: I use the expanded Adobe RGB color space.

When you are using one of the Creative Zone modes, you can select one of two different color spaces (also called *color gamuts*) using this menu entry. One color space is named *Adobe RGB* (because it was developed by Adobe Systems in 1998), while the other is called *sRGB* (supposedly because it is the *standard* RGB color space). These two color gamuts define a specific set of colors that can be applied to the images captured.

The Color Space menu choice applies directly to JPEG/HEIF images shot using P, Tv, Av, and M exposure modes. When you're using Scene Intelligent Auto mode, the camera uses the sRGB color space for all the JPEG/HEIF images you take. RAW images are a special case. They have the information for *both* sRGB and Adobe RGB, but when you load such photos into your image editor, it will default to sRGB (with Scene Intelligent Auto or Creative Auto shots) or the color space specified here, unless you change that setting while importing the photos. (See the "Best of Both Worlds" sidebar that follows for more information.)

You may be surprised to learn that the camera doesn't automatically capture *all* the colors we see. Unfortunately, that's impossible because of the limitations of the sensor and the filters used to capture the fundamental red, green, and blue colors, as well as that of the elements used to display those colors on your camera and computer monitors. Nor is it possible to *print* every color our eyes detect, because the inks or pigments used don't absorb and reflect colors perfectly. In short, your sensor doesn't capture all the colors that we can see, your monitor can't display all the colors that the sensor captures, and your printer outputs yet another version.

On the other hand, quite a few more colors are captured than we need. A 14-bit RAW image contains a possible 281 *trillion* different hues (16,384 colors per red, green, or blue channel), which are condensed down to a mere 16.8 million possible colors when converted to a 24-bit (eight bits per channel) image.

The set of colors, or gamut, that can be reproduced or captured by a given device (scanner, digital camera, monitor, printer, or some other piece of equipment) is represented as a color space that exists within the larger full range of colors. That full range is represented by the odd-shaped splotch of color shown in Figure 11.19, as defined by scientists at an international organization back in 1931. The colors possible with Adobe RGB are represented by the black triangle in the figure, while the sRGB gamut is represented by the smaller white triangle. The location of the corners of each triangle represents the position of the primary red, green, and blue colors in the gamut.

A third color space, ProPhoto RGB, represented by the yellow triangle in the figure, has become more popular among professional photographers as more and more color printing labs support it. While you cannot *save* images using the ProPhoto gamut, you can convert your photos to 16-bit ProPhoto format using Adobe Camera RAW when you import RAW photos into an image editor. ProPhoto encompasses virtually all the colors we can see (and some we can't), giving advanced photographers better tools to work with in processing their photos. It has richer reds, greens, and blues,

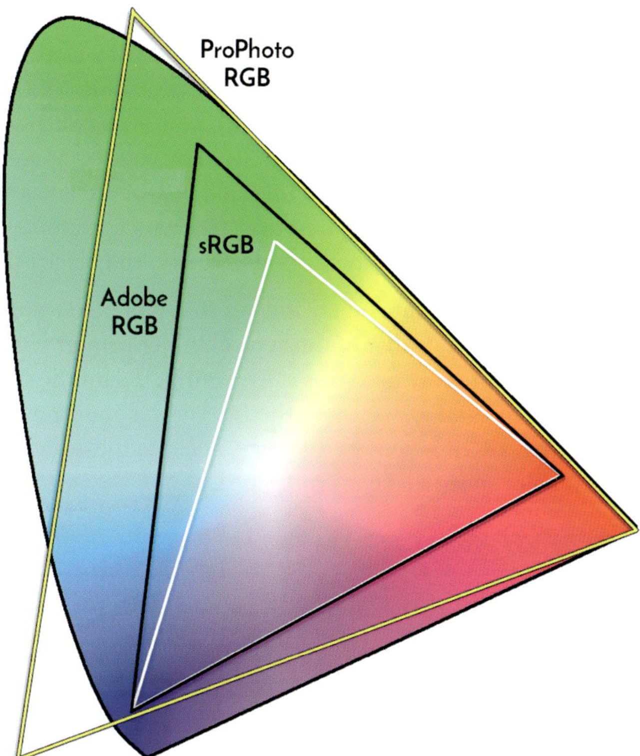

Figure 11.19 The outer curved figure shows all the colors we can see; the outlines show the boundaries of Adobe RGB (black triangle), sRGB (white triangle), and ProPhoto RGB (yellow triangle).

although, as you can see from the figure, its green and blue primaries are imaginary (they extend outside the visible color gamut). Those with exacting standards need not use a commercial printing service if they want to explore ProPhoto RGB: many inkjet printers can handle cyans, magentas, and yellows that extend outside the Adobe RGB gamut.

Regardless of which triangle—or color space—is used, you end up with some combination of 16.8 million different colors that can be used in your photograph. (No one image will contain all 16.8 million! Think about it: the only way an image could include that many colors would be if two-thirds of the pixels were each a unique hue!) But, as you can see from the figure, the colors available will be *different*.

Adobe RGB, like ProPhoto RGB, is an expanded color space useful for commercial and professional printing, and it can reproduce a wider range of colors. It can also come in useful if an image is going to be extensively retouched, especially within an advanced image editor, like Adobe Photoshop, which has sophisticated color management capabilities that can be tailored to specific color spaces. As an advanced user, you don't need to automatically "upgrade" to Adobe RGB, because images tend to look less saturated on your monitor and, it is likely, significantly different from what you will get if you output the photo to your personal inkjet. (You can *profile* your monitor for the Adobe RGB color space to improve your on-screen rendition using widely available color-calibrating hardware and software.)

While both Adobe RGB and sRGB can reproduce the exact same 16.8 million absolute colors, Adobe RGB spreads those colors over a larger portion of the visible spectrum, as you can see in the figure. Think of a box of crayons (the jumbo 16.8 million crayon variety). Some of the basic crayons from the original sRGB set have been removed and replaced with new hues not contained in the original box. Your "new" box contains colors that can't be reproduced by your computer monitor, but which work just fine with a commercial printing press. For example, Adobe RGB has more "crayons" available in the cyan-green portion of the box, compared to sRGB, which is unlikely to be an advantage unless your image's final destination is the cyan, magenta, yellow, and black inks of a printing press.

The other color space, sRGB, is recommended for images that will be output locally on the user's own printer, as this color space matches that of the typical inkjet printer fairly closely. You might prefer sRGB, which is the default for most cameras, as it is well suited for the range of colors that can be displayed on a computer screen and viewed over the Internet. If you plan to take your image file to a retailer's kiosk for printing, sRGB is your best choice, because those automated output devices are calibrated for the sRGB color space that consumers use.

BEST OF BOTH WORLDS

If you plan to use RAW+JPEG for most of your photos, go ahead and set sRGB as your color space. You'll end up with JPEGs suitable for output on your own printer, but you can still extract an Adobe RGB version from the RAW file at any time. It's like shooting two different color spaces at once—sRGB and Adobe RGB—and getting the best of both worlds.

Of course, choosing the right color space doesn't solve the problems that result from having each device in the image chain manipulating or producing a slightly different set of colors. To that end, you'll need to investigate the wonderful world of *color management*, which uses hardware and software tools to match or *calibrate* all your devices, as closely as possible, so that what you see more closely resembles what you capture, what you see on your computer display, and what ends up on a printed hardcopy. Entire books have been devoted to color management, and most of what you need to know doesn't directly involve your camera, so I won't detail the nuts and bolts here.

To manage your color, you'll need, at the bare minimum, some sort of calibration system for your computer display, so that your monitor can be adjusted to show a standardized set of colors that is repeatable over time. (What you see on the screen can vary as the monitor ages, or even when the room light changes.) I use the SpyderX Pro monitor color correction system from Datacolor (www.datacolor.com) for my computer's 32-inch main screen and two 26-inch displays. The unit checks room light levels every five minutes and reminds me to recalibrate every week or two using a small sensor device, which attaches temporarily to the front of the screen and interprets test patches that the software displays during calibration. The rest of the time, the sensor sits in its stand, measuring the room illumination, and adjusting my monitors for higher or lower ambient light levels.

Picture Style

Options: Auto (default), Standard, Portrait, Landscape, Fine Detail, Neutral, Faithful, Monochrome, three User Styles

My preference: Auto

This feature is one of the most important tools for customizing the way your photos are rendered. Picture Styles are a type of fine-tuning you can apply to your photos to change certain characteristics of each image taken using a particular Picture Style setting. The parameters you can specify for full-color images include the amount of sharpness, degree of contrast, the richness of the color, and the hue of skin tones. For black-and-white images, you can tweak the sharpness and contrast, but the two color adjustments (meaningless in a monochrome image) are replaced by controls for filter effects (which I'll explain shortly), and sepia, blue, purple, or green tone overlays.

There are preset Picture Styles for Standard, Portrait, Landscape, Fine Detail, Neutral, and Faithful pictures, plus Auto, and three user-definable settings called User Def. 1, User Def. 2, and User Def. 3, which you can define to apply to any sort of shooting situation you want, such as sports, architecture, or baby pictures. There is also a seventh, Monochrome, Picture Style that allows you to adjust filter effects or add color toning to your black-and-white images. See Figure 11.20 for the main Picture Style menu.

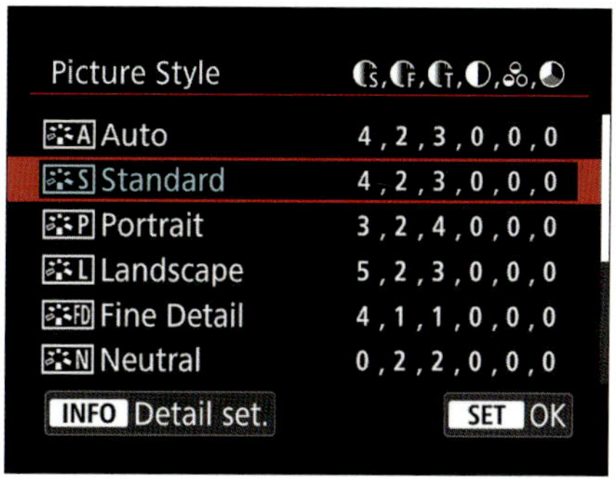

Figure 11.20 Picture Styles are available from this scrolling menu; these six, plus Faithful, Monochrome, and three User Def. styles that become visible when you scroll down the list.

Picture Styles are extremely flexible. Canon has set the parameters for Auto and the predefined color Picture Styles and the single monochrome Picture Style to suit the needs of most photographers. But you can adjust any of those "canned" Picture Styles to settings you prefer. Better yet, you can use those three User Definition files to create brand-new styles that are all your own. If you want rich, bright colors to emulate Velvia film or the work of legendary photographer Pete Turner, you can build your own color-soaked style. If you want soft, muted colors and less sharpness to create a romantic look, you can do that, too. Perhaps you'd like a setting with extra contrast for shooting outdoors on hazy or cloudy days.

The current settings for each are arrayed along the top in Figure 11.20 as icons, left to right: S (sharpness strength), F (sharpness fineness), T (sharpness threshold), Contrast (a half white/half black circle), Saturation (a triangle composed of three circles), and Color Tone (a circle divided into thirds). When you scroll down within the Monochrome Picture Style, Filter Effect (overlapping circles) and Toning Effect (paintbrush tip) appear. These parameters, applied when using Picture Styles, are described next.

Here are your options:

- **Sharpness.** This parameter determines the apparent contrast between the outlines or edges in an image, which we perceive as image sharpness. When adjusting sharpness, remember that more is not always a good thing. A little softness is necessary (and is introduced by a blurring "anti-alias" filter in front of the sensor) to reduce or eliminate the moiré effects that can result when details in your image form a pattern that is too close to the pattern, or frequency, of the sensor itself. The default levels of sharpening were chosen by Canon to allow most moiré interference to be safely blurred to invisibility, at the cost of a little sharpness. As you boost sharpness (either using a Picture Style or in your image editor), moiré can become a problem, plus, you may end up with those noxious "halos" that appear around the edges of images that have been oversharpened. Use this adjustment with care. You have three individual parameters within this setting that you can adjust individually:

  - **Strength.** Set the intensity of the sharpening on an eight-step scale from 0 (weak outline emphasis) to 7 (strong outline emphasis). Adding too much strength can result in a halo and excess detail around the edges within your image.

  - **Fineness.** This determines which edges will be emphasized, on a scale of 1 (sharpens the finest lines in your image) to 5 (sharpens only larger, coarser lines). Use a lower number if you anticipate your image will have a wealth of fine detail that you want to emphasize, such as a heavily textured subject. A larger number might be better for portraits, so that eyes and hair might be sharpened, but not skin defects. Changes in Fineness and Threshold (which follows) do not apply when shooting movies.

  - **Threshold.** This setting uses contrast between the edges being sharpened and the surrounding areas, to determine the degree of sharpening applied to the outlines. It uses a scale from 1 to 5, with lower numbers allowing sharpening when there is less contrast between the edge and surroundings. There is an increase in noise when a low threshold is set. Higher numbers produce sharpening only when the contrast between edge and adjacent pixels is already high. The highest numbers can produce excessive contrast and a poster-like effect.

- **Contrast.** Use this control, with values from −4 (low contrast) to +4 (higher contrast), to change the number of middle tones between the deepest blacks and brightest whites. Low-contrast settings produce a flatter-looking photo, while high-contrast adjustments may improve the tonal rendition while possibly losing detail in the shadows or highlights.

- **Saturation.** This parameter, adjustable from −4 (low saturation) to +4 (high saturation) controls the richness of the color, making, say, a red tone appear to be deeper and fuller when you increase saturation, and tend more toward lighter, pinkish hues when you decrease saturation of the reds. Boosting the saturation too much can mean that detail may be lost in one or more of the color channels, producing what is called "clipping." You can detect this phenomenon when using the RGB histograms, as described in Chapter 4.

- **Color tone.** This adjustment has the most effect on skin tones, making them either redder (0 to −4) or yellower (0 to +4).

- **Filter effect (Monochrome only).** Filter effects do not add any color to a black-and-white image. Instead, they change the rendition of gray tones as if the picture were taken through a color filter. I'll explain this distinction more completely in the sidebar "Filters vs. Toning" later in this section.

- **Toning effect (Monochrome only).** Using toning effects preserves the monochrome tonal values in your image but adds a color overlay that gives the photo a sepia, blue, purple, or green cast.

The predefined Picture Styles are as follows:

- **Auto.** Adjusts the color to make outdoor scenes look more vivid, with richer colors.

- **Standard.** This Picture Style applies a set of parameters, including boosted sharpness, that are useful for most picture taking, and which are applied automatically when using Basic Zone modes other than Portrait or Landscape.

- **Portrait.** This style boosts saturation for richer colors when shooting portraits, which is particularly beneficial for women and children, while reducing sharpness slightly to provide more flattering skin texture. The Basic Mode Portrait setting uses this Picture Style. You might prefer the Faithful style for portraits of men when you want a more rugged or masculine look, or when you want to emphasize character lines in the faces of older subjects of either gender.

- **Landscape.** This style increases the saturation of blues and greens and increases both color saturation and sharpness for more vivid landscape images. The Basic Zone Landscape mode uses this setting.

- **Fine detail.** As you might expect, this setting uses sharpening and contrast to produce an image with optimum detail, at the expense of possibly adding some visual noise.

- **Neutral.** This Picture Style is a less-saturated and lower-contrast version of the Standard style. Use it when you want a more muted look to your images, or when the photos you are taking seem too bright and contrasty (say, at the beach on a sunny day).

- **Faithful.** The goal of this style is to render the colors of your image as accurately as possible, roughly in the same relationships as seen by the eye.

- **Monochrome.** Use this Picture Style to create black-and-white photos in the camera. If you're shooting JPEG only, the colors are gone forever. But if you're shooting JPEG+RAW you can convert the RAW files to color as you import them into your image editor, even if you've shot using the Monochrome Picture Style. Images are displayed in black-and-white on the screen during playback, but the colors are there in the RAW file for later retrieval.

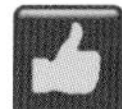

TIP You can use the Monochrome Picture Style even if you are using one of the RAW formats alone, without a JPEG version. The camera displays your images on the screen in black and white and marks the RAW image as monochrome so it will *default* to that style when you import it into your image editor. However, the color information is still present in the RAW file and can be retrieved, at your option, when importing the image.

Selecting Picture Styles

Canon makes selecting a Picture Style for use very easy, and, to prevent you from accidentally changing an existing style when you don't mean to, divides *selection* and *modification* functions into two separate tasks. There are different ways to choose from among your existing Picture Styles:

- **Picture Styles menu.** Use this menu entry and scroll down the list shown earlier in Figure 11.20 with the QCD until the style you want to use is highlighted. Then press SET.
- **Quick Control screen.** Press the Q/SET button and navigate to the Picture Styles icon in the right column. With the icon highlighted, you can rotate either dial or use the directional controls to choose the style you want to use and press Q/SET to confirm.

Defining Picture Styles

Canon makes interpreting current Picture Style settings and applying changes very easy. As you saw in Figure 11.20, the current settings of the visible Picture Style options are shown as numeric values on the menu screen. Some camera vendors use word descriptions, like Sharp, Extra Sharp, or Vivid, More Vivid that are difficult to relate to. You can change one of the existing Picture Styles or define your own whenever the Picture Styles menu is visible. Just follow these steps:

1. **Choose a style to modify.** Highlight the style you'd like to adjust.

2. **Activate adjustment mode.** Press the INFO button to choose Detail Set. The screen that appears next will be like the one shown in Figure 11.21 for the six color styles or three User Def. styles. In addition to the Sharpness and Contrast adjustments shown in the figure, you can scroll down to two more: Saturation and Color Tone. The Monochrome screen looks similar but substitutes Filter Effect and Toning Effect (discussed later) for Saturation and Color Tone.

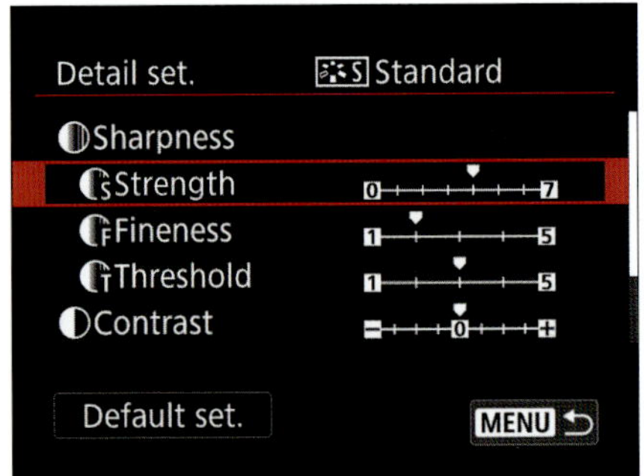

Figure 11.21 Each parameter can be changed separately for color Picture Styles, such as the Standard style pictured.

3. **Choose a parameter to change.** Use the QCD to scroll among the parameters, plus Default Set. at the bottom of the screen, which restores the values to the preset numbers.

4. **Activate changes.** Press Q/SET to change the values of a highlighted parameter.

5. **Adjust values.** Use the QCD to move the triangle to the value you want to use. Note that the previous value remains on the scale, represented by a gray triangle. This makes it easy to return to the original setting if you want.

6. **Confirm changes.** Press the Q/SET button to lock in that value, then press the MENU button three times to back out of the menu system.

FILTERS VS. TONING

Although some of the color choices overlap, you'll get very different looks when choosing between Filter Effects and Toning Effects. Filter Effects add no color to the monochrome image. Instead, they reproduce the look of black-and-white film that has been shot through a color filter. That is, Yellow will make the sky darker and the clouds will stand out more, whereas Orange makes the sky even darker and sunsets more full of detail. The Red filter produces the darkest sky of all and darkens green objects, such as leaves. Human skin may appear lighter than normal. The Green filter has the opposite effect on leaves, making them appear lighter in tone. Figure 11.22, left, shows the same scene shot with no filter, then Yellow, Green, and Red filters.

The Sepia, Blue, Purple, and Green Toning Effects, on the other hand, all add a color cast to your monochrome image. Use these when you want an old-time look or a special effect, without bothering to recolor your shots in an image editor. Figure 11.22, right, shows the various Toning Effects available.

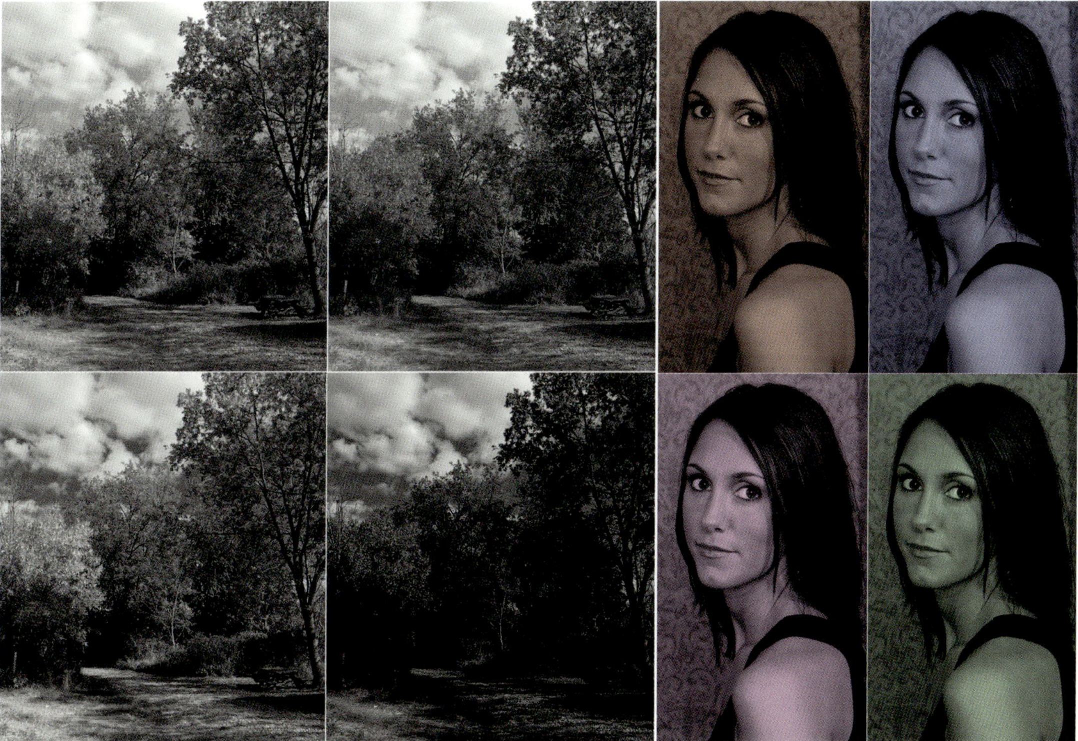

Figure 11.22 Left: Applying color filters: No filter (upper left); Yellow filter (upper right); Green filter (lower left); and Red filter (lower right). Right: Toning: Sepia (top left); Blue (top right); Purple (lower left); and Green (lower right).

Any Picture Style that has been changed from its defaults will be shown in the Picture Style menu with blue highlighting the altered parameter. You don't have to worry about changing a Picture Style and then forgetting that you've modified it. A quick glance at the Picture Style menu will show you which styles and parameters have been changed.

Making changes in the Monochrome Picture Style is slightly different. As I mentioned, the Saturation and Color Tone parameters are replaced with Filter Effect and Toning Effect options. (Keep in mind that once you've taken a JPEG photo using a Monochrome Picture Style, you can't convert the image back to full color.) You can choose from Yellow, Orange, Red, or Green filters, or None, and specify Sepia, Blue, Purple, or Green toning, or None. You can still set the Sharpness and Contrast parameters that are available with the other Picture Styles.

Adjusting Styles with the Picture Style Editor

If you'd rather edit Picture Styles in your computer, the Picture Style Editor supplied for your camera in versions for both Windows and Macs allows you to create your own custom Picture Styles, or edit existing styles, including the Standard, Landscape, Faithful, and other predefined settings already present. You can change sharpness, contrast, color saturation, and color tone—and a lot more—and then save the modifications as a PF2 file that can be uploaded to the camera, or used by Digital Photo Professional to modify a RAW image as it is imported.

To create and load your own Picture Style, just follow these steps:

1. **Load the editor.** Launch the Picture Style Editor (PSE, not to be confused with the *other* PSE, Photoshop Elements).

2. **Access a RAW file.** Load a RAW CR3 image you'd like to use as a reference into the PSE. You can drag a file from a folder into the editor's main window or use the Open command in the File menu.

3. **Choose an existing style to base your new style on.** Select any of the base styles except for Standard. Your new style will begin with all the attributes of the base style you choose, so start with one that already is close to the look you want to achieve ("tweaking" is easier than building a style from the ground up).

4. **Split the screen.** You can compare the appearance of your new style with the base style you are working from. Near the lower-left edge of the display pane are three buttons you can click to split the old/new styles vertically, horizontally, or return to a single image.

5. **Dial in basic changes.** Click the Advanced button in the Tool palette to pop up the Advanced Picture Style Settings dialog box that appears at left in the figure. These are the same parameters you can change in the camera. Click OK when you're finished.

6. **Make advanced changes.** The Tool palette has additional functions for adjusting hue, tonal range, and curves. Use of these tools is beyond the scope of a single chapter, let alone a notation in a list, but if you're familiar with the advanced tools in Photoshop, Photoshop Elements, Digital Photo Pro, or another image editor, you can experiment to your heart's content. Note that these modifications go way beyond what you can do with Picture Styles in the camera itself, so learning how to work with them is worth the effort.

7. **Save your Picture Style.** When you're finished, choose Save Picture Style File from the File menu to store your new style as a PF2 file on your hard disk. Add a caption and copyright information to your style in the boxes provided. If you click Disable Subsequent Editing, your style will be "locked" and protected from further changes, and the modifications you did make will be hidden from view (just in case you dream up your own personal, "secret" style). But you'll be unable to edit that style later. If you think you might want to change your custom Picture Style, save a second copy without marking the Disable Subsequent Editing box.

Uploading a Picture Style to the Camera

Now it's time to upload your new style to your camera into one of your three User Def. slots in the Picture Style array. Just follow these steps:

1. **Link your camera for upload.** Connect your camera to your computer using the USB cable, power up the camera, launch the EOS Utility, and click the Camera Settings/Remote Shooting choice in the splash screen.

2. **Choose the Shooting menu.** It's marked with an icon of a white camera on a red background, from the menu bar located about midway in the control panel that appears on your computer display.

3. **Select Register User Defined Style.** Click on the box to produce the Register Picture Style dialog box.

4. **Choose a User Def. tab.** Click on one of the three tabs, labeled User Def. 1, User Def. 2, or User Def. 3. Each tab will include the name of the current Picture Style active in that tab.

5. **Click the Open File button and choose the Picture Style file to load.** The Picture Styles you've saved (or downloaded from another source) will appear with a PF2 extension. Click on the one you want to use, and then click the Open button in the Open dialog box.

6. **Upload Picture Style to the camera.** The Register Picture Style File dialog box will return. Click OK and the Picture Style will be uploaded to the camera in the User Def. "slot" represented by the tab you've chosen. The name of the Picture Style will appear in the menu in place of User Def. 1 (or User Def. 2/User Def. 3).

Changing a Picture Style's Settings from the EOS Utility

You can modify the settings of a Picture Style that's already loaded into your camera from the EOS Utility when your camera is linked to your computer. Just follow these steps:

1. **Link your camera to the computer.** Connect your camera to your computer using the USB cable, turn the camera on, launch the EOS Utility, and click the Camera Settings/Remote Shooting choice in the splash screen.

2. **Choose the Shooting menu.** It's marked with an icon of a white camera on a red background, from the menu bar located about midway in the control panel that appears on your computer display.

3. **Access the Picture Style.** Click on the Picture Style choice. The currently active Picture Style in the camera will be shown, along with its detail settings.

4. **Choose a Picture Style to modify.** Click the Picture Style box to produce a listing of all the available Picture Styles.

5. **Click Detail Set.** At lower left, Landscape is now highlighted. When you click on Detail Set., a dialog box appears. You can move the sliders to change the settings, as described earlier. You can also click the Default Set. button to return the settings to their original values.

6. **Confirm choice.** Click Return when you've finished making changes, and the Picture Style you've modified will be changed in the camera.

7. **Exit EOS Utility.** Disconnect your camera from your computer, and your modified style is ready to use.

Getting More Picture Styles

I've found that careful Googling can unearth other Picture Styles that helpful fellow EOS owners have made available, and even a few from the helpful Canon company itself. My own search turned up this link:

https://global.canon/en/imaging/picturestyle/file/download.html

Canon offers a half dozen or more useful PF2 files you can download and install on your own. Remember that Picture Style files are compatible between various Canon EOS models (that is, you can use a style created for the Canon 90D with your R8), but you should be working with the latest software versions to work with the latest cameras and Picture Styles. If you owned an earlier EOS and haven't re-installed the software since your camera upgrade, you might need to re-install the software. It's available for download from the Canon website.

Try the additional styles Canon offers. They include:

- **Studio Portrait.** Compared to the Portrait style built into the camera, this one, Canon says, expresses translucent skin in smooth tones, but with less contrast. (Like films in the pre-digital age that were intended for studio portraiture.)

- **Snapshot Portrait.** This is another "translucent skin" style, but with increased contrast.

- **Nostalgia.** This style adds an amber tone to your images, while reducing the saturation of blue and green tones.
- **Clear.** This style adds contrast for what Canon says is additional "depth and clarity."
- **Twilight.** Adds a purple tone to the sky just before and after sunset or sunrise.
- **Emerald.** Emphasizes blues and greens.
- **Autumn Hues.** Increases the richness of browns and red tones seen in fall colors.

Clarity

Options: −4 to +4

My preference: N/A

Leave it to Canon to add an often-misunderstood feature to their cameras, but not tell you what it is in sufficient detail. That's why I'm here. Clarity is a contrast-adjustment process that concentrates on the mid-tones rather than the image as a whole. And, as I emphasized in Chapter 5's discussion of autofocus, increased contrast translates into sharpness, and reduced contrast results in a blurrier appearance. However, Clarity adjustments—whether applied in-camera using this menu entry or in an image editor like Photoshop—differ from sharpness controls. Sharpness increases the contrast between all dark and light tones, while clarity increases the contrast only within the middle tones of the image. The results are similar to sharpening, but textures become more evident, and you don't get as much digital noise.

If you want to increase or decrease Clarity, this menu entry provides a simple slider, with 0 as the default and adjustments available from −4 to +4. I recommend you experiment with the feature before using it widely. The clarity adjustments aren't shown in-camera, so you'll need to send your images to your computer to evaluate your results. Keep in mind that in images that are already high in contrast (that is, those with fewer middle tones), the clarity setting may lighten or darken areas adjacent to the boundaries between portions of your images.

Digest Type (Hybrid Auto Mode Only)

Options: Include Stills (default), No Stills

My preference: N/A

Your R8 is able to create a "digest" movie that provides a snapshot of your day's photographic exploits when the Mode dial is set to the Hybrid Auto position. I'll provide detailed instructions for using this feature in Chapter 16. The Digest can include both still photos and movie clips, or only movie segments. This entry allows you to choose which mode you prefer. This entry is accessible in the Shooting 4 menu *only* when the Mode dial is set to the Hybrid Auto position.

Retain Creative Assist Data (Scene Intelligent Auto Mode Only)

Options: Off (default), On

My preference: N/A

As I described in Chapter 4, when using Scene Intelligent Auto, you can tap the Creative Assist icon in the lower-right corner of the screen and choose from a series of Presets or make adjustments to Background Blur, Brightness, Contrast, Saturation, Color Tone, or Monochrome effects. (Remember that these are different from Creative Filter effects, such as Grainy Black-and-White, or Soft Focus.)

Any changes you make are lost when you exit Scene Intelligent Auto or turn the R8 off. If you'd rather retain your settings, set this entry to On. When activated, you can store current settings as a User 1–3 Preset by pressing the INFO button, as explained in Chapter 4. This entry is accessible in the Shooting 4 menu *only* when the Mode dial is set to the Scene Intelligent Auto position.

Shooting Creative Filters

Options: Off (default), Grainy B/W, Soft Focus, Fish-eye Effect, Art Bold Effect, Water Painting Effect, Toy Camera Effect, Miniature Effect

My preference: N/A

This is just a menu implementation of the Creative Filters available from the Mode dial. It resides here so you can assign this function to a custom key if you want to. Select a filter using the directional controls, and press INFO to choose the intensity of any of the filters other than Miniature Effect.

Lens Aberration Correction

Options: Peripheral Illumination Correction: Enable (default)/Disable; Distortion Correction: Enable/Disable (default); Digital Lens Optimizer (Chromatic Aberration and Diffraction correction): Enable/Disable (default)

My preference: Use the default values

This is the first entry in the Shooting 5 menu (see Figure 11.23). Your camera can automatically partially correct for lens aberrations in several different ways using three different settings if you are using a lens for which correction data is available. Previously, several of these corrections were available only when post-processing the image in Digital Photo Professional or another utility. The three choices (see Figure 11.24), all described in detail in the next section, are as follows:

- **Peripheral illumination correction.** Fixes light fall-off at the edges of an image.
- **Distortion correction.** Adjusts for barrel and pincushion distortion.
- **Digital lens optimizer.** Corrects for a variety of characteristics, taking into account the lens, subject distance, focal length, aperture, and low-pass (anti-aliasing) filter over the sensor. It corrects for both chromatic aberration (color fringes around the edges of subjects) and diffraction for moiré effects produced when shooting at a very small aperture.

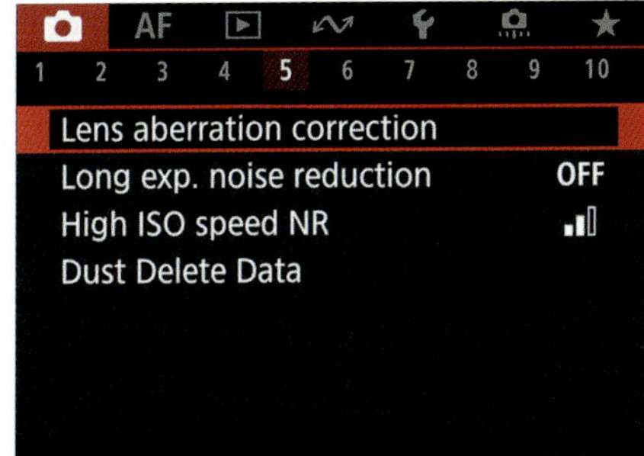

Figure 11.23 The Shooting 5 menu.

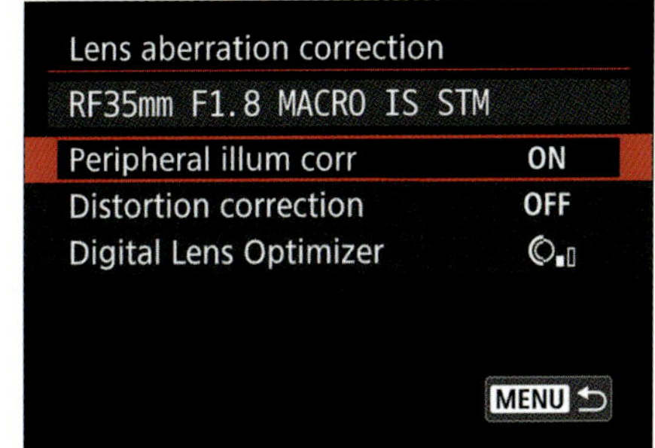

Figure 11.24 The Lens Aberration Correction screen.

I'll explain what each of these components do one at a time and include some examples of those aspects that can be easily illustrated.

Peripheral Illumination Correction

One defect is caused by a phenomenon called *vignetting*, which is a darkening of the four corners of the frame because of a slight amount of fall-off in illumination at those nether regions. This menu option allows you to activate Peripheral Illumination Correction, a clever feature that partially (or fully) compensates for this effect for any lens included in the camera's internal, updateable (through firmware upgrades) database. Depending on the f/stop you use, the lens mounted, and the focal length setting, vignetting can be non-existent, slight, or may be so strong that it appears you've used a too-small hood on your camera. (Indeed, the wrong lens hood can produce a vignette effect of its own.) Vignetting can be affected by the use of a telephoto converter (more on those in Chapter 7, too).

Peripheral illumination drop-off, even if pronounced, may not be much of a problem. I actually *add* vignetting, sometimes, when shooting portraits and some other subjects. Slightly dark corners tend to focus attention on a subject in the middle of the frame. On the other hand, vignetting with subjects that are supposed to be evenly illuminated, such as landscapes, is seldom a benefit.

To minimize the effects of corner light fall-off, you can process RAW files using Digital Photo Professional or, if you want your JPEG files fixed as you shoot them, by using this menu option. Figure 11.25 shows an image at top left without peripheral illumination correction, and a corrected image at bottom left. I've exaggerated the vignetting a little to make it more evident on the printed page. Keep in mind that the amount of correction available with Digital Photo Pro can be a little more intense than that applied in the camera. In addition, the higher the ISO speed, the less correction is applied. If you see severe vignetting with a particular lens, focal length, or ISO setting, you might want to turn off this feature, shoot RAW, and apply correction using DPP instead.

When you select this menu option from the Shooting 5 menu, a screen appears with the name of the lens currently attached to the camera, along with a notation whether correction data needed to brighten the corners is already registered in the camera. (Information about the most popular lenses is included in firmware.) If so, you can use the QCD to choose Enable to activate the feature or

Disable to turn it off. Press the Q/SET button to confirm your choice. Note that in-camera correction must be specified *before* you take the photo, so that the DIGIC X processing engine can lighten the corners of your photo before it is saved to the memory card.

Distortion Correction

This option adjusts to correct barrel and pincushion distortion, based on information in the camera's database.

Barrel distortion is found in some wide-angle lenses, and causes straight lines to bow outward, with the strongest effect at the edges. In fisheye (or *curvilinear*) lenses, this defect is a feature. When distortion is not desired, you'll need to use a lens that has corrected barrel distortion. Manufacturers like Canon do their best to minimize or eliminate it (producing a *rectilinear* lens), often using *aspherical* lens elements (which are not cross-sections of a sphere). You can also minimize less severe barrel distortion simply by framing your photo with some extra space all around, so the edges where the defect is most obvious can be cropped out of the picture. If none of the above work, you can apply this feature, which is disabled by default, to "undistort" your image with some bending of its own.

Pincushion distortion is a trait of many telephoto lenses, producing lines that curve inward toward the center of the frame. You might find after a bit of testing that it is worse at certain focal lengths with your particular zoom lens. Like chromatic aberration, it can be partially corrected using tools like Photoshop's Lens Correction filter and Photoshop Elements' Correct Camera Distortion filter, Digital Photo Professional, or this in-camera feature.

Digital Lens Optimizer

This option is a general-purpose fixer-upper based on a database of lenses and characteristics of the camera and sensor. It applies a whole range of corrections and can apply them separately to the center or edges of the frame, fixing spherical aberration, axial chromatic aberration, curvature of field, astigmatism, chromatic aberration, sagittal halo, and chromatic magnification. Many of these are technical aspects that are beyond the scope of this book. Note that image processing takes longer when these corrections are applied, continuous shooting maximum burst is lower with the High setting, and visual noise may increase. The higher the ISO setting, the lower amount of correction applied.

Another defect fixed by the Digital Lens Optimizer involves fringes of color around backlit objects, produced by *chromatic aberration*, which comes in two forms: *longitudinal/axial*, in which all the colors of light don't focus in the same plane, and *lateral/transverse*, in which the colors are shifted in one direction. (See Figure 11.25, top right.) When this feature is enabled, the camera will automatically correct images taken with one of the supported lenses to reduce or eliminate the amount of color fringing seen in the final photograph. (See Figure 11.25, bottom right.)

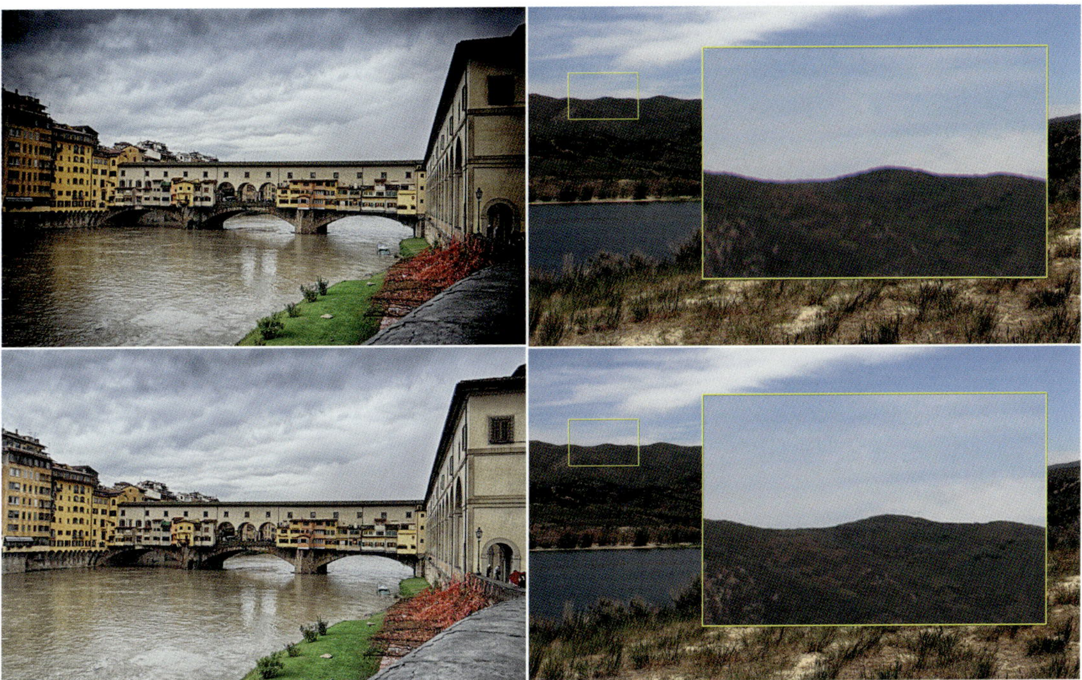

Figure 11.25 Left: Vignetting (top) is undesirable. You can correct this defect in the camera (bottom). Right: Color fringes can be corrected using the Digital Lens Optimizer's chromatic aberration correction feature (right, top and bottom).

The final defect corrected by the Digital Lens Optimizer is *diffraction*, a phenomenon that can cause a reduction in the apparent sharpness of your image due to scattering and interference of photons as they pass through smaller lens openings. In effect, the edges of your lens aperture affect proportionately more photons as the f/stop grows smaller. The relative amount of space available to pass freely decreases, and the amount of edge surface that can collide with incoming light increases.

The best analogy I can think of is a pond with two floating docks sticking out into the water, as shown in Figure 11.26. Throw a big rock in the pond, and the ripples pass between the docks relatively smoothly if the structures are relatively far apart (top). Move them closer together (bottom), and some ripples rebound off each dock to interfere with the incoming wavelets. In a lens, smaller apertures produce the same effect.

Canon has greatly expanded the list of lens data included within the camera itself. However, if lens aberration correction information for your lens is not registered in the camera, you can often remedy that deficit using the most recent version of the EOS Utility.

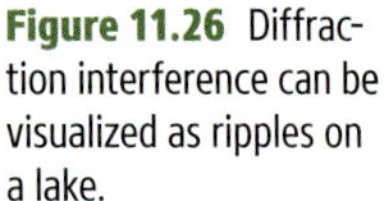

Figure 11.26 Diffraction interference can be visualized as ripples on a lake.

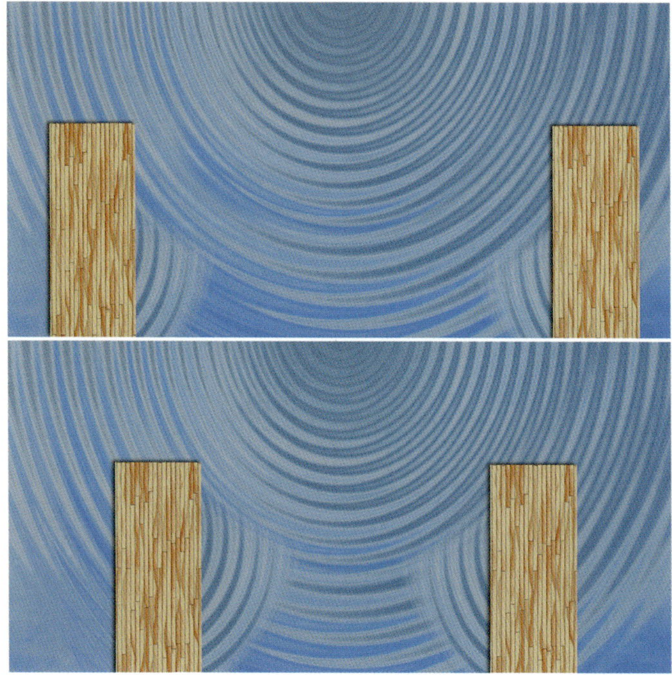

Just follow these steps:

1. **Link up your camera.** Connect to your computer using the USB cable supplied with the camera.

2. **Launch the EOS utility.** Load the utility and click on Camera Settings/Remote Shooting from the splash screen that appears.

3. **Select the Shooting menu.** It's located on the menu bar located about midway in the control panel that appears on your computer display. The Shooting menu icon is the white camera on a red background.

4. **Click on the Lens Aberration Correction choice.** The selection screen will appear.

5. **Choose your lens.** Select the category containing the lens you want to register from the panels at the top of the new screen; then place a checkmark next to all the lenses you'd like to register in the camera.

6. **Confirm your choice.** Click OK to send the data from your computer to the camera and register your lenses.

7. **Activate correction.** When a newly registered lens is mounted on the camera, you will be able to activate the anti-vignetting feature for that lens from the Set-up 1 menu.

Long Exposure Noise Reduction

Options: Off/Disable (default), Auto, On/Enable

My preference: Auto

This entry allows you to enable or disable long exposure noise reduction or allow the camera to evaluate your scene and decide whether to use this noise-canceling adjustment. Visual noise is that graininess that shows up as multicolored specks in images, and this setting helps you manage it. In some ways, noise is like the excessive grain found in some high-speed photographic films. However, while photographic grain is sometimes used as a special effect, it's rarely desirable in a digital photograph.

The visual noise-producing process is something like listening to a CD in your car, and then rolling down all the windows. You're adding sonic noise to the audio signal, and while increasing the CD player's volume may help a bit, you're still contending with an unfavorable signal to noise ratio that probably mutes tones (especially higher treble notes) that you really want to hear.

The same thing happens when the analog signal is amplified: You're increasing the image information in the signal but boosting the background fuzziness at the same time. Tune in a very faint or distant AM radio station on your car stereo. Then turn up the volume. After a certain point, turning up the volume further no longer helps you hear better. There's a similar point of diminishing returns for digital sensor ISO increases and signal amplification as well.

These processes create several different kinds of noise. Noise can be produced from high ISO settings. As the captured information is amplified to produce higher ISO sensitivities, some random noise in the signal is amplified along with the photon information. Increasing the ISO setting of your camera raises the threshold of sensitivity so that fewer and fewer photons are needed to register as an exposed pixel. Yet, that also increases the chances of one of those phantom photons being counted among the real-life light particles, too.

Fortunately, the sensor and its digital processing chip are optimized to produce the low noise levels, so ratings as high as ISO 800 or ISO 1600 can be used routinely (although there will be some noise, of course), and even ISO 3200 can generate good results.

A second way noise is created is through longer exposures. Extended exposure times allow more photons to reach the sensor but increase the likelihood that some photosites will react randomly even though not struck by a particle of light. Moreover, as the sensor remains switched on for the longer exposure, it heats, and this heat can be mistakenly recorded as if it were a barrage of photons. This entry can be used to tailor the amount of noise-canceling performed by the digital signal processor.

Your options are:

- **Off/Disable.** Disables long exposure noise reduction. Use this setting when you want the maximum amount of detail present in your photograph, even though higher noise levels will result. This setting also eliminates the extra time needed to take a picture caused by the noise-reduction process. If you plan to use only lower ISO settings (thereby reducing the noise caused by ISO amplification), the noise levels produced by longer exposures may be acceptable. For example, you might be shooting a river spilling over rocks at ISO 100 with the camera mounted on a tripod, using a neutral-density filter and long exposure to cause the pounding water to blur slightly. To maximize detail in the non-moving portions of your photos, you can switch off long exposure noise reduction. Because the noise-reduction process used with Auto and On can effectively double the time required to take a picture, Off is a good setting to use when you want to avoid this delay when possible.

- **Auto.** With exposures of one second or longer, if long exposure noise is detected, a second, blank exposure is made and compared to the first image. Noise found in the "dark-frame" image is subtracted from your original picture, and only the noise-corrected image is saved to your memory card.

- **On/Enable.** When this setting is activated, dark-frame subtraction is applied to all exposures longer than one second. You might want to use this option when you're working with high ISO settings (which will already have noise boosted a bit) and want to make sure that any additional noise from long exposures is eliminated, too. Noise reduction will be applied to some exposures that would not have caused it to kick in using the Auto setting.

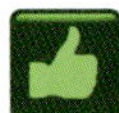 **TIP** While the "dark frame" is being exposed, the display will be blank during Live View mode, and the number of shots you can take in continuous shooting mode will be reduced. White balance bracketing is disabled during this process.

High ISO Speed Noise Reduction

Options: Disable, Low, Standard (default), High, Multi Shot Noise Reduction

My preference: Low, with further noise reduction as required in an image editor

The other type of noise results from using higher ISO settings. This entry allows you to specify just how much or how little of this noise reduction to apply, which can be a valuable option because noise reduction does eliminate detail while blurring the amount of noise. The default is Standard noise reduction, but you can specify Low or High noise reduction, or disable noise reduction entirely. At lower ISO values, noise reduction improves the appearance of shadow areas without affecting highlights; at higher ISO settings, noise reduction is applied to the entire photo. Note that when the High option is selected, the maximum number of continuous shots that can be taken will decrease significantly, because of the additional processing time for the images.

Your options are:

- **Disable.** No additional noise reduction will be applied.
- **Low.** A smaller amount of noise reduction is used. This will increase the grainy appearance but preserve more fine image detail.
- **Standard.** At lower ISO values, noise reduction is applied primarily to shadow areas; at higher ISO settings, noise reduction affects the entire image.
- **High.** More aggressive noise reduction is used, at the cost of some image detail, adding a "mushy" appearance that may be noticeable and objectionable. Because of the image processing applied by this setting, your continuous shooting maximum burst will decrease significantly.
- **Multi Shot Noise Reduction.** When this option is active, the camera takes four separate shots continuously. It then aligns them (in case there was movement between images) and then merges them, using the dark-frame subtraction technique to ignore random pixels caused by noise. The result is an image that is of better quality than the High setting.

  Multi Shot NR works best if the camera is mounted on a tripod and your subject is not moving. It is not available when Image Quality is set to RAW or RAW+JPEG/HEIF or Dual Pixel RAW, nor when using flash, live view, shooting multiple or Bulb exposures, or performing autoexposure/ white balance bracketing.

Dust Delete Data

Options: Store Delete Data

My preference: N/A

This menu choice lets you "take a picture" of any dust or other particles that may be adhering to your sensor. The information about the location of this dust will be appended to your photos, so that the Digital Photo Professional software can use this reference information to identify dust in your images and remove it automatically. You should capture a Dust Delete Data photo from time to time as your final line of defense against sensor dust. When you access this menu entry, the date of your last update will be displayed.

To use this feature, select Dust Delete Data, select OK, and press the Q/SET button. The camera will first perform a self-cleaning operation by applying ultrasonic vibration to the low-pass filter that resides on top of the sensor. Then, a screen will appear asking you to press the shutter button. Point the camera at a solid-white card with the lens set on manual focus and rotate the focus ring to infinity. When you press the shutter release, the camera takes a photo of the card using Aperture-priority and f/22 (which provides enough depth-of-field [in this case, *depth-of-focus*] to image the dust sharply). The "picture" is not saved to your memory card but, rather, is stored in a special memory area in the camera. Finally, a "Data obtained" screen appears.

The Dust Delete Data information is retained in the camera until you update it by taking a new "picture." The information is added to each image file automatically.

Multiple Exposure

Options: Multiple exposure: Disable (default), On (Enable); Multiple exposure control, Number of exposures, Save source images, Continue multiple exposure, Select image for multi-exposure

My preference: N/A

This is the first entry in the Shooting 6 menu. (See Figure 11.27.) This option lets you combine two to nine separate images into one photo without the need for an image editor like Photoshop. It can be an entertaining way to return to those thrilling days of yesteryear when complex photos were created in the camera itself. In truth, prior to the digital age, multiple exposures were a cool, groovy, far-out, hep/hip, phat, sick, fabulous way of producing composite images. Today, it's more common to take the lazy way out, snap two or more pictures, and then assemble them in an image editor like Photoshop.

However, if you're willing to spend the time planning a multiple exposure (or are open to some happy accidents), there is a lot to recommend the multiple exposure capability that Canon has provided. For one thing, you can combine two or more images using the RAW data from the sensor, producing photos that are blended together more smoothly than is likely for anyone who's not a Photoshop guru. In addition, Canon has eliminated one annoying aspect of the feature found in some cameras: it's not necessary to return to the menu to activate multiple exposure for every set. If you want to take a series of pictures, you can set it once, and forget it. (But don't forget to turn it off when you're done!)

Multiple exposures cannot be captured if white balance bracketing, HDR shooting, or movie-making modes are in use. Before you begin snapping your own multi-exposures, you'll need to set your parameters using the options discussed below. The Multiple Exposure command has so many options that each one requires a more detailed explanation that I'm going to supply next. (See Figure 11.28.)

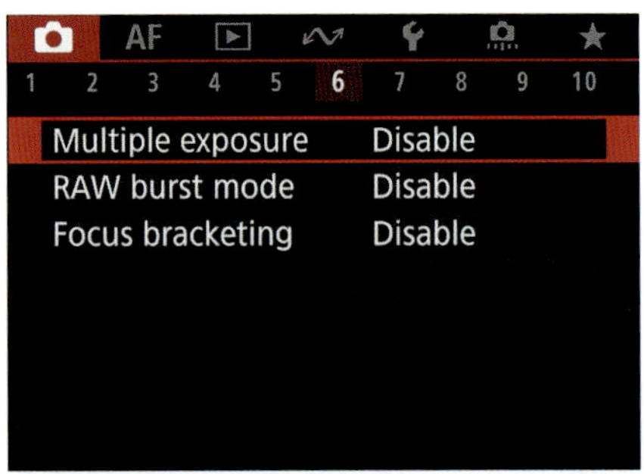

Figure 11.27 The Shooting 6 menu.

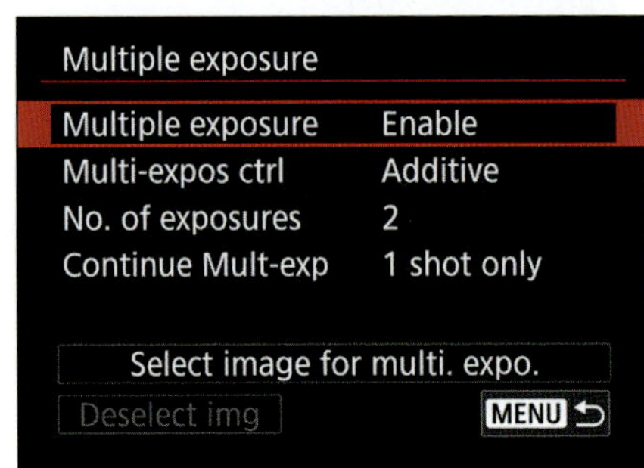

Figure 11.28 Set these parameters to configure your multiple exposures.

Multiple Exposure

The Disable option deactivates the multi-exposure feature, but you can quickly choose either of the two On variations. This is the "master control" that allows you to turn multiple exposure on and off (leaving the other parameters you've set unchanged).

- **Disable.** Deactivates multiple exposure.
- **Enable.** Makes the additional options described next available.

Multiple Exposure Control

This essential parameter can determine how successful your multiple exposure is, by controlling how each individual exposure is merged with the overlapping portions of the other images in the series. Picture an image like the one shown at left in Figure 11.29. The performer, Todd Cooper of the Alan Parsons Live Project, was photographed against a plain, dark background. He happened to be moving, so neither of the two images overlapped with each other, or with any details of the feature- less background. But in Figure 11.29, right, the dancer remained in place, so that each subsequent image overlapped the others slightly. The Multiple Exposure Control feature allows you to specify how the images are combined with these choices:

- **Additive.** Each individual shot in the series is, by default, given the full exposure, which is what I used for Figure 11.29, left. Because the background was totally black and the subject was moving and did not overlap, the cumulative exposure effect was to combine two separate images into one image.

  However, you can manually adjust the amount of exposure each shot is given by dialing in expo- sure compensation, making this mode useful for overlapping images as well. The customary procedure is to specify –1-stop exposure compensation for two shots, –1.5 EV for three-shot multiple exposures, and –2 EV for four-shot multis. Manually calculating the amount of negative exposure compensation allows you to fine-tune the look of overlapping images.

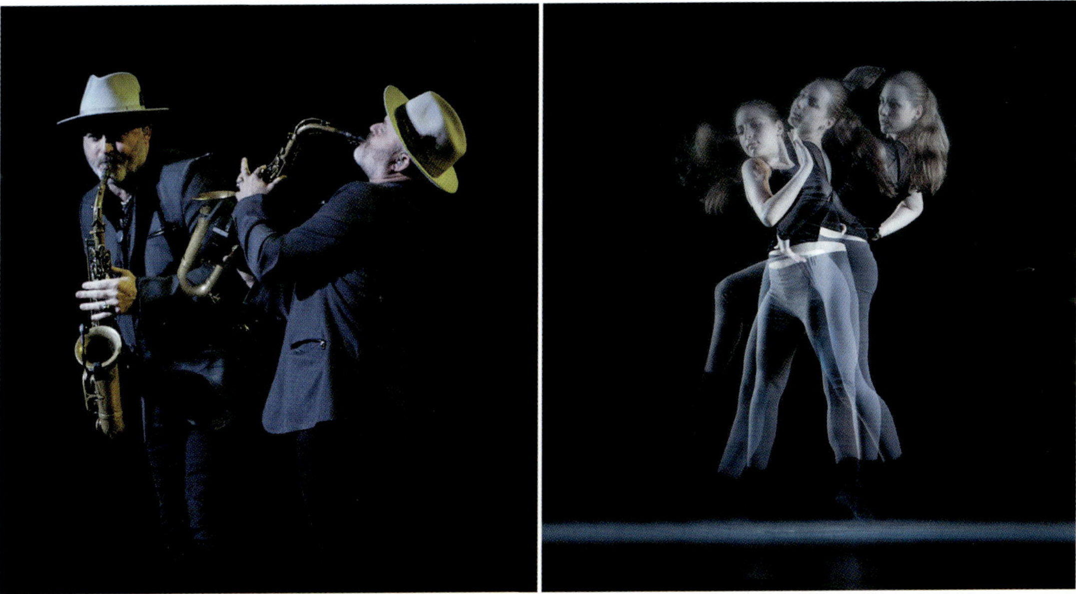

Figure 11.29 Left: Multiple exposure using Additive exposure, and no exposure compensation. Right: Multiple exposure using Average exposure.

- **Average.** Choose this option to apply appropriate negative exposure compensation, based on the number of exposures you're combining into a single image. If your multiple exposures happen to be of the same scene (rather than separate subjects), the camera will attempt to ensure that the background receives the equivalent of a full exposure. I used this option for Figure 11.29, right.
- **Bright.** This mode uses special algorithms to compare the first shot in a series with subsequent images that will be added to that base shot, and then give preference to the brighter parts of the image where pixels overlap. Conceptually, this is like the "lighten" layer merging routines in Photoshop (and other image editors).
- **Dark.** Similar to the Bright option, only preference is given to darker pixels. You may need to use both the Bright and Dark parameters for a while to visualize how they affect your images. I can't really provide hard and fast examples of when to use one or the other; it's a creative process.

Number of Exposures

You can choose from 2 to 9 exposures in each multiple exposure set. Highlight the option, press SET, and spin the QCD to choose the number of exposures. I recommend starting out with three multiple exposures when you begin exploring this tool; you'll quickly discover picture opportunities that call for more or fewer combined shots in a single image.

Continue Multiple Exposure

Choose 1 Shot Only or Continuously. Choose the former if you want to take a single multiple exposure series and then return to normal shooting with Multiple Exposure then disabled. Select Continuously if you plan to shoot a batch of different multiple exposures and don't want to return to the menu system to reactivate the feature after each shot.

Select Image for Multiple Exposure

If you like, you can use an image you already took as the base image for a subsequent multi-exposure. The base image can only be a RAW image. When RAW images *taken with your camera* (other RAW images on the card cannot be used) are available, this option will be selectable. However, a RAW image that is already a multiple exposure *can* be used as your base image (the mind boggles at the possibilities).

With the option highlighted, press Q/SET and choose the image you want to use. Rotate the QCD to view compatible RAW images and press Q/SET to choose one. Press OK. You can then take the *remaining* exposures in your set. That is, if you've chosen to combine three shots in a multiple exposure, the base image counts as one, so you'll be able to add two more by pressing and holding the shutter release.

Note that images using Highlight Tone Priority or an Aspect Ratio other than 3:2 cannot be used as your base image, and Lens Aberration Correction and Auto Lighting Optimizer will not be applied to your set. If the RAW image specifies the Auto Picture Style, the camera will revert to Standard for the rest of the images.

MULTI NOTES

Some special conditions are required to shoot multiple exposures. Some features are disabled, and others are locked in at particular values.

- Auto Lighting Optimizer, Highlight Tone Priority, and Lens Aberration Correction are disabled, and the Standard Picture Style will be used if you've chosen the Auto Picture Style setting. Multiple exposures are disabled if your camera is connected to a computer or printer via the USB cable.

- Most settings used for the first shot in a series are locked in for all subsequent images in that series, including image recording quality, ISO sensitivity, Picture Style, High ISO Noise Reduction, and Color Space.

- Other functions that cannot be changed while shooting multiple exposures will be dimmed in the camera menu.

RAW Burst Mode

Options: RAW Burst Mode: Enable, Disable (default); Pre-Shooting: Enable, Disable (default)

My preference: N/A

Have you ever missed a shot and wished you could travel back in time to the decisive moment? RAW Burst Mode is a clever feature that allows you to capture a photo that happened up to half a second *before* you pressed the shutter release. You'll never miss a bat striking a baseball or a bride tossing her bouquet again... more or less.

This capability takes advantage of the EOS R8's generous memory buffer, which stores the images you take until they can be written to the memory card. It has two options, shown in Figure 11.30. When RAW Burst Mode setting (the top entry in the screen) is enabled, you can use the R8's continuous shooting mode to capture RAW images at high speed. When pre-shooting is enabled, a half-press of the shutter release button tells the camera to start capturing images continuously and holding it in its buffer for a short time, replacing it with new images as you continue to hold the release down. When the shutter release button is pressed down all the way, the burst is saved to your memory card, *including the images remaining in the buffer from the half-second before you pressed the release fully.* In effect, you've captured a photo of action that happened just before you triggered the shutter. Figure 11.31 provides an example of the kinds of shots you can obtain.

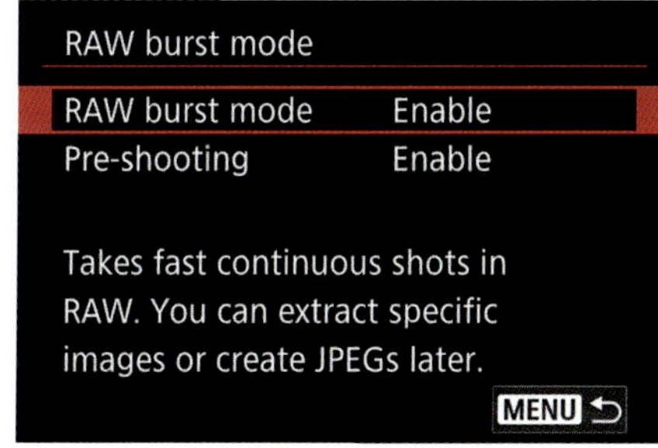

Figure 11.30 RAW Burst Mode settings.

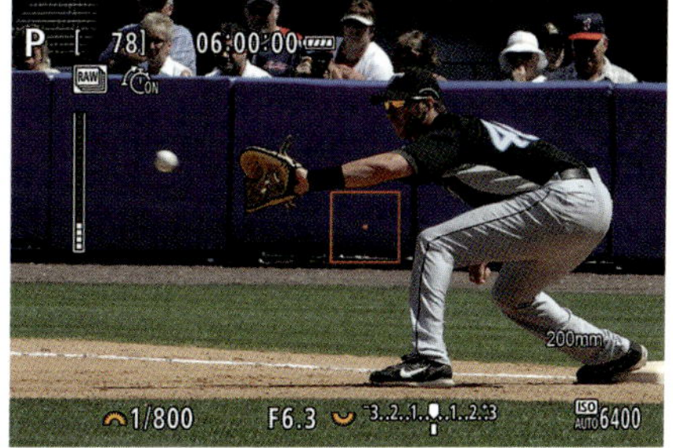

Figure 11.31 Pre-shooting lets you capture a critical moment.

Focus Bracketing

Options: Focus Bracketing, Number of Shots, Focus Increment, Exposure Smoothing
My preference: N/A

If you are doing macro (close-up) photography of flowers or other small objects at short distances, the depth-of-field often will be extremely narrow. In some cases, it will be so narrow that it will be impossible to keep the entire subject in focus in one photograph. Although having part of the image out of focus can be a pleasing effect for a portrait of a person, it is likely to be a hindrance when you are trying to make an accurate photographic record of a flower, or small piece of precision equipment. One solution to this problem is focus stacking (which Canon calls "Focus Bracketing"), a procedure that can be considered like HDR translated for the world of focus—taking multiple shots with different settings, and, using software as explained below, combining the best parts from each image in order to make a whole that is better than the sum of the parts. Focus bracketing requires a non-moving object, so some subjects, such as flowers, are best photographed in a breezeless environment, such as indoors.

With the camera's focus bracketing feature, the camera takes a series of pictures, adjusting the focus slightly between each image, refocusing from closest to your subject to the farthest point that needs to appear sharp. You end up with a series of up to 999 different images that can be combined using Digital Photo Professional or another application. I find the process much easier in Photoshop, using two simple Photoshop commands, which I will describe shortly. If you prefer to use DPP, you can consult that software's documentation for instructions.

You can visualize how focus stacking works if you examine Figure 11.32, which is cropped versions of three actual frames from one of my own focus bracketing series. All three used an exposure of 1/30th second at f/6.3 with an RF 85mm f/2 Macro IS STM lens. At top is the original exposure, with the lens focused on the nearest die. The center image shows the 35th exposure in the series, in which the focus shift feature had adjusted focus on the last die. In between were 33 intermediate-focus shots that I merged to produce the finished image at bottom. Here are the detailed steps you can take to use focus bracketing for your own deep-focus images:

1. **Set the camera firmly on a solid tripod.** A tripod or other equally firm support is absolutely essential for this procedure. You don't want the camera (or the subject) to move at all during the exposures.

2. **Attach a remote release.** You want to be able to trigger the camera without moving it. However, the procedure does pause for a short period of time once you activate it, perhaps giving your tripod/camera time to settle down even if you begin by pressing the shutter release button with your finger.

3. **Attach a lens with an appropriate focus range.** Focus bracketing uses the lens's built-in autofocus motor.

4. **Set the focus modes.** Choose One-Shot AF operation and Single-point AF. Focus bracketing cannot be used when the lens is set to manual focus.

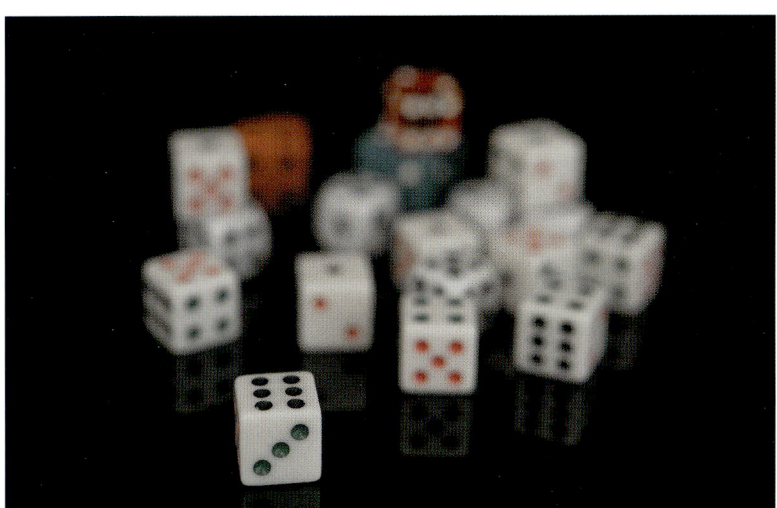

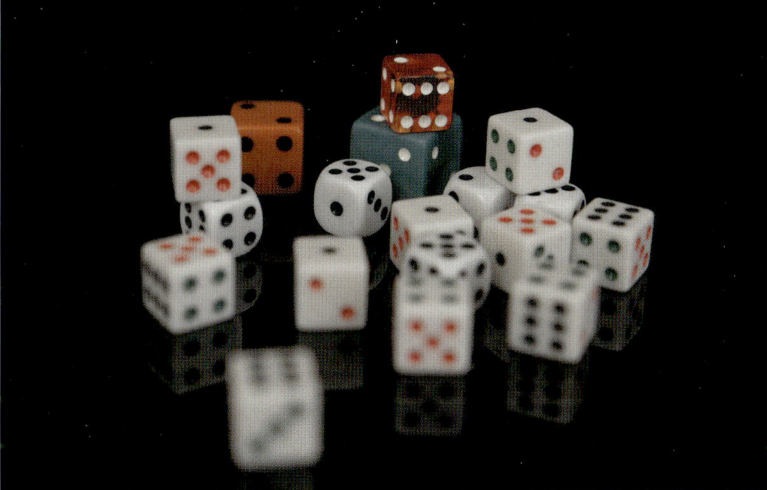

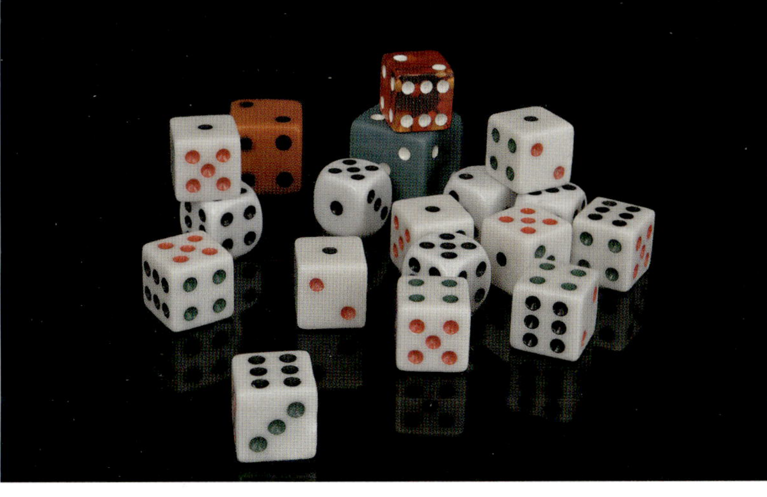

Figure 11.32 Closest focus (top), farthest focus (center), merged image (bottom).

5. **Set the quality of the images to JPEG.** Use the Shooting 1 menu to make this adjustment.

6. **Set the exposure, ISO, and white balance manually.** Use test shots, if necessary, to determine the best values. This will help prevent visible variations from arising among the multiple shots that you'll be taking. You don't want the camera to change the ISO setting or white balance between shots.

    Note: Even though you'll be effectively increasing depth-of-field through focus stacking, you should still avoid the widest apertures of your lens, as they are rarely the sharpest f/stops. I always stop down at least 1.5 f/stops—using f/6.3 in the example. Shutter speed is not as important, because the camera is on a tripod, but I tend to avoid very slow speeds anyway. You can manually set a slightly higher ISO sensitivity, if needed, to obtain the shutter speed/aperture combination you want to use.

7. **Turn off image stabilization.** You want straight exposures with no IS applied.

8. **Access the Focus Bracketing menu.** It's shown at upper left in Figure 11.33. Select an appropriate setting for each of the following parameters, using my guidelines:

    - **Focus Bracketing.** Set to Enable to activate focus bracketing.

    - **Number of Shots.** You can choose from 1 to 999 individually refocused shots. (See Figure 11.33, upper right.) The number of images captured will depend on how finely you want to have the camera change focus between shots (and you'll combine this with the step increment option described next). I rarely need more than 50 shots and used only 35 for the example shown earlier in Figure 11.32.

Figure 11.33 Focus Bracketing Shooting options.

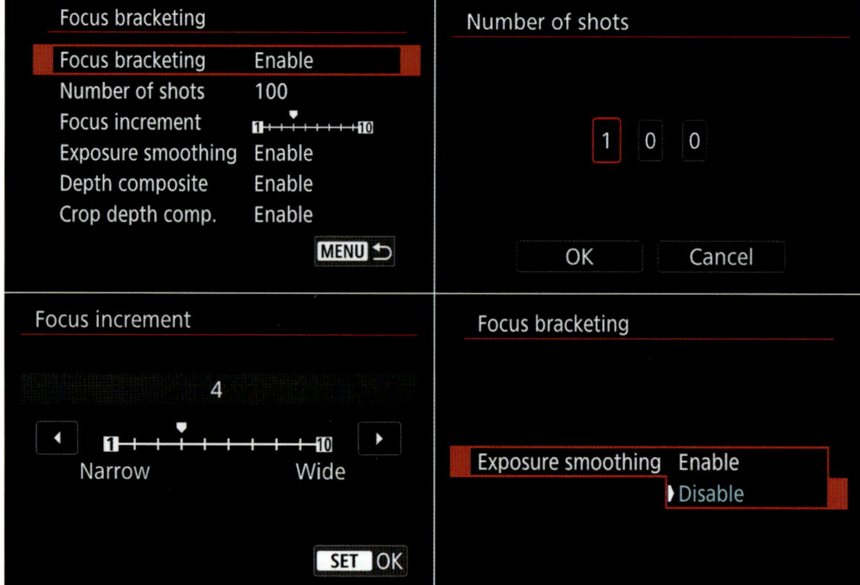

- **Focus Increment.** You can specify values from 1 (a narrow slice per adjustment) to 10 (a much wider focus change). (See Figure 11.33, lower left.) Canon does not specify how much each increment changes the focus, for a very good reason: it *can't*. Depending on the focal length of your lens and your f/stop, the effective plane of apparent focus may vary from narrow, to very narrow, to super-narrow in macro shooting environments. (If you're confused, see "Circles of Confusion" in Chapter 5.)

  You may need some trial-and-error to choose the correct number of shots and focus step width. For example, with 50 shots and a wide focus step, the first 10 may encompass your entire subject and the last 40 may be wasted on completely out-of-focus images. It's often worthwhile to take a test shot, view a slide show of all your images, and decide whether to increase/decrease the number of shots and/or focus step width.

- **Exposure Smoothing.** This option minimizes changes in image brightness when set to Enable, compensating for differences in the actual aperture value as focus changes. The distance between the lens's iris and the sensor focal plane can change as you change focus from near to far, producing a slightly different effective f/stop. Exposure smoothing takes that into account and adjusts. (See Figure 11.33, lower right.)

- **Depth Composite.** You can opt to let the camera create a composite image for you by enabling this option. You can use this if you don't want to take the time to create your composite in an image editor. This is not an all-or-nothing choice; both the composited image and the original images you capture are saved, so you always have the option to take the original images and composite them manually if you are dissatisfied with the camera's rendition or want to fine-tune the image.

- **Crop depth composite.** Enable this option and the camera will crop images if necessary to achieve the required field of view for compositing.

9. **Choose MENU to exit.** When finished, choose MENU to exit the focus bracketing setup screens.

10. **Create a new folder.** I highly recommend depositing your bracketed images in a new folder. When you exit the focus bracketing settings, a Folder icon appears at lower left on the LCD screen. Tap it to create a new folder using the next highest number increment.

11. **Set focus point to nearest object.** Use the directional controls to position the red focus box on the subject nearest the camera lens. Press the shutter button halfway to focus.

12. **Capture images.** Press the shutter button down all the way to begin capture. The shots are captured continuously, with the focal position moving toward infinity with each shot by the increment you've specified.

13. **Combine your images (optional).** If you didn't elect to have the R8 create a composite image, you can combine the original shots yourself, as I'll describe next.

Here are the instructions for Photoshop. Transfer the images to your computer, and then follow these steps:

1. In Photoshop, select File > Scripts > Load Files into Stack. In the dialog box that then appears, navigate on your computer to find the files for the photographs you have taken, and highlight them all.

2. At the bottom of the next dialog box that appears, check the box that says, "Attempt to Automatically Align Source Images," then click OK. The images will load; it may take several minutes for the program to load the images and attempt to arrange them into layers that are aligned based on their content.

3. Once the program has finished processing the images, go to the Layers panel and select all the layers. You can do this by clicking on the top layer and then Shift-clicking on the bottom one.

4. While the layers are all selected, in Photoshop go to Edit > Auto-Blend Layers. In the dialog box that appears, select the two options, Stack Images and Seamless Tones and Colors, then click OK. The program will process the images, possibly for a considerable length of time.

5. If the procedure worked well, the result will be a single image made up of numerous layers that have been processed to produce a sharply focused rendering of your subject. If it did not work well, you may have to take additional images the next time, focusing very carefully on small slices of the subject as you move progressively farther away from the lens.

6. You'll want to flatten the final image before saving it. Given the 24MP resolution of the camera, the stack of individual shots will easily be more than 2GB, which exceeds the maximum file size of some storage media and/or OS file systems.

Although this procedure can work very well in Photoshop, you also may want to try it with Digital Photo Professional, as well as programs that were developed more specifically for focus stacking and related procedures, such as Helicon Focus (www.heliconsoft.com), PhotoAcute (www.photoacute.com), or CombineZM (https://combinezm.informer.com/). Note that focus bracketing is not "sticky" and the setting reverts to Disable when the camera is powered down.

Drive Mode

Options: Single Shooting, High Speed Continuous +, High Speed Continuous, Low Speed Continuous, Self-timer: 10 second/Remote, Self-timer: 2 second/Remote, Self-timer: Continuous

My preference: N/A

This is the first entry in the Shooting 7 menu. (See Figure 11.34.) This duplicates other Drive mode settings, providing a menu entry, typically so you can assign the function to a custom key.

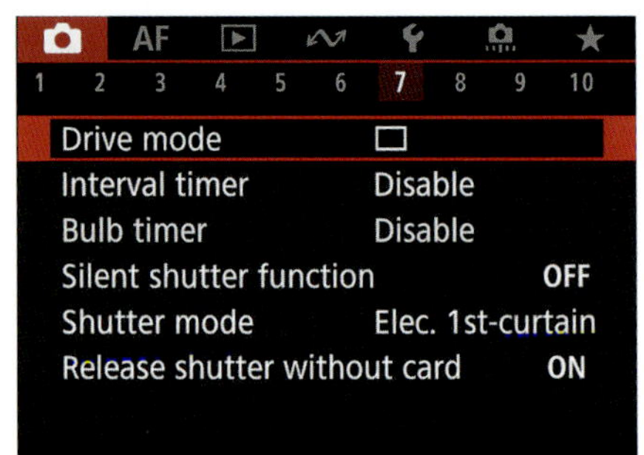

Figure 11.34 The Shooting 7 menu.

Interval Timer

Options: Disable (default), Enable, Interval, Exposure Time

My preference: N/A

This entry allows you to specify exposure times up to 99 hours, 59 minutes, and 59 seconds. Simply press the INFO button to access a screen that allows you to specify the number of shots and the interval between them. I described use of this feature in detail in Chapter 6, and won't repeat those instructions here.

Bulb Timer

Options: Disable (default), Enable; Times from 00:00:00 to 99:59:59 seconds

My preference: N/A

When you've enabled the feature using this menu entry, and have set the Mode dial to Bulb, you can press the INFO button to specify a long exposure time up to 99 hours, 59 minutes, and 59 seconds. It's unlikely that your battery will last that long and your camera won't overheat with an ultra-long exposure (I haven't tested the extreme settings), but longer exposures are helpful for star trails and other shots that require more than 30 seconds. While the Mode dial must be set to B (Bulb) to use this feature, unlike traditional Bulb exposures, you do not need to keep the shutter button depressed the entire time.

Silent Shutter Function

Options: On, Off (default)

My preference: N/A

When enabled, this allows you to take pictures in stealth mode, with reduced sounds and visual indications that photos are being captured. The electronic shutter is used and audio signals such as shutter release sound, focusing beep, touch operations, and self-timer sounds are all squelched. The self-timer lamp does not blink, electronic flash is disabled, and the AF-assist beam does not fire. Long exposure noise reduction is disabled. If you turn off the camera, the shutter remains open. Headphone output remains active, so if you're recording video, you'll be able to monitor the audio. With all that (not) going on, the only sounds that may be heard are likely to be the autofocus motor of the lens and your own breathing.

Shutter Mode

Options: Electronic 1st-Curtain, Electronic

My preference: Enable when needed

This entry allows you to choose between the electronic first-curtain shutter (which allows using flash) and the all-electronic shutter (which disables flash). Your camera can shoot completely silently using the camera's electronic shutter. I explained first- and second-curtain shutters and electronic shutters in detail in Chapter 9 and will not repeat that information here.

Here's what you need to know to use the Shutter Mode entry:

- **Electronic 1st-curtain shutter.** The EOS R8 does not have a physical first curtain, which can potentially eliminate the loss of sharpness that can occur from mechanical shutter "bounce" during
longer exposures. The shutter opens and then the sensor is "cleared" electronically, just as if a
mechanical first curtain has opened. The exposure continues until the conventional mechanical
second curtain descends after 30 to 1/200th second.

- **Electronic shutter.** This mode starts and ends exposure electronically, providing exposure times
of one-half second to 1/8000th second (in Fv, P, or Av mode), or 1/16,000th second (in Tv and
M mode). There are trade-offs in exchange for this mode's silence:

  - For complete silence, you'll need to turn off Beep in the Set-up 2 menu, as the camera uses the
  beep to let you know a picture has been taken in electronic shutter mode.

  - Electronic flash or automatic exposure bracketing cannot be used. A flash burst tends to be
  more disruptive than even the loudest camera shutter anyway, so the electronic shutter's
  silence wouldn't provide much of an advantage.

  - Because of the length of time required to capture the full frame using the camera's rolling
  shutter, your images may exhibit banding artifacts, especially under flickering light sources.
  Images of fast-moving subjects may look distorted because the first portion of the subject
  captured will have moved by the time the last portion is exposed.

  - The camera drops from 14-bit to 12-bit readout mode, which helps reduce the rolling shutter
  effect, but also limiting the dynamic range to capture tones in the darkest shadow areas. This
  is especially noticeable at ISO settings higher than ISO 400. So for best results use lower ISOs
  and/or stick to the mechanical shutter.

Release Shutter without Card

Options: Enable (default), Disable

My preference: Disable

This entry in the Shooting menu gives you the ability to snap off "pictures" without a memory card
installed—or to lock the camera shutter release if that is the case. It is sometimes called Play mode,
because you can experiment with your camera's features or even hand your camera to a friend to let
him/her fool around, without any danger of pictures being taken. Back in our film days, we'd sometimes finish a roll, rewind the film back into its cassette surreptitiously, and then hand the camera to
a child to take a few pictures—without wasting any film. It's hard to waste digital film, but Release
Shutter without Card mode is still appreciated by some, especially camera vendors who want to be
able to demo a camera at a store or trade show, but don't want to have to equip every demonstrator
model with a memory card. Choose this menu item, press SET, select Enable or Disable, and press
Q/SET again to turn this capability on or off.

IS (Image Stabilizer) Mode

Options: Off (default), On, Enhanced
My preference: N/A

This is the first entry on the Shooting 8 menu. (See Figure 11.35.) Optical image stabilization (OIS) is included in some RF/RF-S and EF mount lenses. This setting allows you to turn image stabilization off (as recommended when the camera is on a tripod) or on. It is used to enable/disable IS with lenses that do not have an IS switch (if present, you should use the lens switch instead). If the lens has an IS switch, this entry is used to enable/disable Movie mode's digital image stabilization (discussed in Chapter 16) instead. When the Stills/Movie switch is in the Movie position, an additional option, Enhanced, appears.

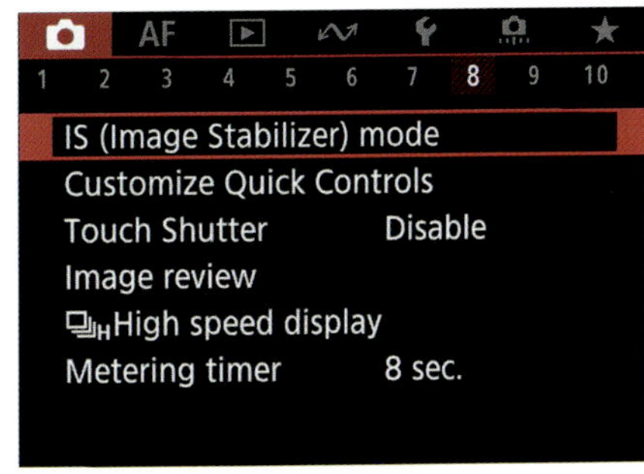

Figure 11.35 The Shooting 8 menu page.

The Enhanced setting available in Movie mode applies *electronic IS* in addition to OIS. Electronic image stabilization moves a slightly cropped version of each frame around within the boundaries of the sensor, allowing stronger shake correction. The result is a slightly magnified image due to the cropping. This enhanced IS works best with wide-angle lenses and not at all with lenses over 1000mm. It can also produce a slight amount of blurring caused by the pixel movement, as well as additional grain. You should avoid using the Enhanced setting when the camera is mounted on a tripod.

Customize Quick Controls

Options: Edit Layout, Reset Settings, Clear All Items
My preference: N/A

The Quick Controls screen provides fast access to what Canon considers to be the 11 most-used functions of the EOS R8: AF Area, AF Operation, Subject to Detect, Image Quality, Drive Mode, Metering Mode, Anti-Flicker Shooting, White Balance, Picture Styles, Creative Filters, and Cropping/Aspect Ratio. If you're like me, those 11 aren't even *close* to the roster of functions I'd elect to have on the Quick Controls screen. Right off the bat, Anti-Flicker, Picture Styles, and Creative Filters are not features I frequently need instant access to. Fortunately, Canon allows you to customize your Quick Controls. You can select the 11 functions of your choosing or trim the list to fewer than 11 if you want to streamline the screen. It's actually possible to create a Quick Controls screen with only one entry, or even none at all. (I don't recommend this as an April Fool's joke. No, really, I don't.)

The entry has just three commands, shown at left in Figure 11.36. Edit Layout, Reset Settings (restores the factory default arrangement), and Clear All Items (deletes every item quickly so you can start from scratch, or prepare for April 1). When you select Edit Layout and press SET, the current Quick Controls are shown (see Figure 11.36, right).

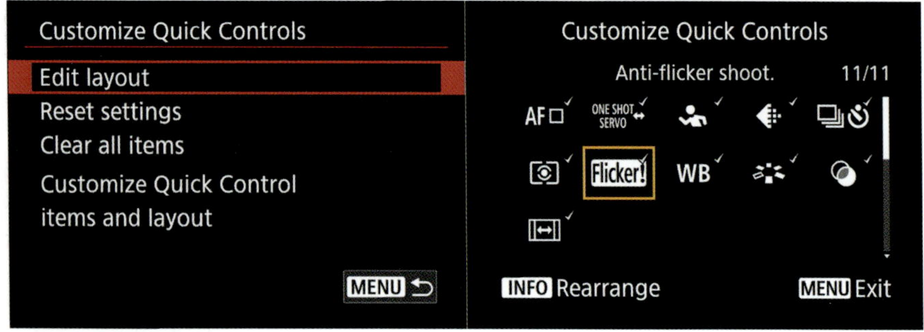

Figure 11.36 Customize Quick Controls screen (left). Current settings (right).

To create your own custom Quick Controls screen, just follow these steps:

1. **Access Edit Layout.** The screen at right in Figure 11.36 appears with the current settings. A checkmark appears next to active functions.

2. **Unmark settings to be removed.** Highlight each of the current settings you would like to replace and press Q/SET to remove its check. As items are removed, the numeric indicator at upper left will change from 11/11 (11 of 11) to 10/11, 9/11, and so forth.

3. **Choose settings to add.** Scroll through the list of available settings and highlight those you want to add, as seen at left in Figure 11.37. A colored box appears next to each icon in red, magenta, purple, or amber, which indicates whether that function is from the Shooting, AF, Wireless, or Set-up menus, which are also highlighted in those colors.

4. **Confirm each addition.** Press Q/SET to add a checkmark to each new function, up to the number you deleted.

5. **Exit or rearrange order.** When finished, you can press MENU to exit, or press INFO if you'd like to rearrange the order in which the items appear in the Quick Controls menu.

6. **Rearrange order (optional).** To move an item, press INFO, highlight the entry (see Figure 11.37, right), press Q/SET and then use the QCD or left/right directional controls to relocate the item. Press Q/SET again to confirm.

7. **Save Settings.** Press INFO to return, MENU to exit, highlight Save and Exit, and press Q/SET to exit.

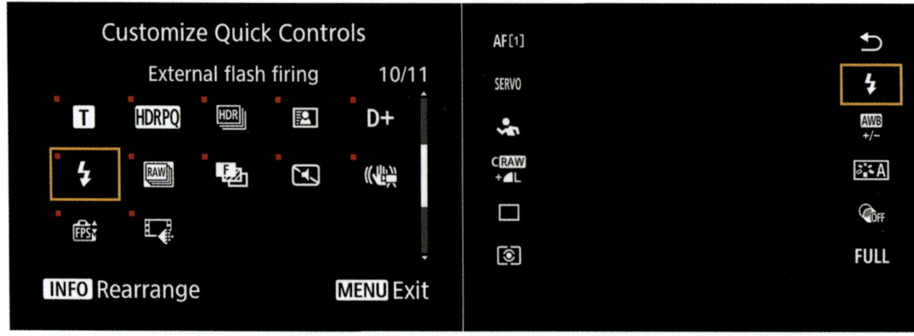

Figure 11.37 Customizing the Quick Controls screen.

Touch Shutter

Options: Enable (default), Disable

My preference: Disable

The Touch Shutter feature allows you to tap the LCD screen to focus and snap a picture with one gesture. It's easy to accidentally trigger the Touch Shutter, so I generally leave it off. However, it's quite useful when your camera is on a tripod and you want to be able to snap a picture of some portion of your scene quickly and with minimal vibration. An icon appears in the lower-left corner of the screen. You can tap to toggle to turn the touch shutter on and off once you've enabled it here. When you've turned it off, touching the screen will instead perform focusing on the spot tapped. You'd need to press the shutter release down all the way to take the picture.

In Touch Shutter mode, the camera performs in single-shot mode even when continuous shooting has been specified; touch focus uses One-Shot AF, even if AF Operation has been set to Servo AF. To shoot with a Bulb exposure, tap the screen twice: first to start the exposure and a second time to stop it.

Image Review

Options: Review Duration: 2 sec. (default), Off, 4 sec., 8 sec., Hold; Viewfinder Review: Disable (default), Enable

My preference: 2 sec., Disable

This setting has two options: Review Duration, and whether you want to playback review images in the viewfinder.

- **Review Duration.** You can adjust the amount of time an image is displayed for review on the LCD after each shot is taken. You can elect to disable this review entirely (Off), or choose display times of 2, 4, or 8 seconds. You can also select Hold, an indefinite display, which will keep your image on the screen until you use one of the other controls, such as the shutter button, Main dial, or QCD, or the time set for Display Off in the Power Saving entry of the Set-up 2 menu elapses.

  Turning the review display off or choosing a brief duration can help preserve battery power. However, the camera will always override the review display when the shutter button is partially or fully depressed, so you'll never miss a shot because a previous image was on the screen. Choose Image Review and select Off, 2 sec., 4 sec., 8 sec., or Hold. If you want to retain an image on the screen for a longer period, but don't want to use Hold as your default, press the Erase button under the LCD monitor. The image will display until you choose Cancel or Erase from the menu that pops up at the bottom of the screen. A longer review time gives you an opportunity to delete a non-keeper quickly without a visit to the menu system.

- **Viewfinder Review.** If you enable viewfinder review, you can see a playback of the shot you just took in the viewfinder.

High-Speed Display

Options: Enable, Disable (default)

My preference: Enable

This function activates a high-speed display that is more responsive, switching between the shot you've taken and the live image. It is always activated when working with the electronic shutter. Sports shooters will find it particularly useful when they're trying to follow action. To use high-speed display, these conditions must be met:

- **Using RF lens.** High-speed display does not work when an adapted EF/EF-S lens is mounted.
- **Servo AF.** You must set AF Operation to Servo AF to allow continuous focusing of your moving subject.
- **High-Speed Continuous.** Drive mode must be set to High-Speed Continuous (not High-Speed Continuous+). You don't need this feature at slower shooting speeds, anyway, and the fastest speed is too rapid for even the high-speed display to keep up.
- **No Anti-Flicker Shooting.** Set Anti-Flicker to Disable.
- **Exposure Simulation.** You must enable Exposure Simulation.

High-speed display is not used at shutter speeds slower than 1/30th second and apertures smaller than f/11, during flash photography, or when expanded (L or H) ISO settings are used.

Metering Timer

Options: 4 sec., 8 sec. (default), 16 sec., 30 sec., 1 min., 10 min., 30 min.

My preference: 8 sec. most of the time; I switch to 10 min. when shooting sports.

This option allows you to specify how long the metering system will remain active before switching off. Tap the shutter release to start the timer again after it switches off.

Display Simulation

Options: Exposure+Depth-of-Field, Exposure, Exposure Only During Depth-of-Field

My preference: Exposure+Depth-of-Field Preview

This option is the first on the Shooting 9 menu (see Figure 11.38). It allows you to choose whether the live view image mimics the exposure level of the final image, or whether the screen displays a bright image (dependent on the Screen Brightness setting you've specified in the Set-up 4 menu) that may be easier to view under high ambient lighting conditions.

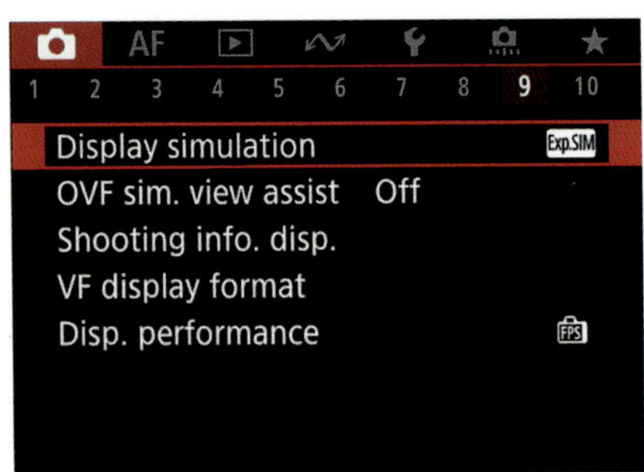

Figure 11.38 The Shooting 9 menu page.

Your choices are as follows:

- **Exposure+Depth-of-Field.** The image on the screen corresponds to the brightness level of the actual image based on the current exposure settings, including any exposure compensation you've specified. Use this option when you want to be able to roughly (but not precisely) monitor the effects of your exposure settings in live view. The display will also show the effective depth-of-field at the currently selected aperture.

- **Exposure.** The image brightness is adjusted to represent the actual exposure, including any exposure compensation, but depth-of-field will not be shown. Use this option when you want to see how your exposure is affecting an image, but don't need to see exactly what is or is not in focus.

- **Exposure Only During DOF Preview.** The view image is displayed at standard brightness but will be adjusted to simulate your exposure settings *only* when you press any button you may have defined as a depth-of-field preview button. This is your best option when you might want to check exposure from time to time during a shooting session. It's the setting I use most often, because I can compose with a big, bright screen, but still stop down to the aperture that will be used and view exposure and depth-of-field effects.

OVF Sim View Assist

Options: On, Off (default)
My preference: Off

If you miss the "optical viewfinder experience," this feature will effectively give it back to you. It's only recently that the electronic viewfinder found in mirrorless cameras have had the resolution and viewability approaching that of the big, bright optical viewfinders provided by digital (and film) SLR cameras. It takes advantage of the enhanced dynamic range offered by the OLED (organic light-emitting diode) viewfinder inside the Canon EOS R8. First introduced in the upscale EOS R3, the feature automatically adjusts the overall brightness of the scene shown through the EVF giving you a preview that's similar to what you get with a conventional optical viewfinder, assuming you haven't specified a large exposure compensation adjustment. While using this feature, Display Simulation, described above, is disabled, and both highlights and shadows appear brighter in comparison to the midtones in your scene, thanks to an adjusted, more linear tone curve.

When OVF simulation is not used, the EVF preview instead resembles the more limited dynamic range and extra contrast seen in the JPEG version, which uses a more S-shaped tone curve. I generally leave this feature turned off, because I'd rather see a rendition that will more closely resemble the JPEGs I will end up with. If you prefer the optical viewfinder look, enable OVF simulation and see if it suits your needs. Note that if you are viewing your preview on an external monitor through the HDMI port, simulation is disabled both for the EVF and LCD screen.

Shooting Information Display

Options: Screen Info. Settings, VF Info/Toggle Settings, VF Vertical Display, Grid Display, Histogram Display, Lens Information Display, Reset

My preference: N/A

This multi-layered entry allows you to customize what is displayed while you're shooting. Your camera is able to display a wealth of information right in your viewfinder or on the LCD screen while you shoot. Unfortunately, having all that data presented constantly can be distracting. The sub-settings in this entry let you specify exactly what you do or do not view while you're taking pictures. (See Figure 11.39, left.)

- **Screen Information Settings.** You can choose to enable or disable any of five different types of LCD screen information, as shown in Figure 11.39, right, activated by pressing the INFO button.

    1. Basic information
    2. All information except live histogram
    3. All information including live histogram
    4. Only autofocus point/zone display
    5. Graphic shooting information screen

- **Viewfinder Information/Toggle Settings.** Choose to enable/disable three different viewfinder displays, equivalent to screens 1 to 3 listed above.

- **VF Vertical Display.** Choose On, and when you rotate the camera to a vertical orientation, your viewfinder information rotates as well.

- **Grid Display.** You can choose 3 × 3, 6 × 4, or 3 × 3 with diagonal grids or turn grids off on the LCD screen and viewfinder.

Figure 11.39 Shooting Information Display (left); Screen Information Settings (right).

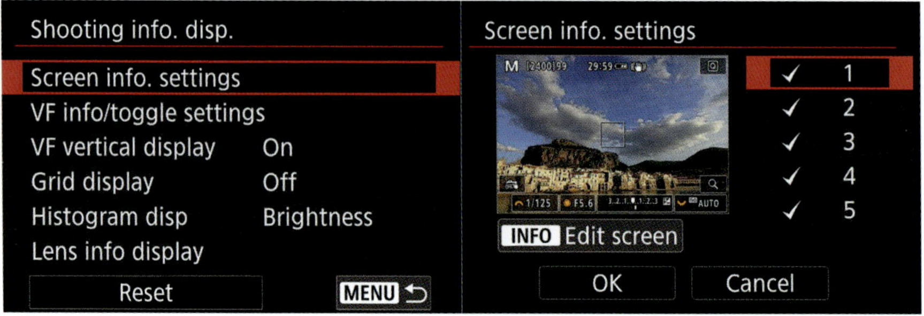

- **Histogram Display.** This parameter has two options:
  - **Brightness/RGB.** Choose the Brightness (luminance) live histogram or RGB (all three primary colors) live histogram.
  - **Display Size.** Choose Large or Small.
- **Lens Information Display.** This parameter has four options:
  - **Focus Distance Display.** Determines *when* focus distance will be shown: In manual focus mode only, While focusing only, Always, or Never (disable).
  - **Unit.** Determines focus distance units, either Meters or Feet.
  - **Focal Length Display.** You can enable or disable having the current focal length shown in the display.
  - **SA Variable Amount.** Shows the amount of correction for spherical aberration with lenses, such as the RF 100mm f/2.8 Macro, that are compatible with this adjustment. As I explained in Chapter 7, spherical aberration control can be used to fine-tune the bokeh (appearance of out-of-focus highlights).
- **Reset.** Restores the above parameters to their default values.

Viewfinder Display Format

Options: Display 1, Display 2

My preference: Display 2

Even if you don't completely declutter your viewfinder, you can make it a little easier to view. You can choose from two viewfinder display formats. (See Figure 11.40.) Display 1 fills the viewfinder with your image, with some information located in a black bar below the frame, but the rest overlaid on the frame itself. Choose Display 2, and black bars appear at left and right sides and above the frame, and the additional information is included within those bars rather than overlaid on a somewhat smaller image frame. Pressing INFO cycles among the viewfinder information displays you've activated in the Shooting Information Display entry described above.

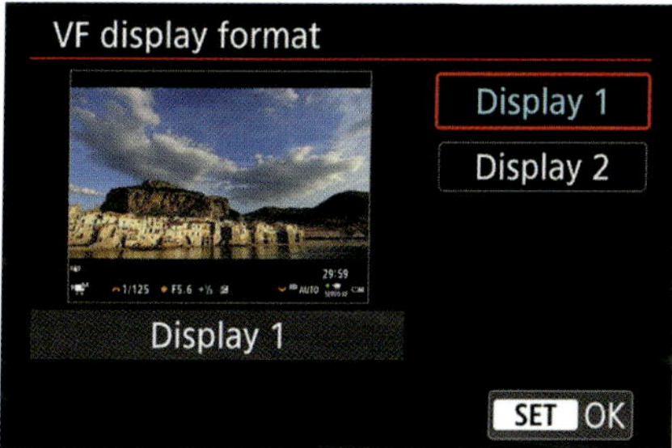

Figure 11.40 Choose from two viewfinder display formats.

Display Performance

Options: Power Saving, Smooth

My preference: Smooth

This setting determines whether the display uses more power or displays quick-moving subjects more smoothly. I always carry extra batteries and am not concerned about power-saving, so I always use the Smooth setting.

Customizing with the Autofocus Menu

12

This chapter contains descriptions of some of the more esoteric options available for the complex autofocus systems found in the EOS R8. Many of these are the settings that you'll probably set once and forget for a while, or, at least until you decide to make a significant change in your camera's autofocus behavior.

As much as I would have liked to present one huge, 100-page chapter on autofocus, it made more sense to describe the basic functions and settings in-depth in Chapter 5, and retain the lesser-used AF menu descriptions here with the camera's other menus. I think the need to jump back and forth will be minimal, although, as with any camera guide, you may need a review of other chapters from time to time as a refresher.

AF Menu Options

The entries listed in the AF menus vary, depending on your shooting mode. In still photography Creative Zone modes, the full list of items is distributed among AF tabs numbered AF 1 to AF 6. In Basic Zone modes, a simplified roster is available.

The settings accessible when using Basic Zone modes are marked with an asterisk below. The AF 2 menu does not appear at all in Basic Zone modes, and the AF 3–6 menus are renumbered 2–5 to account for that.

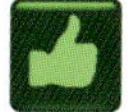 **NOTE** I'll explain the use of the 20 AF entries available in Movie mode in more detail in Chapter 16. Some 18 of them are the same as their still photo counterparts, with two additional settings to adjust Movie Servo AF speed and tracking sensitivity.

AF 1

- AF Operation
- AF Area *
- Whole Area Tracking Servo AF *
- Subject to Detect *
- Eye Detection *
- Switching Tracked Subjects
- Focus Mode *

AF 2

- Case 1
- Case 2
- Case 3
- Case 4
- Case Auto

AF 3

- One-Shot AF Release-priority
- Preview AF *
- Lens Drive when AF Impossible
- AF-Assist Beam Firing *

AF 4

- Touch & Drag AF Settings *
- Limit AF Areas
- Orientation Linked AF Point
- Limit Subject to Detect
- Left/Right Eye Detection

AF 5

- MF Peaking Settings *
- Focus Guide *
- Movie Servo AF *

AF 6

- Electronic full-time MF
- Lens Electronic MF
- Focus/Control Ring
- Focus Ring Rotation *
- RF Lens MF Focus Ring Sensitivity *

AF Operation

Options: One-Shot AF (default), AI Focus AF, Servo AF

My preference: N/A

This menu entry, the first in the AF 1 menu (see Figure 12.1) is an alternative to using the Quick Control screen or M-Fn button options to set autofocus operation. If the AF/MF switch on the lens is set to MF, then only MF appears in this entry and the other two are not available. **Reminder:** when focus is achieved, the focus point turns green or blue (in Servo mode); if focus cannot be achieved, the point turns orange. To recap:

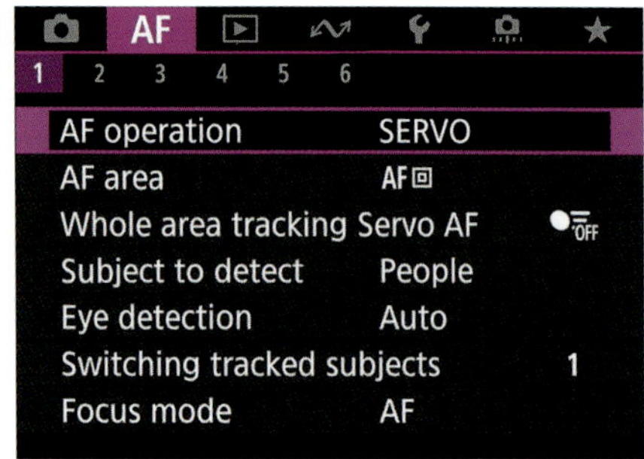

Figure 12.1 The AF 1 menu.

- **One-Shot AF.** Single autofocus locks in a focus point when the shutter button is pressed down halfway. Green boxes will appear when the image is in focus at the active focus points, or orange if the camera is unable to achieve sharp focus. You'll hear a beep when focus is locked in if Beep is not disabled in the Set-up 2 menu. The focus will remain locked until you release the button or take the picture. If sharp focus cannot be achieved, a picture will not be taken even if you press down the shutter release all the way.

- **AI Focus AF.** When you press the shutter button halfway and hold it there, the camera uses One-Shot mode to lock in focus, as described above. But, if the subject begins moving, it will switch automatically to Servo AF (described next) and change the focus to keep the subject sharp. AI Focus AF is a good choice when you're shooting a mixture of action pictures and less dynamic shots and want to use One-Shot AF when possible. The camera will default to that mode, yet switch automatically to Servo AF when it would be useful for subjects that might begin moving unexpectedly.

- **Servo AF.** This continuous autofocus mode sets focus when you partially depress the shutter button, but continues to monitor the frame and refocuses if the camera or subject is moved. The focus area turns blue when focus is achieved (there is no beep), or orange if the camera is unable to focus. Pressing the shutter release down all the way takes a picture even if sharpest focus has not been achieved. Exposure is not calculated and set until you take the picture.

AF Area

Options: Spot AF, 1-point AF, Expand AF area, Expand AF area: Around, Flexible Zone AF 1, Flexible Zone AF 2: (Vertical), Flexible Zone AF 3 (Horizontal), Whole area AF (default)

My preference: Whole area AF

You can use this menu entry instead of the Quick Controls screen or M-Fn button options. You can check focus with 5X/10X magnified views by pressing the Magnify/Reduce button in all modes. When the setting screen appears, rotate the QCD dial to cycle among these choices, as explained in more detail in Chapter 5:

- **Spot AF.** Allows you to manually select a single, reduced-size AF point.
- **1-point AF.** Allows you to manually select a single AF point.
- **Expand AF area.** You can manually select a single AF point, as well as the four points located above, below, and to the left/right of it. In Servo mode, the camera will first focus using a single point, then track using the surrounding points if needed.
- **Expand AF area: Around.** You can manually select a single AF point, as well as *up to* eight points surrounding it (above, below, left, right, and diagonally from the selected point).
- **Flexible Zone AF 1.** AF points are segregated into square-shaped zones that cover about one-sixth of the frame, and you can select which zone to use. In this Zone mode and the two that follow, the camera will seek out faces and attempt to focus on them.
- **Flexible Zone AF 2 (Vertical).** AF points are segregated into larger, vertically oriented zones, and you can select which zone to use.
- **Flexible Zone AF 3 (Horizontal).** The AF points are located with a larger horizontally oriented zone that you specify.
- **Whole area AF.** The camera selects the focus area for you, using the entire frame. For many subjects, I prefer to use this mode as my default, as it does a good job of finding subjects, particularly people, animals, or vehicles, that are moving around within the frame. It also takes into account subject motion and distance.

When any of these eight AF area modes are active, you can enable/disable spot tracking by pressing the AF point selection button, followed by the INFO button. Tracking will take place when the shutter button is held down halfway in Servo focus mode, and will commence with AI Focus *when your subject starts to move.*

As I mentioned in Chapter 5, each of the three Flexible Zone AF areas can be resized. Press the AF point selection button, then the RATE button. Then you can make the zone wider using the Main dial or taller with the QCD. Press the Q/SET button to confirm. To revert back to the original size, press the AF point selection button, the RATE button, and then the INFO button.

Whole Area Tracking Servo AF

Options: On (default), Off

My preference: On

As I noted above, Whole area AF can usually correctly identify and focus on your subject. By default, this entry is set to On. In that case, when AF operation is set to Servo and tracking is not disabled, when you press the shutter release halfway, the R8 switches to tracking using Whole area AF, over-riding any choice you've made using the AF area.

In effect, you can choose an AF area for use with non-moving subjects, and switch automatically to Whole area AF only when Servo is active. This entry can be confusing, so I've summarized the camera's behavior:

- **On.** Switches to Whole area tracking if AF operation is set to Servo and tracking is enabled. If AF operation is set to One-Shot AF or AI Focus, the area specified in the AF area entry is used instead.
- **Off.** The area specified with the AF area entry above will be used consistently for One-Shot, AI Focus, or Servo focus methods.

As an option, you can assign the behavior Start/Stop Whole area AF tracking to a particular button, such as the AF-ON button, using the Customize Buttons entry of the Custom Functions menu, as described in Chapter 15. You would then be able to toggle between your preferred AF area and Whole area tracking by pressing that defined button.

Subject to Detect

Options: Auto, People (default), Animals, Vehicles, None

My preference: Auto

This entry determines the priority for tracking subjects. If you rarely shoot one particular type of subject, you can hide that choice in this menu entry using the Limit Subject to Detect entry in the AF 4 menu, described later in this chapter. You'll find a full discussion of subject detection and tracking in Chapter 5. Your choices are:

- **Auto.** The camera will look for people, animals, or vehicles in the frame and make its own decision as to which is the main subject, based on proximity to the camera and movement.
- **People.** The camera first looks for faces or heads of humans on which to focus. At some distances or shooting angles, it may have problems locating faces, and may then focus on and track parts of human bodies, such as torsos, instead. Very large or small faces, or those that are partially hidden (say, by a hat) or extremely bright or dark may not be detected.

- **Animals.** The camera is most successful seeking out faces or heads of dogs, cats, horses, or birds, and then focusing on/tracking them, or parts of their bodies. If people are in the frame, the animals are given priority, so keep that in mind when photographing people and their active pets.

- **Vehicles.** The R8 may ignore your family sedan, but will do an excellent job of identifying the typical motor sports vehicle, including race cars or motorcycles, along with aircraft and trains. Press the INFO button to enable or disable Spot detection of typical key details of vehicles, such as headlights, wheels, the front of trains, etc. Spot detection can be useful for finding a particular vehicle if there aren't too many overlapping.

- **None.** The camera doesn't give focus/tracking preference to people or animals; all types of subjects have equal priority.

Eye Detection

Options: Disable, Auto (default), Right eye, Left eye

My preference: Auto

This setting lets you turn eye detection on and off, choose whether to give priority to left or right eyes, or allow the camera to decide which eye to focus on. These options are more important than you might think. Here's how it works:

- **Disable.** The R8 does not look for eyes, but it will search for humans if appropriate. You may find this option to be slightly faster, especially if your frame will contain human subjects that are so small that their eyes may not be readily detected.

- **Auto.** Eye detection is enabled, and once eyes are found, the camera will decide which to focus on, generally choosing the one closest to the camera. That's especially desirable for portraits if the depth-of-field is shallow and the entire face may not be in focus.

- **Right eye/Left eye.** In some cases, you may want to specify giving priority to either the left or right eye, as in portrait situations like the one above where you will know that a particular eye will be closest to the camera. If the specified eye is not detected, the camera will still use the other eye instead.

When Whole area AF is active, you can choose an eye manually by tapping the screen or moving the focus frame using the directional controls. Note that you can hide any three of the four choices from this menu entry (but not all of them) using the Left/Right Eye Detection entry found in the AF 4 menu. I'll describe that entry later in this chapter.

Switching Tracked Subjects

Options: Initial-priority, On Subject (default), Switch Subject

My preference: On Subject

This entry determines how quickly the camera switches from one subject to another when the initial tracked subject moves out of the frame, moves behind an obstruction, or turns away from the camera. For example, if you're shooting a football game as a running back is breaking through the line and a referee bolts along the sideline in front of you. With this feature set to Enable, the camera will very quickly switch to the ref, and then should return its attention to the running back—but often, not quickly enough. A better choice would be to use Disable, so that the camera briefly ignores the referee, who is likely to have moved on in a second or two. Focus tracking will remain on your running back. With the default value, On Subject, response is delayed. Your options include:

- **Initial-priority (0).** At the 0 setting, the camera will lock onto the initial subject and follow it until it leaves the frame. Use this setting when you know you'll have intervening subjects often and are certain that you want to ignore them. Many sports events fall into this category.

- **On Subject (1).** At the 1 setting, response to movement is a bit slower, so that the camera doesn't constantly refocus as subjects move about the frame. This is the default and should be used when there is only moderate movement, and especially if the movement is across the width or height of the frame (rather than coming toward you or away from you), and when you're using a small f/stop, because the increased depth-of-field will eliminate the need for most re-focusing.

- **Switch Subject (2).** At the 2 setting, the camera quickly responds to new subjects that cross the frame. This is the best setting to use for fast-moving subjects, such as sports or frenetic children, *as long as you don't expect intervening subjects.* The camera will smoothly follow your subjects. It works well when subjects within the frame are at significantly different distances.

Focus Mode

Options: AF (default), MF

My preference: N/A

This entry on the AF 1 menu appears only if you have a lens mounted on the camera that does not have an AF/MF switch. In that case, you'll need to use this option to toggle between autofocus and manual focus.

Servo AF Characteristics

Options: Case 1 (default), Case 2, Case 3, Case 4, Case A (Auto)

My preference: N/A

This entire menu, shown in Figure 12.2, is used to select from among four different factory preset "Cases," plus Auto, each with autofocus settings suitable for various types of action scenes. You can also modify the presets to adjust the sensitivity of the camera during tracking of moving objects, its response to acceleration and deceleration.

The icons for a selected Case provide pictogram reminders showing the types of action each Case is designed to cover. Highlight the Case you want to use and press Q/SET to confirm. The camera provides helpful information about each Case at the press of the INFO button, and you can read my own detailed recommendations for this menu in Chapter 5. To recap, the parameters you can change are listed below. To reset these parameters to their default values, highlight the Case, press RATE, and then press the Trash button.

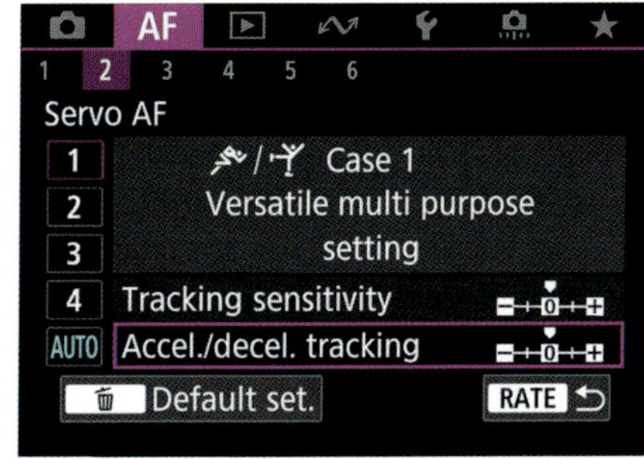

Figure 12.2 The AF 2 menu.

- **Tracking sensitivity.** Determines how swiftly the AF system refocuses on a new subject that enters the focus area. Your choices are –2 (Locked On) to +2 (Responsive). Negative numbers allow you to retain focus on the original subject even if it briefly leaves the area covered by the focus points, making tracking easier. Positive numbers switch more quickly to a new subject.
- **Acceleration/deceleration tracking.** Determines how the AF system responds to sudden acceleration, deceleration, or stopping. Your choices are 0 (constant speed) to 2 (sudden changes).

While you can adjust these parameters for any Case, you may find their default values useful:

- **Case 1: Versatile multi-purpose setting.** All-purpose setting that works well with many moving subjects, including motor sports and track, especially with subjects moving toward or away from you.
- **Case 2: Continue to track subject, ignoring possible obstacles.** Excellent for football and other sports where an intervening subject may pass in front of your primary subject. The camera will delay refocusing on the new object long enough to resume following the original subject.
- **Case 3: Instantly focus on subjects suddenly entering AF points.** Ideal when you're photographing a static scene, waiting for a moving subject, such as the winner of a race, a skier, or bicyclist.
- **Case 4: For subjects that accelerate or decelerate quickly.** I prefer this Case for basketball and soccer because you can have players racing toward you one instant, and crossing your field of view the next.
- **Case A: For erratic subjects moving quickly in any direction.** This Automatic setting is my choice for hockey games and anything that involves skates—as well as small children and pets. It's also excellent for that most difficult of subjects: birds in flight.

To change either of the two parameters, press the RATE button and use the QCD or touch screen to select Tracking Sensitivity or Accel/Decel Tracking. Press Q/SET to produce a sliding scale that can be adjusted using the QCD, the touch screen, or directional controls. See Chapter 5 for more information on using any of the five AF Cases.

One-Shot AF Release-Priority

Options: Release-priority, Focus-priority (default)

My preference: Release-priority for sports, Focus-priority for most other subjects

This is the first entry in the AF 3 menu. (See Figure 12.3.) This setting can be used to specify whether One-Shot AF uses focus-priority (the default) or release-priority. I explained the use of these alternatives in Chapter 5.

Preview AF

Options: Enable, Disable (default)

My preference: Disable

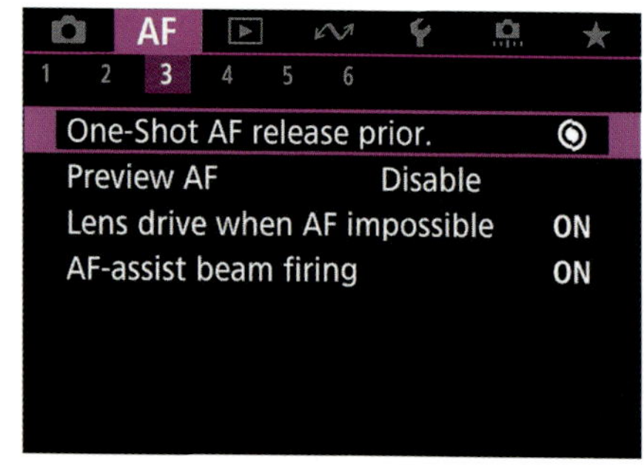

Figure 12.3 The AF 3 menu.

When Preview AF is enabled, the camera refocuses all the time (even in One-Shot mode) until you press the shutter release halfway. Then it refocuses (and locks, in One-Shot mode) and resumes refocusing (in Servo mode) until you press the shutter release all the way. The net effect is that when you're ready to take a picture, the camera has focused and refocused continually and therefore should be ready for the final focusing when you take the photo. You'll find that you get fewer shots per battery charge in this mode, because the continuous focus drains power as refocusing continues. Canon called this continuous focus in previous cameras, but it was too easily confused with Servo focus, hence the name change.

Lens Drive when AF Impossible

Options: On: Continue focus search (default); Off: Stop focus search

My preference: Stop focus search

When a scene has little inherent contrast (say, a blank wall or the sky) or if there isn't enough illumination to allow determining contrast accurately (in low light levels, or with lenses having maximum apertures of less than f/5.6), a lens may be unable to achieve autofocus. Very long telephoto lenses suffer from this syndrome because their depth-of-field is so shallow that the correct point of focus may zip past during the AF process before the AF system has a chance to register it.

Use this setting to tell the camera either to keep trying to focus if AF seems to be impossible or to stop seeking focus. Your choices are as follows:

- **On: Continue focus search.** The camera will keep trying to focus, even if the effort causes the lens to become grossly out of focus. Use this default setting if you'd prefer that the lens keep trying. Sometimes you can point the lens at an object with sufficient contrast at approximately the same distance to let the AF system lock on, then reframe your original subject with the hope that accurate focus will now be achieved.
- **Off: Stop focus search.** When this option is selected, the camera will stop trying to focus uselessly, allowing you to attempt to manually bring the subject into focus. This setting is best for very long telephoto lenses (around 400mm and up), because they encounter AF difficulties more than most lenses, and are less likely to benefit from extended "hunting."

AF-Assist Beam Firing

Options: Enable (default), Disable, LED AF-assist beam only
My preference: LED AF-assist beam only

This setting determines when bursts from a compatible external electronic flash or the camera's built-in LED are used to emit a pulse of light that helps provide enough contrast for the camera to focus on a subject. You can select Enable to use the camera's LED or an attached Canon Speedlite to produce a focus assist beam. Use Disable to turn this feature off if you find it distracting. Keep in mind that if you select Enable and the Speedlite's own AF-assist beam firing is set to Disable, the AF-assist beam will not be emitted (the flash's setting takes precedence).

- **Enable.** The AF-assist light is emitted by the camera's LED or an attached, powered-up external flash whenever light levels are too low for accurate focusing using the ambient light.
- **Disable.** The AF-assist illumination is disabled. You might want to use this setting when shooting at concerts, weddings, or darkened locations where the light might prove distracting or discourteous.
- **LED AF-assist beam only.** Some Canon flash units have an LED AF-assist lamp. Select this option to activate only the Speedlite's beam. If your flash does not have an LED, the camera's LED will be used instead. Again, if you've turned off the external flash's AF-assist beam using its own controls, this function is disabled. If you've used any of Canon's conventional dSLRs, you may recall that some flash units have an infrared AF-assist beam. That won't work with mirrorless cameras because focusing is done on the sensor rather than a dSLR's separate AF sensor. So, you'll want to rely only on the LED version with your R8.

Touch & Drag AF Settings

Options: Touch & Drag: Enable, Disable (default); Tap to select subject to detect: On (default), Off; Positioning method: Absolute, Relative (default); Active touch area: Whole panel, Right (default), Left, Top, Bottom, Top right; Relative sensitivity: –1, 0 (default), +1

My preference: When enabled, I prefer Relative positioning and Whole panel active touch area.

This is the first entry in the AF 4 menu. (See Figure 12.4.) As I've mentioned before, your touch screen can be useful even when you're working exclusively with the electronic viewfinder. When you access this entry, the screen shown at left in Figure 12.5 appears, giving you five options:

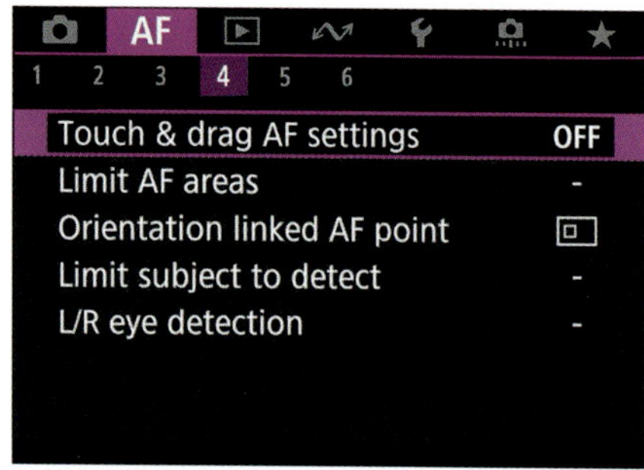

Figure 12.4 The AF 4 menu

- **Touch & Drag AF.** Choose Enable to activate, or Disable to turn the feature off. When enabled, you can touch and drag according to the parameters that follow. A round orange frame appears in the viewfinder while you are dragging. As soon as you are satisfied with that position, lift your finger and the frame changes to a square frame and tracking of the subject begins. Press the Trash button to cancel selection of that subject.

- **Tap to Select Subject to Detect.** To switch to a different subject when several subjects are found within the frame, you can tap the area within the Active Touch Area (discussed shortly). Note that this option is available *only* when Touch & Drag AF is set to Off.

- **Positioning method.** You have two options for this setting:

  - **Absolute.** While looking through the viewfinder, touch the LCD screen with a finger on the active area and drag to any position on the screen. The AF point will move to that location. This option may be more precise, but it requires you to be aware of approximately where you are touching the screen. When the active touch area (as described next) is the whole panel, that's not difficult, but the behavior is more touch and go (so to speak) with smaller screen active areas.

  - **Relative.** You can touch and drag *anywhere* within the active area and move the AF point in that direction by an amount corresponding to the *size* of the motion, regardless of where you tap on the screen.

Figure 12.5 Touch & Drag options (left); Active touch area (right).

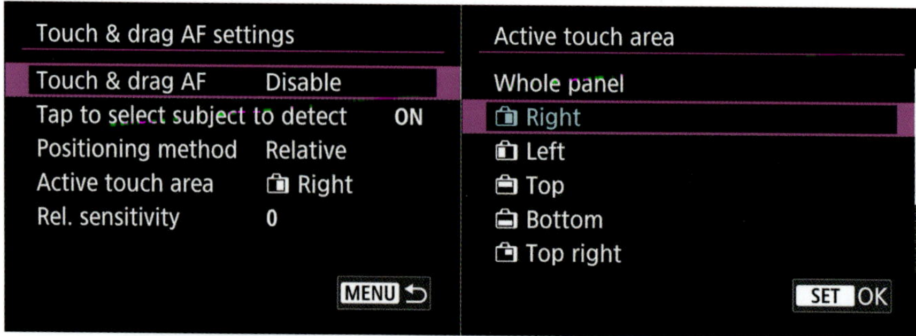

- **Active touch area.** It's simplest if you select Whole panel, so the entire LCD screen is active for the Touch & Drag feature. However, you can choose to make only the left, right, top, or bottom halves active, or the top-right corner. (See Figure 12.5, right.) A smaller area requires less dragging to move the focus point to a particular location but is also less precise. The Whole panel choice is generally more accurate, even if a bit slower than the alternatives.
- **Relative sensitivity.** This allows you to set the touch screen's sensitivity when dragging the AF point. The default value is 0, but you can also lower sensitivity (–1) or enhance it (+1).

Limit AF Areas

Options: Spot AF, 1-point AF, Expand AF area, Expand AF area: Around, Flexible Zone AF 1, Flexible Zone AF 2 (Vertical), Flexible Zone AF 3 (Horizontal), Whole area AF (Default: All enabled)

My preference: All options checked

Here you can choose which of the AF area selection modes are available. In effect, you can enable the modes you use most often, and disable those that you rarely or never work with. The 1-point AF mode cannot be disabled, however, and is displayed with a permanent checkmark.

When you access this entry, a screen with all modes is displayed (see Figure 12.6). Use the QCD or directional controls to highlight a mode you want to activate/deactivate and press SET. A checkmark above the icon indicates that the mode will be available. Select OK to confirm your choices. To cycle among the modes you've checked, press the AF point selection button on the upper-right corner of the back of the camera and press the M-Fn button until the mode you want to use is selected.

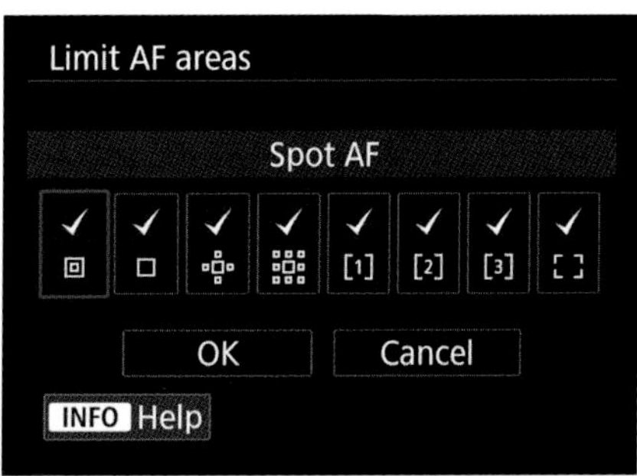

Figure 12.6 Enable or disable any AF-area selection modes.

Orientation Linked AF Point

Options: Same for both vertical and horizontal (default), Separate AF points: Point only

My preference: Separate AF Points: Point only

If you have a preference for a particular manually selected AF point or Zone AF frame when composing vertical or horizontal pictures, you can specify that preference using this menu entry, by choosing Separate AF points. Or, you can indicate that you want to use the same mode/point in all orientations (same for both vert/horizontal).

If you'd like to differentiate, there are different orientations to account for:

- **Same for both vertical and horizontal.** The AF area selection mode *and* the AF point or zone that you select manually are used for both vertical and horizontal images.
- **Separate AF points: Point only.** The AF area mode remains the same regardless of camera orientation, but you can specify a different AF point in manual point selection modes for each of three orientations. The specified point will remain in force even if you switch from one manual selection mode to another. The orientations are as follows:
  - **Camera held horizontally.** This orientation assumes that the camera is positioned so the viewfinder/shutter release are on top.
  - **Camera held vertically** with the grip/shutter release above the Mode dial.
  - **Camera held vertically** with the Mode dial above the grip/shutter release.

I provided instructions for setting your focus points and illustrations in Chapter 5 and won't repeat that information here.

Limit Subject to Detect

Options: Auto, People, Animals, Vehicles, None, Default: All checked

My preference: All checked

This entry functions similarly to the Limit AF Areas option. Its screen, shown in Figure 12.7, arrays the three types of subjects—People, Animals, and Vehicles—plus Auto and None. You can hide any four of the five choices; at least one checkmark must remain. If you have disabled any type of subject, an asterisk appears in the AF 4 menu next to this entry as a reminder; otherwise, a dash appears.

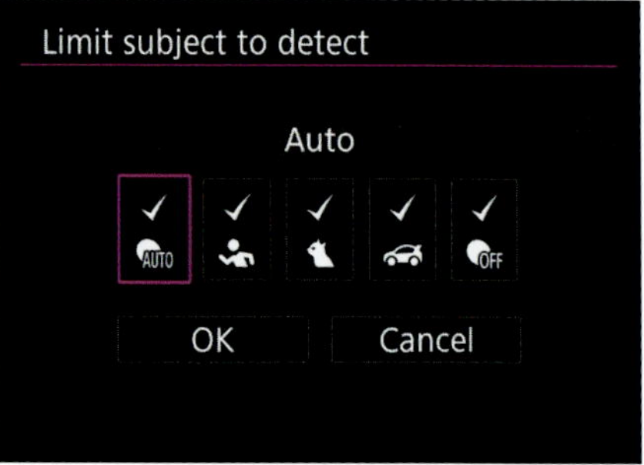

Figure 12.7 Hide up to four subject types.

Left/Right Eye Detection

Options: Off, Auto, Right eye, Left eye; Default: All checked

My preference: All checked

This is another "choice limit" option. You can hide any three of the four eye detection options; at least one must remain checked and not hidden.

MF Peaking Settings

Options: Peaking: On, Off (default); Level: High (default), Low; Color: Red (default), Yellow, Blue

My preference: On, High, Red

Although located as the first entry in the AF 5 menu, (see Figure 12.8), MF Peaking Settings deals only with manual focus. *Focus peaking* is a technique that emphasizes the outlines of the area in sharpest focus with a color that can be red, blue, or yellow. The colored area shows you at a glance what will be very sharp if you take the photo at that moment. If you're not satisfied, simply change the focused distance (with manual focus). As the focus gets closer to ideal for a specific part of the image, the color outline develops around hard edges that are in focus. You can choose how much peaking is applied (High and Low), select a specific accent color (Red, Yellow, or Blue), or turn the feature off.

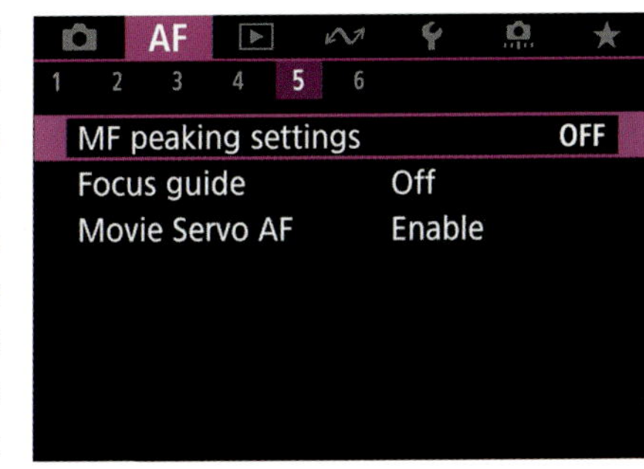

Figure 12.8 The AF 5 menu.

Peaking color allows you to specify which color is used to indicate peaking when you use manual focus. Red is the default value, but if that color doesn't provide enough contrast with a similarly hued subject, you can switch to a more contrasting color, such as blue or yellow. Peaking is not shown in magnified view or in the HDMI output you direct to an external monitor or recorder. It may be difficult to see the outlines at high ISO settings or when Canon Log is activated.

Focus Guide

Options: On, Off (default)

My preference: On

This is another useful manual focus (only) tool that overlays a guide within the image frame that shows you which direction you need to move the focus ring, and roughly how much. You can relocate the focus guide to a desired portion of the screen (press the AF point button and use the directional controls) or tap the screen to move it. Pressing the multi-controller button (or the Return icon at the upper-right corner of the touch screen) places the guide frame in the center. I provided more information on using the Focus Guide, along with illustrations, in Chapter 5.

Movie Servo AF

Options: Enable (default), Disable

My preference: Enable

This is the movie equivalent of the Preview AF feature described earlier. When active, the camera focuses on your subject all the time, without the need to press the shutter down halfway. If you temporarily don't want the camera to focus continually, tap the Servo AF icon in the lower-left corner of the screen. Tap again to resume, or simply press the MENU or Playback buttons. It will also resume if you change the AF area. When this feature is disabled, you'll need to hold the shutter button down halfway to focus continually; or press the AF-ON button to focus just once.

Electronic Full-Time MF

Options: Enable, Disable

My preference: N/A

This setting is the first in the AF 6 menu. (See Figure 12.9.) It enables or disables manual focus adjustment using the focusing ring when certain lenses, shown under the Lens Electronic Manual Focus entry (discussed next), are attached.

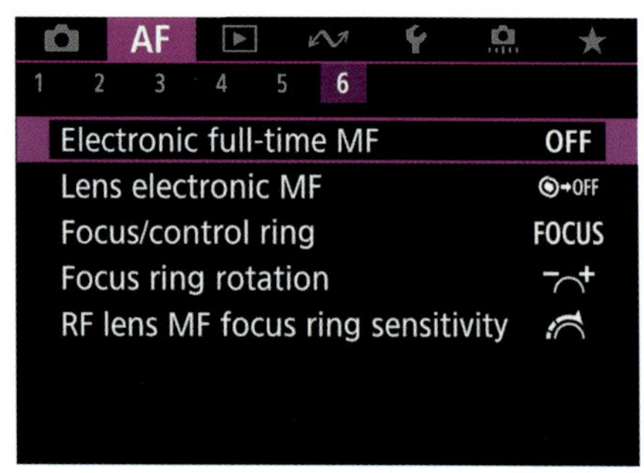

Figure 12.9 The AF 6 menu.

- **Enable.** Manual focus adjustment is available at all times when the camera is powered up, no matter what your setting is under Lens Electronic Manual Focus. In effect, this means you can always use manual focus with the listed lenses whether the camera is set for One-Shot or Servo AF.

- **Disable.** Manual focus adjustment is available only according to the settings you have made under the Lens Electronic Manual Focus setting.

Lens Electronic MF

Options: Disable after One-Shot AF (default), One-Shot AF → Enabled, One-Shot AF → Enabled (Magnify), Disable in AF

My preference: One-Shot AF → Enabled

You may need this entry's capabilities if you frequently use EF-/EF-S-mount lenses with an adapter. A limited number of extra-fast Canon prime lenses and one zoom—all of them L lenses with USM or STM motors—feature super-sensitive electronic manual focusing rings you can use to fine-tune focus after focus has been locked in using One-Shot AF. You might want to disable the use of this ring when using one of the compatible lenses, because even a casual bump against the ring can change focus significantly.

> **NOTE**
>
> Even if you've enabled One-Shot AF → Enabled (Magnify), the LCD screen or viewfinder display may not be magnified when you turn the focus ring while pressing the shutter button halfway following a shot. If that happens, release the shutter button, wait for the magnified display, and then press the shutter release halfway again while turning the focus ring. (This is a rather esoteric capability; I don't expect many readers of this book to need it.) The lenses in question are as follows as of this writing:
>
> | | | |
> |---|---|---|
> | EF50mm f/1.0L USM | EF300mm f/2.8L USM | EF600mm f/4L USM |
> | EF85mm f/1.2L USM | EF400 f/2.8L USM | EF1200 f/5.6L USM |
> | EF85mm f/1.2L II USM | EF400mm f/2.8L II USM | EF200mm f/1.8L USM |
> | EF500mm f/4.5L USM | EF28-80mm f/2.8-4L USM | EF40mm f/2.8 STM |
> | EF50mm f/1.8 STM | EF24-105mm f/3.5-5.6 STM | |

You have four choices:

- **Disable after One-Shot AF.** After AF operation is completed, manual focus is disabled. Use this when you are satisfied with the focus set by the camera's autofocus system and don't want to manually tweak it. Remember that if you truly want to use manual focus and bypass the AF system entirely, just slide the AF/MF switch on the lens to the MF position.

- **One-Shot AF → Enabled.** Once the camera has achieved focus, you can continue to hold the shutter release halfway, while adjusting focus manually. I use this when shooting portraits with my EF 85mm f/1.2 lens at a large aperture, allowing me to zero focus in on the near eye of a subject seated on a diagonal angle.

- **One-Shot AF → Enabled (Magnify).** After AF is achieved, you can continue to hold the shutter release halfway, while adjusting focus manually. Rotate the lens focus ring to magnify the area being focused as you make adjustments. If the display does not magnify on cue, release the shutter button, then press the shutter release halfway again while rotating the focus ring.

- **Disable in AF.** The camera autofocuses, and manual adjustments are disabled.

Focus/Control Ring

Options: Use as focus ring (default), Use as control ring

My preference: Use as focus ring

All RF-mount lenses have either a control ring and a focus ring or only a single ring that can be used for either function. This entry appears in the AF 6 menu only if you have mounted a lens that has a single focus/control ring, but no switch to toggle between the two functions. You can use it to specify how you want the ring to behave. (See Figure 12.10.)

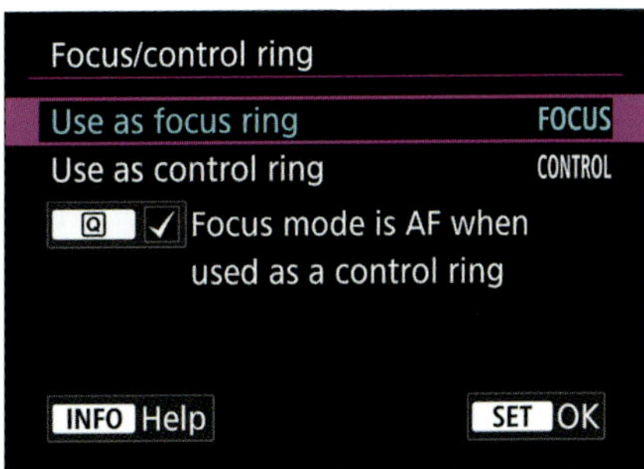

Figure 12.10 Choose control ring function.

Focus Ring Rotation

Options: Normal (clockwise), Reverse direction (counterclockwise)

My preference: Normal

Some shooters prefer to have the focus ring rotate in the opposite direction when changing focus from near to far. Usually, they are photographers coming from another vendor, such as Nikon, that uses the reverse rotation. If you want your R8 to focus more closely when rotating clockwise, choose Normal. If you would prefer to rotate counterclockwise to focus more closely, choose Reverse direction. My day job involves extensive use of both Canon and Nikon cameras, as well as Sony (which conforms to the Canon convention). I've learned to work with the rotational direction native to the system I happen to be using.

RF Lens MF Focus Ring Sensitivity

Options: Varies with rotation speed (default), Linked to rotation degree

My preference: Varies with rotation speed

Because your RF lenses use *focus by wire*, it was easy for Canon to program your R8 to change the degree of focus adjustment during manual focus, based on how quickly you are rotating the focus ring. When you turn the ring slowly—usually because you are fine-tuning the focus plane, perhaps during macro or portrait photography—the point of focus changes slowly. But when you turn the ring rapidly—say to follow-focus a speedy athlete—the camera focuses over a larger range for each degree you rotate the focus ring. That behavior is usually ideal, and is the default for your camera.

However, videographers have found this feature not helpful under some conditions. That's because, unless a lens is optimized for video shooting, zooming with a particular lens may not necessarily be *linear*. Alternating between small focus jumps and large ones, depending on the speed of rotation, doesn't work well when the goal is to pull or push focus. That's a technique used during a shot to focus the viewer's attention first on one object, and then on another one that gradually (or quickly) snaps into focus. In such cases, it's preferable to have a given amount of rotation produce the same amount of focus change. Videographers often use accessories around the focus ring and markings that show where focus should begin and end during a shot. Linking sensitivity to rotation ensures that this refocusing happens smoothly regardless of speed.

I tend to use the default setting to vary sensitivity with rotation speed, when I am shooting stills and most video, and switch to the other option only when a more linear behavior is important.

13

The Playback and Communication Functions Menus

In the last two chapters, I introduced you to the layout and general functions of the menu system used in the R8, with specifics on how to customize your camera with the Shooting and Autofocus menus. In this chapter, you'll learn how to work with the Playback and Communication Functions menus. If you're jumping directly to this chapter and need some guidance in how to navigate the menu maze, review the first few pages of Chapter 11. Otherwise, you're welcome to dive right in.

Playback Menu Options

The four blue-coded Playback menus are where you select options related to the display, review, transfer, and printing of the photos you've taken. Most of these entries are *functions* rather than *settings*, and thus only a few have actual default values, such as Image Jump with Main dial (10 images). The choices you'll find include:

Playback 1

- Protect Images
- Erase Images
- Rotate Stills
- Change Movie Rotate Info
- Rating
- Print Order
- Photobook Set-up

Playback 2

- RAW Processing (RAW/DPRAW)
- Creative Assist
- Quick Control RAW Processing
- Cloud RAW Image Processing
- Playback Creative Filters
- Resize
- Cropping

Playback 3

- HEIF-->JPEG Conversion
- Slide Show
- Set Image Search Conditions
- View From Last Seen
- Magnification
- Image Jump with Main Dial

Playback 4

- Playback Information Display
- Highlight Alert
- AF Point Disp.
- Playback Grid
- Movie Play Count
- HDMI HDR Output

Protect Images

Options: Select Images, Select Range, All Images in Folder, Unprotect All Images in Folder, All Images on Card, Unprotect All Images on Card

My preference: N/A

This is the first of seven entries in the Playback 1 menu (see Figure 13.1). If you want to keep an image from being accidentally erased (either with the Erase button or by using the Erase Images entry in the Playback menu), you can mark that image for protection. Use the Protect entry in the Playback version of the Quick Control menu (described next), or use this menu item. To protect one or more images, press the MENU button while viewing an image and choose Protect from the Playback 1 menu.

One of two screens will appear:

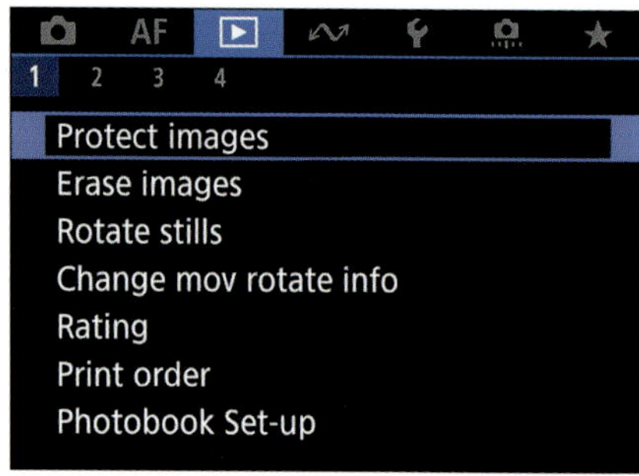

Figure 13.1 The Playback 1 menu.

- **Default screen.** By default, the screen shown at left in Figure 13.2 appears with these choices:
  - **Select Images.** Choose individual images from the current card by scrolling through an array of thumbnail previews.
  - **Select Range.** Specify a continuous range of images by selecting the first image, pressing SET, then scrolling to the last image and pressing Q/SET again.
  - **All Images in Folder.** Select all the images in a folder. You'll be shown a list of available folders (if more than one is available). Press Q/SET to specify the highlighted folder.
  - **Unprotect All Images in Folder.** Select a folder and unprotect all images within that folder.
  - **All Images on Card.** Protect all images in the active card.
  - **Unprotect All Images on Card.** Unprotect all images in the active card.

Figure 13.2 Default Protect Images screen (left). Protect/Unprotect only images meeting search conditions (right).

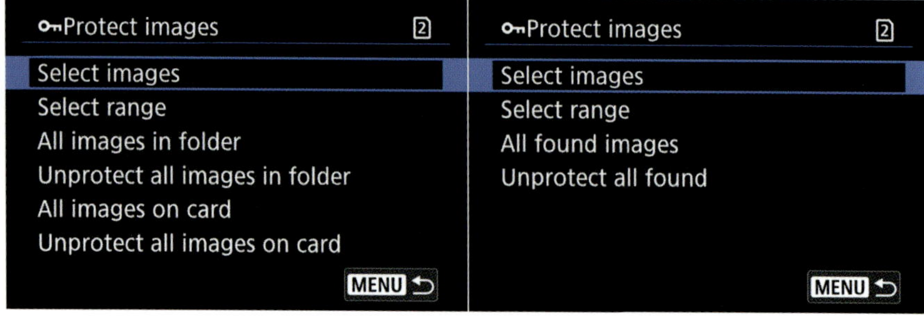

- **Specified Search screen.** As I'll explain later in this chapter, you can tell the camera to use specified parameters when searching for images during playback. If you have set up these search conditions, the screen shown in Figure 13.2, right, appears. You can then select images to protect using these options:
  - **Select Images.** Choose any of the individual images on the current card by scrolling through an array of thumbnail previews.
  - **Select Range.** Specify a continuous range of images on the card, as described earlier.
  - **All Found Images.** Protect *all* the images located using the parameters you chose in the Set Image Search Conditions entry in the Playback 3 menu, as described later. You could, for example, protect all images with a particular Rating, those taken on a particular date, only Still photos, or only Movies.
  - **Unprotect All Found Images.** Remove protection from the images meeting your image search conditions.

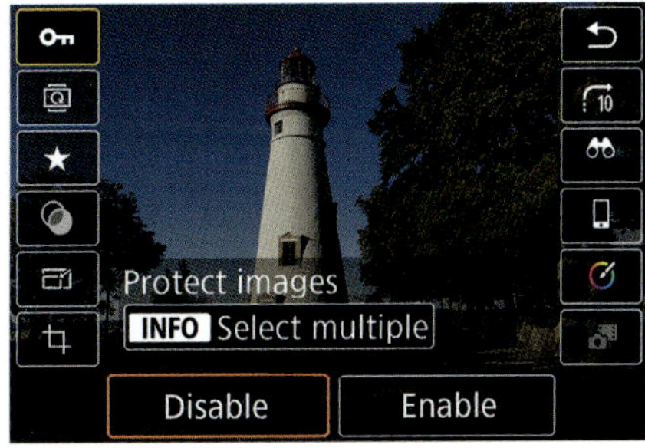

Figure 13.3 Protected images can be locked against accidental erasure (but not preserved from formatting) using the Q menu.

> ### FAST PROTECTION
>
> A fast way to protect images is to press the Q/SET button when an image is displayed, then navigate to the Protect "key" icon that appears at top in the left-hand column. (See Figure 13.3.) When Enable is highlighted, press Q/SET to protect the current image, or press INFO to select multiple images using the Select Range, All Images on Card, or Unprotect All Images on Card options that appear.

Erase Images

Options: Select and Erase Images, Select Range, All Images in Folder, All Images on Card
My preference: N/A

Choose this menu entry and you'll be given four choices: Select and Erase Images, Select Range, All Images in Folder, and All Images on Card. You can use the first three to selectively remove images, while the fourth option deletes all the pictures on a card. Protected images will not be erased. But, using the Format command is usually faster and more thorough.

This function works similarly to the Protect Images function described above. If no Image Search Conditions have been set, the default screen appears with these choices:

- **Select and Erase Images.** View the images on your card by pressing the left/right directional controls to scroll through them. To mark an image for deletion or to remove a checkmark, press the Q/SET button. When you're finished selecting, press the Q/SET button and you'll be asked to confirm. Choose Cancel or OK and Q/SET to finish.

- **Select Range.** Operates similarly to the range protect option listed earlier. Choose Select Range and you can mark the first of a string of images by highlighting it and pressing Q/SET. Then navigate to the last image to be erased and press Q/SET again. Press Q to confirm and delete the images.

- **All Images in Folder.** You'll be shown a list of the available folders on your memory card. Select SET, and a prompt will appear asking you to confirm, and reminding you that Protected images will not be removed.

- **All Images on Card.** A prompt will ask you to confirm this step. The All Images on Card choice removes all the pictures on the card, except for those you've marked with the Protect command. This step only removes images and does not reformat the memory card.

If you have set Image Search Conditions in the Playback 3 menu, your choices are as follows:

- **Select and Erase Images.** Choose any of the individual images on the current card by scrolling through an array of thumbnail previews.

- **Select Range.** Specify a continuous range of images on the card, as described earlier.

- **All Found Images.** Delete all images located using the parameters you chose in the Set Image Search Conditions entry, except for Protected images.

Rotate Stills

Options: Rotate Image

My Recommendation: N/A

While you can set the camera to automatically rotate images taken in a vertical orientation using the Auto Rotate option in the Set-up 1 menu (as described in Chapter 14), you can manually rotate an image during playback using this menu selection. Select Rotate Stills from the Playback 1 menu, use the QCD to page through the available images on your memory card until the one you want to rotate appears, then press Q/SET. The image will appear on the screen rotated 90 degrees. Press Q/SET again, and the image will be rotated 270 degrees. (See Figure 13.4.) Note that you can also rotate images from the Quick Control menu that appears when you press the Q/SET button during playback. It's the second icon from the top in the left column, as shown earlier in Figure 13.3.

Figure 13.4 A vertically oriented image that isn't rotated appears larger on the LCD (left), but rotation allows viewing the photo without turning the camera (right).

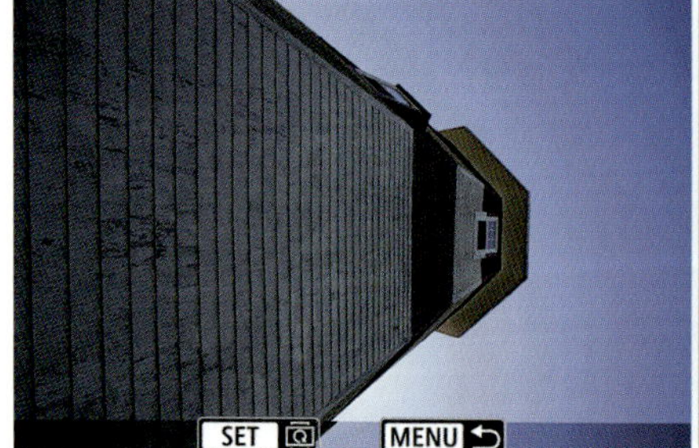
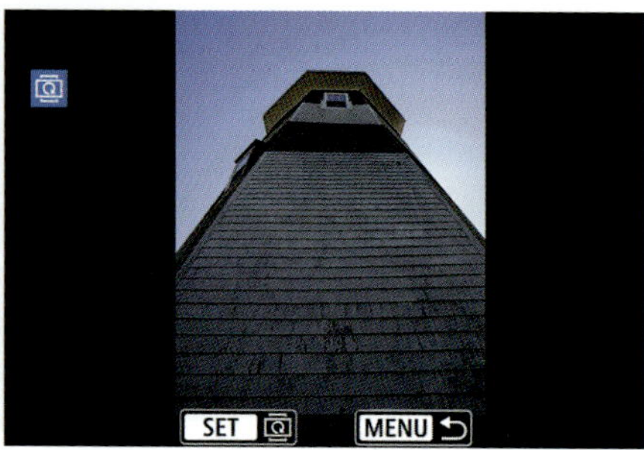

Change Movie Rotate Info.

Options: Change playback orientation

My recommendation: N/A

Those of us who have used smartphones to record movies know that the orientation of the device can vary from horizontal to vertical and upside down. This entry allows you to change the orientation of your camera's videos when viewed on other devices. Your movies will always be shown horizontally on the camera's display; this option only affects display on your smartphone and other devices. You'll need to activate the Add Movie Rotate Info option in the Set-up 1 menu, as described in Chapter 14.

Just select this entry from the Playback 1 menu, then choose a movie by rotating the QCD. An icon at the upper-left corner of the screen includes an arrow indicating which side of the movie frame will appear at the top when the video is played back. Each time you press SET, the orientation changes from top (the default) to right side, to left side.

Rating

Options: Select Images (Individual Images, Range, All Images in Folder, All Images on Card); One to five stars, None

My recommendation: N/A

If you want to apply a quality rating to images or movies you've shot (or use the rating system to represent some other criteria), you can use this entry to give images one, two, three, four, or five stars, or remove a rating. The Image Jump function can display only images with a given rating. Suppose you were photographing a track meet with multiple events. You could apply a one-star rating to jumping events, two stars to relays, three stars to throwing events, four stars to hurdles, and five stars to dashes. Then, using the Image Jump feature, you could review only images of one type.

With a little imagination, you can apply the rating system to all sorts of categories. At a wedding, you could classify pictures of the bride, the groom, guests, attendants, and parents of the couple. If you were shooting school portraits, one rating could apply to first grade, another to second grade, and so on. Given a little thought, this feature has many more applications than you might think. Ratings can be used to specify images for a slide show, too, or to select images in Digital Photo Professional.

There are three ways to apply ratings to an image or movie:

- **Assigned button.** You can assign the Rating function to a button using the Customize Buttons entry in the Custom Functions 3 menu, as described in Chapter 15. However, this setup only allows assigning one rating of your choice (one to five stars, or off) rather than the full range. You might use this capability to quickly mark images during playback so they can be searched using that rating.
- **Quick Control menu.** You can also apply ratings from the Quick Control menu that appears when you press the Q/SET button during Playback. It's the third icon from the top in the left column, as shown earlier in Figure 13.3.
- **This menu entry.** To apply a rating using this entry, use the steps described next, if you want to apply ratings to more than a few images or movies quickly.

To use the Ratings menu entry, just follow these steps:

1. Choose the Rating menu item.
2. Choose Select Images, Select Range, All Images in Folder, or All Images on Card to specify images to be rated.
3. When an image or movie you want to rate is visible, press Q/SET. You can also select a range of images, all those in a folder, or all on a card, as described under the Protect and Erase Images entries earlier.
4. Now rotate the QCD to apply a one- to five-star rating, or turn a rating off. You can rate up to 999 images.
5. When finished rating, choose MENU to exit.

Print Order

Options: Select Image; Multiple: Select Range, Mark/Clear All in Folder, Mark All/Clear All on Card; Set Up: Print type (Standard, Index, Both); Date (On/Off); File Number (On/Off)

My preference: N/A

Your camera supports the DPOF (Digital Print Order Format) that is now almost universally used by digital cameras to specify which images on your memory card should be printed, and the number of prints desired of each image. This information is recorded on the memory card, and can be interpreted by a compatible printer. Photo labs are also equipped to read this data and make prints when you supply your memory card to them.

Once marked for DPOF printing, you can print the selected images, or take your memory card to a digital lab or kiosk, which is equipped to read the print order and make the copies you've specified. (You can't "order" prints of RAW images or movies.) To create a DPOF print order, just follow these steps:

1. **Access Print Order screen.** In the Playback 1 menu, navigate to Print Order. Press SET.
2. **Access Set-up.** The Print Order screen will appear. (See Figure 13.5.) Use the directional controls to highlight Set Up. Press Q/SET.
3. **Select Print type.** Choose Print Type (Standard, Index/Thumbnails print, or Both), and specify whether Date or File Number imprinting should be turned on or off. (You can turn one or the other on, but not both Date and File Number imprinting.) You cannot set print type individually; all images in the print order will use the same print type. Press MENU to return to the Print Order screen.

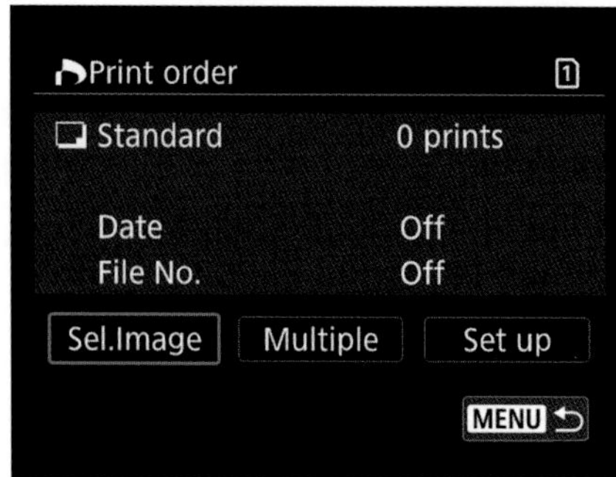

Figure 13.5 Select the images to be printed individually, by folder, or all the images on your memory card.

4. **Choose selection method.** Highlight Sel. Image (choose individual images) or Multiple:

   - **Select individual images.** With Sel. Image, use the directional controls to view the images, and press Q/SET to mark or unmark an image for printing and choose the number of prints to be made. If you'd rather view thumbnails of images, press the Thumbnail/Zoom In button. Press the Magnify/Zoom Out button to return to single-image view.

   - **Multiple.** Allows you to select a Range, Mark All in Folder, Clear All in Folder, Mark All on Card, or Clear All on Card. Press Q/SET to choose a range or folder, and MENU to return to the print order screen.

5. **Choose number of prints.** If you've selected individual images (rather than a range, folder, or card) as an image is selected, you can press the up/down directional controls to specify 1 to 99 prints for that image. (For Index prints, you can only specify whether the selected image is included in the index print, not the number of copies.) Press Q/SET to confirm. You can then use the up/down buttons to select additional images. Press MENU when finished selecting to return to the Print Order screen.

6. **Output your hardcopies.** If the camera is linked to a PictBridge-compatible printer, an additional option appears on the Print Order screen—Print. You can select that; optionally, adjust Paper Settings as described in the previous section, and start the printing process. Alternately, you can exit the Print Order screen by tapping the shutter release button. Then turn off the camera and printer, remove the memory card, and insert it in the memory card slot of a compatible printer, retailer kiosk, or digital minilab.

Photobook Set-up

Options: Select Images, Multiple

My preference: N/A

You can select up to 998 images on your memory card, and then use the EOS Utility to copy them all to a specific folder on your computer. This is a handy way to transfer only specific images to a particular folder, and is especially useful when you're collecting photos to assemble in a photobook. RAW images and movies cannot be chosen for a photobook. Your choices include:

- **Select images.** You can mark individual images from any folder on your memory card.

- **Multiple.** You can choose Select Range, All Images in Folder, Clear All in Folder, All Images on Card, or Clear All on Card. Note that movies or RAW images will not be collected when using the Multiple option.

Once you have marked the images you want to transfer to the specified folder, use the EOS Utility to copy them.

RAW Image Processing

Options: Select Images, Select Range; Use Shot Settings; Set Up Processing: JPEG; Set Up Processing: HEIF

My recommendation: N/A

This is the first entry on the Playback 2 menu page (see Figure 13.6). This entry can perform functions on standard RAW and C RAW files, with the exception that creating HEIF files is not possible with images captured using expanded L or H ISO sensitivity settings.

This option allows you to produce JPEG or HEIF versions of your full-size RAW images right in the camera. The original RAW shot is not modified. When you select this menu entry, only compatible RAW images are offered for your selection. Just follow these steps:

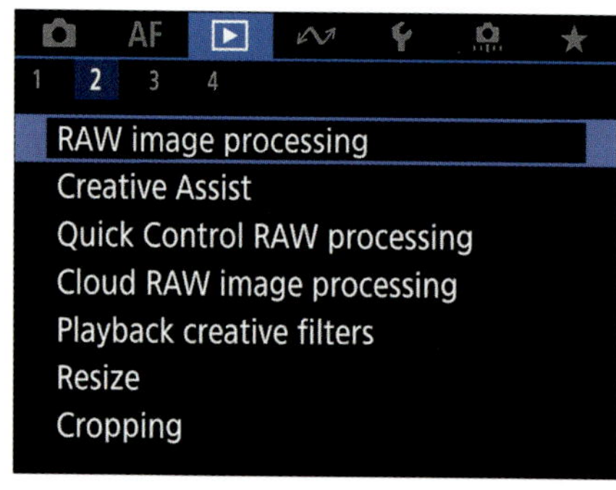

Figure 13.6 The Playback 2 menu.

1. **View RAW images.** From the first screen that appears, select either Select Images (to choose individual RAW images) or Select Range (to choose a continuous series of images). Rotate the QCD to scroll through compatible images. Press the Magnify button and rotate the Main dial counterclockwise to activate a selection of index images instead.

2. **Select image to process.** Press Q/SET to select an image for processing. A checkmark will appear next to it. When you are done choosing, press the Q/SET button to move on to the next step.

3. **Use Shot Settings or Set Up Processing (JPEG or HEIF).** If you select Use Shot Settings in the next screen, the camera will immediately create JPEG copies of the RAW image(s) you specified, asking you to confirm that you want to save as a new file. If you want to customize settings, proceed to Step 4.

   Note: If you elect the default Use Shot Settings, the image settings in effect at the time the picture was taken will be used. If HDR PQ Settings was set to Disable, JPEGs are created; if set to Enable, HEIFs are created instead.

4. **Specify parameters.** A screen appears with a selection of parameters you can adjust. (See Figure 13.7.) Navigate to the parameter you want to manipulate using the directional controls. Your choices include:

   - Brightness
   - White balance
   - Picture Style
   - Clarity (JPEG only)
   - Auto Lighting Optimizer
   - High ISO Noise Reduction
   - Image quality
   - Color space
   - Lens aberration correction

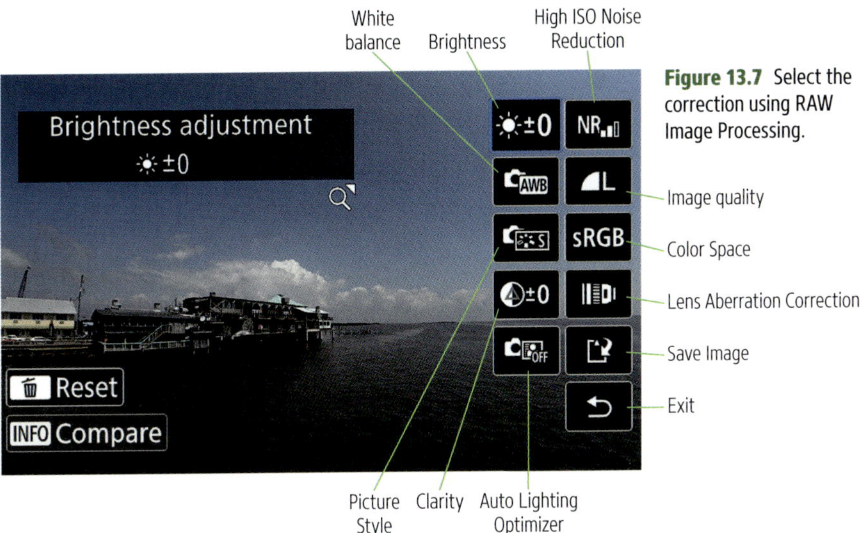

Figure 13.7 Select the correction using RAW Image Processing.

5. **Make adjustments.** All parameters will already be set to those specified when you exposed the RAW file. When a parameter you want to change is highlighted, press SET, then rotate either the Main dial or QCD to select an option. Some changes are difficult to see; press the Magnify button to enlarge a portion of the image for review. Press Q/SET to confirm your option, and return to the main screen.

6. **Repeat Step 5 (optional).** You can continue making adjustments to any or all of the other parameters. At any time you can press the Trash/Erase button to cancel all the changes you've made so far.

7. **Compare before/after.** Here's the cool part. After you've made adjustments, you can press the INFO button to compare your before and after images. The image will be shown in the After Change version (and labeled as such) with the parameters you've modified highlighted in orange in the upper-right corner of the screen. Rotate the QCD to toggle between the After Change image and the Shot Settings (original) version. (Digital Lens Optimizer effects are shown only in magnified view.) Press MENU to exit Compare mode.

8. **Save JPEG/HEIF.** When you're satisfied with your changes, navigate to the Save icon at the bottom right of the screen (just above the Return arrow) and press Q/SET. Choose OK to save as a new file, or Cancel to abort the process. If the original was shot using an aspect ratio other than 3:2, the image will be displayed in those proportions, and the JPEG or HEIF will be saved in that aspect ratio.

9. **Continue processing?** If you've selected several images, you'll be asked whether you want to continue processing them. Choose Yes to continue.

10. **Select image to display.** You can tell the camera which of the two versions to display, the Original Image or the Processed Image.

11. **Repeat.** If you have more images selected, continue processing all the images you want to work with.

Creative Assist

Options: Presets: Vivid, Soft, Warm, Cool, Green, Shine, Lime, Peach, Black-and-White, Blue, Purple, Normal, and Auto 1–3; Effects: Background Blur, Brightness, Contrast, Saturation, Color Tone 1, Color Tone 2, Monochrome

My recommendation: N/A

You don't have to apply Scene Intelligent Auto's Creative Assist when taking photos. This Playback menu option lets you apply those effects to images *after* they have been captured. Just follow these steps:

1. **Select image.** Press the Playback button, highlight the image you want to process using Creative Assist and press the Q/SET button.

2. **View Effects.** A horizontal scrollable list appears. It has icons representing Effects ranging from Background Blur, Brightness, Contrast, Saturation, Color Tone 1, Color Tone 2, and Monochrome. (See Figure 13.8, top row). You can also select Presets, seen in the bottom row of the figure, and which include Vivid, Soft, Warm, Cool, Green, Shine, Lime, Peach, Black-and-White, Blue, Purple, Normal, and Auto 1–3.

3. **Adjust Effect.** Highlight the effect you want to use, press Q/SET to access the adjustment screen, each equipped with an appropriate adjustment slider. Press the AF point selection button to apply the effect.

4. **Confirm and save.** Select Cancel or OK and press the Q/SET button to save the image as a new file.

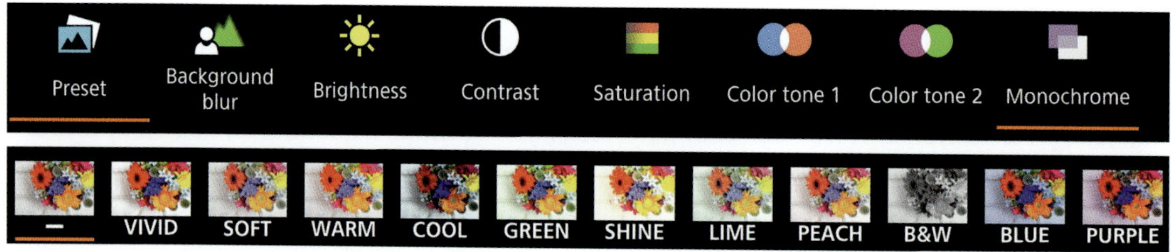

Figure 13.8 Creative Assist Effects (top row) and Presets (bottom row).

Quick Control RAW Processing

Options: Creative Assist, RAW Processing

My recommendation: N/A

RAW Image Processing and Creative Assist, described above, can be accessed directly from the Playback version of the Quick Controls screen (shown in Figure 13.3, earlier). This entry allows you to specify *which* of the two is active. By default, the Creative Assist icon is displayed in the Quick Controls screen as the second from the bottom of the right column. If you'd prefer to summon RAW Processing instead, highlight it on the screen that appears when you access this menu, and press Q/SET.

Cloud RAW Image Processing

Options: Quantity Selected, Processing Capacity, Last Updated, Check Processing Capacity (Refresh), Add Images to Process, Check/Remote Selected images, [Send]

My recommendation: N/A

Strictly speaking, this menu entry is not actually an R8 feature. It is a gateway to Canon's subscription service that provides cloud-based RAW image processing that is theoretically better than what the camera can accomplish internally. The service uses neural network processing and can reduce noise, false color, moiré, and jagged lines and perform other functions. Canon says the service is most effective for images such as night scenes and astronomical images taken with a high ISO, images taken with a moving subject in a dark place, images with fine stripes, and images of buildings with tile/brick patterns.

Pre-processed RAW images and processed images will be stored in Canon's cloud storage for 30 days in original qualities, and they can be transferred to your computer or other services, such as Google Photos. A free account to image.canon (lowercase is their usage, not mine) is available, but Cloud RAW Image Processing requires a paid monthly subscription, which costs $4.99 and allows you to process up to 80 images. If you use up your allowance in any month, additional processing in 80-image increments can be purchased for $4.99 each.

This menu entry is used to check the status of your account, select images, and send them to the Canon server while the R8 is connected to the Internet. When processing is finished, Canon will send you an email notifying you that your images are ready.

This service is too new to estimate how many R8 users want it or need it, or will be willing to pay the monthly fee. My guess is that Canon will be adding features in the future that will make it more useful.

Playback Creative Filters

Options: Grainy B/W, Soft Focus, Fish-eye Effect, Art Bold Effect, Water Painting Effect, Toy Camera Effect, and Miniature Effect

My recommendation: N/A

This entry allows you to apply any of the Creative Filter effects described in Chapter 4 to images that you've already taken. All but Miniature Effect and the HDR Art filters allow you to modify the effect by pressing the up directional button and using the left/right controls to change parameters. Your choices include: Grainy B/W (Contrast), Soft Focus, Fish-eye Effect (strength of the effect), Art Bold Effect (strength of the effect), Water Painting Effect (color density), Toy Camera Effect (color tone), and Miniature Effect (location of blur).

Resize

Options: Medium, Small 1, Small 2 image sizes

My recommendation: N/A

If you've already taken an image and would like to create a smaller JPEG or HEIF version (say, to send by e-mail), you can create one from this menu entry. Just follow these steps:

1. **Choose Resize.** Select this menu entry from the Playback 2 menu.

2. **View images to resize.** You can scroll through the available images with the touch screen or directional controls. Only images that can be resized are shown. They include JPEG or HEIF Large, Medium, and Small 1 images. Small 2 and RAW images of any type and movies cannot be resized.

3. **Select an image.** Choose Q/SET to select an image to resize. A pop-up menu will appear on the screen offering the choice of reduced-size images: M, S1, or S2 sizes. Rotate the QCD to select:

   Medium: 3984 × 2656, 11MP; Small 1: 2976 × 1984, 5.9MP; Small 2: 2400 × 1600, 3.8MP.

   You cannot resize an image to a size that is larger than its current size; that is, you cannot save a Medium image as Large.

4. **Resize and save.** Choose Q/SET to save as a new file, and confirm your choice by selecting OK from the screen that pops up, or cancel to exit without saving a new version. The old version of the image is untouched.

As with some other entries in the Playback menu, you can also resize images from the Quick Control menu that appears when you press the Q/SET button during Playback. It's the fifth icon from the top in the left column, as shown earlier in Figure 13.3.

Cropping

Options: Crop, Aspect Ratio

My recommendation: N/A

If you need to crop an image, you can do it here. You don't have as much control as you would have in an image editor, but if you, say, need to crop an image for emailing or uploading to a social media site, this may do the job. You can crop *only* JPEG or HEIF images. This function does not work on RAW images, or frames grabbed from 4K or 8K movies.

Simply select this menu entry and press Q/SET. A compatible image appears. Use the QCD to select an image for cropping. Press Q/SET when you've chosen your image and go to the screen shown in Figure 13.9. (Note that you can also crop images from the Quick Control menu that appears when you press the Q/SET button during Playback. It's the sixth icon from the top in the left column, as shown earlier in Figure 13.3.)

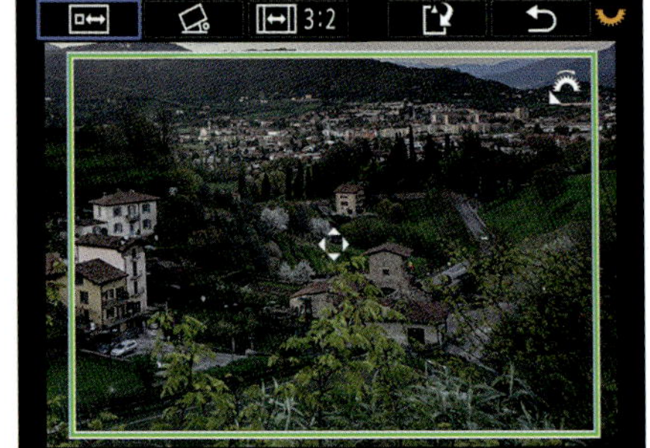

Figure 13.9 The green frame represents the cropped area.

In the cropping screen you can apply one of these tools:

- **Select adjustment.** Arrayed along the top row of the screen are function icons. Rotate the QCD to highlight any of these (from left to right):
  - **Change the crop view.** Enlarge/reduce crop. When this option is highlighted, rotate the Main dial to enlarge and reduce the green cropping frame, seen in Figure 13.9. Use the directional controls to relocate the position of the cropping frame within the image.
  - **Straighten the image.** Correct for tilt. When this option is highlighted, press Q/SET to produce a grid overlaid on your image. Up to plus/minus 10 degrees of tilt can be corrected. Rotating the QCD will adjust orientation in 0.1-degree increments. Rotational arrows appear in the top row that you can tap on the touch screen to adjust in 0.5-degree increments. The grid helps you straighten your image. Press Q/SET to finish this correction and confirm.
  - **Change aspect ratio.** When this option is highlighted, press Q/SET repeatedly to cycle the cropping frame's proportions among 3:2, 16:9, 4:3, 1:1, 2:3, 9:16, or 3:4 aspect ratios.
- **Save cropped image.** Highlight this option and press Q/SET, select OK, and press Q/SET again to save your cropped image as a new file. Your original image is retained unharmed.

HEIF-->JPEG Conversion

Options: Convert to JPEG
My recommendation: N/A

This is the first entry in the Playback 3 menu (see Figure 13.10). You can convert HEIF images captured during HDR Shooting with PQ (perceptual quantization) enabled (as discussed in Chapter 11) to JPEG format if you need a conventional image. Select this menu entry and you'll be shown only compatible HDR images. Press Q/SET and a message Converting to JPEG appears, followed by a Save As New File prompt. That's all there is to it. Your original file is unchanged.

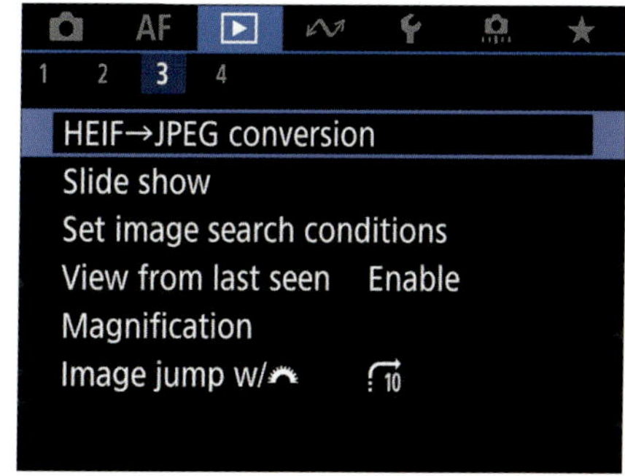

Figure 13.10 The Playback 3 menu.

Slide Show

Options: Image Selection, Display Time, Repeat, Transition Effect
My recommendation: N/A

Slide Show is a convenient way to review images or movies one after another, without the need to manually switch between them. To activate, just choose Slide Show from the Playback 5 menu. During playback, you can press the Q/SET button to pause the "slide show" (in case you want to examine an image more closely), or the INFO button to change the amount of information displayed on the screen with each image. For example, you might want to review a set of images and their histograms to judge the exposure of the group of pictures.

To set up your slide show, follow these steps:

1. **Choose images.** By default, the Slide Show feature chooses all images on the card. If that's what you want, proceed to Step 3. If you want to choose specific images, continue to Step 2.

2. **Specify certain images.** You can "filter" which images will be displayed in your slide show. The parameters can include Rating, Date, Folder, Protected, and File Type (RAW, RAW+JPEG, JPEG, or Movie). You'll find instructions for filtering images in the entry described after Slide Show: Set Image Search Conditions.

3. **Choose Set Up.** Highlight the Set Up option and press Q/SET to begin choosing display parameters.

4. **Choose Display Time.** Highlight Display Time and press Q/SET to produce a screen with a choice of playing times (1, 2, 3, 5, 10, or 20 seconds per image). Press Q/SET to confirm.

5. **Repeat.** If you want the show to keep playing, highlight Repeat, press Q/SET, and Enable.

6. **Exit Set Up.** Press MENU to exit Set Up.

7. **Start the show.** Highlight Start and press Q/SET to begin your show. (If you'd rather cancel the show you've just set up, press MENU instead.) **Note:** the display time of each slide will vary, depending on the file size of the image.

8. **Use show options during display.** Press Q/SET to pause/restart; INFO to cycle among the information displays for still photos; and MENU to stop the show. The auto power-off feature will not turn the camera off during playback. The sound volume of movies can be adjusted by rotating the Main dial, and during playback or pause, you can rotate the QCD to view a different slide.

Set Image Search Conditions

Options: Filter by: Rating, Date, Folder, Protection, or File Type

My preference: N/A

You don't need to see every image on your memory card as you play them back or perform functions like Protect or Erase. This entry allows you to specify which images are shown during image review, available in a slide show, or subject to the Protect and Erase features.

Just follow these steps:

1. **Choose Set Image Search Conditions.** Highlight the entry and press SET.

2. **Select condition.** A vertical column at left appears with the conditions available, listed, from top to bottom: Rating, Date, Folder, Protection, or File Type. Use the QCD to scroll to and highlight a condition. (See Figure 13.11.)

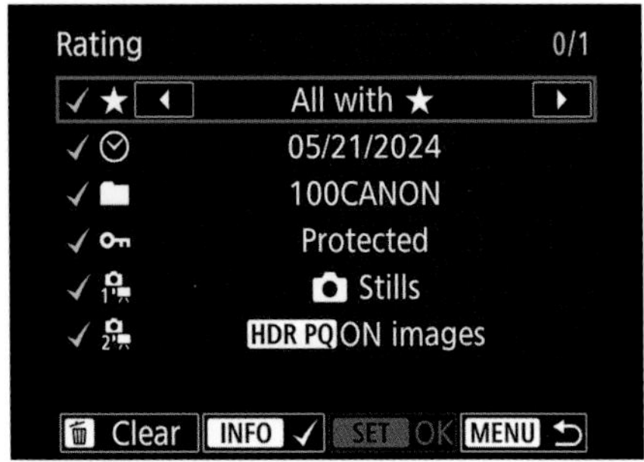

Figure 13.11 Image search conditions.

3. **Enter parameter.** Use the Main dial to set the parameter for a particular condition:

   - **Rating.** You can choose one to five stars.
   - **Date.** Select a specific date *that includes photos taken.* (That is, you cannot select a date on which no images were taken with this card.)
   - **Folder.** Select from among the various folders on your card. If only one folder is available, that is chosen by default.
   - **Protected.** Choose Protected or Unprotected images.
   - **Type of File 1 and 2.** Choose to show only stills, various combinations of RAW, RAW+JPEG, and JPEG, plus movie files. You can set two different specifications, numbered 1 and 2.

4. **Set condition.** When parameters are set for a condition, press INFO to add it to your conditions. You can press INFO again to unselect it. Mix and match conditions, choosing any one, or any combination of the five parameters. Press Trash to remove/clear all conditions.

5. **Confirm.** Press Q/SET to exit. An informational screen will appear. Press OK to confirm. If no images meet the conditions you specified, you will be unable to apply them.

View From Last Seen

Options: Enable (default), Disable
My preference: Disable

This entry determines what happens when you resume playback review of your images. When you select Enable, playback starts with the last image displayed during review. When disabled, playback shows the last image you shot. Most of the time, when I am actively shooting, I want to see my most recent images immediately, so I leave this set to Disable. However, if you were reviewing a large group of images and performing some other function (say, cropping or resizing them), you'd want to return to the last image you were already working with.

Magnification

Options: 2X (default), 4X, 8X, 10X, Actual size, Same as last magnification
My recommendation: Same as last magnification

This setting allows you to specify the initial magnification for magnified view during playback, as well as the starting position on the screen. Choose your starter magnification based on how often you tend to take a close-up look at your images during review. If you're a pixel-peeper, you might want an in-depth 10X view each time you magnify your image. I like to use the same magnification I most recently used, because I am likely to examine a series of similar images at the same zoom level during a shooting or review session.

Your options are as follows:

- **Magnification.** You have three choices:
  - **2X, 4X, 8X, 10X (from the center of the frame).** The initial magnified view will be 2X, 4X, 8X, or 10X (your choice), centered around the middle of the frame.
  - **Actual Size (from selected point).** Magnified view starts at 100 percent, centered around the auto-focus point used to achieve focus; if manual focus was used, the image will be centered around the middle of the frame.
  - **Same as last magnification (from the center point).** The camera uses the same magnification value you last used, centered around the middle of the frame.
- **Magnified position.** This determines the initial position around which magnification will be applied. You can choose From Center or From Focus Point.
- **Maintain position.** You can choose to maintain your current position in the frame when browsing images. This is useful when you want to compare the same area of an image—say a subject's face—in a series of shots captured consecutively.

Image Jump with Main Dial

Options: 1 Image, 10 Images (default), Specified number (1–100), Date, Folder, Movies, Stills, Protected, Rating, First Image of Scene

My preference: 10 Images

As first described in Chapter 2, you can leap ahead or back during picture review by swiping across the touch screen with two fingers, or by rotating the Main dial. You can select from a variety of increments that will be used with this menu entry. The Jump method is shown briefly on the screen as you leap ahead to the next image displayed, as shown in Figure 13.12. Your options are as follows:

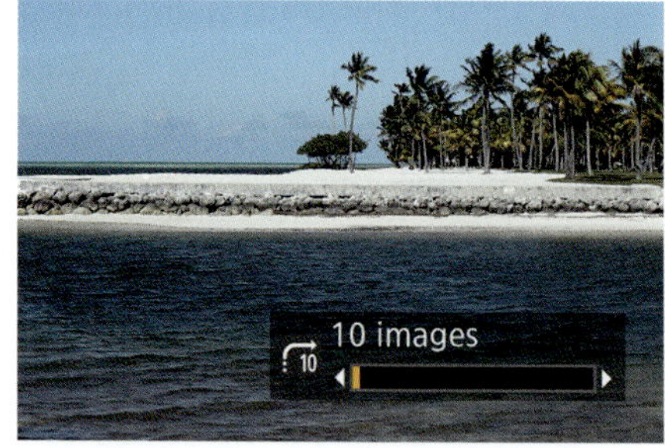

Figure 13.12 The Jump method is shown on the LCD briefly—when you leap forward or back using the Main dial or a two-fingered touch-screen swipe.

- **1 image.** Rotating the Main dial one click or swiping jumps forward or back 1 image.
- **10 images.** Rotating the Main dial one click or swiping jumps forward or back 10 images.
- **Specified number.** When this option is highlighted, rotate the Main dial to choose the increment between jumps, from one image to 100.
- **Date.** Rotating the Main dial one click or swiping jumps forward or back to the first image taken on the next or previous calendar date.

- **Folder.** Rotating the Main dial one click or swiping jumps forward or back to the first image in the next folder available on your memory card (if one exists).

- **Movies.** Rotating the Main dial one click or swiping jumps forward or back, displaying movies you captured only.

- **Stills.** Rotating the Main dial one click or swiping jumps forward or back, displaying still images only.

- **Protected.** Rotating the Main dial jumps between Protected images only. This is a good way to review images you deemed worthy of protection, or which you have marked with the protected attribute for some other reason (say, you wanted to group some favorite shots for review, but not apply a specific star rating).

- **Rating.** Rotating the Main dial one click or swiping jumps forward or back, displaying images by the ratings you've applied (as described earlier). Tap the touch screen or rotate the Main dial to choose the rating parameter. You can choose to jump between images with a particular rating (1 to 5 stars) or all images that have been assigned any of those ratings (choose the large star icon).

- **First Image of Scene.** Jumps to the first shot of a continuous sequence.

Playback Information Display

Options: Enable or Disable 11 informational screens

My recommendation: Screens 1 and 2 only

This is the first entry on the Playback 4 menu. (See Figure 13.13.) When you press the INFO button during playback, the camera cycles among three different screens, shown in Figure 13.14. They include an uncluttered screen with no overlaid information, a basic information screen, and a shooting information screen that provides more complete information, and can include several additional optional panels of data. Use this entry to specify which of the optional screens you want to display using the INFO button.

I opt to display only screens 1 (Basic Information) and 2 (Shooting Information). In that mode, pressing the INFO button cycles among the No Information (just a plain screen with the image), Basic Information, and Shooting Information. *All of the other screens described below are still available.* Just use the directional controls to scroll down to them when the Shooting Information screen is displayed. Activate any of the other screens for INFO button display only if you really need to see it quickly during picture review.

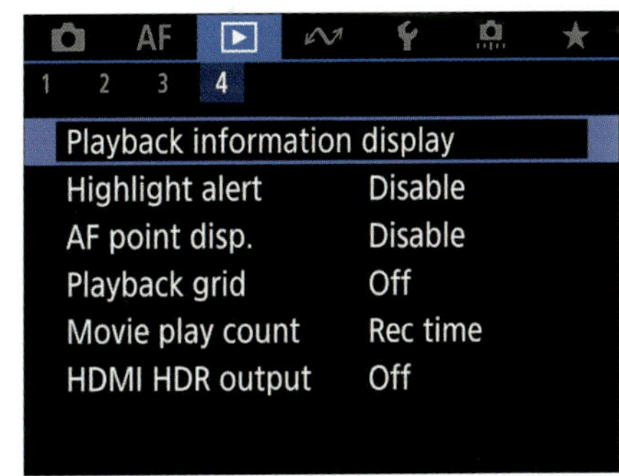

Figure 13.13 The Playback 4 menu.

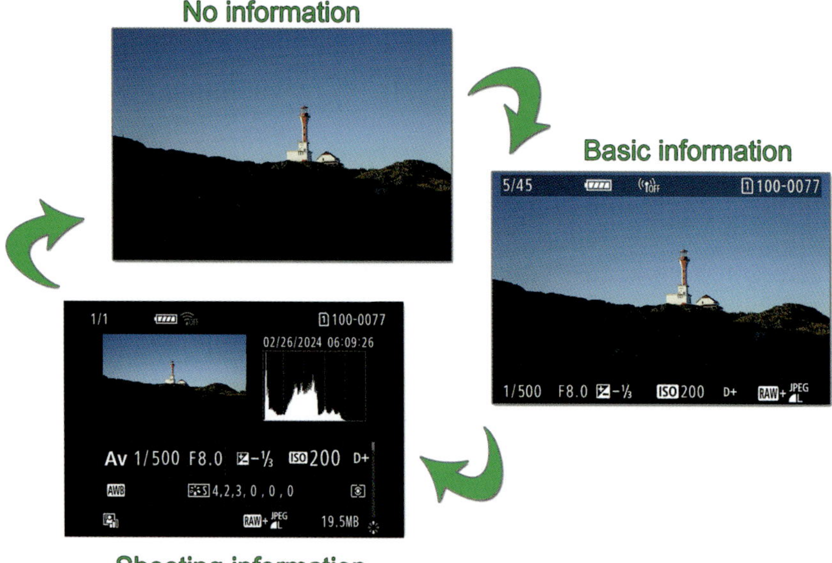

Figure 13.14 Press INFO to cycle among these three screens: No information (upper left); Basic Information (center right); Shooting Information (lower left). You can enable or disable all but the No Information version.

Just follow these steps to include/exclude the available displays:

1. Access with menu entry. A screen similar to the one shown in Figure 13.15 appears. Checkmarks appear next to any of the screen options.

2. Highlight the screens that you want to see using the INFO button, and press Q/SET to add a checkmark. To hide a display, highlight a checkmarked option and press Q/SET to unmark it. **Reminder:** you can still view unchecked screens by scrolling down with the directional controls when viewing the Shooting Information screen.

3. You can mark or unmark any or all. If none are selected, only the No Information screen will be displayed during Playback. (See Figure 13.14, upper left.)

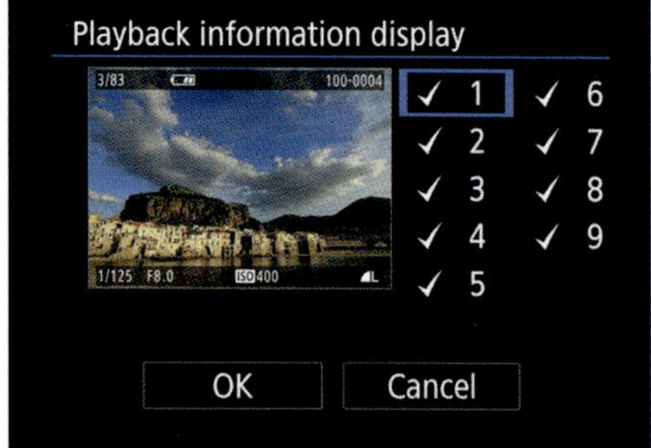

Figure 13.15 Mark any, all, or none of the Playback display options using this screen.

4. The available screens are as follows (numbers correspond to Figure 13.15):

   1. **The Basic Information screen.** (See Figure 13.14, right.) This shows a limited amount of information, such as battery status, picture number, shutter speed, aperture, exposure compensation, ISO setting, highlight-priority, and image quality.

   2. **The Shooting Information screen**, which provides more detailed information like that shown in Figure 13.14, lower left. Note the scroll bar at lower right. Options 2 to 11 in the Playback Information Display represent additional panels, described next. By default, a brightness/luminance histogram is displayed at upper right in the Shooting Information Screen. You can press INFO while activating this entry to substitute an RGB histogram instead. I showed you how to work with histograms in Chapter 4.

3. **Lens information/alternate histogram.** Activating this option and scrolling down from the main Shooting Information screen displays information about the lens used to take the current photo, as well as the *other* histogram display. (If the main screen shows the Brightness histogram, the RGB histogram appears here, and vice versa.) You can press INFO and exchange the order of the two histograms if you wish.

4. **White balance.** Adds WB information to the scrolling screen, including a color bias display.

5. **Picture Control.** Displays current Picture Control settings.

6. **Color Space/Noise Reduction.** Appends these details to the display.

7. **Peripheral Illumination/Distortion Correction.** You can choose which corrections to apply.

8. **Image Sent To.** Lets you know that the image has been transferred to your smart device.

9. **GPS Information.** Appears if the image was taken using a GPS device.

5. When finished adding screen options, highlight OK at the bottom left of the Playback Information Display screen and press Q/SET.

6. During Playback, when the Shooting Information screen is displayed (press INFO to make it appear, if necessary), you can scroll among the activated options using the directional controls.

Highlight Alert

Options: Enable, Disable (default)

My recommendation: Enable

Choose Enable, and overexposed highlight areas will blink on the LCD screen during picture review (these are commonly known as "blinkies"). Set to Disable if you find this alert distracting. Many users access the histogram displays during playback as a more precise indicator of over- (and under-) exposure.

AF Point Disp.

Options: Enable, Disable (default)

My recommendation: N/A

Select Enable, and the exact AF point(s) used to determine focus will be highlighted in red. If automatic AF point selection was used, you may find multiple points highlighted.

Playback Grid

Options: 3 × 3, 6 × 4, 3 × 3+ diagonal lines, Off (default)

My recommendation: N/A

You can superimpose a 3 × 3, 6 × 4, or 3 × 3 plus diagonal lines grid over your image during playback, or disable the grid display entirely. (See Figure 13.16.) The same selection of grids can be displayed as you shoot, using the Shooting 9 menu entry Shooting Information Display, explained in Chapter 11.

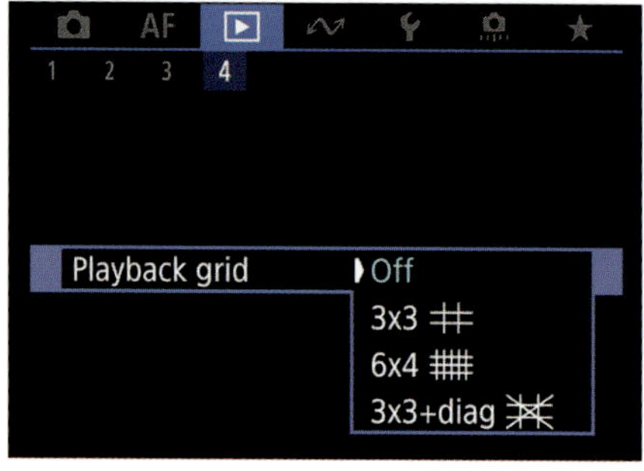

Figure 13.16 Playback grid options.

Movie Play Count

Options: Record Time (default), Time Code

My recommendation: N/A

Determines whether the movie recording and playback time (Rec Time) is shown on the screen, or whether the Time Code (an absolute positional marker/index) is displayed instead. If you change the Movie Play Count setting in the Movie Shooting menus or here, the other will be changed automatically. You'll find additional Time Code options in the Movie Shooting menus, described in Chapter 16.

HDMI HDR Output

Options: Off, On (default)

My recommendation: N/A

This entry allows you to view RAW or HEIF images in high dynamic range mode when the camera is connected to an HDR TV using an HDMI cable. Television innovations come and go, but some are more likely than others to catch on, and Canon is keeping abreast of the curve. Unlike, say, 3D TV (which suffered from a lack of content and consumer desire and had mercifully died by 2018), High Dynamic Range (HDR) TV is here to stay. If your current television doesn't have HDR, it's likely your next one will (along with 4K display). In that case, you'll be able to output your camera's RAW images for display on your nifty new set. They'll look mar-velous (at least, that's what I'm told).

In addition to an HDR-compatible TV, you'll need to remember to set up your television's input to accept HDR images. While viewing HDR output from your camera, some features, such as RAW processing, are not available. The camera will also send JPEG images instead of RAW to your HDR TV when displaying multiple-exposure RAW images and photos shot with the L (ISO 50 equivalent) sensitivity setting.

Communications Functions Menu

Your Canon EOS R8 has some of the most sophisticated communications functions the company has ever offered in a camera, with the capability of connecting to multiple devices over Wi-Fi, Bluetooth, and direct connections. You can operate your camera remotely, transfer images, upload them to the web, direct them to a wireless printer, and integrate the GPS capabilities of external devices with your photos.

Activating and using all these functions involves a robust suite of software utilities, including those built into the camera's Network (Communications Functions) menu, the Canon Camera Connect app installed on your smart device, as well as the EOS Utility and Digital Photo Professional (DPP) that you install on your Windows or Macintosh computer. Detailed step-by-step instructions for using all these functions amount to more than 300 pages, and are beyond the scope of this book, which concentrates on still photography and movie-making rather than information technology. So, I'm not going to go into fine detail on LAN configuration and the techie side of Bluetooth and Wi-Fi connectivity. However, I think you'll find enough information in the following overview sections to get you up and running with the basics.

Your first step is to download the latest software, or make sure the software you already have is up to date, along with accompanying instructions. Visit the Canon website for your country for more information and/or downloadable utilities and manuals:

- **EOS R8 Firmware Update.** You'll want to make sure your camera has the most recent firmware update with the latest fixes and features. I always recommend waiting a few weeks after new firmware becomes available (allowing other users to beta test it for you), as there have been firmware "recalls" in the past. But after that, it's usually best to go ahead and obtain the most recent firmware even if you aren't having any problems. Firmware installation is easy and requires no documentation other than the instructions Canon provides on its web page.

- **EOS R8 Advanced User Guide.** The downloadable PDF version includes a full 108 pages of descriptions and instructions for using all the communications functions of your camera. As I noted earlier, the techie stuff included therein is far beyond the scope of this book. It's important to make sure you have the latest version of this guide as Canon can, and does, update its documentation as new features and options are added to the camera through firmware updates.

- **EOS Utility for Windows and Macintosh.** As I write this, Version 3.16.11 is the latest update. Canon offers a downloadable PDF manual that will help you use its functions. With this utility, you can download and display images, perform remote shooting, and adjust camera controls after you've connected to the camera.

- **Digital Photo Professional (DPP)/Express for Windows and Macintosh.** The application for your Windows or Mac computer, in Version 4.17.20 as I write this, is a powerful RAW processor. Canon provides a manual for it on its website. However, you may not be familiar with DPP Express, a wireless tool for recent iPads that works in conjunction with the Camera Connect app that installs on your smartphone. You can use DPP to view images and adjust settings on your camera, and save files to the cloud, a computer, or your camera.

- **Canon Camera Connect app.** This app is available for both iOS and Android and allows connecting your camera to your smart device. The user interface was changed when the version supporting the R8 was introduced, so if you've worked with it in the past, you may have to adjust to the latest layout. As I write this, the current iOS edition is Version 3.0.11.24 (Build 1341).

Here is a list of the menu entries you can use to connect to a smartphone or tablet, connect your camera to your computer over Wi-Fi or USB cable, print images directly to a PictBridge-compatible printer, or use the Canon image.canon gateway to share your images with colleagues, family, or friends over the Internet once you've registered for a free account. If you have previously used a Canon R-series model, you see that Canon has completely revamped its wireless/networking menu structure. Instead of a single page of options, Canon has elevated many of the sub-entries to the top level, spread over two pages, making them faster to access while exposing just how complex the camera's communications capabilities are. (See Figure 13.17.) At the same time, the company did a favor for more technical types by including the 100-plus pages of instructions for these features in the camera's main PDF guide rather than in a document that had to be located and downloaded separately.

Communication Functions 1

- Connect to Smartphone (Tablet)
- Connect to Wireless Remote
- Connect to EOS Utility
- Upload to image.canon
- Advanced Connection

Communication Functions 2

- Airplane Mode
- Wi-Fi Settings
- Bluetooth Settings
- Camera Name
- GPS Device Settings
- Error Details
- Reset Communications Settings

If you don't want to wade through the thicket of Canon's documentation, I'm going to help you get started with some overview instructions, described by logical function rather than as a listing of each and every menu entry in the order presented on the camera.

Figure 13.17 The two Communications Functions menus.

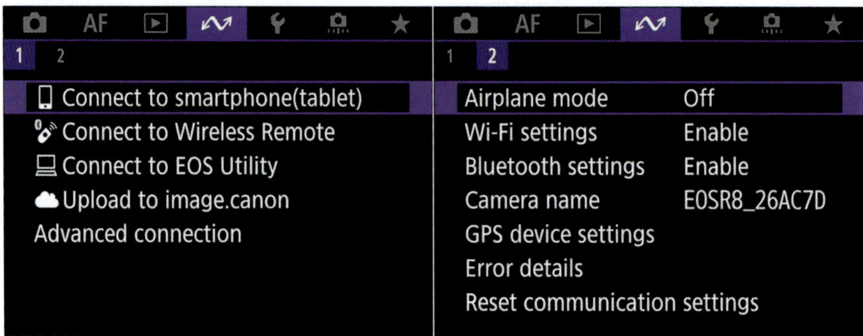

I'll explain all of these in the next sections, but the first step is helping you get connected using the most common methods. You have your choice of linking your camera using Bluetooth, Wi-Fi using the camera's built-in access point ("hot spot"), or your existing home/office network that operates using a router.

Connecting to a Smartphone via Bluetooth

Connecting your smart device to your camera is most easily done using a Bluetooth connection, which is available on virtually all smart devices introduced within the last five years. After making sure Bluetooth is enabled on your smartphone, and you have installed the Camera Connect app, just follow these steps:

1. **Choose to connect.** In the Communication Functions 1 menu, select Connect to Smartphone (Tablet), as seen in Figure 13.18, upper left, and press Q/SET. **Note:** If Wi-Fi has not been enabled on the camera, you'll be prompted to activate it; otherwise, the screen shown in the next step appears.

2. **Add device.** Select Add Device to Connect To and press Q/SET again (see Figure 13.18, upper right). **Note:** If Bluetooth has not been enabled on the camera, you'll be prompted to turn it on; the prompt does not appear if Bluetooth is already active.

3. **Bluetooth notice.** The Bluetooth reminder shown at lower left in Figure 13.18 appears. Press Q/SET to continue.

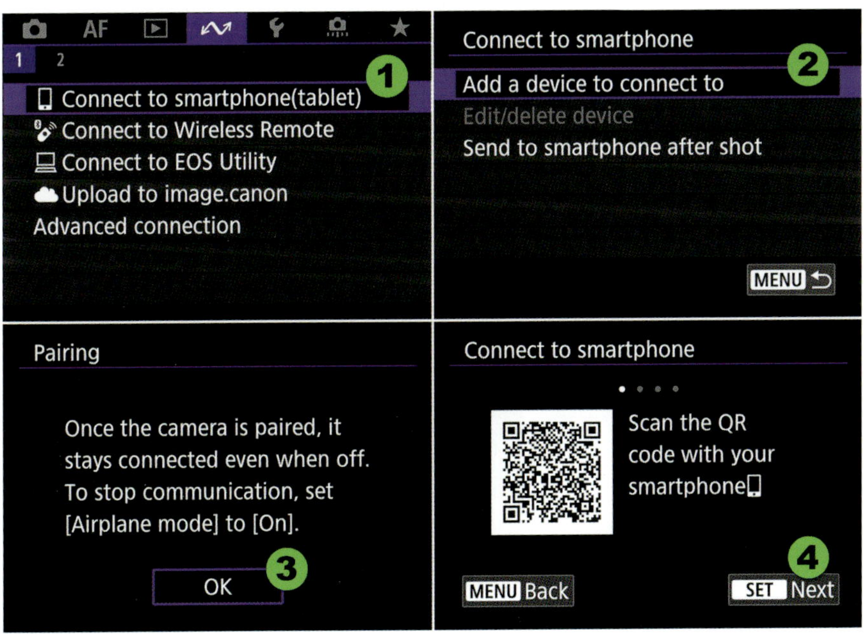

Figure 13.18 Initial Bluetooth connection steps on the camera.

4. **Connect using Camera.** While it is possible to link your camera to your smart device using the Camera Connect app by scanning the QR code that appears on this screen (see Figure 13.18, lower right), I find it's easier to initiate the link from the camera. Ignore the Scan QR prompt and press Q/SET instead to proceed to the next steps.

5. **Open Camera Connect.** Launch Camera Connect on your smart device. It will display a message like the one shown at far upper left in Figure 13.19. Tap the name of your camera as shown.

6. **Pairing begins.** Camera Connect will display the pairing request from the camera (see Figure 13.19, center upper left). Tap Pair to confirm.

7. **Confirm on camera.** Your R8 will display the screen shown in Figure 13.19, upper right. Press Q/SET to confirm and continue.

8. **Pairing completes.** As the camera and smart device link up, you'll see progress screens like the one seen in Figure 13.19, lower left.

9. **Bluetooth connection established.** When pairing is finished, confirmation messages will appear on both the smart device and camera, as seen in Figure 13.19, lower center and right.

10. **If pairing fails.** Pairing may fail if you wait too long between steps or your connection is dropped. If that happens, you can begin again, but you must go to your device's Settings screen and tell it to *Forget any previous connection that might have been partially established.* This is usually the only connection step you'll need to perform outside the Camera Connect and camera menus.

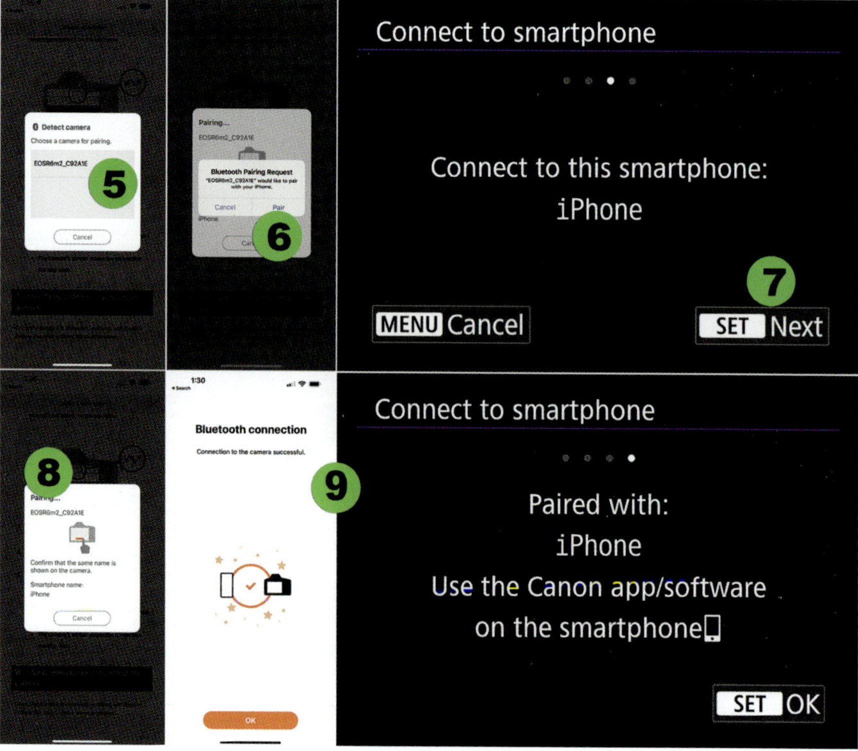

Figure 13.19 Connection steps on the smart device and camera.

Once you've connected using Bluetooth you can easily keep in touch. The camera will remain connected to your device *even if you turn the camera off.* Low-energy Bluetooth requires little power, so you can safely enable the camera and device to remain connected when they are in range of each other. Just launch Camera Connect on your device, select Images on Camera (tap Join if using iOS), and you'll be able to view a list of images on the camera.

You can even command the camera to send each image taken to your smart device automatically, using the Send to Smartphone After Shot option seen previously in Figure 13.18, upper right. You can choose whether to send an Original Size image, or, to save time and bandwidth, to transmit only a Reduced Size version. The figure also shows the Upload to image.canon option, which can be used after you've installed the image.canon app on your device.

Other Connection Options

Although a Bluetooth connection between your smart device and your R8 is easy, versatile, and quick to set up, you can also connect using Wi-Fi and a wired USB connection (which are both faster than Bluetooth for image transfer). If you initiate a connection from Camera Connect, you can choose which type of connection to make, as shown in Figure 13.20. The app and camera will guide you step-by-step through setup.

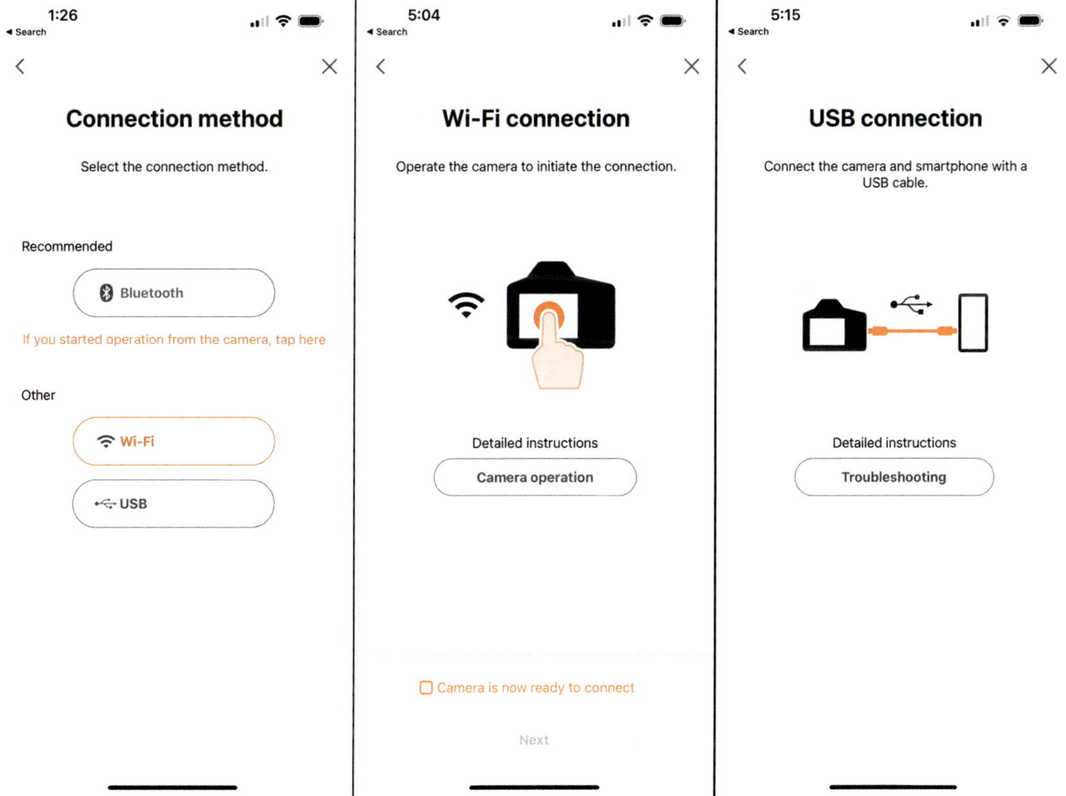

Figure 13.20 The Camera Connect app can guide you through a connection.

Other options include:

- **Bluetooth Remote.** If you're using the optional Wireless Remote Control BR-E1, you can link that to the R8 using the easy pairing procedure in the Connect to Wireless Remote entry of the Communication Functions 1 menu. When you reach the Add a Device to Connect To screen, choose Wireless Remote. When the Pairing screen appears, hold down the W and T buttons on the BR-E1 remote simultaneously for at least three seconds, until a message appears confirming the pairing. Then press Q/SET to exit. Set the camera Drive mode to one of the Remote Self-Timer settings when shooting stills, and set the Remote Control entry in the Shooting menu to Enable when capturing movies.

- **EOS Utility.** With the Connect to EOS Utility entry in the Communication Functions 1 menu, you can set up a Wi-Fi connection from your R8 to a desktop or laptop computer and use the Windows/Mac versions of the EOS utility, or third-party tethering software. Then use the Wi-Fi connection or an interface cable and Direct Transfer to send images from your camera to the computer, including RAW+JPEG/HEIF images. You can also create and register captions. This process is a bit more technical, but can be navigated by those who are comfortable with WPS and/or manually connecting to networks and access points.

- **Upload to image.canon.** Once you have a subscription, this option allows you to upload photos to the image.canon cloud-based service discussed earlier.

- **Transfer to FTP server.** This advanced capability allows using Wi-Fi to connect to an FTP server using basic File Transfer Protocol (FTP), a more secure FTPS link using a root certificate, or through an SSH connection (SFTP). You'll need the relevant address setting, port number, and FTP server's IP address.

- **GPS Device.** If you have the Canon GPS-E2 receiver or a smart device with GPS capabilities you can automatically embed location information in your image files. For most of us, using a phone's GPS feature is usually the easiest and least expensive route to go, and doesn't require mounting an extra gadget on the accessory shoe. When active, an additional screen containing geotagging information (latitude, longitude, elevation, and UTC [Coordinated Universal Time]) will be added to your photos' EXIF data.

Ready to Go

Canon has considerably simplified the interface and operation of the Camera Connect app, making it much easier to access the mind-boggling full range of wireless capabilities your camera offers, especially with a Bluetooth link. If Wi-Fi is needed, the app will guide you through making a connection. Figure 13.21 shows you some of the key screens you'll be using.

- **Main screen.** At upper left in Figure 13.21 is the Home screen, which is your gateway to a variety of features, including importing images and remote shooting, along with editing RAW images with DPP Express, tagging and transferring images with FTP, and cloud-based image.canon features.

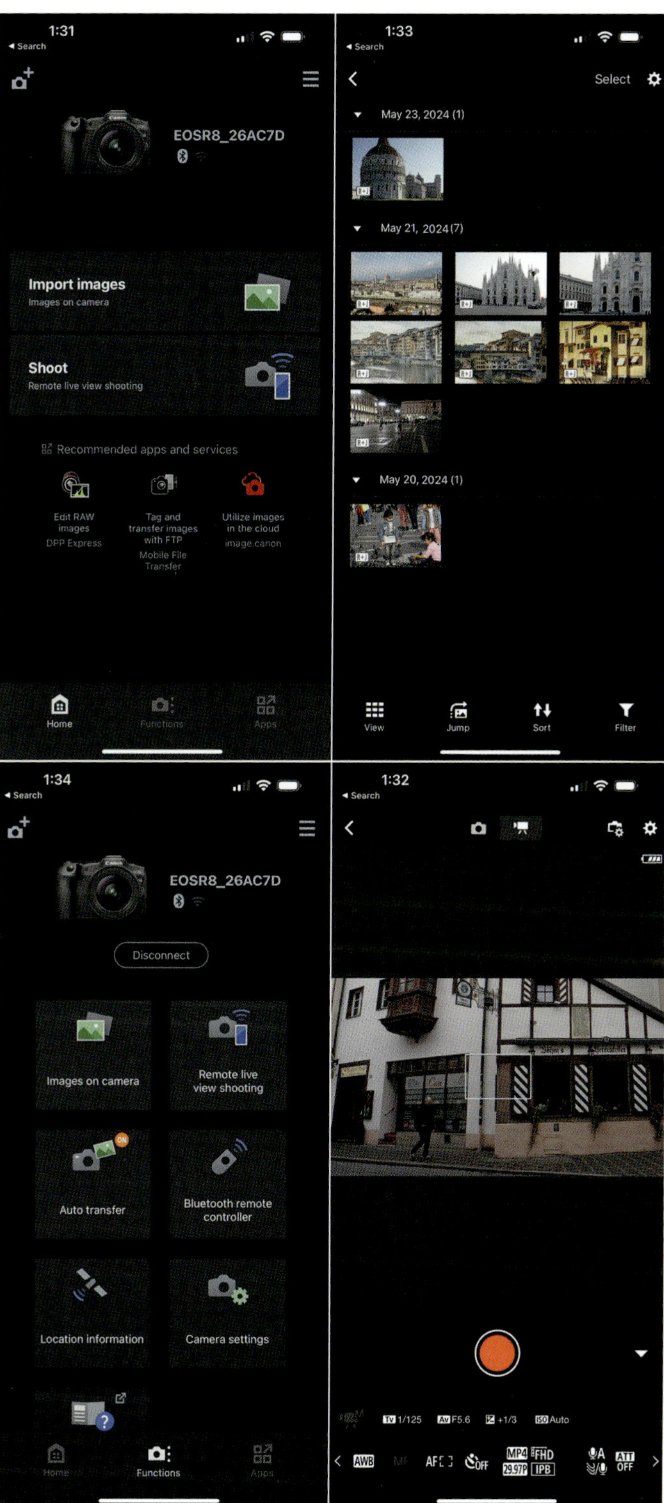

Figure 13.21 Camera Connect main screen (upper left); Importing images (upper right); Accessing functions (lower left); and Remote shooting (lower right).

- **Importing images.** At upper right in Figure 13.21 is the sleek image-transfer screen, which you can use to preview and download images on the camera directly to your smart device. There are viewing and image jumping options, as well as tools to sort and filter images right from your smart device before making the transfer.

  You can view information about an image, apply a star rating, and choose Reduced or Original Size for JPEG/HEIFs as they are transferred, whether to save RAW images as JPEGs, and the quality of saved movies.

- **Functions.** The Functions screen, seen in Figure 13.21, lower left, gives you additional access to Auto Transfer features, GPS location information, options for your Bluetooth remote controller, and ability to make a variety of camera settings. There's also access to the R8's online camera guide if you forget to take this book along with you.

  Auto Transfer is useful for transporting still images from the camera to your device. You have the option of reducing the image size (to save space and speed transfer) and including or deleting location information during transfer. Note that RAW images can be transferred in JPEG format, again because of their size and because most smart devices don't handle RAW files well.

- **Remote shooting.** Remote Live View shooting is probably the second-most popular function of Camera Connect (after image transfer). Separate Still and Movie modes are available. This screen lets you preview the same image your camera's sensor sees, adjust exposure settings and other parameters, and take a picture by tapping the red circle at the bottom. (See Figure 13.21, lower right.)

14

Set-up Menu

In the last three chapters, I introduced you to the layout and general functions of the menu system, with specifics on how to customize your camera with the Shooting, Autofocus, Playback, and Communications Functions (Network) menus. In this chapter, you'll learn how to work with the Set-up menu. If you're jumping directly to this chapter and need some guidance in how to navigate the menu system, review the first few pages of Chapter 11. Otherwise, you're welcome to dive right in.

Set-up Menu Options

There are six amber-/yellow-coded Set-up menu screens where you adjust how your camera *behaves* during your shooting session, as differentiated from the Shooting menu, which adjusts how the pictures are taken. Your choices include:

Set-up 1
- Select Folder
- File Numbering
- Format Card
- Auto Rotate
- Add Movie Rotate Information
- Date/Time/Zone
- Language

Set-up 2
- Video System
- Help Text Size
- Mode Guide
- Feature Guide
- Beep
- Volume
- Headphones

Set-up 3
- Power Saving
- Screen/Viewfinder Display
- Screen Brightness
- Viewfinder Brightness
- Fine-Tune Viewfinder Color Tone
- UI Magnification
- HDMI Resolution

Set-up 4
- Touch Control
- Multi-Function Lock
- Sensor Cleaning
- Choose USB Connection App

Set-up 5
- Reset Camera
- Custom Shooting Mode (C1, C2)
- Battery Information
- Copyright Information
- Manual/Software URL
- Certification Logo Display
- Firmware

Select Folder

Options: Select Folder, Create Folder

My preference: N/A

This is the first entry in the Set-up 1 menu (see Figure 14.1). Choose this menu option to create a folder where the images and video you capture will be stored on your memory card, or to switch between existing folders. By default, folders are given a three-digit number followed by five letters. A folder can contain up to 9999 images. When full, a new folder is created automatically. Folder numbers from 100 to 999 can be created. You can also create folders on a properly formatted memory card within the main DCIM folder. Just follow these steps:

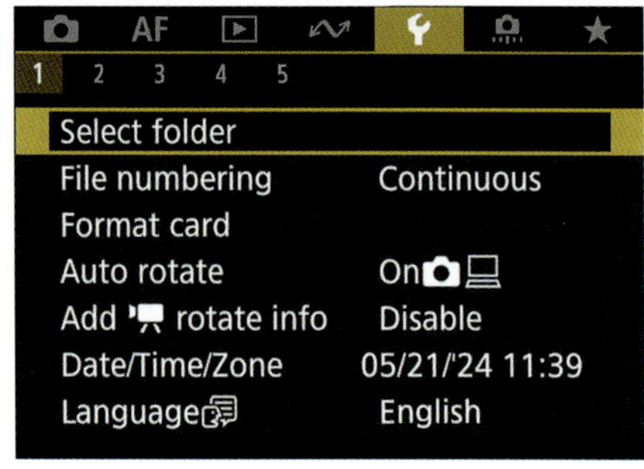

Figure 14.1 The Set-up 1 menu.

1. **Select Folder.** Access the option from the Set-up 1 menu.

2. **View list of available folders.** The Select Folder screen pops up with a list of the available folders on your memory card, with names like 100CANON, 101CANON, etc. (See Figure 14.2, left.)

3. **Choose a different folder.** To store subsequent images in a different existing folder, use the touch screen or directional controls to highlight the label for the folder you want to use. When a folder that already has photos is selected, two thumbnails representing images in that folder are displayed at the right side of the screen, as shown at left in the figure.

4. **Confirm the folder.** Choose Q/SET to confirm your choice of an existing folder.

5. **Create folder.** If you'd rather create a new folder, highlight Create Folder in the Select Folder screen and choose Q/SET. The name of the folder that will be created is displayed, along with a choice of Cancel or OK (creating the folder). Choose Q/SET to confirm your choice.

6. **Exit.** Press MENU to return to the Set-up 1 menu.

Figure 14.2 Choose a folder or create a new one.

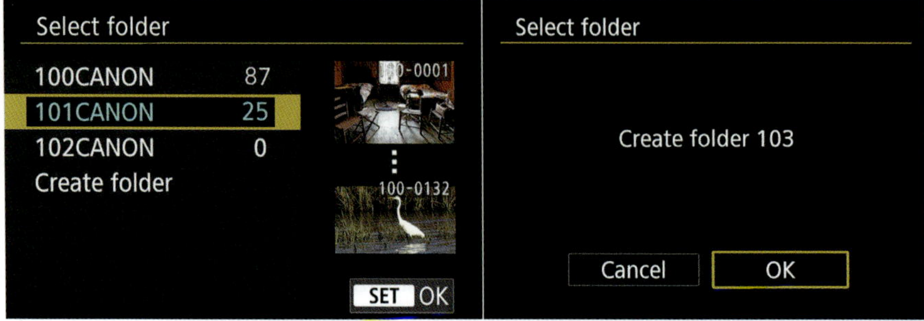

File Numbering

Options: Numbering: Continuous (default), Automatic Reset; Manual Reset

My recommendation: Continuous

A file number will be automatically applied to each picture you take, using consecutive numbering for all your photos over a long period, spanning many different memory cards, starting over from scratch when you insert a new card, or when you manually reset the numbers. Numbers are applied from 0001 to 9999, at which time the camera creates a new folder on the card (100, 101, 102, and so forth), so you can have 0001 to 9999 in folder 100, then numbering will start over in folder 101.

The camera keeps track of the last number used in its internal memory. That can lead to a few quirks you should be aware of. For example, if you insert a memory card that had been used with a different camera, numbering may start with the next number after the highest number used by the previous camera. (I once had a brand-new Canon camera start numbering files in the 8,000 range.) I'll explain how this can happen next.

On the surface, the numbering system seems simple enough: In the menu, you can choose Continuous, Automatic Reset, or Manual Reset. Here is how each works:

- **Continuous.** If you're using a blank/reformatted memory card, the system will apply a number that is one greater than the number stored in the camera's internal memory. If the card is not blank and contains images, then the next number will be one greater than the highest number on the card *or* in internal memory. (In other words, if you want to use continuous file numbering consistently, you must always use a card that is blank or freshly formatted.) Here are some examples:

  - You've taken 4,235 shots with the camera, and you insert a blank/reformatted memory card. The next number assigned will be 4,236, based on the value stored in internal memory.

  - You've taken 4,235 shots with the camera, and you insert a memory card with a picture numbered 2,728. The next picture will be numbered 4,236.

  - You've taken 4,235 shots with the camera, and you insert a memory card with a picture numbered 8,281. The next picture will be numbered 8,282, and that value will be stored in the camera's menu as the "high" shot number (and will be applied when you next insert a blank card).

- **Automatic Reset.** If you're using a blank/reformatted memory card, the next photo taken will be numbered 0001. If you use a card that is not blank, the next number will be one greater than the highest number found on the memory card. Each time you insert a memory card, the next number will either be 0001 or one higher than the highest already on the card. Note that when your Folder number reaches 999 (that's potentially a lot of folders on one card!) and that folder has 9999 images, you will not be able to continue shooting until you replace the card with a different one.

- **Manual Reset.** A new folder is created numbered one higher than the last folder, and restarts the file numbers at 0001. Then, the camera uses the numbering scheme that was previously set, either Continuous or Automatic Reset, each time you subsequently insert a blank or non-blank memory card. When performing a manual reset, you are offered the option to change the folder name used to something other than the default CANON, or whatever five characters you have specified previously.

Format Card

Options: Format Card, Low-Level Format

My recommendation: N/A

Use this item to erase everything on your memory card and set up a fresh file system ready for use. The screen shown in Figure 14.3 pops up when you access this menu entry, displaying the capacity of the card, how much of that space is currently in use, and two choices at the bottom of the screen to Cancel or OK (proceed with the format). Press the Trash button if you'd like to do a low-level format. That's a more basic format that removes all sectors from the card and creates new ones, which can help speed up a card that seems to be slow (because the camera must skip over "bad" sectors left behind from previous uses). An orange bar appears on the screen to show the progress of the for-matting step.

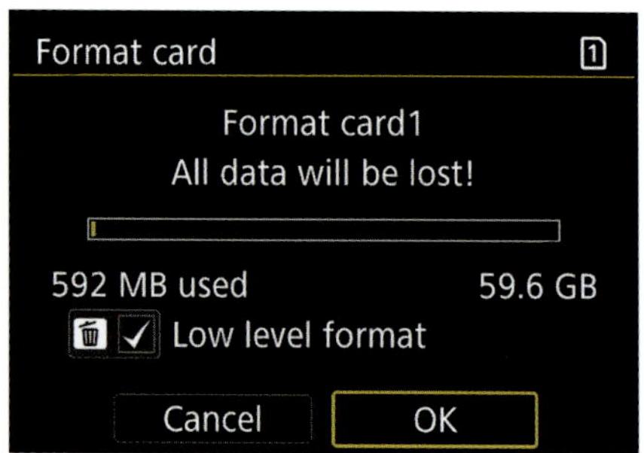
Figure 14.3 Formatting a memory card.

Auto Rotate

Options: On: Camera, Computer (default); On: Computer Only; Off

My recommendation: Camera+Computer

You can turn this feature On or Off. When activated, pictures taken in vertical orientation are rotated on the display screen so you don't have to turn the camera to view them comfortably. However, this orientation also means that the longest dimension of the image is shown using the shortest dimen-sion of the display, so the picture is reduced in size. You have three options. The image can be auto-rotated when viewing in the camera *and* on your computer screen using your image-editing/viewing software (this choice is represented by a pair of camera/computer screen icons). The image can be marked to autorotate *only* when reviewing your image in your image editor or viewing software (just a computer screen icon is used). This option allows you to have rotation applied when using your computer, while retaining the ability to maximize the image on your display in the camera. The third choice is Off. The image will not be rotated when displayed in the camera or with your computer. Note that if you switch Auto Rotate off, any pictures shot while the feature is disabled will not be automatically rotated when you turn Auto Rotate back on; information embedded in the image file when the photo *is taken* is used to determine whether autorotation is applied.

Add Movie Rotate Information

Options: Enable, Disable (default)

My recommendation: Disable if you don't transfer your video to smart devices often

Thanks to smartphones, movies aren't all horizontal anymore. While video has traditionally been shot in landscape orientation, users of smart devices have been happily rotating their phones and tablets to record movies in both horizontal and vertical modes. This setting allows you to automatically add information to your video clips that indicate which side is up, so they can be played back in the same orientation on their devices. This setting does not apply to video played back on the camera or through an external monitor connected via an HDMI cable.

Date/Time/Zone

Options: Date, Time, Zone, Daylight Savings

My recommendation: N/A

Use this option to set the date and time, which will be embedded in the image file along with exposure information and other data. As first outlined in Chapter 1, you can set the date and time by following these steps:

1. Access this menu entry from the Set-up 1 menu.
2. Rotate the QCD to move the highlighting down to the Date/Time entry.
3. Press the Q/SET button in the center of the QCD to access the Date/Time setting screen.
4. Rotate the QCD to select the value you want to change. When the gold box highlights the month, day, year, hour, minute, or second format you want to adjust, press the SET button to activate that value. A pair of up/down pointing triangles appears above the value.
5. Rotate the QCD to adjust the value up or down. Press the Q/SET button to confirm the value you've entered.
6. Repeat steps 4 and 5 for each of the other values you want to change. The date format can be switched from the default mm/dd/yy to yy/mm/dd or dd/mm/yy; you can turn Daylight Savings time on or off, and choose an appropriate time zone.
7. When finished, rotate the QCD to select either OK (if you're satisfied with your changes) or Cancel (if you'd like to return to the Set-up 1 menu without making any changes). Press Q/SET to confirm your choice.
8. When finished setting the date and time, press the MENU button to exit, or just tap the shutter release.

Language

Options: 29 languages

My recommendation: N/A

Choose from 29 languages for menu display, rotating the Quick Control dial or using the directional controls until the language you want to select is highlighted. Press the Q/SET button to activate.

Video System

Options: For NTSC, For PAL

My recommendation: N/A

This is the first entry on the Set-up 2 menu. (See Figure 14.4.)

This setting controls the output through the HDMI cable when you're displaying images on an external monitor. You can select either NTSC, used in the United States, Canada, Mexico, many Central, South American, and Caribbean countries, much of Asia, and other countries or PAL, which is used in the UK, much of Europe, Africa, India, China, and parts of the Middle East.

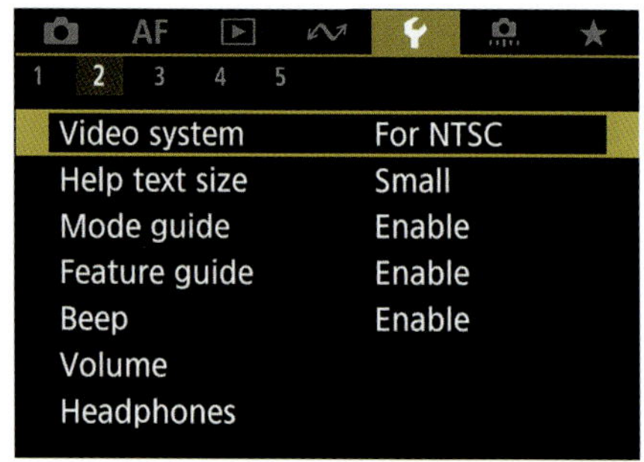

Figure 14.4 The Set-up 2 menu.

VIEWING ON A TELEVISION

Canon makes it quite easy to view your images on a high-definition television (HDTV). Purchase the optional HDMI Cable HTC-100 (or equivalent HDMI Micro C cable) and connect it to the HDMI OUT terminal just below the USB Type-C port on the left side of the camera.

Connect the other end to an HDMI input port on your television or monitor (my 42-inch HDTV has three of them; my 26-inch monitor has just two). Then turn on the camera and press the Playback button. The image will appear on the external TV/HDTV/monitor and will not be displayed on the camera's LCD. Most HDTV systems automatically show your images at the appropriate resolution if you set HDMI Resolution to Auto using the Set-up 4 entry described later in this chapter.

Help Text Size

Options: Small (default), Large

My recommendation: Large

When you first begin using your camera, you may find yourself pressing the INFO button when the INFO Help message is displayed below a menu. Pressing it will pop up a screen with information on how to choose options for that menu item. You won't need this help after you've had your camera for a while, but as long as you avail yourself of this aid, you might as well have it displayed in large, clear text. You can press the up/down directional controls to scroll within the help text display.

Mode Guide

Options: Enable (default), Disable

My preference: Disable

When Mode Guide is enabled, a graphic screen appears each time you rotate the Mode dial to a new setting, providing you with a brief description of what that mode does. It's useful only for the first few weeks you own the camera, at most. After that, you don't need the reminder and can begin working with the new mode immediately. To select options for Scene Intelligent Auto, SCN, or Creative Filter modes when the Mode Guide is disabled, just press the Q/SET button after choosing that Mode dial position to access the Quick Controls screen for that mode.

Feature Guide

Options: Enable (default), Disable
My preference: Disable

When enabled, presents a brief description of the functions of the options in the Quick Control screen. As with the Mode Guide, you won't need it after using your R8 for a few weeks.

Beep

Options: Enable (default), Disable
My preference: Disable

An internal beeper provides a helpful chirp to signify various functions, such as the countdown of your camera's self-timer, when an image is in focus, and during touch operations. You can switch it off entirely if you want to avoid the beep because it's annoying, impolite, or distracting (at a concert or museum), or undesired for any other reason. In the Beep screen, choose Enable to activate, Disable to silence all beeps, as you prefer. Press Q/SET to activate your choice and exit.

Volume

Options: Set Volume for Shutter, Focused Beep, Touch Sounds, Self-timer Volume, and Time Exposure Beeps
My recommendation: N/A

You can choose volume levels from 0 (off) to 8 (loudest) for shutter sounds, the beep emitted when the camera achieves focus, touch control actions, self-timer volume, and the sound used to signal that an exposure is being made when using the Time Exposure function. The default value is 2 for each one, except Touch Sounds, which are set at 0 (off) by default. Highlight the volume item, press SET, and rotate the QCD to make the adjustment. Press Q/SET again to confirm and exit. See Figure 14.5.

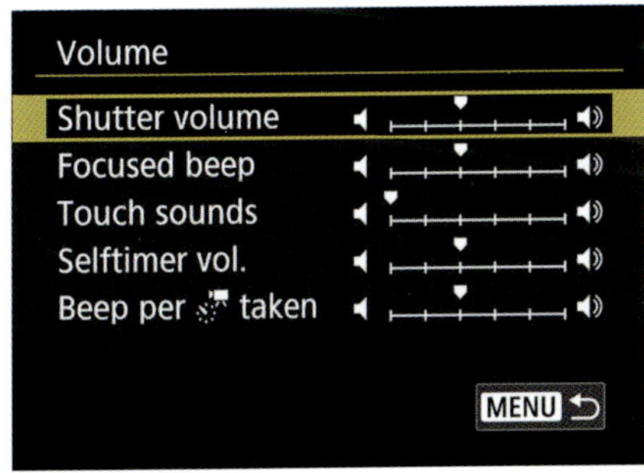

Figure 14.5 Setting volume levels.

Headphones

Options: Volume: 16 levels from 0 to 15 (default is 8); Audio Monitoring: Real-time Audio (without Noise Reduction), Recorded Audio (Noise Reduction applied)

My recommendation: N/A

You can change the volume of audio sent to headphones through the camera's headphone port by rotating the QCD, or using the directional controls. There are 16 levels available from 0 to 15. You'll find headphones particularly useful to check the sound quality being recorded by your camera's built-in microphone or an external mic when Sound Recording is enabled and High Frame Rate is disabled. (Both settings are located in the Movie Shooting 1 menu.)

You have two options for the *source* of the sound directed to the headphones under the Audio Monitoring setting:

- **Real-time Audio (without NR).** With this setting you hear the audio live without any noise reduction signal processing applied. The audio you listen to will be in exact sync with the video you are viewing through the camera as the movie is captured.

- **Recorded Audio (NR applied).** Choose this option, and you'll hear the audio as it will sound when played back, with any noise reduction applied. Being able to monitor the sound you are capturing is an advantage, but be aware that the video you are seeing may be slightly out of sync with the audio, because of the additional time needed for audio processing. However, when you play back the captured video (that is, you are not viewing it live), the video and audio will be in sync.

Power Saving

Options: Screen Dimmer (default: 10 seconds), Screen Off (default: Disable), Auto Power Off (default: 30 seconds), Viewfinder off (default: 1 minute)

My recommendation: Screen Dimmer: Disable; Screen Off: 5 minutes; Auto Power Off: 5 min.; Viewfinder Off: 3 min.

This is the first entry in the Set-up 3 menu (see Figure 14.6). Your mirrorless camera is inherently more power hungry than traditional dSLRs you may have used. The sensor is energized any time you are using the viewfinder or LCD screen (rather than only when capturing a photo), and the EVF and LCD themselves suck up juice. This setting allows you to adjust how long your camera remains active before features are turned off to save power. Intelligent power saving can be crucial with mirrorless cameras.

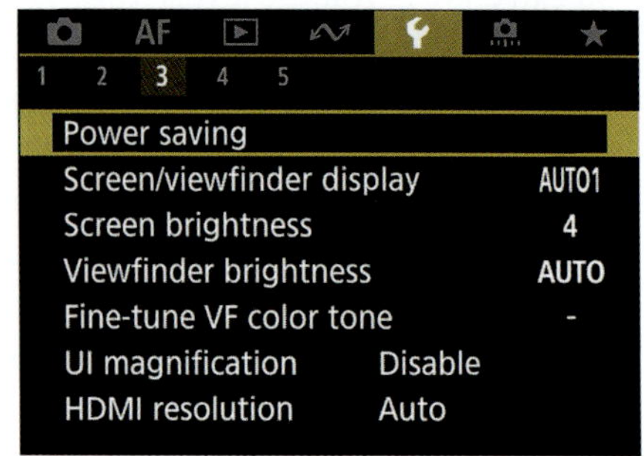

Figure 14.6 The Set-up 3 menu.

You have four choices:

- **Screen Dimmer.** When enabled, the LCD screen darkens drastically if the camera is not used after a delay you specify from 5 to 30 seconds. It can also be disabled completely. To reactivate, tap the shutter release, bring the camera up to your eye, or simply wave your hand in front of the viewfinder's eye sensor to gain yourself another interval of LCD viewing. While this is a thoughtful feature on Canon's part, in practice it can be a major inconvenience, especially if you are using the LCD to compose your image (say, the camera is mounted on a tripod). In such cases, you'd definitely want to make sure the screen dimmer is turned off. Even better, you can turn it off and leave it off for the rest of your life though the simple expedient of buying a reasonable number of batteries. Swapping power cells every few hours is preferable to losing your LCD image at a critical moment. I use this feature only when I am down to my last battery (due to unforeseen circumstances, or, stupidity) and want to squeeze every bit of juice I can out of my remaining LP-E17.

- **Screen Off.** You can specify a delay of 5 seconds to 30 minutes. As long as I have a spare battery or two with me, I'm more comfortable with a longer delay of 5 minutes. That gives me time to stop and think about what I am doing if I am working with menus or reviewing an image on the LCD. In special cases, longer delays are appropriate, say, if you have the camera on a tripod and are monitoring a live scene while waiting for wildlife or another subject to appear before taking a picture.

- **Auto Power Off.** This setting controls the amount of time the camera can remain idle before powering down. You can bring the system back to life by tapping the shutter button. I usually set this option for five minutes, but set a longer delay when shooting sports or taking street photos and I want the camera to be ready for a quick shot.

- **Viewfinder Off.** Power savings from switching off the electronic viewfinder are relatively minimal, which is why your only options are 1 minute, 3 minutes, and Disable. Regardless of the setting, the viewfinder reactivates when you bring the camera up to your eye, so a three-minute delay is reasonable. If you're in sports or photojournalism mode, you might want to disable automatic power down.

Screen/Viewfinder Display

Options: Adjust viewfinder/LCD screen switching

My recommendation: N/A

Canon has managed to fix an annoyance that has vexed many mirrorless camera owners—the tendency of the display to automatically switch from LCD screen to viewfinder at inopportune moments. The eye sensor located under the viewfinder window can activate the viewfinder when your face—or, unfortunately, anything else—approaches the eyepiece. If your camera is mounted on a tripod, just reaching for the MENU button can trigger the switch.

This setting has four useful modes:

- **Auto1.** If the LCD screen is swiveled out from the camera body, always use the LCD, even if something approaches the eye sensor. When the screen is folded back to the normal position, switch to the viewfinder when your eye nears the sensor. Effectively, this disables switching to the EVF *only* when the screen is swiveled out.

- **Auto2.** Use the LCD for display whether the screen is in the normal position or swiveled out, but switch to the viewfinder if your eye or something else approaches the viewfinder/eye sensor. In other words, the display switches regardless of the position of the screen.

- **Viewfinder.** Always use the viewfinder for display.

- **Screen.** Always use the LCD screen for display. If you'd like to toggle between this setting and the last, you can define a button to perform the switch, using the Customize Buttons entry in the Custom Functions 3 menu, described in Chapter 15.

Screen Brightness/Viewfinder Brightness

Options: Adjust brightness of viewfinder and/or LCD screen

My recommendation: N/A

These next two entries function identically, to let you adjust the LCD screen and viewfinder, respectively. In general, you'll find yourself tweaking the LCD screen more frequently, to make it more visible under bright illumination outdoors—or less visible indoors. At concerts, I tend to review my images using the electronic viewfinder; if I want to share images with a companion, I often dial down the brightness of the LCD screen to the minimum to avoid disturbing the other paying customers who might not be as interested in my results.

Use the example image and the gray patches shown (see Figure 14.7) to decide whether the brightness is satisfactory. The thumbnail shows the last image viewed during Playback, so you can actually "calibrate" your display for your current shooting environment. You want to be able to see both the lightest and darkest steps at top and bottom of the gray scale, and not lose any of the steps in the middle. Brighter settings use more battery power, but can allow you to view an image on the LCD outdoors in bright sunlight. When you have the brightness you want, press the Q/SET button to lock it in and return to the menu.

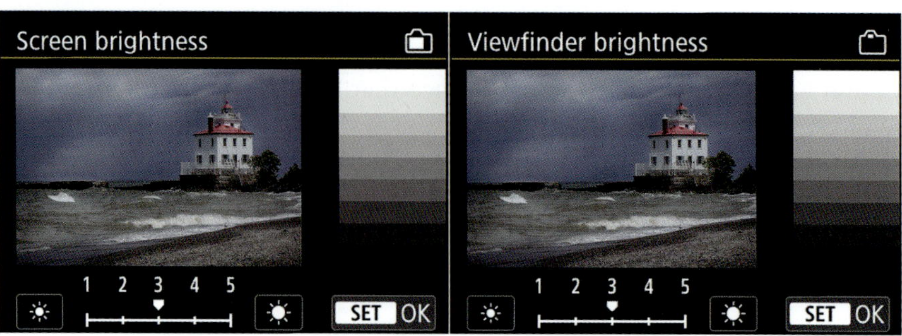

Figure 14.7 Adjust electronic viewfinder and LCD screen brightness for easier viewing under varying ambient lighting conditions.

Fine-Tune Viewfinder Color Tone

Options: Blue/Amber, Green/Magenta adjustments

My recommendation: N/A

If you want to really tweak your viewfinder's color tone, this entry allows you to adjust bias along the blue/amber and green/magenta axes, just as you can do with color balance settings (described in Chapter 11). As you evaluate the playback image through the viewfinder, you can use the directional controls to move the color balance zero point in all four directions. A grayscale is displayed at the bottom of the screen for reference. Press Q/SET to confirm when you're satisfied with the setting.

UI Magnification

Options: Enable, Disable (default)

My recommendation: Disable

If you find you sometimes have trouble viewing menus under less than perfect viewing conditions with the standard user interface (UI), you can double the size of menu screens by enabling this option. Then, just double-tap the LCD screen to increase the size of the display, and double-tap again to return to the normal display. When the user interface is enlarged, other touch screen operations are disabled and you must use the camera controls to make your settings.

HDMI Resolution

Options: Auto (default), 1080p

My recommendation: 1080p if your device accepts it

As I mentioned earlier, you can output to an external monitor or video recorder using a cable that has an HDMI Mini-C connector to fit the camera and a standard HDMI connector on the other end to link to your device. You can set this option to Auto, in which case the camera will attempt to ascertain the correct resolution for the connected device, and then direct its output in that format. There may be some delay while the appropriate resolution is achieved, but if you know your device can accept 1080p video, you can go ahead and select that setting to avoid the time lag.

The only problem with this procedure is that the system has a nasty habit of *not* adjusting to the correct resolution for some devices, complicated by the fact that you cannot then select the right setting yourself. I've encountered several devices, including my BlackMagic Intensity Shuttle capture device, that the camera is unable to recognize automatically, and which require a setting that Canon does not allow you to make manually. I checked with Canon and they offer no solution; there is no way to manually specify a resolution other than 1080p. I ended up using a $20 MavisLink USB-to-HDMI video capture device, and the free OBS Studio software to grab the screens shown in this book.

Touch Control

Options: Standard (default), Sensitive, Disable

My recommendation: Standard

This is the first entry in the Set-up 4 menu. (See Figure 14.8.) Here you can specify how sensitive the touch screen is to your taps and strokes. Note that the screen responds to changes in capacitance (changes in an electrical charge), rather than pressure, so using a stylus or other object instead of a finger isn't advised. Moisture or protective covers for the LCD screen may also interfere with touch operation, although I've had no problems with GGS screens available from Amazon and elsewhere. If you find that your everyday handling frequently triggers unwanted actions, you can disable touch control entirely if you never want to use it. Otherwise, set the amount of sensitivity that works best for digital control, so to speak. While Standard works best for most, those who use touch control frequently may want to try the Sensitive setting. However, at that setting, very rapid, light movements may not register.

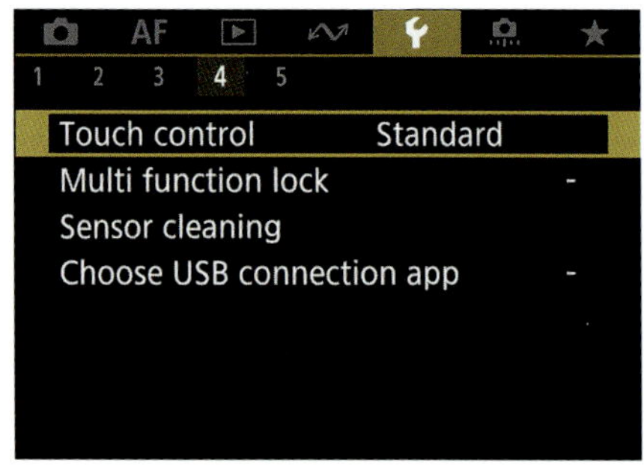

Figure 14.8 The Set-up 4 menu.

Multi-Function Lock

Options: Main dial, Quick Control dial, Touch Control, Control Ring

My recommendation: N/A

Your camera includes a multi-function lock center position of the On/Off switch, used when you want to prevent the use of the Main dial, Quick Control dial, Touch Controls, or control ring from accidentally changing a setting.

You can select any or all four of the controls to lock, while freeing the others (or none) to act normally. I use this sometimes when I am using manual exposure, especially when I'm fumbling around in a darkened environment, and don't want to unintentionally manipulate my settings. The Multi-Function Lock screen has one option for each control; highlight the control and press Q/SET to lock or unlock it. A checkmark appears next to the control's name when it's locked, and an L/Lock indicator appears in your displays. In Scene Intelligent Auto mode, only touch control can be locked. (See Figure 14.9.)

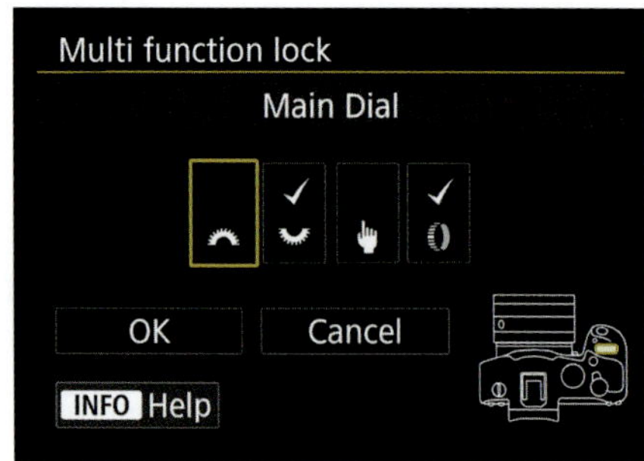

Figure 14.9 Lock any or all of these four: Main dial, Quick Control dial, Touch Control, or control ring.

Sensor Cleaning

Options: Auto Cleaning, Clean Now (default), Clean Manually

My recommendation: N/A

One very useful feature is the automatic sensor cleaning system that reduces or eliminates the need to clean your camera's sensor manually using brushes, swabs, or bulb blowers. Canon has applied anti-static coatings to the sensor and other portions of the camera body interior to counter charge build-ups that attract dust. A separate filter over the sensor vibrates ultrasonically each time the camera is powered off, shaking loose any dust, which is captured by a sticky strip beneath the sensor.

Use this menu entry to enable or disable automatic sensor cleaning on power up (select Auto Cleaning to choose) or to activate automatic cleaning during a shooting session (select Clean Now). You can also choose the Clean Manually option to open the shutter and clean the sensor yourself with a blower, brush, or swab. If the battery level is too low to safely carry out the cleaning operation, the camera will let you know and refuse to proceed.

Choose USB Connection App

Options: Photo Import/Remote Control, Canon App(s) for iPhone

My recommendation: N/A

You'll use this entry to choose how you will transfer images to an Android or iOS smartphone or computer using a compatible USB cable. Choose Photo Import/Remote Control to use computer apps such as EOS Utility, dedicated Android apps available from the Google Play Store, or the Apple iOS version of Photos. Select Canon App(s) for iPhone if you'll be connecting the camera to your iPhone using a USB cable.

Reset Camera

Options: Basic Settings, Other Settings

My recommendation: N/A

This, the first entry in the Set-up 5 menu, includes choices to let you return most settings to their default values. (See Figure 14.10.) You can choose Basic Settings, which restores the default adjustments for camera shooting functions and menu settings. Regardless of how you've set up your camera, it will be adjusted to One-Shot AF mode, Evaluative metering, Single Shot drive mode, JPEG Fine Large image quality, Automatic ISO, sRGB color mode, Automatic White Balance, Auto Lighting Optimizer Off, and Standard Picture Style. Any changes you've made to exposure compensation, flash exposure compensation, and

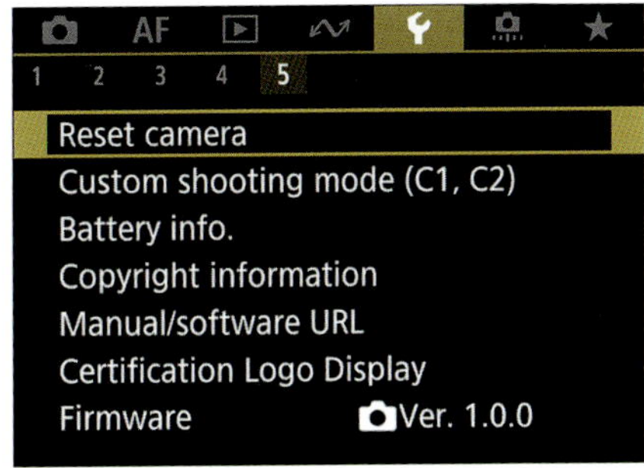

Figure 14.10 The Set-up 5 menu.

white balance will be canceled, and any bracketing for exposure or white balance nullified. Custom white balances and Dust Delete Data will be erased.

The other settings that can be reset here include Root Certificate, Communications Settings, Shooting Information Display, Custom Shooting Modes, Copyright Information, Custom Functions (Customize Buttons and Customize Dials will be retained), Custom Controls (clears Customize Buttons and Customize Dials), and My Menu. You'll also find a Clear Customized Settings in the Custom Functions 3 menu and Clear All Custom Functions in the Custom Functions 5 menu, as explained in Chapter 14.

Custom Shooting Mode (C1, C2)

Options: Register Settings; Clear Settings; Auto Update Settings; Enable, Disable

My recommendation: N/A

Custom Shooting modes are not cancelled by the Reset Camera commands. This entry allows you to register your current camera shooting settings and file them away in the C1 or C2 positions and access them when pressing the MODE button. Doing this overwrites any settings previously stored at that position. You can also clear the settings for any of the three MODE positions individually, returning them to their factory default values.

Register your favorite settings for use in particular situations. I have stored settings for sports, portraits, and landscapes. If you switch to C1 or C2 and forget what settings you've made for that slot, just press the INFO button to view the current settings. Keep in mind that My Menu settings are not stored individually. You can have only one roster of My Menu entries available for all the Mode dial's positions.

This menu choice has only three options: Register Settings (which stores your current settings in your choice of C1 or C2), Clear Settings (which erases the settings in C1 and C2), and Auto Update Settings. When the latter is set to Enable, any changes you make to your settings in C1 and C2 modes will be stored in that memory slot; use Disable to preserve your registered setting as-is, ignoring any changes you made while using that Custom Shooting mode. Note that you must use this menu entry to clear your settings.

To perform these tasks, just follow these steps:

1. **Make your settings.** Set the camera to an exposure mode other than Scene Intelligent Auto.
2. **Access Camera user settings.** Navigate to the Custom shooting mode option in the Set-up 6 menu, and press SET.
3. **Choose function.** Choose Register Settings if you want to store your camera's current settings in C1 or C2; or select Clear Settings if you want to erase the settings stored in either location. Press Q/SET to access the settings screen for your choice.
4. **Store/Clear settings.** The individual screens for storing/clearing are virtually identical. Use the QCD to highlight Custom Shooting Mode: C1 or Custom Shooting Mode: C2 and press Q/SET to store or clear the settings for that position. (You'll be given a choice to proceed or cancel first.)

5. **Auto update.** Keep in mind that if you change a setting while using one of the custom shooting modes and want to retain the new settings, your stored settings can be automatically updated to reflect the modifications. Select Auto Update Set. and choose Enable to activate this option. If you'd rather retain your custom settings until you manually decide to update, select Disable instead.

6. **Exit.** When you confirm, you'll be returned to the Set-up 6 menu. Press the MENU button or tap the shutter release button to exit the menu system entirely.

Battery Information

Options: None
My recommendation: N/A

This is an informational screen only, and shows the remaining capacity and recharging performance of your battery. You can use this as a rough gauge of how much power you have remaining. If you're in the middle of an important shooting session, you might want to switch to a fully charged battery at the 25–33 percent level to avoid interruptions. The recharge performance indicator shows how well your battery pack is accepting and holding a charge. Three green bars mean that the pack's performance is fine; two bars show that recharge performance is degraded a little. A red bar indicates that your pack is on its last legs and should be replaced soon. To lengthen the service time of your batteries, you might want to rotate usage among several different packs, so they all "age" at roughly the same rate.

Copyright Information

Options: Display Copyright Information, Enter Author's Name, Enter Copyright Details, Delete Copyright Information
My recommendation: N/A

Here's where you can give yourself credit for the great photos you're shooting with your camera:

- **Display Copyright Info.** Enable or disable embedding copyright information in your image files. If you're a double-naught secret agent who wants to submit spy photos anonymously, you'll definitely want to disable copyright information.

- **Enter Author's Name.** You can add your own name (up to 63 characters) to each image file.

- **Enter Copyright Details.** You can add more information using an expanded character set. Up to 63 characters can be entered. Note that no copyright symbol is available. While some use a lower-case **c** within parentheses, technically the correct notification would be (Copyright) or (Copr.).

- **Delete Copyright Information.** This removes all the data you've entered and gives you a clean slate, so to speak.

Manual/Software URL

Options: None

My recommendation: N/A

This entry displays a URL you can type in to access manuals and software for your camera, as well as a QR code you can scan with your smart device to whisk you off to the same web page.

Certification Logo Display

Options: None

My recommendation: N/A

This is an information-only screen, which allows Canon to add certification data (similar to what is printed on the bottom panel of the camera) via a firmware upgrade, and without the need to manufacture new stickers for the camera bottom.

Firmware

Options: Update Firmware

My recommendation: N/A

You can see the current firmware release for camera-compatible accessories in the menu listing. If you want to update to a new firmware version, insert a memory card containing the binary file, and press the Q/SET button to begin the process.

The Custom Functions and My Menus

15

Custom Functions let you tailor the behavior of your camera in a variety of different ways, such as the function carried out when the Q/SET button is pressed. If you don't like the default way the camera carries out a particular task, you may be able to do something about it. You can find the Custom Functions in their own menu, color-coded orange-brown, and visible whenever you are using P, Fv, Tv, Av, M, and B exposure modes.

Custom Functions 1

- Exposure Level Increments
- ISO Speed Setting Increments
- Speed From Metering/ISO Auto
- Bracketing Auto Cancel
- Bracketing Sequence
- Number of Bracketed Shots
- Safety Shift

Custom Functions 2

- Same Exposure for New Aperture
- AE Lock Metering Mode After Focus
- Set Shutter Speed Range
- Set Aperture Range

Custom Functions 3

- Dial Direction to Set Tv/Av
- Control Ring Direction to Set Tv/Av
- Switch Dials When Shooting
- Customize Buttons
- Customize Dials
- Clear Customized Settings

Custom Functions 4

- Add Cropping Information
- Audio Compression
- Default Erase Option
- Release Shutter Without Lens
- Retract Lens on Power Off

Custom Functions 5

- Clear All Custom Func. (C.Fn)

Custom Function Settings

I've often suspected that the Custom Function category was invented by Canon in order to keep the Set-up menu from approaching a dozen pages in length. Many of these are "set-up" type adjustments that you specify once and forget about for long periods. Are Touch Control options (Set-up 4) and Customize Buttons (Custom Functions 3) really that much different? Your choices start out with the first of the five C.Fn menu pages, where you can set the increments for exposure and ISO, define bracketing parameters, and change a few other settings. See Figure 15.1.

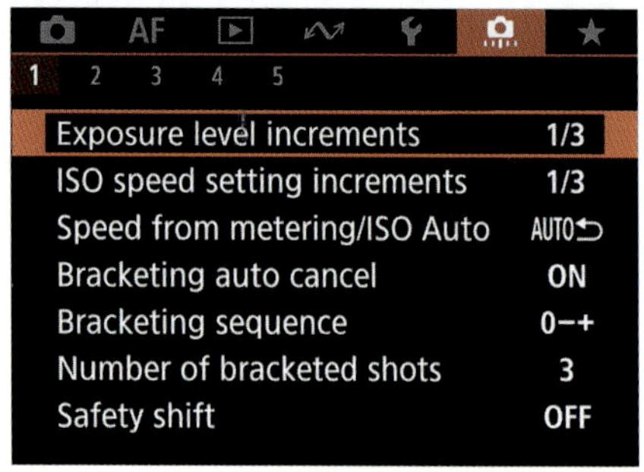

Figure 15.1 The Custom Function 1 menu.

Exposure Level Increments

Options: 1/3 stop (default), 1/2 stop

My preference: 1/3 stop

This setting tells the camera the size of the "jumps" it should use when making exposure adjustments—either one-third or one-half stop. The increment you specify here applies to f/stops, shutter speeds, EV changes, and autoexposure bracketing.

- **1/3 stop.** Choose this setting when you want the finest increments between shutter speeds and/or f/stops. For example, the camera will use shutter speeds such as 1/60th, 1/80th, 1/100th, and 1/125th second, and f/stops such as f/5.6, f/6.3, f/7.1, and f/8, giving you (and the autoexposure system) maximum control.

- **1/2 stop.** Use this setting when you want larger and more noticeable changes between increments. The camera will apply shutter speeds such as 1/60th, 1/125th, 1/200th, and 1/500th second, and f/stops including f/5.6, f/6.7, f/8, f/9.5, and f/11. These coarser adjustments are useful when you want more dramatic changes between different exposures.

ISO Speed Setting Increments

Options: 1/3 stop (default), 1 stop

My preference: 1/3 stop

This setting determines the size of the "jumps" made when adjusting ISO—either one-third or one full stop. At the one-third stop setting, typical ISO values would be 100, 125, 160, 200, and so forth. Switch to the one-stop setting, and ISO values would be 100, 200, 400, 800, and so forth. The larger increment can help you leap from an ISO setting to one that's twice (or half) as sensitive with one click.

Speed From Metering/ISO Auto

Options: Restore Auto after Metering (default), Retain Speed after Metering

My preference: Restore Auto after Metering

ISO Auto has the ability to change your ISO to a different value once it has evaluated your scene and determined an appropriate exposure. This entry determines what happens if ISO Auto changes to a different sensitivity for a particular photo when using P, Tv, Av, M, or Bulb modes.

- **Restore Auto after Metering.** With this setting, after the metering timer expires, the camera returns to the Auto setting.
- **Retain Speed after Metering.** In this case, after the metering timer expires, the new ISO setting is retained. You'd want to use this in situations where you expect to take several more exposures under the same lighting conditions and want them all to be consistent in terms of ISO.

Bracketing Auto Cancel

Options: Enable (default), Disable

My preference: Enable

When Auto Cancel is activated (the default), AEB (Auto Exposure Bracketing) and WB-BKT (White Balance Bracketing) are cancelled when you power down, change lenses, use the flash, or change memory cards; when Auto Cancel is deactivated, bracketing remains in effect until you manually turn it off or use the flash. When Auto Cancel is switched off, the AEB and WB-BKT settings will be kept even when the power switch is turned to the OFF position. The flash still cancels autoexposure bracketing, but your settings are retained.

I prefer the Enable setting, because I generally shoot a series of bracketed exposures and then turn off the camera when I am finished.

Bracketing Sequence

Options: 0–+ (default), –0+, +0–

My preference: –0+

You can define the sequence in which AEB and WB-BKT series are exposed. For exposure bracketing, you can determine whether the order is metered exposure, decreased exposure, increased exposure; decreased exposure, metered exposure, increased exposure; or increased exposure, metered exposure, decreased exposure. Or, with white balance bracketing, if your bias preference is set to Blue/Amber in the WB SHIFT/BKT adjustments in the Shooting 4 menu, the white balance sequence when option 0 is selected will be current WB, more blue, more amber. If your bias preference is set to Magenta/Green, then the sequence for option 0 will be current WB, more magenta, more green. Because I shoot so many HDR images to merge in Photoshop, I prefer the –0+ sequence, which starts with less exposure, metered exposure, and plus exposure, as that is the way I bracketed back in the film days.

Here are your options:

- **0–+.** Exposure sequence is metered exposure, decreased exposure, increased exposure (0,–,+). White balance sequence is current WB, more blue/more magenta (depending on how your bias is set), more amber/more green (ditto).
- **–0+.** The sequence is decreased exposure, metered exposure, increased exposure (–,0,+). White balance sequence is more blue/more magenta, current WB, more amber/more green.
- **+0–.** The sequence is increased exposure, metered exposure, decreased exposure. White balance sequence is more amber/more green, current WB, more blue/more magenta.

Number of Bracketed Shots

Options: 2, 3 (default), 5, 7 shots
My preference: 3

Your choices are 2, 3, 5, or 7 shots in a bracket sequence. I find that with an increment of 2/3 or one full stop, three bracketed exposures are enough that one of them will be close to optimum.

Safety Shift

Options: Disable (default), Shutter Speed/Aperture, ISO Speed
My preference: Disable

Ordinarily, both Aperture-priority and Shutter-priority modes work fine because you'll select an f/stop or shutter speed that allows the camera to produce a correct exposure using the other type of setting (shutter speed for Av; aperture for Tv). However, when lighting conditions change, it may not be possible to select an appropriate setting with the available exposure options, and the camera will be unable to take a picture at all. (**Note:** for this and other similar discussions, Fv mode is considered the same as Av or Tv mode when you select either aperture or shutter speed manually.)

For example, you might be at a concert shooting the performers and, to increase your chances of getting a sharp image, you've selected Tv or Fv mode and a shutter speed of 1/200th second. Under bright lights and with an appropriate ISO setting, the exposure system might select f/5.6, f/4, or even f/2.8. Then, in a dramatic moment, the stage lights are dimmed significantly. An exposure of 1/200th second at f/2 is called for, but your lens has an f/2.8 maximum aperture. If you've used this Custom Function to allow the camera to override your own selection, it will automatically switch to 1/125th second to allow the picture to be taken at f/2.8.

Safety Shift will make similar adjustments if your scene suddenly becomes too bright; although, in practice, you'll find that the override will be needed most often when using Tv mode. It's easier to "run out of" f/stops, which generally range no smaller than f/22 or f/32, than to deplete the available supply of shutter speeds, which can be as brief as 1/8000th second. For example, if you're shooting at ISO 400 in Tv mode at 1/1000th second, an extra-bright beach scene could easily call for an f/stop smaller than f/22, causing overexposure. However, Safety Shift would bump your shutter speed up to 1/2000th second with no problem.

On the other hand, if you were shooting under the same illumination in Av mode with the preferred aperture set to f/16, the camera could use 1/1000th-, 1/2000th-, 1/4000th-, or 1/8000th-second shutter speeds to retain that f/16 aperture under conditions that are 2X, 4X, 8X, or 16X as bright as normal daylight. No Safety Shift would be needed, even if the ISO were (for some unknown reason) set much higher than the ISO 400 used in this example. These are your options:

- **Disable.** Turn off Safety Shift. Your specified shutter speed or f/stop remains locked in, even if conditions are too bright or too dim for an appropriate exposure. Use this option if you'd prefer to have the shot taken at the shutter speed, aperture, or ISO you've selected under all circumstances, even if it means an improperly exposed photo. You might be able to salvage the photo in your image editor.

- **Shutter Speed/Aperture.** Safety Shift is activated for Tv and Av modes. The camera will adjust the preferred shutter speed or f/stop to allow a correct exposure. If you don't mind having your camera countermand your orders, this option can save images that otherwise might be incorrectly exposed. Use when working with a shutter speed or aperture that is *preferable,* but not critical.

- **ISO Speed.** This option operates in Program AE (P) mode as well as Tv and Av modes. Think of it as an "emergency" Auto ISO option. You can manually select your preferred ISO setting, and the camera will generally stick with that, but you can adjust the ISO setting if required to produce an acceptable exposure. If you've selected a minimum and maximum allowable ISO range in the ISO Speed Settings entry of the Shooting 2 menu (as explained in Chapter 11), this setting will honor those limits *unless* your current manually selected ISO is outside those boundaries.

  For example, if you've chosen a minimum and maximum Auto ISO range of ISO 200 to ISO 800, this setting will stay within that range when adjusting ISO (even though you have Auto ISO off), but if your camera is currently manually set to ISO 100 or a value higher than ISO 800, it will go ahead and use the extra values, too.

Same Exposure for New Aperture

Options: Disable (default), ISO Speed, ISO Speed/Shutter Speed, Shutter Speed
My preference: Disable

This entry, the first in the Custom Function 2 menu (see Figure 15.2), works in Manual exposure mode to allow you to keep the same exposure when you switch lenses, attach a teleconverter, or use a zoom lens that doesn't have a constant maximum aperture (say, it varies from f/3.5 at the wide end to f/5.6 at the telephoto setting). In all three cases, the reason the manual exposure you've set changes is because your lens (or lens/converter combination) may have a maximum aperture that is different from that when you made your original setting. For example, if you switch from a lens with an f/2.8 maximum aperture to one that

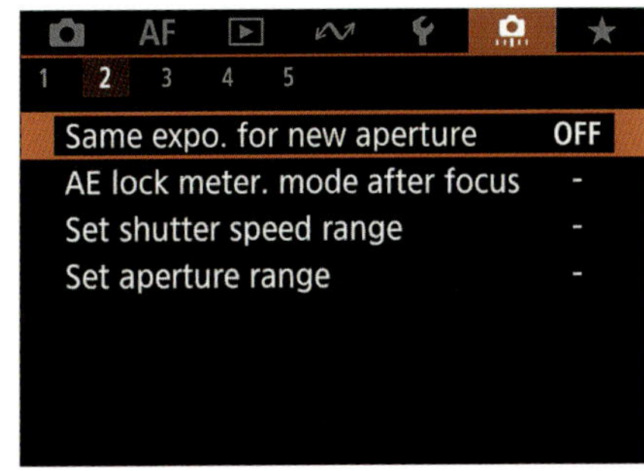

Figure 15.2 The Custom Function 2 menu.

opens no wider than f/4, or use, say, a 1.4X tele extender that changes the effective maximum aperture by one stop, your manually set exposure may be wrong. Similarly, a lens that has a maximum aperture of f/3.5 at its widest setting may have the equivalent of just f/5.6 at its longest telephoto setting. Unless you've set ISO Auto for Manual mode, your exposure can differ from what you intended.

This setting allows you to account for these effects and retain your desired exposure in Manual mode. Note that it does not work with macro lenses that change their effective aperture value as their focus magnification changes. Your choices are as follows:

- **Disable (default).** No automatic compensation is applied. If you switch lenses, use a tele extender, or have a variable aperture lens, you may need to manually adjust your exposure to allow for the "slower" lens speed. This setting displays as OFF in the Custom Function 2 menu.
- **ISO Speed.** Choose this setting, and the camera will set a higher ISO speed to compensate so your exposure remains the same. The ISO sensitivity will be adjusted within the boundaries you've set for the Range for Stills option in the ISO Speed Settings entry of the Shooting 2 menu, as explained in Chapter 11.
- **ISO Speed/Shutter Speed.** In this case, a higher ISO speed will be set first. If the upper boundaries specified in Range for Stills is exceeded, the camera will then change the shutter speed within the range specified for Set Shutter Speed Range on the Custom Functions 2 page (described next).
- **Shutter Speed.** The camera will compensate by using a slower shutter speed to keep the same exposure you set manually. The Set Shutter Speed Range boundaries will be observed, so this setting does not guarantee that your desired exposure will be achieved.

Which should you select? I generally don't use this setting at all, partially because I own very few lenses with variable maximum apertures, and, when I change lenses or add a teleconverter, I am (usually) smart enough to know I need to recalculate my manual exposure. You probably do the same. The most common scenario for needing this feature is when you want to use a lens that does have an aperture that changes when you zoom. It's not only cheap lenses that change their aperture: Canon's two EF 100-400mm zooms have an effective aperture of f/4.5 at 100mm, and f/5.6 at 400mm. There are several good lenses in the 70-300mm range (including one L lens) with f/4-5.6 variable apertures. If you do decide to implement this feature, decide which is most important to you: constant ISO speed or shutter speed. For sports, especially in low-light situations, the ISO Speed/Shutter Speed option is likely to be your best bet.

AE Lock Metering Mode After Focus

Options: Lock: Evaluative (default), Partial, Spot, Center-weighted Average metering (Any or all)
My preference: N/A

If you find yourself frequently using the * button to lock exposure, you may find this entry handy. You can order the camera to automatically lock the exposure as soon as autofocus is achieved in One-Shot AF mode by pressing the shutter release halfway. There is no need to press the * button; simply keep the shutter release depressed halfway until you press it all the way down to take a picture, or release it. Highlight any of the four metering mode options (Evaluative, Partial, Spot, Center-weighted Averaging) and press Q/SET to enable exposure lock for that mode. A checkmark appears above the metering mode, and you can enable any, all, or none of them. (See Figure 15.3.) The exposure lock does not apply to Servo AF mode.

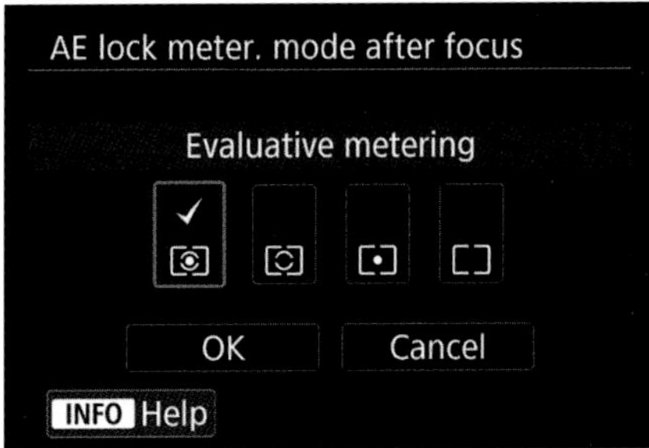

Figure 15.3 Lock exposure after autofocusing for any of the four metering modes.

Set Shutter Speed Range

Options: Highest speed: 1/4000th sec. to 15 sec.; Lowest speed: 30 sec. to 1/4000th sec.
My preference: N/A

There are times when you want to limit shutter speed range when using Tv or M exposure modes, or the value chosen automatically by the camera in P and Av modes. For example, if you're shooting motor sports and want to maintain a bit of blur in the vehicle tires (to avoid that "frozen in time" look), you might want to lock out any shutter speeds higher than 1/500th second. In that case, you might not mind if your aperture changes when the upper limit is reached, or you might let Auto ISO kick in lower sensitivity a notch or two to allow optimum exposure. Going the other way, you might want to avoid shutter speeds lower than, say, 1/60th second because you know that's the slowest speed at which a hand-held image is going to be acceptably sharp. This setting lets you specify a "top" shutter speed from 1/4000th second to 15 seconds, and a "bottom" speed from 30 seconds to 1/2000th second, depending on your creative needs.

Set Aperture Range

Options: Minimum Aperture (smallest lens opening): f/91 to f/1.4; Maximum Aperture (largest lens opening): f/1.0 to f/64

My preference: N/A

This entry allows you to specify an aperture range. When using Av, M, and Bulb exposure modes, you can set the aperture manually within the range you specify here. In P and Tv, the aperture will be set automatically within this range when shooting stills. Minimum apertures (the smallest f/stops) can be specified for f/91 to f/1.4, and a maximum aperture of f/1.0 to f/64. These "limits" all depend on the maximum and minimum apertures of your lenses, of course. Use this entry when you want to limit the available f/stops, say, to preserve selective focus or, going the other direction, to maximize depth-of-field (even if it costs you some sharpness because of diffraction). I explained diffraction in Chapter 11.

Dial Direction to Set Tv/Av

Options: Normal (–+) (default), Reverse direction (+–)

My preference: Normal

This setting, the first in the Custom Function 3 menu (see Figure 15.4), reverses the result when rotating the Quick Control dial and Main dial when using Shutter-priority or Aperture-priority (Tv and Av). That is, rotating the Main dial to the right will decrease the shutter speed rather than increase it; f/stops will become larger rather than smaller. Use this if you find the default rotation scheme in Tv and Av modes are not to your liking. Activating this option also reverses the dial direction in Manual exposure mode. In other shooting modes, only the Main dial's direction will be reversed.

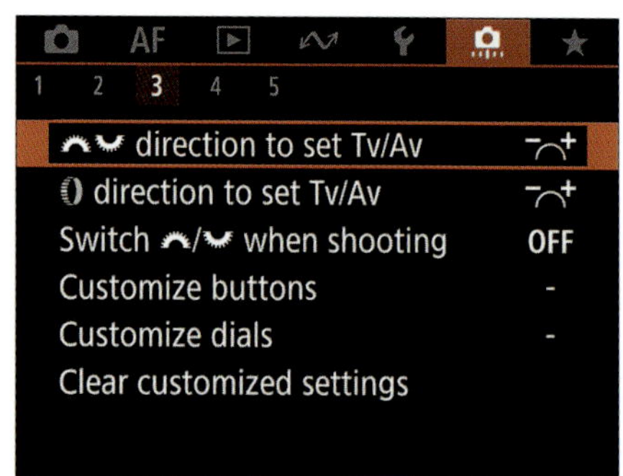

Figure 15.4 The Custom Functions 3 menu.

- **Normal.** The Main dial and Quick Control dial change shutter speed and aperture normally.

- **Reverse direction.** The dials adjust shutter speed and aperture in the reverse direction when rotated.

Control Ring Direction to Set Tv/Av

Options: Normal (–+) (default), Reverse direction(+–)

My preference: Normal

This setting reverses the rotational direction of the control ring on RF-mount lenses and the control ring mount adapter, as well, when using either ring to set shutter speed (Tv mode) or aperture (Av mode).

Switch Dials When Shooting

Options: Disable (default), Enable

My preference: Disable

Swaps the functions of the Main dial and Quick Control dial. This is primarily useful to those coming from other camera platforms that used the front and rear dials differently.

Customize Buttons

Options: Redefine 11 buttons

My preference: N/A

If you're eager to totally confuse any poor soul who is not equipped to deal with a custom-configured camera (or, perhaps, even yourself), Canon allows you to redefine the behavior of no less than 10 different buttons (many of them in different configurations for still and movie modes) in interesting, and potentially hilarious ways. Just highlight any of the options (some are shown in Figure 15.5), press Q/SET to view the functions you can assign, and make your choice. You'll need to scroll down using the directional controls or QCD to view them all.

If you see the INFO icon at bottom left when viewing the available functions, there are even more decisions to make.

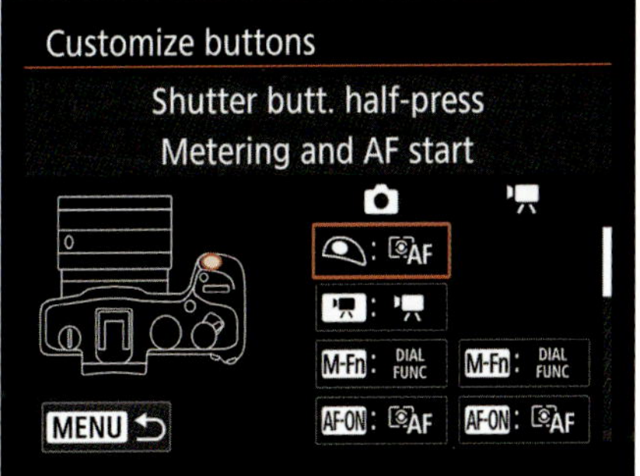

Figure 15.5 Scroll down the list to view all of the assignable buttons.

You can truly manipulate your camera to work in a way that's fastest and most efficient for you. There are dozens of combinations of control possibilities, spelled out in a huge matrix+legend description starting on page 844 of your factory manual. Those huge tables and explanations would take up half this chapter, so I won't duplicate that information here. The default values are shown in Table 15.1.

TABLE 15.1 Default Button Assignments

CONTROL	DEFAULT FUNCTION: STILLS	DEFAULT FUNCTION: MOVIES
Shutter button half-press	Metering and AF Start	None
Movie button	Movie Recording	None
M-Fn button	Dial Functions	Dial Functions
AF-ON button	Metering and AF Start	Metering and AF Start
AE Lock/FE Lock button	AE Lock/FE Lock	AE Lock (Hold)
AF Point button	AF Point Selection	AF Point Selection
Up button	Reset Selected Item in FV mode	Digital Zoom
Left button	Reset Selected Item in FV Mode	None
Right button	Reset Selected Item in FV Mode	None
Down button	Reset Selected Item in FV Mode	Digital Zoom
Q/SET button	Quick Control Screen	Quick Control Screen
Lens AF stop button	AF Stop	AF Stop
Speedlite Menu Direct button	Flash Function Settings	None

Here's how to modify a control to perform another function, using the AE/Lock button as an example:

1. **Select AE Lock button.** In the Customize buttons screen seen at left in Figure 15.6, use the directional controls to highlight AE Lock Button in the left column, which is under the camera icon. Note that you can also select AE Lock Button in the right (movie camera) column to assign a different behavior in Movie mode.

2. **Press SET.** The screen shown in Figure 15.6, center, appears.

3. **Choose function.** Use the directional controls to scroll down to the function you want to add. In this case, I chose Eye Detection, as seen at right in Figure 15.6. There are a total of 65 functions to choose from, plus Off.

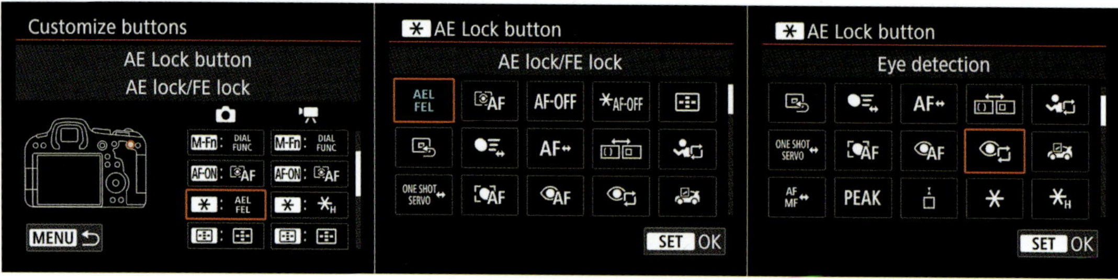

Figure 15.6 Highlight a button (left), access functions (center), and choose new function (right).

4. **Press INFO for options.** Many of the available functions are simply turned on and off. A few have additional parameters, which are indicated by an INFO: Detail Set. option. For example, if you assign Rating to a button, you can specify how stars are assigned when the button is pressed. The One-Touch Image Quality setting can be assigned to switch to the RAW and/or JPEG settings you prefer. Press Q/SET to confirm your options.

5. **Exit.** Press Q/SET to exit to the Customize Buttons screen.

Other buttons are customizable with their own behaviors, and not all are assignable to every control. For example, Shutter button half-press can invoke Metering and AF Start, Metering Start (only), or AE Lock (while button is pressed), and no other functions. The best way to learn what each button can do is to work your way through the Customize Buttons screen.

Customize Dials

Options: Redefine Main dial, QCD, and Control Ring

My preference: N/A

Each of these three can also be redefined with a customized behavior, but, fortunately, the possibilities are more limited. All these are a matter of personal taste, and don't need to be changed to "improve" anything. Your choices are as follows:

- **Redefine Main dial.** By default, the Main dial adjusts the shutter speed in Tv and Manual exposure modes, and in Fv mode if you haven't set the camera to adjust shutter speed automatically. The dial's behavior can be changed *only* for Manual exposure mode. You can set it to adjust shutter speed (the default), aperture, or disable it so that the dial does nothing in Manual exposure mode.

- **Quick Control dial (QCD).** By default, the QCD adjusts the aperture in Av and Manual exposure modes, and in Fv mode if you haven't set the camera to adjust aperture automatically. The dial's behavior can be changed *only* for Manual exposure mode. You can set it to adjust aperture (the default), switch it to change the shutter speed, or disable it so that the dial does nothing in Manual exposure mode.

- **Control ring.** The control ring on the lens or mount adapter has a little more flexibility. By default, you can use it to change the aperture of the lens by rotating it as you hold the shutter release (or other Metering Start button you may have defined). In effect, this gives you an old-school lens aperture adjustment ring, and is very convenient if you want to adjust the f/stop while cradling the lens in your left hand. (That may be more comfortable than using a thumb on the QCD for some users.)

  If you prefer, the control ring can be defined to set aperture, shutter speed, ISO, or exposure compensation when rotated, and you can choose to require holding down the shutter release, or skip so that any of these adjustments can be performed just by spinning the dial, with no need to hold a button down. The no-hold options are faster, but make it easier for you to accidentally adjust a setting when you grip the control ring instead of the focus ring by mistake. Like the other two, the control ring can also be set to Off to disable it.

Clear Customized Settings

Options: Clear Customize Buttons and Customize Dials settings
My preference: N/A

This entry can be used to erase all your customization of controls, should you need to do that. Note that the Clear All Custom Functions entry (the only one in the Custom Function 5 menu) does *not* reset these settings (fortunately); you have to do it here.

Add Cropping Information

Options: Off (default), Aspect ratios: 6:6, 3:4, 4:5, 6:7, 10:12, 5:7
My preference: Varies depending on print size

This is the first setting in the Custom Functions 4 menu. (See Figure 15.7.) If you want to use image crops other than the default 3:2 aspect ratio in live view, but don't want to lock the settings down in stone, this Custom Function may help you. Available only when *not* using one of the camera's built-in crop settings, it allows you to specify one of the optional available crops, such that vertical lines will appear on the live view image to delineate that cropping—but the image you take will be saved in its full-frame form, *without* the actual crop being applied. However, the cropping information *is* embedded in the image file and can be retrieved by compatible software (including Canon's Digital Photo Pro) and used to apply the crop in post-processing.

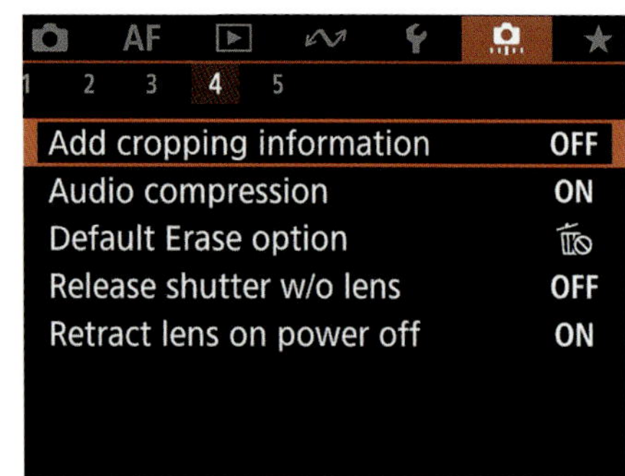

Figure 15.7 The Custom Function 4 menu.

If you're saying, "Wha?" about now, I can clarify. One of the coolest things about a mirrorless camera's live view is that it mimics the ground glass screen of the medium format (say, 120/220 roll film models) or large format (4 × 5, 5 × 7, or larger-sheet film cameras) that many of us grew up with (although our numbers are dwindling rapidly). That is, as with a medium-format or large-format film camera, the actual film/sensor plane image is there for you to view (although, not necessarily reversed left to right or reversed and inverted as in the good old days).

Canon gives you a variety of optional cropping proportions so you can compose and expose your image just as if you were using a camera from those thrilling days of yesteryear—or simply want to use an alternate aspect ratio for creative effect. Your choices include the 6:6 and 6:7 proportions used to create 6cm × 6cm and 6cm × 7cm film images (think Hasselblad or Pentax 67); 4:5 and 5:7 ratios used with 4 × 5-inch, 8 × 10-inch, and 5 × 7-inch sheet film cameras; plus other formats as well. These include 3:4 and 10:12 (the latter perfect for 20 × 24-inch wall prints).

Of course, these days, cameras have enough resolution that you can easily crop the full-frame image to any proportions you like, but many photographers still enjoy composing within a given aspect ratio. This feature can be used only when the Cropping/Aspect Ratio in the Shooting 1 menu is set to Full Frame.

Audio Compression

Options: ON: Enable, OFF: Disable

My preference: OFF: Disable

Specifies the amount of audio compression when recording video. I like to set this option to Disable to achieve higher audio quality, even though the file sizes are somewhat larger. Even if Disable is set, audio is compressed in Scene Intelligent Auto (A+) mode when Movie Recording Quality is set to FHD: 29.97p IPB/25p Low Quality.

Default Erase Option

Options: Cancel Selected (default), Erase Selected/Erase RAW+JPEG Selected, Erase RAW Selected, Erase JPEG Selected

My preference: Erase Selected/Erase RAW+JPEG Selected

Specify what happens during image review and playback when you press the Trash button and the Erase Image screen appears. This entry determines which choice is the default. You'll want to choose the option you use most often, either for convenience or to avoid accidentally erasing an image you mean to keep.

- **Cancel Selected.** Pressing the Q/SET button backs you out of the screen with no harm done. You'd choose this if you find you accidentally press Trash from time to time and want to avoid losing your shot.
- **Erase Selected/Erase RAW+JPEG Selected.** With this option enabled, when you press SET, the current image will be deleted. If you're shooting RAW+JPEG, both versions will be removed. It's your choice, but I prefer speed over caution, so I use this setting most of the time.
- **Erase RAW Selected.** Only the RAW file will be deleted; if you shot both formats, the JPEG file is retained. This choice and the one below provide a safety net.
- **Erase JPEG Selected.** Only the JPEG/HEIF file will be deleted; if you shot both formats, the RAW file is retained. When I am shooting RAW+JPEG or RAW+HEIF but intend to process mostly JPEG or HEIF files (as at an event where I will be selecting large numbers of images and don't plan to do much post-processing), I use this option so I can quickly delete the non-RAW version of the file. Back home, I can delete any RAW file that doesn't have a matching JPEG or HEIF file, but if I've changed my mind, I still have the RAW version as a backup.

Release Shutter without Lens

Options: Enable, Disable (default)

My preference: Enable

Ordinarily, you don't want the camera to be capable of actuating the shutter when no lens is attached. However, if you are using optics that the R8 does not recognize as a lens—such as a microscope, telescope, or a lens mounted on a bellows, you do want to take a photo using your manual exposure controls (ISO, shutter speed, and whatever aperture your device offers).

Retract Lens on Power Off

Options: Enable (default), Disable

My preference: Enable

Some lenses that focus using a gear mechanism (such as the EF40mm f/2.8 STM) can retract when the camera is turned off. The retracted lens is smaller and its reduced surface area is better protected against bumps, so I usually leave this setting enabled.

Clear All Custom Func. (C.Fn)

Options: Clear

My preference: N/A

This is the only entry on the Custom Functions 5 page (not shown in a figure). Select this entry and choose Cancel (if you chicken out) or OK to return all your Custom Functions to their default values. But don't panic—your matrix of customized buttons and dials are retained. You must reset them using their specific entries, described earlier.

My Menu

Options: Add My Menu Tab, Delete All My Menu Tabs, Delete All Items, Menu Display

My preference: N/A

Your camera has a great feature that allows you to define your own menu with multiple tabs, each with just the items listed that you want. Remember that the camera always returns to the last menu and menu entry accessed when you press the MENU button. So, you can set up My Menu to include just the items you want, and jump to those items instantly by pressing the MENU button. Or, you can set your camera so that My Menu appears when the MENU button has been pressed, regardless of what other menu entry you accessed last.

To create your own My Menu, you have to *register* the menu items you want to include. When no items have been registered, the initial My Menu tab looks like the one at left in Figure 15.8. Just follow these steps:

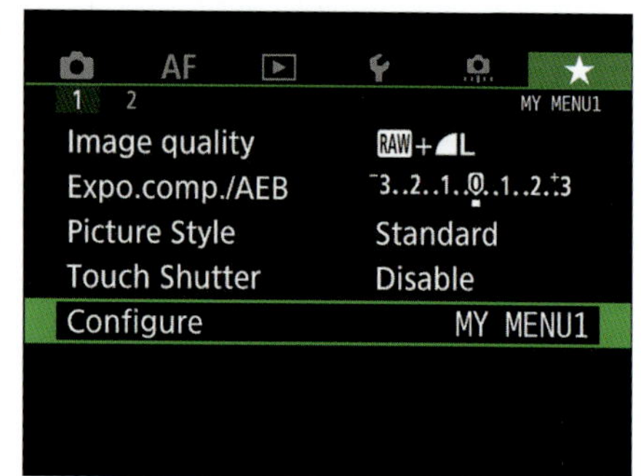

Figure 15.8 Typical user-created My Menu tab.

1. Press the MENU button and use the Main dial or directional controls to select the My Menu tab. When you first begin, the personalized menu will be empty except for the My Menu settings shown in the figure.

2. Rotate the Quick Control dial to select Add My Menu Tab, then press the Q/SET button. Highlight OK in the screen that appears, and press Q/SET once again.

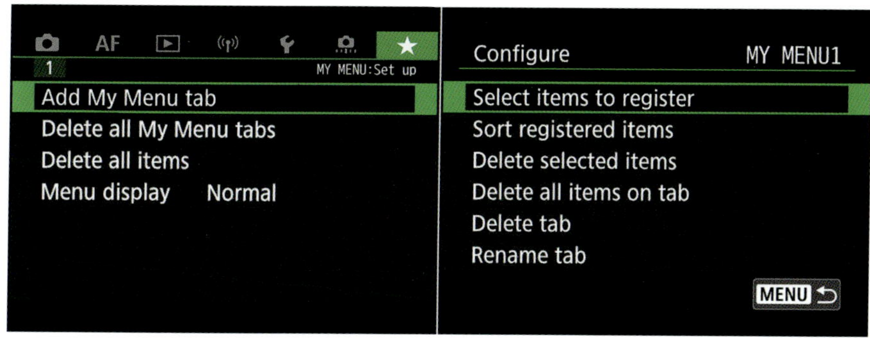

Figure 15.9 Initial My Menu screen (left); Configure tab screen (right).

3. The Configure choice will appear. Press Q/SET to view a list of options. Choose Select Items to Register, located at the top of the options screen. (See Figure 15.9, right.)

4. Use the Quick Control dial to scroll down through the continuous list of menu entries to find one you would like to add. Press Q/SET.

5. Confirm your choice by selecting OK in the next screen and pressing Q/SET again.

6. Continue to select more entries for your My Menu tab. You can add up to six for each tab. If you try to add a seventh, you'll be told that you cannot register more items for the current tab.

7. When you're finished, press the MENU button twice to return to the My Menu screen to see your customized menu.

The Configure choice now appears at the bottom of the My Menu tab you have just created (and will be repeated at the bottom of any additional My Menu tabs you add). If you want to modify this tab (or any tabs created later), just select Configure and use the options that appear in the screen. Those items include:

- **Select items to register.** Use this entry to add additional items to My Menu. As a tab fills up, a new tab will be created, and will be assigned names, like MY MENU1, MY MENU2, etc. The original MY MENU: Set-up tab will move to the farthest position in the tab lineup. You can have a maximum of five new tabs, plus the sixth Set-up tab.

- **Sort registered items.** Choose this entry to reorder the items in each My Menu tab. Select the menu item and press the Q/SET button. Rotate the Quick Control dial to move the item up and down within the menu list. When you've placed it where you'd like it, press the MENU button to lock in your selection and return to the previous screen. When finished, press MENU again to exit.

- **Delete selected items, Delete all items on tab, Delete tab.** Use these to remove an individual menu item or all menu items on a tab, or to delete the entire tab itself.

- **Rename tab.** You're not stuck with the MY MENU1, MY MENU2... monikers. This entry allows you to apply a new name for a tab with up to 16 characters. For example, if you created customized Shooting or Autofocus settings, you could name them My Shooting and My Autofocus, respectively. As with any of the text-entry screens, this is one example of when the touch screen is highly preferable.

The Configure entry operates only on the currently selected tab. However, once you've created your first tab, a new Set-up tab appears automatically. It looks like Figure 15.10, left, and contains the following options:

- **Add My Menu Tab.** Use this to create a new, blank tab, which will be assigned the next available number.
- **Delete All My Menu Tabs.** Removes your existing tabs and all the items in them so you can start fresh.
- **Delete All Items.** This deletes all the registered items on all the tabs you have added. The options in the MY MENU: Set-Up tab remain. When you delete all items, each will still contain a Configure choice, which allows you to register more entries. The tabs themselves are not removed.
- **Menu Display.** This determines which menu screen appears first when the MENU button is pressed (see Figure 15.10, right). You can choose:
  - **Normal display (default).** Shows the *most recently displayed* menu tab from the Shooting, AF, Playback, Set-up, Custom Settings, and My Menu choices. You'd want this if you prefer to jump back to whichever menu you were working with recently.
  - **Display from My Menu tab.** Shows the My Menu tab only. Use this if you want to bypass the conventional menus and make your menu choices only from your custom My Menu tabs. The other menu tabs are still shown and can be selected.
  - **Display only My Menu tab.** Only the My Menu tabs are available. The others are hidden. Use this only if you do not need to use the conventional menus as you work. You can return to this entry and restore Normal display at any time.

The customizing process will be easier if I lead you through a typical session, using the M-Fn button as an example. Its default behavior is Dial Functions: if you press the M-Fn button (without first pressing the AF point button), a scrollable list appears with functions arranged in two rows. The top row includes White Balance, Drive Mode, Flash Exposure Compensation, and Picture Style. The bottom row includes Metering Mode, Focus Operation, ISO Sensitivity, and AF Area mode.

To access any of these controls, press the M-Fn button repeatedly, until the pair you want to use is highlighted: White Balance/Metering Mode, Drive Mode/Focus Operation, Flash Exposure Compensation/ISO Sensitivity, or Picture Style/AF Area mode. You can then rotate the Main dial to make adjustments to the upper control, or the QCD to adjust the lower control.

If you don't use a particular function, say, Picture Control, very often, you can substitute one of the other options.

Figure 15.10 Add or delete tabs (left) and customize My Menu display (right).

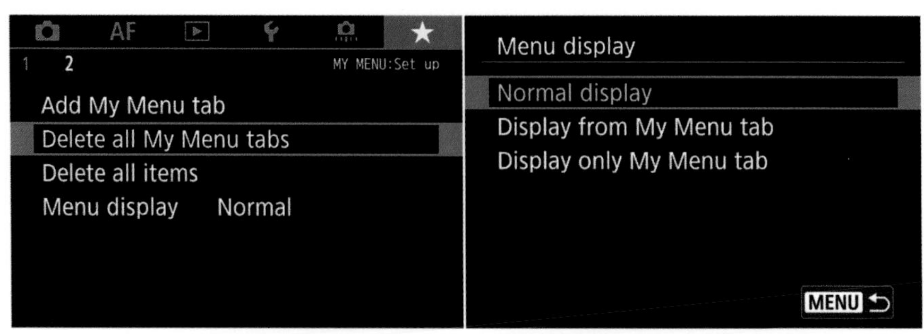

Capturing Video 16

The Canon EOS R8 has some great features that will be especially prized by professional videographers. It has headphone and microphone jacks, focus peaking and zebra exposure indicators, and can capture both Canon Log (C-log) or HDR PQ video with view assist for both (so you can play back high-dynamic range clips on the camera or an HDMI monitor). Although videography merits a book of its own, I hope to provide you with a good introduction to your camera's movie-making prowess in this chapter.

Shooting movies on the spur of the moment is easy, even if you are currently in any still shooting mode. All you need to do is press the Movie button (located on top of the camera to the southwest of the shutter release button and marked with a red dot). Press the INFO button multiple times to change the information overlaid on the screen. (See Figure 16.1.) To stop shooting, press the button again. That's all there is to it.

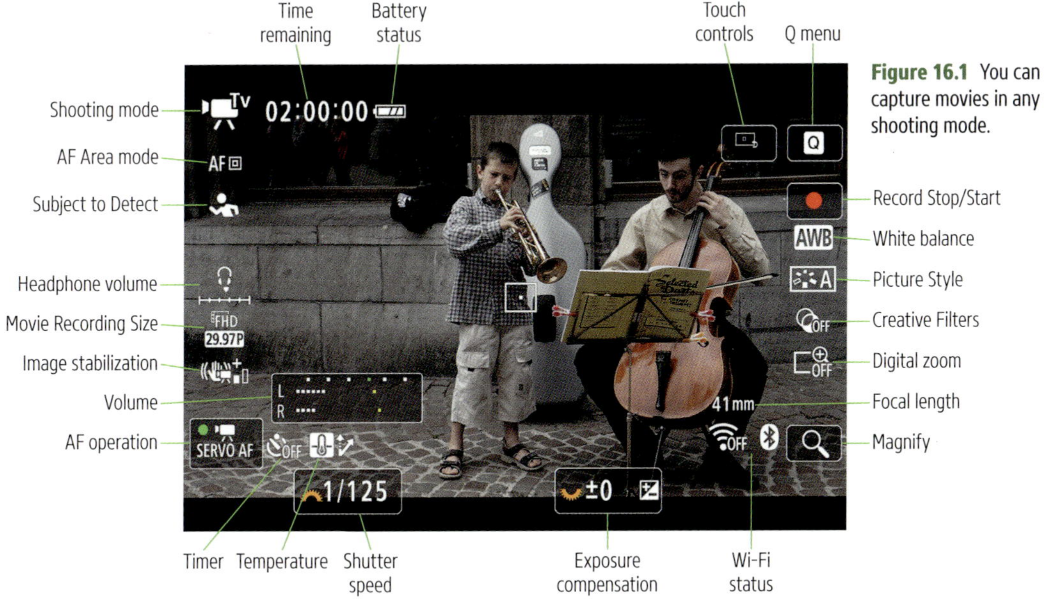

Figure 16.1 You can capture movies in any shooting mode.

If Scene Intelligent Auto is selected as your movie mode, the camera tries to detect what type of scene is being captured and displays an icon representing the selected scene in the upper-left corner of the display. There are many possible icons. Scene selection takes into account background (bright, bright/backlit, blue sky, blue sky/backlit, sunset, spotlight, and dark), as well as subject (people, people in motion, nature/outdoors, in motion, and close-up). The camera can also detect when the camera is mounted on a tripod and activate scene modes with longer shutter speeds to help brighten the background.

While Scene Intelligent Auto is fine for casual use, if you need the most flexibility and full control over your settings, you'll want to switch to the "official" movie mode. Flip the R8's Still/Movie switch located on the left shoulder of the camera to movie mode and you'll have access to a fully featured set of movie-oriented menus. I'll discuss each of the options available to you in the sections that follow.

Using the Movie Shooting Menus

In Chapter 11, I mentioned that in Still photography mode, the R8 has a tenth Photo Shooting menu, dedicated to movie-shooting functions. I did not describe that menu page there, because its settings are more readily available in the full Movie Shooting menus that appear when your camera is switched to Movie mode. In that mode, a revised set of eight Movie Shooting menus are available. (In Scene Intelligent Auto and other Basic Zone modes, there are only four, with a subset of the features I'll describe next.)

Some of the entries in the Movie Shooting menus have exact counterparts for those available for still shooting. As they were explained in detail in Chapter 11, I won't repeat that information here. Those duplicate entries that I don't address in this chapter are marked with an asterisk in the list below. The remaining entries are new or different, and I'll explain them in more detail later in this chapter. Here are the options found in the Movie Shooting menus:

Movie Shooting 1

- Movie Recording Size
- High Frame Rate
- Movie Cropping
- Digital Zoom
- Sound Recording

Movie Shooting 2

- Exposure Compensation *
- Movie ISO Speed Settings
- HDR Shooting [HDR PQ] *
- HDR Movie Recording
- Auto Lighting Optimizer *
- Highlight Tone Priority *
- High Frequency Anti-Flicker Shooting *

Movie Shooting 3

- Av 1/8-stop Increments
- Movie Auto Slow Shutter

Movie Shooting 4

- White Balance *
- Custom White Balance *
- WB Correction *
- Picture Style *
- Canon Log Settings
- Clarity *
- Shooting Creative Filters *

Movie Shooting 5

- Lens Aberration Correction *
- High ISO Speed Noise Reduction *

Movie Shooting 6

- Pre-recording Settings
- Time-lapse Movie
- Movie Self-timer

Movie Shooting 7

- IS (Image Stabilizer Mode)
- Customize Quick Controls *
- Shutter Button Function for Movies
- Metering Timer *
- False Color Settings
- Zebra Settings
- Shooting Information Display

Movie Shooting 8

- VF Display Format*
- Standby: Low Resolution
- HDMI Display
- Time Code

Movie Recording Size

Options: Image Size, Frame Rate, Compression Method

This is the first entry in the Movie Shooting 1 menu (see Figure 16.2). Your camera has a large number of video recording quality settings, including ultra-high-resolution 4K video. (See Figure 16.3.) I'll explain the use of these settings in more detail later in this chapter, but, in brief, your choices include the following:

- **Image size.** This is the resolution of the movie: 4K and Full HD. The actual resolution and movie area varies, depending on recording quality, movie crop settings, and lens used.

- **Frame Rate.** The number of individual frames or fields captured per second. These are commonly expressed as 180 fps, 120 fps, 60 fps, 30 fps, and 24 fps (in NTSC mode, used in North America, Japan, and other countries); frame rates (150 fps, 100 fps, 50 fps, and 25 fps) are different in Europe and other areas using the PAL specification. Note that the actual frames-per-second is a fraction less than the nominal value, as I'll explain below.

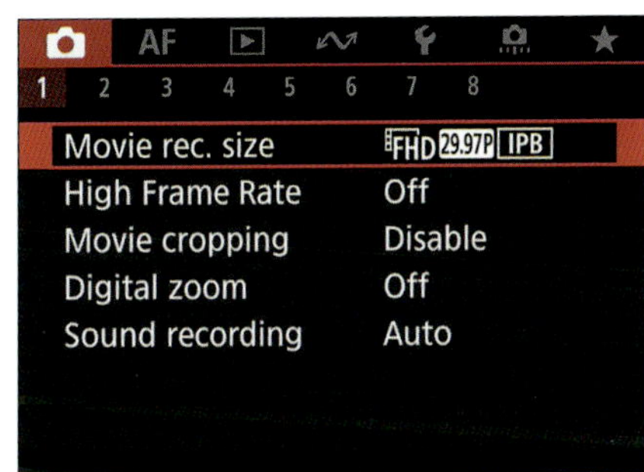

Figure 16.2 Movie Shooting 1 menu.

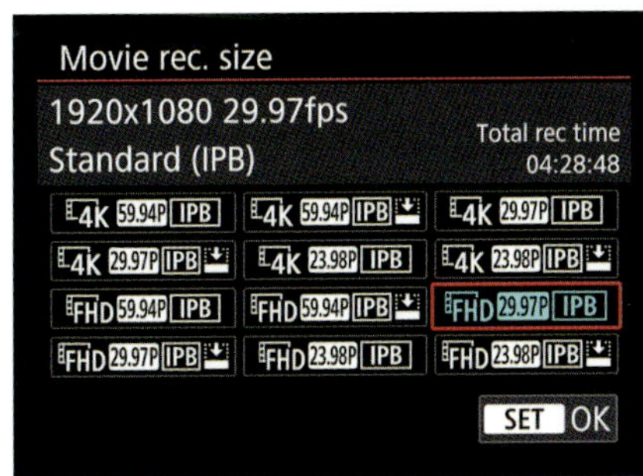

Figure 16.3 Movie Recording Quality settings.

- **Compression Method.** To save space and reduce demands on the transmission rates of the captured frames to your storage device, each frame is compressed, using either ALL-I (for time-lapse movies) or IPB formats. "IPB Lite" versions using lower bit-rate capture are represented by an icon with a downward-pointing arrow like the one shown at far right in the bottom row of Figure 16.3. I'll explain these in more detail later.

All movies are stored using the MP4 format as the "container" for your video files, with the MPEG4 AVC/H.264 codec (coder/decoder). MP4 is an international standard and widely supported/used and recorded using progressive scan, described shortly. MP4 files receive the .MP4 extension.

High Frame Rate

Options: Disable (default), Enable

When you enable High Frame Rate movies, your video is captured at 179.8 and 119.9 (NTSC) or 150.0 and 100.0 (PAL), but is played back at 29.97/25.00 fps speeds, resulting in 6X and 4X slow motion (one second of action takes six or four seconds to play back). However, if you output your video from the camera through the HDMI port, it will be displayed in 2X slow-motion format, instead.

Sound is not recorded, and clips are limited to 1 hour, 30 minutes. Flickering may be noticeable under fluorescent or LED light sources, and ISO speeds are limited to ISO 100 to 12,800 (or ISO 25,600 if extended settings are enabled in the Shooting menu). You'll find High Frame Rate video useful for slow-motion action sequences in your movies, or for analyzing movement.

The High Frame Rate slow-motion video option allows you to capture movies that play back at 1/4 or 1.6 speed—not slow enough to highlight the flaws in your golf swing, but enough of a special effect to allow you to add *Baywatch*-style running sequences to your next Dwayne Johnson (or David Hasselhoff) parody.

The cool feature comes at a cost. Your high-definition video is Standard HD (1280 × 720) resolution and is silent. The maximum recording time is 7 minutes, 29 seconds, which should be sufficient for most purposes; a longer slo-mo clip would be excruciating to watch. Autofocus is disabled, so Movie Servo AF is out of the picture, and the high frame rate renders digital IS non-functional as well. High Frame Rate movies cannot be recorded with RF-S or EF-S lenses, which already produce a cropped image area.

The slow-motion secret, of course, is that the video is recorded at nominally 180p/120p for NTSC and 150p/100p (PAL), and then *played back* as if it were captured at 30/25 fps. So, each frame is displayed for 6X or 4X longer than the time at which it was actually captured. The resulting sequences are pretty good, although you can expect some flickering when shooting under fluorescent or LED lighting, and other weirdness when outputting to HDMI. Time codes are not recorded when Count Up is set to Free Run. Canon cautions you to check your Movie Recording Size setting once you've disabled High Frame Rate video.

Movie Cropping

Options: Disable (default), Enable

The actual area of the sensor's full image size that is captured is always cropped to a certain extent when shooting movies. Because the FHD and 4K aspect ratios are 16:9 rather than the 3:2 ratio used for still photography, a certain amount is cropped off the top and bottom of your frame. The remaining area may be further cropped depending on your movie mode and the lenses you are using. This setting gives you some control over the image crop used.

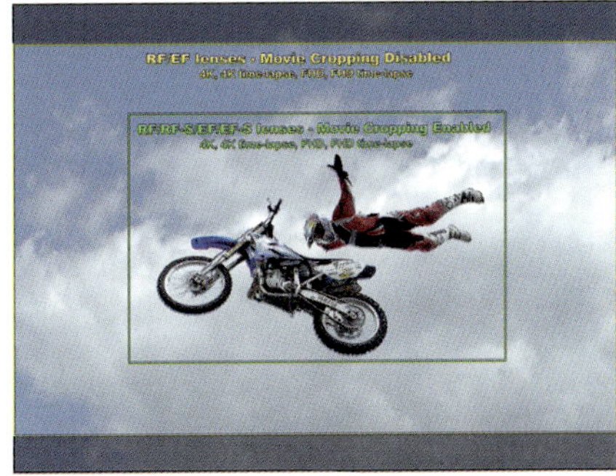

Figure 16.4 Video image areas for the R8 with Movie Cropping disabled (yellow box) and enabled (green box).

- **Movie Cropping: Disable.** This mode is suitable for use with RF-mount and EF-mount lenses attached using an adapter (typical full-frame lenses). The image area for the R8 with Movie Cropping disabled is shown in Figure 16.4, represented by the yellow box.

- **Movie Cropping: Enable.** With this setting, your video is *always* cropped, and the resulting image area corresponds to that of Canon APS-C lenses with the RF-S or EF-S designation. The image area for the R8 with Movie Cropping enabled is shown in Figure 16.4, represented by the green box.

Note: As I noted earlier, High Frame Rate movies cannot be captured with the R8 when using RF-S or EF-S lenses or when Movie Cropping is set to Enable. An additional slight crop is applied when using Movie Digital IS.

Digital Zoom

Options: Disable (default), Enable

When Movie Size is set to FHD 29.97, 23.98 (NTSC), or FHD 25 (PAL), you can activate a digital zoom feature with up to 10X magnification. When enabled, it takes pixels from the center of the sensor and enlarges them to fill the movie frame. Because it functions by cropping the image, you can expect to see increased noise and decreased image quality, and the live view while shooting may become grainy. This feature adds zooming capability to any lens, including fixed focal length prime lenses.

When enabled, you can tap the W/T icon in the lower-right corner of the LCD screen to activate the zoom. (See Figure 16.5, left.) It's a good idea to assign a button to activate zoom, using the Customize Buttons entry of the Custom Functions 3 menu, as described in Chapter 15. That will allow you to zoom while composing your image with the viewfinder, without the need to look at the LCD screen. Once the zoom is active, you can zoom in and out using the directional controls. (See Figure 16.5, right.)

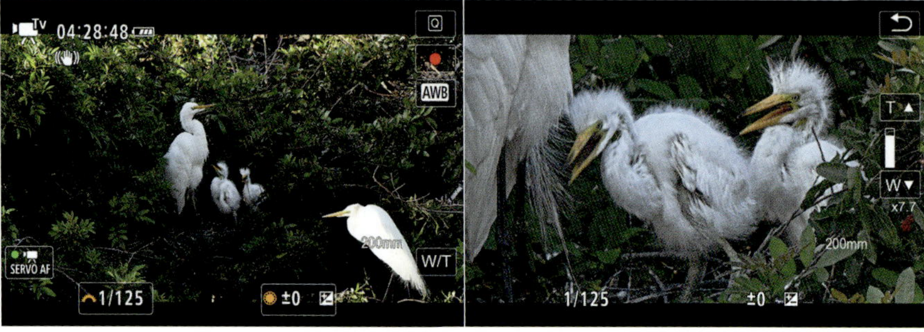

Figure 16.5 Tap the W/T icon or press a defined Zoom button to activate the digital zoom (left), then use the directional controls to zoom in or out (right).

You may want to use a tripod to reduce camera shake beyond what the R8's image stabilization features provide, particularly if you are adding digital zoom to a long focal length, say, 200mm or more. When digital zoom is active, the maximum ISO speed available is ISO 25,600, and time-lapse movies, Creative Filters, and magnified view are not available. Digital zoom can cause the sensor to heat up more rapidly, which can reduce the available recording time.

Sound Recording

Options: Sound Recording: Auto (default), Manual, Disable; Recording Level; Wind Filter: Auto (default), Disable; Audio Noise Reduction: Disable (default), Enable, High

This setting lets you choose Auto, Manual, or Disable sound recording levels; plus, Enable or Disable the wind filter, and set audio noise reduction to Disable, Enable, or High. (See Figure 16.6, left.) In Movie Scene Intelligent Auto (A+) mode, only On (Auto level) or Off are available. Left/right balance cannot be adjusted.

- **Auto.** Audio level is set for you.
- **Manual.** Choose from 64 different sound levels. Select Rec Level and rotate the QCD while viewing the decibel meter at the bottom of the screen to choose a level that averages –12 dB for the loudest sounds. (See Figure 16.6, right.) If the recording level reaches the 0 point at the far right of the scale, your sound will be quite distorted.

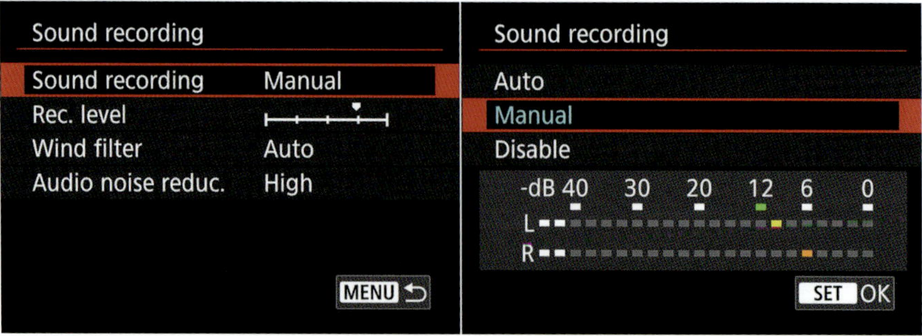

Figure 16.6 Sound recording options.

- **Disable.** Shoot silently, and add voice over, narration, music, or other sound later in your movie-editing software. Note that if you are connected to an external device, including recorders using HDMI, sound is not output when sound recording is disabled in the camera.

- **Wind Filter.** Enable to reduce the effects of wind noise on the built-in microphone. This also reduces low tones in the sound recording. If wind is not a problem, you'll get better-quality audio with this option disabled. Even better is to use an external microphone with a wind shield.

- **Audio Noise Reduction.** This option suppresses noise caused by the motors built into your lenses and white noise, which tends to mask the actual audio you want to capture. But keep in mind that this reduction can sometimes make background sounds more obtrusive, because they are no longer hidden by the white noise.

You can use the built-in stereo microphone or plug in a stereo microphone into the 3.5mm jack on the left side of the camera. An external microphone is a good idea because the built-in microphone can easily pick up camera operation, such as the autofocus motor in a lens. Headphones are useful for monitoring sound. Press the Q button, select Headphone, and rotate the Main dial to adjust headphone volume.

Movie ISO Speed Settings

Options: ISO Speed, ISO Speed Range, Max for Auto, Time-lapse Max for Auto

This is the first of only two movie-specific entries in the Movie Shooting 2 menu. (See Figure 16.7.) (The first entry, Exposure Compensation, as well as several others in this menu, function the same as in Still photo mode and are not covered in this chapter.) You can separately specify ISO parameters for movie shooting using this entry. Select a specific ISO speed or specify limits on the range of ISO settings that the camera selects for you in Auto ISO mode.

Although the Movie ISO Speed Settings resemble its Still photography counterpart, there are several differences:

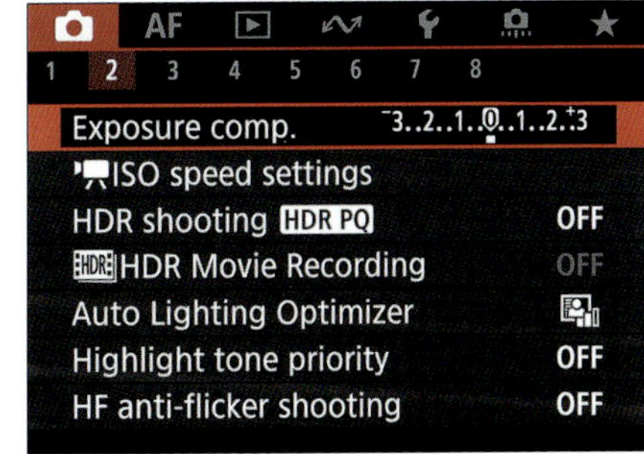

Figure 16.7 The Movie Shooting 2 menu.

- **Manual ISO settings.** You can choose specific ISO values *only* when the camera is set for Manual exposure mode. If you choose another exposure mode, including Av, Tv, P, or Fv, an appropriate ISO is set for you automatically.

- **No Auto Range.** In Movie mode, you cannot choose a *range* of ISO values for Auto ISO. You can only specify the maximum ISO that will be enabled.

- **Maximum ISO.** You can set *separate* maximum ISO values for conventional video and time-lapse video.

- **Cannot set Minimum Shutter Speed.** As you'll learn, the shutter speed used for video capture has an additional aspect when shooting movies: speeds that are too slow or too fast can affect the appearance of the video. So, unlike Still mode, you cannot choose a minimum shutter speed that will trigger boosting the ISO sensitivity.

The options available for each of the subentries shown in Figure 16.8 are described next. They include:

- **ISO Speed.** In Movie Scene Intelligent Auto (A+), P, Av, and Tv modes, ISO is set automatically in the range of ISO 100 to ISO 25,600. As I noted above, specific ISO speeds can only be set if the R8 is using Manual exposure.

  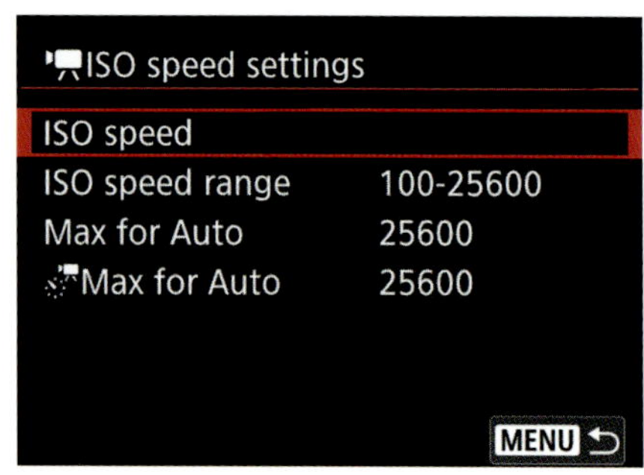

  Figure 16.8 Movie ISO Speed Settings.

  In Manual exposure mode, you can select a specific ISO speed from ISO 100 to 25,600. However, you can expand the manual setting range to add ISO 51,200 or ISO 102,400 using the ISO Speed Range setting described next. Oddly enough, Manual exposure mode also has an Auto setting. The latter effectively gives you an autoexposure mode when using manual exposure: you select the *shutter speed* and *aperture* manually, and the camera adjusts the ISO to produce the right exposure.

- **ISO Speed Range.** You can specify an ISO range for both minimum available settings and the maximum available settings.

  - **Minimum.** You can set the minimum sensitivity from ISO 100 to ISO 12,800. The high end remains at 12,800 even if Highlight Tone Priority (found in both the Movie and Still Shooting 2 menus) is set for an expanded range.

    Note: The minimum speed is set to ISO 400 for Auto exposure when Canon Log is enabled. The ISO 100 and ISO 200 settings can still be specified manually, but they are labeled as expanded L settings, indicating that some quality loss should be expected.

  - **Maximum.** You can specify a maximum available ISO of up to ISO 51,200 or ISO 204,800. Note that the highest settings are all labeled with an H indicator to remind you that they are expanded settings. The Highlight Tone Priority setting has no effect on this.

  I find myself using this feature frequently to keep me from accidentally switching to a setting I'd rather (or need to) avoid. For example, at concerts I may switch from ISO 1600 to ISO 6400 as the lighting changes, and I set those two values as my minimum or maximum. Outdoors in daylight, I might prefer to lock out ISO values lower than ISO 100 or higher than ISO 800.

- **Max for Auto.** This is the equivalent "safety net" for Auto ISO operation for a maximum setting.

- **Time-lapse Max for Auto.** Set the maximum ISO for 4K/Full HD time-lapse movie shooting in Program, Tv, Av, or Manual exposure mode and ISO Auto. The default maximum is 25,600, but you can specify another value between ISO 400 and ISO 25,600.

HDR Movie Recording

Options: Disable (default), Enable

This is the only other entry in the Movie Shooting 2 menu that is exclusive to Movie mode. This setting simply turns HDR movie recording on or off. There are no additional settings to make. I'll discuss HDR movie making later in this chapter, but the important things to note here are the other settings that preclude HDR shooting. Highlight Tone Priority, Canon Log, Movie Digital IS, and Movie Cropping must be disabled. Movie recording quality is fixed at FHD 29.97P IPB. You'll find more HDR movie information near the end of this chapter.

Av 1/8-stop Increments

Options: Disable (default), Enable

This is the first of only two entries in the Movie Shooting 3 menu. (See Figure 16.9.) RF-mount lenses have apertures that can be controlled much more precisely than those found in EF/EF-S lenses, and Canon takes advantage of that by offering the ability to adjust f/stops in increments of 1/8th stop. While such fine increments are not essential for still photography, when movie shooting it's important to have consistent exposure, especially with sequences of shots. This feature is available only in the two Movie exposure modes in which you have full control over the aperture—Av and M modes. Choose Enable to allow selection in 1/8th-stop increments rather than the 1/2- or 1/3-stop jumps you may have set in the Custom Functions 1's Exposure Level Increments entry. This feature does not work with EF or EF-S lenses.

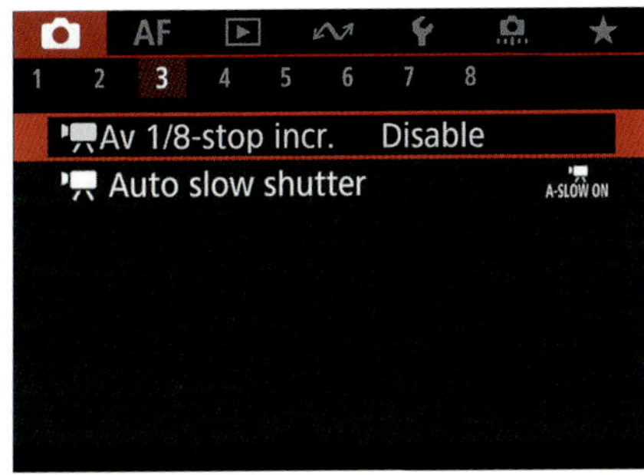

Figure 16.9 The Movie Shooting 3 menu.

Movie Auto Slow Shutter

Options: Auto Slow On (default), Auto Slow Off

Use this setting to allow the camera to select a slower shutter speed no faster than 1/30th second when shooting with Program or Av (Aperture-priority) at a frame rate of 60p. (I'll provide more detail on how choice of frame rates affects your movies later in this chapter.) You can select Enable or Disable.

Here's the difference:

- **Disable.** Frame rates of 1/60th second or faster will be chosen in Program and Av exposure modes when shooting 60p video. The video will be smoother and more natural looking, and individual frames will be sharper because of this "higher" shutter speed. However, under low light, your video may appear to be underexposed.

- **Enable.** Shutter speeds of 1/30th second or slower are enabled, producing better-exposed movies that may have less noise (because a lower ISO setting may be used). However, moving subjects may be blurry or leave a visible "trail" caused by the longer exposure.

Canon Log Settings

Options: Canon Log, View Assist, Characteristics, Color Space

This is the only entry in the Movie Shooting 4 menu that is movie-specific (see Figure 16.10). Canon Log, or *C-log3* is a type of *gamma* adjustment, which allows capturing as much useful tonal information as possible, thanks to the non-linear way in which humans perceive light and color. In plain English, C-log allows the camera to squeeze as much of the original scene's dynamic range as possible into a video file with as many as 10 bits of information. It produces a "flat"-looking, low-contrast image that looks horrible when viewed before it's post processed in a suitable professional video-editing program, such as DaVinci Resolve, Adobe Premiere Pro, or Apple Final Cut Pro. It's then processed during editing to create a rich, full-range video.

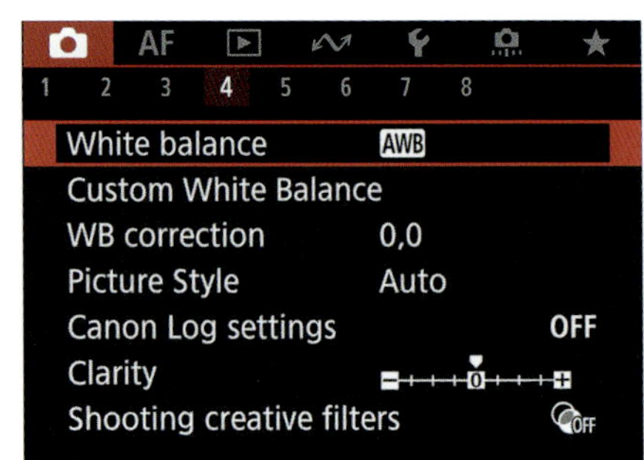

Figure 16.10 The Movie Shooting 4 menu.

Theoretically, the basic Canon Log profile allows an increased tonal (dynamic) range of about 800 percent, or 12 f/stops at sensitivity settings of ISO 400 or above. (The ISO boost is needed to allow the Dual Pixel CMOS sensor to capture the extra detail in the highlights and shadows.) Canon has added a "View Assist" function available from the Canon Log Settings entry in the Shooting 4 menu that allows you to view a "corrected" version in the camera before actual processing (called *grading*) has taken place. Log profiles space the data captured more equally among the number of stops of exposure captured, using a predetermined number of stops, with colors desaturated ("flatter"-looking) to eliminate over-saturated parts of the scene that would interfere with corrective grading.

The technology underlying Canon Log is beyond the scope of this book, which emphasizes camera features over software processing, but videographers who perform post-processing grading will appreciate the ability to use a system of 10 "look-up tables" (called LUTs in video parlance) that substitute appropriate values to correct the recorded image's gamma and color space for viewing on an external monitor. Canon provides useful LUT data on their website for downloading.

The latest (at this writing) Canon Log 3 profile provides additional advantages over the original basic Canon Log profile. C-Log3 doubles the base ISO rating to 800, which effectively tells the camera to use one stop less exposure to capture a greater number of highlights. C-Log3 does a better job of not clipping black values, producing better results in shadows during grading. Compared to Canon Log, C-Log3 offers a bit more dynamic range, improved shadows, and is more compatible with the look-up tables used with Canon's Cinema EOS models.

To capture movies with Canon Log, follow these steps:

1. **Use Manual exposure.** Change the Movie Shooting mode to Manual exposure.

2. **Navigate to Canon Log Settings.** In the Movie Shooting 4 menu, access the Canon Log Settings entry.

3. **Select Canon Log** (shown in Figure 16.11) and choose:

   Canon Log: On—C.LOG3. Use C-Log3 when recording 10-bit video to the internal memory card or to an external recorder. The output will be at the recording quality specified in the Movie Shooting 1 menu. Output will be "clean" uncompressed YCbCr 4:2:2 video using the BT709/BT2020 color space. I'll explain these later on. To disable Canon Log recording, choose Off.

4. **Optionally, set View Assist.** Your C-Log video saved to your memory card will appear darker and lower in contrast when viewed on the camera's LCD screen. Turning View Assist On provides a clearer display, although it does not affect the video files themselves. It is not used during playback.

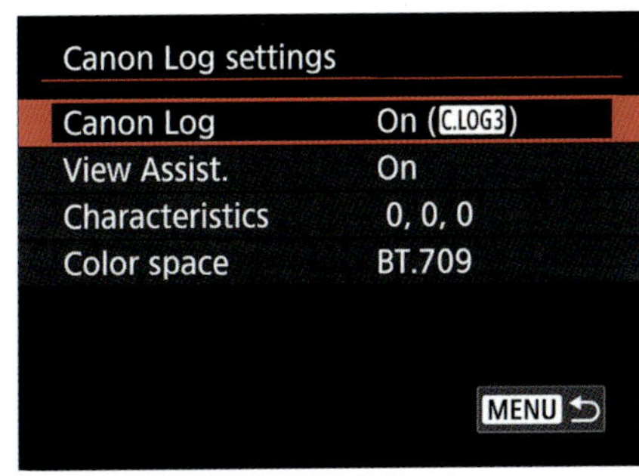

Figure 16.11 Canon Log options.

5. **Adjust Characteristics.** Think of these characteristics as additional Picture Controls for Canon Log video. You can specify Sharpness, Strength, Saturation, or Hue using familiar Picture Control-style sliders.

6. **HDMI Color Space.** Choose BT.709, BT.2020, or Cinema Gamut as your color space for HDMI output. These are definitions defined by ITU-R (International Telecommunication Union Radio Communication Sector, if you're an acronym junkie) to define characteristics of high-definition television signals, including resolution, frame rates, bit depth, and various color specifications. If you need to choose among them, you'll already know why and don't need further instruction from me. **Note:** There have been reports of color shifts when using Cinema Gamut with the Atomos Ninja V recorder/monitor. It may be fixed by the time this book is published.

7. **Other settings.** Choose ISO speed, shutter speed, and aperture.

8. **Record.** Capture your video, storing on the internal memory card or an external video recorder.

Pre-recording Settings

Options: Pre-recording: Off (default), On; Recording Time: 5 seconds (default), 3 seconds

There are no movie-specific entries in the Movie Shooting 5 menu, so I'm going to skip that one completely. This entry is the first of three video-oriented options in the Movie Shooting 6 menu. (See Figure 16.12.) Having your camera record the action a few seconds before you actually want capture to begin can help ensure you don't miss important action. Say, you're waiting for a toddler to do something cute, but find you don't react quickly enough. When on Standby in Movie mode, the sensor is creating a video signal anyway, so it's no big feat to include the last 5 or 3 seconds of footage (at your option) in the video captured. You may also find the extra few seconds gives you more flexibility when editing a clip.

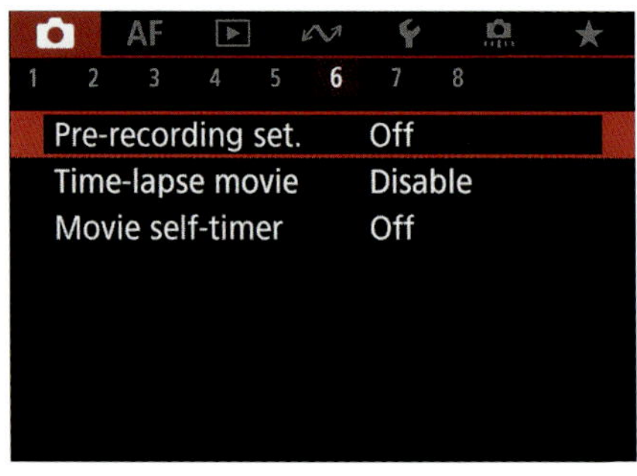

Figure 16.12 The Movie Shooting 6 menu.

Time-lapse Movie

Options: Disable (default), Enable; Interval, Number of Shots, Movie Recording Size, Auto Exposure, Screen Auto Off, Beep As Image Taken

Time-lapse photography isn't just for nature photographers who want to show the miracle of a flower bud gradually opening to its full blossoming glory. Time-lapse has hit the mainstream, and an amazing number of movies and television shows use it to represent the passage of time, whether it's the march of the sun across the sky in the daytime or the changing seasons. Canon has placed this technique within your grasp, as well.

I explained the process in some detail in Chapter 6, and won't repeat that information here. I'll give you just a quick recap of the key settings, the first five of which are shown in Figure 16.13.

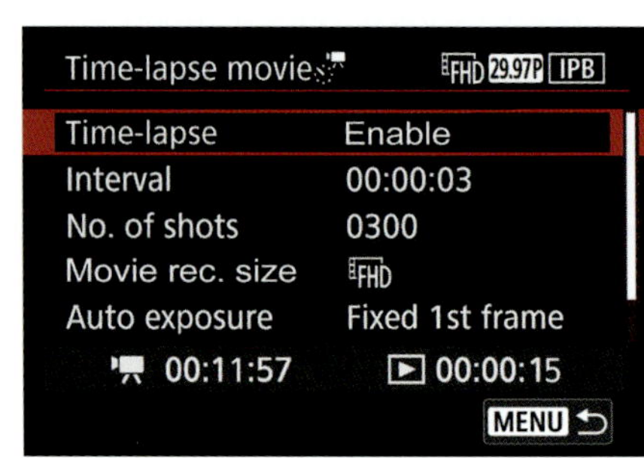

Figure 16.13 Time-lapse options.

- **Time-lapse Movie.** Choose Enable to begin setup, or Disable to deactivate the option.

- **Interval.** You can choose the interval between shots, up to 99 hours, 59 minutes, and 59 seconds.

- **Number of Shots.** Enter the number of shots you want in the sequence, from 2 up to 3,600. The expected elapsed time for the entire sequence will be shown near the bottom of the screen. If the playback time is displayed in red, that means the memory card doesn't have enough space, or, if the card is not formatted in exFAT, your settings will result in a file size greater than 4GB. (Don't worry; all SDXC cards are automatically formatted in the camera in exFAT. Only SDHC and cards not formatted in the camera are susceptible.) Recording will stop when the card is full or the maximum file size is reached.

- **Movie Recording Size.** You can choose 4K 29.97P (NTSC)/4K 25.00P (PAL), or FHD 29.97P/25.00P (NTSC/PAL, respectively).

- **Auto Exposure Setting.** You can choose:

  - **Fixed 1st Frame.** Metering takes place and the exposure is set for the first frame and used for all subsequent frames. You'd use this setting when you want the exposure to remain constant, even if lighting changes.

  - **Each Frame.** Metering is performed for each shot in the sequence. A time-lapse movie of a city skyline from dawn to dusk will reflect the correct exposure for each stage of the day.

- **Screen Auto Off.** You'll need to scroll down to see this entry and the next. Here you can Disable automatic dismissal (the screen will turn off after about 30 minutes), or choose Enable to turn off the screen 10 seconds after shooting begins and you've had time to check your framing and exposure.

- **Beep as Image Taken.** Enable or disable the Beep As Image Taken feedback feature (the electronic shutter used is silent). You can select the volume level for the sound.

Movie Self-timer

Options: Off (default), 10 seconds, 2 seconds

This is a handy feature that delays the beginning of movie capture for either 10 or 2 seconds. It gives you time to get in front of the camera yourself (choose 10 seconds if you need to comb your hair; 2 seconds if you're ready to go or don't care). If you don't have a remote release, this setting also can be used to let the camera settle down after you've stabbed the Movie button with your index finger. (**Tip:** Don't stab!)

Vloggers could also use this feature for an impromptu session, but probably wouldn't need it, as those serious enough to use an R8 (instead of a smartphone) probably also are adept at using editing tools to snip out the offending rush to make the scene.

IS (Image Stabilizer Mode)

Options: Off (default), On, Enhanced

This is the first entry in the Movie Shooting 7 menu, which contains five movie-specific entries (the Customize Quick Controls and Metering Timer entries function like their Still counterparts described in Chapter 11). (See Figure 16.14.)

Because your camera lacks in-body image stabilization (IBIS), it relies on the image stabilization built into some RF/RF-S and EF/EF-S-mount lenses. It can supplement this optical image stabilization (OIS) with an electronic version called Movie Digital IS that can be activated when shooting video.

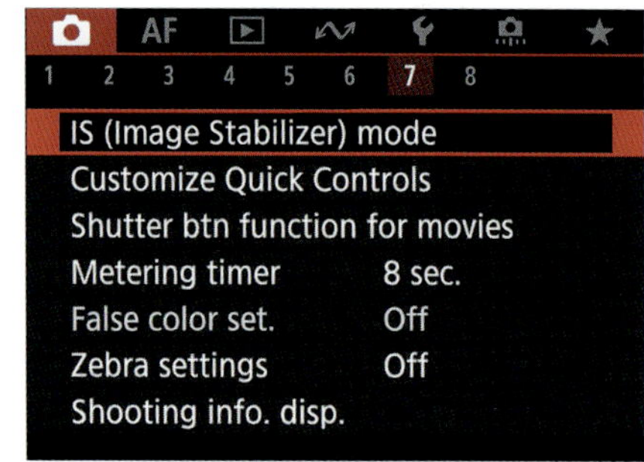

Figure 16.14 The Movie Shooting 7 menu.

Movie digital image stabilization takes advantage of the fact that cropped video frames contain some image information outside the boundaries of the actual frame displayed. The camera is able to monitor movement and compensate for it by shifting the pixels of the entire frame slightly so that subject matter that is not moving remains in the same relative position in the frame. That is, if the camera image shakes a few pixels to the left, the frame area is moved an equivalent amount the same number of pixels to the right. Because some pixels at the edges of the frame must be trimmed to compensate for this adjustment, the resulting movie is slightly cropped, adding a small amount of magnification.

An advantage of Movie Digital IS is that it works with any lens, at your option. It provides vibration reduction with lenses that lack built-in IS, and if the lens does have IS, Digital IS will work in tandem with the lens and camera's in-body stabilization to provide even better results.

Use this feature in conjunction with the built-in optical image stabilization of your lenses that have stabilization; if your lens has IS and it is turned off, the camera will remind you to turn it back on. Canon provides a list of lenses that are compatible with what it terms "combination IS" (when both digital and optical image stabilization are combined). Movie IS does not work with lenses with a focal length greater than 800mm and is not recommended with tilt/shift (TS-E), fisheye, or third-party lenses.

Your options are as follows:

- **IS Mode (On, Off).** This option appears *only* if your lens does not have built-in IS. It allows you to turn the *camera's* in-body image stabilization on or off. You might want to turn it off when the camera is mounted on a tripod, because the R8 might still make unwanted adjustments while you are capturing video. For hand-held-use, you can leave the IBIS active.

- **Movie Digital IS (Off, On, Enhanced).** This option appears whether your lens has built-in IS or not, and is the *only* entry if you are using an IS-equipped lens.
  - **On.** A great deal of camera shake will be corrected; the image will be slightly cropped, producing a slight magnification effect. This setting works best with wide-angle lenses.
  - **Enhanced.** Even more pronounced camera shake is compensated for, and the image will be magnified a bit more. Use this as a last resort, as there may be a noticeable blurring of the image *while viewing* and an increase in visual noise.

Shutter Button Function for Movies

Options: Half-press: Meter+Movie Servo AF (default), Meter+One-Shot AF, Metering Only; Fully press: Start/Stop Movie Recording, No Function (default)

This entry allows you to define a function for the shutter button during movie shooting, overriding any setting you may have specified using the Custom Functions 3 menu's Customize Buttons options. Separate behaviors can be set for a half-press and full press of the button.

- **Half-press.** You can choose:
  - **Metering plus Movie Servo AF.** Use this default setting to initiate metering and autofocus using the shutter button when you want the camera to continually track and refocus on a moving subject.
  - **Metering plus One-Shot AF.** Constant refocusing may be distracting, especially in static shots in which only the camera moves. If you'd prefer that focus remain on your initial subject, use this entry to start metering and AF using the shutter release button.
  - **Metering Only.** Choose this option when you want to use the shutter button solely to initiate metering.
- **Fully press.** You can choose:
  - **Start/Stop Movie Recording.** This definition allows you to use a full press of the shutter release to start/stop movie recording. You may find it convenient to use the same button to trigger both still photos and movies. Since it's not possible to shoot stills while shooting movies, assigning the movie function to the shutter release is a viable option. (You can, however, extract single frames from your videos if you need a still.)
  - **No function.** With this default setting, a full press has no function.

False Color Settings

Options: False Color: Off (default), On; False Color Index: White Clipping, Just below White Clipping, One Stop over 18% Gray, 18% Gray, Just above Black Clipping, Black Clipping

This is a very cool tool. Like Zebra Settings, described next, it is somewhat akin to the flashing "blinkies" you may have been using with previous cameras to see what areas of an image are badly overexposed. While it may be a new feature for those just exploring video, cinematographers have been using false color displays to judge exposure for quite a while. Instead of just the flashing black blinkies you are used to, false color translates various exposure levels into colors that you can use to see roughly just how over- or underexposed parts of your subjects are.

The feature actually has just one setting: On or Off, as seen at left in Figure 16.15. The second "option" shown on that screen, False Color Index, is actually just an informational screen that familiarizes you with what the various colors mean. The false color display can only be viewed on your LCD screen or viewfinder. The actual image is shown, instead, on an external monitor linked to the R8 with an HDMI cable or though Canon's Camera Connect or EOS Utility software.

As with any new type of display, you'll need to learn what each of the individual colors represent. Pink, Yellow, and Red indicate increasing degrees of overexposure (in that order), with Red representing noticeable clipping of white tones. Green represents a satisfactory 18% gray tone, with blue and purple indicating increasing amounts of underexposure (in that order). Once you've mastered the color coding, you can add or subtract exposure until your image has the desired range of tones.

When using False Color, several other exposure tools, such as the Zebra display and Auto Lighting Optimizer, are disabled, along with View Assist for Canon Log. Also, you won't be able to use the manual focus Peaking feature (its colors would conflict with false color, natch) or create time-lapse movies.

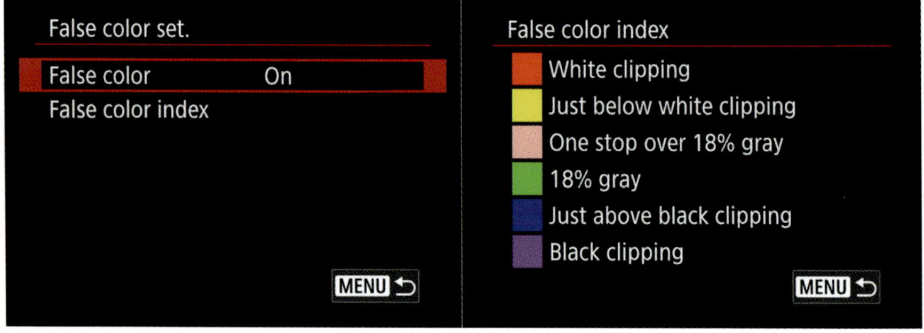

Figure 16.15 False Color selection (left). The informational False Color Index screen (right).

Zebra Settings

Options: Zebra: Off (default), On; Zebra Pattern (Zebra 1, Zebra 2, Zebra 1+2); Zebra 1 Level (5–95 percent), Zebra 2 Level (50–100 percent)

This feature warns you when highlight levels in your image are brighter than a setting you specify in this menu option. It's somewhat comparable to the flashing "blinkies" that digital cameras have long used during image review to tell us, after the fact, which highlight areas of the image we just took are blown out.

Zebra patterns are a much more useful tool because you are given an alert *before* you take the picture and can specify exactly how bright *too bright* is. The Zebra feature has been a staple of professional video shooting for a long time, as you might guess from the moniker assigned to the unit used to specify brightness: IRE, a measure of video signal level, which stands for *Institute of Radio Engineers.*

When you want to use Zebra pattern warnings, access this menu entry, choose your pattern, and specify an IRE brightness value from 5 to 100 (depending on the pattern selected). Once you see the results on your display, you can adjust your exposure settings to reduce the brightness of the highlights, as described in Chapter 4.

So, exactly how bright *is* too bright? A value of 100 IRE indicates pure white, so any Zebra pattern visible when using this setting indicates that your image is extremely overexposed. Any details in the highlights are gone and cannot be retrieved. Settings from 70 to 90 can be used to make sure facial tones are not overexposed. Generally, Caucasian skin falls in the 80 IRE range, with darker skin tones registering as low as 70, and very fair skin or lighter areas of your subject edging closer to 90 IRE. Once you've decided the approximate range of tones that you want to make sure do *not* blow out, you can set the camera's Zebra pattern sensitivity appropriately and receive the flashing striped warning on your display. The pattern does not appear in your final image, of course—it's just an aid to keep you from blowing it, so to speak. Maximum brightness value can vary, depending on your Canon Log, Highlight Tone Priority, Picture Style, and HDR-PQ settings.

Your adjustments, shown in Figure 16.16, include:

- **Zebra.** Choose On or Off to enable/disable display of Zebra patterns during movie shooting.
- **Zebra Pattern.** There are two Zebra patterns to choose from: right-slanting diagonal lines as seen in Figure 16.17, and left slanting. These appear over areas that exceed your specified brightness level. You can also elect to show Zebra 1+2, which shows an overlapping pattern where the two warnings merge. That allows you to see areas that represent a combination of the two levels.
- **Zebra 1 Level.** You can set the Zebra 1 display from 5 to 95 percent (with plus/minus 5 percent tolerance).
- **Zebra 2 Level.** The Zebra 2 level can be specified from 50 to 100 percent. (See Figure 16.17.)

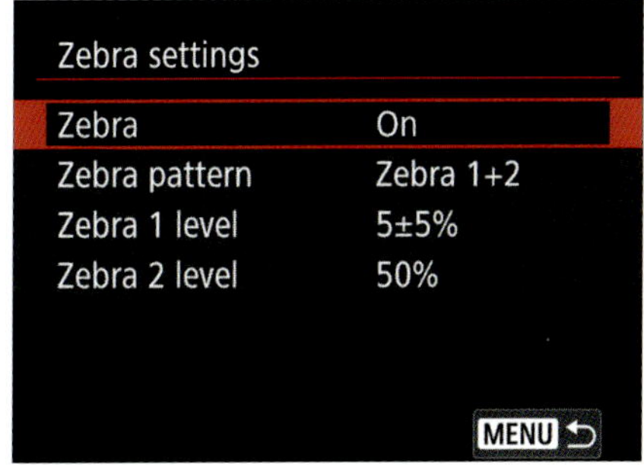

Figure 16.16 Zebra options.

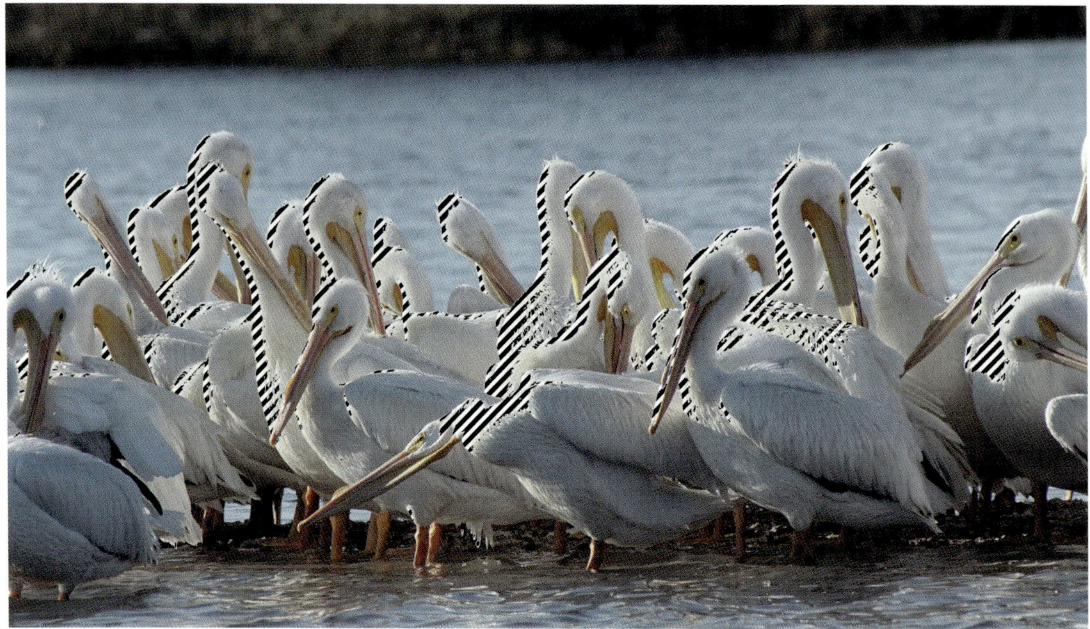

Figure 16.17 The flashing stripes show an area is overexposed using this Zebra 2 warning.

Shooting Information Display

Options: Screen Info. Settings, VF Info/Toggle Settings, Grid Display, Histogram Display, Lens Information Display, Recording Emphasis, Aspect Marker, Reset

My preference: N/A

This multi-layered entry is similar to the one provided for Still photography mode, with a couple of differences. Like its Still counterpart, it allows you to customize what is displayed in the viewfinder or LCD screen while you're shooting. The seven sub-settings in this entry let you specify exactly what you do or do not view while you're taking pictures. Five of the settings are the same as in the Still version (the VF Vertical Display option in the Still entry is not available in Movie mode). There are two new options for movie-shooting: Recording Emphasis and Aspect Marker. Here's an overview:

- **Screen Information Settings (same as Still version).** You can choose to enable or disable any of five different types of LCD screen information, each activated by pressing the INFO button. The screen was illustrated earlier in Figure 11.39, and won't be repeated here. You can choose from Basic information, All information except live histogram, All information including live histogram, Only autofocus point/zone display, and Graphic shooting information screen.

- **Viewfinder Information/Toggle Settings (same as Still version).** Choose to enable/disable three different viewfinder displays.

- **Grid Display (same as Still version).** You can choose 3 × 3, 6 × 4, or 3 × 3 with diagonal grids or turn grids off on the LCD screen and viewfinder.

- **Histogram Display (same as Still version).** This parameter has two options, allowing you to choose live histograms for Brightness (luminance) or RGB (all primary colors), and large or small display size.

- **Lens Information Display (same as Still version).** This parameter has four options:

  - **Focus Distance Display.** Determines *when* focus distance will be shown: In manual focus mode only, While focusing only, Always, or Never (disable).

  - **Unit.** Determines focus distance units, either Meters or Feet.

  - **Focal Length Display.** You can enable or disable having the current focal length shown in the display.

  - **SA Variable Amount.** Shows the amount of correction for spherical aberration with lenses, such as the RF 100mm f/2.8 Macro, that are compatible with this adjustment. As I explained in Chapter 7, spherical aberration control can be used to fine-tune the bokeh (appearance of out-of-focus highlights).

- **Recording Emphasis (Movie mode only).** Set to On, and a red frame blinks on the screen while movie recording is active. It's a useful indicator when the camera is set on a tripod, as you can confirm that video capture is underway by glancing at the screen. Choose Off, and no frame appears. Use that option if you don't want to make it obvious when the camera is recording, or if you find the blinking frame distracting.

- **Aspect Marker (Movie mode only).** This option allows you to choose from 1:1, 4:5, 5:4, 9:16, or 2:35 marker frames in the display. These frame guides are a useful way of visualizing the area that will be captured during video capture within a larger visible display. They are a popular tool for videographers because they allow viewing the area outside the actual frame that will be captured (the "look-around area") so you can monitor moving subjects before they enter the frame. In professional productions, it's useful to look at the region outside the captured frame to detect when boom microphones, careless crew members, or other objects threaten to intrude on the frame.

  It's common to shoot movies knowing in advance that they will be cropped down eventually for display in a slightly different format. The director simply makes sure that the important parts of the frame are included in the "safety zone" that will never be cropped out. For example, you wouldn't want to put two characters who are talking to each other at opposite ends of the entire frame but would instead locate them in the safety zone so both would be visible.

  You can use the R8's Aspect Markers to frame your image so the important subject matter is contained within a desired aspect ratio, or to frame the image for later cropping to that aspect ratio. You can select Off, 1:1, 4:5, 5:4, 9:16, or 2.35:1. (*Star Wars*, for example, was filmed in CinemaScope, with a 2.35:1 aspect ratio.) (See Figure 16.18.)

- **Reset.** Restores the above parameters to their default values.

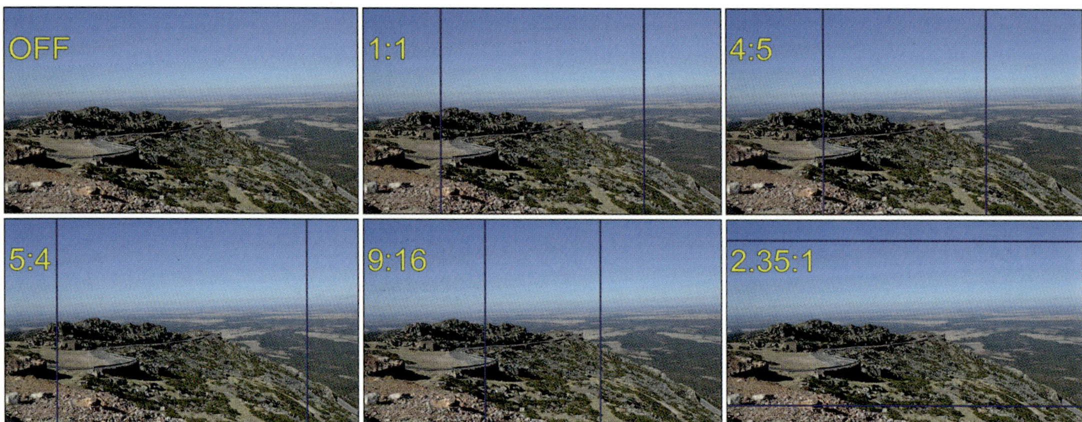

Figure 16.18 Aspect Markers.

Standby: Low Resolution

Options: On (default), Off

This is the second entry in the Movie Shooting 8 menu, and the first one with functions dedicated to movie shooting. (See Figure 16.19.) Think of this setting as an overheating/power-saving mode. The R8's sensor is energized and memory card storage is active continuously as you preview or capture video. Autofocus, exposure metering, and other functions are also hard at work. Shooting 4K video at high speeds and fast transfer rates generates a lot of heat. This control provides a modest amount of help to prevent the camera from becoming over-warm, and, perhaps, damaging the sensor while idling, by displaying the preview image at a reduced refresh/quality setting. It also saves power and may allow you to shoot longer, particularly if you have the camera on, but on standby, for longer periods of time. Image quality while on standby isn't that critical, in any case, even if there is a noticeable difference between the preview and your actual recorded video.

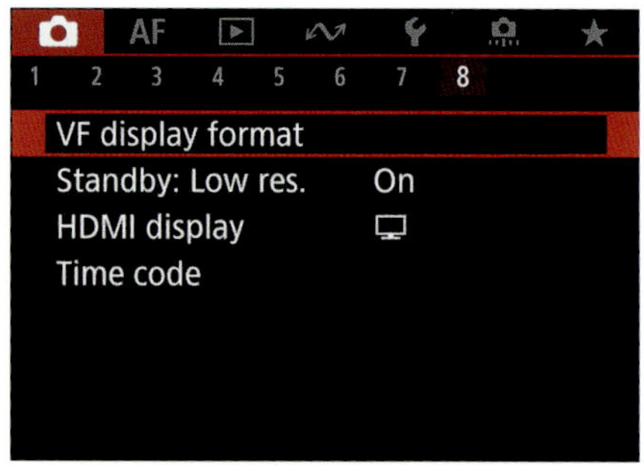

Figure 16.19 The Movie Shooting 8 menu.

This setting cannot be used when Digital Zoom is enabled or Pre-Recording is set to On. If overheating doesn't concern you, switch from the default On setting to Off. Your chief gain is faster response when you resume capture, and improved display on the standby screen.

HDMI Display

Options: Camera+External (default), External Only

When directing video to an external device, you can choose whether your output is displayed on your camera *and* on the external device, or *only* on the external recorder or monitor.

- **Camera+External.** Movie display is shown on the camera and the other device connected through the HDMI port. In this mode, recording on the camera's memory card is not possible. The HDMI shows the video only, with no information overlays, and is used to display menus and playback. The camera displays the video as it's being captured, along with informational overlays summoned by the INFO button. Menus and playback aren't shown on the camera.

  You might want to use this mode to be able to monitor your recording at the camera, as well as on the HDMI device (which may be physically separated and connected by a long cable).

- **External Only.** This shows video, information, menus, and playback image on the external device only, and nothing on the camera itself.

Time Code

Options: Count Up, Start Time Setting, Movie Rec. Count, Movie Play Count, HDMI, Drop Frame

Advanced video shooters find SMPTE (Society of Motion Picture and Television Engineers)-compatible time codes embedded in the video files to be an invaluable reference during editing. To oversimplify a bit, the time system provides precise *hour:minute:second:frame* markers that allow identifying and synchronizing frames and audio. The time code system includes a provision for "dropping" frames to ensure that the fractional frame rate of captured video (remember that a 24 fps setting actually yields 23.976 frames per second while 30 fps capture gives you 29.97 actual "frames" per second) can be matched up with actual time spans.

As I noted in the introduction to this book, I won't be covering the most technical aspects of movie shooting in great detail (including time codes, raw HDMI streaming, etc.). If you're at the stage where you're using time codes, you don't need a primer, anyway. However, the Time Code submenu, shown in Figure 16.20, does include the following options:

- **Count Up.** Choose Rec Run, in which the time code counts up only when you are actually capturing video, or Free Run (also known as Time of Day), which allows the time code to run up even between shooting clips. The latter is useful when you want to synchronize clips between multiple cameras that are shooting the same event. When using Free Run, even if the cameras record at different times, you'll be able to match the video that was captured at the exact same moment during editing. When Free Run is selected, the time code will always be recorded to the movie file (except for HFR clips).

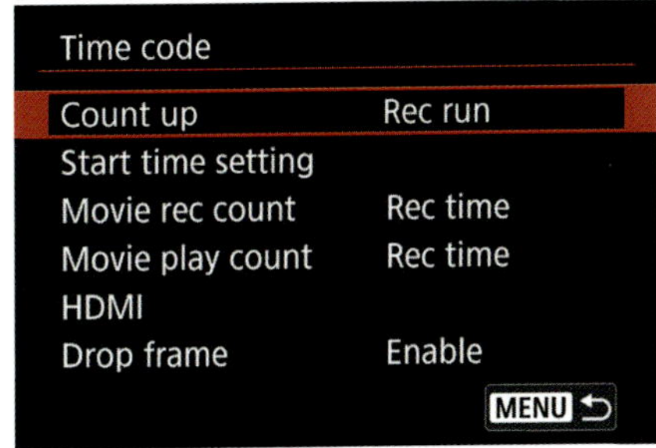

Figure 16.20 Time Code options.

- **Start Time Setting.** Normally, the camera uses its internal clock to specify the hours:minutes:seconds, with frames set to :00 when you begin shooting. This entry allows you to manually enter any hour:minute:second:frame of your choice, or to Reset the start time to 00:00:00:00.
- **Movie Rec. Count.** Here you can decide whether to display the elapsed time for the current clip on the LCD, or the Time Code while capturing video.
- **Movie Play Count.** This gives you the same choices during playback, allowing you to choose elapsed time or Time Code.
- **HDMI.** You can select Enable to append the time code to the HDMI video output, or Disable to not add it to the output. The Record Command output, when Enabled, allows the camera's Stop/Start action to sync with the external recording device. When Disabled, starting and stopping are controlled by the external recording device.
- **Drop Frame.** As I mentioned, the 30 fps setting yields 29.97 actual frames per second, 60 fps gives you 59.95 frames per second, and HFR provides 119.9 fps, causing a discrepancy between the actual time and the time code that's recorded. Choose Enable, and the camera will skip some time code numbers in drop-frame mode at intervals to eliminate the discrepancy. When disabled, you may notice a difference of several seconds per hour.

Movie Autofocus Menus

When you've switched to one of the movie shooting modes, a revised set of six Movie Autofocus menus appear with a total of 20 entries. All but three of those entries are identical to their exact counterparts for still shooting and were explained in Chapter 12, and, again, I won't repeat those descriptions here.

Instead, I'll explain the differences and describe the three new entries, which relate to differences in autofocus when shooting movies. Your other movie AF settings, such as AF Method, will be familiar to you from still shooting.

Movie Servo AF

Options: Movie Servo AF: Enable (default), Disable; Subject Detection AF: Detection-priority (default), Detection Only

This function operates similarly to Continuous AF described in Chapter 12, but, when enabled, uses *only* Movie Servo AF.

Your options include:

- **Movie Servo AF.** When disabled, you can initiate autofocus by pressing the shutter button half-way or the AF-ON button (the latter button initiates AF only once). When enabled, focus is adjusted constantly without the need to press the shutter release halfway. The continuous auto-focus pauses when using digital zooming or magnified view. This mode consumes more battery power and may reduce recording time.

  To lock focus or pause continuous focusing (say, to eliminate the sound of the lens's motor as it refocuses), tap the Servo AF icon at the lower left of the LCD screen. Tap again to resume. Movie Servo AF will also be reactivated if you press the MENU or Playback buttons, or change the AF method. You can specify how the camera responds using the Movie Servo AF Speed entry, described shortly.

- **Subject Detection AF.** You can specify certain types of subjects (people, animals, or vehicles) using the AF: Subject to Detect entry of the AF 1 menu. This option allows you to set whether Movie Servo AF is used all the time, or only when your preferred subject is found.

  - **Detection-priority.** Autofocus will continually search for subjects within the frame if they are within the current AF area, and give priority to people, animals, or vehicles, if specified.

  - **Detection Only.** Movie Servo AF will pause if your preferred Subject to Detect is not found.

Movie Servo AF Speed

Options: When Active, AF Speed

This choice is available from the Movie AF 2 menu when Movie Servo AF is set to Enable. The function is also enabled when using lenses released after 2009 that have USM or STM motors. Your choices are as follows:

- **When Active.** Always On activates the AF adjustment speed setting automatically before and during movie shooting. The During Shooting AF choice makes the speed adjustment active *only* when you are capturing video. (See Figure 16.21, top.)

- **AF Speed.** Highlight this option and press SET. You can then adjust the AF speed using the touch screen, QCD, or directional controls along a sliding scale from Slow (–7 to 0) to Standard (0) to Fast (+1 to +2). (See Figure 16.21, bottom.)

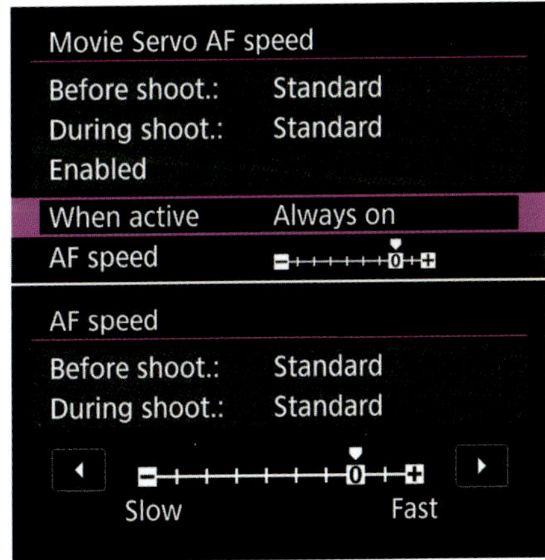

Figure 16.21 Movie Servo AF speed settings.

Movie AF Tracking Sensitivity

Options: –3 (Locked On) to +3 (Responsive)

Here you can specify how quickly the Movie Servo AF tracking locks onto a moving subject. Movie Servo AF must be enabled. It's similar to the Tracking Sensitivity that you can set in the Autofocus 1 menu, as described in Chapter 12. As with its still photo counterpart, changing the tracking sensitivity can come in useful when an intervening subject passes through the frame in front of the subject you were capturing. It's also helpful when panning. A sliding scale can be adjusted from Locked On (–3 to –1) to Responsive (+1 to +3) or standard at the 0 position. (See Figure 16.22.) Locked On tells the camera to stick with the subject

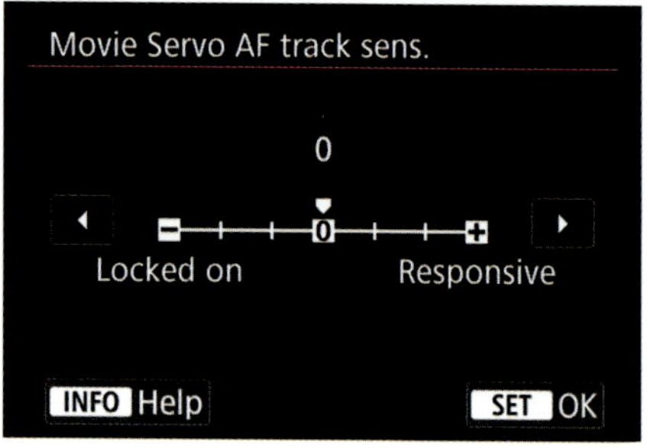

Figure 16.22 Movie Servo AF tracking sensitivity.

currently in focus—like that referee at a football game, or a passerby in an urban scene. Responsive settings tell the camera to switch to track a subject located at the current focus point, even if it's the same subject now moving toward you at a rapid rate, or a different subject that comes into view.

Compression, Resolution, and Frame Rates

I've explained how to make and use settings first, and saved explanations of some of the technical terms for now. The information in this section will help you make your choices. Even intermediate movie shooters can be confused by the number of different options for compression, resolution, and frame rates. This section will help clarify things for you.

Compression

Compression is easiest to understand, so I'll get it out of the way first. As I mentioned earlier, the camera stores files using the standard H.264/MPEG-4 codec ("coder-decoder").

- **ALL-I (All Intraframe).** This mode is available only when shooting time-lapse and digest movies. The camera takes each individual frame that you shoot and attempts to compress it before writing the frame to your memory card. You can think of ALL-I compression as a series of still images (which is what time-lapse clips consist of), each squeezed down by discarding (hopefully) redundant information. While this compression method is not the most efficient way to reduce file size, because individual frames are stored in their entirety, the resulting files are easier to edit.

  Your R8 cannot use this compression method for conventional movie shooting. The reduced compression puts extra demands on your camera and memory card as video is stored, especially when shooting 4K movies. Canon says that transfer rates average 480Mb/s when using ALL-I for UHD video. IPB compression (discussed next) requires only one-quarter that transfer rate—120Mb/s, so your camera uses it for conventional video capture.

- **IPB (Standard).** This is a newer compression method that uses *interframe* compression; that is, only certain "key" frames are saved, with other frames "simulated" or interpolated from information contained in the frames that precede and succeed them. I-frames are the complete or *intraframes* (the only kind used by ALL-I compression); P-frames are "predicted picture" frames, which record *only the pixel changes* from the previous frame (say, a runner traveling across a fixed background); B-frames are "bi-predictive picture" frames, created by using the differences from the preceding *and* following frames. This interpolation produces image quality that is a bit lower and which requires more of your camera's DIGIC X processing power, but file sizes are smaller.

  Video encoded using IPB must be converted, or transcoded to a format compatible with your video-editing software. The compression scheme can produce more artifacts, particularly in frames with lots of motion throughout the frame.

- **IPB (Light).** It is recorded at a bit rate that is lower than IPB (Standard), producing files that are smaller, transfer more quickly, have higher playback compatibility, and provide longer maximum shooting times. If you don't need the maximum resolution possible, this choice can be very useful.

"CLEAN" HDMI OUTPUT

The video is directed through the HDMI port with embedded time code to an external monitor or recorder. As mentioned earlier, you can simultaneously display the video on the color LCD as it is recorded to your memory card. You can choose whether to display the captured image and scene and camera shooting information on the LCD as you shoot. This capability allows professional videographers (or other advanced shooters) more latitude in color correction through the enhanced color space, improved monitoring during the shoot, and more versatile post-production workflow. You can, for example, synchronize the camera's video capture with the start/stop of the external video recorder.

Movie files are limited to 4GB in size if you are using an SDHC card (those with a capacity of 32GB or less). Such cards are formatted using the FAT32 file system, which cannot store files larger than 4GB. If a clip stored on such a card reaches that size, the camera will create a new file and continue shooting. The separate files must be viewed separately and/or combined in a movie editor.

On the other hand, SDXC cards (with capacities of 64GB or more) are formatted in the camera using the exFAT file system and files can exceed 4GB. However, your *computer's operating system* may have some restrictions on file size.

Resolution

Resolution choices are a little less techie:

- **4K (3840 × 2160).** This ultra-high-definition format is the wave of the future, even if content and display choices are limited at present. As you advance in the video world, you'll probably find yourself shooting 4K a lot, even if you intend to distribute Full HD video. Many editors swear that 4K video converted to Full HD is better than Full HD video captured natively.

- **1920 × 1080 (1080p).** This resolution is so-called "full HD" and is the maximum resolution displayed when using the HDTV format. Many monitors and most HD televisions can display this resolution, and you'll have the best image quality when you use it. Use this resolution for your "professional" productions. However, the top-of-the-line resolution requires the most storage space, approximately 235 to 685 megabytes per minute, as mentioned earlier. This means you can fit a collection of individual clips amounting to no more than about 1 hour 4 minutes on a single 16GB memory card.

Frame Rate

In the digital camera world, in which all video is shot using *progressive scan* with no *interlaced scan* option, frame rates are easy to choose. (Interlacing is a capture method in which even/odd numbered lines of each frame are captured alternately; with progressive scan, all the lines in a frame are captured consecutively.) Fortunately, one seemingly confusing set of alternatives can be dispensed with quickly: The 50/25 fps and 60/30 fps options can be considered as pairs of *video*-oriented frame rates. The 60/30 fps rates are used only where the NTSC television standard is in place, such as North America, Japan, Korea, and a few other places. The 50/25 frame rates are used where the PAL standard reigns, such as Europe, Russia, China, Africa, Australia, and other places. For simplicity, I'll refer just to the 60/30 frame rates in this section; if you're reading this in India, just convert to 50/25.

The third possibility is 24 fps, which is a standard frame rate used for motion pictures. Keep in mind that the rates are *nominal*. A 24 fps setting yields 23.976 frames per second; 30 fps gives you 29.97 actual "frames" per second. As I mentioned earlier, the R8's High Frame Rate option captures video at 179.8/119.99 fps or, nominally, 180/120 fps for NTSC and 150/100 fps for PAL.

The difference lies in the two "worlds" of motion images—film and video. The standard frame rate for motion picture film is 24 fps, while the video rate, at least in the United States, Japan, and those other places using the NTSC standard, is 30 fps. Computer-editing software can handle either type and convert between them. The choice between 24 fps and 30 fps is determined by what you plan to do with your video.

The short explanation is that shooting at 24 fps gives your movie a "film" look, excellent for showing fine detail. However, if your clip has moving subjects, or you pan the camera, 24 fps can produce a jerky effect called "judder." A 30 or 60 fps rate produces a home-video look that some feel is less desirable, but which is smoother and less jittery when displayed on an electronic monitor. I suggest you try both and use the frame rate that best suits your tastes and video-editing software.

Another consideration that we can't do much about is the difference between a *rolling shutter* and *global shutter*. In progressive scan mode, each line is captured one after another, so that a moving subject may have perceptibly relocated (part of it anyway) during the capture of a frame. The rolling shutter may produce Jell-O-like effects with such motion. A global shutter, like those used in professional video cameras, captures the entire frame at once, eliminating that problem. Without benefit of a global shutter, we at least need to be aware of the possible result when shooting action.

HDR Movies

You can extend the dynamic range of your movies in high-contrast situations by shooting HDR movies. Effectively, this mode is a type of in-camera bracketing to provide an expanded dynamic range and improved highlight rendition. The Movie Recording Size setting under Movie Recording Quality must be set to Full HD 29.9P IPB or Full HD 25.00P IPB. Highlight Tone Priority and Time Lapse Movies must be disabled.

Then, press the Q button to produce the movie version of the Quick Control screen, and navigate to the HDR setting at the bottom of the right-hand column. Scroll down to the HDR Movie Shooting entry and enable it. Then shoot a movie conventionally. Multiple frames are merged to create an HDR movie. You may see excessive noise or some distortion, so you'll want to experiment with this feature to see how useful it is to you.

You should be using an RF- or EF-mount lens to shoot HDR movies in Full HD. If you're using EF-S lenses with an adapter or when you use the Movie Cropping entry, movies are recorded in Standard HD. HDR movies are not available when using Highlight Tone Priority, Canon Log, or when shooting time-lapse movies.

Exposure Options

You can select fully automatic exposure, elect to specify exposure manually, or choose a shutter speed or aperture setting that you prefer for creative reasons. The system will select an ISO speed for you automatically in all cases, generally sticking to the range ISO 100 to ISO 12,800. (Some oddball exceptions are applied for various combinations of exposure mode and ISO speed settings made in the Shooting 2 menu.) Exposure can be locked with the * button, and cancelled with the AF point selection button located to the right of the * button.

The R8 offers a complete range of exposure adjustments. Here are your options:

- **Fully automatic exposure.** The camera will automatically select an appropriate exposure for you if the mode selected is Scene Intelligent Auto, P (program auto exposure), or B (bulb exposure). Note that B will not produce a bulb or time exposure; the camera defaults to P when you use the B position. The idea is to prevent you from losing video capture capabilities if you accidentally select B by mistake. In Scene Intelligent Auto, the camera will analyze your subject and select a Scene type and display it on the upper-left corner of the LCD monitor.

- **Shutter-priority AE.** You can choose Tv, exactly as you do when shooting still photographs, and specify a shutter speed, with some limitations. The camera will select an appropriate aperture for you. The available shutter speeds will depend on the frame rate, primarily because you can't (logically) choose a shutter speed that is longer than the length of time needed to expose an individual frame. Any shutter speed slower than 1/8th second is locked out.

  Choosing the shutter speed yourself offers two advantages. Even though each frame is captured in about 1/60th–1/30th second, slicing up the time the sensor is exposed to light allows capturing video in a much broader range of lighting conditions. Outdoors in full daylight, 1/30th second would produce an overexposure even with a very small f/stop and an ISO 100 sensitivity setting. In addition, opting for a higher shutter speed allows you to freeze action within each individual frame, reducing or eliminating blur, but with the (usually) unwanted side effect of unnatural-looking "judder."

- **Aperture-priority AE.** Select Av, and you can choose an f/stop that will allow you to maximize or minimize depth-of-field for creative effects. There is no limitation on your f/stop selection. However, you should avoid switching to a different aperture while capturing video, as the sudden change can provide a jarring effect.

- **Manual exposure.** Choose M and you can specify ISO speed, shutter speed, and aperture. When choosing shutter speed or aperture, you can monitor exposure using the exposure level scale at the bottom of the LCD screen. For an additional check, you can press the INFO button to view a live histogram.

More on Shutter Speeds

You might think that setting your camera to a faster shutter speed will help give you sharper video frames. But the choice of a shutter speed for movie making is a bit more complicated than that. As you might guess, it's almost always best to leave the shutter speed at 1/30th or 1/60th second, and allow the overall exposure to be adjusted by varying the aperture and/or ISO sensitivity. We don't normally stare at a video frame for longer than 1/30th or 1/24th second, so while the shakiness of the *camera* can be disruptive (and often corrected by your camera's in-lens and in-body image stabilization), if there is a bit of blur in our *subjects* from movement, we tend not to notice. Each frame flashes by in the blink of an eye, so to speak, so a shutter speed of 1/30th or 1/60th second works a lot better in video than it does when shooting stills. Even shots with lots of movement are often sufficiently sharp at 1/60th second.

Higher shutter speeds introduce problems of their own. If you shoot a video frame using a shutter speed of 1/200th second, the actual moment in time that's captured represents only about 12 percent of the 1/30th second of elapsed time in that frame. Yet, when played back, that frame occupies the full 1/30th of a second, with 88 percent of that time filled by stretching the original image to fill it. The result is often a choppy/jumpy image, and one that may appear to be *too* sharp.

The reason for that is more social imprinting than scientific: we've all grown up accustomed to seeing the look of Hollywood productions that, by convention, were shot using a shutter speed that's half the reciprocal of the frame rate (that is, 1/48th second for a 24 fps movie). Professional movie cameras use a rotary shutter (achieving that 1/48th-second exposure by using a 180-degree shutter "angle"), but the effect on our visual expectations is the same. For the most "film-like" appearance, use 24 fps and 1/60th-second shutter speed.

Faster shutter speeds do have some specialized uses for motion analysis, especially where individual frames are studied. The rest of the time, 1/30th or 1/60th of a second will suffice. If the reason you needed a higher shutter speed was to obtain the correct exposure, use a slower ISO setting, or a neutral-density filter to cut down on the amount of light passing through the lens. A good rule of thumb is to use 1/60th second or slower when shooting at 24 fps; 1/60th second or slower at 30 fps; and 1/125th second or slower at 60 fps.

Creating Digest Movies

Some earlier Canon cameras included a novel "video snapshot" feature, which captured short movie clips (2 to 8 seconds) that could be assembled into a video snapshot "album." It eventually migrated to its current form in subsequent PowerShot and EOS M-series interchangeable-lens mirrorless cameras. Your R8 is one of the first EOS R-series model to include the updated capability, which Canon now dubs "Hybrid Auto." It is enabled whenever the Mode dial is set to the Hybrid Auto position.

Thereafter, each time you take a still photo, the camera will record 2 to 4 seconds of video and add it to a movie digest "album" that summarizes the images you capture that day. The digest can consist of only the video clips, or, at your option, include the still photographs, too. The process can be a little confusing, so I'm going to provide step-by-step instructions.

1. **Choose Still Mode.** Hybrid Auto does not operate when the R8's Still/Movie dial is set to Movie mode.

2. **Access Hybrid Auto.** Rotate the Mode dial to the Hybrid Auto position.

3. **Choose Digest Type.** Navigate to the Shooting 4 menu that is available only when the Mode dial is set to Hybrid Auto. Select either Include Stills or No Stills.

4. **Compose your Still shot.** Make any adjustments for exposure and focus and frame the still photo you will be taking.

5. **Hold the camera steady.** The video clip, including audio, is recorded *before* you press the shutter release down all the way. It begins when you press the shutter button halfway, so you don't want the R8 moving before the shot.

6. **Press shutter release halfway.** At this point, the camera begins capturing the scene in its internal buffer. The camera does not beep, but will begin recording other sounds.

7. **Take the still photo.** Press the shutter release down all the way. The R8 will capture the still image, and save the final 2 to 4 seconds of video before that.

8. **Capture more photos/video.** As you continue to take pictures, the camera will save the still photo versions and add each subsequent video clip to the digest album.

9. **Review.** At any time you can press the Playback button to locate, review, or edit the digest, which is stored as a Full HD 29.97 (NTSC) or 25.00 (PAL) MP4 movie using ALL-I compression. It will consist of the video clips captured so far, and, if you've chosen Include Stills as the Digest Type, your still pictures, too.

Playback and Editing

To review or edit a movie, press the Playback button and rotate the QCD to select a video to play. In single-image display mode, a movie-camera/SET icon appears in the upper-left corner of the screen when a video is selected. If you're using Index view, a set of film perforations appears at the left of each thumbnail. Press Q/SET to view that movie in single-image display.

Once the movie you want to play back is visible in the single-image display, press Q/SET to produce a screen of options in the Movie Playback Panel, shown in Figure 16.23. The Digest Playback Panel is similar, but the functions are slightly different, as I'll explain. You'll use either panel to set a location for editing within a movie or digest.

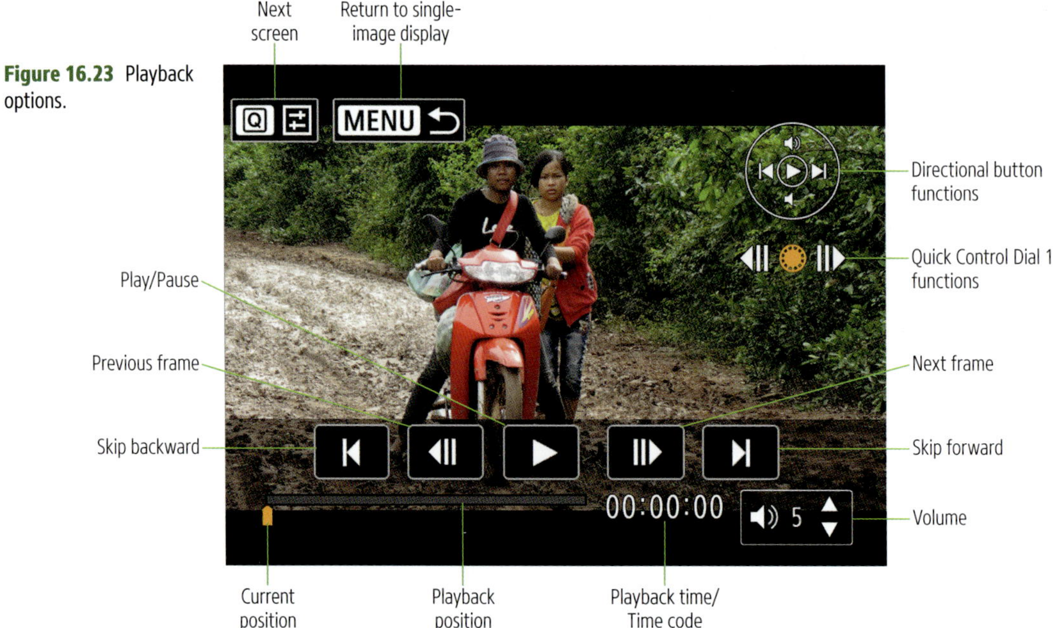

Figure 16.23 Playback options.

Once a Playback Panel is visible, you can press Q/SET to begin playback of the movie/digest, and press Q/SET again while viewing to return to the Playback Panel. The icons in the upper-right corner of the panel are reminders of the functions of the directional controls and QCD.

- **Adjust volume.** Press the up or down directional buttons to increase or decrease volume emitted by the speaker (even during playback). Or, tap the Volume icon on the lower-right corner of the touch screen. If your camera is connected to a television, you may have to use that device's controls to adjust volume.

- **Skip ahead/Skip back.** Press the left/right directional buttons to skip ahead to the next movie or, if working with a digest, the next clip within the digest. You can also tap the Skip Forward/Skip Backward icons located above the Playback Position bar at the bottom of the screen.

- **Next frame/Previous frame.** The QCD can be rotated clockwise to move ahead one frame, or counterclockwise to move back one frame. You can also tap the Next Frame/Previous Frame icons located above the Playback Position bar at the bottom of the screen.

- **Edit clip.** When you've reached the position in the video where you want to trim, press the Q button to proceed to the next screen, described below.

- **Playback time/Time code.** The numbers at lower right represent the elapsed time of the current clip when Move Play Count, described earlier, is set to Record Time. If you've chosen Time Code instead, the Record Time is replaced with the Time code. Digest movies always show the playback time.

After pressing the Q button, you'll see a screen similar to the one shown in Figure 16.24, left. It will show several icons, depending on the Movie/Digest format selected. Three of them, from left to right are:

- **Edit.** Takes you to an editing screen (see Figure 16.24, center), where you can trim off the beginning or ending of the clip, move the progress point, or save your edited clip.

- **Slow motion.** A slider (not shown) appears in the upper-right corner of the screen, allowing you to adjust the slow-motion rate.

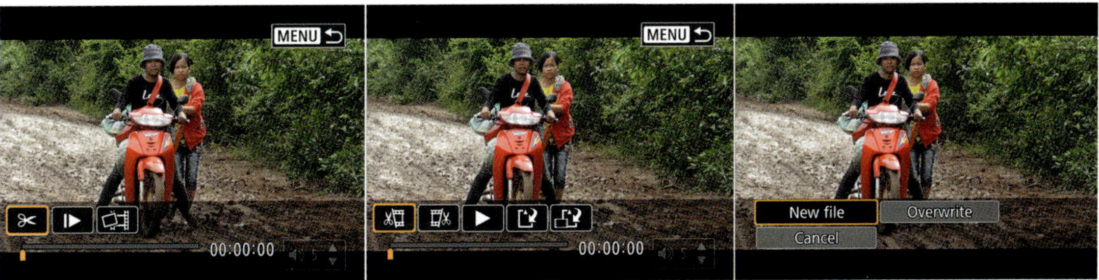

Figure 16.24 Editing options.

- **Frame Grab.** This icon appears *only* when reviewing 4K movies. You cannot capture stills while shooting movies. You must stop video capture first, take your stills, and then resume movie shooting.

  However, you *can* grab an 8.3-megapixel 3840 × 2160 JPEG still image from any 4K video or 4K time-lapse movie (as long as Canon Log options haven't been used). This capability can be valuable if you can settle for relatively low-resolution stills. You'll be asked "Save as a New Still Image?" Choose OK to save that frame as a still JPEG or HEIF.

- **Erase Clip.** This icon (not shown) appears only when editing a Digest Movie. It removes the current clip ("chapter") from the digest. This is a good way to cull less-than-interesting clips from your movie digest. Once a chapter has been deleted, it cannot be restored.

As I noted above, when you select Edit, the screen shown at center in Figure 16.24 appears. While reviewing your video, you can trim from the beginning or end of your video clip. Press Q/SET to pause the video at the edit position, and select the scissors symbol. The icons that appear have the following functions:

- **Cut beginning.** Trims off all video prior to the current point.
- **Cut end.** Removes video after the current point.
- **Play video.** Play back your video to reach the point where you want to trim the beginning or end. Edit is performed in roughly one-second increments.
- **Save.** Saves your video to the memory card. A screen appears offering to save the clip as a New File, or to Overwrite the existing movie with your edited clip. (See Figure 16.24, right.)
- **Save compressed version.** Saves a compressed version of your movie to the memory card. This option is not available for movies recorded with HDR PQ, Canon Log options, and "light" versions of FHD IPB movies (which are already compressed).
- **Menu.** Exits editing mode.

Using an External Recorder/Monitor

If you're truly becoming an advanced videographer, you'll probably be working with the ability to output "clean" non-compressed HDMI video to an external monitor or video recorder, including the Atomos Shogun lineup, which includes versions that are quite affordable, at least in terms of professional video gear. You can choose models both with and without an external LCD monitor, and capture to solid-state drives (SSD), a laptop's internal or connected hard drive or memory card.

Probably the best of the lot is the Atomos Ninja V, an extremely portable unit with a 5.2-inch screen and a $500 price tag that's currently the lowest for this type of device. Its size is a definite plus—if you're shooting video with a smaller, lightweight camera, you're going to need an equally compact recorder/monitor, such as the roughly 13-ounce Ninja V. Add a battery, HDMI cable, and a 2.5-inch solid-state drive, and you're ready to go.

The Ninja V has HDMI input and output jacks on its left edge, which you can see in Figure 16.25. The latter allows you to daisy-chain an even larger monitor or other device. A power button, headphone jack, microphone/audio input, and remote jack reside on the other edge. The touch screen enables you to view your video and access the monitor/recorder's menus and controls, which is convenient (except outdoors in cold weather when you're wearing gloves and might wish you had a few buttons to press instead). The only other "defect" of the unit is the noise produced by its fan; even when you're using an external microphone, the fan noise may be picked up in a quiet room.

If you simply want a monitor and don't want to record your camera's output, the $300 Atomos Shinobi is a lightweight 1920 × 1080 HDMI monitor introduced in February 2019 that has the same display as the Ninja V, but lacks recording capabilities. It does have a headphone jack so you can output to an external recorder if you want. Like the screen on the Ninja V, the Shinobi can display full HD or 4K video (despite its native 1920 × 1080 resolution) with 10 stops worth of dynamic range, and includes a preset to adjust the display for Canon Log output.

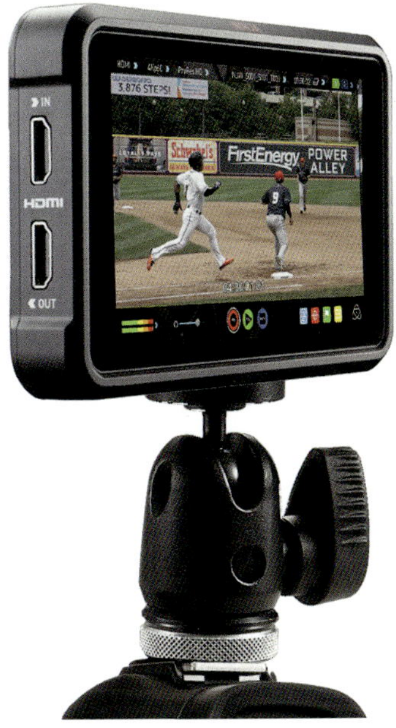

Figure 16.25 The Atomos Ninja V monitor/recorder.

Why use an external monitor or a monitor/recorder like the Ninja V, when your camera has its own nifty monitor and can store quite a lot of video on its memory card? From a monitor standpoint, an external unit's screen is larger, easier to see, and offers more flexibility in positioning. The Ninja V's screen tilts up or down; mounted on a ballhead like the one in the figure, you can adjust an external screen to any angle, including reversing it to point in the same direction as the lens, so vloggers can monitor themselves as they record or stream their video blog.

But the best value may come from the recording capabilities of such a device. Internal video is saved to your memory card in the standard H.264/MPEG-4 as an MP4 file, which compresses that stream of images as much as 50X. Standard video has only 8 bits of information: good, but somewhat limited in the dynamic range that can be included. Depending on your scene, you may lose some detail in the highlights or shadows.

Fortunately, your camera can record 4:2:2 10-bit Canon Log-3 (H.265) video plus 4:2:2 10-bit HDR PQ (H.265) video internally, and direct video output through the HDMI port in "clean" uncompressed 4:2:2 10-bit resolution. You really get your two-bits' worth of information: 8-bit output gives you 16.8 million possible colors; 10-bit output is capable of more than 108 billion hues. If your video stream to the external device uses Canon Log or Log-3, the dynamic range (overall different tones that can be captured) increases dramatically. The View Assist feature I described earlier in this chapter enables you to view Canon Log footage with a more contrasty "normal" rendition.

The HDMI port on the camera accepts an HDMI mini-C cable. Canon offers the HTC-100, but I prefer to purchase less-pricey third-party cables, which I buy in convenient lengths of 3 feet, 6 feet, 10 feet, or longer. The cable can be connected to the monitor, recorder, or other device of your choice.

> **TECH ALERT**
>
> Unless you're venturing into professional videography, you probably aren't obsessed with all those numbers in the previous paragraph. However, if you're terminally curious, the important things to keep in mind are:
>
> - **Transfer bit rate.** This is the speed the camera outputs its video to your memory card or external recorder. High transfer rates (such as the 144 megabits per second required for 4K ALL-I video, as mentioned in Chapter 15) require fast memory cards; an external recorder should be able to suck up video as quickly as your camera can deliver it.
> - **Encoding.** Although the "clean" video output to the HDMI port is not compressed, it is *encoded* using a procedure called *chroma subsampling,* which does reduce the amount of information that needs to be transferred. Chroma subsampling takes advantage of the fact that human beings don't detect changes in color (chroma) as easily as they do for brightness (luma). The designation 4:2:2 simply indicates that the full amount of brightness information is passed along ("4") while the two chroma values are sampled at half that rate ("2:2"). Subsampling in this way reduces the bandwidth of the otherwise uncompressed video signal by as much as one-third with no visual difference.

But producing good-quality video is more complicated than just buying good equipment. There are techniques that make for gripping storytelling and a visual language the average person is very accustomed to seeing, but also unaware of. After all, by comparison we're used to watching the best productions that television, video, and motion pictures can offer. While this book can't make you a professional videographer, there is some advice I can give you that will help you improve your results with the camera.

There are many different things to consider when planning a video shoot, and when possible, a shooting script and storyboard can help you produce a higher-quality video.

Lens Craft

I covered the use of lenses in more detail in Chapter 7, but a discussion of lens selection when shooting movies may be useful at this point. In the video world, not all lenses are created equal. The two most important considerations are depth-of-field, or the beneficial lack thereof, and zooming. I'll address each of these separately.

Depth-of-Field and Video

One thing that makes digital still cameras so attractive for professional video shooters—especially now that cameras support 4K video—is that they have relatively large sensors, which provides improved low-light performance and results in the oddly attractive reduced depth-of-field, compared with many professional video cameras.

But wait! you say. No matter what size sensor is used, isn't the number of pixels in that video frame exactly the same—1920 × 1080 pixels for, say, full HD? That's true—the final resolution of the FHD video image is precisely 1920 × 1080 pixels, whether you're capturing that frame with a point-and-shoot camera, a professional video camera, or a full-frame digital model like the R8. But that's only the *final* resolution. The number of pixels used to capture each video frame varies by sensor size.

For example, your camera does *not* use only its central 1920 × 1080 pixels to capture a full HD video frame. If it did that, you'd have to contend with a significant "crop" factor, and the field of view of a wide-angle lens would be sharply curtailed. Instead, it captures a full HD video frame using the full width of its full-frame sensor, trimmed to the proportions of a 16:9 area, producing a negligible crop factor. Other crops are available and used for different video image sizes. Your wide-angle and telephoto lenses retain roughly their same fields of view, and you can frame and compose your video through the viewfinder normally, with only the top and bottom of the frame and a little off each side cropped off to account for the wider video aspect ratio. That's why your camera gives you such great video quality, and why your video images retain roughly the same field of view and exact same depth-of-field you get with full-frame still images in Full HD mode.

Figure 16.26 shows at upper left the approximate capture areas for still photos, and video captured using the full width of the sensor. Also shown in lower and right sides of the picture are the video capture areas for some professional video sensors, the sensor in many snapshot cameras, and the APS-C sensor found in non-full-frame models.

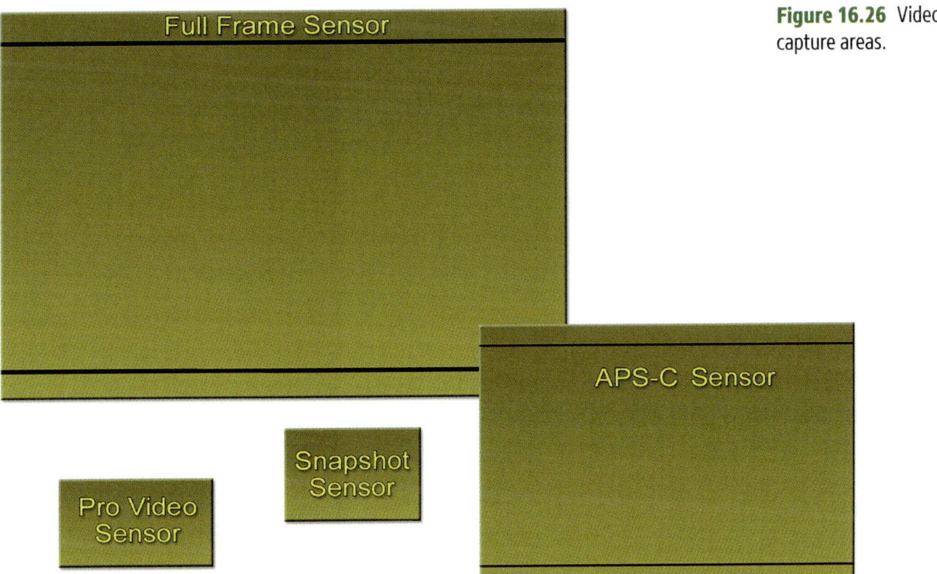

Figure 16.26 Video capture areas.

As I noted in Chapter 7, a larger sensor calls for the use of longer focal lengths to produce the same field of view, so, in effect, a larger sensor has reduced depth-of-field. And *that's* what makes full-frame cameras attractive from a creative standpoint. Less depth-of-field means greater control over the range of what's in focus. Your camera, with its larger sensor, has a distinct advantage over consumer camcorders in this regard, and even does a better job than many professional video cameras. With a really fast lens, such as the Canon 85mm f/1.2 or 50mm f/1.2, some sensational selective focus effects can be achieved.

Optical Zooming and Video

When shooting still photos, a zoom is a zoom is a zoom. The key considerations for a zoom lens used only for still photography are the maximum aperture available at each focal length ("How *fast* is this lens?"), the zoom range ("How far can I zoom in or out?"), and its sharpness at any given f/stop ("Do I lose sharpness when I shoot wide open?").

When shooting video, the priorities may change, and there are two additional parameters to consider. The first two I listed, lens speed and zoom range, have roughly the same importance in both still and video photography. Zoom range gains a bit of importance in videography, because you can always/usually move closer to shoot a still photograph, but when you're zooming during a shot most of us don't have that option (or the funds to buy/rent a dolly to smoothly move the camera during capture). But, oddly enough, overall sharpness may have slightly less importance under certain conditions when shooting video. That's because the image changes in some way many times per second (24/30/60/120 times per second in NTSC mode), so any given frame doesn't hang around long enough for our eyes to pick out every single detail. You want a sharp image, of course, but your standards don't need to be quite as high when shooting video.

Here are the remaining considerations:

- **Zoom lens maximum aperture.** The speed of the lens matters in several ways. A zoom with a relatively large maximum aperture lets you shoot in lower light levels, and a big f/stop allows you to minimize depth-of-field for selective focus. Keep in mind that the maximum aperture may change during zooming. A lens that offers an f/3.5 maximum aperture at its widest focal length may provide only f/5.6 worth of light at the telephoto position. If shooting wide open, you may want to retain the same maximum aperture regardless of focal length, so depth-of-field (and, along with it, focus) will increase or decrease more predictably from shot to shot, because the *focal length* has changed (that is, going from wide-angle to tele, or the reverse), and not because the *effective aperture* has changed, too.

  In that case, you'll want to use a *constant aperture* lens (sometimes called a *fixed aperture* lens, which can be interpreted two ways). Often, such lenses are Canon L lenses; with less expensive optics with a similar focal length range having a variable maximum aperture. A typical example is the RF 24-105mm f/4L. The L lens's maximum aperture is f/4 from 24mm right up to 105mm.

- **Zoom range.** Use of zoom during actual capture should not be an everyday thing, unless you're shooting a kung-fu movie. However, there are effective uses for a zoom shot, particularly if it's a "long" one from extreme wide angle to extreme close-up (or vice versa). Most of the time, you'll use the zoom range to adjust the perspective of the camera *between* shots, and a longer zoom range can mean less trotting back and forth to adjust the field of view. Zoom range also comes into play when you're working with selective focus (longer focal lengths have less depth-of-field), or want to expand or compress the apparent distance between foreground and background subjects. A longer range gives you more flexibility.

- **Linearity.** Interchangeable lenses may have some drawbacks, as many photographers who have been using the video features of their digital SLRs have discovered. That's because, unless a lens is optimized for video shooting, zooming with a particular lens may not necessarily be linear. Rotating the zoom collar manually at a constant speed doesn't always produce a smooth zoom. There may be "jumps" as the elements of the lens shift around during the zoom. Keep that in mind if you plan to zoom during a shot, and are using a lens that has proved, from experience, to provide a non-linear zoom. (Unfortunately, there's no easy way to tell ahead of time whether you own a lens that is well-suited for zooming during a shot.)

Keep Things Stable and on the Level

Camera shake's enough of a problem with still photography, but it becomes even more of a nuisance when you're shooting video. The image-stabilization feature found in many Canon lenses (and some third-party optics) can help minimize this. Any of them make an excellent choice for video shooting if you're planning on going for the hand-held cinema verité look.

Just realize that while hand-held camera shots—even image stabilized—may be perfect if you're shooting a documentary or video that intentionally mimics traditional home movie making, in other contexts it can be disconcerting or annoying. And even IS can't work miracles. It's the camera movement itself that is distracting—not necessarily any blur in our subject matter.

If you want your video to look professional, putting the camera on a tripod will give you smoother, steadier video clips to work with. It will be easier to intercut shots taken from different angles (or even at different times) if everything was shot on a tripod. Cutting from a tripod shot to a hand-held shot, or even from one hand-held shot to another one that has noticeably more (or less) camera movement can call attention to what otherwise might have been a smooth cut or transition.

Remember that telephoto lenses and telephoto zoom focal lengths magnify any camera shake, even with IS, so when you're using a longer focal length, that tripod becomes an even better idea. Tripods are essential if you want to pan from side to side during a shot, dolly in and out, or track from side to side (say, you want to shoot with the camera in your kid's coaster wagon). A tripod and (for panning) a fluid head built especially for smooth video movements can add a lot of production value to your movies.

Shooting Script

A shooting script is nothing more than a coordinated plan that covers both audio and video and provides order and structure for your video when you're in planned, storytelling mode. A detailed script will cover what types of shots you're going after, what dialogue you're going to use, audio effects, transitions, and graphics. A good script needn't constrain you: as the director, you are free to make changes on the spot during actual capture. But, before you change the route to your final destination, it's good to know where you were headed, and how you originally planned to get there.

When putting together your shooting script, plan for lots and lots of different shots, even if you don't think you'll need them. Only amateurish videos consist of a bunch of long, tedious shots. You'll want to vary the pace of your production by cutting among lots of different views, angles, and perspectives, so jot down your ideas for these variations when you put together your script.

If you're shooting a documentary rather than telling a story that's already been completely mapped out, the idea of using a shooting script needs to be applied more flexibly. Documentary filmmakers often have no shooting script at all. They go out, do their interviews, capture video of people, places, and events as they find them, and allow the structure of the story to take shape as they learn more about the subject of their documentary. In such cases, the movie is typically "created" during editing, as bits and pieces are assembled into the finished piece.

Storyboards

A storyboard makes a great adjunct to a detailed shooting script. It is a series of panels providing visuals of what each scene should look like. While the storyboards produced by Hollywood are generally of very high quality, there's nothing that says drawing skills are important for this step. Stick figures work just fine if that's the best you can do. The storyboard helps you visualize locations, placement of actors/actresses, props and furniture, and also helps everyone involved get an idea of what you're trying to show. It also helps show how you want to frame or compose a shot. You can even shoot a series of still photos and transform them into a "storyboard" if you want, such as in Figure 16.27.

Composition

In movie shooting, several factors restrict your composition, and impose requirements you just don't always have in still photography (although other rules of good composition do apply). Here are some of the key differences to keep in mind when composing movie frames:

- **Horizontal compositions only.** Some subjects, such as basketball players and tall buildings, just lend themselves to vertical compositions. But movies are shown in horizontal-format only. So, if you're interviewing a local basketball star, you can end up with a worst-case situation like the one shown in Figure 16.28. If you want to show how tall your subject is, it's often impractical to move back far enough to show him full-length. You really can't capture a vertical composition. Tricks like getting down on the floor and shooting up at your subject can exaggerate the perspective, but aren't a perfect solution.

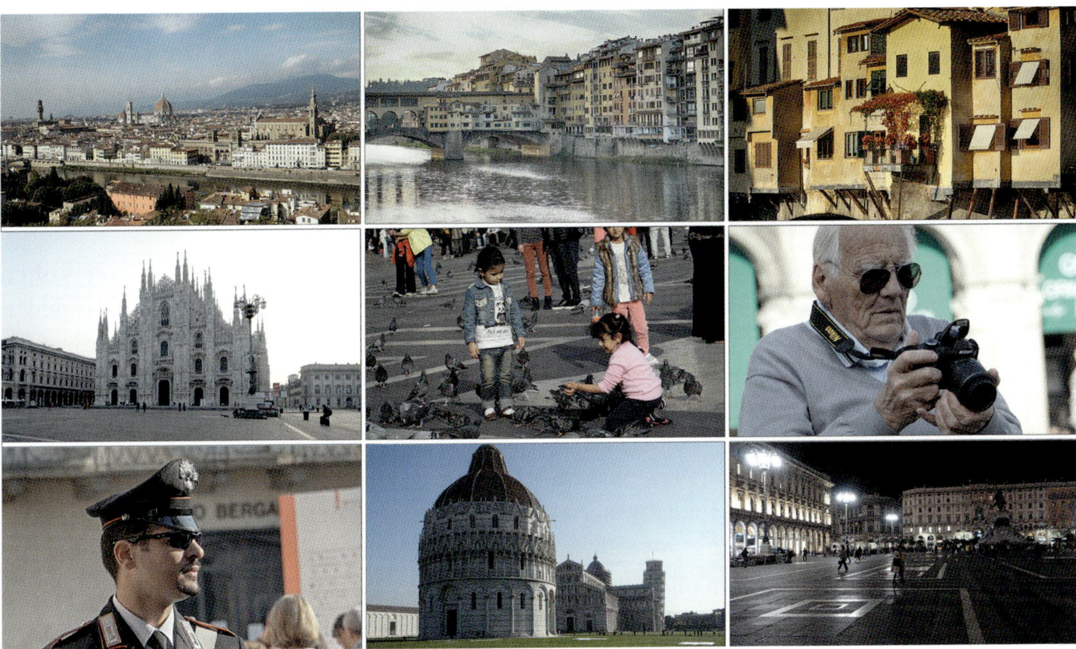

Figure 16.27 A storyboard is a series of simple sketches or photos to help visualize a segment of video.

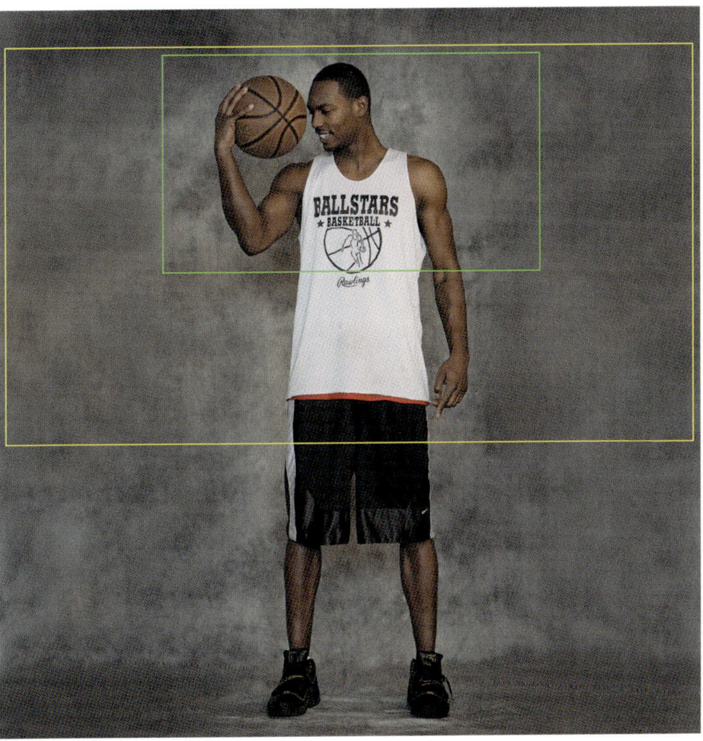

Figure 16.28 Movie shooting requires you to fit all your subjects into a horizontally oriented frame.

- **Wasted space at the sides.** Moving in to frame the basketball player as outlined by the yellow box in Figure 16.28 means that you're still forced to leave a lot of empty space on either side. (Of course, you can fill that space with other people and/or interesting stuff, but that defeats your intent of concentrating on your main subject.) So, when faced with some types of subjects in a horizontal frame, you can be creative, or move in *really* tight. For example, if I were willing to give up the "height" aspect of my composition, I could have framed the shot as shown by the green box in the figure, and wasted less of the image area at either side.

- **Seamless (or seamed) transitions.** Unless you're telling a story with a photo essay, still pictures often stand alone. But with movies, each of your compositions must relate to the shot that preceded it, and the one that follows. It can be jarring to jump from a long shot to a tight close-up unless the director—you—is very creative. Another common error is the "jump cut" in which successive shots vary only slightly in camera angle, making it appear that the main subject has "jumped" from one place to another. (Although everyone from French New Wave director Jean-Luc Goddard to Guy Ritchie—Madonna's ex—have used jump cuts effectively in their films.) The rule of thumb is to vary the camera angle by at least 30 degrees between shots to make it appear to be seamless. Unless you prefer that your images flaunt convention and appear to be "seamy."

- **The time dimension.** Unlike still photography, with motion pictures there's a lot more emphasis on using a series of images to build on each other to tell a story. Static shots where the camera is mounted on a tripod and everything is shot from the same distance are a recipe for dull videos. Watch a television program sometime and notice how often camera shots change distances and directions. Viewers are used to this variety and have come to expect it. Professional video productions are often done with multiple cameras shooting from different angles and positions. But many professional productions are shot with just one camera and careful planning, and you can do just fine with your camera.

Here's a look at the different types of commonly used compositional tools:

- **Establishing shot.** Much like it sounds, this type of composition, as shown in Figure 16.29, upper left, establishes the scene and tells the viewer where the action is taking place. Let's say you're shooting a video of your offspring's move to college; the establishing shot could be a wide shot of the campus with a sign welcoming you to the school in the foreground. Another example would be for a child's birthday party; the establishing shot could be the front of the house decorated with birthday signs and streamers or a shot of the dining room table decked out with party favors and a candle-covered birthday cake. I wanted to show the studio where the video was shot.

- **Medium shot.** This shot is composed from about waist to head room (some space above the subject's head). It's useful for providing variety from a series of close-ups and makes for a useful first look at a speaker. (See Figure 16.29, upper right.)

■ **Close-up.** The close-up, usually described as "from shirt pocket to head room," provides a good composition for someone talking directly to the camera. Although it's common to have your talking head centered in the shot, that's not a requirement. In Figure 16.29, center left, the subject was offset to the right. This would allow other images, especially graphics or titles, to be superimposed in the frame in a "real" (professional) production. But the compositional technique can be used with videos, too, even if special effects are not going to be added.

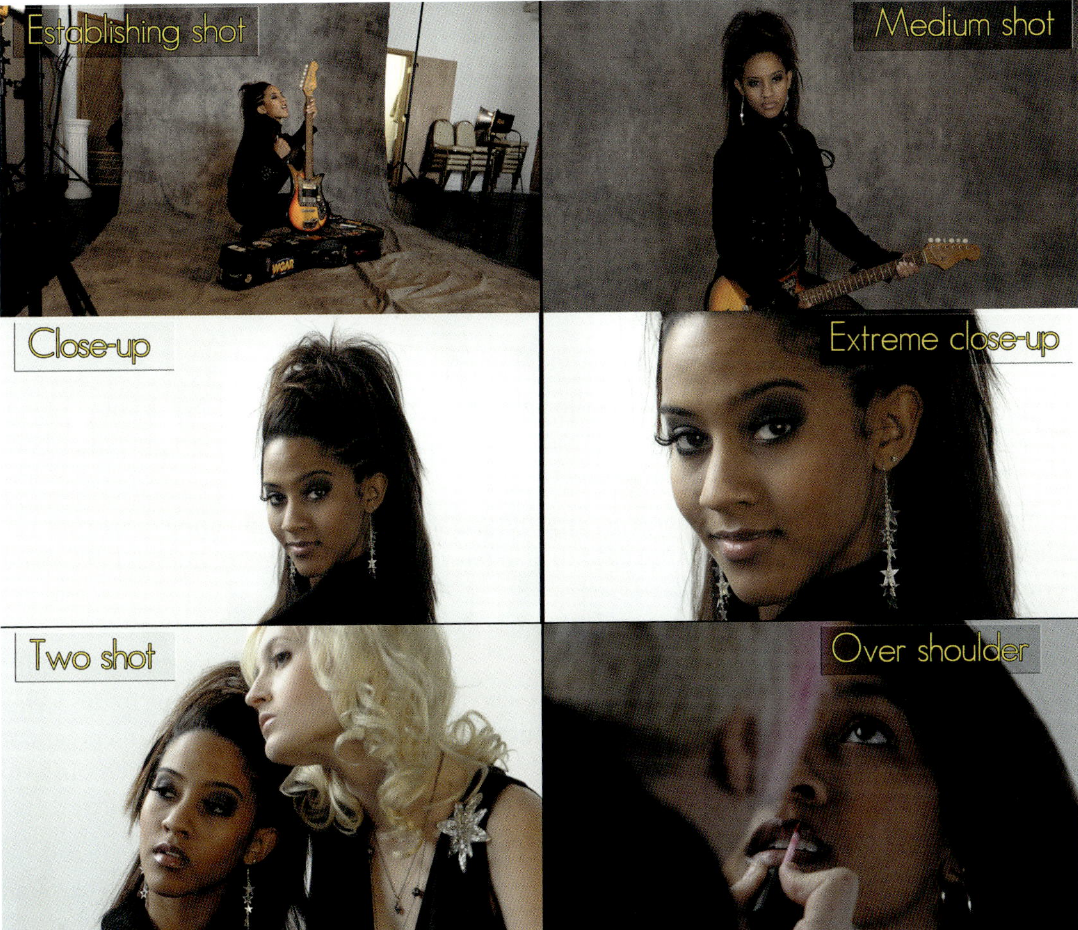

Figure 16.29 Shot choice provides different perspectives on a scene.

- **Extreme close-up.** When I went through broadcast training back in the '70s, this shot was described as the "big talking face" shot and we were actively discouraged from employing it. Styles and tastes change over the years and now the big talking face is much more commonly used (maybe people are better looking these days?) and so this view may be appropriate. Just remember, the camera is capable of shooting in high-definition video and you may be playing the video on a high-def TV; be careful that you use this composition on a face that can stand up to high definition or 4K resolution. (See Figure 16.29, center right.)

- **"Two shot."** A two shot shows a pair of subjects in one frame. They can be side by side or one in the foreground and one in the background. (See Figure 16.29, lower left.) This does not have to be a head-to-ground composition. Subjects can be standing or seated. A "three shot" is the same principle except that three people are in the frame.

- **Over-the-shoulder shot.** Long a composition of interview programs, the "over-the-shoulder shot" uses the rear of one person's head and shoulder to serve as a frame for the other person. This puts the viewer's perspective as that of the person facing away from the camera. (See Figure 16.29, lower right.)

Lighting for Video

Much like in still photography, how you handle light pretty much can make or break your videography. Lighting for video can be more complicated than lighting for still photography, since both subject and camera movement are often part of the process.

Lighting for video presents several concerns. First off, you want enough illumination to create a useable video. Beyond that, you want to use light to help tell your story or increase drama. Let's take a better look at both.

Illumination

You can significantly improve the quality of your video by increasing the light falling in the scene. This is true indoors or out, by the way. While it may seem like sunlight is more than enough, it depends on how much contrast you're dealing with. If your subject is in shadow (which can help them from squinting) or wearing a ball cap, a video light can help make them look a lot better.

Lighting choices for amateur videographers are a lot better these days than they were a decade or two ago. An inexpensive incandescent video light, which will easily fit in a camera bag, can be found for $15 or $20. You can even get a good-quality LED video light for less than $100. Work lights sold at many home improvement stores can also serve as video lights since you can set the camera's white balance to correct for any color casts. You'll need to mount these lights on a tripod or other support, or, perhaps, to a bracket that fastens to the tripod socket on the bottom of the camera.

Much of the challenge depends upon whether you're just trying to add some fill-light on your subject versus trying to boost the light on an entire scene. A small video light will do just fine for the former. It won't handle the latter. Fortunately, that versatility comes in quite handy here. Since the camera shoots video in Auto ISO mode, it can compensate for lower lighting levels and still produce a decent image. For best results, though, better lighting is necessary.

Creative Lighting

While ramping up the light intensity will produce better technical quality in your video, it won't necessarily improve the artistic quality of it. Whether we're outdoors or indoors, we're used to seeing light come from above. Videographers need to consider how they position their lights to provide even illumination while up high enough to angle shadows down low and out of sight of the camera.

When considering lighting for video, there are several factors. One is the quality of the light. It can either be hard (direct) light or soft (diffused) light. Hard light is good for showing detail, but can also be very harsh and unforgiving. "Softening" the light, but diffusing it somehow, can reduce the intensity of the light but make for a kinder, gentler light as well.

While mixing light sources isn't always a good idea, one approach is to combine window light with supplemental lighting. Position your subject with the window to one side and bring in either a supplemental light or a reflector to the other side for reasonably even lighting.

Lighting Styles

Some lighting styles are more heavily used than others. Some forms are used for special effects, while others are designed to be invisible. At its most basic, lighting just illuminates the scene, but when used properly it can also create drama. Let's look at some types of lighting styles:

- **Three-point lighting.** This is a basic lighting setup for one person. A main light illuminates the strong side of a person's face, while a fill light lights up the other side. A third light is then positioned above and behind the subject to light the back of the head and shoulders. (See Figure 16.30, top.)
- **Flat lighting.** Use this type of lighting to provide illumination and nothing more. It calls for a variety of lights and diffusers set to raise the light level in a space enough for good video reproduction, but not to create a mood or emphasize a scene or individual. With flat lighting, you're trying to create even lighting levels throughout the video space and minimize any shadows. Generally, the lights are placed up high and angled downward (or possibly pointed straight up to bounce off a white ceiling). (See Figure 16.30, bottom.)
- **"Ghoul lighting."** This is the style of lighting used for old horror movies. The idea is to position the light down low, pointed upward. It's such an unnatural style of lighting that it makes its targets seem weird and "ghoulish."

- **Outdoor lighting.** While shooting outdoors may seem easier because the sun provides more light, it also presents its own problems. As a general rule of thumb, keep the sun behind you when you're shooting video outdoors, except when shooting faces (anything from a medium shot and closer) since the viewer won't want to see a squinting subject. When shooting another human this way, put the sun behind her and use a video light to balance light levels between the foreground and background. If the sun is simply too bright, position the subject in the shade and use the video light for your main illumination. Using reflectors (white board panels or aluminum foil–covered cardboard panels are cheap options) can also help balance light effectively.

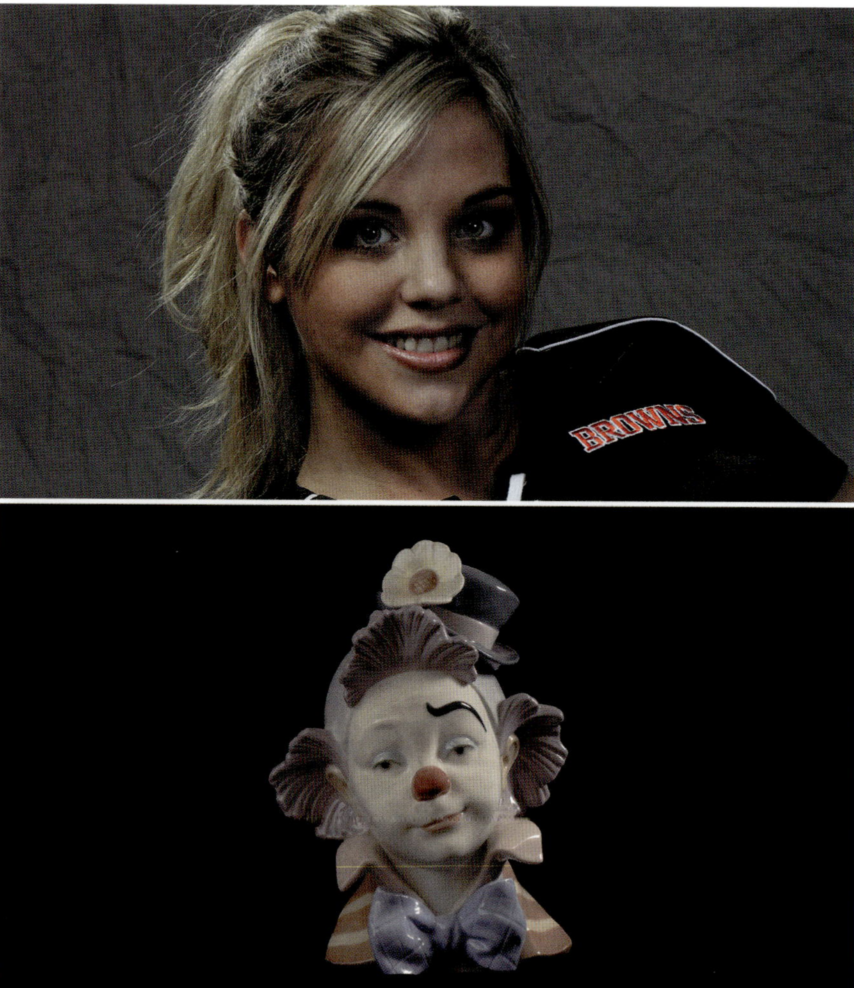

Figure 16.30 With three-point lighting (top) and flat lighting (bottom).

Audio

When it comes to making a successful video, audio quality is one of those things that separates the professionals from the amateurs. We're used to watching top-quality productions on television and in the movies, yet the average person has no idea how much effort goes in to producing what seems to be "natural" sound. Much of the sound you hear in such productions is recorded on carefully controlled sound stages and "sweetened" with a variety of sound effects and other recordings of "natural" sound.

Tips for Better Audio

Since recording high-quality audio is such a challenge, it's a good idea to do everything possible to maximize recording quality. Here are some ideas for improving the quality of the audio your camera records:

- **Get the camera and its microphone close to the speaker.** The farther the microphone is from the audio source, the less effective it will be in picking up that sound. While having to position the camera and its built-in microphone closer to the subject affects your lens choices and lens perspective options, it will make the most of your audio source. Of course, if you're using a very wide-angle lens, getting too close to your subject can have unflattering results, so don't take this advice too far. It's important to think carefully about what sounds you want to capture. If you're shooting video of an acoustic combo that's not using a PA system, you'll want the microphone close to them, but not so close that, say, only the lead singer or instrumentalist is picked up, while the players at either side fade off into the background.

- **Use an external microphone.** You'll recall the description of the camera's external microphone port in Chapter 2. As noted, this port accepts a stereo mini-plug from a standard external microphone, allowing you to achieve considerably higher audio quality for your movies than is possible with the camera's built-in microphones (which are disabled when an external mic is plugged in). An external microphone reduces the amount of camera-induced noise that is picked up and recorded on your audio track. (The action of the lens as it focuses can be audible when the built-in microphones are active.)

The external microphone port can provide plug-in power for microphones that can take their power from this sort of outlet rather than from a battery in the microphone. Canon provides optional compatible microphones such as the Canon Directional Microphone DM-E1 (around $180); you also may find suitable microphones from companies such as Shure and Audio-Technica. If you are on a quest for superior audio quality, you can even obtain a portable mixer that can plug into this jack. Or, you might be using an Atomos recorder with professional microphone jacks. One good thing about Canon still cameras is that so many pro videographers are using them that a wealth of add-on video gear, from monitors to cages, and stabilizers are available for it.

- **Hide the microphone.** Combine the first few tips by using an external mic, and getting it as close to your subject as possible. If you're capturing a single person, you can always use a lapel microphone (described in the next section). But if you want a single mic to capture sound from multiple sources, your best bet may be to hide it somewhere in the shot. Put it behind a vase, using duct tape to fasten the microphone, and fix the mic cable out of sight (if you're not using a wireless microphone).

- **Turn off any sound makers you can.** Little things like fans and air handling units aren't obvious to the human ear, but will be picked up by the microphone. Turn off any machinery or devices that you can plus make sure cell phones are set to silent mode. Also, do what you can to minimize sounds such as wind, radio, television, or people talking in the background.

- **Make sure to record some "natural" sound.** If you're shooting video at an event of some kind, make sure you get some background sound that you can add to your audio as desired in post-production.

- **Consider recording audio separately.** Lip-syncing is probably beyond most of the people you're going to be shooting, but there's nothing that says you can't record narration separately and add it later. It's relatively easy if you learn how to use simple software video-editing programs like iMovie (for the Macintosh) or Windows Movie Maker (for Windows PCs). Any time the speaker is off-camera, you can work with separately recorded narration rather than recording the speaker on-camera. This can produce much cleaner sound.

External Microphones

The single most important thing you can do to improve your audio quality is to use an external microphone. The camera's internal stereo microphones on the front of the camera will do a decent job, but have some significant drawbacks, partially spelled out in the previous section:

- **Camera noise.** There are plenty of noise sources emanating from the camera, including your own breathing and rustling around as the camera shifts in your hand. Manual zooming is bound to affect your sound, and your fingers will fall directly in front of the built-in mics as you change focal lengths. An external microphone isolates the sound recording from camera noise.

- **Distance.** Anytime your camera is located more than 6 to 8 feet from your subjects or sound source, the audio will suffer. An external unit allows you to place the mic right next to your subject.

- **Improved quality.** Obviously, Canon wasn't able to install a super-expensive, super-high-quality microphone, even on an advanced camera. Not all owners of the camera would be willing to pay the premium, especially if they didn't plan to shoot much video themselves. An external microphone will almost always be of better quality.

- **Directionality.** The camera's internal microphone generally records only sounds directly in front of it. An external microphone can be either of the directional type or omnidirectional, depending on whether you want to "shotgun" your sound or record more ambient sound.

You can choose from several different types of microphones, each of which has its own advantages and disadvantages. If you're serious about movie making with your camera, you might want to own more than one. Common configurations include:

- **Shotgun microphones.** These can be mounted directly on your camera, although, if the mic uses an accessory shoe mount, you'll need the optional adapter to convert the camera's shoe to a standard hot shoe. I prefer to use a bracket, which further isolates the microphone from any camera noise. One thing to keep in mind is that while the shotgun mic will generally ignore any sound coming from *behind* it, it will pick up any sound it is pointed at, even *behind* your subject. You may be capturing video and audio of someone you're interviewing in a restaurant, and not realize you're picking up the lunchtime conversation of the diners seated in the table behind your subject. Outdoors, you may record your speaker, as well as the traffic on a busy street or freeway in the background.

- **Lapel microphones.** Also called *lavalieres*, these microphones attach to the subject's clothing and pick up their voice with the best quality. You'll need a long enough cord or a wireless mic (described later). These are especially good for video interviews, so whether you're producing a documentary or grilling relatives for a family history, you'll want one of these.

- **Hand-held microphones.** If you're capturing a singer crooning a tune, or want your subject to mimic famed faux newscaster Wally Ballou, a hand-held mic may be your best choice. They serve much the same purpose as a lapel microphone, and they're more intrusive—but that may be the point. A hand-held microphone can make a great prop for your fake newscast! The speaker can talk right into the microphone, point it at another person, or use it to record ambient sound. If your narrator is not going to appear on-camera, one of these can be an inexpensive way to improve sound.

- **Wired and wireless external microphones.** This option is the most expensive, but you get a receiver and a transmitter (both battery powered, so you'll need to make sure you have enough batteries). The transmitter is connected to the microphone, and the receiver is connected to your camera. In addition to being less klutzy and enabling you to avoid having wires on view in your scene, wireless mics let you record sounds that are physically located some distance from your camera. Of course, you need to keep in mind the range of your device, and be aware of possible signal interference from other electronic components in the vicinity.

WIND NOISE REDUCTION

Always use the wind screen provided with an external microphone to reduce the effect of noise produced by even light breezes blowing over the microphone. Many mics include a low-cut filter to further reduce wind noise. However, these can also affect other sounds. You can disable the low-cut filters for some units by changing a switch on the back from L-cut (low cutoff) to Flat.

Index

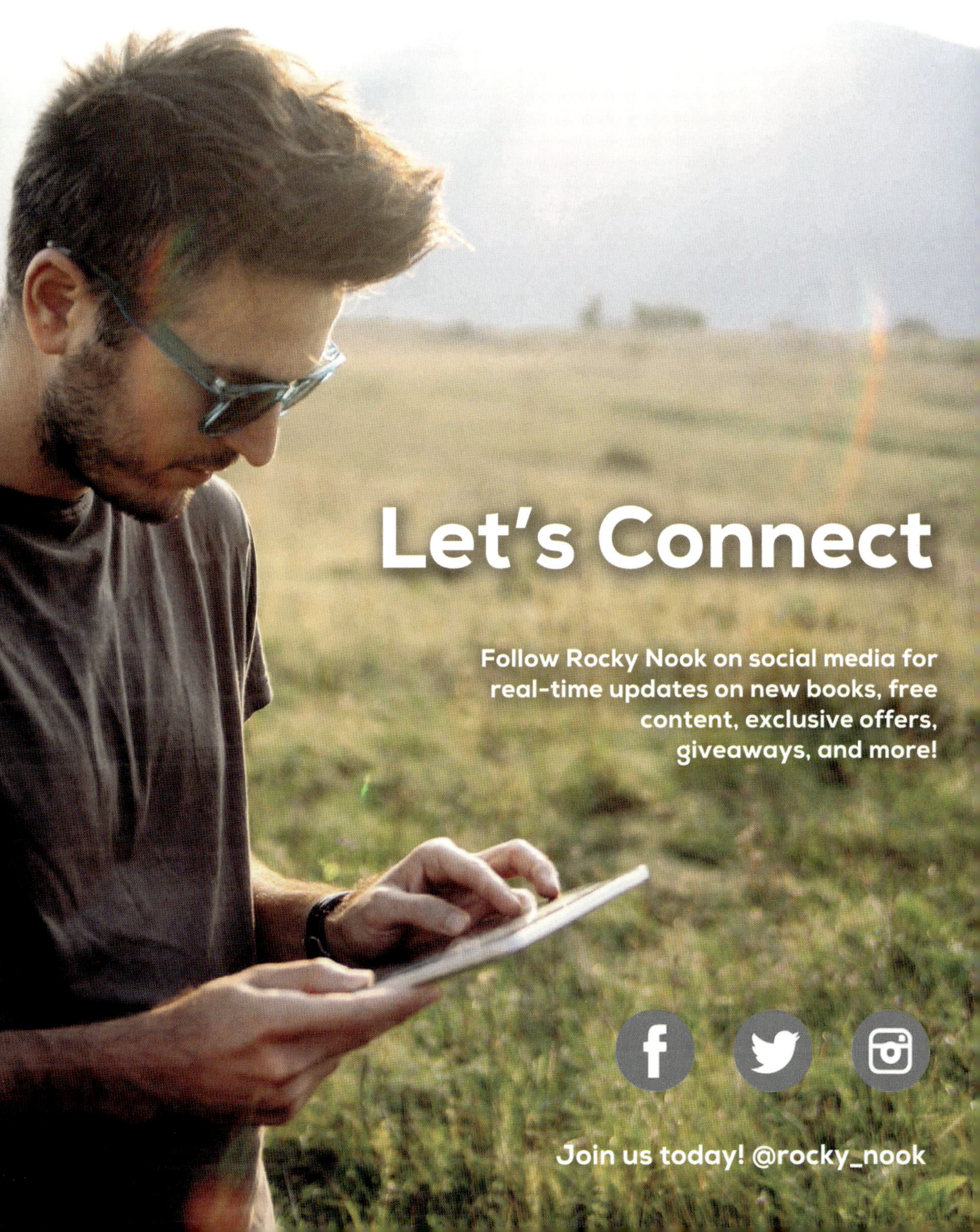

rockynook
Let's Connect
Follow Rocky Nook on social media for real-time updates on new books, free content, exclusive offers, giveaways, and more!
Join us today! @rocky_nook

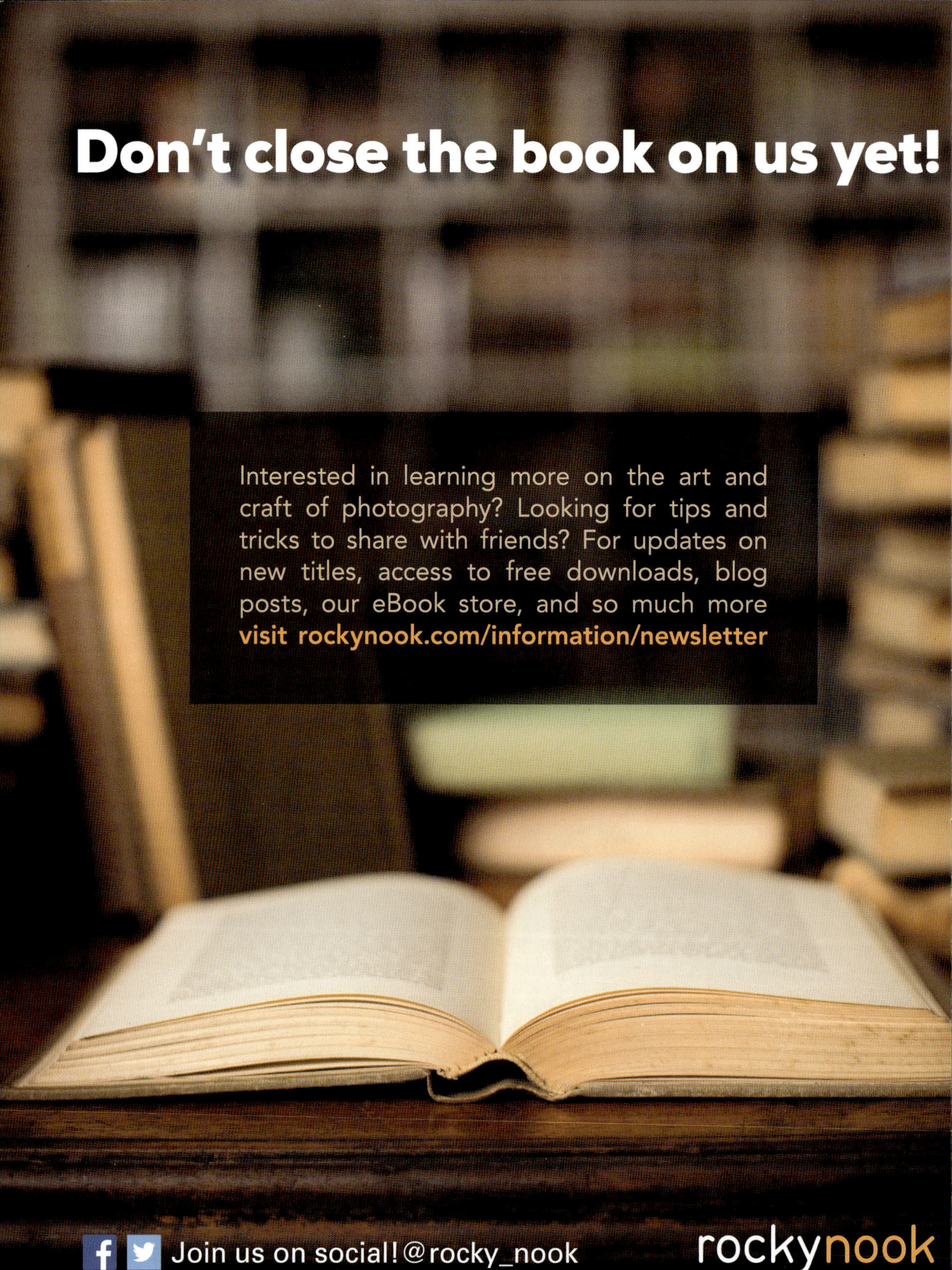